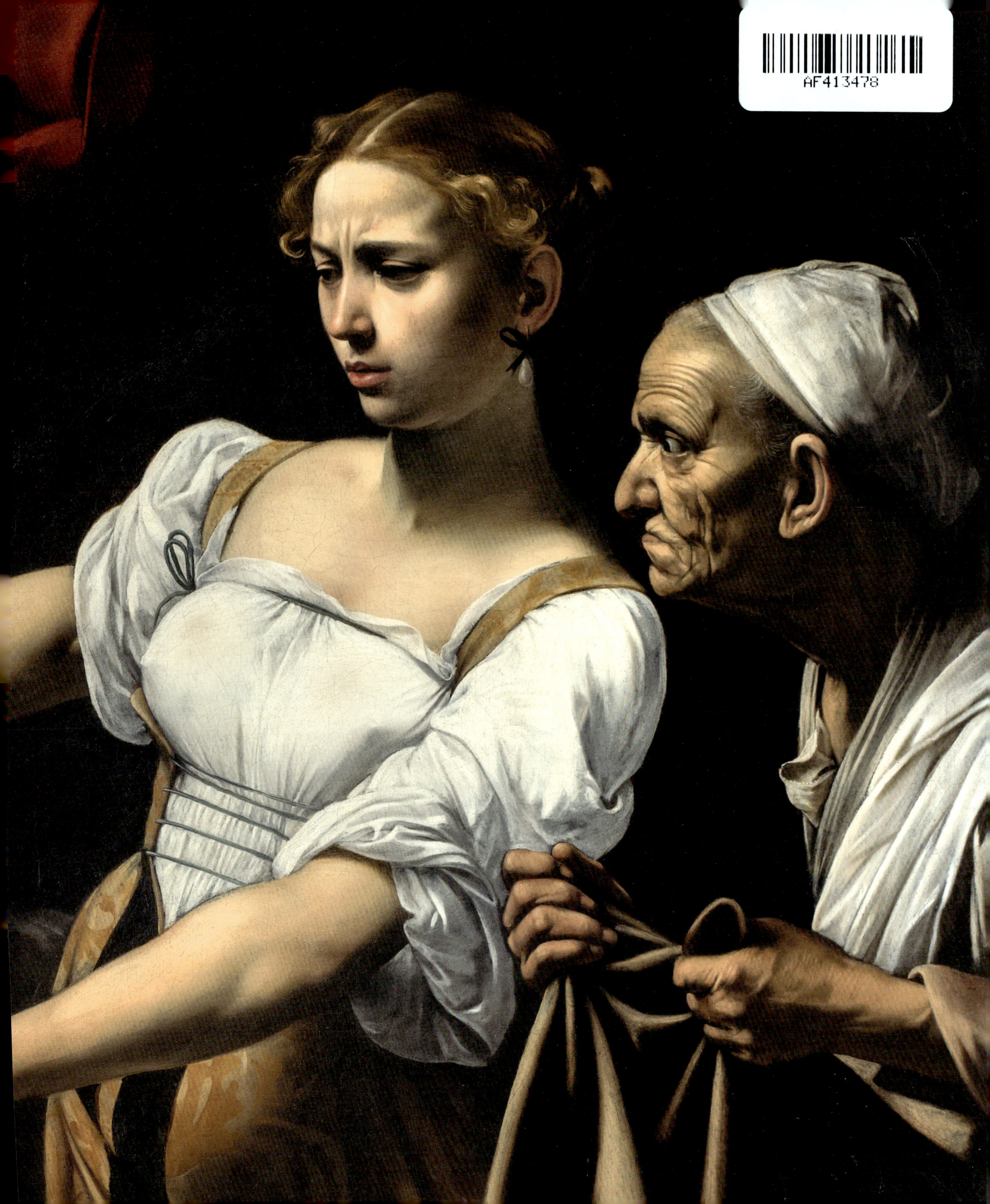

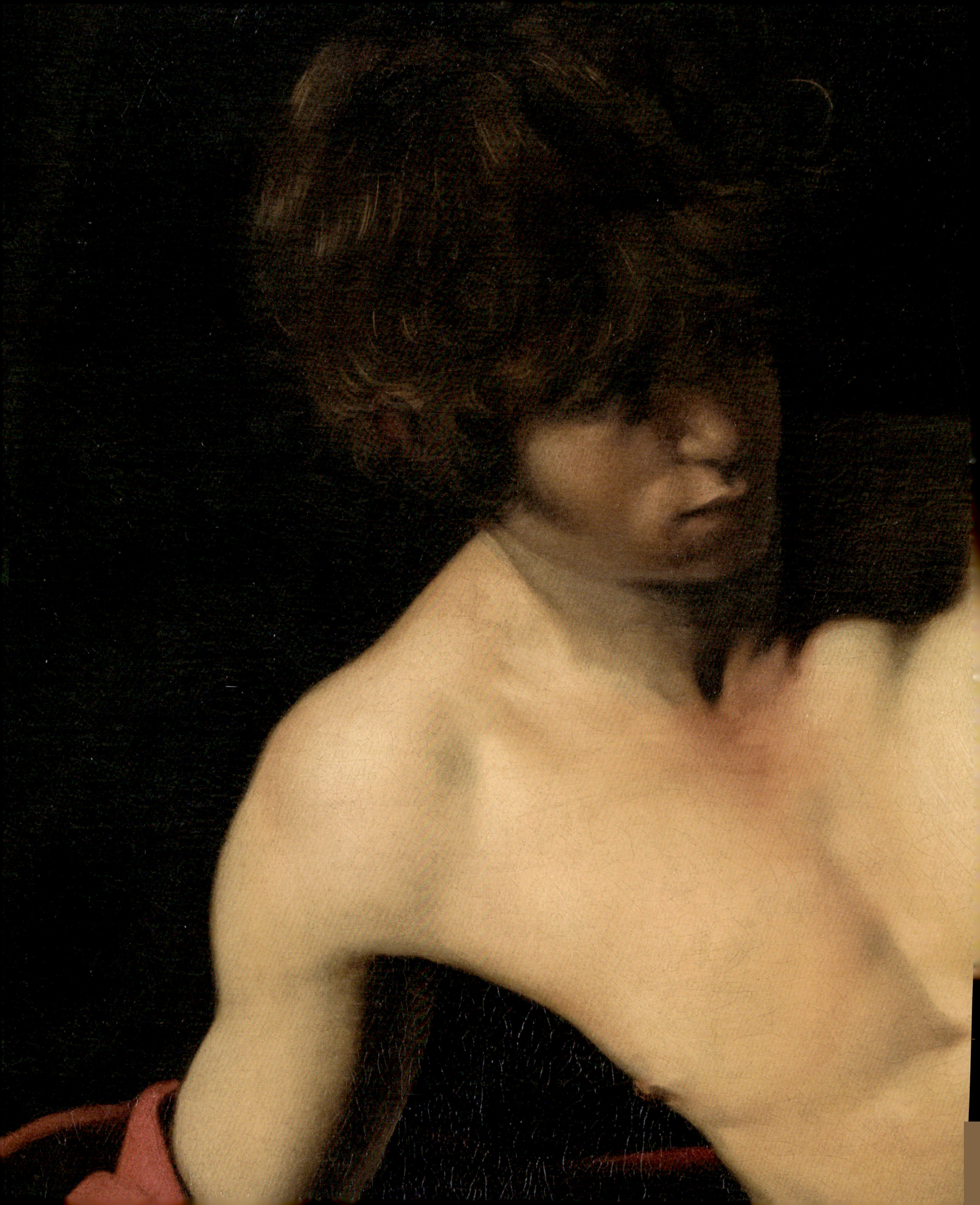

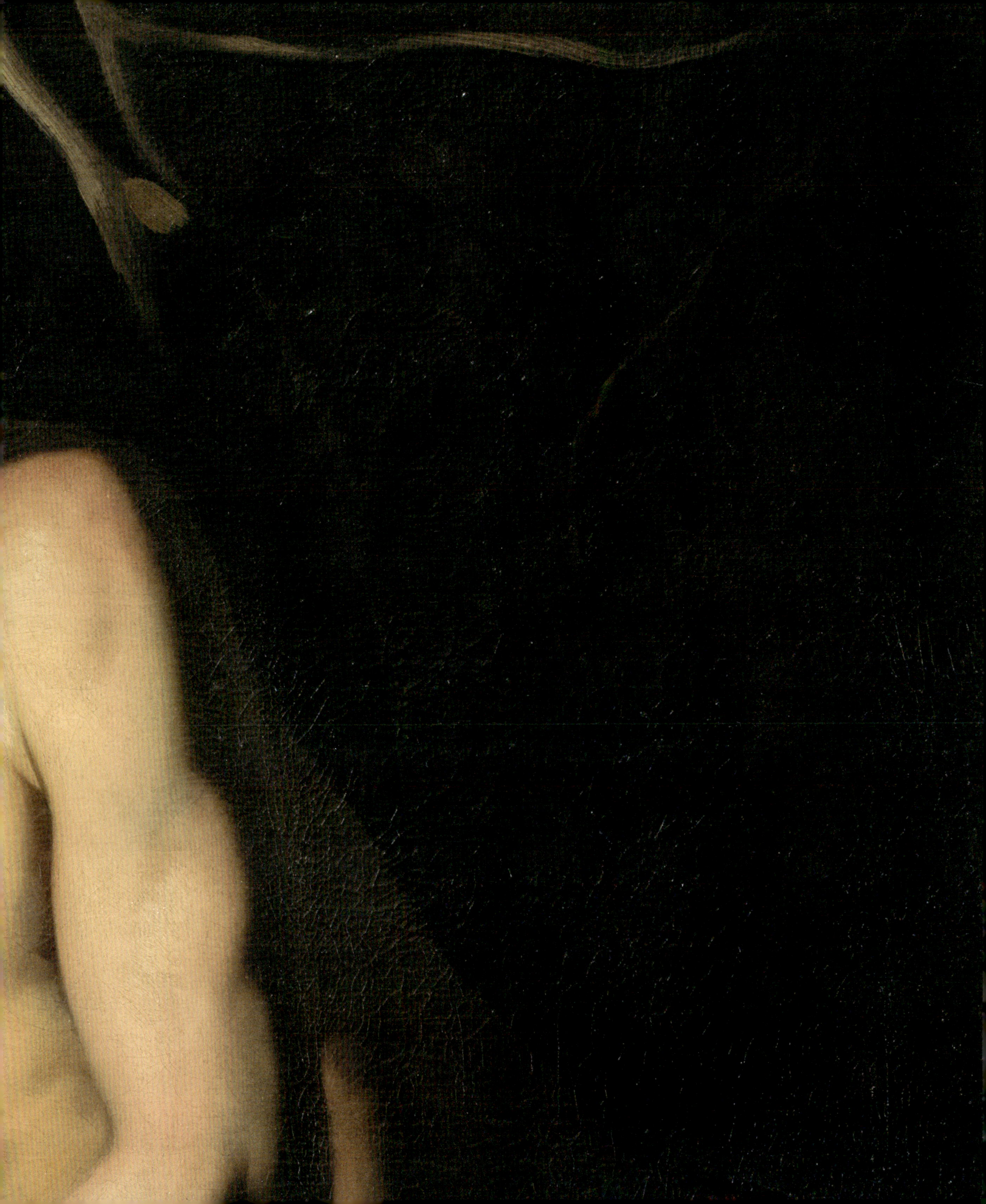

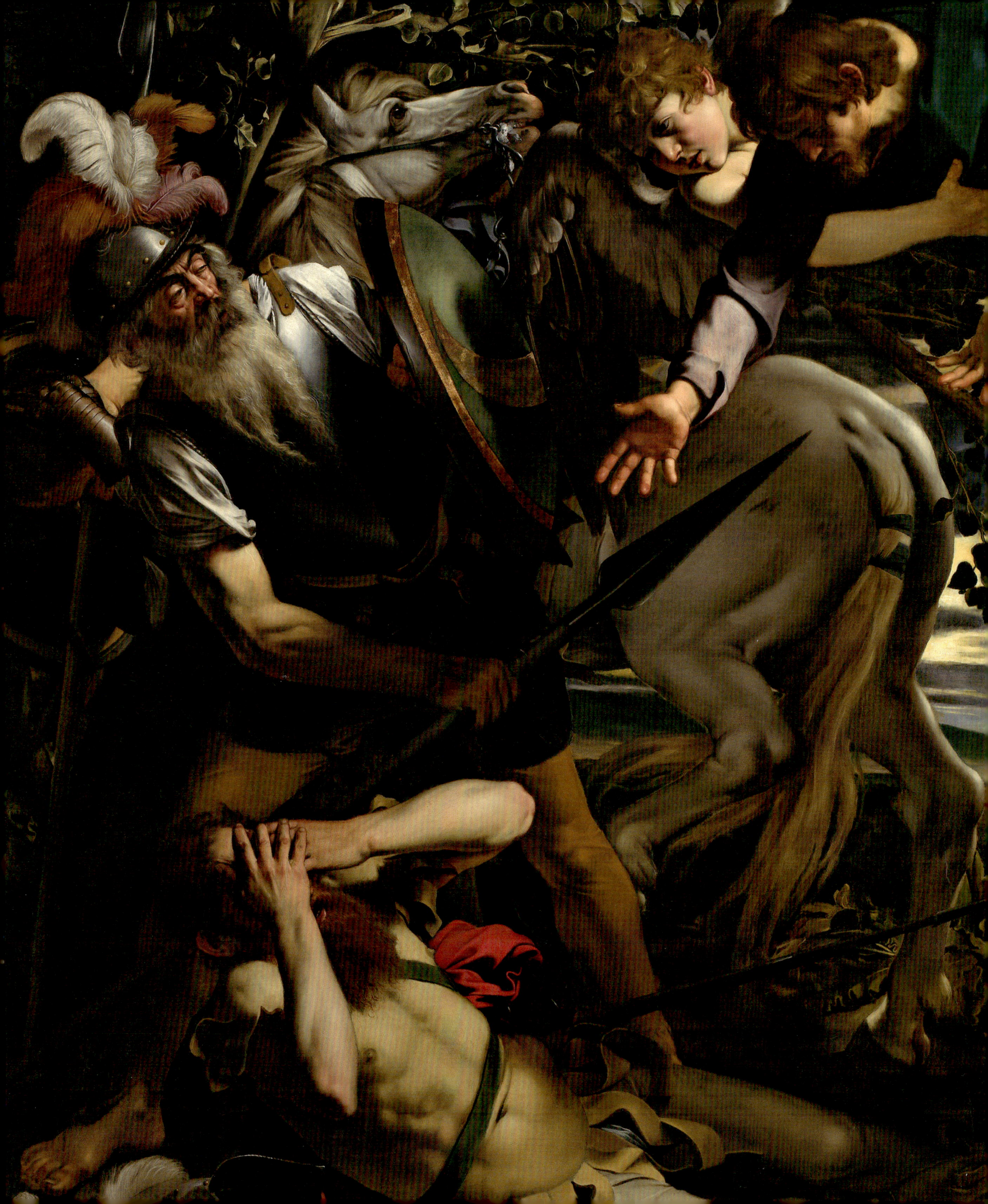

CARAVAGGIO 2025

edited by
Francesca Cappelletti
Maria Cristina Terzaghi

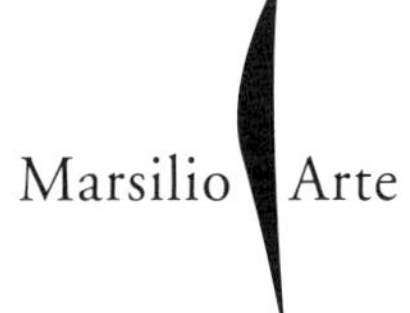

Marsilio Arte

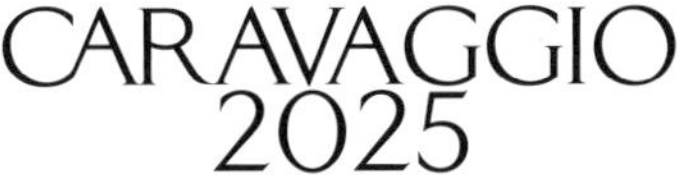

CARAVAGGIO 2025

Gallerie Nazionali di Arte Antica
Palazzo Barberini
07.03.2025 – 06.07.2025

curated by Francesca Cappelletti,
Maria Cristina Terzaghi
and Thomas Clement Salomon

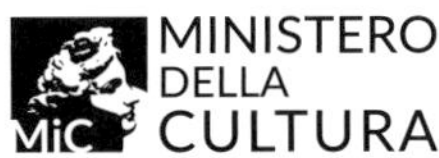

MINISTERO DELLA CULTURA

Minister
Alessandro Giuli

Undersecretaries of State
Lucia Borgonzoni
Gianmarco Mazzi

Chef de Cabinet
Valentina Gemignani

*Deputy Chef de Cabinet
and Economic Adviser
to the Minister*
Giorgio Carlo Brugnoni

*Head of the Minister's
Secretariat*
Chiara Sbocchia

*Head of the Minister's
Technical Secretariat*
Emanuele Merlino

*Head of Press and
Communication Office*
Piero Tatafiore

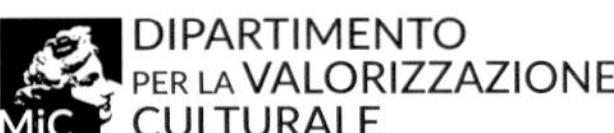

DIPARTIMENTO PER LA VALORIZZAZIONE CULTURALE

Head of Department
Alfonsina Russo

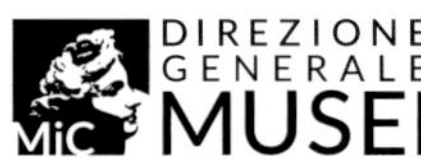

DIREZIONE GENERALE MUSEI

Director General
Massimo Osanna

*Director of Service II
"Sistema museale nazionale
e valorizzazione del patrimonio
culturale"*
Roberto Vannata

*Director of Service III
"Fruizione e comunicazione
del patrimonio culturale"*
Luca Mercuri

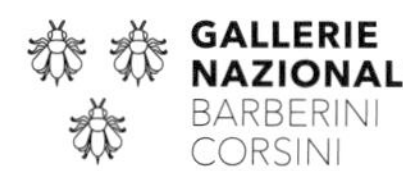

GALLERIE NAZIONALI BARBERINI CORSINI

Director
Thomas Clement Salomon

Director's Office
Cinzia Ammannato, *Head*
Simona Baldi

Secretariat to the Direction
Francesco Canto
Cristina Lio

Project Manager
Alessandro Cosma

General Coordination
Claudia Sarpi
with the collaboration of
Michela Ulivi

Administrative Coordination
Chiara Di Marco, Ales
Emanuel Tarquini, Ales

Estates and Management
Fulvio Favro

Legal Support
Donatella Viscogliosi
Nicoletta Di Pucchio

Restoration Laboratory
Pilar Grazioli
Grazia Del Giudice
Laura Di Vincenzo
Alessandra Percoco
Vega Santodonato
Paola Surace

Registrar
Giuliana Forti

*Image Collection
and Reproductions*
Valeria Danesi

Technical Department
Dario Aureli
Marco Corsi
Gabriele Mari
Antonio Massa, Ales

Events and Ceremonies
Simona Baldi
with Luca Galano
Annarita Margani

Promotion and Communication
Paola Guarnera, *Head*
with Maria Francesca Castaldo
Maura Garofalo

Marketing
Diego Giacomelli

Digital Media
Dinamica Studio
Giuseppe Perrino

Press Office
Lara Facco

*Education, Reception
and Services to the Public*
CoopCulture

Room Texts
Camilla Iacometti

*Concept and Installation
Design*
PANSTUDIO architetti
associati
Paolo Capponcelli / Mauro
Dalloca / Cesare Mari
with Carlotta Mari

Graphic Design
Alessandro Mele

Installation
Articolarte

Translations
Byron Tree Srl

Photography
Alberto Novelli
and Alessio Panunzi

Special thanks to

Nesta Alexander
Andrea Benedetti
Alice Bertolazzo
Stefania Bisaglia
Beatriz Blanco
Aoife Brady
Mary Busick
Caroline Campbell
Maria Laura Chiacchio
Jorge Coll
Michele Coppola
Alessandro Coscia
Angelo Crespi
Beatrice Cristini
Noemia d'Amico
Anna De Angelis
Stefano Del Lungo
Antonio Ernesto Denunzio
Giovanni Maria de' Spuches
Anastasia Diaz della Vittoria
  Pallavicini
Patricia Fernández Lorenzo
Antonio Fonzi
Francesca Franciolini
Eleonora Fusco
Valentina Gemignani
Cinzia Guglielmi
Max Hollein
Camilla Iacometti
Cristina Intelisano
Tim Knox
Raffaella Lanino
Eric M. Lee
Luana Lovisetto
Alberto Magni
Martina Massarelli
Gianmarco Mazzi
Martina Mian
Fabrizio Moretti
Agnese Murrali
Mariella Nuzzo
Nicoletta Odescalchi
Massimo Osanna
Federica Maria Papi
Luigi Pomponio
Dario Porcini

Daniela Porro
Sara Pozzato
Valentina Rosetta
Chiara Rostagno
Eugenia Rumi
Xavier F. Salomon
Salvador Salort-Pons
Livia Sanminiatelli Branca
Eike Schmidt
Benedetta Scialanga
Samantha Sizemore
Michelle Smith
Guillermo Solana
Jill Thompson
Simone Verde
Madeleine Whicheloe
Stephan Wolohojian
Julian Zugazagoitia

For the loan of the *Flagellation*
we would like to thank the
Patrimonio del Fondo Edifici
di Culto, administered by
the Direzione Centrale degli
affari dei culti, and for the
administration of the Fondo
edifici di culto of the Ministry
of the Interior, on the occasion
of the 40th anniversary this year
of its establishment.

To speak of Michelangelo Merisi da Caravaggio as one of the greatest masters
of painting goes without saying. It is enough to leaf through any art history manual
to reconstruct in detail the aesthetic and cultural revolution that is unanimously
attributed, at the turn of the seventeenth century, to the genius of Caravaggio.
But the *Caravaggio 2025* exhibition, brilliantly staged at the Gallerie Nazionali di
Arte Antica in Palazzo Barberini, between 7 March and 6 July 2025, takes us further,
telling us something more about the power and modernity of the great Lombard artist.
And it has done so by proposing an original and ambitious exhibition itinerary that for
the first time has brought together an extraordinary number of autograph paintings
and unpublished masterpieces from all over the world, to one of the symbolic places that
is the very embodiment of the connection between Caravaggio and the city of Rome.
The project was made possible thanks to the generous loans from some of the most
prestigious museums in the world, not to mention the contribution of Intesa Sanpaolo,
which has long distinguished itself for its commitment to the world of culture, with
programmes for the restoration and recovery, protection and enhancement of Italy's
artistic heritage.
Caravaggio 2025 presents to the general public an authentic Caravaggio, "at his purest",
to cite the words of Francesca Cappelletti, curator of the exhibition together with
Maria Cristina Terzaghi and Thomas Clement Salomon.
It is a previously unseen Caravaggio such as the *Portrait of Maffeo Barberini*, a work
from a private collection, loaned for the first time; it is a 'rediscovered' Caravaggio
such as the autograph *Ecce Homo* which came to light in 2021; and it is a Caravaggio
that 'returns home', with many of his masterpieces dispersed around the world that
have arranged to meet in Palazzo Barberini, offering new perspectives and suggesting
new points of discussion. Suffice it to mention, above all, the *Saint Catherine of
Alexandria*, from the Thyssen-Bornemisza Museum in Madrid exhibited alongside
the *Martha and Mary Magdalene* from the Detroit Institute of Arts and the *Judith
with the Head of Holophernes* from Palazzo Barberini: three paintings that Merisi
painted using the same model.
With its collection of 'Caravaggisti', the largest in the world, Palazzo Barberini could
not but be the ideal setting in which to bring together and rediscover the immense
innovations introduced by the Lombard painter, who, centuries later, continues
to inspire us and all contemporary art.
The undertaking was a courageous one, also because it was accompanied by a particular
historical sensitivity, evident in the reference to 2025, the year of the Jubilee, and in
the decision not to exhibit works housed in churches, thus leaving to the visitor
the honour and the responsibility of continuing the Caravaggio itinerary within
the broader cultural context of the city.
An unsurpassed 'master of light', Caravaggio found in Rome the thread of a great revolt
against Mannerism and its stale and backward-looking ideals. In opposition to a by
now exhausted Humanism, which had long persisted in the representation of the human
figure as an abstract aspiration, Caravaggio chose to look at men and things with fresh,
disenchanted eyes, and at the same time at life, its beauty and its truth.
The catalogue that follows, bringing together the themes and motifs that inspired
the exhibition, is a fitting fulfilment of what is an impressive and preeminently
successful cultural project.

ALESSANDRO GIULI
Minister of Culture

THOMAS CLEMENT
SALOMON
*Gallerie Nazionali
di Arte Antica,
Palazzo Barberini*

Artist at the heart of European figurative culture whose pictorial revolution
and overwhelming humanity have taken on a mythical character, Caravaggio
is central to the collections of the Gallerie Nazionali di Arte Antica in Rome.
True pride of place in the Galleries goes to the *Judith with the Head of Holophernes*,
a capital work, archetype for dozens of representations of the macabre biblical subject,
and the last painting by Caravaggio to be acquired by the Italian State in 1971.
No less important are the *Saint John the Baptist* in the Corsini Collection,
the *Saint Francis in Meditation*, and also the splendid *Narcissus*, attributed to
Caravaggio since 1913, when Roberto Longhi rediscovered it in the home of art historian
Paolo d'Ancona, and the attribution of which has long wavered between Caravaggio
and Giovanni Antonio Galli known as Spadarino.
The two sites of Palazzo Barberini and the Galleria Corsini also house the richest
collection of paintings in the world by Caravaggio's followers—the 'Caravaggeschi'.
Over a hundred works painted in Rome between 1600 and 1630 by Orazio Gentileschi,
Giovanni Baglione, Simon Vouet, Valentin de Boulogne and Giuseppe de Ribera,
among the most renowned painters who drawing inspiration from Caravaggio's
stylistic revolution, reinterpreted it in their own works.
Fifteen years after the last exhibition dedicated to Caravaggio in Rome (Scuderie
del Quirinale), the project we are presenting here today stems from the research
and scientific discoveries of recent years, with the intention of sharing the results
with scholars and the general public.
The Gallerie Nazionali, which I have had the honour of directing for just over a year,
cannot ignore the fact that they are at the forefront of studies dedicated to the work
of the artist, as demonstrated with the first 'historic' exhibition of what Longhi called
Caravaggio's "real Maffeo Barberini", which—for the first time, sixty years
after its rediscovery—has been on display in recent months in the Sala Paesaggi
of Palazzo Barberini, as a preview for this exhibition.
It will be possible to compare this rediscovered *Portrait of Maffeo Barberini*
in the exhibition display with other examples of Caravaggio's rare portraits,
such as the *Knight of Malta* from Palazzo Pitti and the 'other' *Portrait of Maffeo
Barberini* from the Corsini Collection, the attribution of which sees scholars divided.
Another unprecedented loan is the *Ecce Homo* recently rediscovered in Spain,
and until now exhibited at the Prado Museum. There are few exhibitions dedicated
to the titans of art history that can boast as many as two recently rediscovered
paintings exhibited for the first time within a conspicuous number of autograph works,
especially when by Caravaggio, a painter too often dragged into the limelight with
unfounded attributions.
Another objective of the exhibition is to present and bring back to Palazzo Barberini
the masterpieces that belonged to the collections of the papal family, such as
the *Musicians* from the Metropolitan Museum in New York and the *Cardsharps*
now in Texas (Fort Worth, Kimbell Museum), and above all the *Saint Catherine
of Alexandria* which is now in Madrid, a painting that formerly graced the Baroque
palace before entering the Thyssen-Bornemisza collection in the 1930s; it is a work
that one had dreamed for decades to see once more in Rome; included in the catalogue
of the 2010 exhibition, to which, in the end, it did not come. This unprecedented loan
moreover allows us an to make an extraordinary comparison with the Detroit Institute
of Art's *Martha and Mary Magdalene* and the *Judith*, that is all three works that feature

the same model, perhaps *Fillide Melandroni*, whose portrait, painted by Caravaggio, was lost in Berlin during the war.

Building on this solid and rigorous scientific approach and research, the museum is at the forefront of the continuation of Caravaggio studies. The exhibition was conceived with this in mind: an important opportunity to study, research, and share the work, not only of one of Europe's greatest artists, but of one who is today considered a mythical figure by the community at large, an outstanding artist whose paintings succeed in resonating in our present, in which time slips away from us with ever-increasing speed.

This exhibition has been specially conceived for the Universal Jubilee of 2025, an important date for the Capital in which the Ministry of Culture cannot fail but play a central role with such an ambitious project offering citizens and guests of Rome the opportunity to admire and study over twenty paintings by Caravaggio, some of them from remote locations in the United States, not easily accessible even for the most affluent travellers.

With his stark realism, dramatic lighting, and unparalleled emotional depth, Caravaggio, through action, knew how to portray the deepest facets of the human soul, from innocence to violence, from hope to despair. His paintings succeed today, for those to whom they speak, in bringing to a standstill this hastening of the time in which we live.

It is in this spirit of service to the Gallerie Nazionali di Arte Antica, to Rome, and to Italian culture that we have worked with great determination and passion over the last few months to bring to fruition this great project which, only a year ago, seemed impossible to many.

What we hope will be the most important exhibition in Italy in 2025, a complex project of international standing, would not have been possible without the fundamental support of the General Directorate for Museums and the Galleria Borghese. I deeply thank the Director General, Professor Massimo Osanna, for having believed in this exhibition and in the rehanging project of the Gallerie Nazionali; the Director of the Galleria Borghese, Professor Francesca Cappelletti, curator of this exhibition, a partner in the project who has supported it with enormous generosity through the loan of three works and with a substantial contribution both from a scientific and an organisational point of view; Professor Maria Cristina Terzaghi, also curator of the exhibition and editor of this catalogue, with whom we have shared a great deal of work over the past months, overcoming considerable difficulties; all of my esteemed colleagues in the Gallerie who have worked with laudable ambition on this exhibition, brilliantly overcoming the obstacles, in particular Alessandro Cosma (project manager), Claudia Sarpi, Michela Ulivi, Paola Guarnera, Dario Aureli, Gabriele Mari, Marco Corsi, Cinzia Ammannato, Simona Baldi, Chiara Di Marco, Cristina Lio, Francesco Canto, Emanuel Tarquini, Giuliana Forti, and Diego Giacomelli.

The ambitious nature of this project could only have had the support of a principal sponsor such as Intesa Sanpaolo, testifying to a true synergy between the public and private sectors, and for which I would like to profoundly thank Michele Coppola, who believed in and supported the project; we could not have had a better partner.

GIAN MARIA
GROS-PIETRO
President
Intesa Sanpaolo

GIOVANNI BAZOLI
President Emeritus
Intesa Sanpaolo

Intesa Sanpaolo, through its contribution and the loan of a fundamental work, has participated in the realisation of this prestigious exhibition project, which will without any doubt have a great impact, given the enormous popularity of the Lombard master who is here being displayed for the admiration of the international public present in Rome during the Jubilee Year.

The return of Caravaggio to the Capital, after the 2010 exhibition at the Scuderie del Quirinale, is a not-to-be-missed opportunity, for its quality and the importance of the works arriving from museums all over the world, but in particular for the presence of two recently rediscovered masterpieces: the moving *Ecce Homo*, which reappeared in Spain and is now in the Prado, and the *Portrait of Maffeo Barberini*, future Pope Urban VIII, which has been on display since last November in Palazzo Barberini, the venue for this present exhibition.

Exceptionally, we have granted the loan of the *Martyrdom of Saint Ursula*, convinced of the excellence of an initiative that will contribute to broadening the knowledge of Caravaggio's genius, also thanks to the recognised authority of the curators—Francesca Cappelletti, Maria Cristina Terzaghi, Thomas Clement Salomon—and of all the scholars involved.

The *Martyrdom of Saint Ursula* became part of the collection of the Banca Commerciale Italiana in 1972 as a work by Mattia Preti. Its real identity was only recognised a few years later, thanks to a complex restoration, and was definitively ascertained and confirmed also through documentary evidence. It is the last work by the hand of Caravaggio, painted just over a month before his tragic death.

The masterpiece is normally exhibited in the new Gallerie d'Italia in Naples and has become the image that identifies our collections: in a certain sense it is the symbol of the Culture Project that for decades has seen Intesa Sanpaolo's involvement at the forefront of the protection and promotion of the immense artistic heritage of our country.

In the four museum locations of the Gallerie d'Italia, in Milan, Naples, Turin and Vicenza, important collections belonging to the bank are on permanent display to the public, and temporary exhibitions are periodically organised, inspired by the *genius loci* of the cities that host them. All this in the belief that we should go beyond the promotional and ephemeral logic of the event, to offer the public opportunities for cultural enrichment.

In the name of Caravaggio we hope to unite Rome and Naples in the minds of those who visit the exhibition. These are the two cities that preserve his greatest works and to which the artist's extraordinary path, both artistic and human, was particularly linked.

After all, it may be that perhaps when the artist was painting the *Martyrdom of Saint Ursula* in Naples, on the run and physically exhausted, he had a premonition that this painting would be his pictorial testament. This is how the painting appears to us in its tormented and dramatic religiosity, but also in the absolute originality with which the artist has depicted a subject often represented in the history of art. The work, as with many other paintings by Caravaggio, involves the spectator both in its formal elements and in its spiritual message. It is a kind of descent into darkness, because of the power with which the increasingly tragic and current theme of martyrdom has been portrayed, but it is also an ascent towards the light.

The *Martyrdom of Saint Ursula* brings the exhibition to a close, an exhibition which allows visitors to admire an exceptional sequence of masterpieces.
In this high-level cultural initiative, Intesa Sanpaolo is working alongside the Gallerie Nazionali di Arte Antica in Rome, the Galleria Borghese and the Directorate General of Museums of the Ministry of Culture, confirming its constant presence alongside public institutions in support of our country's historical and artistic heritage.

CONTENTS

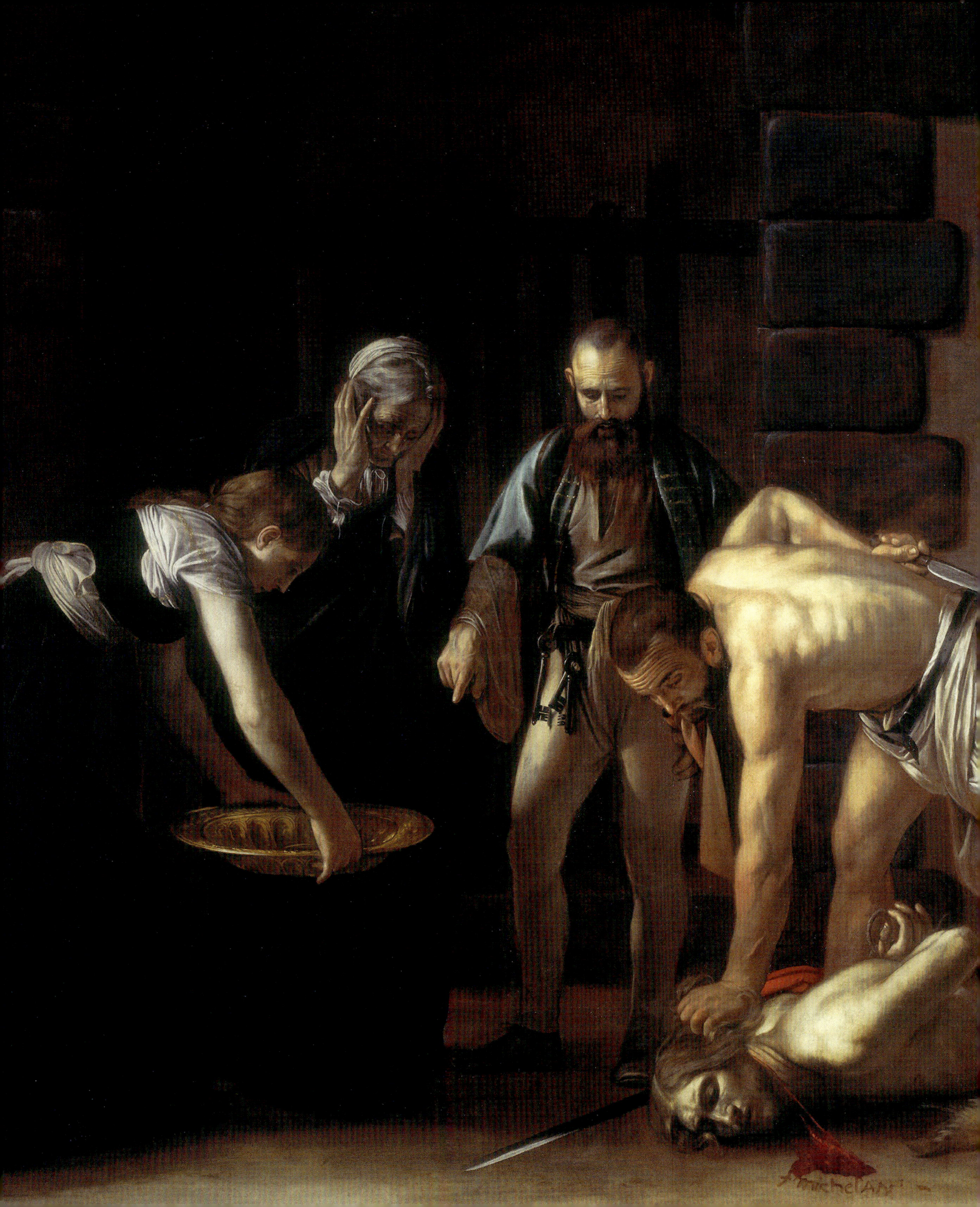

Keith Christiansen

ENCOUNTERING THE ART OF CARAVAGGIO

In the 1980s I was so fortunate as to be part of the international team organizing *The Age of Caravaggio*, held successively in 1985 at The Metropolitan Museum of Art and the Museo Nazionale di Capodimonte.[1] What a formative experience! I had the good fortune to meet virtually all the major Caravaggio scholars and had the enormous privilege of working closely with Mina Gregori, the author of the entries on Caravaggio. Her work, built on the legacy of Roberto Longhi, with whom she had studied and to whose memory the exhibition was dedicated, opened new ways of thinking about the artist and his paintings. It's difficult to recall how controversial many of her ideas were and the enormous contribution she made. To take but two examples, her insistence on Caravaggio's authorship of the ceiling in Cardinal del Monte's camerino [fig. 2], today universally considered a key work for understanding the Lombard painter and his relationship with his major patron and supporter, met with loudly voiced skepticism, while her no less provocative arguments for the *Toothpuller* [fig. 3]—a work I unhesitatingly accept as a late work by the master—still inspires controversy.[2] Since then, study of Caravaggio—now practically an industry—has been further transformed by archival discoveries and the technical examination of his paintings.[3] Moreover, the data of his increasingly documented biography has provided fodder for multiple popular biographies, some of dubious credibility.[4] The catalyst for this intense interest—by both the public and by scholars of the Seicento—was the landmark exhibition *Mostra del Caravaggio e dei caravaggeschi* held in the Palazzo Reale in Milan in 1951. Organized by Roberto Longhi, who also wrote the introductory essay and the following year came out with his influential monograph,[5] the exhibition resulted in

[fig. 1]
The Beheading of Saint John the Baptist, 1608, detail, St. John's Co-Cathedral, Valletta (Malta)

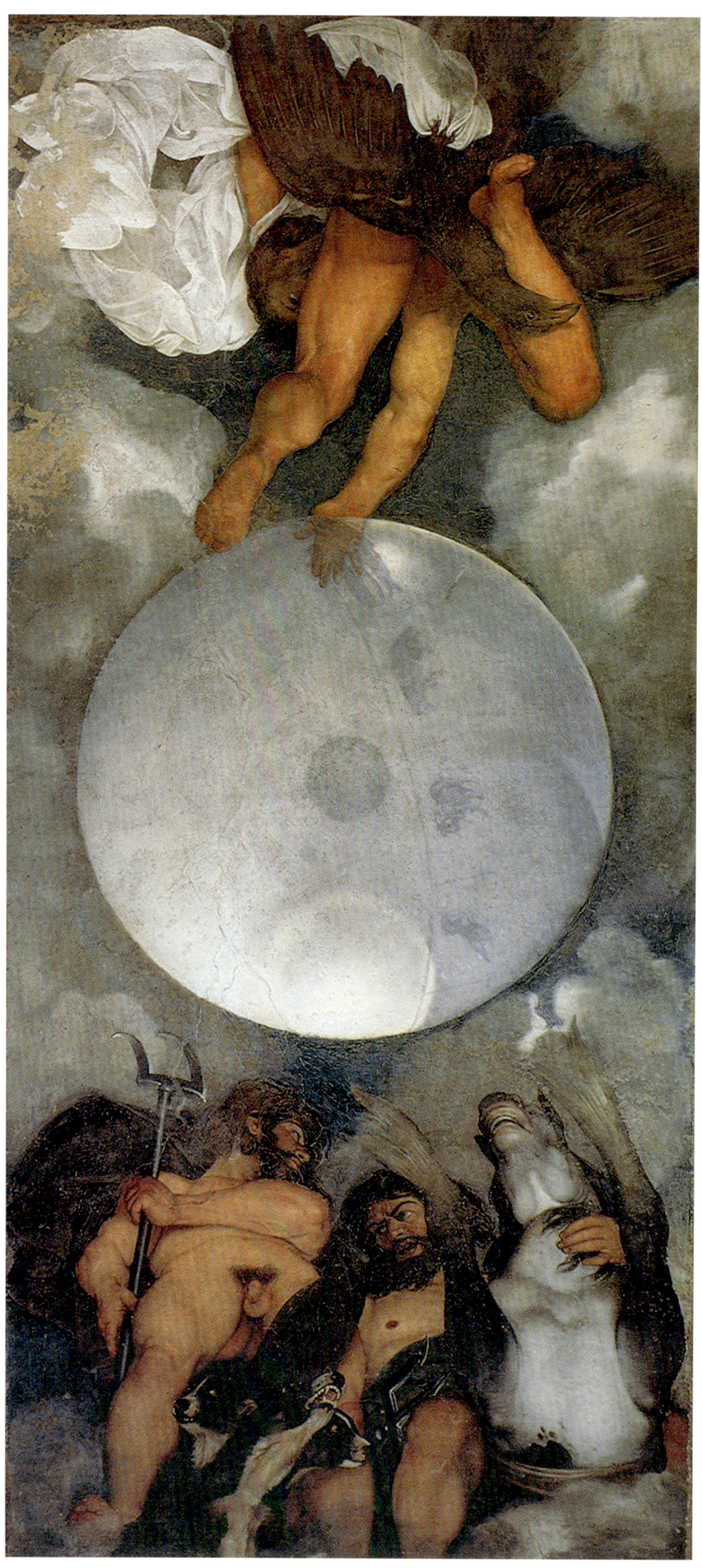

[fig. 2]
Jupiter, Neptune and Pluto,
c. 1598–1599
Ceiling of the Camerino,
Villa Boncompagni Ludovisi,
Rome

Keith Christiansen

an explosion of interest that has burgeoned during the last seventy-five years, to the point that Caravaggio has become the most studied of all so-called Old Masters. It's difficult to recall just how much has changed since the early years of the century. Had you been a tourist in Rome in 1909 with your latest edition of a Baedecker guidebook in hand and decided to visit the church of San Luigi dei Francesi, you would have been directed as the highpoint not to Caravaggio's canvases in the Contarelli Chapel but Domenichino's fresco cycle of the life of Saint Cecilia, which from the moment it was completed in 1615 asserted a resurgent Raphaelesque classicism and, it is well to remind ourselves, commanded almost universal admiration.[6] Suffice it to say that in 1993, in the 8th edition of *Touring Club Italiano*, mention is made of Domenichino's cycle but attention focuses on the Contarelli Chapel. It was in no small part through Roberto Longhi's influential articles written between 1913 and 1951 that this transformation gained traction and Caravaggio came to be viewed as the fountainhead of modernity.[7] But it's well to remember that this new status, embraced by both scholars and an increasingly fascinated public, was not accepted by everyone.

One of the most puzzled observers of the artist's newfound popularity was Bernard Berenson, who at 86 years of age was a holdover from an earlier era—that of Walter Pater's aesthetic vision of the Renaissance. In response to the 1951 exhibition and

[fig. 3]
Toothpuller, c. 1608–1610, Palazzo Pitti, Galleria Palatina, Florence

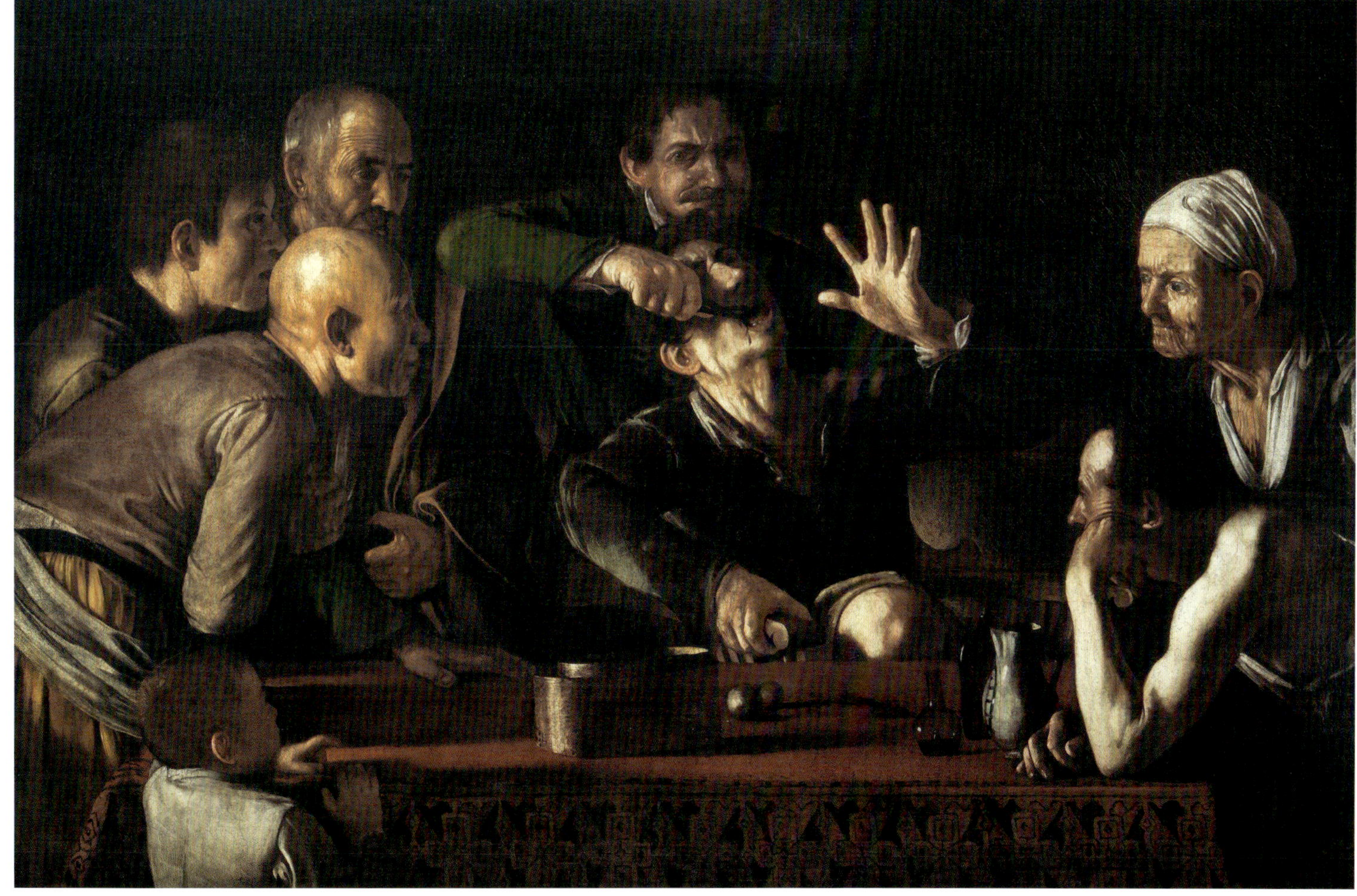

its enormous popularity, Berenson published what even then must have seemed an anachronistic book titled *Del Caravaggio, delle sue incongruenze, e della sua fama*.[8] It's not read anymore, both because its premise that Caravaggio was a flawed artist runs counter to our current views, and because there are now so many books on the artist that, quite frankly, who has time for the ruminations of an old-fashioned critic lamenting the taste of a younger generation? Yet some of the ideas expressed by this out-of-step critic are still worth reflecting upon. Above all, what Berenson identified as Caravaggio's "incongruenze": figures or elements in his paintings that, as with so many seventeenth-century critics, from Giulio Mancini to Giovan Pietro Bellori, seemed to him arbitrary, indecorous, or out of place. After judiciously distributing his guarded praise on certain paintings and elaborating on his reservations about others, Berenson went on to pose a question still worth thinking about: "Why are . . . writers today so excited over Caravaggio and not over the most compendious exponent of his age, Rubens, or over such an exemplar of what was most distinguished in that same period as Velázquez? The reason, perhaps is simple enough. Neither of those geniuses lived a disorderly life; nor after a turbid, squalid, chequered career, died in his prime, and died sordidly. It is," Berenson declared, "the character and career of Caravaggio that attracts today, and not, I venture to suggest, his quality as an artist, and even less as a painter. The fallacy of most men of letters, philosophers and critics, is that they will read the private life of the artist into the kind and quality of his art."[9]

This essay is aimed against the reduction of Caravaggio's enormous artistry and his achievement as a painter—something that Berenson, not unlike his British contemporary Roger Fry, were reluctant to acknowledge—to a reflection of the external facts of his biography.[10] Not an easy task, for with what other pre-nineteenth century artist are we so persistently encouraged to read his biography into his work? The only serious contender is Artemisia Gentileschi, who rose to popularity and today overshadows even the singular achievement of her father, as a sort of female Caravaggio: rebellious to the conventions of her day and prefiguring the cause of feminism.[11] What we encounter in both cases is the confusion of realism as a polemical style—a means of questioning the status quo as well as establishing a reputation—and realism as the language of auto-biography.[12]

That said, Caravaggio's life and art do sometimes seem to intersect, and the one unquestionably informs the other. But not in the ways popular biography would have it. Temperament and character—as well as sexual orientation—certainly informed Caravaggio's art in many of the same ways as they did his experience of the world. But there is no evidence that Caravaggio thought of his art as a vehicle for self-expression. Nor is there evidence of an artist obsessed with self-examination, as with Rembrandt, in whose unparalleled series of self-portraits we seem to see his evolving sense of himself as an artist and as a human being. By contrast, even Caravaggio's depiction of *David with the Head of Goliath* (Galleria Nazionale di Villa Borghese; cat. 17)—a work often interpreted as a confessional, psychologically revealing, tragic self-portrait done at the end of his career, following the laceration of his face—belongs to a poetic convention: the lover as victim of his beloved, in this case a young man identifiable as Cecco di Caravaggio, himself to become a talented painter.[13] When artists employ a realist style, we are too easily tempted simply to read their art in terms of biography. Yet I would suggest that it is not so much Caravaggio's life that we see inscribed into his art but, rather, the artist's deepened sense of the tragic dimension of life—which

Keith Christiansen

is quite another thing. It is this that makes his art so fascinating, and at times seemly so modern.

When Caravaggio arrived in Rome from Milan—an event now placed in 1595 instead of 1592[14]—he was an artist with no reputation and few enough connections. He found a congested and competitive art world unlike anything he had experienced in Milan and struggled to support himself, let alone establish a reputation. The legacy of the past—of Raphael and Michelangelo and the Antique—was overwhelming; indeed, inescapable. It had been embraced by Caravaggio's contemporary, Annibale Carracci, despite the fact that Annibale was famous when he transferred to Rome to work for the Farnese. In his early work in Bologna, he had promoted a naturalism based on Lombard and Venetian traditions that in many respects was as radical as Caravaggio's, and he had received some of the same criticism levelled at him by his older colleagues as had Caravaggio. Yet once in Rome, he embraced the illustrious legacy of the great figures of the Renaissance and Antiquity as well as the informed opinions about what serious, or high, art is and what it should aim to achieve, as pointedly explicated by one of the Caravaggio's admirers, Vincenzo Giustiniani, in his *Discorso sulla pittura*.[15] We should also remember that apart from the reigning conventions, increasing importance also attached to art as a vehicle for communicating the truths of Catholicism, as articulated by the Council of Trent. By contrast with Annibale, and in an informed and boldly provocative way, Caravaggio created a naturalistic style that looked to break down the aesthetic assumptions of Renaissance painting and the distinctions habitually made between an idealizing, artistic fiction and the world of everyday experience.

Caravaggio's recorded pronouncements on art make his intentions quite clear. For example, Marchese Vincenzo Giustiniani, who owned fifteen works by the artist, records in his *Discorso* that Caravaggio once proclaimed that it took as much work to make a good painting of flowers as one of figures. The painting this sophisticated collector owned of a *Lute Player* (The State Hermitage Museum, St. Petersburg, fig. 11 on p. 38) would seem an illustration of this declaration. Another contemporary, the painter-biographer Giovanni Baglione, states that Caravaggio declared that a painting he had done of a vase of flowers for his protector and patron, Cardinal Francesco Maria del Monte, "was the most beautiful thing he had ever done."[16] The paradox is that Caravaggio had no intention of being sidelined as a painter of genre scenes and still lives—works he painted to gain a foothold in the art market. Rather, he aspired to be a master of grand, figural compositions. So we must understand these statements as polemical darts aimed at dismantling those hierarchies of art that ascribed more importance to complex figural compositions, less to landscapes and still lives, and still less to portraiture, which was viewed as involving the mere, craftsman-like ability to copy what was before your eyes—the very system Caravaggio was accused of embracing. Still-life painting, too, was thought to reveal no particular critical faculty or ability to reconfigure visual data. To these comments from sources close to Caravaggio we can add the report of the informed and influential but highly disapproving Bellori, who tells the story (unquestionably embellished) of how, "when shown the most famous statues by Phidias and Glicon as things worthy of study, he had no other response than to stretch his hand towards a multitude of men, ascerting that Nature had provided quite enough masters."[17] Bellori's was a critical judgment that encompassed not only an artistic hierarchy but a social one tracing its origins to Aristotle. To these comments we should add the much-cited one of the northern painter-biographer Karl van Mander, written as early as 1603. "[Caravaggio] holds that all works are nothing but bagatelles, child's work, or trifles, whatever their subject and by whomever painted, unless they be done and painted after life and nothing could be good and nothing better than to follow Nature."[18] This was, of course, heresy to most Roman artists.

It has long been recognized that Caravaggio's painting of *Saint John the Baptist* (Rome, Musei Capitolini, fig. 3 on p. 105), commissioned by a member of the Mattei family, is a provocative response to one of Michelangelo's much admired "ignudi" on the Sistine ceiling. Taking a paradigm of high style, Caravaggio inverted its poetics and gave it a low life treatment by insisting on the figure as a posed studio model (as did Velázquez decades later in his depiction of Mars). There is, in other words, an intentional "incongruity" (to use Berenson's term) between the compositional source and its naturalistic treatment; an incongruity exploited to undercut the idealizing premise of Michelangelo's art and land a broadside at Renaissance aesthetics. *Épater le bourgeois?* To a degree, yes. One contemporary, the expatriate Italian living in Spain, Vincencio Carducho, had this to say of Caravaggio: "Has anyone else managed to paint as successfully as this evil genius, who worked naturally, almost without precepts, without doctrine, without study, but only with the strength of his talent, with nothing but nature before him, which he simply copied in his amazing way? . . . Thus this anti-Michelangelo, with his showy and superficial imitation, his stunning manner, and liveliness, has been able to persuade such a great number and variety of people that his is good painting, and his method and doctrine the true ones, that they have turned their backs on the true way of achieving eternity. . ."[19] I don't think there could be a more eloquent encapsulation of the impact Caravaggio had on his contemporaries, both amateurs and painters, and the response it elicited from conservative artists like Carducho. Quite literally, he created a new arena for artistic achievement outside the parameters of Renaissance aesthetics and he did this by engaging in a persistent, polemical dialogue with the most admired artists and ideas in Rome. His achievement would have been impossible without the expanding Roman art market, which provided a new means of establishing a reputation outside the prevailing system of patronage.[20] For artists of the next generation such as Ribera and Valentin, Caravaggio's example was crucial (during his ten years in Rome, Ribera established his fame without a single public commission in the city!). Indeed, I believe that all sorts of otherwise enigmatic aspects of Caravaggio's paintings carried out during his years in Rome gain urgency if we remember the polemical point Caravaggio makes over and over in them, each time with fresh insight and vigor and insistence: that painting must refer to the world around us rather than to a received tradition. Take, for example, those nude figures who occupy and frame the foreground of Caravaggio's *Martyrdom of Saint Matthew* [fig. 4]. They have been ingeniously interpreted by some scholars as neophytes: figures awaiting baptism in a pool at the foot of the altar.[21] This activity is not mentioned in the highly detailed contract for the painting, nor is the treatment of the baptismal pool—if that is what it is—very convincing from an architectural or antiquarian point of view. Moreover, the nude figures don't seem to have been planned in the first version of the composition—at least so far as can be made out from x-rays of the existing canvas. And while the identification of the figures as neophytes would account for their nudity, it does not explain the impassivity of the two onlooking figures in the righthand side of the composition, in which Caravaggio lays emphasis on beauty

Keith Christiansen

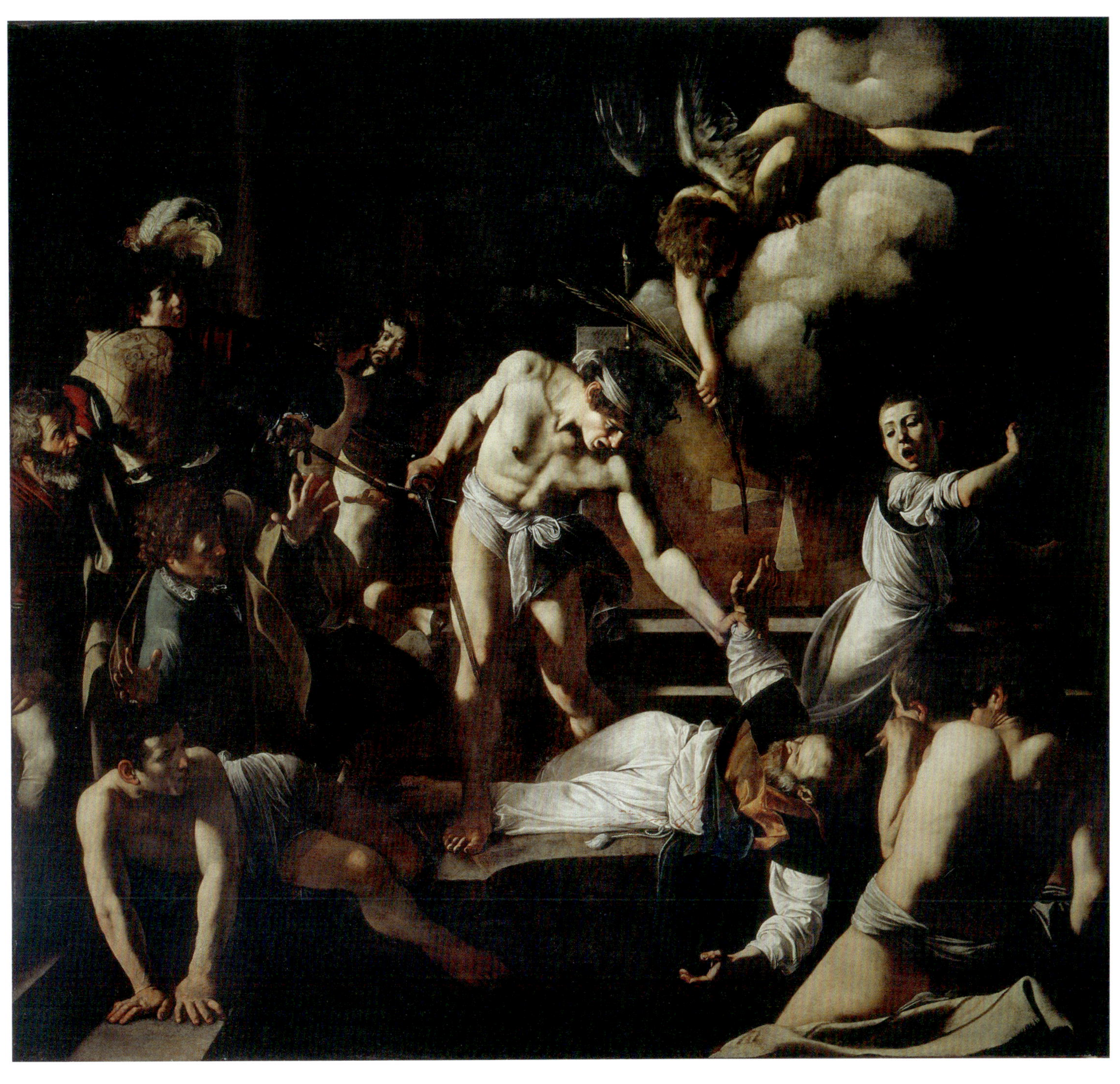

[fig. 4]
Martyrdom of Saint Matthew, 1599–1600, Church of San Luigi dei Francesi, Contarelli Chapel, Rome

of posture and body, recalling the model set by Michelangelo's *ignudi* on the Sistine ceiling, where nude male figures frame the Biblical scenes of the Creation. Through engravings these *ignudi* had become a central part of a young artist's training and the tradition of introducing nude or semi-nude figures to frame the foreground of a composition had become *de rigueur* in the sixteenth century. Here are just a few examples. Large figures in deshabille frame Simone Peterzano's fresco of *Christ Chasing the Money Changers from the Temple* on the counter-façade of San Maurizio Maggiore in Milan—the point of departure for Caravaggio's initial composition for the *Martyrdom of Saint Matthew*). In Taddeo Zuccari's fresco of *Christ presented to the People* in the Mattei Chapel of Santa Maria della Consolazione, we find quasi-nudes in the foreground that, significantly, have nothing to do with the narrative. Rather, they serve to enhance the composition as a work of art. The cycle dates from 1556. Not long before Caravaggio began work on the *Martyrdom of Saint Matthew*, Giovanni Baglione completed a fresco cycle in the church of Santa Maria dell'Orto in the Trastevere in which the principal action of the *Presentation of the Virgin in the Temple* has been pushed into the background while in the foreground an elaborately dressed dandy gives alms to two semi-nude beggars. Later, in the chapel adjacent to the Contarelli's in San Luigi dei Francesi, Baglione had an opportunity to compete directly with Caravaggio by including a nude figure in an *Adoration of the Magi*, the figure's placement exposing perfectly the intention to challenge his rival. When we recall that the paintings in the Contarelli Chapel constituted the first major public commission of Caravaggio's—his entrée onto the Roman stage—I think we must allow that he took the opportunity to display his mastery of just those parts of *Arte* that were most appreciated by artists and connoisseurs—and to undercut that expectation through his radical painting "dal naturale". We should also remember that the pose of Saint Matthew's executioner lunging forward with an upraised arm is derived from a print designed by Raphael of the *Massacre of the Innocents*, while that of the fleeing acolyte, who looks back, his arms visually describing an arched cry, is inspired—in reverse—from a print copying a famous painting by Titian. In other words, these nude figures at once assert Caravaggio's understanding of *Arte* and critique the idealizing style of revered artists in a way that puts forward a new credo of realistic drama.

The *Martydom of Saint Matthew* was unveiled in the summer of 1600. By the time Caravaggio fled the city six years later, this sort of persistent challenging of established artistic conventions was no longer the primary driver of Caravaggio's poetics of painting.[22] Gone are those elegantly posed figures that recall an aesthetics of *bellezza* yet are treated in an insistently naturalistic style, such as the back-viewed angel of the *Rest on the Flight into Egypt* (Rome, Galleria Doria Pamphilj, fig. 5) or those astonishing foreshortenings and "in your face" displays of bravura painting, such as one finds in the great Mattei *Supper at Emmaus* in the National Gallery, London [fig. 6], where the sleeve of one of the disciples has a conspicuous tear at the point of maximum projection, the gestures explode outwards, and the basket of fruit protrudes precariously over the edge of the table. This extraordinary painting is plainly a work that was meant to astonish—and provoke. Painting as a Bellorian fiction, appealing above all to the intellect through a studied use of formal gesture and expression, is rejected in favor of painting as an emulation of temporal reality, appealing to the senses. Light is used not only dramatically but also descriptively to assert the physical reality of the objects and assert the destabilizing moment of recognition. The overripe fruit

Keith Christiansen

(Bellori objected to the "out-of-season grapes, figs and pomegranates"[23]) testifies to the corruptibility of matter, while Christ is provocatively shown with sensually thick lips and full, beardless cheeks. Christ is sometimes shown beardless on early Christian sarcophagi, but I think it is wrong to interpret Caravaggio's figure in terms of Christian antiquarianism, as practiced in the circle of the great Oratorian Cardinal Baronio. Precisely this detail had been included by Michelangelo in his *Last Judgment* in the Sistine Chapel, and it had been singled out for censure by Counter-Reformation ecclesiastics and critics such as Giovanni Andrea Gilio in his 1564 *Dialogo degli errori e degli abusi dei pittori*. I believe we must understand Caravaggio's image as an intentional breech of decorum and a baiting of traditionalists (how his sophisticated patrons, the Mattei, must have enjoyed this polemic of naturalism—just as they had relished the undercutting of idealist principles in his *Saint John the Baptist*, now in the Musei Capitolini). When seventeenth-century critics refer to Caravaggio's extravagant or twisted imagination, they were not alluding to someone who introduced theologically arcane references in his work. As his fame grew and he was lauded as "egregius in Urbe Pictor", as he is called in the contract for his work in the Cerasi Chapel of Santa Maria del Popolo, Caravaggio allowed himself ever greater freedom to experiment and by 1609 a patron in Palermo, Nicolao di Giacomo, specified that the four scenes of Christ's Passion that Caravaggio was to paint for him were to be "a capriccio del pittore"—that is, they were to manifest Caravaggio's marvelous powers of invention—his "twisted brain"—and his ability to produce works that defied expectations, which is a more complex idea than the mere undercutting of tradition.[24]

Following his flight from Rome in 1606, the transformation in Caravaggio's approach to critiquing tradition is apparent in that extraordinary remake of the theme of the *Supper at Emmaus* [cat. 17] that he painted to be sent back to the papal city for sale during his convalescence at Zagarolo, southeast of Rome. How noisy and dissonant the earlier painting seems by comparison! I remember the impression made when the two pictures hung in adjacent rooms at the Metropolitan Museum in 1985, and then, again, in the 2004–2005 exhibition *Caravaggio. L'ultimo tempo 1606–1610* in Naples and London. In the Mattei picture everything is exclamation and dazzling, tour-de-force painting that contemporaries associated with the artist's radical naturalism. In the later, Brera, version there is a new, laconic use of the brush to create a pervasive and penetrating quality of meditative quietness, with gestures used in a sparing but ultimately more eloquent fashion. Emphasis is on psychological probity rather than dramatic moment. And, of course, Christ is now bearded. The very terms of Caravaggio's art seem to have undergone a transformation. Naturalistic painting as a polemical tool is discarded in favor of exploring the psychological dimension of a particular story. It is worth noting that in 1606, Caravaggio was thirty-five, not in his rebellious twenties. He still did not have a handle on his temper (he never did), but he seems to have acquired some of that intellectual distance that is born of experience.

The indicators of the new direction in Caravaggio's art are already present in his mature Roman paintings, but a new creative force was released following his flight from Rome in 1606, and this had less to do with any imagined remorse he felt over the killing of his tennis opponent Ranuccio Tomassoni—a remorse that is the invention of modern biographers—than to the entirely different situation Caravaggio discovered in Naples. In Rome he had fought hard to create a distinctive presence and become one of the principal players on a crowded stage. He was constantly on the alert to what other artists were doing and we know that he felt his reputation (what, in the hands of his critics, became notoriety) was in constant danger of being challenged. When the young and enormously talented Guido Reni painted an altarpiece—*The Crucifixion of Saint Peter* (Pinacoteca Vaticana)—that at once emulated Caravaggio's style and simultaneously critiqued it, the volatile Lombard wasted no time in confronting his Bolognese competitor in the street and challenging him to a duel.[25] To which the cool-minded Reni is reported to have replied that he had "come to Rome to paint—not to duel."[26] Reni went on to become the highest paid artist in Italy and in demand across Europe.

In Naples, Caravaggio encountered no comparable competition, and this new situation had a liberating effect, enabling him to de-polemicize his art and to profit in a new way from a tradition against which he had persistently railed but to which, in fact, he was deeply indebted. Increasingly, Caravaggio explores the psychological dimension of the subject of his paintings and to do this he increasingly employs the rhetorical devices of classical painting, though without the idealist aesthetic of an artist such as Poussin, who, after all, declared that Caravaggio had been born to destroy art. There is an increased clarity to his compositions and the use of formalized gesture as the conveyor of meaning. There is also a new sense of the importance of subordinating peripheral detail to achieve a greater concentration and expressive effect. It is in the post-Roman works that we feel the full justice of Longhi's observation, made as long ago as 1935: "It was precisely the ethical attitude towards man, his history, his myths that changed with Caravaggio."[27]

It is important to remember that in the years following his fight with Ranuccio Tomassoni on May 31, 1606, Caravaggio was neither abandoned by his high-placed friends nor undirected in his movements. He first took refuge on the Colonna estates southeast of Rome, where he convalesced. Then, by October, he moved on to Naples, where he was evidently provided with quarters by Costanza Colonna, widow of Francesco Sforza, the marquis of the artist's native town of Caravaggio and the employer of Caravaggio's father as majordomo and architect. She must have known Caravaggio when he was a boy and she remained a mainstay during these years.[28] Indeed, when Caravaggio died on a hot summer day in 1610, his last effects were returned to her Neapolitan residence, the Palazzo Carafa on the riviera di Chiaia. But well before then, the machinery had been set in motion to procure Caravaggio a papal pardon. Meanwhile, the artist did not have to look far for employment. Nor is there any indication that he attempted to maintain a low profile. He had arrived in Naples, which was under Spanish rule, a celebrated artist, and commissions poured in, not least for an altarpiece of the *Flagellation* for the church of San Domenico [cat. 21], delivered before he left the city in the summer of 1607. [29]

Perhaps more clearly than in the other works, especially the *Seven Acts of Mercy* [fig. 2 on p. 63], which required combining multiple, unrelated events within a relatively narrow picture field, the *Flagellation* reveals the direction of Caravaggio's art. Christ is shown bound to the column, assailed by three torturers, each of whom has been allotted a specific identity by the task he performs. One binds Christ to the column. Another grasps his hair with one hand while he prepares to strike with the other. The third, with his profile defining the foreground space in much the same way as one of the disciples in the Brera *Supper at Emmaus*, binds a scourge of twigs. In a fashion completely consonant with notions of *contrapposto*—that is, the principle of striking artistic contrasts—Caravaggio draws a distinction between the brutality of the torturers

Keith Christiansen

and the beauty of Christ, whose torso is surely based on an antique statue. Just how far he has traveled from his Lombard roots is perhaps best seen by comparing the picture to one painted some sixty years earlier by an artist whose works Caravaggio surely knew. The picture—actually a processional banner for a Franciscan confraternity—is by Girolamo Romanino (Metropolitan Museum of Art), and I am quite confident that Caravaggio saw this picture during his study years in northern Italy and was haunted by its expressive power as well as the balletic poses of the figures. But if this was so, how clearly he declares his Roman experience: indeed, his picture reads like a reformulation in a naturalistic vein of Sebastiano del Piombo's mural in San Pietro in Montorio, for which drawings were provided by Michelangelo, and it sets the stage for the extraordinary achievement of the greatest of the Caravaggisti, Ribera.

Caravaggio sailed from Naples to Malta in early July 1607, evidently with the help of Constanza Colonna and her son Fabrizio, who was himself a knight and captain general

Rest on the Flight into Egypt, c. 1597, Galleria Doria Pamphilj, Rome. Trust Doria Pamphilj

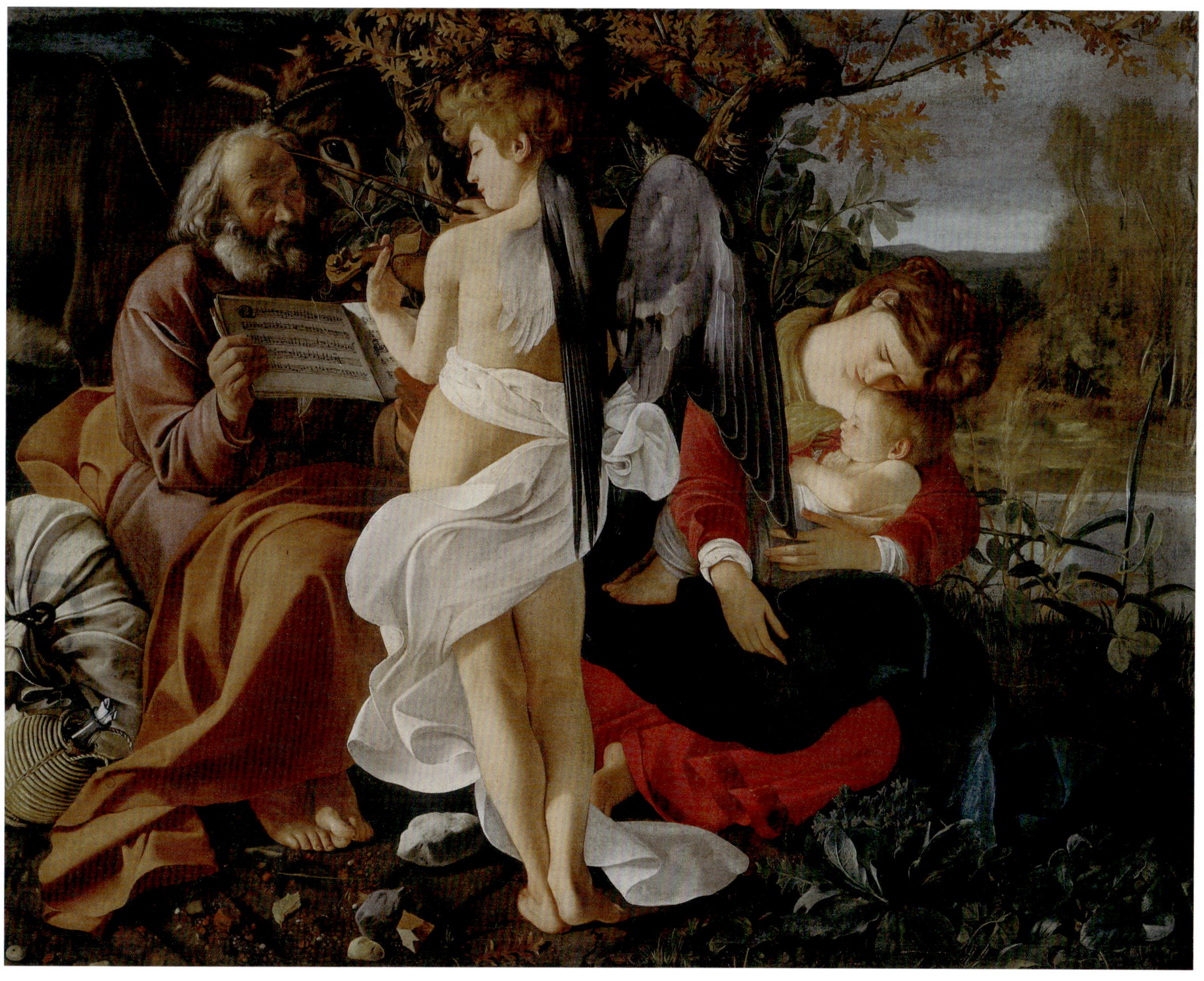

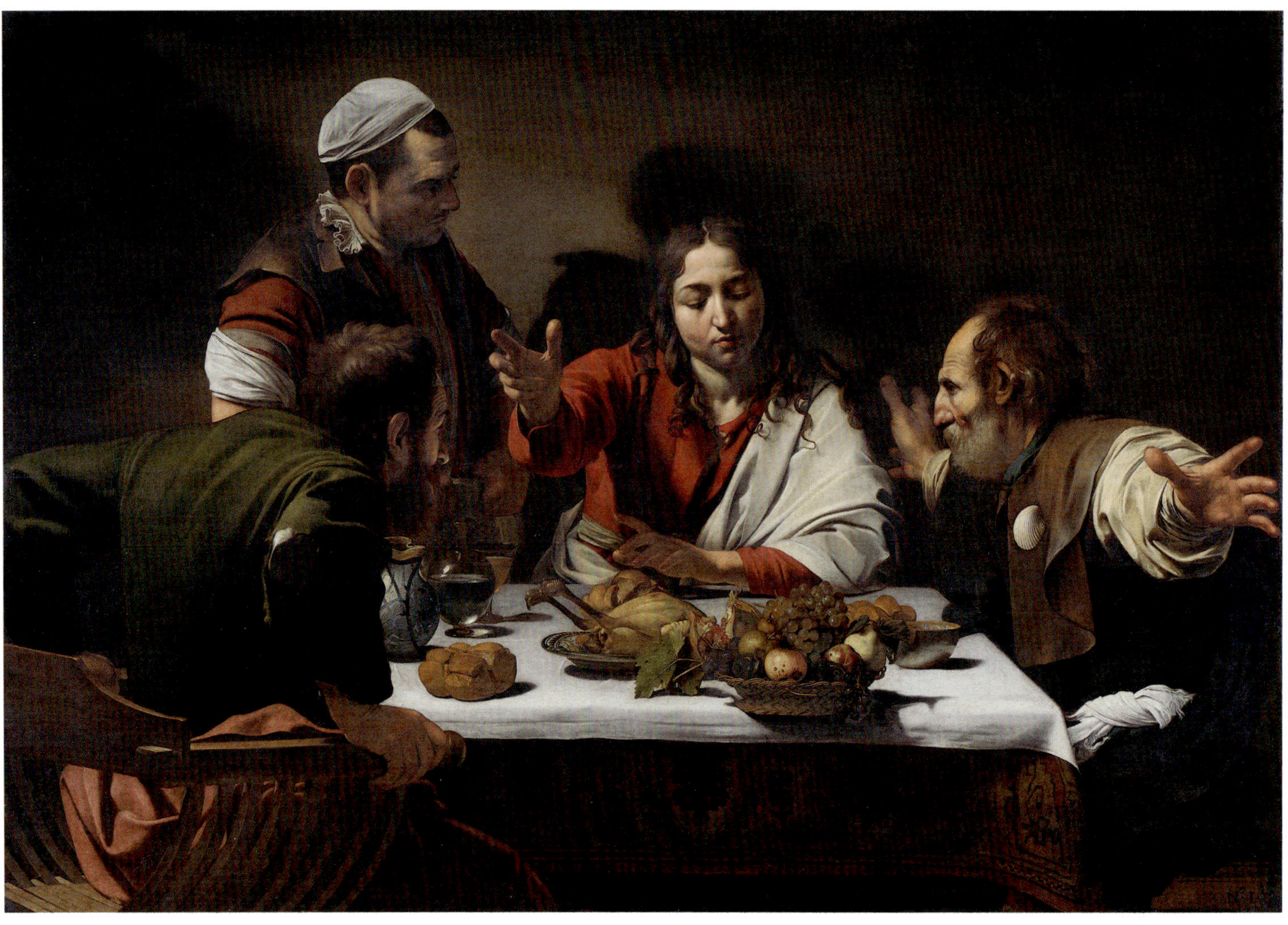

of the order's galleys from 22 August 1606. The move has all the earmarks of a pre-arranged step in the negotiations undertaken by several high-placed people to secure a pardon for Caravaggio. The object was clearly to have the painter knighted, which required papal permission and amounted to a tacit pardon for the crime that would normally have excluded him from membership. Caravaggio completed the mandatory year's residence and was admitted. The Grand Master, Alof de Wignacourt, whose portrait Caravaggio painted [fig. 9 on p. 114], had sent a letter of inquiry to the Pope in February 1608, but his letter had been preceded by the solicitations of other supporters of Caravaggio the previous December—only five months after Caravaggio's arrival on the fortified island. Throughout all of this, Caravaggio was busy painting pictures that maintained his fame and helped to pay off favors. One of these, a *Sleeping Cupid* [fig. 7] painted for the sophisticated Florentine Francesco dell'Antella, is of special interest as it took up a subject the young Michelangelo had famously sculpted and that had been passed off in Rome as an actual antiquity—and it did so by approaching the subject in rigorously naturalistic terms.[30] The picture (now in the Gallerie di Palazzo Pitti) is quite clearly calculated to respond to a topos of Renaissance art: the

Keith Christiansen

paragone, or comparison between the arts of painting and sculpture. In Caravaggio's picture, painting conquers sculpture—even that of his acclaimed namesake—by its incomparable ability to suggest a real, sleeping child. Caravaggio further insists on the contradiction inherent the fine facture and the homeliness of the model, for not only is the brushwork delicate but the Ottoman-style bow is embellished with shell gold—a technique the artist used only one other time: for Vincenzo Giustiniani's *Amor Vincit Omnia* of 1601 [fig. 2 a p. 105]. Caravaggio has obviously borne in mind the reigning poetics of Florentine literary tastes, dominated by the personality of Michelangelo's great-nephew, the poet-playwright Michelangelo Buonarroti the younger. Indeed, the poet's opinion on the picture was openly solicited and we know that some sonnets were composed in praise of it. The literary style of the time was based on a poetics of contradiction.[31] Such was the admiration the picture elicited in Florence that in 1619 a copy of it was painted in fresco on the façade of Palazzo dell'Antella in Piazza Santa Croce; in 1667 the painting was acquired for the Grand Ducal collections.

The monumental canvas of the *Beheading of Saint John the Baptist* [figs. 1, 8] that Caravaggio painted for the oratory of the Knights of Malta takes a completely different tack.[32] Unquestionably one of the great masterpieces of European painting, it has the geometric clarity of a Giottesque fresco and the concentrated pathos of a work of the nineteenth century. The scene is staged outside the prison where John the Baptist had been held by King Herod. In few other pictures by Caravaggio does architecture play such a conspicuous role, with the rusticated arch framing the principal figural group, the figures of which are arranged so as to emphasize carefully calibrated contrasts, or *contrapposti*: four figures—two young, two older; two men and two women; one man bent over the dead John to finish cutting through his neck, the other standing erect and expressionless, gesturing towards the platter onto which John's head is to be placed to bring into the banquet hall; one of the women (probably Salome) bent over with the platter while an old woman, standing erect, clasps her hands to her head in a gesture of horror. Behind these figures are the slats of a closed door, adding to the atmosphere of desperation. The composition is bilateral and in brilliant counterpoint to the action downstage right, we see two prisoners pressing against a barred window opening for a view of the grisly scene—their probable future fate. The rectangular prison window is like a picture within the picture and acts as a comment on our own view through the frame. This magisterial composition possesses the narrative clarity of a work by Domenichino but has no need of the elevated, abstracting vocabulary of the most cerebral of Annibale Carracci's pupils. It is worth comparing this magisterial composition with the packed, confused action of the *Martyrdom of Saint Matthew* painted less than a decade earlier. Uniquely, Caravaggio scrawled his name on the ground with the Baptist's blood. Should we understand this as biographical confession of some sort? A provocative assertion of authorial engagement? Regardless, in this work, as in the sublime *Salome with the Head of Saint John the Baptist* [fig. 15 on p. 74] in the Spanish Royal Collections, Caravaggio seems to discover the expressive power of the void and the way, as with a pause in a musical composition, it can set off the performance of the solo voices of the protagonists and enhance the mood and structures their recitatives.

Barely had the *Beheading of Saint John the Baptist* been installed and Caravaggio been inducted into the Order of Malta than there occurred one of those incidents Caravaggio seems to have been unable to avoid. He evidently got into an altercation with a superior knight and was thrown into prison. We know few details, but his escape from his cell on the impregnable island must have been carefully arranged. Two months later he was stripped of his honorary knighthood and before the very picture he had painted he was degraded *in absentia*. So far from ingratiating himself with the Pope, he was now a doubly condemned man and fugitive from justice.

We next find him at Syracuse, in Sicily, where he painted an altarpiece showing the burial of Saint Lucy that, despite its ruinous state, is as remarkable in its compositional structure as the *Beheading of Saint John the Baptist*. In the *Burial of Saint Lucy* [fig. 9] the contrast is between the two powerful grave-diggers who occupy the foreground and the row of spectators who, like a Greek chorus arranged along a gradually declining diagonal, stand behind the pathetic corpse of Lucy, each figure epitomizing a different and complimentary state of reaction to the burial, with the group dominated by the blessing gesture of the mitred bishop. The poses of the gravediggers may well have been taken from life, but the rest of the picture incorporates a repertory of figure types. In other words, what we encounter are abstractions growing from a poetics of naturalism rather than idealizations. This marks yet a further removal from the principles of his Roman paintings, where the models are so individualized that they have given rise to studies attempting to identify them with real people in Caravaggio's life: painting as biography. The altarpiece marks Caravaggio's arrival at something very like Aristotle's insistence in the *Poetics* that, "The plot is the first essential and the soul of tragedy; character comes second. Pretty much is the same of painting: the most beautiful colors, laid on at random, give less pleasure than a black-and-white drawing. It is the action which is the object of the imitation; the individual characters are subsidiary to it."[33]

A comment on the astonishing abrupt changes in figure scale in this picture is in order. It had become commonplace among artists in late sixteenth-century Rome to set off the main narrative by framing it with oversized figures striking remarkable attitudes. In Federico Zuccaro's *Flagellation* in the Oratorio del Gonfalone, which was unquestionably familiar to Caravaggio, the principle figures are out-scaled by the soldiers in the foreground. It is completely in character with Caravaggio's post-Roman art that he should not have hesitated to take what for a previous generation of painters was a means of demonstrating the sophistication of their art through a conceitful inversion of expectations and employed it instead as an expressive device. The idea— the "capriccio" or "idea stravagante"—of placing Saint Lucy's pitiful corpse in an exaggerated, foreshortened position in the middle ground makes a powerful impact that the composition would have lacked had she been depicted decorously supported.

From Syracuse, it was on to Messina, where, in June 1609 he was commissioned to paint the extraordinary *Raising of Lazarus* [fig. 11] and the *Adoration of the Shepherds* [fig. 10; overall fig. 5 on p. 88]. It would be difficult to imagine two more different pictures, and this fact underscores the degree to which the compositions of Caravaggio's post-Roman pictures grow out of his sense of their theme and the appropriate mode of his poetics of naturalism. The frieze-like composition of the *Raising of Lazarus* may have been inspired by Caravaggio's study of Roman sarcophagi. He employs light as a master of stagecraft, its dramatically life-giving beams falling full face on the body of Lazarus, whose outstretched arms and back-bent head express the shock of being summoned back from the dead. We are told by one of Caravaggio's biographers that in painting this marvelous composition, he used a real corpse for Lazarus and that he had trouble controlling his other models, who were disgusted by the rotting body. There is unquestionably narrative embellishment at work in this story, but the fact

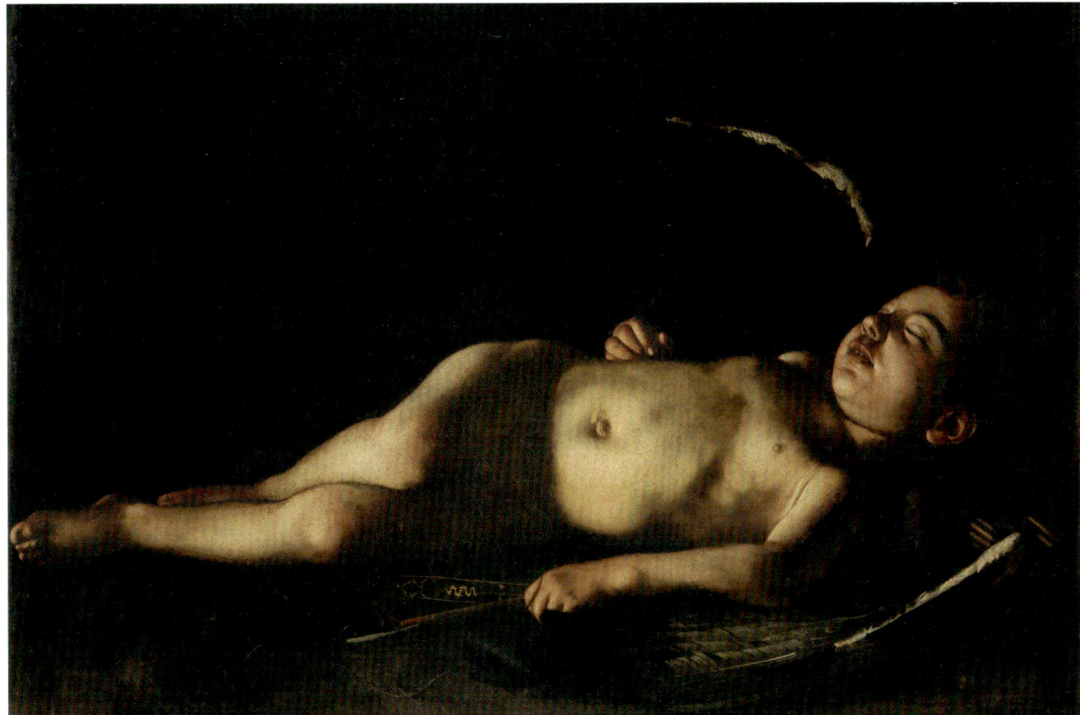

remains that the figure of Lazarus is outlined with incisions inscribed into the preparation of the painting: incisions similar to those we encounter in his Roman paintings, which we know were done to record the pose of a model. The other figures are clearly types—painted from his imagination—but it would seem that for the Lazarus Caravaggio felt he could only get the dramatic charge he wished by using a model. Whether the model for Lazarus was actually dead is another story. The abbreviated style of the picture has an almost unfinished quality when compared to the densely descriptive style of the Roman paintings and it is well to remember that by the early seventeenth century an unfinished, or *non-finito*, look was a recognized means of artistic expression; an artistic strategy that had been famously explored by Titian and Tintoretto. Caravaggio uses it brilliantly to achieve a spectral effect.

The *Adoration of the Shepherds* could not be more different. The scene is staged in a carefully described interior space, with the figures set well back in the middle ground, beneath the beams of the ceiling. The figures of Joseph and the shepherds, their heads aligned along a descending diagonal, are gathered in mute reverence at the miracle of Christ's birth. A humble still life of Joseph's carpenter's tools is situated in the foreground while a donkey and ox at the back of the stable complete the aura of sacred poverty and set off the touching figure of the Virgin reclining against the wooden manger, protectively cuddling her newborn child. A quality of vulnerability pervades the picture. Our best early source on Caravaggio's Sicilian paintings, Francesco Susinno, described the altarpiece as Caravaggio's finest and admired the way Caravaggio employed naturalism without resorting to darkness or broken brushwork—what he called "tingere di macchia". After describing the still life and the Virgin and animals, Susinno went on to describe it as follows: "The Virgin is seen stretched

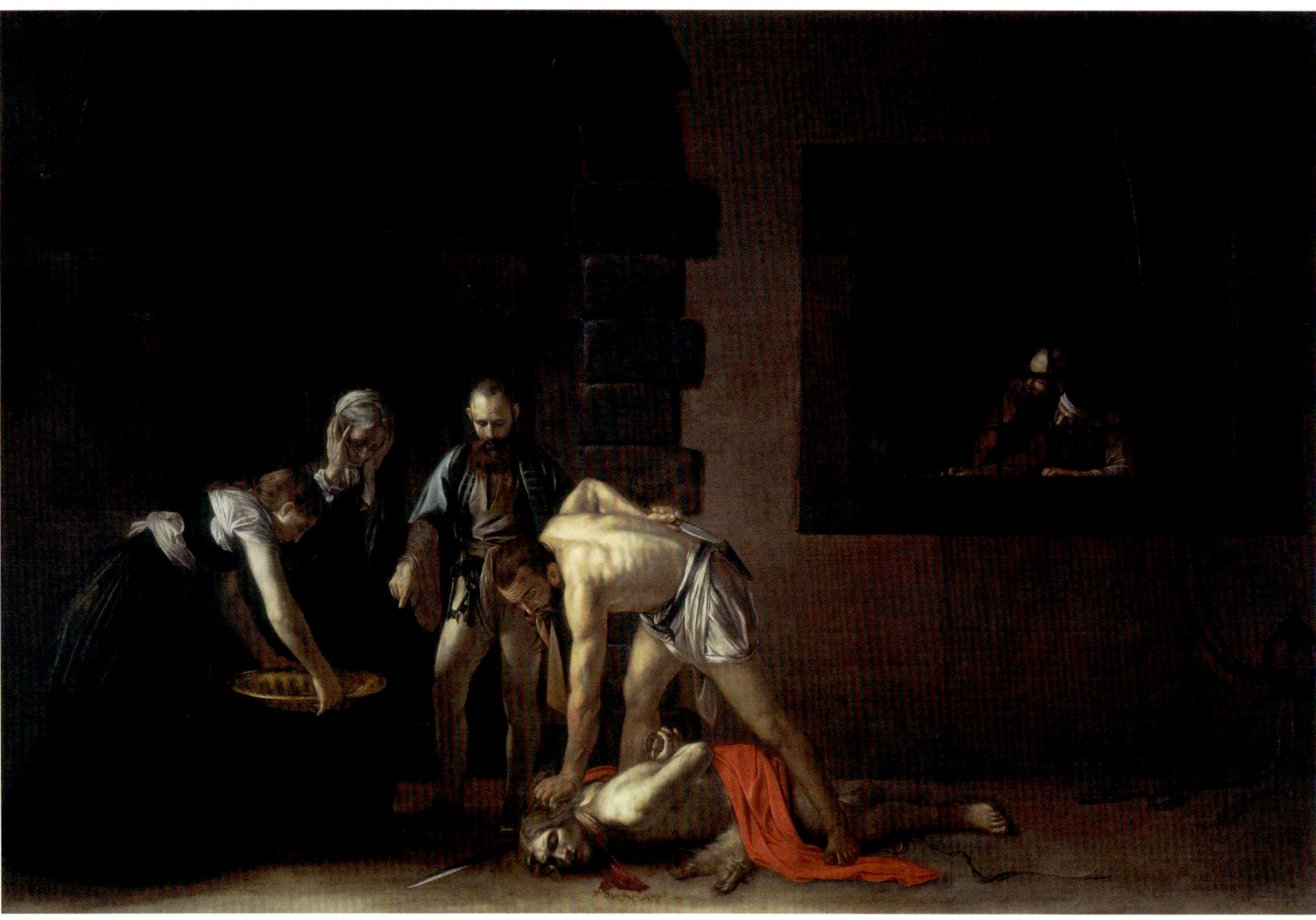

out on the ground looking at the Christ Child wrapped in cloth and caressing him. She is leaning on a manger, behind which those animals are grazing; on the left side, at the foot of the Virgin, St. Joseph is seated, deep in thought. Nearby, three shepherds adore the newborn child; the first one has a staff in his hand and is dressed in white; the second, with his two hands joined in prayer, shows a bare shoulder that looks like real flesh; and the third one looks on admiringly, his bold head marvelously painted. The rest of the canvas consists of a black background with rough wood that forms the shed."[34] What Susinno understood was that Caravaggio employed contrasting types and differentiated gestures in a fashion no less calculated and communicative than those great classicists, Annibale Carracci and Poussin.

It has been argued—I think rightly—that in painting this most tender of all of his altarpieces, the artist was inspired by the ideals of the Capuchins for whose church it was destined. The Capuchins were a reforming branch of the Franciscans, bent on recovering the simplicity of the life of their founder, Saint Francis. Understandably, they revived all those early, thirteenth- and fourteenth-century biographical sources about Saint Francis. It's in one of these early sources—*Le Meditationes vitae Christi*—that we read that Joseph, "rising, took the straw from the manger and put it at the woman's

Keith Christiansen

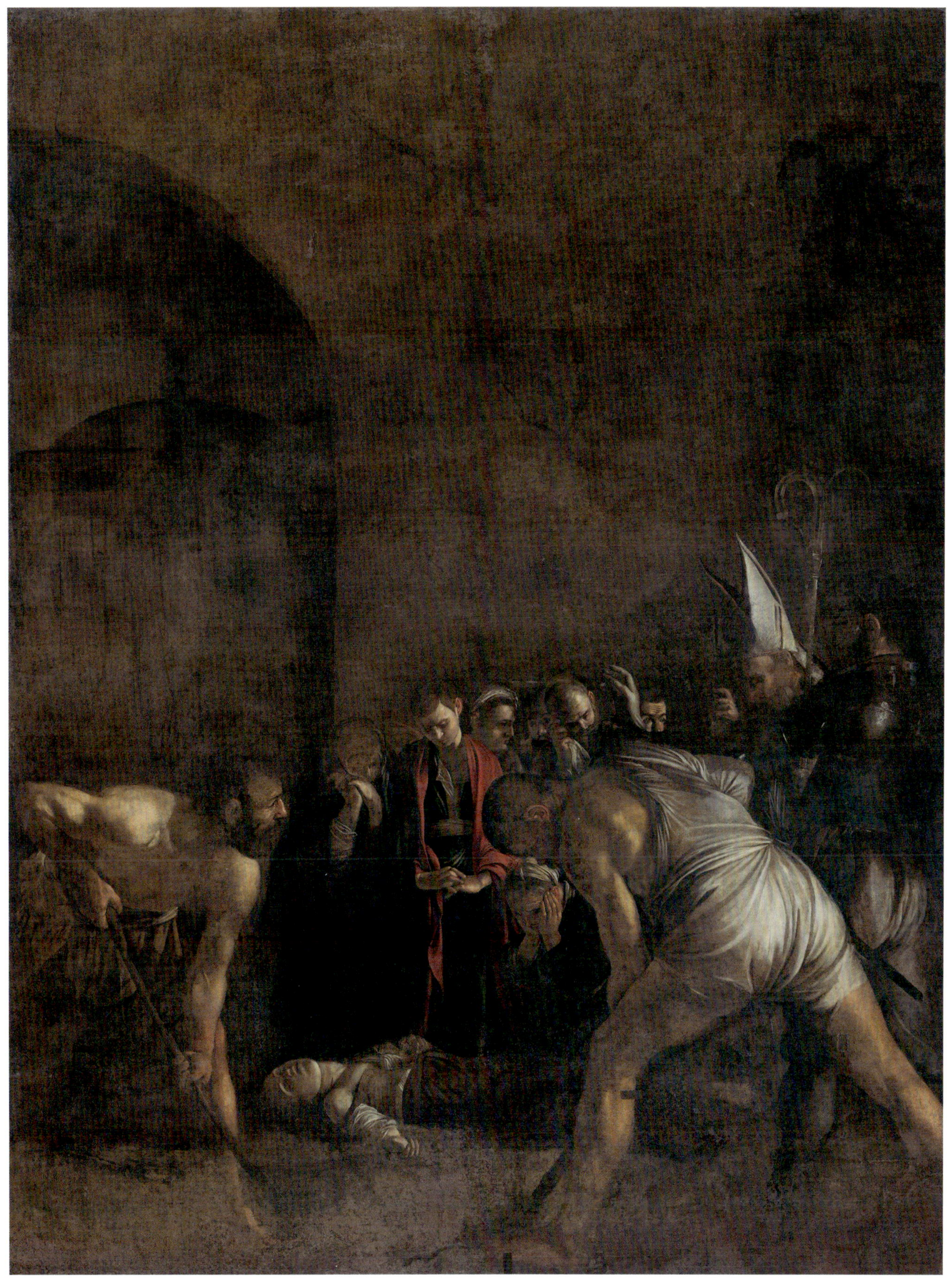

feet and she turned away . . . and the mother bent down and picked up the child and gently placed her arms around him in her lap."[35] As indicated in this popular text, in the fourteenth-century the Virgin is sometimes shown reclining on the ground, in an attitude of humility, and it is this that Caravaggio has revived in his painting. There is a fascinating analogy with an unfinished picture by Federico Barocci (private collection)—an artist belonging to an older generation from that of Caravaggio and one closely associated with the Franciscans and much influenced by the ideas of the Capuchins (the movement originated in Barocci's native Urbino). Years before, around 1600, when he was experiencing the first flush of success in Rome, Caravaggio had painted an altarpiece of this theme for a Franciscan confraternity in Palermo (stolen in 1969) in which can be seen how some of the same ideas were already present, reminding us how responsive Caravaggio was to the themes he painted and the viewers for whom they were intended.[36] But the differences are no less clear. Especially the artist's dependence in the earlier picture on posed models that he renders with specificity, collaging the composition together from its individual parts.

This brings us back to Naples, where Caravaggio arrived for the second time before October 1609. We are told that he painted a gift for the Grand Master of the Knights

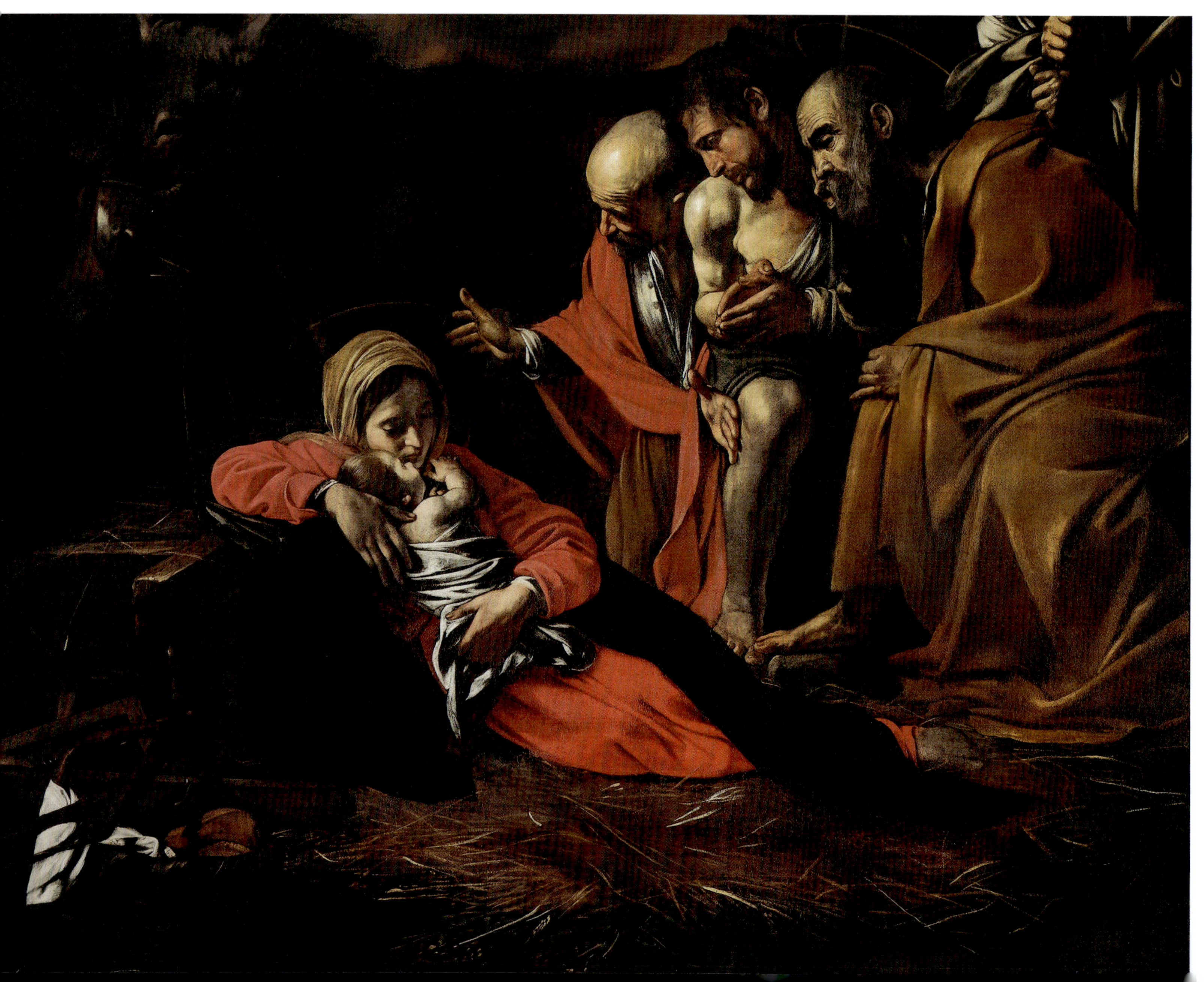

of Malta in an effort to placate him. The picture showed *Salome with the Head of Saint John the Baptist* [fig. 6 on p. 66] and it may, in my view, be the picture now in the National Gallery, London. In any case, shortly after his return to Naples, Caravaggio's enemies caught up with him outside an inn—the Osteria del Cerriglio. He was beaten, his face disfigured, and he was left for dead.

We don't know much about his activity as a painter at this time. There is notice of three paintings—two of Saint John the Baptist and one of the Magdalene—that were returned to Costanza Colonna's palace in Naples following the artist's death. One of these—a *Saint John the Baptist* [cat. 23]—was claimed by Scipione Borghese and is now in the Galleria Borghese. The work about which we are best informed during this time is a badly damaged painting of the martyrdom of Saint Ursula (Naples, Collezione Intesa SanPaolo Gallerie d'Italia; cat. 24). We first hear of it in May of 1610—two months before Caravaggio's death. The agent of Marcantonio Doria, for whom it was painted, wrote his employer in Genoa that he had intended to send the picture but first had set it in the sun to make certain the varnish was completely dry. Instead, the sun spoiled the varnish and the picture was returned to the artist to put aright. An art expert had been brought to see the picture, and, we are told, "he saw it and was stupified, like everyone else who saw it."[37] This is, I think, a notice of the greatest interest, recalling as it does Petrarch's famous description of a painting of the *Madonna and Child* by Giotto. "Its beauty," Petrarch wrote in 1370, "was not understood by the ignorant, but it stupefied those who understand about art"—*magistri artis stupent*. The implication is that Giotto's painting, like Caravaggio's, went beyond normal expectations. In the case of Giotto, I think this had to do with his insistence on the figures as being physically present rather than mere images. In the case of Caravaggio, I believe it had to do with the abbreviated means by which he probed the theme.

All the traits we have discussed thus far are condensed in this painting as in few others: figures—none painted from life—are arranged in a frieze and set against a dark, forbidding background. The emphasis is on contrasts of emotion. The action is stilled to the point that the picture becomes a meditation on a tragic event: the prince of the Huns has had his amorous advances spurned by the Christian virgin and has shot her at close range with an arrow. Ursula seems almost to contemplate the source of her martyrdom, while the face of the prince registers stunned remorse. This is not realist painting—at least not in the sense of Caravaggio's Roman works. It is something quite new. Indicatively, when the picture re-appeared in this century, the painting was not immediately recognized as a work by Caravaggio. Fortunately, confirming letters were discovered together with an inscription on the reverse of the canvas identifying it as the painting commissioned by Marcantonio Doria.

As early as December 1609 it was rumored that Caravaggio's return to Rome was immanent. On Christmas day the papal physician and art critic Giulio Mancini wrote to his brother, "It is said that Caravaggio is safe near here and wants to return to Rome soon and that he has strong support."[38] Among these supporters who had the pope's ear were Cardinals Ferdinando Gonzaga and Scipione Borghese, and it is in a letter to the latter that we have our most detailed information on Caravaggio's last days.

In mid July 1610, the artist ill-advisedly packed his belongings and set sail from Naples. The boat put in at Pola, on the coast north of Rome, where the artist was arrested by the papal guard. He had enough money to get himself released, but by that time the ship had already left, taking his belongings with it. Once again, the artist's temper

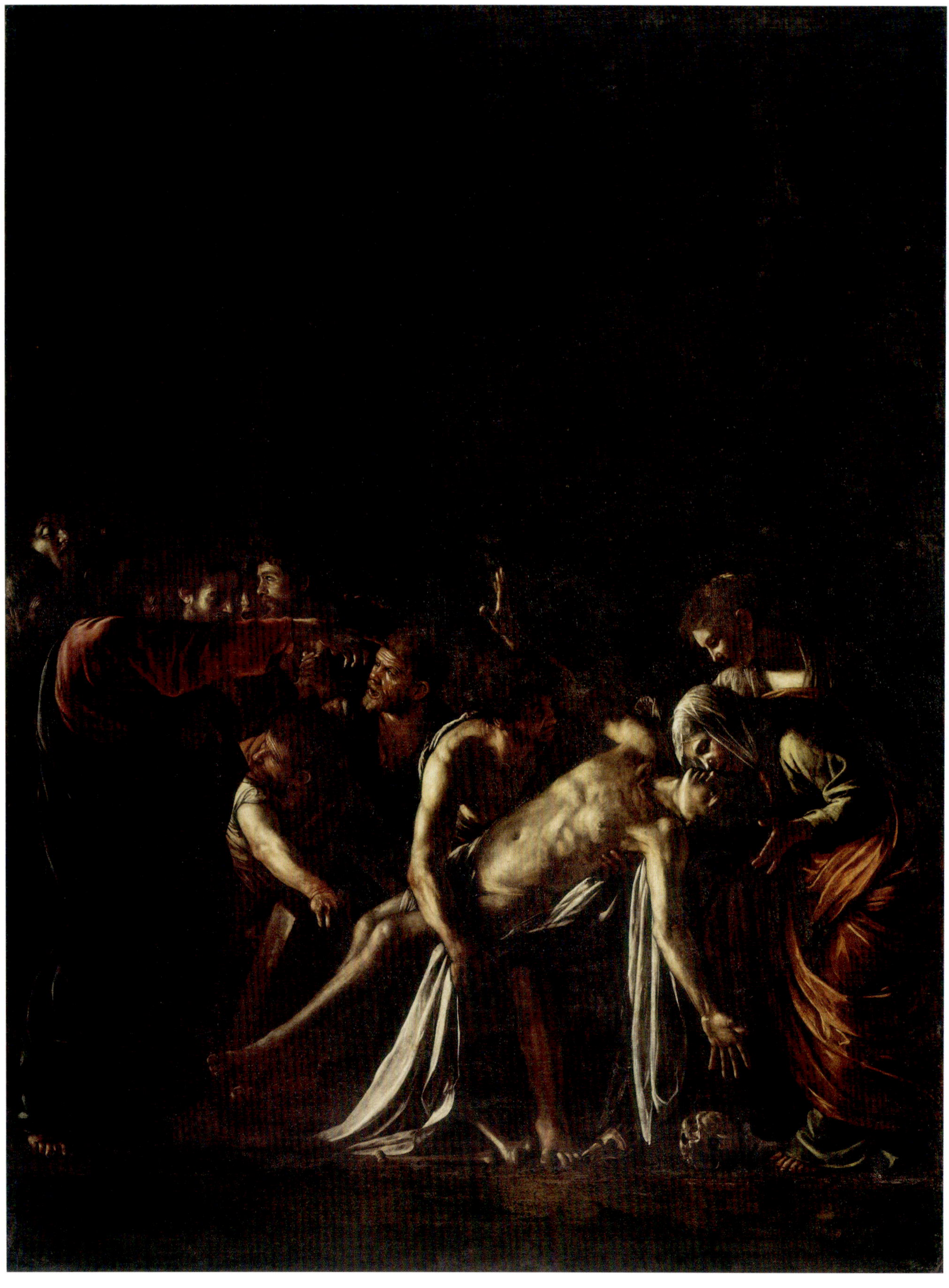

Keith Christiansen

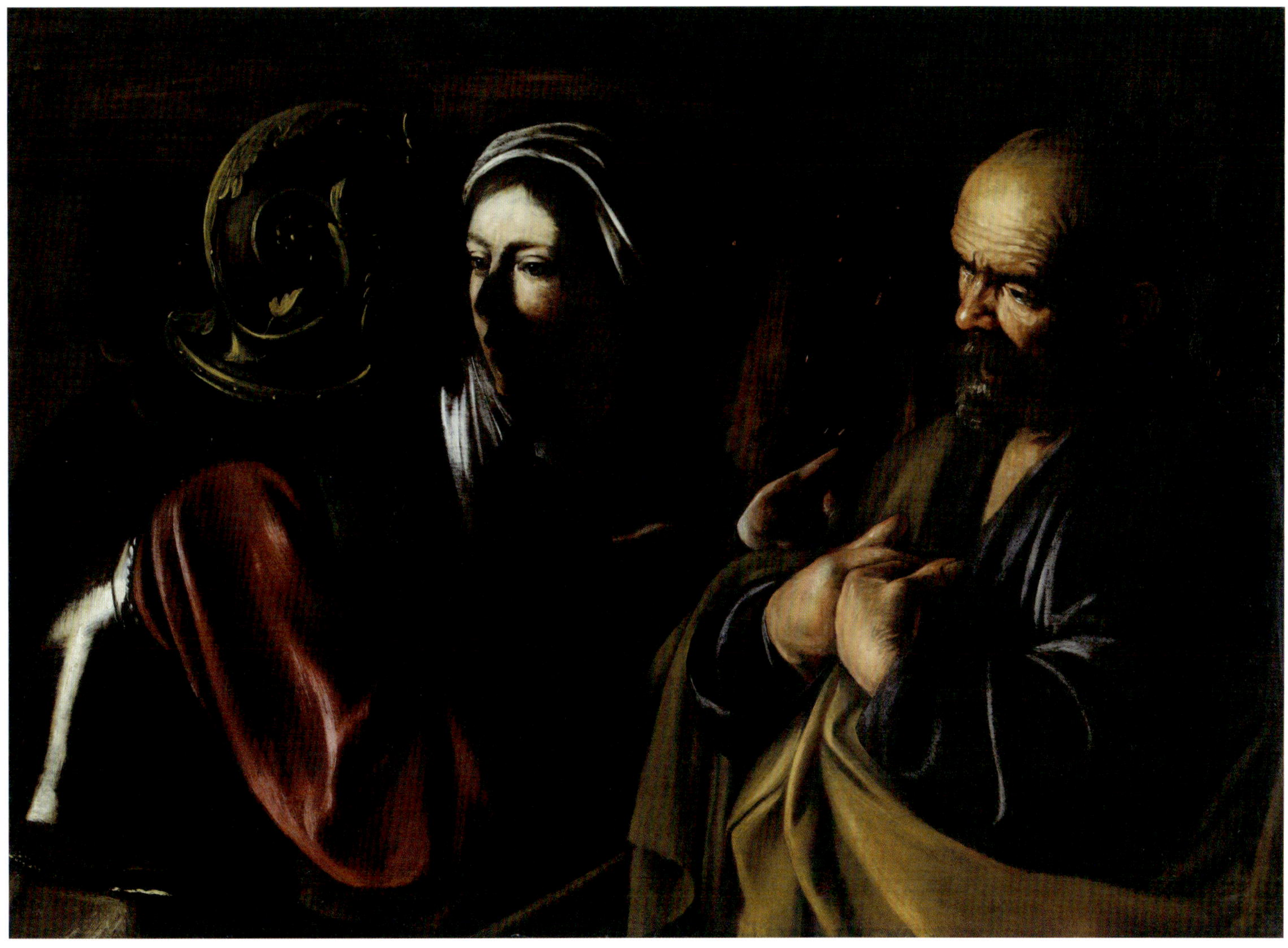

got the better of him, and he foolishly struck out for Porto Ercole, to the north, evidently unaware that the ship had returned to Naples. En route he contracted malaria and on July 18 died—three days before the long-sought papal pardon was published. Scipione Borghese's agent was able to discover that the belongings, including some pictures, had been returned to Costanza Colonna in Naples, but by that time—the agent wrote to Scipione on July 29—the only ones left were the three already mentioned above: two of Saint John the Baptist and one of the Magdalene. Attention has understandably focused on identifying these three paintings, but the wording of the letter strongly suggests that there had been more, and some of these—including the *Denial of Saint Peter* in The Metropolitan Museum—must have made their way back to Rome.

The *Martyrdom of Saint Ursula*, like the National Gallery *Salome* and the *Denial of Saint Peter* [fig. 12], epitomizes in an extraordinary way that moment in Caravaggio's career when he seems to have looked beyond the emerging world of seicento art to put forward a vision of painting not as mimesis—a description of the world we see—but as a probing of the tragic events that shape life. It proposes painting as expression and it embraces an economy of means that seems utterly modern. The relationship of these half-length compositions painted in a *quasi non-finito* style to Caravaggio's altarpieces in Roman churches is a bit like Beethoven's late string quartets to the symphonies: the private versus the public statement; the artist's eye directed inwards rather than outwards.

Caravaggio's Roman paintings had a pervasive influence on a young generation of painters in Rome. But works such as the *Martyrdom of Saint Ursula* really were inimitable: they took painting into a new frontier that had been explored by the late Titian but for which there are otherwise few analogies. For those who believe that painting is about ideas and psychological insight; about extending the boundaries of expression as well as displaying brilliant pictorial effects, Caravaggio's last paintings constitute his most challenging legacy, and they remind us that the pictures—far more than the biography of Caravaggio—repay serious study.

1   *The Age of Caravaggio | Caravaggio e il suo tempo* 1985.

2   Gregori's arguments on behalf of the ceiling in the camerino were presented at a scholars' day during the run of the exhibition in New York. For the *Toothpuller*, see her entry in *The Age of Caravaggio | Caravaggio e il suo tempo* 1985, pp. 341–344 cat. 98.

3   For the documents, see the essential compilation of Stefania Macioce (Maciocie 2010b). For technical studies, see: Falcucci 2006, pp. 39–46; Falcucci 2008, pp. 71-101; *Caravaggio. La bottega del genio* 2010; *Caravaggio's Painting* 2012; *Caravaggio. Opere a Roma* 2016; and, most recently, C. Falcucci, in Vodret 2021a, pp. 102–105. Vodret's 2021 monograph provides an updated, overview of Caravaggio's career.

4   I cite among the most extreme and recent examples of an openly popular approach, Volpe 2023.

5   Longhi [1952] 1982.

6   Baedeker 1909, p. 252. Caravaggio's *Madonna dei pellegrini* in Sant'Agostino does not merit mention, nor does the Cerasi Chapel in Santa Maria del Popolo (pp. 245; 178–180)!

7   See Previtali in Longhi [1952] 1982, pp. 9–30, for Longhi's contributions in the context of those of his contemporaries.

8   Berenson 1951; Berenson 1953. For an interesting response, see Gombrich 1953, p. 1134.

9   Berenson 1951, pp. 69–70.

10   For Fry's devastating critical posture towards Caravaggio, see Fry 1922, pp. 158–169.

11   For a fine review of Artemisia as a famous woman, see Cropper 2001 pp. 262–280.

12   For my thoughts on the way Artemisia's life—or perhaps, better, her body—and her art sometimes intersect in a poetics of biography, see Christiansen 2004, pp. 10, 101–126.

13   For an overview of Cecco and his possible sexual relationship with Caravaggio, see Papi 2023b, pp. 15–51. The beheaded victim as rejected lover is a conceit found in various media, from fifteenth-century majolica plates to Cristofano Allori's celebrated painting of Judith with the head of Holofernes, for which see Christiansen 2004, pp. 115–116.

14   See the review of the documentary information and the current reconstruction of Caravaggio's first yeas in Rome in Vodret 2021a, pp. 29–37. It is worth remembering, however, that lack of a documented presence in Rome is not the same thing as proof of absence. One remembers that Ribera is

Keith Christiansen

first documented in Rome in 1611, but in Naples in 1616 he declared he had worked in Rome for ten years, which places his arrival in the eternal city around 1606–1607. Moroeover, we have it from Gaspare Celio that when Cardinal del Monte sought Caravaggio, "alla fine lo trovò a dormire nel poggiolo attaccato a Pasquino, che non haveva panni a torno." This sort of vagabond existence would have escaped the normal means of census taking. See Gandolfi 2021, p. 321.

15 Giustiniani [c. 1620-1630] 1981.

16 Baglione 1642, p. 136: "& anche vn giouane, che fonaua il Lauto; che viuo, e vero il tutto parea con vna caraffa di fiori piena d'acqua, che dentro il refleffo d' vna fineltra eccellentemente fi fcorgeua con altri ripercotimenti di quella camera dentro l'acqua; e fopra quei fiori eraui vna viua rugiada con ogni efquifita diligenza finta. E quelto (diffe) che fu il più bel pezzo, che faceffe mai." Whether the passage refers exclusively to one picture or, through a lapsus, combined a painting of a lute player in Del Monte's collection with a still life of a vase of flowers that is also described by Bellori [1672] 1976, p. 213, is not altogether clear. It should be noted that there is no reflection of a window in the Hermitage picture.

17 Bellori [1672] 1976, p. 214

18 Van Mander 1604, f. 191*r*. Van Mander was provided this information by his Dutch colleague Floris van Dijck, who was in Rome in 1600.

19 Carducho 1638, p. 89.

20 Study of the art market in Rome has transformed our understanding of the artistic life in seicento Rome. See, among the many contributions, Cavazzini 2008; Spear, Sohm 2010; Spear 2016. Of particular importance for Caravaggio is, *inter alias*, Curti 2011a, pp. 167–197; Curti 2017a, pp. 109–120. Elsewhere I have commented on my notion of the market and the experimentation it allowed Caravaggio: Christiansen 2019, pp. 35–44.

21 The suggestion that the half-clad figures are neophytes was first proposed by Trinchieri Camiz 1990, pp. 89–105. Ebert-Schifferer 2012, p. 126, goes so far as to imagine that the killer of Saint Matthew, "dressed only in loincloth and headband . . . may have sneaked into the sanctuary under the pretense of seeking baptism."

22 We are indebted to Pacelli 2002, for laying the basis for a firmer understanding of the artist's post-Roman career, subsequently celebrated in *Caravaggio. L'ultimo tempo* 2004. See, more recently, *Caravaggio Napoli* 2019.

23 Bellori [1672] 1976, p. 231.

24 The document, which no longer exists, was published by Saccà 1906, p. 56: "quattro storie della passione di gesù cristo da farli a capriccio del pittore dalli quali ne finì uno che rappresenta Christo colla croce in spalla, la Vergine addolorata e due manigoldi uno sona la tromba riuscì veramente una bellissima opera . . . e l'altri tre s'obligò il pittore portarmeli nel mese di agosto con pagarli quanto si converrà da questo pittore che ha il cervello stravolto."

25 Spear 1997, pp. 282–288, gives a good analysis of Reni's critical approach of "evoking [Caravaggio's] revolutionary style and then surpassing it." In essence, he appropriated the tactic Caravaggio had employed to undermine the reigning idealist Roman style.

26 The story of Caravaggio's threatening encounter with Guido is told by Malvasia 1688, II, pp. 15–16.

27 Longhi [1935] 1972, p. 15.

28 Among the more recent studies of Caravaggio and the Colonna, see Berra 2021b.

29 For a review of these years, with bibliography, see Vodret 2021a, pp. 61–75. See also: *Caravaggio a Napoli* 2021.

30 Stone 1997, pp. 165–177.

31 For a brilliant examination of the intersection of Caravaggio's poetics and literary taste, see Cropper 1991, pp. 193–212.

32 Sciberras 2007, pp. 759–766.

33 Aristotle 1958, p. 14. The poetics were widely read, not least by Bellori.

34 Susinno [1724] 1960, p. 113. Susinno's description should be compared to Bellori's on the *Entombment*—the picture by Caravaggio he most admired: Bellori [1672] 1976, p. 221.

35 *Le Meditationes vitae* 2021, pp. 119–120.

36 On the redating of this picture to Caravaggio's Roman period after having long been considered by most scholars as contemporary with Caravaggio's other Sicilian paintings, see, most recently, Vodret 2021a, p. 184.

37 The letter is published in Pacelli 2002, p. 104.

38 Maccherini 1997, p. 86, n. 17.

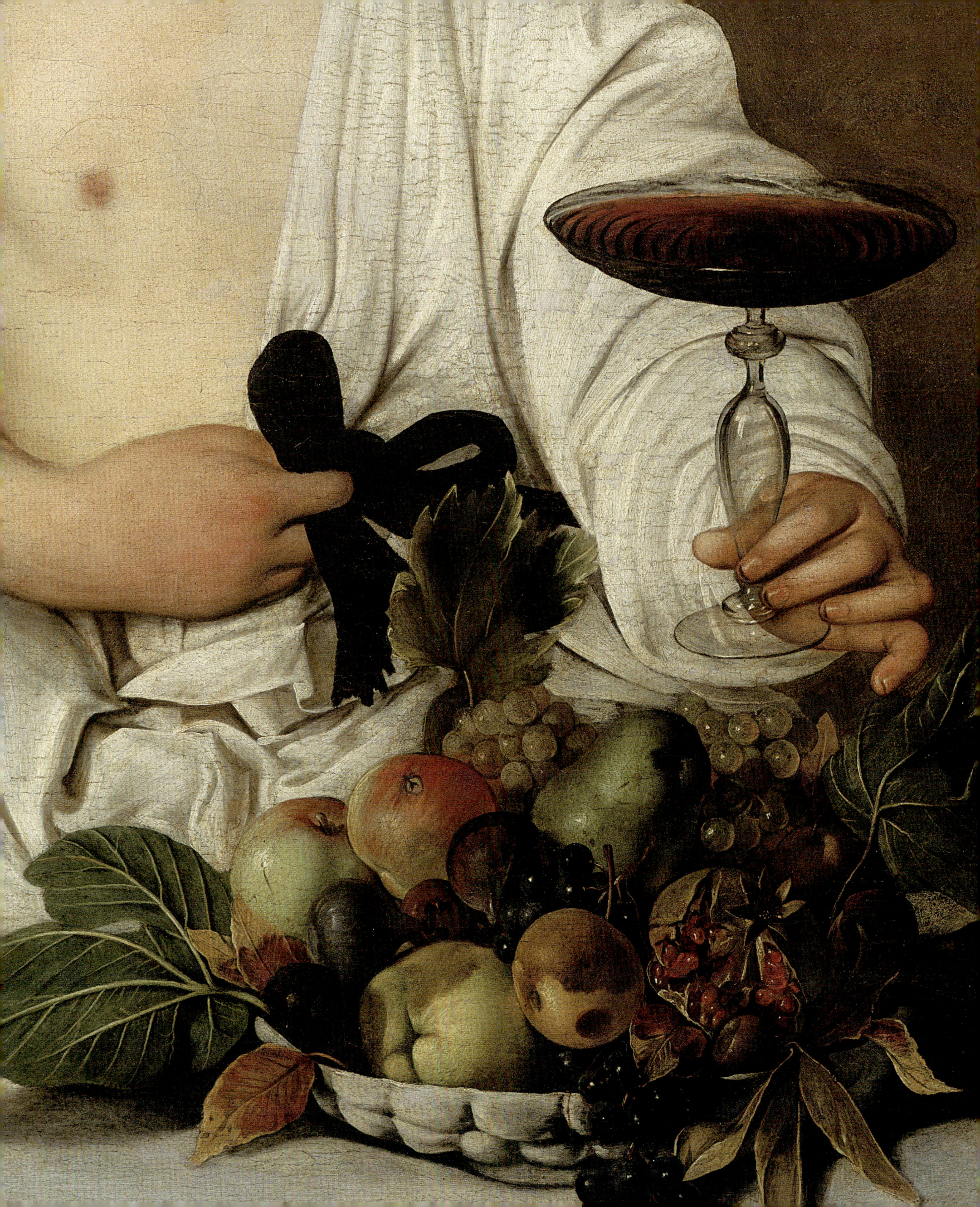

Maria Cristina Terzaghi

CARAVAGGIO IN ROMAN WORKSHOPS

(ROME, C. 1595 – SPRING 1597)

More was paid for his paintings of Heads than for the figure compositions of others.
Giovanni Baglione, *Life of Michelangelo da Caravaggio*, 1642

[fig. 1]
Bacchus, c. 1596–1597, detail,
Gallerie degli Uffizi, Florence

Caravaggio arrived in Rome from the North in search of fortune, "poorly provided with money,"[1] and without a fixed abode; on these two points the pictures painted by the accounts in the sources are broadly in agreement.[2] There is no such agreement as to how the artist was able, within the space of four or five years, that is by the autumn of 1600, to become: "Egregius in Urbe pictor", that is literally: "the most excellent painter in Rome."[3] Great strides have been taken on the reconstruction of this segment of the personal history and career of the great master thanks to the research of the last fifteen years,[4] so that it now seems to me that it is finally possible to include, alongside the protagonists, also the paintings, the execution of which marked turning points, impulses, pauses and milestones in the artist's early career.

Once in Rome, probably in 1595,[5] in what was a huge and socially very different city not only from the small village of Caravaggio where he had been raised from the age of six to twelve, but also from Milan, which he frequented as a boy between the ninth and tenth decade of the sixteenth century,[6] the young Caravaggio was faced with two closely related problems: to find a roof over his head and work, in other words where to live and how to exercise his profession. The Milanese apprenticeship from which he had emerged was excellent, with an artist of the calibre of Simone Peterzano [fig. 3] who, for at least four years, from 1584 to 1588, had taught him all the painting techniques then in use among first-rate artists (from drawing to painting in oil on canvas, via painting in fresco). In that

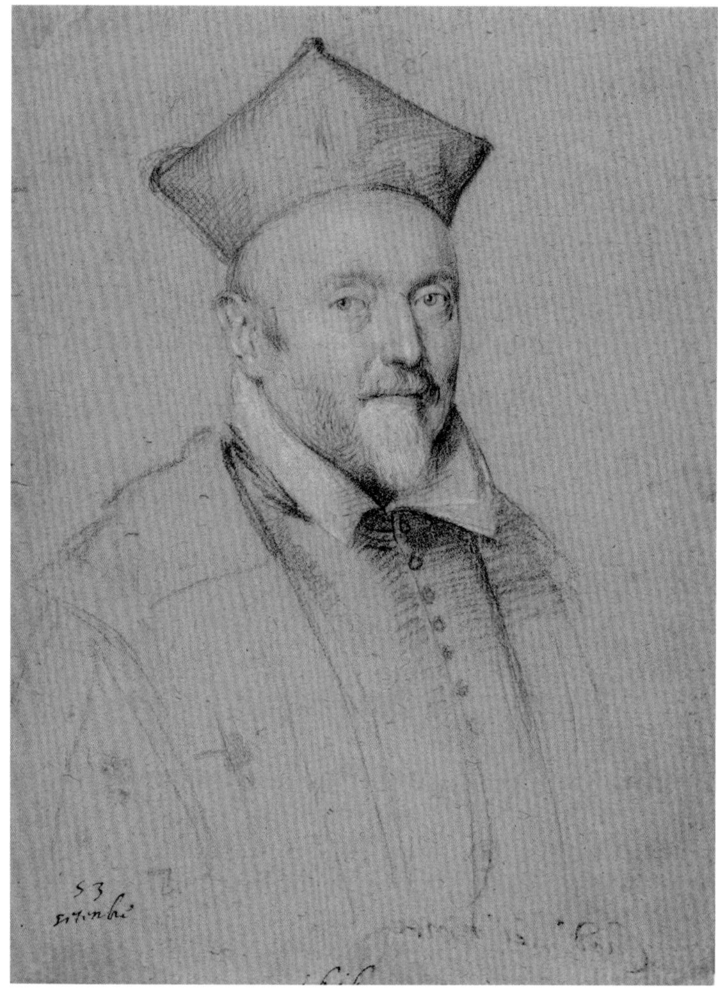

workshop, he had almost certainly also come into contact with Venetian painting, in particular Titian, as Peterzano was exceptionally proud to have been the latter's pupil; with Leonardo, whom all the artists then active in Milan studied with veneration; and, through Giovan Paolo Lomazzo who knew Peterzano well, also with the world of theatre and literary and scenic fiction, a context that would leave an indelible mark on Caravaggio's conception of painting.[7]

In Rome, therefore, the young Caravaggio would not have been looking for further training, but rather a context in which to measure himself against what he had already learnt and the novelties offered by the capital of all arts, in the hope of being able to manifest his talent.

Because of the way the profession of painting was organised in the papal city, the opportunities for a young artist were basically of two kinds: either to join the family of a powerful patron, cardinal or aristocrat, and work in his service; or to grab a slice of the market by frequenting the workshops that produced works of art on a large scale and in great number to satisfy the demand for "Heads", that is for paintings depicting saints, prophets, sibyls, emperors and empresses, illustrious men and women, commonly executed on a small canvas known precisely as "tela da testa"—'canvas for Heads.'[8] Roman painters

Maria Cristina Terzaghi

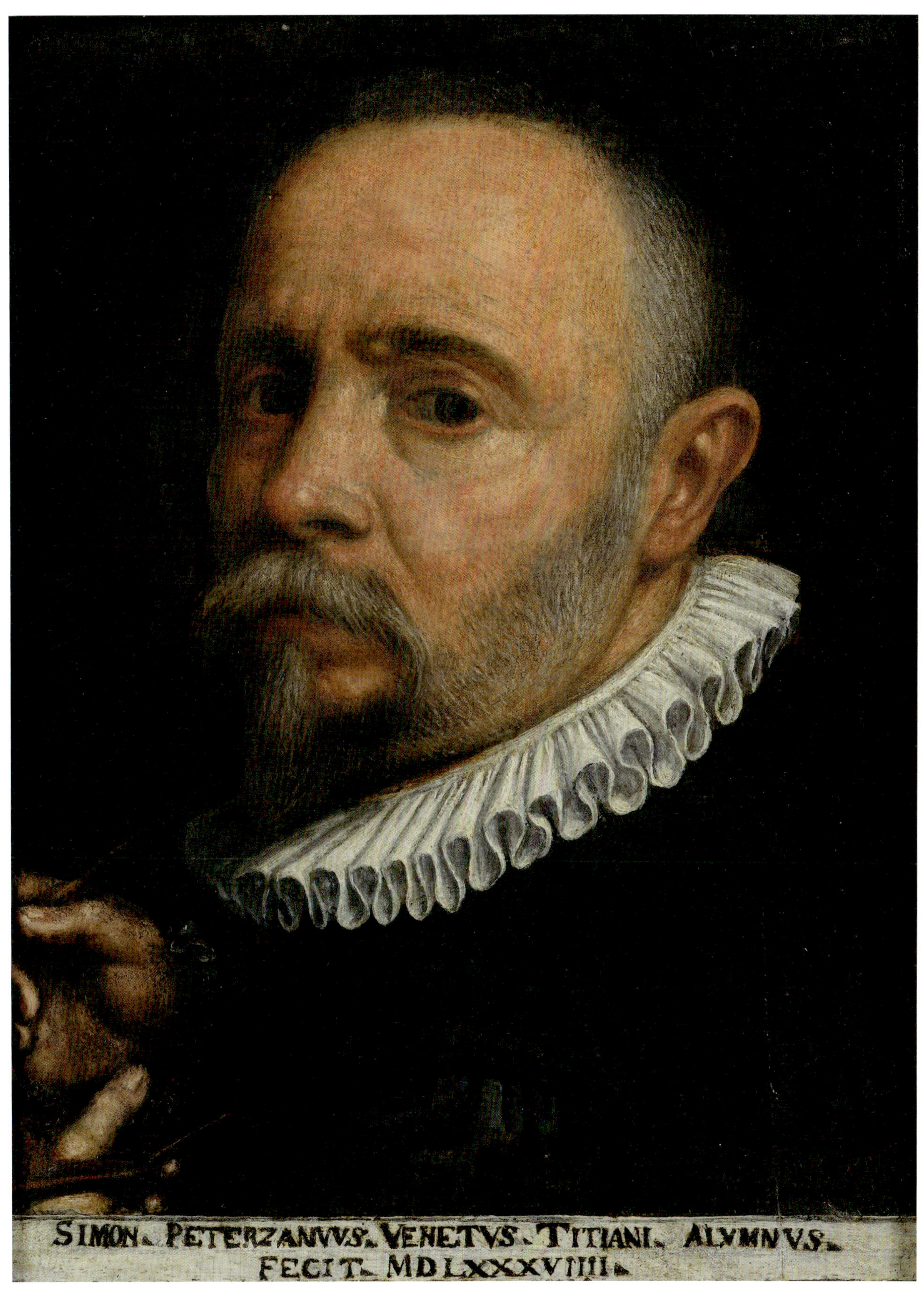

SIMON. PETERZANVS. VENETVS. TITIANI. ALVMNVS.
FECIT. MDLXXXVIIII.

were highly specialised in this field because of the great demand that was not only local, but international. The risk was considerable since, Giulio Mancini said it well when dealing with the beginnings of Jusepe de Ribera only a few years later: "Having come to Rome, he began to work 'by the day' with those who run workshops and sell paintings from the labours of young men such as he."[9] Caravaggio therefore played on multiple tables; in the words of a colleague and eyewitness, the Flemish painter Karel van Mander, who in 1603–1604 wrote of him: ". . . he has risen from poverty through his indefaticable industry, and by tackling and accepting everything with farsightedness and audacity. . . ."[10]

Before the summer of 1597, when he landed his first great patron, Cardinal Francesco Maria del Monte [fig. 2], a turning point in the artist's career, one that will therefore also mark the end of our discussion, we are certain that Caravaggio had already frequented the workshops of Tarquinio Ligustri, the Sicilian painter Lorenzo Carli, Antiveduto Gramatica, and Cavalier d'Arpino; it is also highly probable that he worked with the Spaniard Cristoforo Orlandi, Vittorio Travagni and perhaps Giovan Mario Gherardi[11]. He lived in the palaces of Monsignor Pandolfo Pucci da Recanati and Monsignor Fantino Petrignani da Amelia, and finally had a host who acted as his talent scout, partner, colleague, friend and brother, the Roman painter Prospero Orsi, his *"turcimanno"*, interpreter, but also intermediary, who, probably in partnership with Costantino Spada, "dealer of paintings in San Luigi dei Francesi," was what we would today call his first (and perhaps only) art dealer.[12]

FROM MORNING TO NIGHT

With such an overlap of data, it is well to clear the field of misunderstandings: if these contacts can be established with certainty, their chronology is much less clear, and it is useless, and even misleading, to imagine a real sequence of events, since many of them must have taken place simultaneously. For an adult artist, in fact, frequenting the workshops in Rome at that time did not necessarily imply lodging, but was more generally equivalent to finding employment and, by learning how to manoeuvre, a painter could also work in more than one venture.[13] On the other hand, Caravaggio was little inclined to bind himself univocally not only to a workshop, but also to a patron, or any other form of affiliation: even when he was in place with Cardinal del Monte, he continued to work for other patrons, and despite his protector's liberality, he did not remain with him for long. Finally, a source of exceptional importance for the reconstruction of Caravaggio's biography, is very eloquent in this regard. The Sienese physician Giulio Mancini, an *amateur*, free of all professional partiality, who knew Caravaggio at first hand, provides us with an extraordinary image of the voracity with which the young Caravaggio threw himself into the fray of the art world of the capital: "In the morning he worked with Tarquinio and in the night in the workshops. On leaving, he comes to Pandolfo's."[14] In the mornings, therefore, the artist was employed by the painter from Viterbo Tarquinio Ligustri, while in the evenings he worked in the painters' workshops which, as we shall see, were located on the axis of Via della Scrofa, and then he would find a roof over his head in the home of Monsignor Pandolfo Pucci da Recanati.[15]

Ligustri had not been in Rome for a long time; a good fresco painter, creator of grotesques, he took part in many important city projects in the last five years of the sixteenth century. As difficult as it is to imagine that Caravaggio could have had much in common with a robustly late-Mannerist painter such as Ligustri, I think that such a workshop may

Maria Cristina Terzaghi

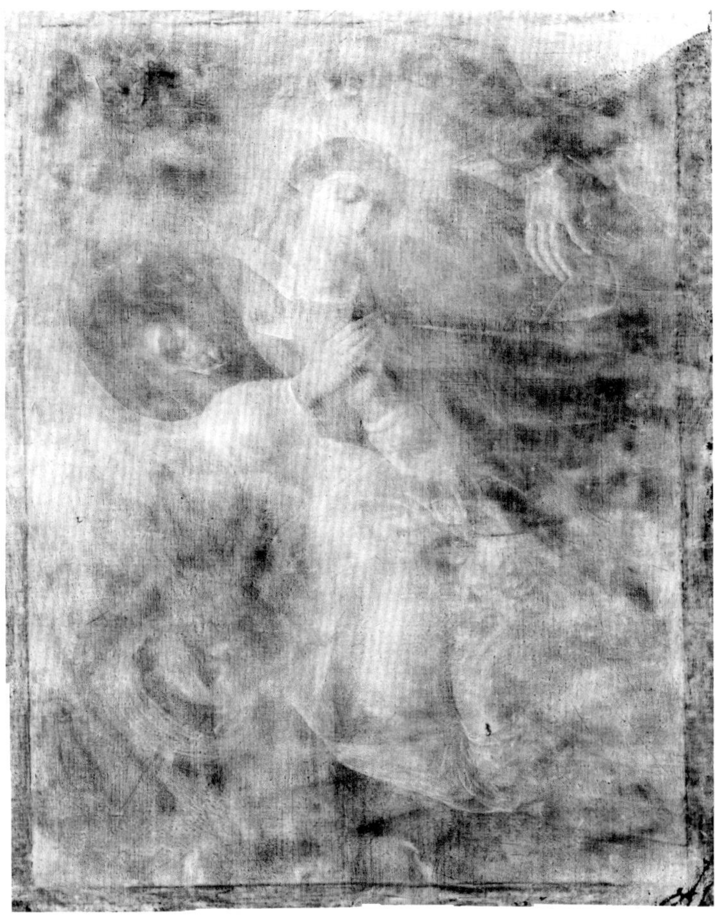

have somehow seemed familiar to him, not too far removed from the Milanese one in which he had been trained.[16] In any case, it seems likely that it was as one of Ligustri's acquaintances that Prospero Orsi, who was a fellow countryman of the artist and, like him, specialised in grotesque decoration, probably entered the scene.[17] It has been established that the two painters were simultaneously active in 1596, if not earlier, on the project in the palazzo of Monsignor Fantino Petrignani, under the direction of the architect Ottaviano Mascarino, Giulio Mancini's informant, who therefore also in this instance had first-hand information.[18] In addition, we have reason to believe that Caravaggio's relationship with Monsignor Pandolfo Pucci da Recanati was also fostered by Orsi himself.[19] However, a traditional artist and furthermore one devoted to fresco painting such as Tarquinio Ligustri could not have provided the right openings for the talented Caravaggio, who, out of necessity, sought his fortune in other circles.

VIA DELLA SCROFA

Less usual, but perhaps more stimulating for a young man trained in Milan to paint portraits, must have been the production of the ateliers in Via della Scrofa where Caravaggio spent his evenings, as recounted not only by Mancini, but also by Gaspare Celio, who was evidently struck by the detail of the evening work: "He went to Rome, where, being in

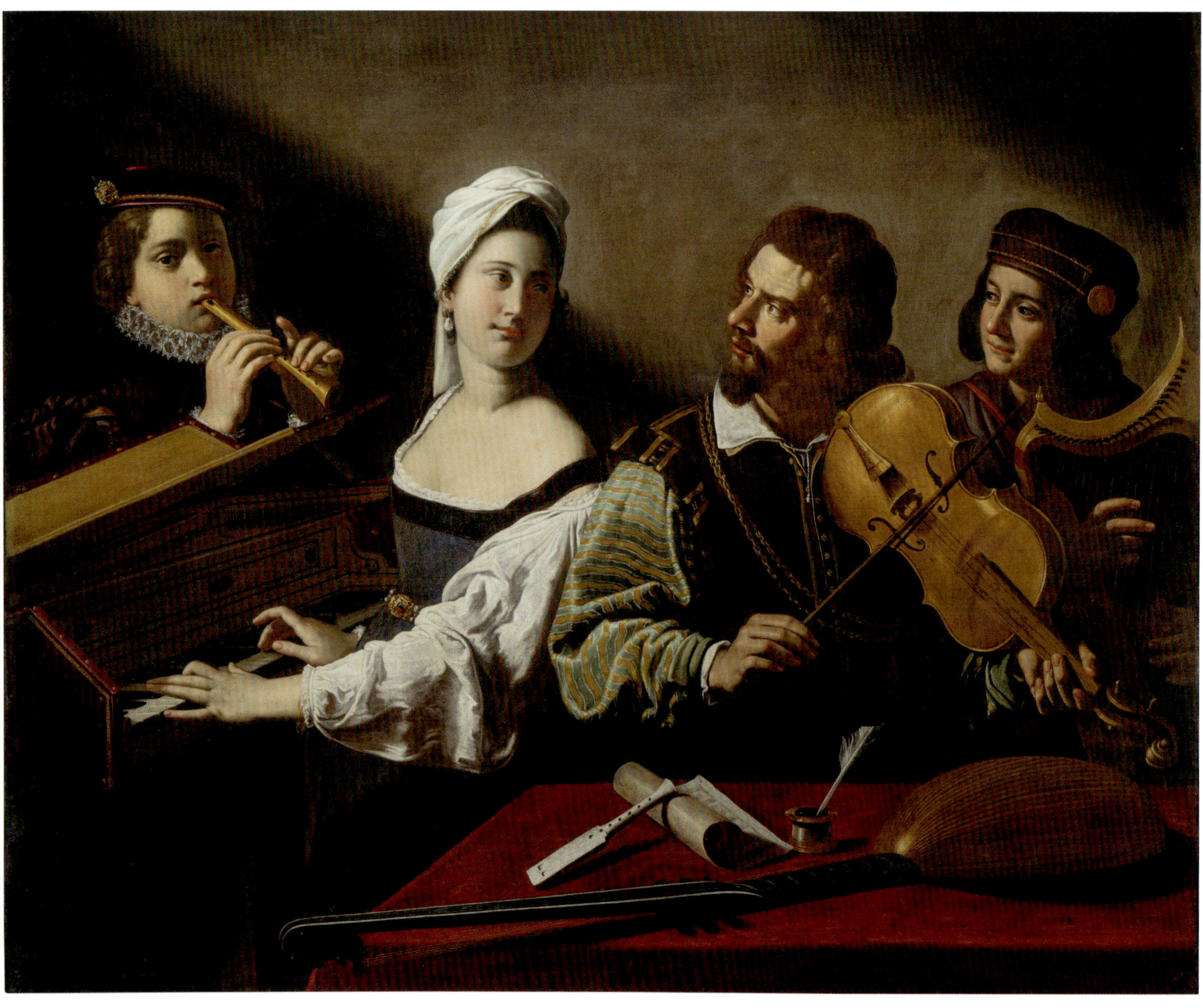

great need, he went to paint some heads of saints in the workshop [of a painter] known as Lorenzo Siciliano, for five *baiochi* each; he would paint two, and would go off to eat."[20]

The trial involving the musician Angelo Tanconi, at which Caravaggio was a silent witness in July 1597, confirms his acquaintance with these figures, identifying their chronological boundaries and giving us a physical description of the painter: a young man around 25 years old, dark, with a sparse beard and a distinct Milanese—or rather—Lombard accent. The description appears in the deposition at the trial by Pietropaolo Pellegrini, the apprentice of barber Luca Benni, who had frequented Caravaggio during Lent 1596, when his employer had helped Caravaggio by treating a bad wound to a leg, caused by the kick of a horse, the accident forcing Caravaggio to go to the Ospedale della Consolazione.[21] At the time, Pellegrini recounts, Caravaggio frequented the neighbouring workshop, that of the Sicilian painter Lorenzo Carli on Via della Scrofa near the church of Sant'Agostino.

Maria Cristina Terzaghi

Carli, originally from Naso in the province of Messina, had been in Rome since at least 1589, when he lived in Piazza Nicosia. From 1591 he had settled in Via della Scrofa, and he would die there, still young, between March and April 1597, leaving behind two children, one of whom was on the way.[22] Amidst easels, chassis and canvases in large numbers, drawings and casts, Carli, who specialised in the making of copies of Marian icons, used to display his works outside the door to attract customers. I wonder if it was at his friend's death, or shortly before, that Caravaggio recuperated a canvas painted with the image of a *Virgin in Prayer*, the *Virgin Oditrigia* much venerated in Sicily [fig. 4], which he re-used to paint the beautiful *Fortune Teller* in the Capitoline Museums [cat. 4].[23] The execution of the painting would have taken place not long after the spring of 1597, as it is unlikely that Caravaggio would keep an already used canvas for years without doing anything with it. Moreover, Mancini tells us that such a work was sold for a derisory sum, 8 *scudi*, when a few years later in 1613 it was worth 300[24] on the market.

In Via della Scrofa, Carli and Caravaggio were in good company. Just a few steps away was another painting atelier, that of Antiveduto Gramatica, specialised in the same genre as the Sicilian, the so-called '*Teste*', to such a degree that he earned the nickname "Gran Capocciante."[25] The premises and probably also the tools of the trade had been left to him by his master Domenico Angelini, at a time when Gramatica had already been working for a few years in partnership with Vittorio Travagni, an artist by whom, alas, no works have come down to us, but who appears to be very much involved with the protagonists in the narrative of Caravaggio and Caravaggism.[26] Vittorio Travagni was in fact the brother-in-law of Giovanni Morelli, his master, and master of Giovanni Baglione and Tommaso Salini, all of whom he had frequented since he was a boy, and he too had settled in Via della Scrofa at the corner of Sant'Agostino, specialising in the execution of *Illustrious Men*. As we have

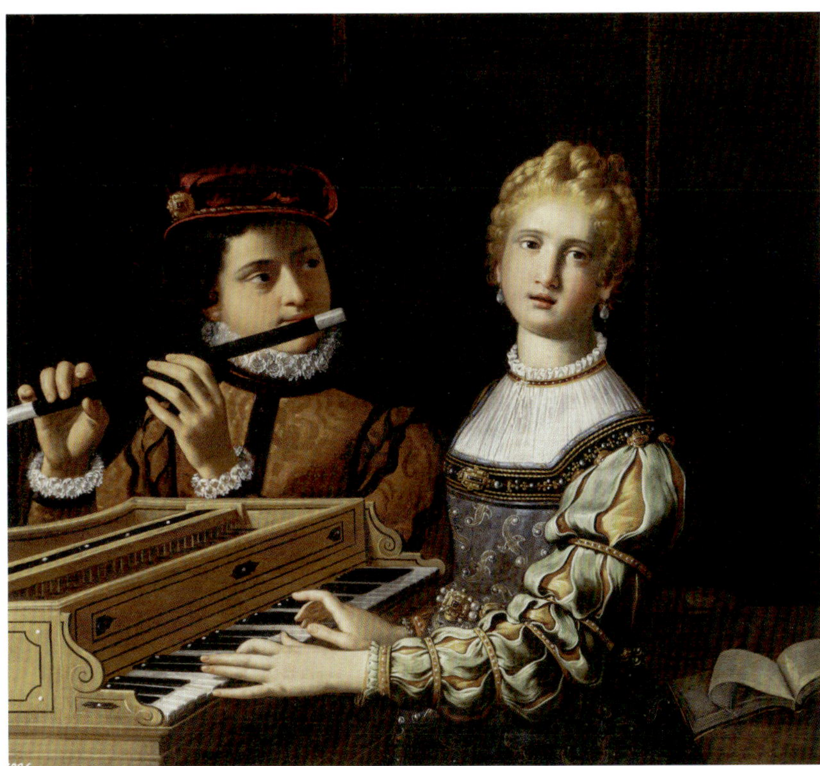

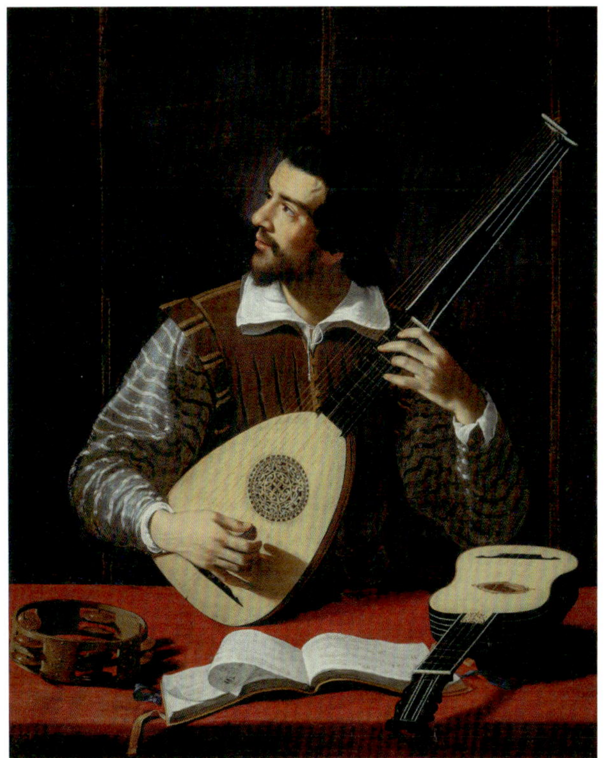

[fig. 6]
Antiveduto Gramatica, *Concert*, c. 1610–1612, Musei Reali, Galleria Sabauda, Turin

[fig. 7]
Antiveduto Gramatica, *Theorbo Player*, c. 1610–1612, Musei Reali, Galleria Sabauda, Turin

observed above, and at this point we need not be surprised given the convenience of the location, Caravaggio also frequented Gramatica by whom he was employed, Bellori tells us, to execute the famous *Heads*, thanks to which he made ends meet, one day at a time.[27] The fact remains that the young Caravaggio left an indelible impression in that workshop, as can be judged by Antiveduto Gramatica's own later Caravagesque direction. Gramatica and Caravaggio, not long after, were in fact to share the favours of Cardinal del Monte,[28] and I do not believe that the opportunity to imitate Caravaggio—his erstwhile assistant— escaped Gramatica's notice, perhaps precisely in order to propose himself to the patron. In this context, Antiveduto's execution of *Concerts* and *Musicians* [figs. 5–7][29] makes much more sense. These are the first paintings that echo Caravaggio's musical paintings for the cardinal in 1597, *The Musicians* [cat. 6] and the *Lute Player* [fig. 11].[30]

Gramatica collaborated until 1599 with Travagni, who soon afterwards would become the associate of Giovan Mario Gherardi and Adriano Monteleone from Perugia, with whom—and in this instance also, it cannot be a coincidence—one of Caravaggio's best-known copyists and interpreters, the young Milanese Giuseppe Vermiglio[31] worked, more or less from 1600. The fact that Vermiglio was so familiar with almost all of Caravaggio's Roman works, and provided paintings that were free interpretations rather than actual copies, invites one to believe that he had seen the paintings in the making, the inventions of which he then felt free to imitate after Caravaggio's departure from Rome.

On the other hand, even the hitherto little-known Giovanni Mario Gherardi does not seem immune to the influence of Caravaggism. The documentary evidence on the possibility that Gherardi may have been involved (and perhaps identified?) with the Hartford Master, the author, as we know, of a series of still-life paintings which, in the past have been attributed to Caravaggio himself, have now become too numerous not to be taken into serious consideration.[32] Although it is difficult to identify works by Gherardi, and thus to definitively unravel the mystery, the attribution of two still-life paintings portrayed in a detailed manner and very similar to those paintings by the Master in the inventory of the possessions belonging to Scipione Borghese and Stefano Pignatelli;[33] the hospitality granted in his workshop to the Spaniard Giovanni Quinsa[34] whose works have often been confused with those of the Master; Gherardi's attested production of copies of Jacopo Bassano's *Stories of Noah*, work reserved for skilled still-life painters[35] and his almost certain presence in a project such as that of the cloister of Santa Maria sopra Minerva in the company of Francesco Nappi, where festoons of fruit and flowers overflow;[36] all of these things suggest that it may have been he, Gherardi, together with his team, who took as their models the still-life paintings of Caravaggio, whom he had met in Via della Scrofa, thus popularising the genre.[37]

The common location of workshops selling similar products between Piazza Nicosia, Sant'Agostino and San Luigi dei Francesi thus leads one to think that many of these artists would have shared the richest commissions: *Illustrious Men*, but also the *Four Elements*; the *Four Seasons*; the *Five Senses* and the *Apostles*[38]; that is, that corporate enterprise amongst painters was the most widespread practice. From the contracts of these 'companies' that have come down to us, we learn that each artist brought with him a specific asset: whether the tools of the trade, the commissions, the labour, or all of these things together. It would seem that only a few ran the business on their own: setting up on one's own was evidently a luxury, and while working by the day could lead to one's talent being exploited, going it alone risked bankruptcy and starvation.[39] The decision to get along "on one's own"[40] was a target that the young Caravaggio achieved in stages, and besides, it was not even a stable solution.

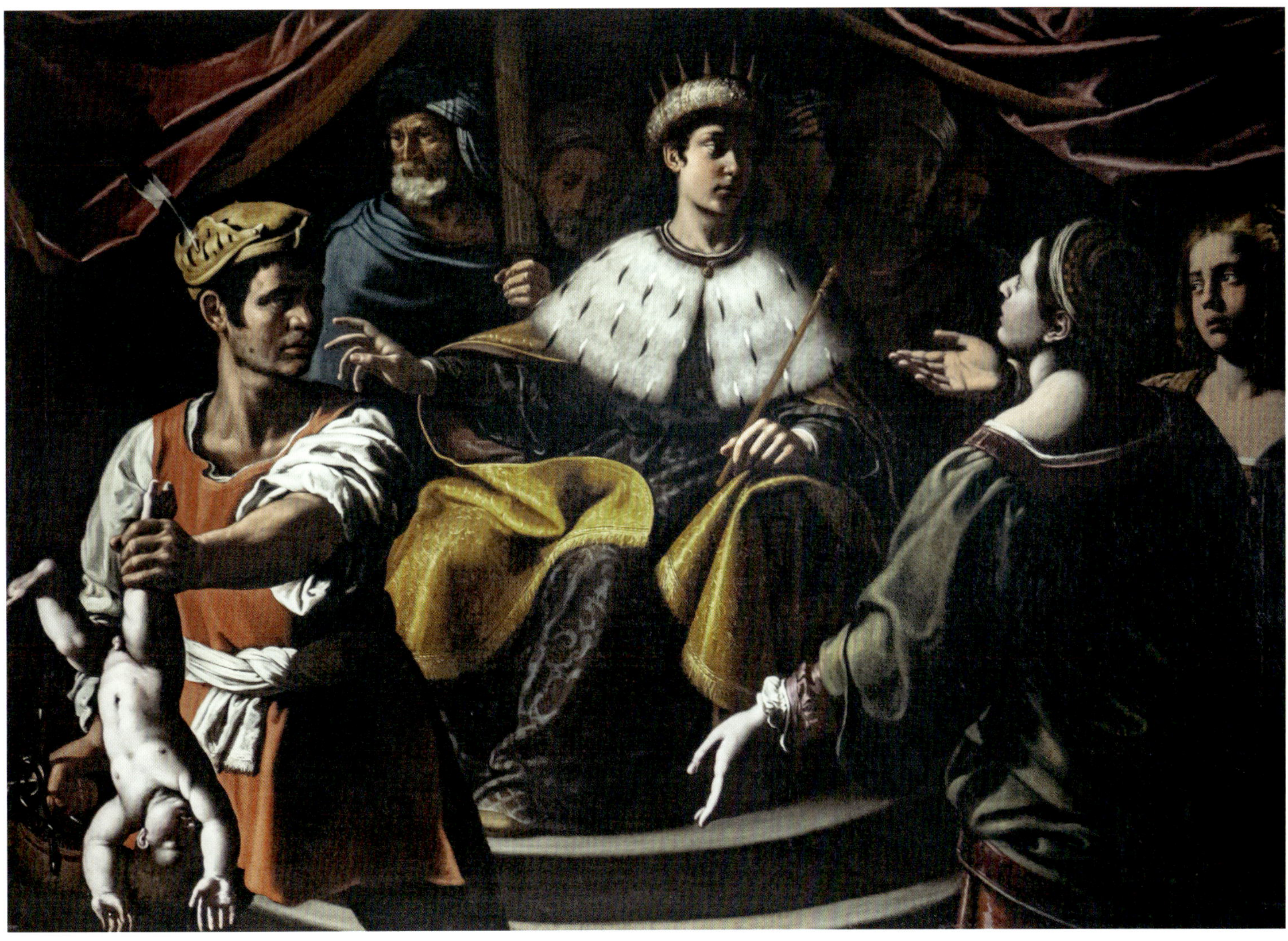

It is extraordinary to imagine that among the hundreds of *Heads* produced in Via della Scrofa by artists of extremely unequal skill, there are those produced by the young Caravaggio; identifying these will be the challenge for studies to come. However, bearing in mind that a part of this production—albeit limited—was taken up by the portraits of contemporaries (Ottavio Leoni, a friend of Caravaggio, would soon corner the market, even producing numbered series[41]), and that in the workshops the division of labour proceeded by specialisation also on the basis of ability—heads and hands to the masters or the most gifted of the painter-workers, the busts and dresses prepared in series by the apprentices[42]—I believe that something of the kind may have taken place for the *Portraits of Francesco* and of *Maffeo Barberini* [cat. 9], the former attributed to a Roman painter of the late sixteenth century, but which Gianni Papi now proposes to assign to the master,[43] the latter to Caravaggio himself.[44] The format and pose in fact suggest that the works were created as pendants, and could easily have been executed in the context of a workshop that produced this kind of painting in series, with the same system of the division of roles even within the same painting. The quality of Maffeo's head and face in particular is in fact so high, that I believe one can see in it the hand of the young Caravaggio, while the

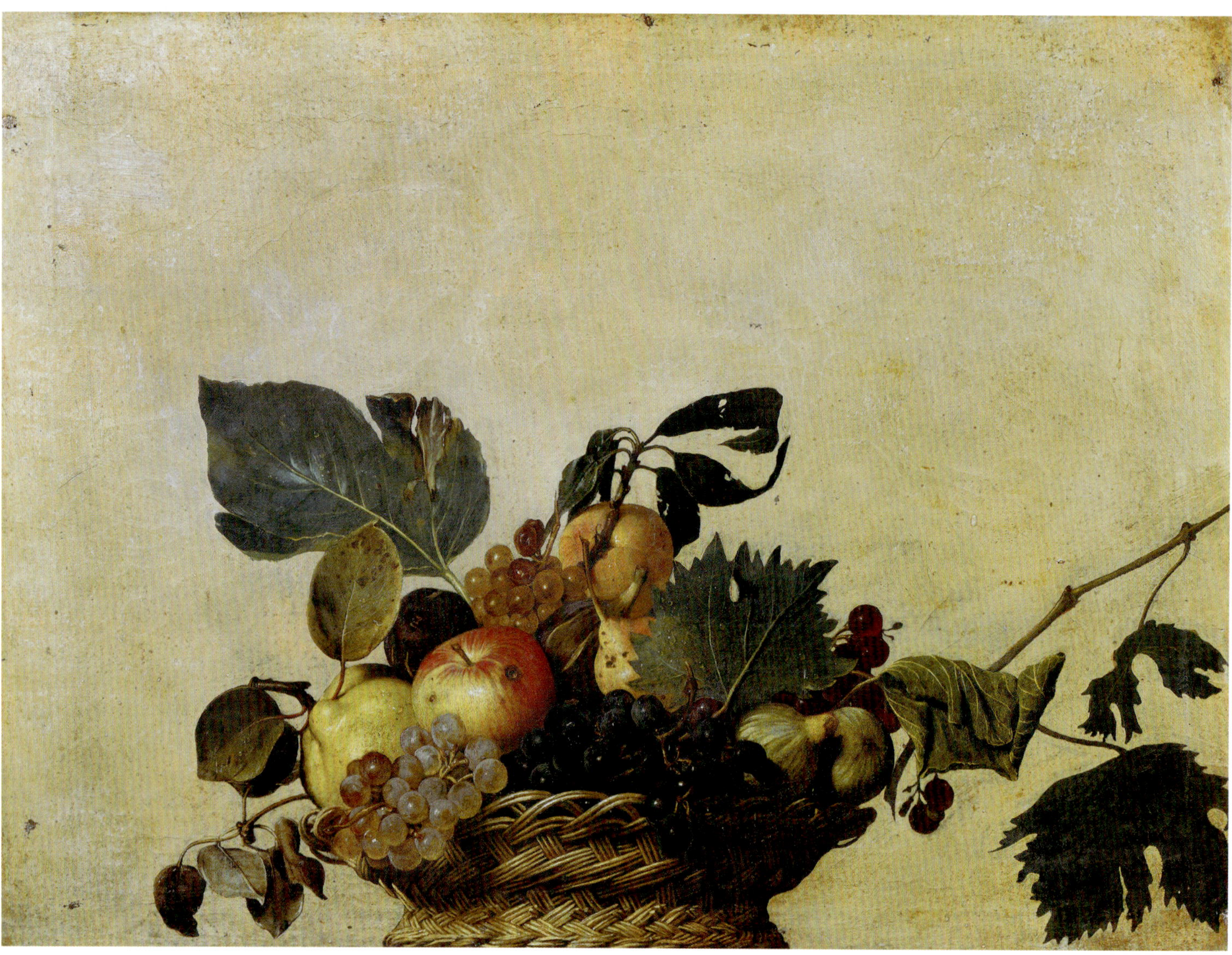

somewhat rigid drapery of the cassock and the stiffness which characterises the still-life hardly correspond with the naturalism of the fruit and flowers inserted in the half-length figures by the Lombard master, who in the Rome of 1595–1596 was undoubtedly peerless in the painting of *naturalia*.

LIVING NATURE

Among the artists frequented by Caravaggio, the Cavalier d'Arpino undoubtedly stands out: all the sources agree on this point, while the inventory of the Cavaliere's paintings, seized in 1607 and ending up in the hands of Scipione Borghese, attests that three of the five half-length figures by Caravaggio known to date were in his possession at that time: the *Sick Bacchus* [cat. 1], the *Boy with a Basket of Fruit* [fig. 2 on p. 160] and the *Boy with a Carafe of Roses*[45]. Cavalier d'Arpino's—'Giuseppino's'—workshop made a real leap in

Maria Cristina Terzaghi

career from 1598, when he became painter to the Aldobrandini, the family of the pope. Three years earlier, when Caravaggio was involved with his atelier in Piazza Nicosia, the Cavaliere seemed to be conducting more or less the same ménage as his colleagues, although his name hovered and was treated with great respect among the painters of Via della Scrofa, and many, including Costantino Spada himself, chose him as godfather to their children, as a guarantee of future protection.[46] The Cavaliere was in fact a real entrepreneur. Within a short time, he had won many important commissions in Rome and had also worked in Naples, gaining an international prestige that other colleagues barely enjoyed. The period of the working relationship between the young Caravaggio and the Cavaliere is now reasonably clear; possibly the summer 1595. Indeed, Mancini specifies that Caravaggio spent eight months with Cavalier d'Arpino, which can be calculated in reverse from the spring of 1596 when Caravaggio ended up in the Ospedale della Consolazione. As we have noted, Caravaggio's hospitalisation marked the break between him and the Cavalier d'Arpino, and I think an abrupt one at that: on the pretext that neither Giuseppe (d'Arpino) nor his brother Bernardino came to the aid the injured painter, once he was discharged from the hospital, Caravaggio never set foot again in Piazza Nicosia.[47]

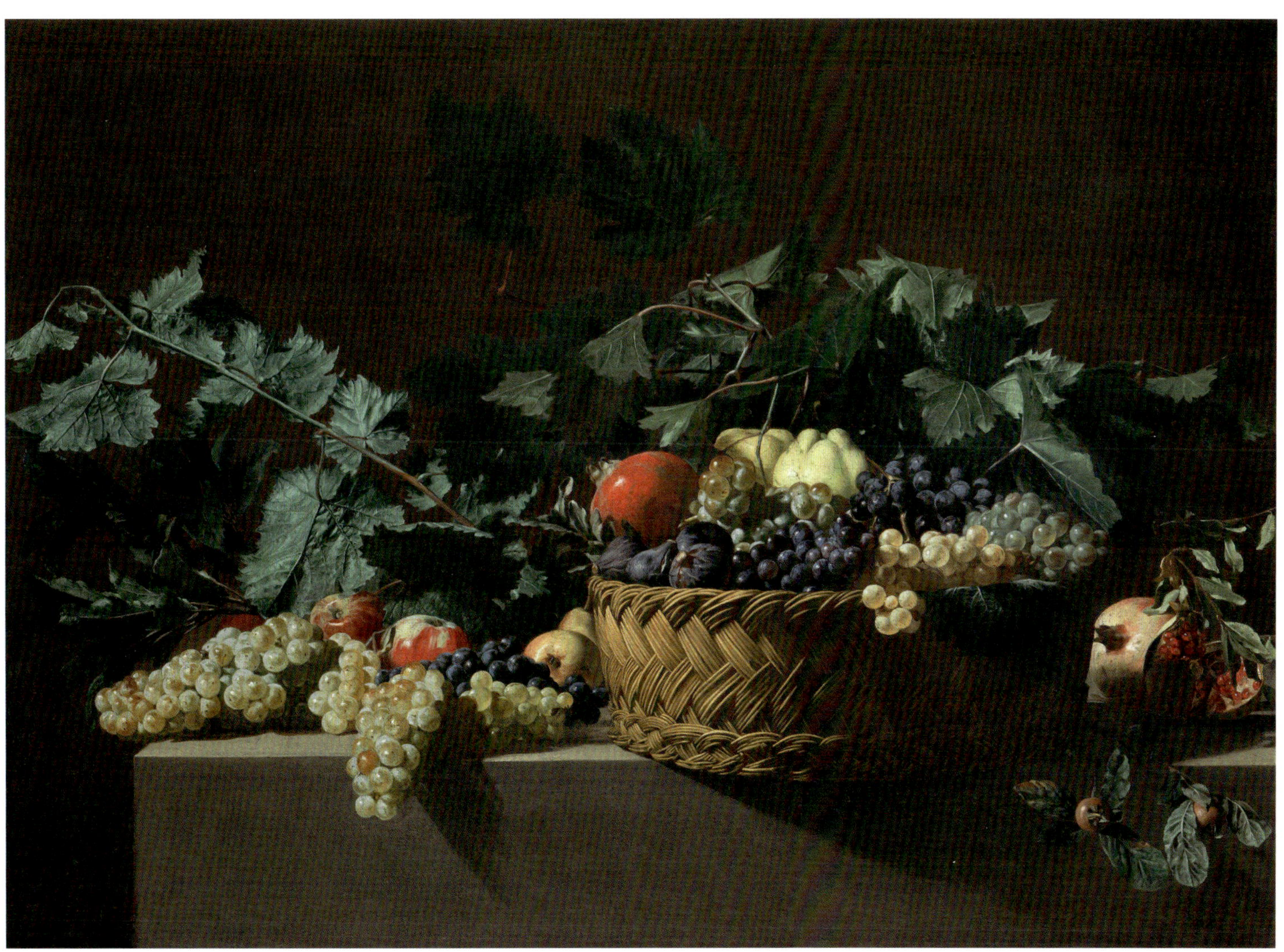

[fig. 10]
Bartolomeo Cavarozzi, *Basket of Fruit*, before 1613, Fondation Palatin, Vaduz, inv. FP 0051

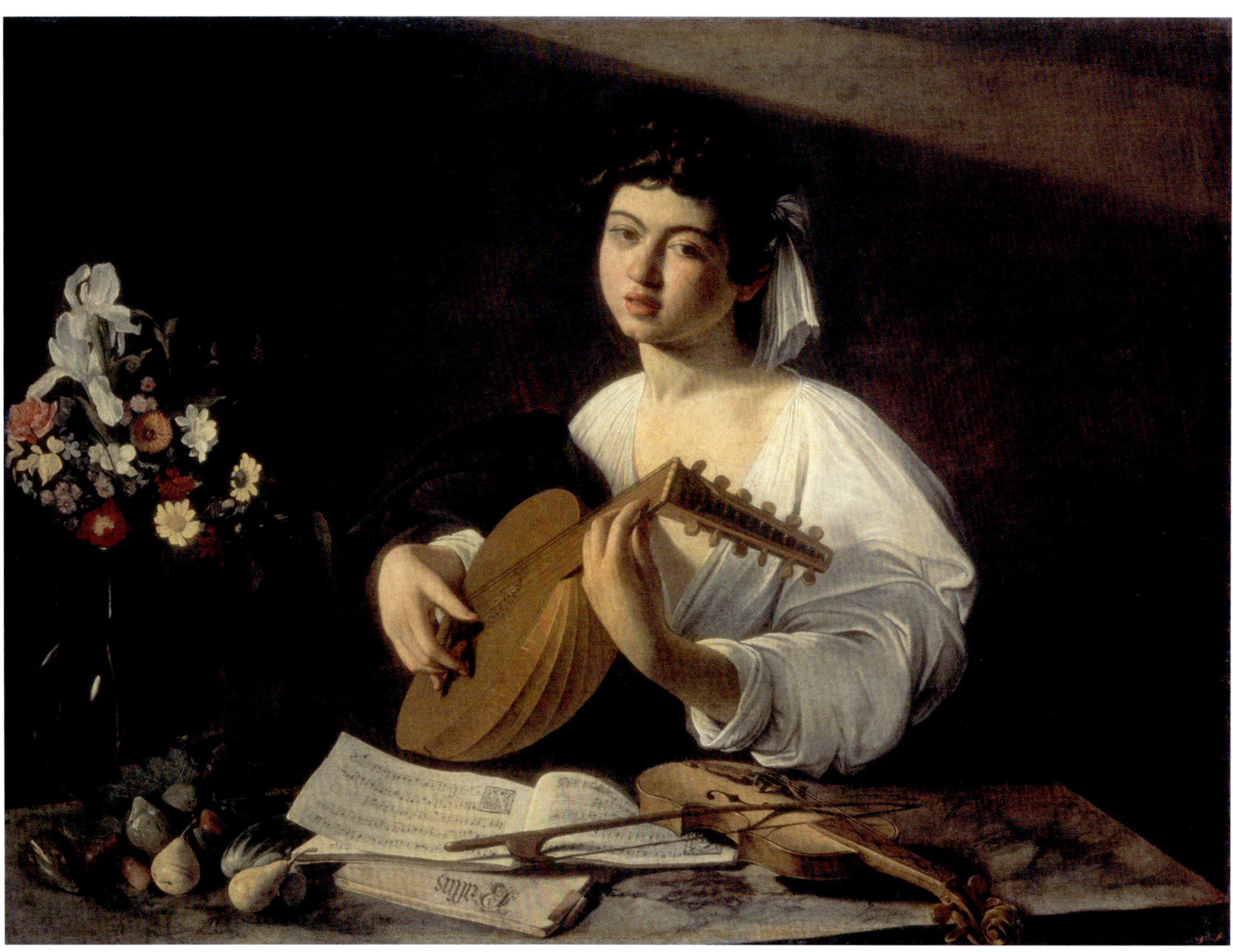

[fig. 11]
Lute Player, c. 1597,
The Hermitage State Museum,
St. Petersburg

But perhaps there was more to it than that. In fact, Bellori recounts that the artist in the workshop was: "Set to painting flowers and fruits, which he imitated so well that through him they attained the superior beauty that affords such delight nowadays"; a well-defined task that probably earned the artist the reputation of having invented a genre.[48]

Despite the proliferation of studies and the emergence of probable parallel experiments, no independent still-life has yet been identified with certainty that precedes the *Basket of Fruit* by Caravaggio, now in the Pinacoteca Ambrosiana, a piece that is undoubtedly early, but at the same time perfectly accomplished [fig. 9]. In this respect, the judgement of its owner, Cardinal Federico Borromeo, based in Rome between the end of 1596 and 1601, seems to me of extraordinary importance. Many years later in Milan, he would say of the painting: "Caravaggio's painting of fruit has that excellence which by comparison has always drawn me away from buying."[49] Whether the illustrious ecclesiastic bought the painting on the market, received it as a gift, or commissioned it,[50] the painting is not the only autonomous still-life by Caravaggio which is recorded. A "Carafe of flowers" is in fact admirably described in the collection of Cardinal del Monte,[51] there-

Maria Cristina Terzaghi

fore also at a time which seems to post-date his involvement with the Cavaliere. What, on the other hand, has remained of his production during his time in the Arpino workshop? Federico Zeri with extraordinary acumen provided an answer to this question by proposing an attribution to the hand of the young Caravaggio of the *Still Life with Fruit, Two Carafes of Flowers and Butterflies* [fig. 12] from the Wadsworth Atheneum in Hartford, present in the Cavaliere's inventory of 1607, and a series of paintings previously attributed to the anonymous Master named after that painting.[52] The great scholar's reasoning was based not only on stylistic grounds, but also on the assumption that the canvases were the production of an artist who worked alongside the Cavalier d'Arpino, which would be entirely plausible, but the reality appears more complicated.

With the idea of a Caravaggio somewhere between the bohemian and the romantic, who on leaving the Cavaliere's house, slammed the door to "vie with him for the glory of the brush,"[53] moreover leaving behind some of his canvases as hostages, with the danger that they might be used as models to be copied, we have a clash with a very interesting piece of information which definitively undermines this interpretation of the events. Contrary to what the inventory of the seizure of the Cavaliere's assets[54] would lead one to suppose, in fact, Mancini informs us that the *Sick Bacchus* [cat. 1] was for sale *chez* Costantino Spada: "In the meanwhile he painted a Bacchus and he was beardless, Borghese has it, Constantino had it,"[55] positioning the canvas at the beginning of Caravaggio's autonomous career (he executed it when "beardless"), an idea also shared by Giovanni Baglione: "After this [that is after he had left Cavalier d'Arpino's] he tried to get along on his own and painted a few small pictures from his own reflection in a mirror. The first was a *Bacchus* with bunches of various kinds of grapes executed with great care, but a little dry."[56] The painting was therefore designed for the market, and marketed by the shrewd Constantino Spada.

Perhaps not immediately, but certainly at some point in time, the Cavaliere must have bought the painting, and other such works by Caravaggio, and perhaps not only because of the high prices that they were now fetching.[57] I believe that he was planning to open up a market for reproductions of these works, in the same manner as the drawings of the great masters of which he had collected a great number;[58] this was a procedure that was in fact common to other workshops, in particular that of Tommaso Salini, in which incidentally the genre of the still-life was 'at home'.[59] And there is a strong suspicion that the Cavalier d'Arpino also nourished the secret hope of rivalling Prospero Orsi's activity in the field of marketing copies of Caravaggio's works, a project that, alas, went up in smoke with the confiscation.[60]

Prosperino delle Grottesche (as Prospero Orsi was also known) had in fact befriended and collaborated with the Cavaliere whom he frequented at the same time as Caravaggio; however, probably at the end of 1596, the relationship between the Cavaliere and Orsi altered, as Giovanni Baglione openly recounts: "[Prospero] was a great friend of Cavalier Giuseppe Cesari d'Arpino and with great study sought to imitate his manner in his paintings, and was extremely partial to his works, commending them to all with great praise. But after some time, I do not know for what reason, he became unfriendly towards him, and was one of Michelagnolo da Caravaggio's followers (*turcimanni*), and went to great lengths to be in opposition to the Cavaliere."[61]

On the other hand, it is not difficult to imagine that the common quarrels with the Cavaliere in a field of great rivalry such as the artistic milieu were one of the elements cementing Prospero friendship with Caravaggio;[62] both had in fact ended—and without appeal—their relationship with the well-connected Cavaliere, and had decided to embark on their own path.

"THEN HE TRIED TO GET ALONG ON HIS OWN"

It is extraordinary to note how the *Sick Bacchus*, perhaps the first canvas Caravaggio painted as his own work, and the cascade of others that followed: the *Boy Peeling Fruit* [cat. 2], the *Boy Bitten by a Lizard* [fig. 13], the *Boy with a Carafe of Roses*, the *Boy with a Basket of Fruit* and the *Bacchus* in the Uffizi [figs. 1, 14], constitute a synthesis of the genres practiced in the workshops: an *ensemble* of half-length figures and still-life. In the same format, with a similar compositional grammar, instead of saints, illustrious men and emperors, Caravaggio painted young apprentices, portraits of innkeepers and, above all, himself; instead of the traditional iconographic attributes, he inserted beautiful still-life elements that he had executed serially in the Cavalier d'Arpino's workshop. In this context, the direct testimony collected by one of the greatest admirers and collectors of the Lombard master, the Marchese Vincenzo Giustiniani, is doubly significant: "And Caravaggio said that it took as much work to execute a good painting of flowers as one with figures."[63]

Prospero Orsi was the first to grasp the sensational novelty of these works, intuiting their expressive and commercial potential, and he tried in every way to help the talented Caravaggio to emerge, making his home and connections available to the Lombard painter, so much so that he convinced his neighbour, Monsignor Fantino Petrignani, to offer the young artist "the comfort of a room." And it was there that some of his masterpieces were born.[64]

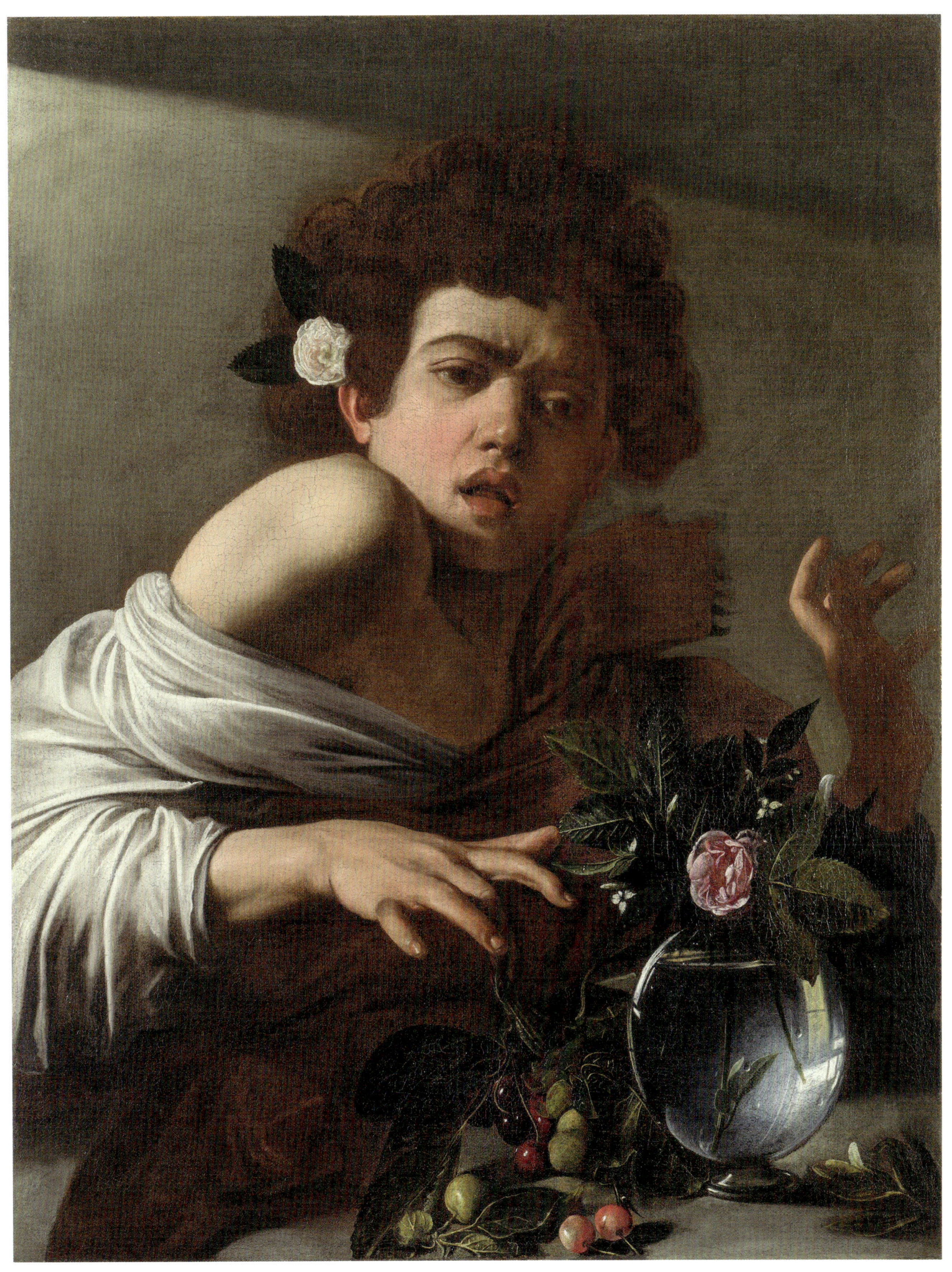

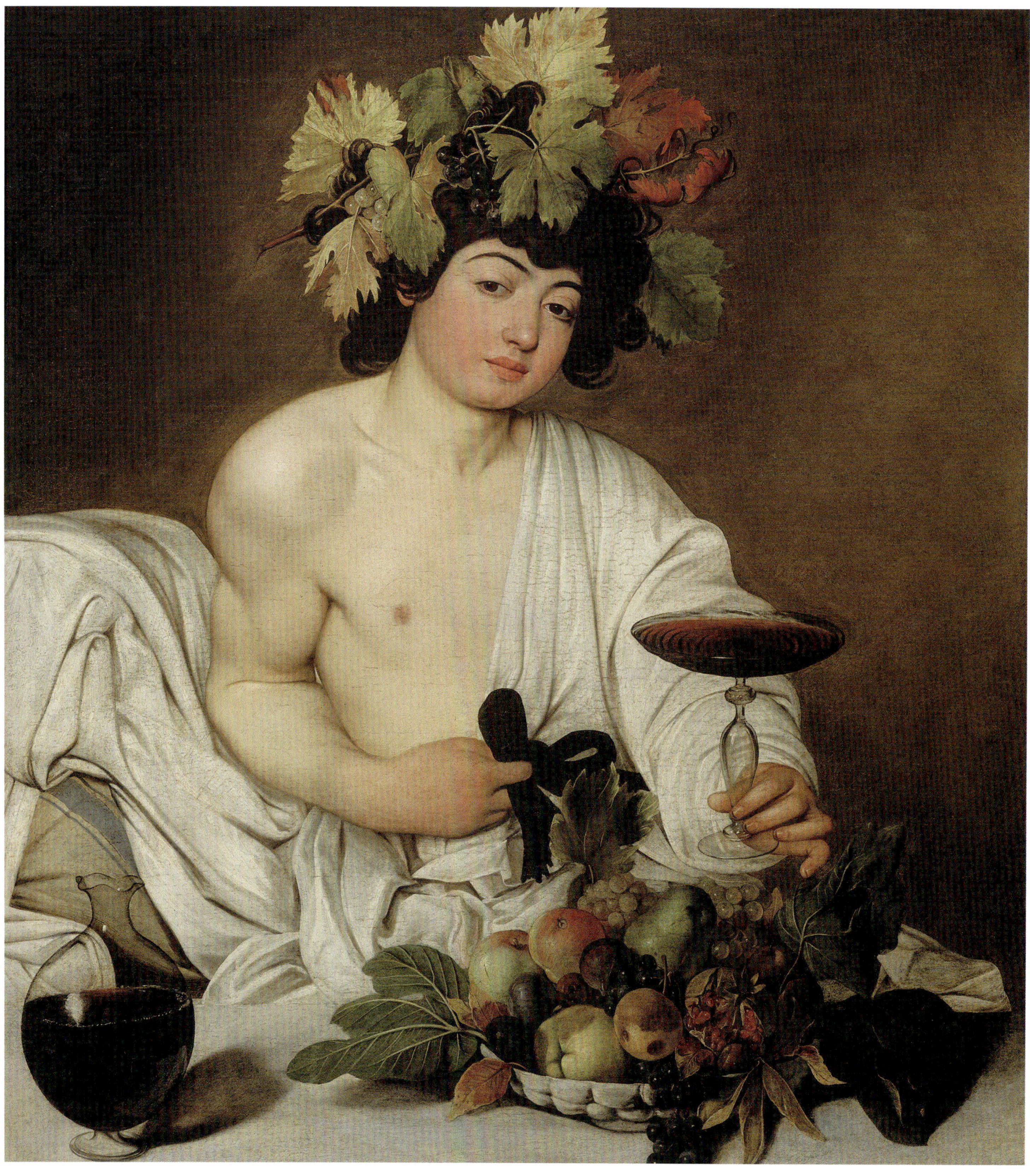

Maria Cristina Terzaghi

Mancini recounts, as we have seen, that the novelties had already begun to appear at Pandolfo Pucci's, when Caravaggio painted the *Boy Bitten by a Lizard*, and the *Boy Peeling Fruit*: "For the market he painted a boy who cries because he is bitten by a lizard which he is holding in his hand, and afterwards one who is peeling a pear with a knife, and a portrait of an innkeeper who had given him a place to live."[65] Baglione, on the other hand, places at the origin of Caravaggio's half-length figures the *Sick Bacchus*, and thus the artist's meditation on his own face as portrayed in a mirror, adding, however, that immediately afterwards he executed the *Lizard*, of which his biographer sings the praise: "He also painted a Boy bitten by a lizard which emerges from some flowers and fruits. The boy actually seems to cry out and the whole was worked with diligence."[66]

Both authors emphasise in essence how the *Boy Bitten by a Lizard* was a turning point in the artist's career, despite the difficulty of placing the painting on the market, which forced Caravaggio to sell it at the extremely low price of 15 *giuli*.[67] The central role attributed to the canvas is not accidental; it is also justified by Prospero Orsi's promotion of it. It is no coincidence, in fact, that copies of the *Boy Bitten by a Lizard* and the *Boy Peeling Fruit*, two works which, as we have said, Orsi probably saw being created, abound;[68] this is so to the degree that for the latter painting the superiority of one exemplar over the other is still a matter of debate, while of the *Lizard* two versions are in existence (London, National Gallery and Florence, Fondazione di Studi Roberto Longhi), both considered to be autograph, although the attribution of the Florentine painting is now highly debated.[69] If, in fact, the paintings were executed at Pucci's and sold with the help of Prospero Orsi, probably through Costantino Spada, Orsi would have been the only one who could have copied them, since Caravaggio, very reluctant to have copies made of his works, would have had qualms about preventing one who had helped him in so many ways from doing so. Proof of this, moreover, is the absence of early copies of the *Sick Bacchus* and the *Boy with a Basket of Fruit*, and the rare examples of copies of the *Boy with a Carafe of Roses*, all works that entered the Cavalier d'Arpino's collection, and thence into the Borghese collection during Caravaggio's lifetime, and thus before the Cavaliere had time to reproduce them or have them reproduced on a large scale.

Over and above the chronology, I think we can agree with Baglione in imagining that Caravaggio's first attempt to free himself from the serial production of the workshops was to take his own face as a model, the most immediate subject for an artist, and that he gave his own features to the heroes of all times or to mythological figures, as for that matter he had seen done in Lombardy, where Lomazzo had disguised himself as a porter (*facchino*) from the Val di Blenio, ivy-crowned like Bacchus, creating his *Self-Portrait as Abbot of the Accademia della Val di Blenio* (Milan, Pinacoteca di Brera). A comparison with another *Bacchus* (fig. 14, Florence, Gallerie degli Uffizi), painted only a few months later, gives a measure of the artist's stylistic evolution; the composition is more studied, while the naturalism of the fruit in the earthenware dish, which is largely over-ripe and rotting, now has the tragic undertones of a *Vanitas*.

Compared to the *Sick Bacchus*, however, the *Boy Bitten by a Lizard* is a work of greater complexity, taking a step forward and giving a central place not to the astonishment of one's own face reflected in the mirror, but to the representation of the sudden motions of the soul, once again in accordance with his Lombard approach and training that looked back to Leonardo himself. To this, Caravaggio adds the extraordinary power of the carafe in which the window is reflected, and the memory of this reflection is vivid in the accounts of biographers who give it a crucial place in the master's career. The painting draws

[fig. 14]
Bacchus, c. 1596–1597,
Gallerie degli Uffizi, Florence

along with it another extraordinary composition, the *Boy with a Carafe of Roses*, hitherto known in four versions, none of which are considered autograph.[70] The two paintings have sometimes been put side by side as pendants, possibly part of a series of the *Senses* (the *Lizard* representing touch, the *Boy with a Carafe of Roses,* the sense of smell).[71] If this were indeed the case, then Caravaggio would have interpreted in an extraordinary and unique way the allegorical personification of the Senses, a subject widespread both in the production of the Roman workshops and, more generally in the European figurative tradition, invigorating and revitalising the iconographic tradition even in the field of allegory, as he had done with Bacchus in the field of myth. In any case, it is a fact that the two compositions present an extraordinary affinity, both characterised not only by the depiction of nature that is anything but still, but almost palpably alive and vibrant, and also with the undoubted meaning of a *vanitas*: pleasure that turns to bitterness, and the fading of youth. For the moment we cannot go any further, also because the two paintings have different collecting histories: the *Carafe with Roses* in the collection of the Cavaliere d'Arpino, while the *Lizard* remained in circulation for a long time through Prospero Orsi. In fact, in 1611, at a very early date, he sold a copy of the painting to the Duca Giovan Angelo Altemps, who bought it as a *Self-Portrait* of Caravaggio, indisputable evidence that this was how the painting was interpreted by his contemporaries.[72] If it is uncertain for the these latter two paintings, for the *Boy Peeling fruit* the allegorical interpretation is amply justified, included as it was (original or copy, we do not know) in the collection of Cesare Crispolti, prince of the Accademia degli Insensati, to which many of Caravaggio's acquaintance belonged, including Maffeo Barberini, Aurelio Orsi, brother of his friend Prospero, and the Cavalier d'Arpino himself.[73] The *Boy with a Basket of Fruit* on the other hand has in its turn been interpreted as Vertumnus, the God of Autumn[74]. Be that as it may, at a far deeper level than the potential allegory, it is the explosive naturalism that dominates in these "Heads", making them "a drama in a nutshell", as Longhi masterfully stated of a slightly later masterpiece, the *Portrait of Maffeo Barberini* [cat. 9]. In the presence of so much truth, Rome would no longer be content with "*bagatelle*" (trifles), the path had been now traced.

1   Mancini [c. 1619–1621] 1956–1957, p. 319. English translation Friedländer [1955] 1976, p. 257.

2   Van Mander 1604, p. 191; Gandolfi 2021, pp. 320–321; Baglione [1642] 2023, p. 401; Bellori [1672] 1976, p. 213.

3   As affirmed in the contract for the lateral paintings for the Cerasi Chapel signed on 24 September 1600 (now in Macioce 2023, doc. 502, with the complete bibliography for the document).

4   I would like to mention with gratitude the work of scholars who have contributed to shed light on a decisive chapter for the understanding of Caravaggio's early period, and more generally for the mechanisms and procedures of painters' workshops in Rome, which until 2010 had been an area almost unexplored (with the exception of the important volume by Cavazzini 2008): Sickel 2009; Calenne 2010; Sickel 2010; Cavietti, Curti 2011, pp. 373–454; Pampalone 2011b, pp. 415–424; Sickel 2011, pp. 77–81; Curti 2014, pp. 313–317; Curti 2017b, pp. 269–275; Curti 2019. I would also like to mention the important collective volume *The Young Caravaggio "Sine ira et studio"* 2018, and in it, in particular, the essay by Papi 2018b, which addresses the problem of the stylistic 'production in series' element in Caravaggio's early works.

5   On the timing of Caravaggio's arrival in Rome see the exhibition catalogue *Caravaggio a Roma. Una vita dal vero* 2011, pp. 235–240. The trial on which the new chronology of Caravaggio's early Roman period is based is discussed by Cesarini 2011, pp. 54–59, and by Curti 2011b, pp. 65–76. Part of the trial was already known thanks to Corradini, Marini 1998, pp. 25–28. A summary of the affair is also in Berra 2018a and Terzaghi 2020b.

6   For Caravaggio in Milan, the research by Berra 2005 is fundamental; updated by Berra 2018a; see also Terzaghi 2020a.

7   For Simone Peterzano, see the recent catalogue of the fine exhibition *Peterzano: allievo di Tiziano* 2020. On the ties with these years in Milan, allow me to refer you to Terzaghi 2020a (with previous bibliography). For the links with the theatre, Terzaghi 2021a (with previous bibliography).

8   65 × 45 cm, usually in a vertical format.

9   Mancini [c. 1619–1621] 1956–1957, I, p. 249.

10   Van Mander 1604, English translation in Friedländer [1955] 1974, p. 260, with slight amendations.

11   For these workshops, see the bibliography cited in footnote 4, and now Terzaghi 2025 in press.

12   The term "turcimanno" is used by Giovanni Baglione both in his biography of Caravaggio (Baglione 1642, pp. 137, 300) and in that of Prospero Orsi, to emphasise the link between the two artists. Synonymous with 'interpreter' according to the Vocabolario della Crusca, the term could also allude to a commercial kind of mediation suggesting an additional lack of transparency (Paliaga 2015, p. 111; Gandolfi, in Baglione [1642] 2023, p. 575, footnote 10). For the figure of Costantino Spada, see Curti 2011a.

13   As studies on workshops—beginning with Cavazzini 2008, pp. 49–70—have shown.

14   The obscure annotation on f. 59*v* of the Marciana manuscript of the *Considerazioni sulla Pittura*, alongside the passage in which Mancini speaks of Caravaggio's sojourn with Monsignor Pandolfo Pucci da Recanati, beneficiary of St. Peter's, already reported in Mancini [c. 1619–1621] 1956–1957, II, pp. 226–227, has been brilliantly unravelled by Curti 2019, pp. 138–145, p. 138. For Pucci, see in particular Teza 2013, pp. 21–32, which also summarises earlier studies.

15   The identification of the 'Tarquinio' cited by Mancini with Ligustri was first proposed by Marini 2001, pp. 14–15; Moretti 2009, p. 82; Moretti 2012a, p. 121; Moretti 2012b, p. 57, and reaffirmed by Curti 2019.

16   On Tarquinio Ligustri, see in particular Guerrieri Borsoi 2000; Nicolai 2001; Sickel 2003b; Nicolai 2007 and now F. Nicolai's commentary and critical notes in Baglione [1642] 2023, pp. 489–491.

17   Prospero Orsi was born in Stabio in the province of Viterbo (Sickel 2003a, pp. 51, 78, footnote 4).

18   On this matter, see Moretti 2009, p. 82: Moretti 2012a, p. 121; Moretti 2012b, p. 57; Curti 2019, p. 141.

19   Orsi as early as the 1590s received payments from cardinal Alessandro Peretti Montalto, nephew of Pope Sixtus V and Camilla Peretti; Pandolfo Pucci had served the latter as steward from 1588 to 1591, and it is therefore probable that the two knew each other well (Terzaghi 2007, pp. 276–279 and Terzaghi 2010b, p. 18).

20   Gandolfi, Zuccari 2017, pp. 250–251; Gandolfi 2019, p. 137; Gandolfi 2021, p. 320. The passage is taken up by Giovan Pietro Bellori in his marginal notes to Baglione's biography of Caravaggio (1642, p. 146): "He took refuge in the workshop of Mss. Lorenzo Siciliano in Rome, where, being extremely destitute and vulnerable (*ignudo*), he painted heads for a *grosso* [giulio] and would paint three in a day, then he worked in the lodgings of Antiveduto Gramatica, half-length figures that were not even painted carelessly".

21   The proceedings of the trial were published in full in *Caravaggio a Roma* 2011, pp. 235–240. The trial is discussed by Cesarini 2011, pp. 54–59, and by Curti 2011b, pp. 65–76. Part of the document was already known thanks to Corradini, Marini 1998, pp. 25–28. For the episode of Caravaggio's wound and his admission to the Ospedale della Consolazione, see Baroncelli 2011.

22   For a description of the workshop, Curti 2011b. When with Carli, Caravaggio met another Sicilian painter, Mario Minniti, one of his earliest admirers, a friendship which—although Minniti returned to Sicily shortly afterwards—the Lombard master would renew in Syracuse years later as he fled from Malta to the north. For Minniti's return to Sicily, see Cuppone 2021b.

23   Perceptively interpreted by Giorgio Leone (Leone 2016), see also R. Vodret, in *Caravaggio. Opere a Roma* 2016.

24   Mancini [c. 1619–1621] 1956–1957, I, p. 140, see now the passage in Macioce 2023, p. 357. For a later assessment of *The Fortune Teller*, see the correspondence between Giulio Mancini and his brother Deifebo, published by Maccherini 1997, p. 75.

25   Baglione [1642] 2023, p. 558 (commentary and critical notes on the biography by Giuseppe Porzio): "In giving shape to the heads there was no one better than he, and he painted them with great skill and likeness. And for copying those illustrious men, who are painted in the palace of the garden of the Medici, there was none more skilful than he; and no prince came to Rome, or personage who did not have great regard for Antiveduto, wishing to have him portray the heads of these illustrious men; and in this practice he advanced, earning well: and in truth they

were beautiful, and executed in a fine manner, so that he acquired the name of great painter of heads (gran capocciante)".

26   For Vittorio Travagni, see Pampalone 2011b. On the close association with other artists, see Calenne 2010, pp. 115–116; Cavietti, Curti 2011; Curti 2014; Curti 2017b; Terzaghi 2025 in press.

27   Baglione 1642, p. 212, in the copy annotated by Giovan Pietro Bellori.

28   Baglione [1642] 2023, p. 559 also emphasises the cardinal's predilection for Antiveduto Gramatica: "For Francesco Maria cardinal of the marchesi del Monte he painted various things, but in particular a large painting of Solomon king of Israel before the evil idolatrous women, very rich; those enticing women were adorned with beautiful garments, and the work was much admired". I believe this painting should be identified with the painting of a similar subject, oil on canvas 145 × 192.5 cm in the Luigi Koelliker collection, published by Gianni Papi, entry in *Orazio Borgianni* 2020, pp. 140–141 [fig. 8]. The painting is still recorded in the cardinal's collection at the time of his death in 1627, where the subject is identified as 'The Idolatry of Solomon', which precisely recurs in Baglione's description. Papi does not refer to the passage in Baglione, but to a work with a similar subject, but 30 cm smaller than the Koelliker painting, in Giovan Angelo Altemps' inventory of 1618–1619 (Nicolai 2008, pp. 71-73). In fact, the 15 *palmi* recorded in Del Monte's inventory, even including the frame, which is described in detail, is larger than the size of the painting, but it should be borne in mind that the description is accurate and paintings in awkward positions were not properly measured, especially in judicial inventories such as the one cited. Nor is it improbable that one of the two canvases was a copy (hardly that of Monte, if this were the case), or else that there were two autograph versions of the painting.

29   The works in the Galeria Sabauda in Turin that came from the del Monte collection formed a single painting (Papi 2022). A more complete version of a concert featuring some of the musicians present in del Monte's painting, first identified by Pulini (2022, pp. 36–37), I think was instead owned by the Marchese Orazio Lancellotti, another illustrious collector and patron in the Rome of the time. In the Lancellotti inventory of 1640, at number 25, there is indeed a: "Picture of a concert with instruments, an original by Ant[...]d[...] with a frame edged with gold", better described in the later inventory of assets as: "another [measuring] seven by five represents a concert with four figures with a frame the colour of walnut with gold fillets, it is believed to be by the hand of Michelangelo del Caravaggio". (Archivio Lancellotto, palazzo, fasc. 26 lettera E, transcribed by Cavazzini 1998, p. 193). As I have been able to ascertain (Terzaghi 2023a, online https://www.youtube.com/watch?v=6PMhLvgT4wU, and forthcoming), the painting probably refers to a concert involving the musicians of Cardinal Alessandro Peretti Montalto, whose star was the Neapolitan singer Ippolita Recupito, together with her husband Cesare Marotta and the very young flutist Orazio Michi.

30   As cited by Baglione 1642, p. 136: English translation adapted from Friedländer [1955] 1976, p. 234: "He painted for the cardinal a concert of youths well portrayed from nature; also a young man playing the lute, who seemed alive, and the whole true [to life], with a carafe of flowers full of water, in which the reflec-

tion of a window could be seen perfectly and the other objects in the room, and on the flowers fresh dew rendered with exquisite accuracy . . . And this he said was the most beautiful painting he ever fashioned." For the various versions and inventory references and for the bibliography, see the critical notes in the cited biography of Caravaggio (Terzaghi in Baglione [1642] 2023, pp. 401–402, notes 12–14). The painting represents the pinnacle of his work in the workshops, admirably uniting still-life and figure, and marking the opening onto musical paintings.

31   On the painter and his Roman phase, *Giuseppe Vermiglio* 2000 remains fundamental; for an update, see Terzaghi 2020b.

32   The biographical details of Giovan Mario Gherardi, a native of Urbino and probably a relative of the more famous Cristoforo Gherardi, are unknown; his figure was first brought into focus by Calenne 2010, pp. 112–132. On the question of his relationship to the Hartford Master, see now Terzaghi 2025 in press.

33   Terzaghi 2025 in press. The inventory held in the Doria Pamphilj Archives which it is difficult to date, between c. 1606 and 1621, was known to Cappelletti 1998; Testa 1998; De Marchi 2016, and can now also be consulted in the Getty Provenance Index database. However, it was thought to list the possessions belonging to Silvestro Aldobrandini, rather than the paintings that would later end up in the collection of Giuseppe Pignatelli, heir of Cardinal Stefano, a close friend of Scipione Borghese. In addition, Gherardi's name had been interpreted as 'Gherardo', and as a result the search was not successful.

34   Terzaghi 2025 in press.

35   Calenne 2010, pp. 127–128.

36   Calenne 2010, p. 122–123.

37   On all of this, see Terzaghi 2025 in press.

38   On the production of the workshops referred to above, see Cavietti, Curti 2011 and Terzaghi 2025 in press. On the production of workshops in Rome in these years more generally, Cavazzini 2008.

39   Cavietti, Curti 2011; Curti 2014; Curti 2017b and Terzaghi 2025 in press, with bibliography.

40   Baglione [1642] 2023, pp. 400–401, critical commentary and notes by M.C. Terzaghi. English translation from Friedländer [1955] 1976, p. 234.

41   On all of this, see Primarosa 2017.

42   Remaining within the sphere of the workshops that Caravaggio frequented, this practice is attested in that of the famous portrait painter Abraham Vinck, partner of Louis Finson, who hosted Caravaggio once he arrived in Naples in the autumn of 1606, as is demonstrated by a payment dated 24 May 1605 from Scipione Cavallo, involving not only Vinck, but also the painter Francesco Bottone: "Al Cl. Scipione Cavallo six ducats, and for him to Francesco Bottone they said part of 16½ ducats that he offered them for a portrait that they will have to paint full-length, and in 15 days time, and the head and the hands will have to be painted by 'Abram fiamengo' (Abraham the Flemish painter), and the rest by the said Francesco" (Pinto 2022, p. 4077). For these Caravaggio-related events, see Terzaghi 2022b, pp. 61–62.

43   See the entry in *L'Immagine sovrana* 2023, pp. 160–161 and Gianni Papi's essay in this catalogue.

44   For the attribution history of the painting, see recently *L'Immagine sovrana* 2023, pp. 158–159 and Gianni Papi's essay in this catalogue.

45   The inventory was first published by De Rinaldis 1936. The seizure followed the trial of the painter in 1607, accused of assaulting and scarring the face of his colleague Cristoforo Roncalli known as Pomarancio. The plea deal led to the confiscation of the property by the Camera Apostolica and the subsequent gift of the collection by Paul V to his nephew Scipione Borghese (Cirinei 2001, pp. 255-305; Sickel 2001, pp. 159–189; Röttgen 2002, pp. 129–135; Cavazzini 2008, pp. 179–180). The Cavaliere also owned an exquisite collection of drawings by various artists, bequeathed to his sons, for which see especially Bolzoni 2013, pp. 148–156.

46   For Costantino Spada, see Francesca Curti's essay in this catalogue; for the other artists, see *Alla ricerca di Ghiongrat* 2011, pp. 399–401.

47   It is again the autograph notes to the Marciano codex of Mancini's *Considerazioni* [c. 1619–1621] 1956–1957, I, p. 340, now in Macioce 2023, p. 355, that mention Caravaggio's chagrin at the Cesari brothers' indifference: "After that a horse's kick swelled up [?] the leg, and no doctor for this was seen. And a Sicilian workshop owner [brought him] to the Consolatione. Neither C.G. nor B. did go, so neither did he return." See also *Caravaggio a Roma* 2011, pp. 399–401.

48   However, according to Bellori ([1672] 2005, pp. 179–180 the being "kept from figures" was regretted by Caravaggio to such a degree that he decided his time with the Cavaliere d'Arpino was over.

49   Rovetta 2006, pp. 109–127. Borromeo's position towards Caravaggio is a matter of much debate, see the discussion in Terzaghi 2018, pp. 108–121.

50   On the painting, see Terzaghi 2018 with previous bibliography. On still-life painting in Caravaggio's time, see *The Origin of Still Life* 2016.

51   On the *Carafe with Flowers*, see in particular Paliaga 2012. Of great importance in relation to this are the numerous references to autonomous still-life paintings attributed to Caravaggio himself in the inventory of the duke Giovan Angelo Altemps' possessions of 1619–1620 (Nicolai 2008, pp. 218–221, 230–233, who also points out those already noted by Spezzaferro 2002). In particular, we know that on 15 February 1613 Prospero Orsi sold to the duke for 40 *scudi*: "two pictures of fruits, one by Caravaggio, the other by Bartolomeo" the latter to be identified with the young Bartolomeo Manfredi, also promoted by the Orsi / Ligustri group (Curti 2019). I believe the citation is highly relevant to the dating of Cavarozzi's autonomous still-life paintings [fig. 10], the only ones that can be said to closely echo the *Canestra* (on this subject see Porzio 2017).

52   Zeri 1976, pp. 92–103; re-edited in Zeri, 1998, pp. 21–27.

53   Bellori [1672] 2005, p.180.

54   Where it is recorded as: "No. 54. Another small picture with a young man with garlands of ivy around him and bunches of grapes in his hand, without a frame," see De Rinaldis 1936, pp. 110, 114, no. 54 and Della Pergola 1959, II, pp. 76–78, cat. 112.

55   For a similar reading of the annotation, see Posner 1971, pp. 315–316; Marini 2001, pp. 14–16; Teza 2013, pp. 14–15.

56   Baglione [1642] 2023, p. 401, and footnote 8 (ed. M.C. Terzaghi). English translation in Friedländer [1955] 1976, p. 234.

57   Maccherini 1997, pp. 80, 84, 86 and Nicolaci, Gandolfi 2011, pp. 55–59.

58   Bolzoni 2013, pp. 134–157.

59   The inventory of Tommaso Salini's workshop, where many canvases that served as "*modelletti*" are recorded, was published by Pegazzano 1997, pp. 131–146.

60   On the subject, see Terzaghi 2025 in press.

61   Baglione [1642] 2023, p. 575, (commentary and critical notes by R. Gandolfi).

62   With a similar idea, Gandolfi, Zuccari 2017, pp. 250–253.

63   The transcription of the passage and of the text in which it is included is by Berra 2018b, pp. 453–479, which differs slightly from the first printed publication of Giustiniani 1667–1675, 3, 1675, III.

64   On Caravaggio and Fantino Petrignani, a native of Amelia, see Moretti 2009, and for further details Moretti, in *Il giovane Caravaggio* 2018, who hypothesises that even the *Bacchus* now in the Uffizi [fig. 14], in 1609 already housed in the villa of Artimino owned by the Grand Duke of Tuscany, may have been executed in the house of Fantino Petrignani who was linked to Antonio Maria Graziani, who in turn was in close contact with the Grand Duke. In terms of style the painting is close to the half-length figures referred to above, while the still-life is as mature as the fruits in the *Basket of fruit* (the *Canestra*) and the *Boy with a Basket of Fruit*.

65   Mancini [c. 1619–1621] 1956–1957, I, p. 224; II, p. 112, notes 884, 885. English translation in Friedländer [1955] 1976, p. 257. For the double *lectio* of this passage in the two manuscripts of the *Considerazioni*, see Teza 2013, p. 18.

66   Baglione [1642] 2023, p. 401, and footnote 9. English translation in Friedländer [1955] 1976, p. 234.

67   Mancini [c. 1619–1621] 1956–1957, I, p. 140. Baglione [1642] 2023, p. 401, footnote 10, also records: "Nor did he find it possible to dispose and make a success of them."

68   They are collected together in Savina 2013, pp. 91–99; 102–106.

69   See discussion in Zuccari 2018.

70   One of these is conserved in Atlanta, High Museum of Art, inv. 8.1; the other is in a private collection in Lugano, considered autograph by Marini 2005, pp. 132–133, no. 2, pp. 370–371, no. 2 (see also Berra 2014, pp. 11–71). The last two versions, of inferior quality, were sold at a Sotheby's auction in 2010 (oil on canvas, 66 × 51.40 cm, Sotheby's New York, 29 January 2010, lot 706, then published by Berra 2016, p. 61) and the other (oil on canvas, 65 × 51.5 cm) the first time at Sotheby's New York, 27 January 2023, lot 435; then again Sotheby's New York, 6 October 2023, lot 12 as "Follower of Michelangelo Merisi called Caravaggio 18th or 19th century". I know of a fifth version of very high quality, recognised by me as autograph, kept in a private collection in France (oil on canvas, 66 × 52.5 cm). It is possible to trace the canvas' provenance from the seizure of Cavalier d'Arpino's collection in 1607, through the Borghese collection, where it remained until at least 1831, while since 1909 it has been in Paris in the collection of a famous bookseller. I will give an account of all the steps and details on this painting in a forthcoming publication.

71   On all of this, see Berra 2016.

72   Spezzaferro 2002, p. 28; Nicolai 2008, p. 238.

73   Teza 2013.

74   Berra 2012.

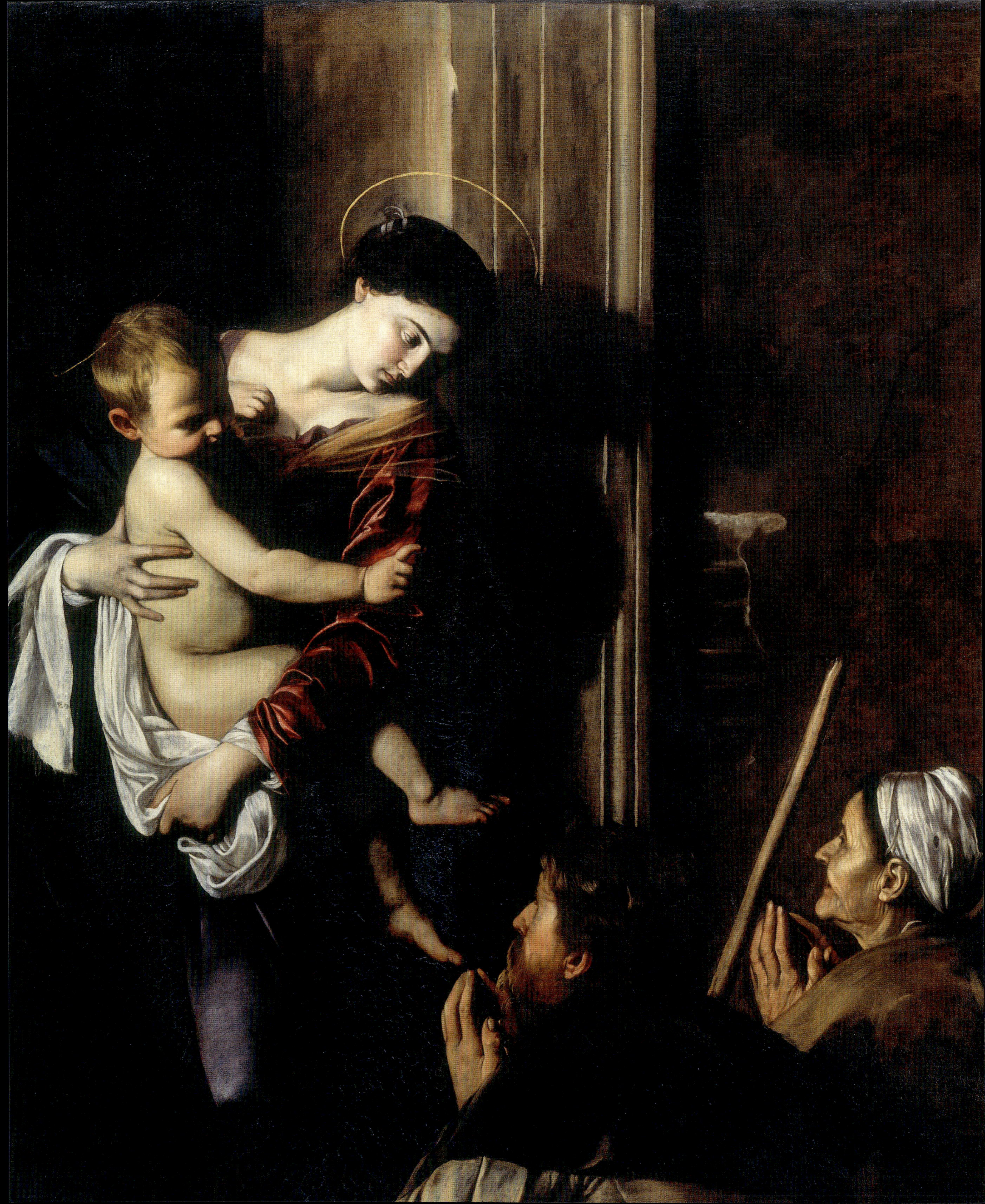

Francesca Cappelletti

"SUCCUMB TO THE CLAMOUR", GRAB THE MAIN CHANCE

A FEW NOTES ON THE COLLECTING OF CARAVAGGIO IN ROME

"Caravaggio's realistic mysticism is the strongest and most persuasive interpretation of the popular religious movements of the period in which he lived."[1] Walter Friedländer's book, from which the quotation is taken, was published in 1955 and represented the first attempt, in Anglo-Saxon scholarship, to interpret systematically, with a *catalogue raisonné*, the course taken by the artistic career of the great Lombard painter who had re-emerged into the spotlight four years earlier with the great Milanese exhibition. The impression aroused by Roberto Longhi's studies, and by the feat he had accomplished with the exhibition at Palazzo Reale in 1951, is already present in the first pages of the book. The 'rediscovery' of Caravaggio was all the more surprising, in Friedländer's eyes, because in his case it was not a question of a fascinating and peripheral seventeenth-century painter, such as Georges de La Tour or Louis Le Nain, but an artist who had disappeared both from scholarship and the public imagination despite having worked for most of his life in a great artistic centre such as the Rome of the popes at the beginning of the seventeenth century; moreover, one who had also deeply impressed artists who were his contemporaries, and those of the following generation, and not just in Italy but throughout Europe. And yet, it was not until the first decades of the twentieth century that his paintings—characterised by dramatic lighting that reclaimed from the darkness the still, humble and grandiose figures—, regained the attention of scholars. According to Friedländer, however, there had not yet been sufficient research into what we would today call today Caravaggio's cultural context or, to be even more contemporary, the social networks[2] within which the artist moved in Rome during the papacies of Clement VIII Aldobrandini (1592-1605), Leo XI Medici (April 1605) and the early days of

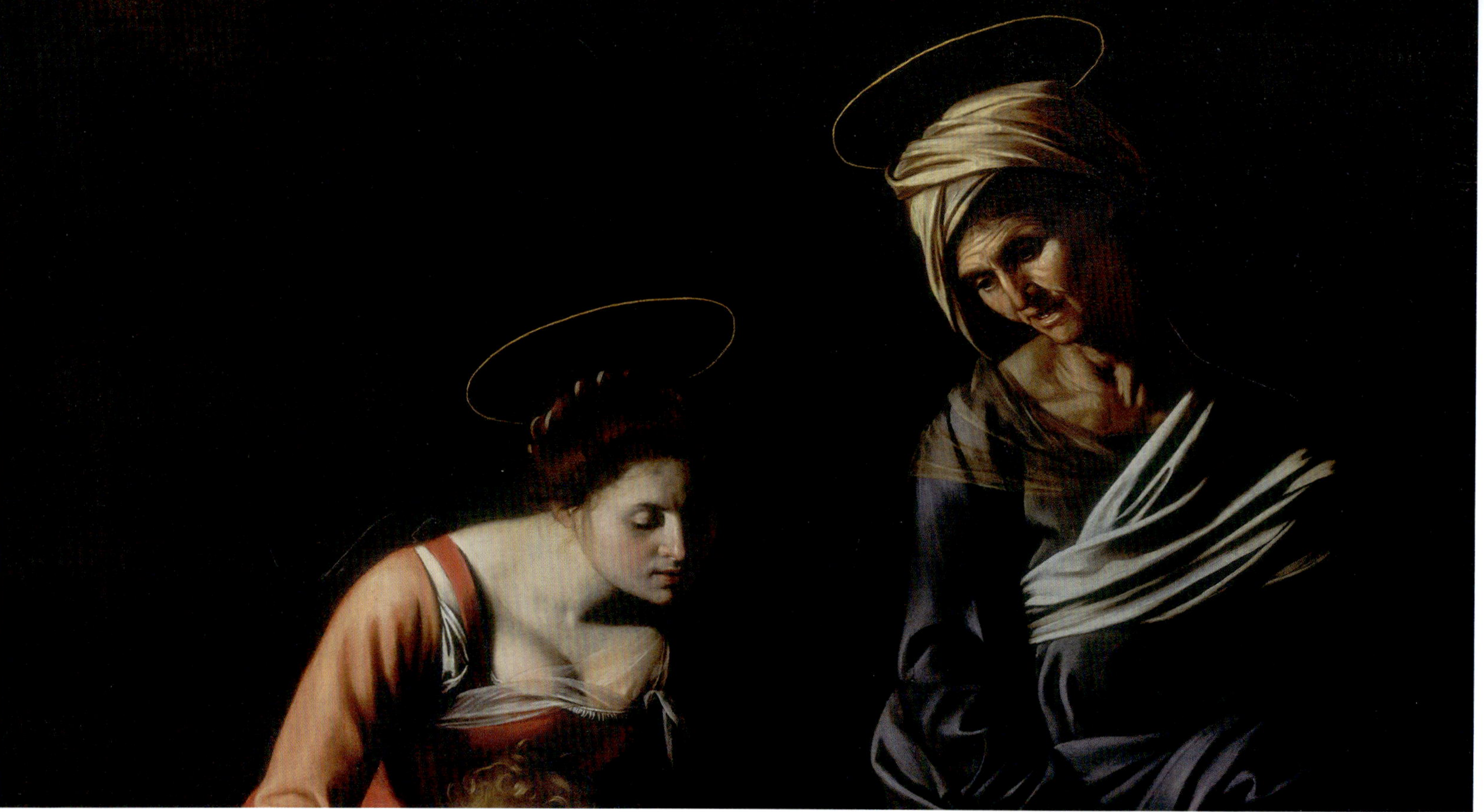

Paul V Borghese (1605-1621) under whom he lived in Rome, fled to the south, and died in Porto Ercole in 1610. Focusing his attention on the artist's mature religious works, that is the altarpieces painted after his experience with the Contarelli chapel, the great scholar saw the emergence of a new form of religiosity, in which the human drama became more important than the celebration of the divine aspects of the events, and the humble faces and contemporary dress of the protagonists were intended to bring about a deep, present-day and ever-renewed meditation on the Christian meaning. While understanding the striking novelty of the Contarelli works, his analysis focused instead on the Roman altarpieces dating from the years before his flight, such as the *Madonna dei Pellegrini* in Sant'Agostino [fig. 1; overall fig. 3 on p. 126] and the *Madonna dei Palafrenieri*, now in the Galleria Borghese [fig. 2; overall fig. 9 on p. 133]. Moving from the diffuzion of the spiritual exercises of Saint Ignatius beyond the restricted Jesuit circle, and from the dissemination of the Catholic practices of Saint Philip Neri and the Oratory, Friedländer began an in-depth study of Caravaggio's works, trying to provide a key to understanding the support the works had enjoyed, at times passionate, and the debate they had aroused in a conspicuous part of Roman society, at least according to his biographers. It was a question of looking beyond the surface of Caravaggio, of making one's way through the darkness, and at a time when, it should not be forgotten, the catalogue of the painter's works was certainly different from the one established in the last decades of the twentieth century. One only has to leaf through the texts from the 1950s to realise to what degree the studies still included works by contemporaries and followers, while the chronology lacked any precise points of reference. The discovery of the contract for the Cerasi Chapel by Denis Mahon in 1951, and the documents found by Herwarth Röttgen in 1965 that finally specified the date of execution of the paintings for the side-walls of the Contarelli

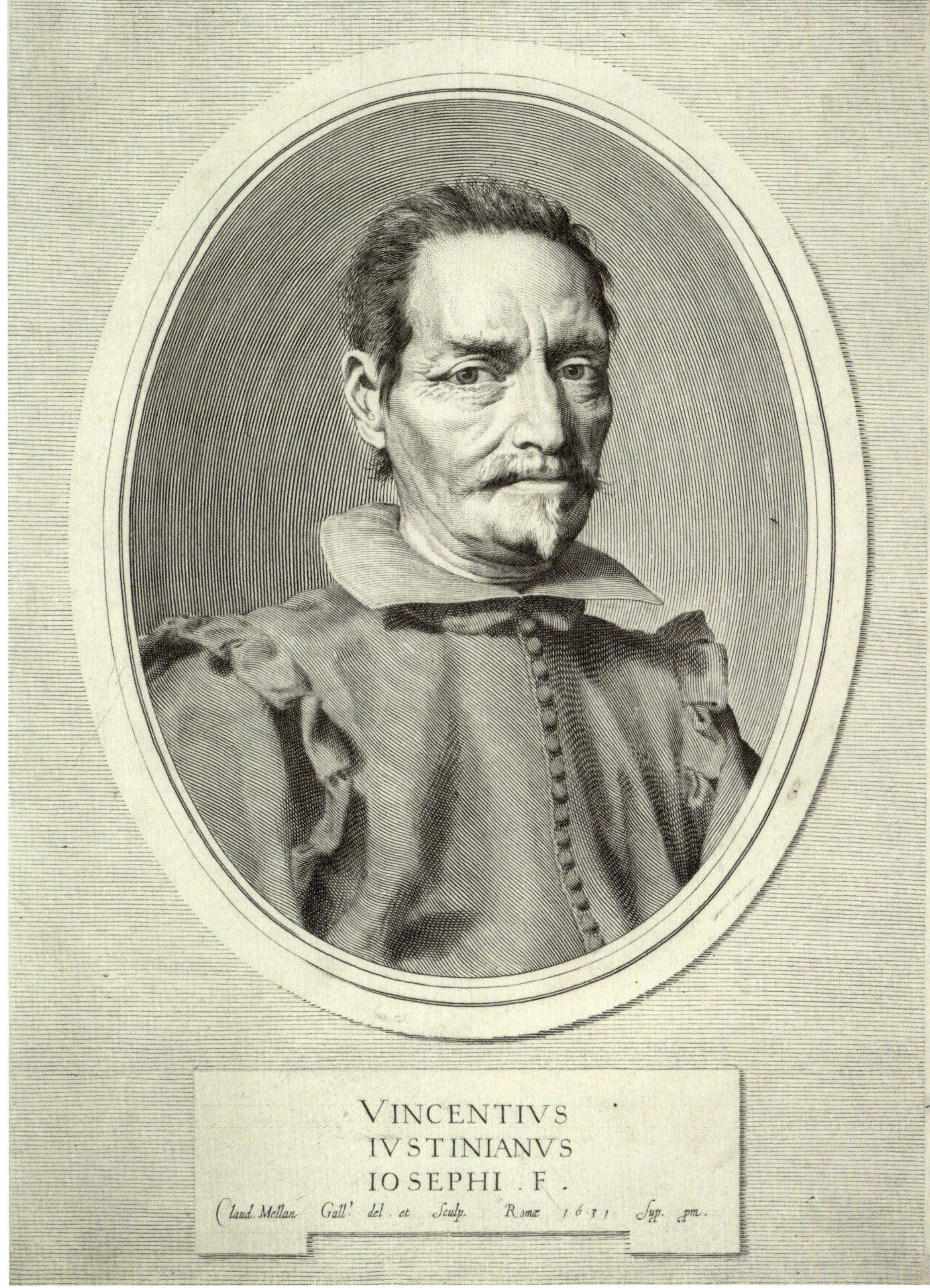

[fig. 3]
Claude Mellan,
Portrait of Vincenzo Giustiniani, 1631,
The Metropolitan Museum of Art, New York, Harris Brisbane Dick Fund, 1928

Chapel, anchoring them to 1599–1600, the turning point between the centuries, were without a doubt findings that were fundamental in order to reflect in an objective manner on the course of the artist's career.[3] Friedländer's insights, although still based on indeterminate material, opened the way to Maurizio Calvesi's reflections on the correspondence between the preaching of Saint Philip Neri and the religious works of Caravaggio, as well as his Christological interpretation of works with profane subjects, and to Alessandro Zuccari's studies on the Oratory and on the re-appropriation of early Christian models by Caravaggio and the artists of the early seventeenth century.[4] Over the decades, this in-depth study of religious and cultural sources has been combined with a deepening interest, which has now become almost maniacal, for patrons and collectors, and in general for the creators of the art collections of the Baroque century. A volume that already prioritised patrons over artists in its title, Francis Haskell's *Patrons and Painters*, first published in 1963, investigated the reasons behind the promotion of the arts in Rome and Venice, and the dynamics involved.[5] Not only religious orders, but also a number of private collectors—rediscovered through the sources, the eighteenth and nineteenth century collections of letters, and the pages of the Rome gazettes (the *avvisi*) published by Orbaan in 1920,[6]—emerged as playing important roles in artistic life, opening up a new

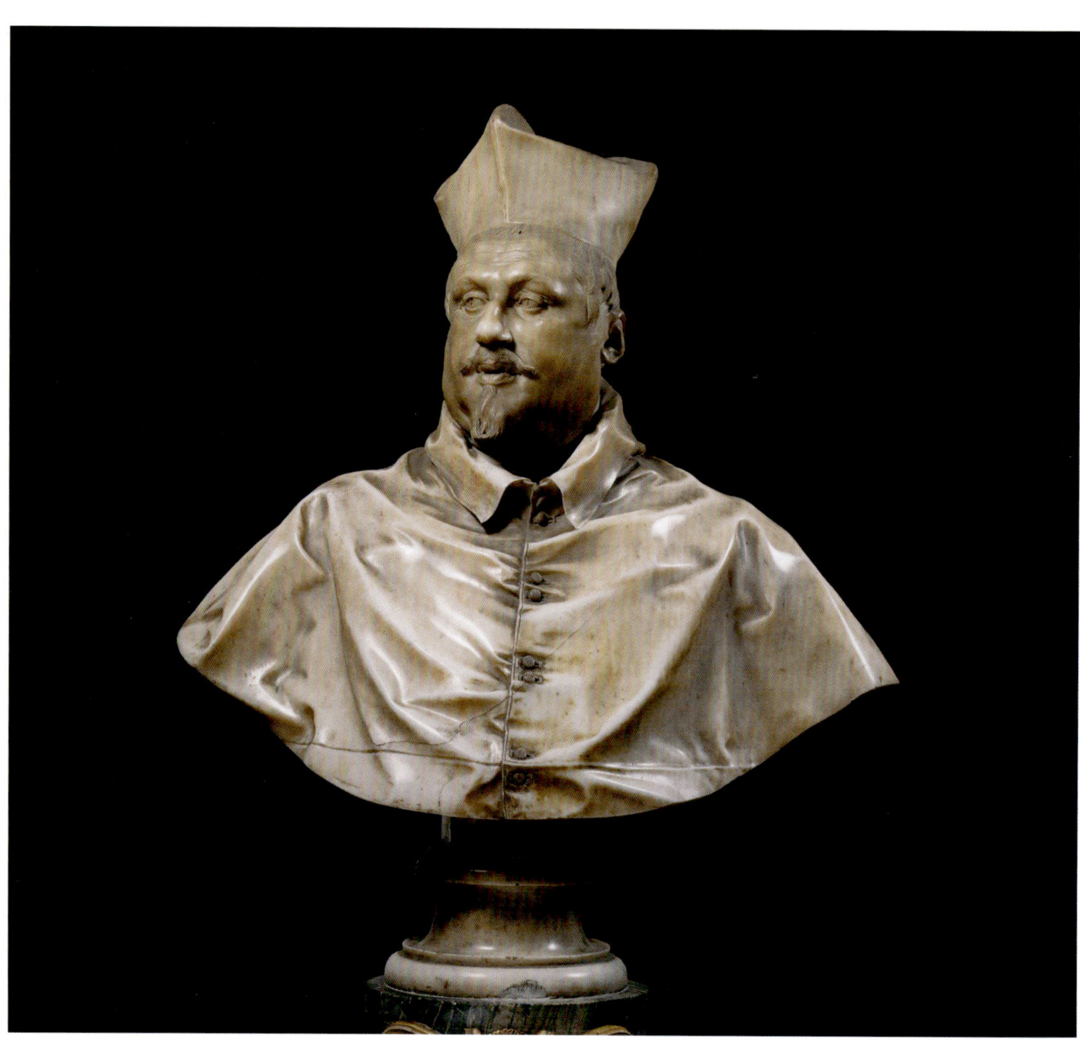

Francesca Cappelletti

perspective for study. Even if not treated as such by Haskell, who was more interested in the erudite environment of scholars such as Cassiano dal Pozzo, some of these private collectors were Caravaggio's patrons: for instance Vincenzo Giustiniani [fig. 3], whose inventories had been published three years earlier by Luigi Salerno and to whom other important monographic studies would be dedicated in the following decades; Maffeo Barberini; Scipione Borghese[7] [fig. 4]. Around Caravaggio, various traditions of scholarship began to coalesce, which—beginning with his paintings—attempted to trace the intellectual dimension of his patrons, their ideas[8] and, more often, the ambitions that animated them; at the same time, studies on provenance and documentary research on 'artistic taste' would lead to new discoveries on the initial owners of Caravaggio's paintings.

Calvesi, in the collection of his writings on Caravaggio's *Realtà*, which had appeared in earlier years and were published together in 1990, reconstructed a context in which figures, such as the Vittrice and del Monte families, the Giustiniani and Massimo families, Federico Borromeo, were all linked to the Oratory and to the return to the religiosity of the early Christians advocated by Philip Neri and his acolytes. This, according to the scholar, contributed to explaining some of the details given prominence in Caravaggio's works, such as the use of the "living model", and which "living model": a humanity made up of wrinkled old men, insolent or sullen teenagers, beautiful girls with somewhat marked features, and dirty feet and blackened nails just about everywhere. It was this reality, this "sangue e incarnatione" (blood and flesh) as Giovan Pietro Bellori summarised Caravaggio's naturalism, that would attract the followers of a more authentic religiosity, of a fervent Catholic Reformation. If poverty and simplicity could induce reflection and draw attention to the church of Christ and the surrounding city, the meaning behind this choice would soon be transformed. Within little more than a decade, painting from life would become a widespread practice, appealing to European painters, a generation of young expatriates from Valentin de Boulogne to Gerrit Honthorst, a practice no longer linked to this potentially devotional root and one that would lead to surprising and sophisticated results. Many of these followers would come together in informal associations, such as the Bent, giving life to a sumptuous and intellectual baroque of beggars.[9] Research on the individuals whose names emerged in the sources as Caravaggio's protectors, and on their families, has shed light on important figures, each of whom has become a kind of monument to patronage, the creator of a complex microcosm, the palazzo, onto which attention shifts to the point of recreating, inside it, potentially complex religious iconographic schemes—such as the entrance hall in the Palazzina Pinciana of the Villa Borghese, the cycle of paintings dedicated to Christ in Palazzo Giustiniani, the Asdrubale Mattei gallery—in which the attention to Caravaggio was part of a context of broader cultural interests. The link with the studies on collecting, in the specialised study of the documents, has made each of these figures a major player on the stage, capturing their specific features and traits as collectors, extracting them from that portrayal of a social group with common interests. Cardinal del Monte, Ciriaco Mattei, Vincenzo Giustiniani and Scipione Borghese shared a passion for Roman antiquities, and their collections, which had a strong antiquarian element, cannot be interpreted solely in the light of Caravaggio's presence. Furthermore, they did not all share the same financial capabilities nor have the same prestige; they encountered Caravaggio at different times in their lives and collected his works in different manners, and their relationship with the painter, based on friendship and trust, was one that lasted for different lengths of time. Some, moreover, such as for instance Ciriaco Mattei, in the words of Giovanni Baglione adopted for the title, were drawn into the sphere of Caravaggio's

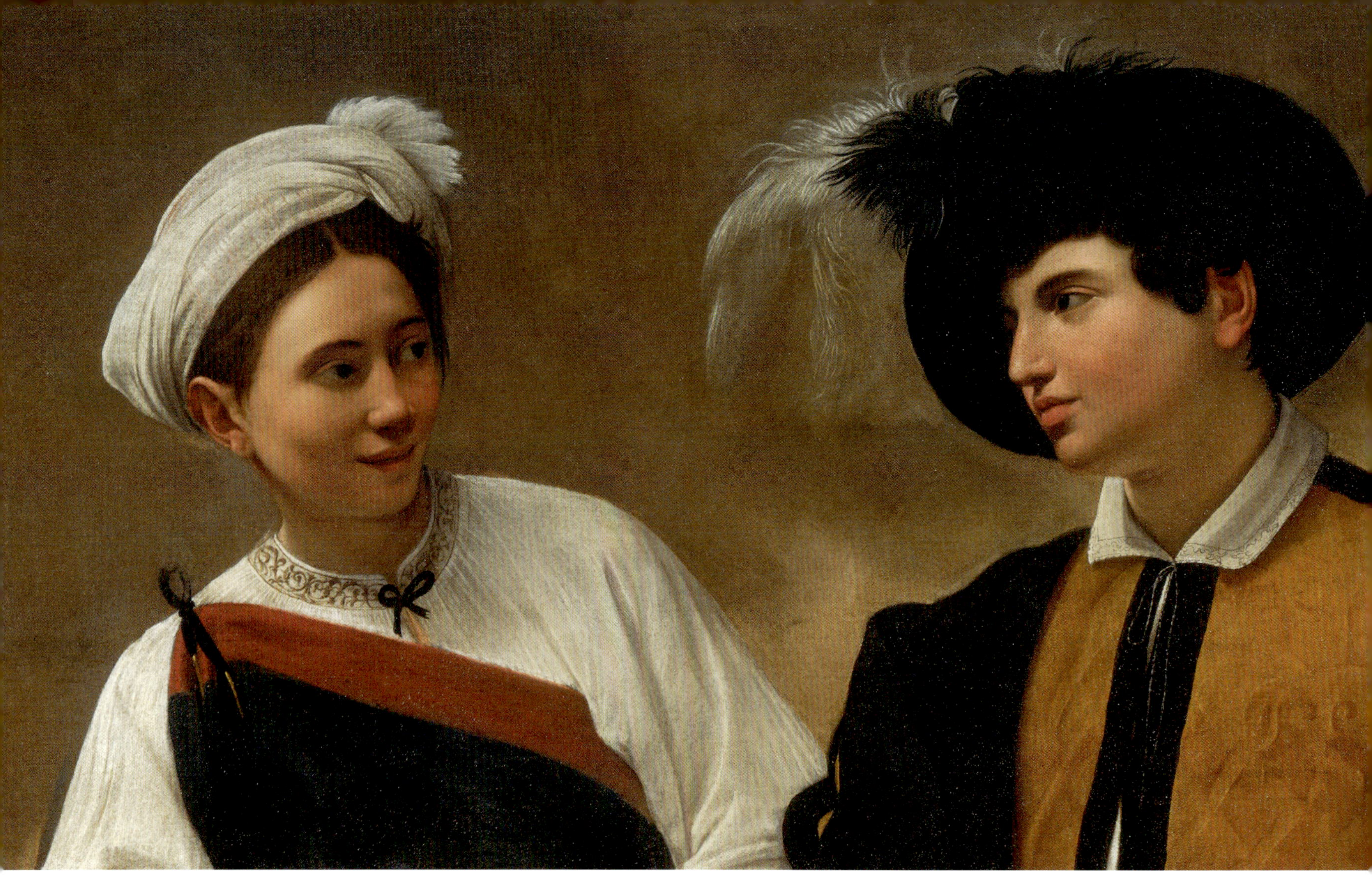

patrons because they succumbed to Prospero Orsi's promotion of Caravaggio: it was he who vociferously, according to the biographer, induced Ciriaco Mattei "to succumb to the clamour", "making him spend many hundreds of *scudi*."[10] The role of Caravaggio's painter friends, the workshops and the dealer, during the early years of the painter's activity and in the dynamics of acquisition, has in recent times revealed a lively context full of micro-stories, not only centred on the relationship between patron and painter; this has given substance to the testimonies of the sources, for example regarding Caravaggio's encounter with Cardinal del Monte, catalysed by a "Gypsy woman" [fig. 5] that the latter had seen *chez* the merchant Costantino Spada,[11] and the rapid and unpredictable passage of works from one workshop to another, or from one collection to another, as for example in the case of Asdrubale Mattei's *Saint Sebastian*, now lost.[12] In short, if today we wanted to reconstruct an overall picture and once again reflect on Caravaggio's clients and collectors in Rome, we would come to realise to what degree the questions we are asking ourselves have changed over the years: we have moved from the why to the how, investigating in greater depth the way in which meetings and acquisitions occurred, the way in which the works were placed within a collection, becoming part of the ever-changing universe of the Roman baroque palazzo, acquiring additional levels of meaning and significance as a result of their location. Caravaggio's paintings, sometimes destined for other displays, as in the case

Francesca Cappelletti

of the first versions of the paintings for the Cerasi Chapel, the *Conversion of Saul* [cat. 13] and the *Crucifixion of Saint Peter* [fig. 5 on p. 108], or the *Madonna of the Palafrenieri*, the destination of which altered dramatically; on other occasions they were covered by a curtain, as in the very different cases of the *Amor Vincit Omnia* in Palazzo Giustiniani [fig. 2 on p. 105] and the *Taking of Christ* in Palazzo Mattei [fig. 6; cat. 14]. Given the different nature of the subjects, it is hard to believe that the curtain had a moralistic function, but rather that the effect sought by the revelation of the painting to the spectator, would lead to the flowering of an erudite discussion in front of the work.

Vincenzo Giustiniani's personality is exceptional in the context of the aristocratic collections of the century, and for the history of the displays. In recent years, there have been very important studies—beginning with the publications and exhibitions of 2000–2001—on the composition of his collections, the role played by his brother Benedetto, his documented relationships with artists, the catalogue of his collection of statues, and the arrangement of sculptures and paintings in his gallery.[13] One of the most productive areas to have attracted the attention of scholars, is Giustiniani's relationships with figures of foreign extraction, and the creation of a kind of international artistic environment in his home. Vincenzo Giustiniani supported Caravaggio even before his public consecration, for a while playing a parallel role to that of Cardinal del Monte and Ottavio Costa,[14] but accumulating a greater number of works and from different phases of his production: in the well-known inventory of 1638, dating from a few weeks after the Marchese's death, there are listed under the name of Caravaggio, portraits, still-life paintings, musical paintings such as the wonderful *Lute Player* in the Hermitage [fig. 11 a p. 38], the *Amor Vincit Omnia* referred to above, and religious subjects such as the *Agony in the Garden*, which was lost in Berlin in 1945, and two celebrated examples of half-length figure paintings, the *Incredulity of Saint Thomas* in Potsdam [fig. 3 on p. 86] and the *Crowning with Thorns* now in Vienna [fig. 7], paintings for the most part obtained from Caravaggio directly, commissioned either by Vincenzo or his brother Benedetto.

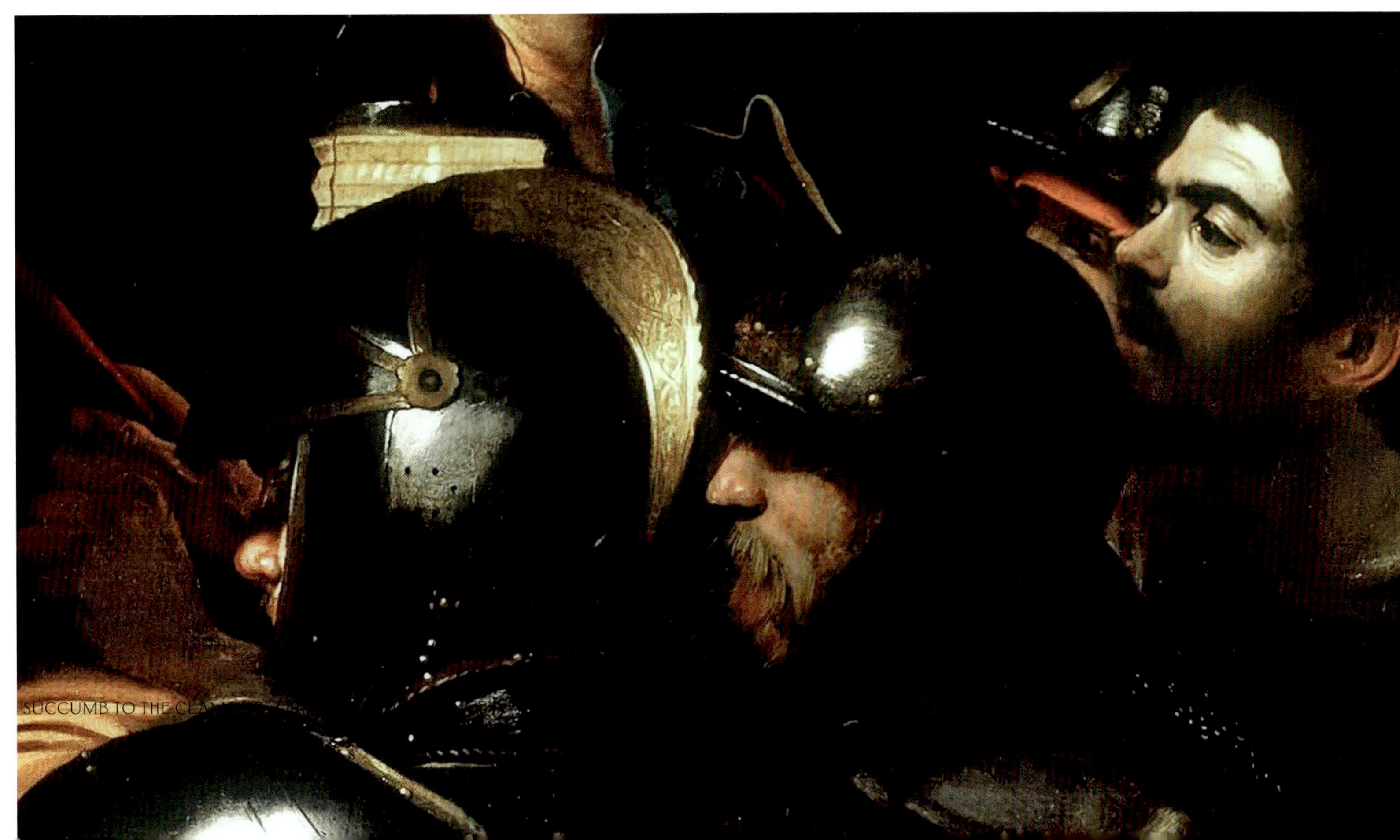

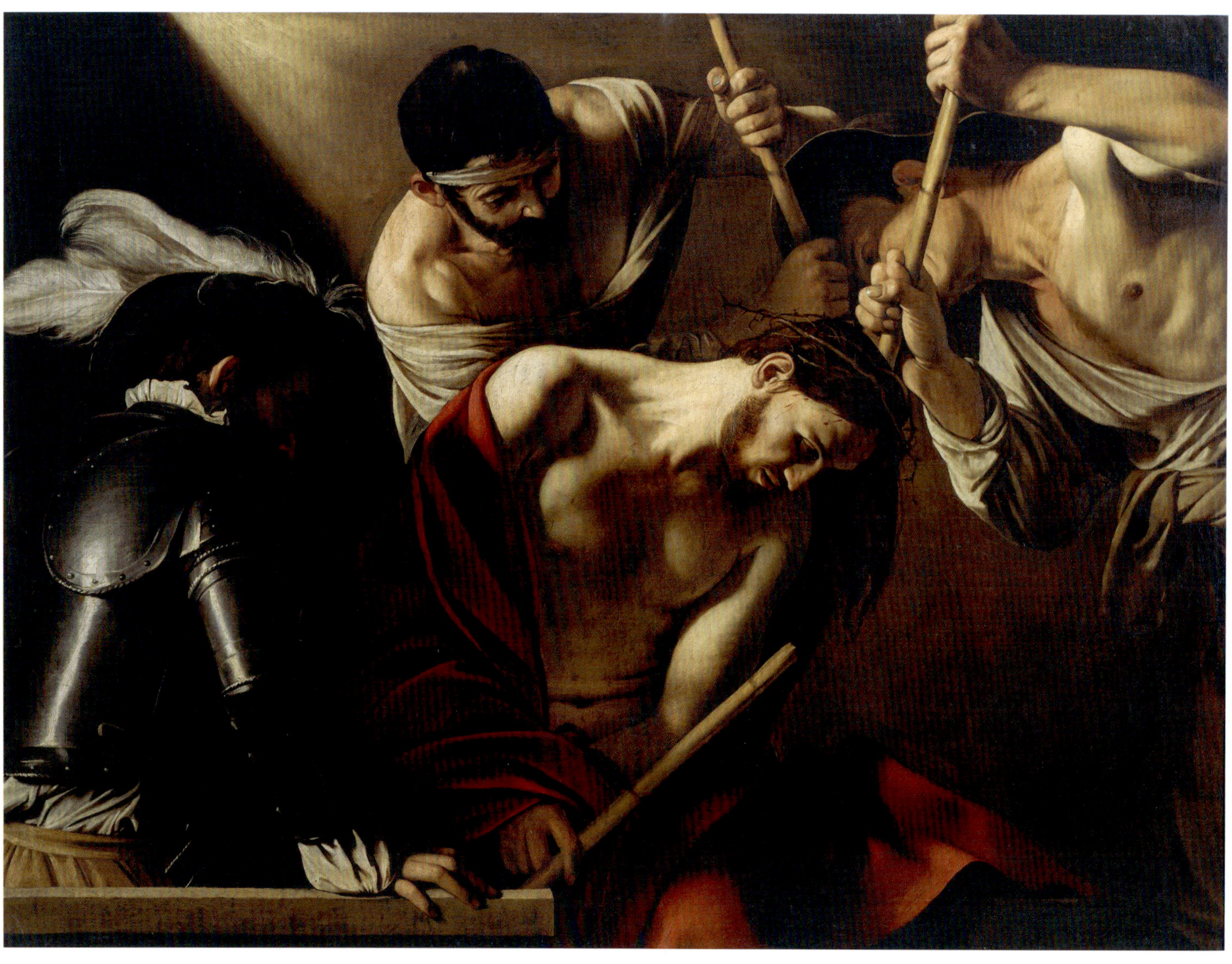

Some aspects that revolve around the composition and the display of the collection, reflected in Palazzo Giustiniani, emerge in some of the other Roman palazzi, such as for instance the use of a curtain, that created expectation, wonder, provoking conversation in front of the paintings,[15] creating the value of the work in relation to its price, to its initial financial worth, as in the case of the *Amor Vincit Omnia*, which had seen its renown and its price increase in an unimaginable way over the years; aspects such as these relaunched—reformulating in a new guise—the *paragone* between the Ancients and the Moderns, between sculpture and painting.[16]

If the relationship between Vincenzo Giustiniani and his family and Caravaggio was based on the direct patronage of the artist, the almost as numerous collection of the artist's paintings belonging to the cardinal nephew of Paul V, Scipione Caffarelli Borghese, was based on completely different premises, established on opportunities, both fortuitous and sought out, on the Roman market. To understand the substance of Scipione's collection of works by Caravaggio,[17] which included early paintings present in Cavalier

Francesca Cappelletti

d'Arpino's collection in 1607, the *Sick Bacchus* [cat. 1] and the *Boy with a Basket of Fruit* [fig. 2 on p. 160], the *Madonna dei Palafrenieri*, the *David with the Head of Goliath* [cat. 19] and the *Saint John the Baptist* [cat. 23], all of which had arrived in the collection by 1613, it is worth taking as a point of reference the seventeenth-century description of the Palazzina inside the Villa Borghese, drawn up by the *guardarobiere* of the Borghese household, Jacomo Manilli, and published in 1650, seventeen years after the cardinal's death.[18] The references to the eight paintings attributed to Caravaggio should be compared with the probable references in earlier lists, those of the Cavalier d'Arpino's possessions transferred to the cardinal in 1607, and the fragmentary and undated inventory published by Sandro Corradini in 1998.[19]

At that time, Manilli attributes eight paintings to Caravaggio, as the two early works, the *Sick Bacchus* and *Boy with a Basket of Fruit*, were missing from the villa and in 1693 were described as being in the palazzo in the city. Their temporary removal from the display is perhaps the reason for the rarity or even lack of copies made of them, a singular fate in comparison to Caravaggio's other early compositions, such as *Boy Peeling Fruit* [cat. 2] and *Boy Bitten by a Lizard*[20] [fig. 13 on p. 41]. A *Portrait of Paul V* [fig. 7 on p. 110], the pope of the family, was instead hanging in the gallery on the ground floor, opposite the image of Innocent X, the reigning pontiff at the time: "Above the Door, opposite the one of the living Pontiff, is the Portrait of Paul V, by Michelagnolo da Caravaggio."[21] For this painting, the existence of which is also mentioned by Bellori, an identification has been proposed as a work now in a private collection.[22] Furthermore, in the villa it was possible to see the *Supper at Emmaus* now in the National Gallery in London [fig. 6 on p. 14], probably to be identified, although it lacks irrefutable documentation, with the painting of the same subject that Caravaggio had painted during 1601 for Ciriaco Mattei, and that he had delivered to him in January 1602. A *Supper at Emmaus* by Caravaggio also appears in the Altemps inventories,[23] a family connected to Scipione Borghese through the purchase of the garden on the Quirinale, and for other notable overlaps in their relationships with artists, as well as in an inventory of the Aldobrandini family with the indication "*che viene da*" ("which comes from"), which is generally the description reserved for copies, a reference that is difficult to classify. Furthermore, to complicate the story further, it should be remembered that, at around the same time as the publication, Richard Symonds saw a *Supper at Emmaus* by Caravaggio in the palazzo in the city, together with other selected masterpieces from the collection (such as Raphael's *Deposition*), although he describes the painting as having a greater number of figures, five or six, which would rather suggest a composition like the *Supper at Emmaus* in the Pinacoteca di Brera [cat. 17], with the elderly woman next to the innkeeper.[24] Also attributed to Caravaggio was a *Christ at the Column*, the history of which has recently been traced.[25] The painting was still present in the Caravaggio bibliography in the 1980s and, with its scholarly history, is reproduced in the various editions of Maurizio Marini's monographs, while later it tends to disappear from scholarship.[26] The *Boy Bitten by a Crab*, another painting cited by Manilli as being attributed to Caravaggio,[27] may well not be an original but a painting modelled on one of the painter's most successful early compositions, the *Boy Bitten by a Lizard*, known through the two versions in Florence and London, which is also a subject found in the Altemps collection.[28] Another citation from the seventeenth-century guide to the Palazzina Borghese lists: "The other, above the alabaster table, of an old man and a young man, with a dove below, is a *capriccio* by Caravaggio, through which he wanted to give expression to the Trinity." This is a reference to what is probably a lost original

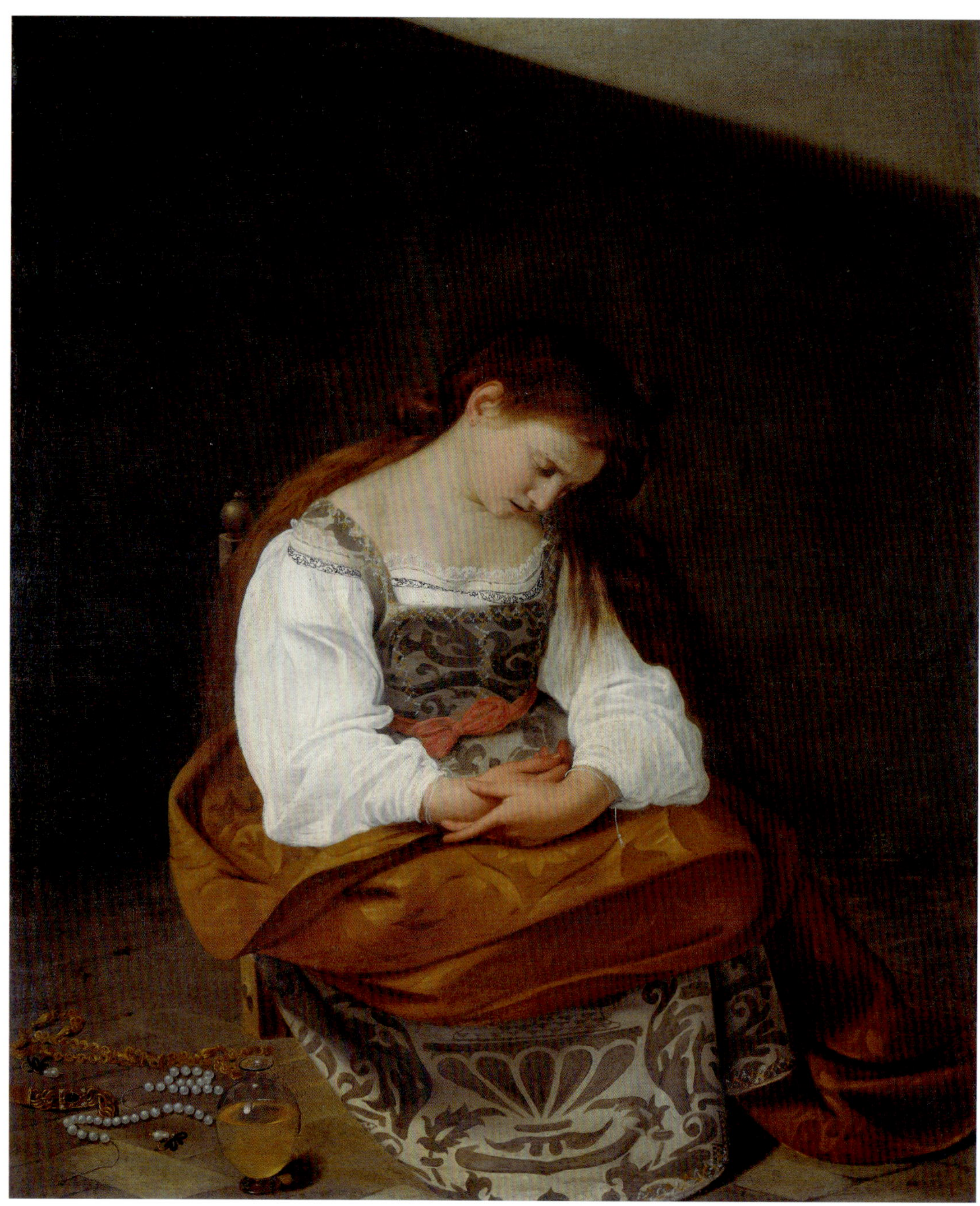

by Caravaggio, an image of the Trinity that must have greatly impressed the author of
the guide and which demonstrates, as has already been emphasised, the same descriptive
method that Bellori would later apply to the Vittrice *Penitent Magdalene* [fig. 8], now in
Palazzo Doria Pamphilj, for example, and from here, Caravaggio's whole manner of constructing the religious image. As is well known, according to the biographer, in order to
paint the *Penitent Magdalene* the artist had "painted a girl . . . in the act of drying her hair
. . . he made her represent the Magdalene."[29] In the instance of the Borghese painting, the
figures are described as their appearance indicates them to be: an old man, a young man
and a dove, through which Caravaggio had "wanted to express" the religious subject, an

                                                                                  Francesca Cappelletti

original vision of the Trinity. With a sensitivity that anticipates Bellori's acutely critical spirit, Manilli begins with the same point of view: Caravaggio stages the scene with human beings, elements in nature and only later is the reference to dogmas and the Scriptures laid over this initial rendering from the live model; a kind of anticipation of the "realistic mysticism"—that mysticism laden with reality—that Friedländer read in Caravaggio, and with which this text begins. However unusual the "*capriccio*" may appear, it corresponds, even in the vocabulary employed, to the terms of a commission entrusted to Caravaggio by the Trinità dei Pellegrini in May 1602, the development of which is not clear.[30] Had it been executed and remained in the painter's hands, it could have been bought by Scipione Borghese.[31] Another example of how Scipione's paintings by Caravaggio originated from different processes and mechanisms: the workshop of a painter, as in the case of the early paintings, a decommissioned altarpiece in Saint Peter's for the *Madonna of the Palafrenieri*, the Palazzo di Chiaia in Naples where the paintings that Caravaggio had brought with him on the boat in his last escape, for the *Saint John the Baptist*. Who knows whether the Marchese Giustiniani—in this latter way of obtaining paintings by the artist he most loved and protected—would have recognised in Cardinal Borghese that skill that he advised everyone to possess if preparing to live at the court of Rome: to unite vigilance with promptness, to seize all the opportunities that presented themselves at the right moment, to always find inspiration in the *Festina lente*.[32]

1   Friedländer 1955, p. 121.

2   Ebert-Schifferer 2012; a systematic contribution to this reinterpretation of Caravaggio's context has been provided by the studies of Lothar Sickel.

3   Mahon 1951; Röttgen 1965.

4   Calvesi 1985a; Calvesi 1990; Zuccari 1984.

5   Haskell 1963; Haskell 2000.

6   Orbaan 1920.

7   Haskell 2019, pp. 38, 181 ff.

8   Bologna 1992; Spezzaferro 2010.

9   Lemoine, Cappelletti 2014.

10   Baglione [1642] 2023, I, p. 404, English translation, amended, in Wittkower [1955] 1976, p. 235; Cappelletti, Testa 1994.

11   Curti 2011b.

12   Sickel 2003; Sickel 2007, pp. 111–117.

13   Danesi Squarzina 2003; Strunck 2001; Pierguidi 2014; *I marmi Torlonia* 2020. For Vincenzo as a traveller, Bizoni 1995, Cappelletti 2016, Danesi Squarzina 2021.

14   Terzaghi 2007.

15   Cappelletti 2016.

16   Danesi Squarzina 2003; Strunck 2001.

17   The most recent summary is in Cappelletti 2023.

18   Manilli 1650.

19   Cappelletti 2023.

20   Versions of these two works can probably also be identified in the list of 1607, and then in Scipione Borghese's collection, Cappelletti 2014.

21   Manilli 1650, p. 77.

22   *Caravaggio a Roma* 2011.

23   Spezzaferro 2010; Nicolai 2008.

24   Brookes 2007, pp. 1–183, in particular pp. 28, 121 note 72, 130 note 310.

25   Puddu 2021, pp. 101-112.

26   *The Age of Caravaggio | Caravaggio e il suo tempo* p. 318; Marini 19837, n. 32, pp. 427–428.

27   In the room of Daphne, Manilli refers to: "The little picture of a putto bitten by a crab, it is by Caravaggio"; Cappelletti 2014.

28   Spezzaferro 2002, pp. 23-50.

29   Bellori 1672, p. 215.

30   Lemoine 1995, pp. 416-429.

30   Röttgen 2002, pp. 345–346, n. 108.

31   Cannatà, Röttgen 1996.

32   Danesi Squarzina, in *Vincenzo Giustiniani* 2021, p. 125.

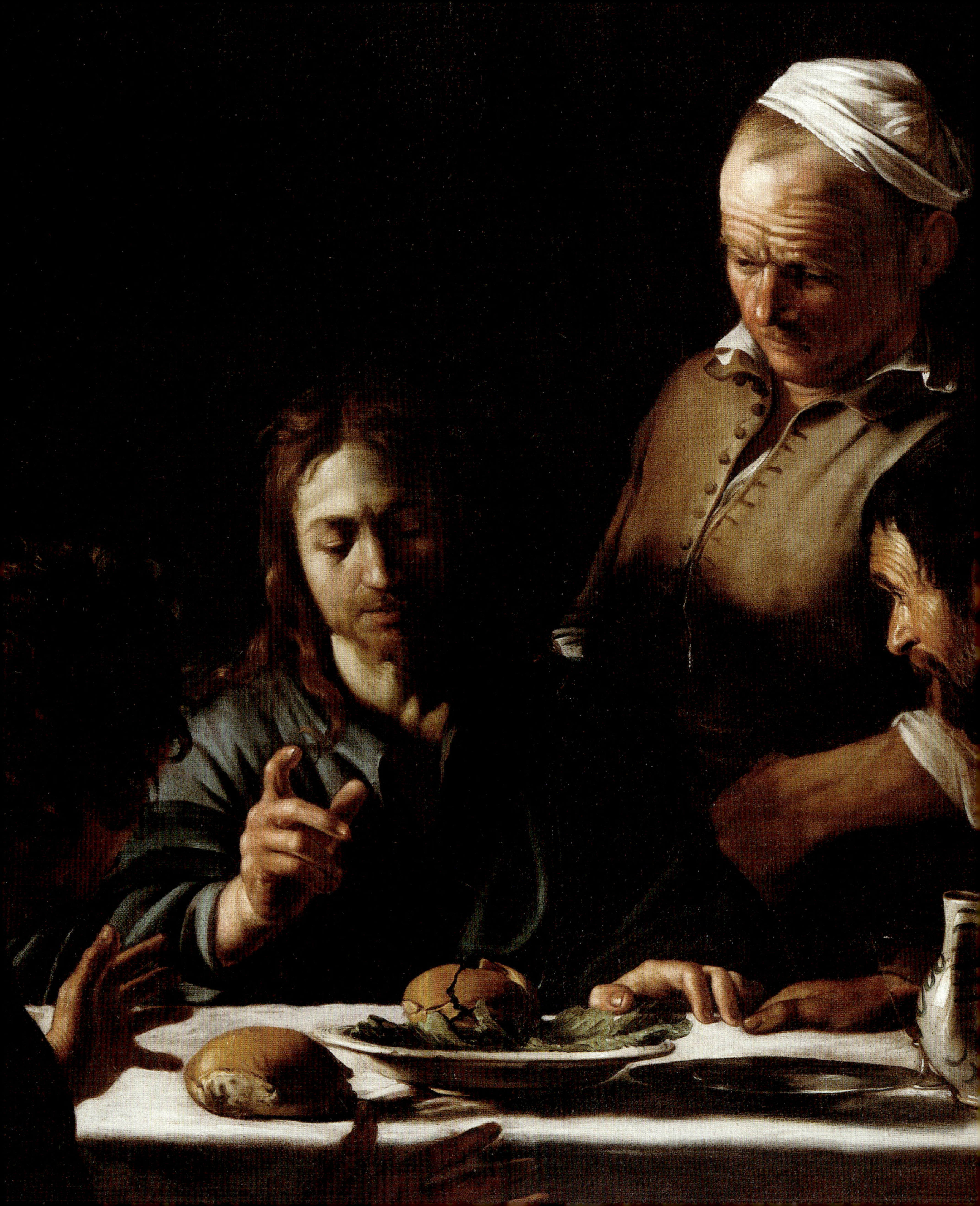

Giuseppe Porzio

CARAVAGGIO: THE YEARS IN THE SOUTH

NAPLES, 1606–1607

It is unanimously agreed that Caravaggio's descent to the South, and in particular his time in Naples, represents a chapter of primary importance in seventeenth-century European art. As a result of the profound cultural integration of the South within the Spanish imperial system, the disruptive power of the new vision introduced by the Lombard master was able to increase in its international resonance, albeit with heterogeneous and often hybrid results. The works produced during this period, continuing along the path of the painter's rethinking of sacred history—for Caravaggio an almost exclusive field of interest—, and in the redefinition of the role of the spectator, are therefore inescapable terms of reference for the transformations of style and figurative models that took place in the Mediterranean area between the first and second decades of the century.[1] Moreover, it has already been observed how the time span of his presence coincides with a moment of re-organisation of the cultural and civic dimensions of Neapolitan life,[2] but also with what one presumes was the breaking point in the uncontrolled demographic and urbanistic growth of the city that had begun in the mid-sixteenth century, which would in the end definitively unbalance its economic and social fabric, projecting onto the image of Naples that characteristic chiaroscuro, which would later became a topos, between the magnificence of the nobility and the misery of the populace,[3] particularly attuned to the tragic naturalism of the late Caravaggio.

The artist's arrival in the capital of the Viceroyalty, where he "he found employment at once, for his style and reputation were already known", takes place (as is well-known) in the autumn of 1606, after a brief period on the run in the Lazio fiefdoms of the Colonna family

[fig. 1]
Supper at Emmaus, 1606, detail, Pinacoteca di Brera, Milan [cat. 17]

following the infamous killing of Ranuccio Tomassoni on 28 May of that year, in a brawl that broke out during a game of "tennis". It is to this interlude that sources date the "Christ at Emmaus between the two apostles" now in the Pinacoteca di Brera in Milan [cat. 17], acquired and brought to Rome by the banker Ottavio Costa, who had been Caravaggio's patron since the end of sixteenth century, and a "half-length figure of the Magdalene", the original of which has yet to be traced.[4]

However, that Caravaggio's innovations were already known in Naples, as claimed by Giovan Pietro Bellori, is a fact that would seem to be a given in view of the geographical proximity and the artistic relations that had always existed between the two cities, and which had recently found their most important focal point in the work on the Carthusian monastery of San Martino, which began in 1589, by the Sistine team of craftsmen under the direction of Giuseppe Cesari (whose birth in Arpino—it should not be forgotten—qualified him as a subject of the Viceroyalty).[5] Moreover, since the beginning of the seventeenth century, Louis Finson and above all Tanzio da Varallo had been active in the city—although their productions remain unknown for this period; they both arrived from Rome, attracted by the prospects of the 1600 Jubilee, and the latter artist, from the workshop of the Cavalier d'Arpino.[6]

It is clear that the more or less intelligent reception of Caravaggio's innovations and their local application with particularly crude interpretations, were made possible chiefly by the widespread Northern influence that had marked the visual culture of the Viceroyalty for decades, as made manifest by the cases of Carlo Sellitto and Filippo Vitale, who, having initially trained with Loys Croys, an established master of a workshop in Mechelen, were to become two of Caravaggio's earliest and most radical followers in Naples.[7]

As is well known, the first conclusive evidence of Caravaggio's presence in the capital of the Viceroyalty, dated 6 October 1606, is the receipt of a payment of 200 ducats for the execution of an altarpiece, which unfortunately has not reached us, painted for Nicolò Radolovich, a merchant from Ragusa [Dubrovnik] who had rapidly risen on the social ladder, becoming the Marchese di Polignano in 1604.[8] A further 150 ducats—according to a second bank entry—would have been received by the painter on 25 October, but the absence of a reference description for this payment does not allow us to establish a possible connection between the two transactions.[9] However, the composition requested by Radolovich, as described in the document, is entirely in line with the iconographic conventions of southern Italian devotion. The standing of the commission, indicated by the considerable cost of the work, and the dynamic potential that the central focus of the composition offered the Lombard master—with the image of the Madonna and Child surrounded by choirs of angels and, in the lower register, between Saint Vitus (patron saint of Polignano) and Saint Nicholas of Bari, the embrace of Saints Dominic and Francis—were already a prelude to the highly celebrated masterpiece that would follow; this was for the church of the newly established Monte della Misericordia, a lay association with charitable aims—among the most important in the city—founded on the initiative of some of the young exponents of the aristocracy of the Viceroyalty, with substantial funding by Radolovich himself.[10]

The chronology of the *Seven Acts of Mercy* [fig. 2], an impressive depiction in terms of its power of veracity and synthesis of the charitable activities put into action by the institution,[11] is demarcated by a payment of 370 ducats in settlement of 400, paid on 9 January 1607 by Tiberio del Pezzo, governor of the Opera dei Morti, with responsibility for the administration of the church.[12] It is probable, however, that Caravaggio's engagement was due to the mediation of Giovan Battista Manso, the future Marchese di Villa,

Giuseppe Porzio

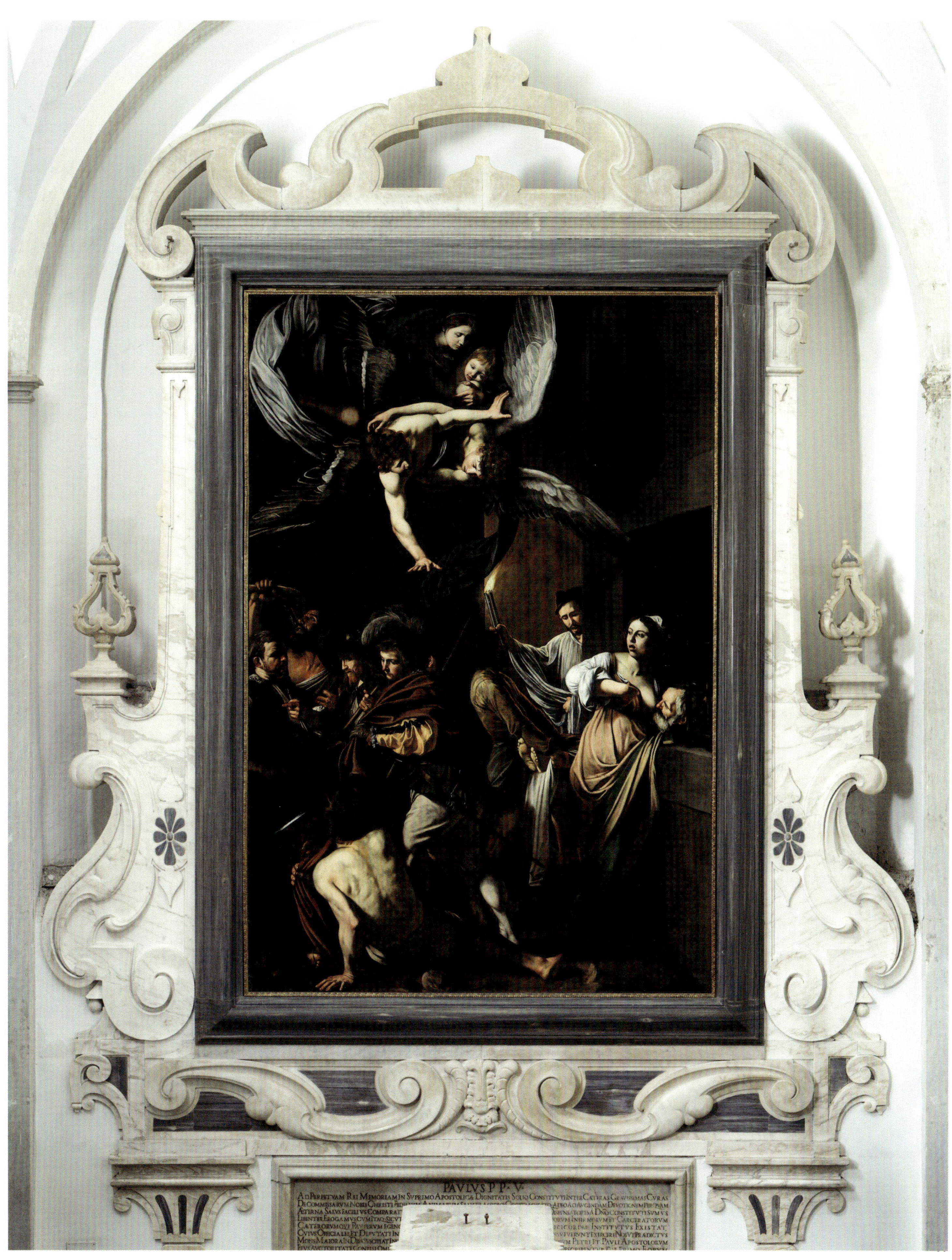

at the time deputy "alla fabrica della casa et chiesa" of the Monte di Pietà as also—as is well known—a close friend of Giovan Battista Marino, himself friend and admirer of the painter from Lombardy.[13]

The impact of this supreme work on the Neapolitan figurative environment, and the mental limitations with which it was received, can be immediately gaged on one of the altarpieces destined for the remaining six altars of the building, namely the *Parable of the Good Samaritan*, that alludes to the "visiting of the sick", painted—immediately after, in 1607—by Giovan Vincenzo Forlì.[14] It is a work that exemplifies the attempt by a then mature artist to adapt his own pictorial language influenced by Corenzo and Bassano, to the novelty of the *Seven Acts*, from which it takes the most superficial and conspicuous aspects (its plastic qualities reinforced by chiaroscuro, the rotating dynamics of the group with the Virgin and the angels, the looming presence of the nude figure, brought to the edge of the visual plane).

At the end of April 1607, the Nolan patrician Girolamo Mastrilli, Marchese di San Marzano since 1612, paid Caravaggio for a painting depicting his own eponymous saint, a work now lost; the sum, 30 ducats in settlement of an unspecified amount, the advance of which had already been paid in cash, was concurrently turned over by the artist to Battistello Caracciolo.[15] It is possible that the ode *Ad un ritratto di San Geronimo, dipinto dal Caravaggio* (*On a depiction of Saint Jerome, painted by Caravaggio*) placed by Orazio Comite from Benevento, academician of the Incauti, at the end of his "dragmatico" poem *La notte overo il nascimento di Christo* (*Night or the birth of Christ*), printed in Naples in 1616 for Lazzaro Scoriggio and dedicated to sister Antonia Avitabile, "nun of the Royal monastery of Santa Chiara" and probably a relative of the painter Girolamo, refers to

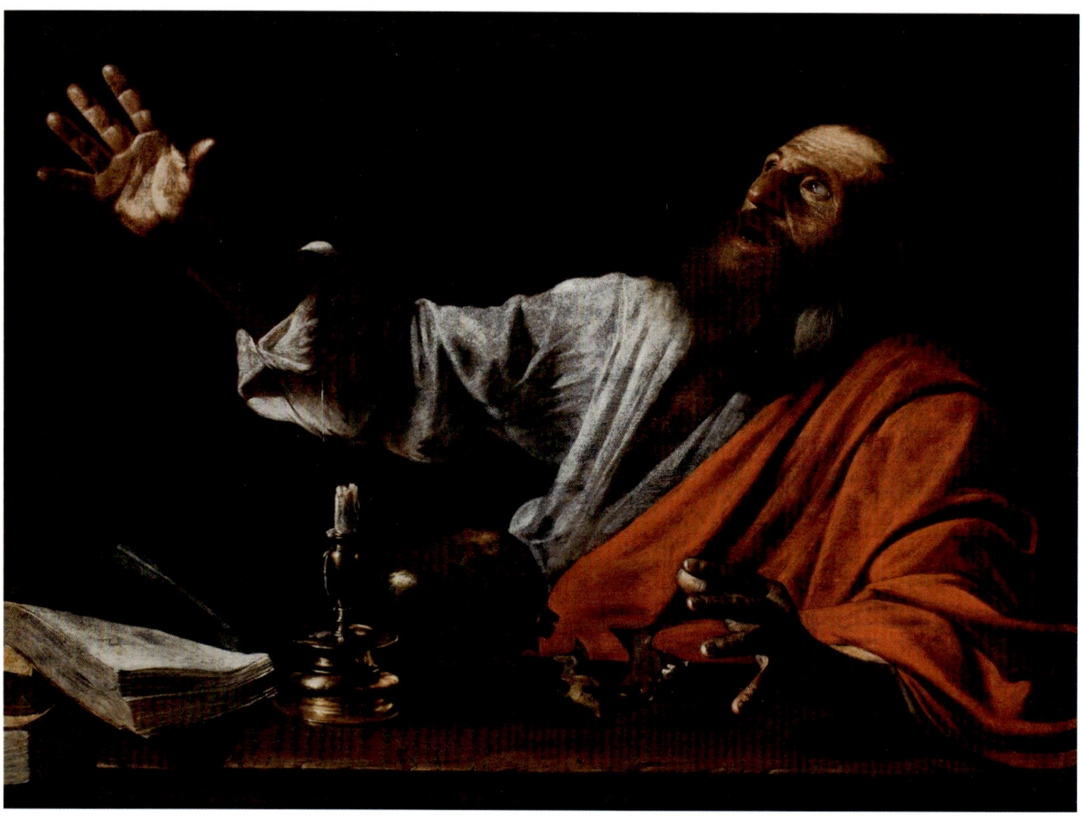

Giuseppe Porzio

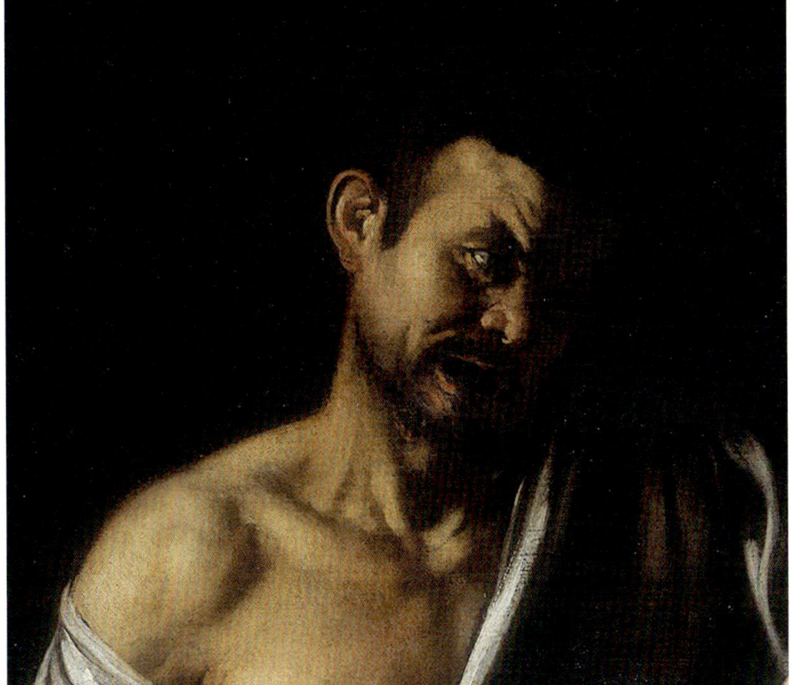 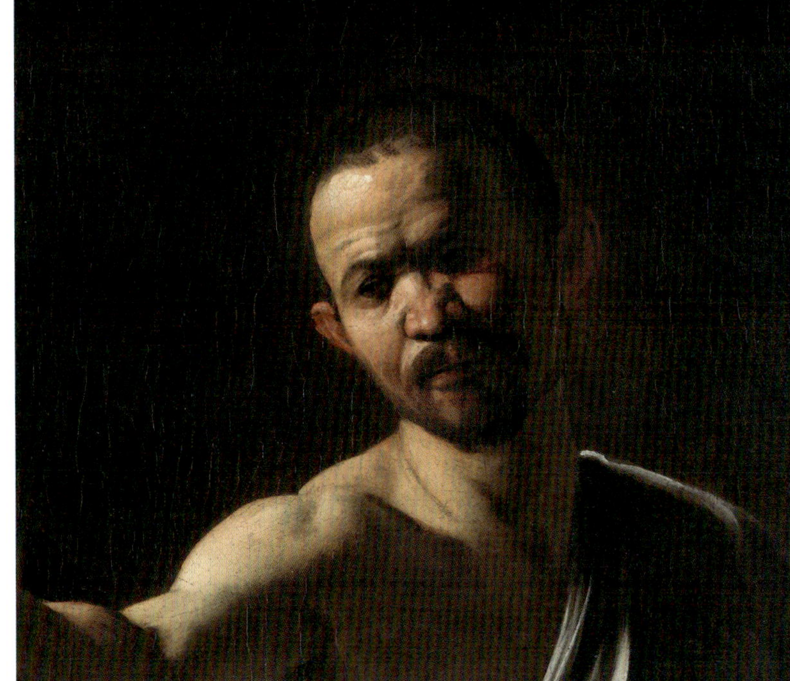

this work. According to the poem, which has been passed over in silence in the literature on Caravaggio, the subject of the painting must have centred on the saint's hearing of the trumpet of the Judgement,[16] an *invenzione* of which clear and old figurative traces remain in Naples, such as the problematic *Saint Jerome* in the Worcester Art Museum [fig. 3],[17] at times itself considered to be an autograph work by the master.[18]

Be that as it may, it is probable that the painting was destined for the residence, located in the Seat of Nido, that Mastrilli was establishing in the same years.[19] But the most important element in the document is undoubtedly the transfer to Caracciolo, which provides us with a glimmer of light as to Caravaggio's professional relations with the local artistic environment, and explains through the direct contact between the artists, the early reception of Caravaggio's models by the Neapolitan painter, whose *Madonna and Child in Glory* in the MARCA–Museo delle Arti di Catanzaro, even implies knowledge of the first draft of the *Seven Acts.*[20]

The following May, a payment on account was made to Caravaggio by Tommaso de Franchis, a member of an important family of jurists, for a work on an unspecified subject; a work which can be identified with the *Flagellation* formerly in San Domenico Maggiore, and now in Capodimonte [fig. 4; cat. 21], on the basis both of Bellori's indication that it was executed for the "chapel of the Di Franco family", and the considerable sum, 250 ducats (of which 150 already received in cash), to which should be added—in all likelihood—a supplement of 40 ducats and 9 grana.[21] However, the discovery of this documentary support did not weaken the debate on the dating of the work, of which the high number of revisions and alterations revealed by diagnostic investigations—noteworthy, in particular, is the elimination in the final draft of a figure of a bystander, revealed by X-ray examination in 1983 and variously interpreted as the portrait of the commissioner, as St. Francis, or even as a self-portrait—has in fact induced some scholars, *in primis* Ferdinando Bologna, to hypothesise (not reliably, in my opinion) its execution in two stages, postponing completion of the painting to Caravaggio's return to Naples after his Sicilian sojourn, insisting, for example, on the similarities between the figure of the henchman [fig. 5] to the right of Christ and the gigantic grave-digger [fig. 9 on p. 19], also on the right-hand side in the *Burial of Saint Lucy* in Syracuse.[22]

[fig. 4]
Flagellation of Christ, 1607, detail, Museo e Real Bosco di Capodimonte, Naples [cat. 21]

[fig. 5]
Salome with the Head of Saint John the Baptist, c. 1607, detail, The National Gallery, London

Such typological cross-references, far from being resolving factors in a creative dynamic such as Caravaggio's, which constantly moves between innovation and repetition, can moreover be more appropriately called upon for the other *Flagellation*, almost contemporary but in a 'room-sized' format, which hangs since 1955 in the Musée des Beaux-Arts in Rouen [fig. 9]. In the *invenzione* of this work, that pivots on the impetuous forward bend of Christ's torso, perhaps a re-surfacing of one of Titian's ideas [fig. 8],[23] as is also the case for the figure of the executioner in *Salome with the Head of Saint John the Baptist* [fig. 7] in the National Gallery in London,[24] which is generally believed to date from the artist's final period due to its synthetic construction, but—in my opinion—is more at home inserted in this sequence.

Should also be situated to a date before the end of Caravaggio's first Neapolitan period (the master's presence in the city is still referred to on 3 July 1607),[25] but with a gaze already turned in the direction of the later Maltese canvases, the sorrow-laden *Crucifixion of Saint Andrew* [fig. 6], now in the Cleveland Museum of Art.[26] It is thought, according once again to what is reported by Bellori, that this work is the same that the Viceroy Juan Alfonso Pimentel Enríquez, Count-Duke of Benavente, brought with him to Spain in 1610, at the end of his Neapolitan mandate.[27] This piece of information is indeed confirmed by the inventory of the family palace in Valladolid, drawn up between 1652 and 1653, which also records, under Caravaggio's name, a "Bishop saint, his head severed" ("Santo obispo, la cabeza degollada"), whose effigy is perhaps transmitted in the *Saint Januarius* now in the Palmer Museum of Art[28]; it remains however to be clarified how the *Saint Andrew* came to

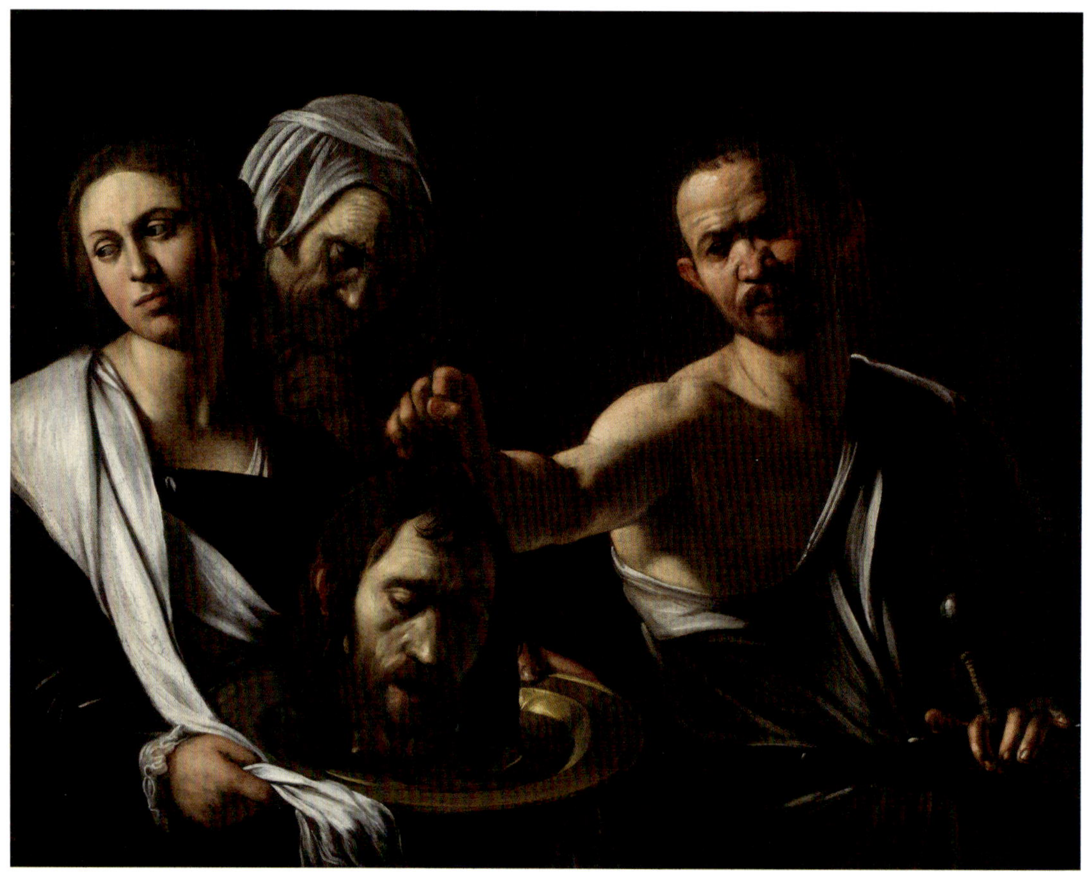

Giuseppe Porzio

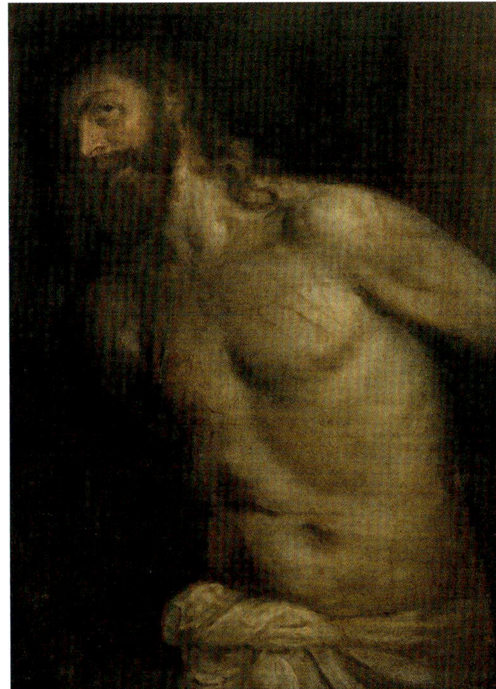
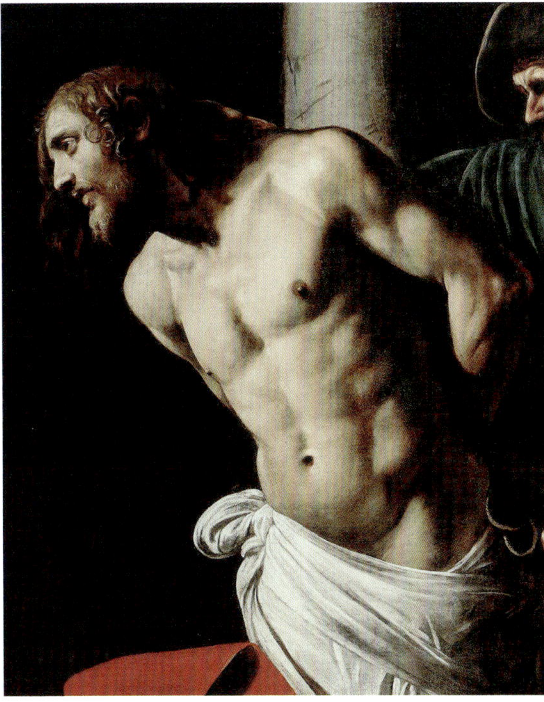

be in the possession of the Viceroy, whether as a direct commission, that is, or purchased on the market.

In the same way as the *Seven Acts*, the Cleveland painting is also notable for its iconographic singularity. First of all, the cross to which the martyr is bound is not decussate, but rather a Latin one; furthermore, the scene depicts not the moment in which the apostle is hoisted up on the cross, but rather the subsequent moment of the vain attempt to untie him in order to interrupt his strenuous preaching.[29]

The dating of the work between the spring and early summer of 1607, on which more recent scholarship has come to focus, is supported by the numerous references to the Pio Monte painting, as well as by the re-proposal of the old woman with the goitre in the maid servant that appears in the disputed *Judith Beheading Holophernes* that appeared in Toulouse in 2016, most probably to be identified—with all the stylistic difficulties that the canvas possesses—in the lost "Holophernes with Judith" brought to the attention of Vincenzo I Gonzaga on the square in Naples—in September of the same year 1607—by the painter Frans Pourbus.[30]

It is precisely the testimony of the Duke of Mantua's agent that raises a question of the greatest importance for understanding the interaction between Caravaggio and the artistic environment of the capital of the kingdom: as we know, in fact, together with the *Judith*, Pourbus also recalled a "Rosary . . . made for an altarpiece", that is the famous altarpiece now in Vienna [fig. 10], the chronology and destination of which are much debated—but which in terms of its style seems to precede the *Seven Acts*.[31]

These "two beautiful paintings by the hand of M[ichel] Angelo da Carravaggio", to which the other emissary of the duke in Naples, Ottavio Gentile, also seems to refer, deeming them—mind you—to have been executed in the city,[32] would reappear exactly ten years later, on 19 September 1617, in Amsterdam.[33] It is here, in fact, that Louis Finson had left his partner Abraham Vinck his share in the co-ownership of the two paintings in his

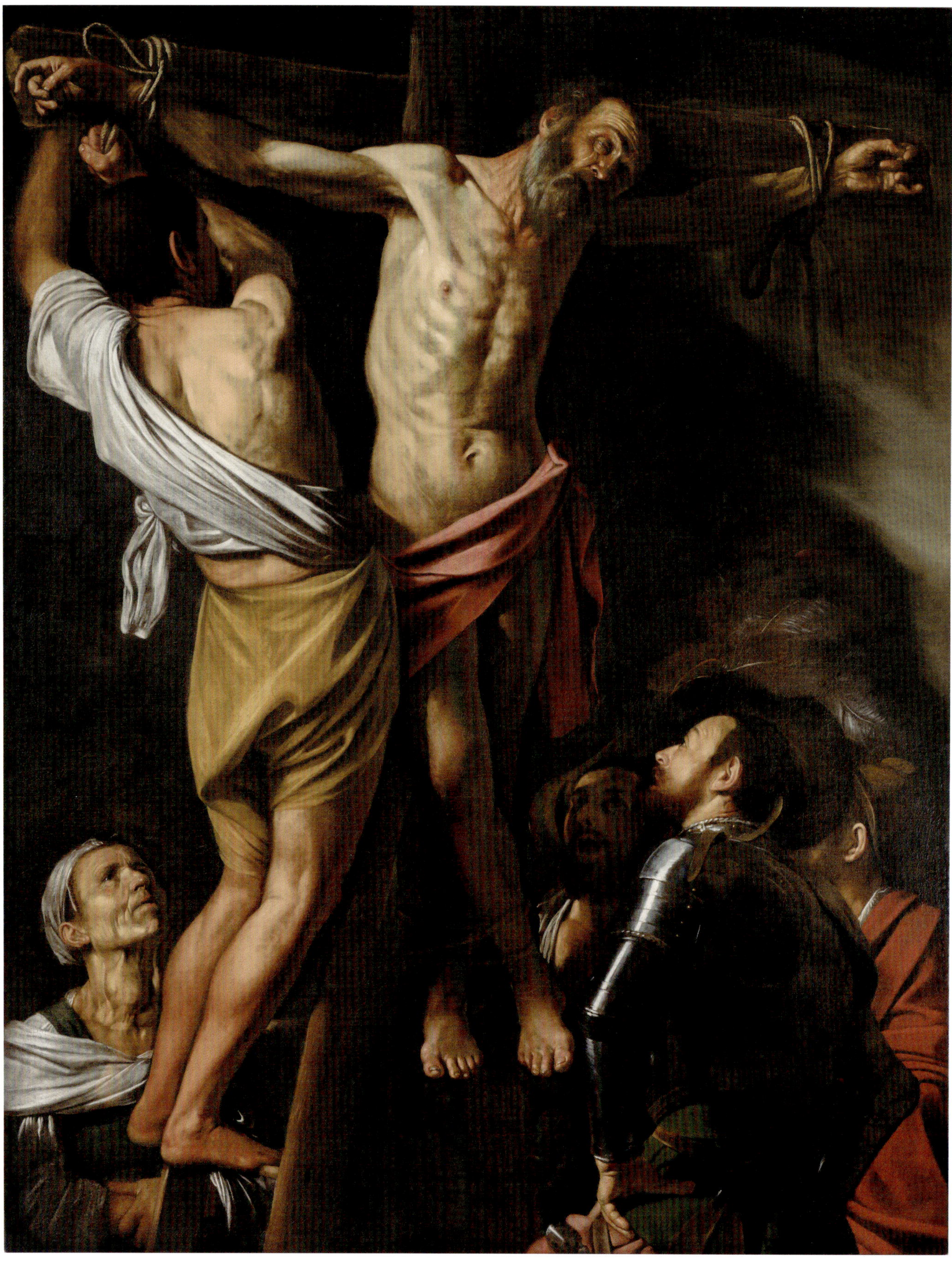

Giuseppe Porzio

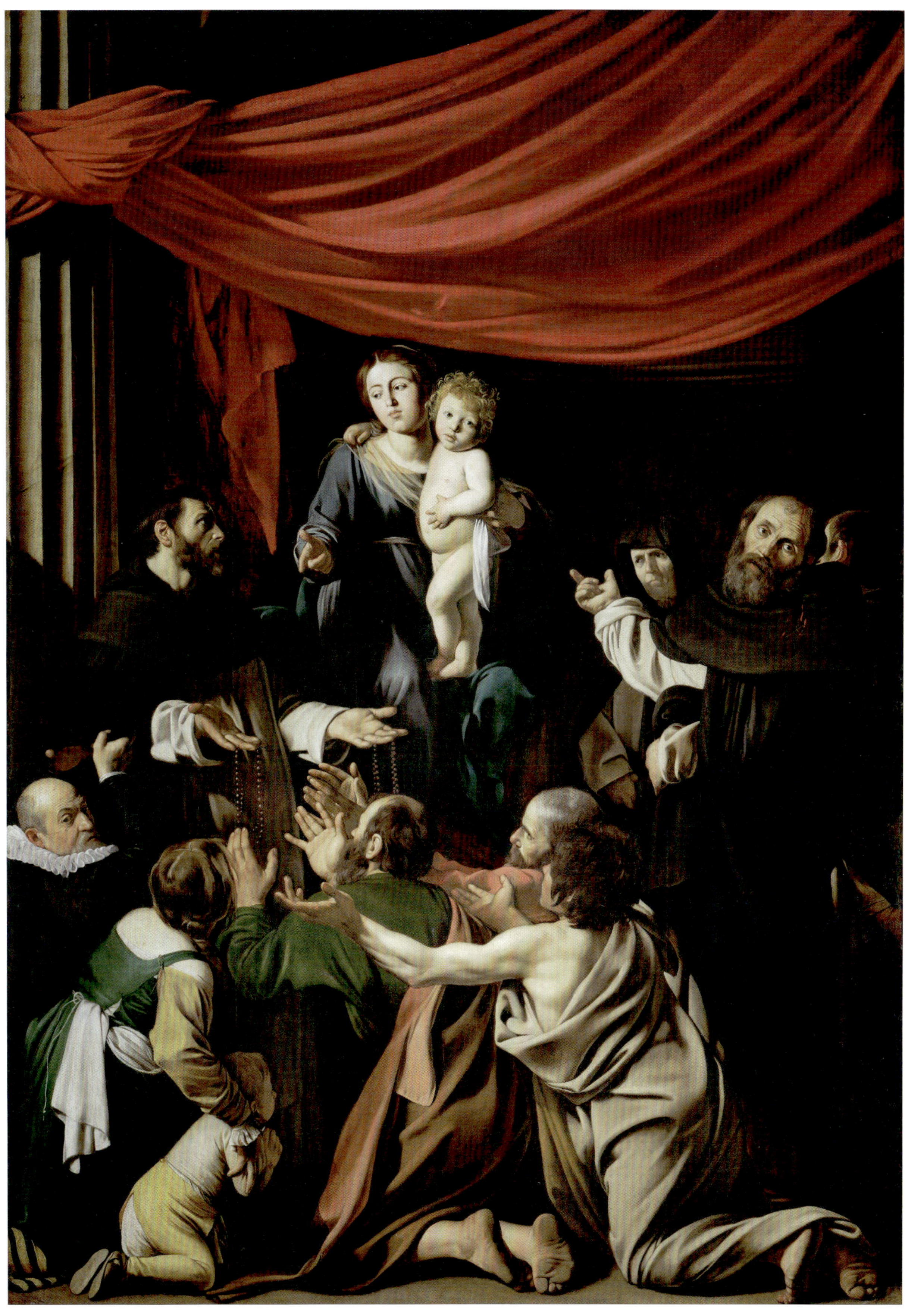

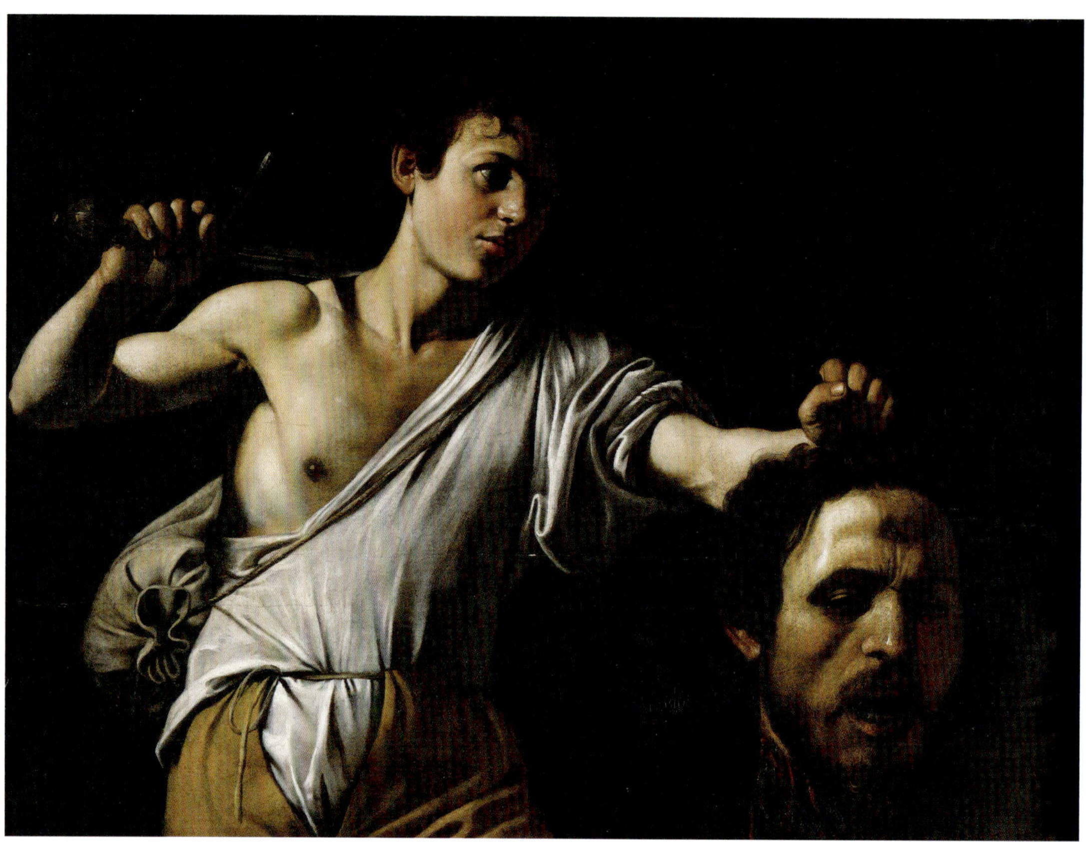

will. It is unclear when and under what circumstances these came into the possession of the two painters, but if we add to this the report of another *Crucifixion of Saint Andrew* from Finson's same inheritance, sold in Amsterdam in 1619 under the name of Caravaggio,[34] as well as that of a copy of the *Rosary* appraised at the beginning of 1630, again in the Netherlandish capital, as the work of Finson himself,[35] it follows that the two Flemish painters must have had a privileged relationship with the Lombard genius, perhaps even before his arrival in the Viceroyal capital, to the point of offering him a foothold in their workshop. The splendid *David with the Head of Goliath* [fig. 11] in the Kunsthistorisches Museum in Vienna,[36] painted by Caravaggio reusing a poplar panel, an unusual support for him, probably dates back to this triangulation. Radiographic investigations, in fact, have revealed an underlying composition with a Mars and Venus with Cupid, attributable to a Northern Mannerist painter, precisely one such as Finson or Vinck.[37]

BETWEEN TWO ISLANDS: MALTA AND SICILY, 1607–1609

We do not know when and why the decision to leave Naples for Malta matured in Caravaggio. However, everything leads us to believe that the move followed the documented route taken by the five galleys belonging to Fabrizio Sforza Colonna, son of the Marchesi di Caravaggio, assiduous protectors of the master, and that therefore the artist embarked for the island around 25 June 1607, to land there on 12 July;[38] in any case, the painter's presence is attested in Malta on 13 July, according to the first of the statements

Giuseppe Porzio

given on the occasion of a trial for bigamy, which took place between the 22nd and 27th of the same month.[39]

His promotion to a Knight of the Order of Saint John, on 14 July 1608, must have been a coveted goal for Caravaggio, perhaps to the point of motivating his departure from Naples. Among the works that will have earned him this honour—apart from an unspecified proof of courage against the Turks, mentioned by Joachim von Sandrart—stand out without a doubt the *Saint Jerome Intent on Translating the Bible* [fig. 12], which still hangs in the co-Cathedral in Valletta, bearing the coat-of-arms of Ippolito Malaspina, bailiff of the Knights of Malta in Naples, and the portrait "standing in armour" of the Grand Master Alof de Wignacourt, now in the Louvre [fig. 9 on p. 114], clearly the same work referred to by Bellori together with another, which is lost, "seated without armour."[40] But the decisive work that Caravaggio painted on the island—the immense *Beheading of Saint John the Baptist* [fig. 8 on p. 18] in the oratory of the same name in Valletta co-Cathedral—, perhaps the artist's absolute masterpiece, was only completed after his investiture as a knight, as indicated by the title that accompanies the signature, "f[ra] Michelang", the only signature ever appended by the artist to his own work, and significantly written in the blood gushing from the neck of the Precursor. The canvas was in all probability inaugurated on 29 August 1608, the feast day of Saint John the Beheaded (San Giovanni Decollato), but in the absence of Caravaggio, who had already been locked up for two days in the prison of Castel Sant'Angelo together with Giovanni Pietro De Ponte for taking part in a violent disturbance that had erupted on the night between 18 and 19 August in the residence of Fra Prospero Coppini.[41] However, the detention did not last long, until the following 6 October, when the artist succeeded in escaping, evidently not without the help of Maltese accomplices.[42]

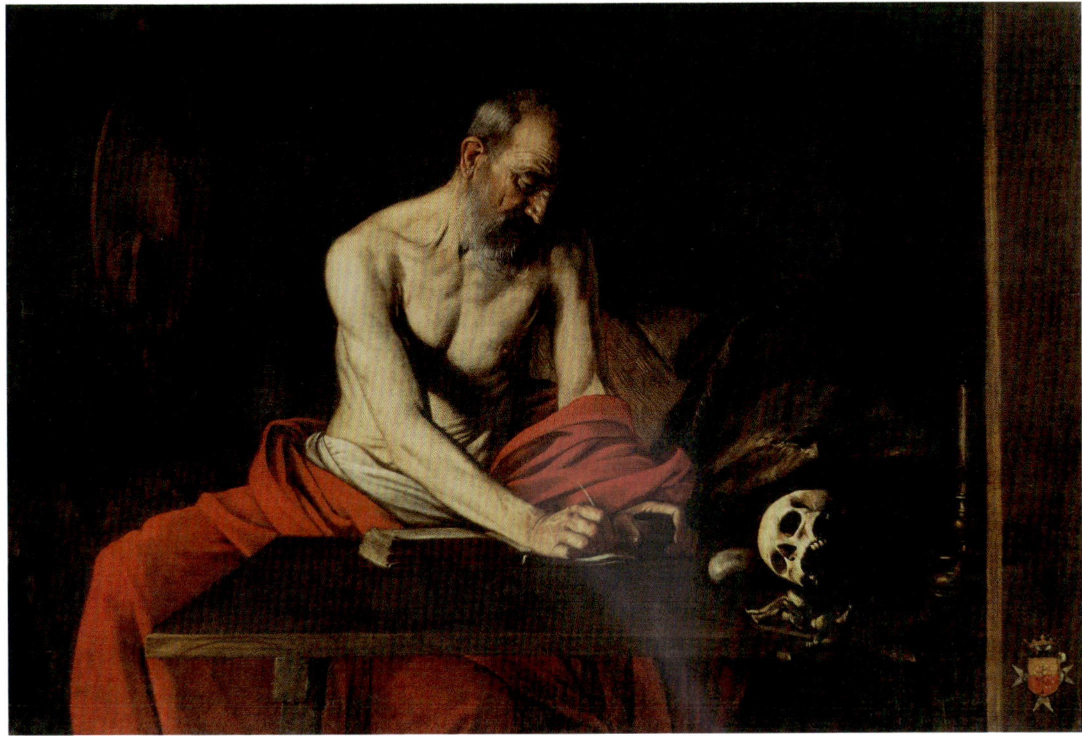

Condemned *in absentia* and officially expelled from the order of Saint John on 1 December 1608,[43] paradoxically in the very oratory dominated by the looming *Beheading*, Caravaggio had already found shelter in Syracuse several weeks earlier. Here, through the mediation of his old associate Mario Minniti, and perhaps the man of letters Vincenzo Mirabella, he soon received the important commission for the celebrated altarpiece with the *Burial of Saint Lucy* [fig. 9 on p. 19] for the *extra moenia* church dedicated to the saint (known precisely as Santa Lucia al Sepolcro), a kind of reworking, in an even more lugubrious key, of the *Death of the Virgin* in the Louvre [fig. 10 on p. 134]. In natural continuity with the *Beheading*, Roberto Longhi observed in the work "the new, great idea of diminishing, in space, the measure of men, in the group of wretches almost oppressed by the gigantic walls", an idea that would be taken up again, fifteen years later, by Battistello Caracciolo for his *Washing of the Feet* in the choir of the Carthusian monastery of San Martino in Naples. The logical *terminus ante quem* for the delivery of this tremendous masterpiece, recalled by Bellori and above all by Francesco Susinno,[44] to whom we owe the most detailed account of the obscure Sicilian interlude, richer however in anecdotes than in documentary evidence, is set by the saint's feast day, 13 December 1608. However, the canvas must have been executed even more rapidly, if Caravaggio is present in Messina as early as 6 December of the same year, for the stipulation of the contract for the altarpiece destined for the main chapel of the local church of the Crociferi, under the patronage of Giovan Battista de' Lazzari.[45] The latter's intention had been that the canvas should depict an "image of the Most Blessed Ever-Virgin Mary, Mother of God, and of Saint John the Baptist and others" ("imago Beatissime semper Virginis Dei genitricis Marie et sancti Iohanni Baptiste et aliorum"); however, apparently at the painter's suggestion, the subject was later modified by linking it to the client's surname instead of his name. The result was the extraordinary *Raising of Lazarus*, now in the Regional Museum in Messina [fig. 11 on p. 23], in which Caravaggio portrays himself as an eyewitness to the mysteries of life and death, making it a further chapter in his own pictorial autobiography, which would end—as we will see later—with the desperate *Martyrdom of Saint Ursula* for Marco Antonio Doria [cat. 24].

The second work Caravaggio painted for Messina, also now housed in the Museo Regionale, is the *Adoration of the Shepherds* [fig. 5 on p. 88] for the Capuchin church of Santa Maria degli Angeli, entrusted to him—according to Susinno—by the city Senate. Yet another profession by the painter of a profound and sincere pauperistic faith, which already emerges from Bellori's description: "colorì a' Capuccini il quadro della Natività, figuratavi la Vergine col Bambino fuori la capanna rotta e disfatta d'assi e di travi" ("he painted the picture of the Nativity for the Capuchins, in which the Virgin is represented with the Child outside a ruined, delapidated hut of boards and beams").[46] We now have an important and unexpected document, published in 2024, that attests that the painting was only paid for in its entirety in Naples, at the end of November 1609, for a fee of 300 ducats.[47] However, it is not certain that the "Nativity" was executed and delivered in the city, to be then sent on to Messina, according to the most immediate and sensationalist interpretation of the document. Indeed, it cannot be ruled out that—about to leave the island and under psychological pressure—Caravaggio had preferred, for practical reasons, to receive such a large sum in the place to which he had decided to return and remain more permanently.

Be that as it may, the lost "Christ carrying the cross, with the Virgin of Sorrows and two henchmen, one sounding the trumpet" ("Christo colla croce in spalla, la Vergine Addolorata e dui manigoldi, uno sona la tromba") is the only work known to have been completed with certainty of a series of four paintings of the Passion of Christ for a certain Nicolao

Giuseppe Porzio

Di Giacomo.[48] With the exception perhaps of the genial *Tooth Puller* [fig. 3 on p. 5] now in Palazzo Pitti,[49] which, in any case, for the present author is a powerful original work from the Sicilian interlude,[50] an archetype for the coarsest strand of tavern scenes, nothing else remains of his sojourn in Messina, just as nothing is known of the painter's later passage through Palermo, referred to by Baglione, Bellori and Susinno.[51] The traditional positioning to this period of the "Nativity" for the Oratory of San Lorenzo, which dates back precisely to Bellori, has now been questioned by more recent studies, which consider the altarpiece to be a work produced in Rome in 1600, and sent from there to the island.[52] In any case, the theft of the work, successfully carried out in October 1969, which was never sufficiently lamented, had already seriously broken the historical bond between the city and the Lombard genius.

THE EPILOGUE. NAPLES, 1609–1610

Caravaggio's return to Naples and his brief sojourn in the city until his death on 18 July 1610 in Porto Ercole, where he had landed in an improbable attempt to reach Rome—or perhaps, according to a new reconstruction,[53] to seal a peace agreement with Tomassoni's heirs—had a severe consequences for him and on his artistic production.[54]

First, however, there is the attack at the hands of unknown assassins in the Cerriglio tavern in October 1609, from which, according to confused contemporary testimonies,

[fig. 13]
Ecce Homo, c. 1609, detail, Icon Trust [cat. 20]

[fig. 14]
David with the Head of Goliath, c. 1606 / 1609, detail, Galleria Borghese, Rome [cat. 19]

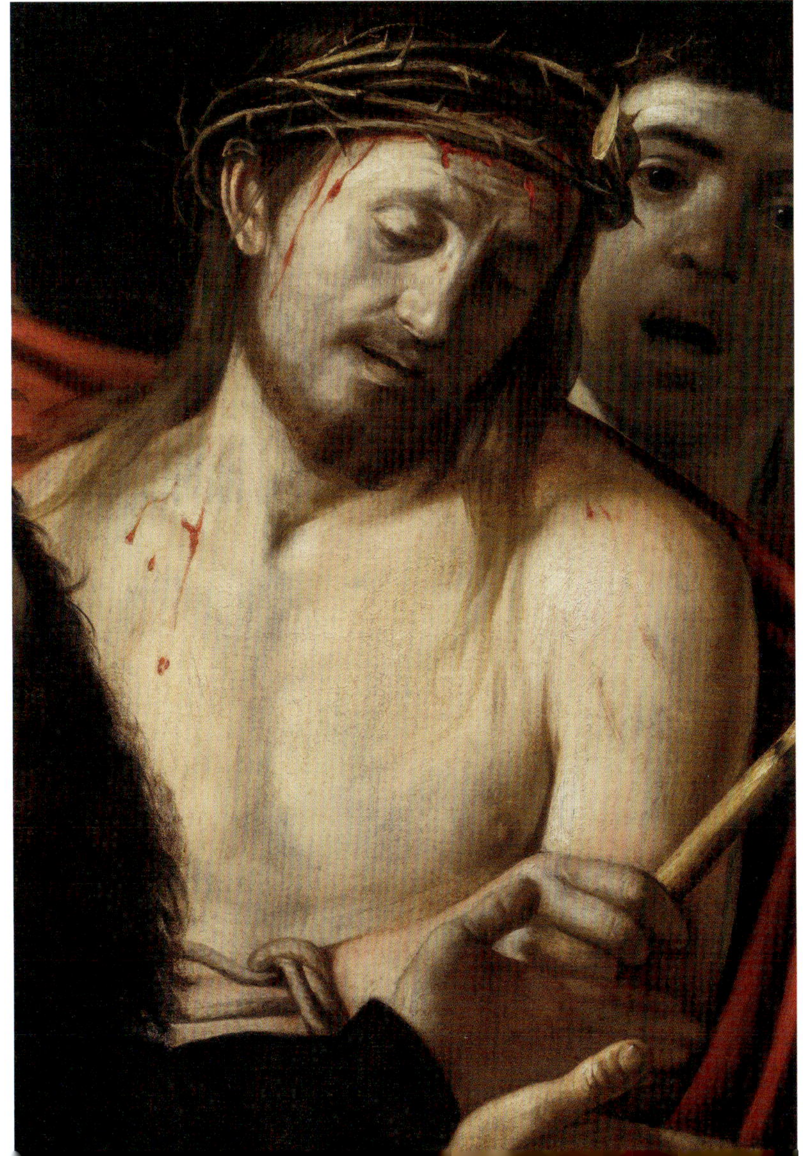

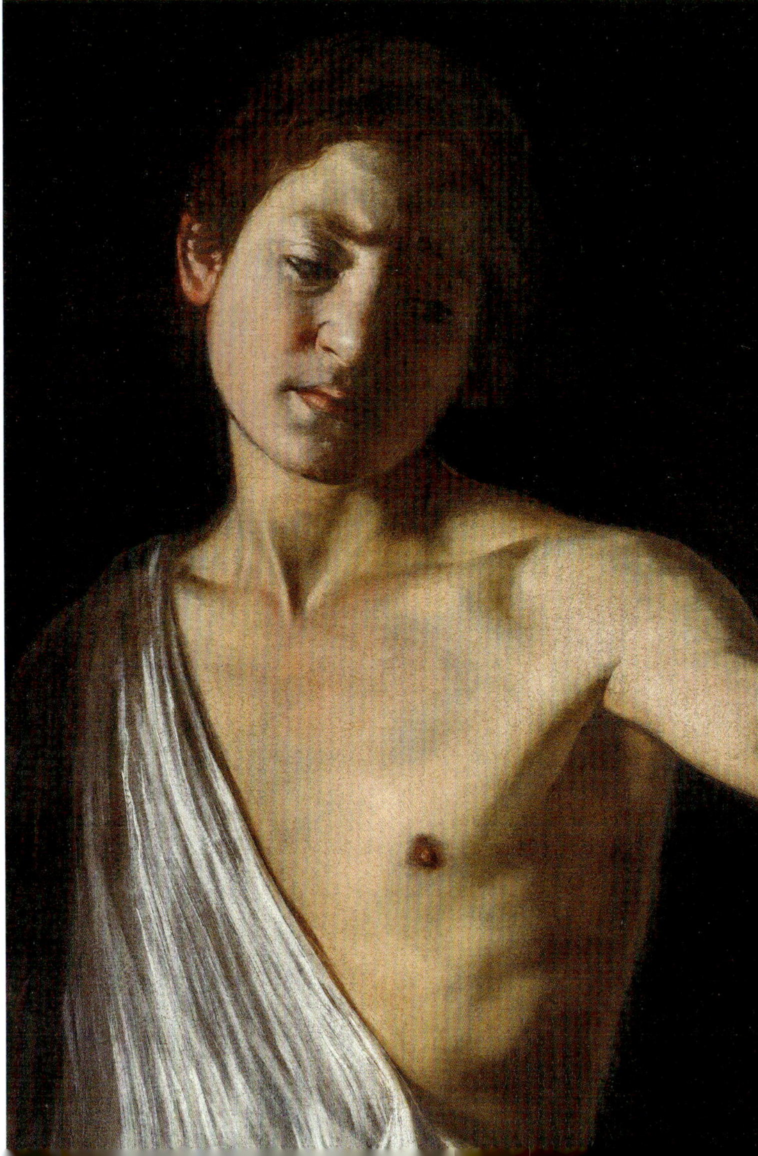

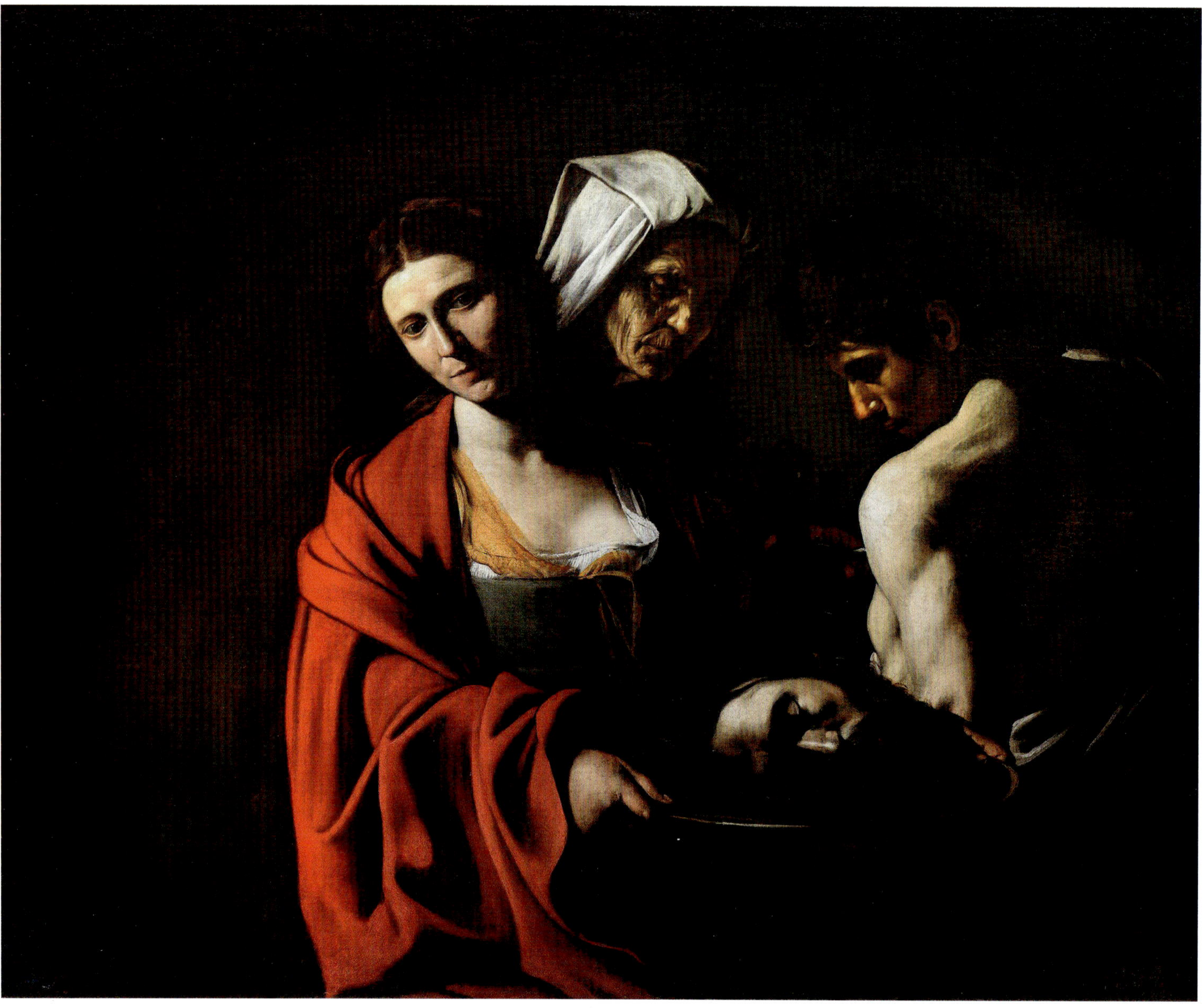

the artist's face was severely disfigured, an episode that would have provoked an even more frantic activity—and for us, one lacking in absolute certainties—to Caravaggio's final production. For the writer, this is perhaps the moment of the *Ecce Homo* in Madrid [fig. 13; cat. 20], first attested in 1657 in Naples in the inventory of the possessions of Viceroy García de Avellaneda y Haro, second Conte di Castrillo, together with the *Salome* from the Spanish royal collections [fig. 15]. In terms of setting and morphological details, in fact, the sorrowful image of Christ seems in every way comparable to that of the *David* in the Galleria Borghese [fig. 14; cat. 19], thus also supporting the typological relationship that Christian exegesis establishes between the two figures. However, the dating of this iconic work is by no means straightforward: the prevailing and, I would say, more solid opinion is that it dates to the second Neapolitan period, especially since Goliath's screaming head makes one think of Caravaggio's disfigured face after the ambush at the Cerriglio. Recently,

Giuseppe Porzio

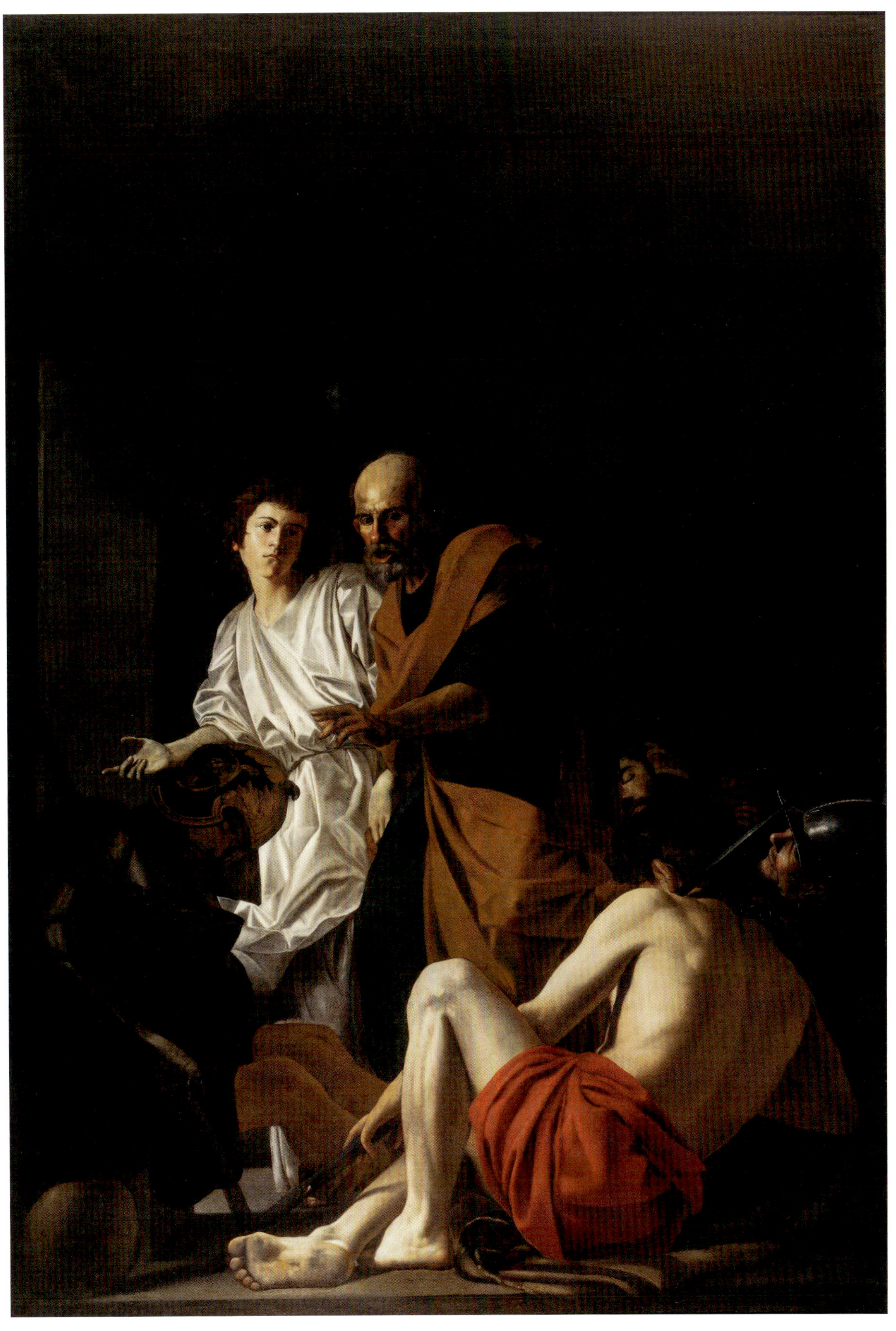

however, an alternative direction in studies has been gaining ground, which tends to anticipate the *David* to the no less feverish period of Caravaggio's transfer from Rome to Naples,
highlighting the similarities with the Brera *Supper at Emmaus*[55] [cat. 17].

It should be stressed, however, that the first hypothesis seems to also agree with the
earliest documentation of the painting in the Borghese collection, dating back to 1613;[56]
furthermore, in 1610, Giulio Cesare Fontana commissioned Baldassarre Aloisi, then in
Naples, to paint two copies of a *David* by Caravaggio,[57] which can be identified, in all likelihood, with the Borghese version of the subject.

Then there is the problem of the lost canvases for the chapel of the Bergamasque
Alfonso Fenaroli in Sant'Anna dei Lombardi, among which a *Resurrection of Christ* would
have stood out, the centre of three works, and the one on which the sources have focused
the most attention.[58] The hypothesis that they should be consigned to Caravaggio's second Neapolitan period, which has also been rejected by some, is based on the fact that the
concession for the chapel dates to 24 December 1607, and therefore the painter could only
have executed the works after his return from Sicily.[59]

Of the main painting, ancient descriptions mainly report the strong sensation aroused by
its unconventional iconography, or rather, as usual, one at the limits of decorum. The most
precise report is that of Charles-Nicolas Cochin, who in the mid-eighteenth century noted
in his diary the image, anything but triumphant, of a gaunt Christ marked by the suffering
he had endured, fleeing the guards as though a thief;[60] an impression that finds confirmation
in the earlier testimonies of Luigi Pellegrino Scaramuccia and Bernardo De Dominici, who
of this "Resurrection of the Lord, who almost with fear emerges from his tomb" blamed the
"base and indecent idea of the [subject] represented".[61] A reworking of this creation by the
master can perhaps be discerned in one of Battistello's most powerful inventions, *Liberation
of Saint Peter from Prison*, painted in 1615 for the Pio Monte della Misericordia [fig. 6].[62]

Either side of the Fenaroli *Resurrection* would have stood a *Saint Francis of Assisi* and
a *Saint John the Baptist*, similarly lost;[63] and in the same way, the various proposals to find
echoes of these among contemporaries, for example in the work of Sellitto and Battistello,
remain at the moment more or less suggestive hypotheses, but ones that cannot be verified.

There is no doubt, however, that the concluding apex of Caravaggio's Neapolitan career
is the spectral *Martyrdom of Saint Ursula* [cat. 24], painted in May 1610 for the Genoese
prince Marco Antonio Doria, just over a month before the artist's death, which now—after
complicated vicissitudes surrounding its attribution and collecting history that are well
known—hangs in the Gallerie d'Italia in Naples.[64]

As is always the case in the Lombard painter's late works, the episode of the saint's martyrdom at the hands of the Hun king is concentrated, with supreme narrative conciseness
and outside the iconographic tradition, to its essential core and factual truth. Isolated from
the execution of her virgin companions, the killing of Ursula, reduced almost to a common
act of bloodshed, is represented in its culminating moment—and among the witnesses to
the drama is the painter himself, on the right of the composition behind the saint—as the violent and instinctive consequence of the woman's final refusal of the barbarian's overtures.

Caravaggio's artistic and existential epilogue is entrusted to a few other works destined
to have important repercussions on naturalism between Naples and Rome, first and foremost in terms of the success of their subject matter: these are, in my opinion, the afore
mentioned *Salome with the Head of Saint John the Baptist* in the Palacio Real in Madrid
[fig. 15], which, however, an authoritative critical interpretation moves back to the first Neapolitan period;[65] certainly the moving *Denial of Saint Peter* in the Metropolitan Museum

of Art in New York [fig. 12 on p. 23],[66] which once belonged to Guido Reni, later ceded to Cardinal Paolo Savelli,[67] and above all the paintings the painter took with him on his last journey to Rome:[68] "the two Saint Johns", the one in the Galleria Borghese [cat. 23], seated amidst the vegetation, and another, depicted lying down, known only through copies,[69] as well as the endlessly replicated half-figure "Magdalene", the original of which has as yet to be identified.[70] The frenzy of his last days did not allow him to execute "the painting he had promised", receiving the considerable sum of almost "one hundred *scudi*", for the new refectory of the Theatine church of Santi Apostoli, to replace a destroyed *Multiplication of the Loaves* by Belisario Corenzio.[71]

What Caravaggio endured in his final days, the circumstances of his arrest and death, are questions that are beyond the scope and concerns of this essay; of greater importance are instead the existence, fate and very identification of the paintings of the "felluca", an affair still shrouded in shadows. However, recent documentary verifications give the impression that it is precisely this line of enquiry, one that further delves into the Naples archives, that may provide the most productive new elements for the understanding of the earliest facts surrounding southern naturalism.[72]

1   This essay revises and expands two of my earlier contributions (Porzio 2019; Porzio 2023), to which I refer you in particular for a more in-depth analysis of contextual issues.

2   It is impossible to compress within the space of a note the vast critical literature that has accumulated on Caravaggio; therefore, since it can only be partial, we will limit ourselves—for the purposes of this study—to indicating only the essential references, in particular those of a documentary nature, on which are based the statements contained in the text. For the archival sources, we refer you—for practical reasons—to the recent re-issue of Stefania Macioce's repertory (2023); for the paintings cited, except in special cases, it is sufficient to refer not only to the entries on the works in the catalogue, but also to the main monographs on Caravaggio: Cinotti 1983; Marini 2005; Bologna [1992] 2006; Schütze 2009; Spike 2010; Vodret 2021a.

3   A useful summary of this transformation is in Galasso 1982, pp. I–VII.

4   For the citations, Bellori [1672] 2005, pp. 182–183. A letter by Fabio Masetti, agent of Cesare d'Este, Duke of Modena and Reggio, sent on 23 September 1606 to the ducal secretary Giovanni Battista Laderchi (Macioce 2023, p. 233, doc. 747), suggests that Caravaggio was still present in Paliano on that date. A detailed analysis of Caravaggio's sojourn in the Lazio as a prelude to his move to Naples can be found in Terzaghi 2022a, pp. 69–87. As for the *Magdalene*, it is Bellori who specifies that it was a half-figure; on the basis of this indication, the majority of scholars—with notable exceptions, for instance Spike 2010, CD-ROM, pp. 390–393, cat. 75, and Papi 2021—have identified the painting with the highly successful archetype that Caravaggio took with him to Naples on his last journey, and from which innumerable copies and variants were derived (for the work most recently accredited as the original—the so-called 'Gregori' *Magdalene*—see the provisional observations of Berra 2021b, pp. 132–134).

5   The necessity for the elucidation of Cavalier d'Arpino's origins was already perceived by Tutini [c. 1664–1666] 2021, pp. 17, 39, and then by De Dominici [1742–1743] 2017, II, p. 935 (commentary by C. Restaino). 28 June 1589 is the date of the contract between the Carthusians and the master (Faraglia 1885, pp. 455–456, doc. I). Generally overlooked, but significant, is the work by Paolo Guidotti, the "Cavalier Borghese", in the apse of the church of Santa Maria del Parto, dated 1593.

6   For Finson in Rome, see Spina 2021; for his presence in Naples, Porzio 2019, pp. 29–30.

7   See Porzio 2022.

8   Macioce 2023, p. 234, doc. 751; for Caravaggio's subsequent moving around of the money, see ibid., pp. 235–236, docs. 755–756. On the commissioning patron see in particular Denunzio 2009, pp. 175–179.

9   Macioce 2023, pp. 235–236, docs. 754–755.

10   For an interpretation of the foundation of the institution in relation to artistic patronage: Gazzara 2003, pp. 51–67; on the building of the church in relation to Caravaggio's altarpiece: Gazzara 2019, pp. 60–69, in particular p. 68 for information on Radolovich's funding; for the broader historical-economic context of the institution in the Naples of the seventeenth century: Casanova 2008.

11   In the description of the subject of the canvas, the seventeenth-century sources all agree on the corporeal nature of the acts of mercy; it is only from the mid-eighteenth century that the iconographic interpretation shifts to the Marian focus of the scene, with the alternative title of "Our Lady of Mercy".

12   Macioce 2023, pp. 242–243, docs. 774–775. On the duties of the "deputy of the Dead": Gazzara 2003, p. 53.

13   Ibid., pp. 52–54. The literature on the relations between Caravaggio and Marino is extensive. Suffice it to recall here that according to Bellori ([1672] 2005, p. 181) it was the poet's benevolence that resulted in Caravaggio receiving the commission for the cycle of the Contarelli chapel in San Luigi dei Francesi.

14   On the altarpiece, see now C. Restaino, in *Pio Monte della Misericordia* 2020, pp. 127–130, cat. I.1.2.

15   Macioce 2023, p. 247, doc. 785A. The name of Forlì was also crossed with that of Caravaggio for the enormous and documented *Circumcision* in the basilica of Santa Maria della Sanità in Naples, ascribed to the Lombard painter by a documentary annotation of 1612, which on closer inspection naturally revealed itself to be an insertion (D'Andrea 1971); the misunderstanding is definitively laid to rest by Restaino 1987, p. 50, note 56.

16   Comite 1616, pp. 42–43, in particular p. 42: "God's trumpet, | which without clamour imprints itself in hearts | this [trumpet], which the world heard | from the cold lands to the dark coasts, | and truthfully painted | this heavenly light that inspires and lights with love the holy face | whose name is Jerome and is divinely resplendent | clothed in purple" ("Quella tromba di Dio, | che senza strepitar s'imprime a i cori, | questa, ch'il mondo udio | da le fredde contrate a i lidi mori, | e dipinta verace, | che spira e accende amor con santa faccia | questo lume celeste | che Geronimo ha nome e divo splende | che di porpora veste . . .").

17   Inv. 1960.13.

18   Marini 2005, pp. 555–557, cat. 100; from the scarce critical fortune of the painting, I should like to highlight the opinion of Previtali 1985, pp. 78–79, fig. 11.

19   Terzaghi 2019, p. 39.

20   For these relationships that can be discerned in the radiographic documentation of the *Seven Acts*: Pacelli 1993, pp. 77–79; see also A. Iommelli, in *Caravaggio Napoli* 2019, pp. 120–121, cat. 4.

21   Macioce 2023, pp. 248–249, docs. 788, 793. For the citation, Bellori [1672] 2018, pp. 40–43.

22   Bologna [1992] 2006, p. 336, cat. 74.

23   For example the *Flagellation*, since at least 1633 in the collections of the Galleria Borghese (inv. 194). Sarti 2022.

24   Inv. NG638. It was Longhi (1959, pp. 21–32) who identified the painting with the "half-length figure of Herodias with the head of Saint John the Baptist in a basin" which, according to Bellori ([1672] 2005, p. 184), Caravaggio sent as a gift to the Grand Master of the Order of Malta to appease his wrath after his escape from the island. Although this is the prevailing scholarly opinion, substantial traces left by the work in early seventeenth-century paintings in Naples seem to contradict the hypothesis.

25   This is the date of a missive sent to the Duke of Mantua by his agent Ottavio Gentile, who intended to take advantage of Caravaggio's availability for an evaluation of Matteo di Capua's collection housed in Vico Equense with a view to a possible purchase (Macioce 2023, p. 251, doc. 799). Given that on the following 12 July the painter was already in Malta, it seems evident that Gentile was not aware of Caravaggio's actual presence in Naples.

26   The dating of the painting to the painter's first sojourn in Naples is the one commonly held in scholarship. However, not lacking in suggestiveness, given the controversial nature of the stylistic elements alone, is the hypothesis of a correlation between the painting and the Viceroy's visit to the relics of Saint Andrew in the crypt of Amalfi cathedral at Easter 1610: Restaino 2012, p. 150. For a presentation of the Cleveland painting after the recent restoration: Benay 2018, in particular pp. 105–138 for the conservation treatment, the technical findings and the comparison with other replicas of the composition, including the one in the Spier collection (formerly Back-Vega), for which a recently misguided attempt has been made to validate it as an autograph work.

27   Bellori [1672] 2018, pp. 60–63.

28   See *The Getty Provenance Index®*, *Archival Inventories*, doc. E86, nos. 10 and 13. The "Santo obispo . . . original de Carabacho" is also present in the earliest inventory of the "pinturas grandes" of the *Fortaleza* of Benavente, dated 1611, which also includes a *Washing of the feet* "orig[ina]l de Carabayo", not otherwise known (Macioce 2023, p. 481, doc. 1).

29   The main source for the episode is Iacopo da Varazze [ms., before 1264] 2007, II, 146, pp. 3839.

30   Macioce 2023, p. 258, doc. 816. It is possible—as also argued by other scholars—that the Toulouse painting, which alternates passages of very high quality—such as the face of the protagonist—with others that are extremely dry and forced, originates from a design by Caravaggio that was followed and completed in the workshop of Finson and Vinck. On the painting, see *Caravaggio. Judith et Holopherne* 2019.

31   Kunsthistorisches Museum Wien, Gemäldegalerie, inv. 147.

32   Thus Gentile's letter to Vincenzo I Gonzaga of 15 September 1607: "[Pourbus] has again seen some good things by Michel Angelo Caravaggio that he has done here, which will be sold" (Macioce 2023, pp. 257–258, doc. 815).

33   Macioce 2023, p. 306, doc. 966.

34   Bredius, Roever 1886, pp. 7–8. It remains unclear whether the work in Finson's possession was in fact an original or rather a copy of Caravaggio's masterpiece now in Cleveland; in recent years, attempts have been made to identify it as the *Crucifixion of Saint Andrew* in the Spier collection (see note 26 above), but promoting it as a certain autograph work.

   Giuseppe Porzio

35   Macioce 2023, p. 321, doc. 1026.

36   Inv. GG 125.

37   For the most complete documentation on the painting: Prohaska, Swoboda 2010, pp. 86–99. For the Finson-Vinck association, Porzio 2019, pp. 27–28 and relative notes, to be integrated with the identification of the true author of the mediocre altarpiece with the *Madonna and Child between Saint Cornelius and Saint Blaise* in the Archbishop's Seminary in Antwerp, attributed to Vinck by Leone de Castris (1991, pp. 97 and 101, note 85) on the basis of a misreading of the convoluted signature, to be read instead as the name of Giuseppe Vitale, a modest painter active in the Neapolitan hinterland between the seventeenth and eighteenth centuries.

38   Denunzio 2004, pp. 48–51; for the landing, see Dal Pozzo 1703–1715, I, 1703, pp. 521–522.

39   Macioce 2023, pp. 252–253, doc. 801. Our knowledge of the painter's troubled Maltese period has now been incorporated in Sciberras 2023.

40   Sandrart 1675, II/2, p. 190; Bellori [1672] 2005, p. 183.

41   Sciberras 2023, pp. 270–271, docs. 851–852.

42   Ibid., p. 271, doc. 854.

43   Ibid., pp. 271-274, docs. 855, 857-860.

44   Bellori [1672] 2005, p. 183; Susinno [1724] 1960, p. 110.

45   Macioce 2023, p. 862, doc. 862.

46   Bellori [1672] 2005, p. 183.

47   Sorrentino 2024b, pp. 60–62, 72, doc. 3; it is worth noting that in the document Caravaggio still boasts of the title "frate", as if he had kept hidden his expulsion from the Order. The contribution also records two other payments to the painter, issued between late October and early November of the same year, for two paintings of an unspecified subject, the first delivered to Lanfranco Massa, Marco Antonio Doria's agent in Naples.

48   Macioce 2023, p. 277, doc. 876.

49   Inv. 1890, 5682.

50   The clear citation from the *Tooth Puller* in a contemporary *Madonna of the Rosary* in the parish church of San Filippo Superiore, attributed to Salvatore Mittica of Messina, is an important clue to the painting's Sicilian origin: Spagnolo 2022a, pp. 37–39; Spagnolo 2022b, pp. 212–213.

51   Baglione [1642] 2023, p. 408; Bellori [1672] 2005, p. 183; Susinno [1724] 1960, p. 115.

52   For the most organic discussion of the work, Cuppone 2023.

53   Curti 2023.

54   The first testimony at present that we have of the painter's return to Naples is the report (dated 24 October) of an assault by some believed to have proved fatal, of which Caravaggio was the victim. Its "source" is in the form of a dispatch sent to the Duke of Urbino Francesco Maria II della Rovere by his correspondents in Rome (Macioce 2023, p. 278, doc. 878). If we take into account the time required for the transmission of information between the two centres, Longhi (1951b, p. 11) considered that the heinous deed (from which the painter must have emerged severely disfigured, as recalled by Baglione [1642] 2023, p. 408 and by Bellori [1672] 2005, p. 184) must have taken place around 20 October. As for the master's death, the date is recorded in two epitaphs composed for the occasion by his jurist friend Marzio Milesi (Macioce 2023, p. 343, doc. F2/17–18).

55   See in this regard G. Papi, in *Cecco del Caravaggio* 2023, pp. 92–95, cat. 2, where the hypothesis of an earlier chronology rests in the first instance on the identification, in the David, of the features of Caravaggio's young companion, Francesco (Cecco) Boneri. For the question of Caravaggio's "Colonna style", that is, circumscribed to his retreat to the Colonna's Lazio fiefs, see Terzaghi 2022a, pp. 69–87.

56   Macioce 2023, p. 295, doc. 923, and pp. 346–347, doc. F10.

57   Ibid., p. 287, doc. 896.

58   At the local level, note in particular Celano 1692, III, pp. 9–10.

59   Prohaska 1975, p. 3, note 9; the current shelf-mark for the document is Archivio di Stato di Napoli, Archivi notarili, Archivi dei notai del XVII secolo, Giovanni Bernardino De Giuliano, 800/2, cc. 361*r*–363*v*.

60   Cochin 1756, p. 132.

61   Scaramuccia 1674, pp. 75–76; De Dominici [1742–1743] 2017, II, p. 969.

62   The painting, initially commissioned to Carlo Sellitto, was then executed, after the latter's death, by Battistello for the sum of one hundred ducats (Porzio 2019, p. 33, note 52, with reference to the relevant documentation). The hypothesis which discerned in it a reflection of the Fenaroli *Resurrection* was put forward by Fagiolo dell'Arco 1969, p. 71, who, however, identified it in the group of sleeping soldiers; I wonder if the echo might not rather be caught in the fleeing motion of the two main figures.

63   The *Saint Francis* is first explicitly described in a seventeenth-century postilla to codex P of Mancini's *Considerazioni sulla pittura* ([c. 1619–1621] 1956–1957, p. 340). For the subject of the other painting: Cochin 1756, p. 133, and with more detail, Puccini [ms., 1783] 2014, p. 103. For the dispersion of the furnishings of Sant'Anna dei Lombardi see Giani 2021, in particular p. 83.

64   For the agnition of the painting: Pacelli, Bologna 1980.

65   See in particular M.C. Terzaghi, in *Da Caravaggio a Bernini* 2017, pp. 126–133, cat. 5.

66   Inv. 1997.167.

67   Nicolaci, Gandolfi 2011.

68   Macioce 2023, pp. 285–286, doc. 891.

69   Of the composition, which seems to have had not insignificant repercussions in the milieu of the Neapolitan naturalists, two replicas in private collections dispute—wrongly, in my opinion—for the privilege of autograph status, one formerly in Munich, the other in Malta (for the latter: *Caravaggio, ultimo approdo* 2022).

70   See note 4 above.

71   The information, taken from Bolvito before 1630, p. 75, is in Delfino 1984, p. 156; initially missed by the specific bibliography on Caravaggio, the information has been exploited by D'Alessandro 2007, pp. XXXV–XXXVI, and by Porzio 2012, pp. 583-584, note 15, and recently confirmed by the payment of 70 ducats to the Theatine house of the Santi Apostoli tracked down by Zappulli 2024, pp. 111–113, to which a second payment of 15 to the fathers of San Paolo Maggiore may be linked. This is precisely the reimbursement to the Theatine fathers of the advance paid to Caravaggio, which the scholar, however, does not connect to Bolvito's report.

72   See Zappulli 2024.

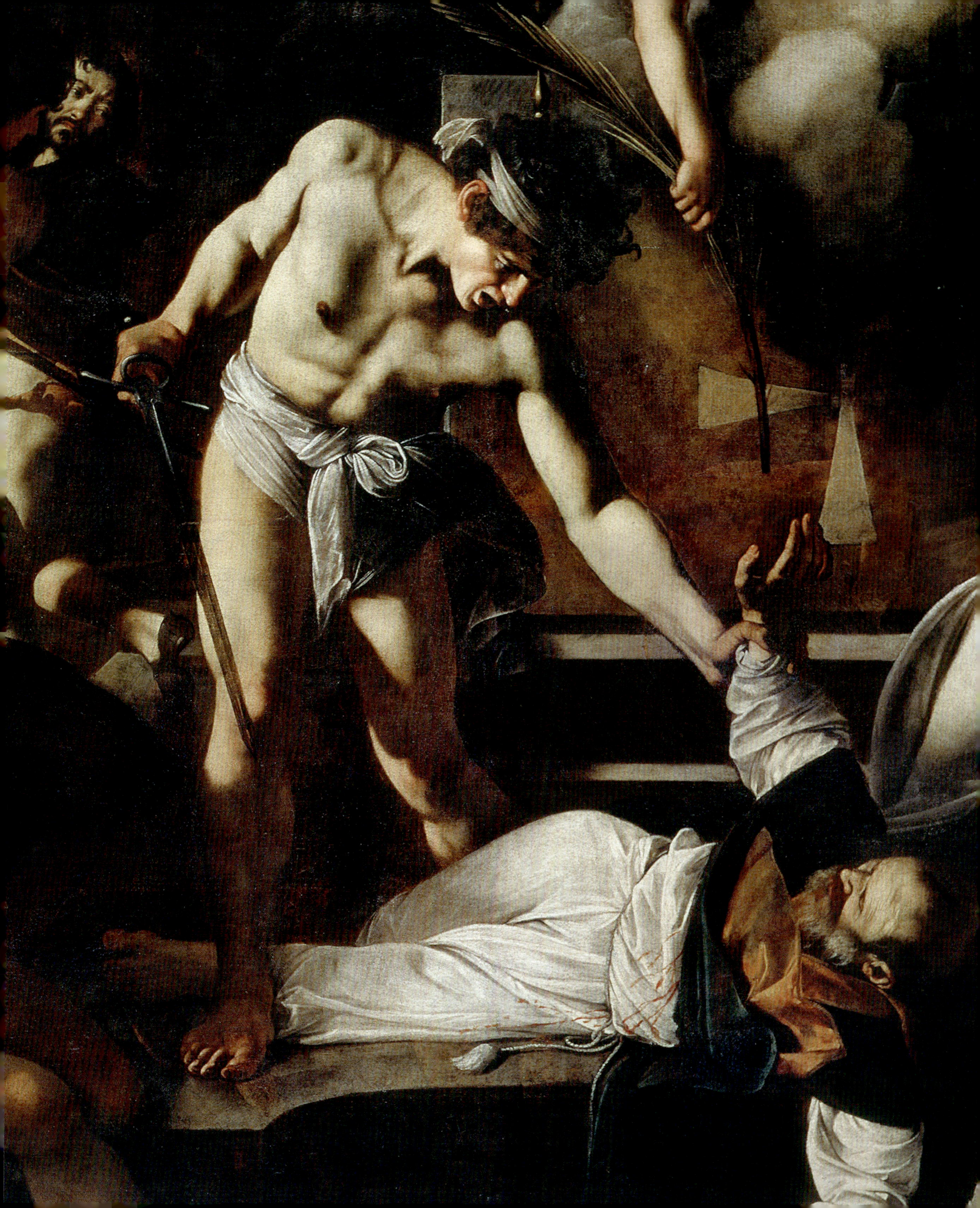

Alessandro Zuccari

CARAVAGGIO AND THE SPIRITUALITY OF HIS TIME

Was Michelangelo Merisi an agnostic or a believer, heterodox or faithful in his own way to the Church of Rome? For a long time scholars have wondered what was the nature of his thought and its relationship with the spirituality of his time, sparking a debate that has lasted for decades, at times polarised into opposing camps.[1] Even beyond the sphere of scholarship, it continues to be a subject of discussion, and this is understandable because Caravaggio's painting is so empathetic and compelling that everyone wants to interpret it in their own way. There is no doubt that he was an unconventional painter, out of tune with the stylistic canons and traditional iconographies of the time; a restless, ingenious, hypersensitive character who it is not easy to bring into focus. Various seventeenth-century biographers have handed down to us a negative image of the artist—whether due to personal rivalry and rancour (Baglione), or artistic militancy in opposition to his anti-academic 'naturalism' (from Celio to Carducho, from Bellori to Susinno)—and for a long time this remained entrenched. Nonetheless, studies and archival research in recent decades have better reconstructed the facts and the historical contexts that marked his existence, from his youth in Lombardy to his intense Roman period, from his wanderings between Naples, Malta and Sicily to his death in Porto Ercole,[2] dismantling the post-Romantic myth of the 'accursed painter' that made of Caravaggio an uncultured, unsociable and an overwhelmingly transgressive subject. The picture that has emerged does not only put before us a prodigious and impetuous painter, one always ready to unsheathe his sword (a habit widespread even among artists), but has revealed a much more complex personality, both in terms of sensitivity and cultural background, as also the importance of the social relations he had succeeded in acquiring.

One need only recall the large number of prelates and members of the aristocracy who procured him prestigious commissions and competed for his paintings, or the relations

[fig. 1]
Martyrdom of Saint Matthew, 1599–1600, detail, Church of San Luigi dei Francesi, Contarelli Chapel, Rome

he entertained with the world of culture (think for instance of his friendship with the poets Marzio Milesi and Giovan Battista Marino, or with the courtier Ainolfo de' Bardi),[3] and the network of protectors who supported him, hosted him and, after his banishment from Rome, did their utmost to obtain his pardon and the longed-for return to the papal capital. Caravaggio, moreover, was not a wild renegade rebelling against all social rules as is demonstrated by his admission into the Knights of Malta, nor was he a penniless vagabond, as is proven by the documents discovered in Naples,[4] where he had opened a bank account, received copious fees, and in his last sojourn in the city lived in the palazzo at Chiaia with Costanza Colonna, his former 'guardian'. Even the observation about "his overwrought brain," recorded by biographers in relation to his last years, can be explained by his condition as a fugitive, hunted by justice for the murder he committed in a game of *pallacorda* that had led to a duel.[5]

These and many other findings redefine the dark and unruly image of Caravaggio conveyed by the biographical sources, fuelled by imposing on the painter nineteenth- and twentieth-century categories and models which, in an historical perspective, are forced and anachronistic. It is no coincidence that the more deeply one studies the painter, the more one understands that Caravaggio was fully a man of his time, and not '*maudit*' as were certain poets and artists of *fin de siècle* France.[6] With these premises in mind, one can try to reconstruct what was his standpoint towards spirituality and the religious institutions of his time.

CARAVAGGIO AND RELIGIOUS PRACTICE: FACTS AND HYPOTHESES

Since we have no direct knowledge of what were Caravaggio's thoughts (he left no writings on the subject), but only fragmentary evidence of his ideas on painting and painters, it is necessary to make a beginning with the archival material at our disposal, to then consider the subjects and the individual compositions of his paintings. In the first instance, we need to take into consideration two documents from the Roman period that indicate that the Lombard master was no stranger to religious practices. The earliest is the well-known 'Lista delle Quarantore', from which it appears that on 18 October 1597 he participated in the vigil of the Blessed Sacrament promoted by the Compagnia dei Virtuosi at the Pantheon, on the occasion of the feast of Saint Luke, the patron saint of painters. Caravaggio's name and that of his friend Prospero Orsi, in fact, appear in the long list of artists who—in pairs—carried out the hour-long vigils.[7] We cannot know whether the painter took part out of social propriety or personal conviction, nevertheless it is a fact that at least outwardly he appeared to be a believer in the Eucharistic cult. It should also be noted that the rite of the Quarantore (the Forty Hours' Devotion) had originated in Milan in 1527 (therefore the painter would have been aware of it), and had been approved by Paul III and successive popes and revived by Clement VIII with the encyclical *Graves et diuturnae* (1592), especially to invoke the end of the wars of religion.[8] Therefore, the presence of Caravaggio in a devotional prayer before the Eucharistic Sacrament runs counter to the idea, repeatedly put forward, that he harboured heterodox sentiments. This may just have been outward adherence, but it must however be borne in mind that this devotional practice, particularly dear to post-Tridentine Catholicism, was instead opposed by the Reformed Churches.

Moreover Caravaggio—as the documents on his father's and mother's families (the Aratori family) demonstrate—had grown up in a Catholic environment linked to local religious practices and devotions, including that for the Marian sanctuary of Caravaggio.[9] He had been baptised with the name Michelangelo, having been born on 29 September 1571, the feast

Alessandro Zuccari

day of the Archangel Michael (a symbol of the fight against the Turks and heretics), and as an adolescent he had received a Christian education that prepared him to receive communion, and was probably also confirmed.[10] His uncle Ludovico Merisi was the canon of San Babila in Milan, and his brother Giovanni Battista was also a priest. He broke with the latter—as Giulio Mancini reports—to the point of not recognising him as his brother, but it has been established that this occurred as a result of disagreements over hereditary matters, and not for religious reasons.[11]

A second document shows that in 1606 the thirty-four-year-old painter observed the Easter precept—the obligation to go to confession and receive communion at least at Easter. The Stati delle Anime of the parish of San Nicola dei Prefetti—the district of which included the house in Vicolo di San Biagio where Merisi lived with Francesco, his apprentice—attest that on 6 June, the parish priest recorded their names with the usual 'c.' for those who had taken communion (and thus confessed).[12] Was this an occasional occurrence or the fruit of custom? We have no way of verifying which because the parish registers are incomplete; in any case, it is evident that this was a more binding and explicit question of choice than participating in a devotional rite involving many of the artists present in Rome.

A HETERODOX DISSIMULATOR?

One could ask whether the painter, while publicly showing himself an observant Catholic, intended to conceal his inner convictions. This question bears in mind that in the Italian territories of the sixteenth and seventeenth centuries, it was not uncommon to dissimulate one's ideas so as not to arouse suspicions of heresy, and not fall into the clutches of the Inquisition. It is well known that in the Catholic states of the ancient regime, those who declared themselves either atheist or heterodox did not have an easy time of it, unless they knew how to cleverly conceal their convictions. We have no evidence of this in relation to Caravaggio, neither from the records of court proceedings, nor from other documents concerning him. On the contrary, it has been noted that in Rome his patrons and collectors were mainly aristocrats, lay members of the curia, monsignors and cardinals. If anything suspicious had come to the surface regarding him, would his patrons— especially the ecclesiastics (including Pope Paul V himself) have acquired or commissioned a quantity of paintings, portraits and altarpieces from him? It is doubtful, at least in the case of some.

Furthermore, if the painter had held a dissenting position from that of the Roman Church, would Cardinal Ferdinando Gonzaga and other figures of importance have worked to obtain his remission of the 'capital' banishment? When delicate doctrinal or philosophical issues were touched upon, everything became more difficult. Therefore, until proven otherwise, one must stick to the documented facts, especially since so far no evidence has emerged of the Lombard master's alleged agnostic or heterodox orientation. In truth, this hypothesis has increasingly affirmed itself over time: indeed, after Vicente Carducho's scathing judgement (which concerns Caravaggio's painting and not his religious inclination),[13] the earliest of the biographers to consider him an "unbeliever" is Francesco Susinno, and he is writing more than a century later and narrates episodes that cannot be relied on, albeit compelling as literature.[14]

In addition to the documents cited above, there is an even more significant biographical element to help us understand what Caravaggio's position was in relation to religious institutions, and that is his firm resolve to join the Order of Malta (a military order notoriously loyal to Rome). The sources, in fact, emphasise the painter's ambitious aspiration for that knighthood, which he obtained on 14 July 1607 thanks to influential backing and the dispensation of Paul V, which enabled him to receive the investiture as a 'Knight of Obedience' even though he lacked the usual requisites of nobility and had "committed murder in a brawl." This choice was no doubt determined by the desire to evade the criminal proceedings pending against him, as well as the aspiration to ennoble himself by becoming a knight; but to achieve this objective he had to demonstrate that he was an observant Catholic [fig. 2]. It is no coincidence that in the investiture ceremony Caravaggio was referred to as "zelo religionis accensus."[15]

Bearing in mind the rules of the Knights Hospitallers of St. John (based on the Rule of Saint Augustine), and Caravaggio's one-year novitiate with them, there can be no doubt that over this period he had manifested his loyalty to the Church of Rome. It is also true that the painter was later imprisoned with other knights and expelled from the Order following a violent brawl in which one of the contenders was seriously wounded; but this does not concern the religious sphere, and once again stems from Michelangelo's passionate and fiery temperament. Then again, the involvement of seven Italian knights in the confrontation demonstrates the extent to which the resort to violence was common.[16]

CARAVAGGIO AND THE NATURALISM OF THE *NOVATORES*

Is it therefore plausible that an immoderate person such as Merisi, during his long sojourn in Malta, could have dissimulated ideas contrary to Catholic thought, especially in that rigid and controlled way of life? Then there is the question as to why the painter, once he had escaped from the impregnable Maltese prison (clearly with someone's help), pursued to the very end his intention of returning precisely to Rome. Had he held unorthodox convictions, he could have sought refuge in Protestant territories, as indeed many Italians had done, for instance by boarding a ship bound for Northern Europe. Instead, he was anxious to obtain a remission of the 'banishment' in order to return to the papal capital, which he evidently felt was his city of choice.[17]

Opinions to the contrary have been expressed in various studies that have attempted to demonstrate Caravaggio's detachment from the Roman Church and, albeit presenting a variety of arguments, his lack of interest in the spiritual currents of his time. In particular, direct or indirect connections have been proposed with renowned thinkers such as Giordano Bruno, Tommaso Campanella and Galileo Galilei, in order to highlight the 'secular' nature of his thought, the affinity of his painting with their respective theoretical concepts and with the experimentalism of the New Science, to the point of seeing in it a "precise equivalent" of the coeval naturalism in philosophy.[18] The greatest commitment in this direction was made

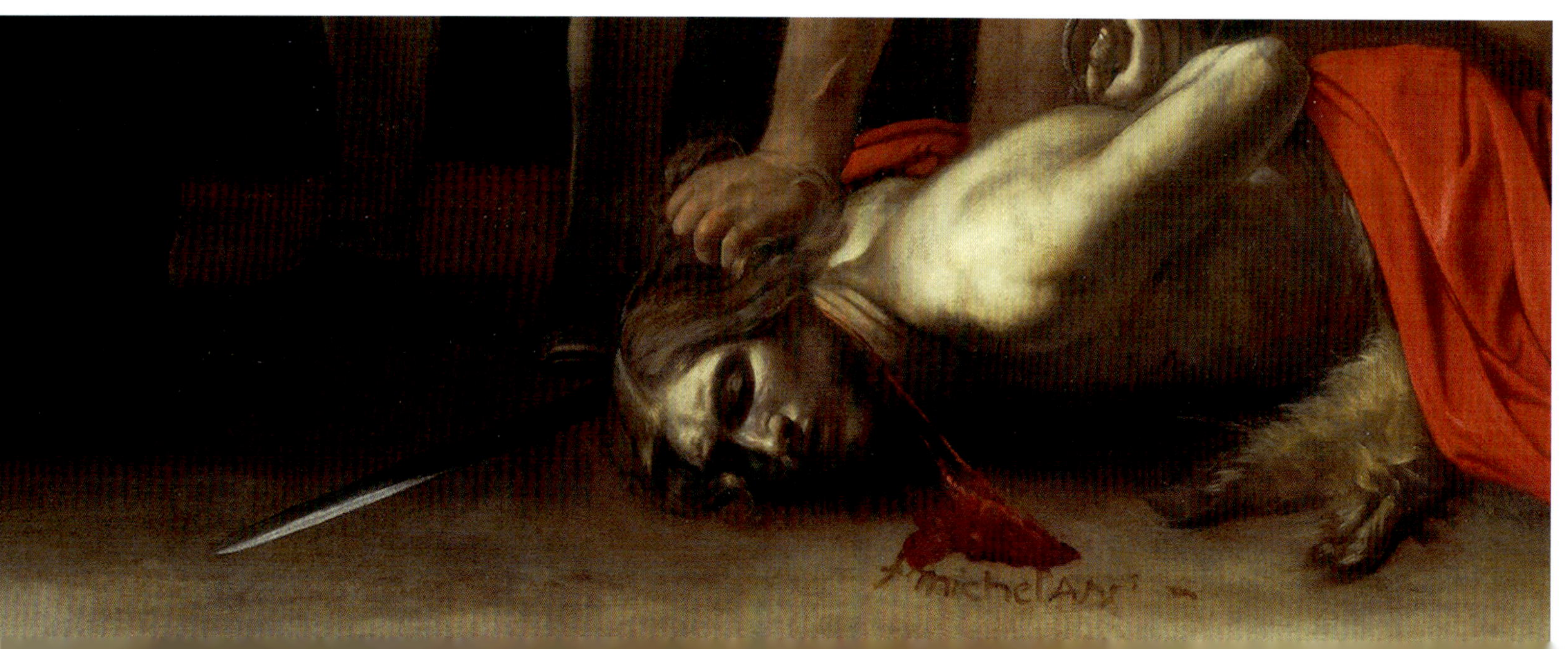

by Ferdinando Bologna, to whom goes the credit of having carried out the cross-checking on the subject, but whose conclusions are not convincing because they are based on historical reconstructions that are not without discrepancies.

Saverio Ricci, in fact, has demonstrated the fallibility of an alignment between Caravaggio and these *novatores*, pointing out that in such studies "Caravaggio's 'naturalism' was established on rather questionable grounds, not only as the 'equivalent' of naturalism in philosophy, presented as homogenous, which in fact it was not, but also as an ethical-religious position consistent with those philosophical values."[19] As a fine scholar of the philosophical and scientific speculations of the early seventeenth century, Ricci laid the emphasis on the different orientation and the considerable divergences between the three thinkers; he made clear that in the early years of the century, the circulation of their writings and knowledge of their content was very circumscribed, and therefore not easily accessible, even to Caravaggio. On the other hand, the painter may have been stimulated and had conversations with Neapolitan scholars of philosophy and science who in those years were involved in the research into the natural world, such as Giovan Battista Manso and Antonio Stigliola, to whom he would however have presented himself "with his own vision of nature and the world already mapped out."[20]

No more can the hypothesis of Caravaggio's contact with Campanella be proven, as both the possibility of their meeting in Rome and the alleged mediation by Cardinal Francesco Maria del Monte—who had met the philosopher in 1592, but had drawn a decidedly negative judgement—are without foundation[21]. The possibility that the painter might have visited Campanella in Naples is also problematic because of the difficulty of gaining access to the prison where the Dominican was being held. For that matter, nor are there affinities between Caravaggio's artistic production and the theories of Giordano Bruno, not only because it is inconsistent and utterly fanciful to compare Caravaggio's "tenebrismo" to Bruno's *De umbris idearum*, but above all because of the evident discrepancy between the designs and conceptions that separates the pictorial 'naturalism' of the former (which moreover had been considered to be "anti-naturalistic") from the philosophical 'naturalism' of the latter. In fact, it has now become clear that there is no confluence between the thought of the essentially "anti-Christian" Giordano Bruno[22] and the religious works of the Lombard painter. These paintings, at times at odds with official formulas, are instead the expression of a distinctive personal spirituality, which is often made manifest through the painter's participation in the sacred subject.

IMMERSION IN BIBLICAL OR HAGIOGRAPHIC SUBJECTS

Various self-portraits of the painter recur in Caravaggio's vast production of religious works—which number significantly more than fifty compared to around twenty autograph works of other subjects—which differ from his youthful ones in that they are set in contexts inspired by biblical subjects and episodes from the lives of the saints.[23] It all begins with the lateral canvases for the Contarelli Chapel (1599–1600), when Caravaggio obtained his first public commission thanks to Cardinal del Monte: in the second version of the *Martyrdom of Saint Matthew,* he places himself among the bystanders who witness this kind of "Murder in the Cathedral" [fig. 1; overall fig. 4 on p. 9]. It is not without reason that Mia Cinotti made the following observation: "The most sensational element is the introduction of the self-portrait—identified by Marangoni—in the figure emerging from the background to the left of the executioner, with a short beard and an expression tormented and doleful, his hand outstretched in strong foreshortening, almost as if to halt the terrible event."[24] This self-representation differs,

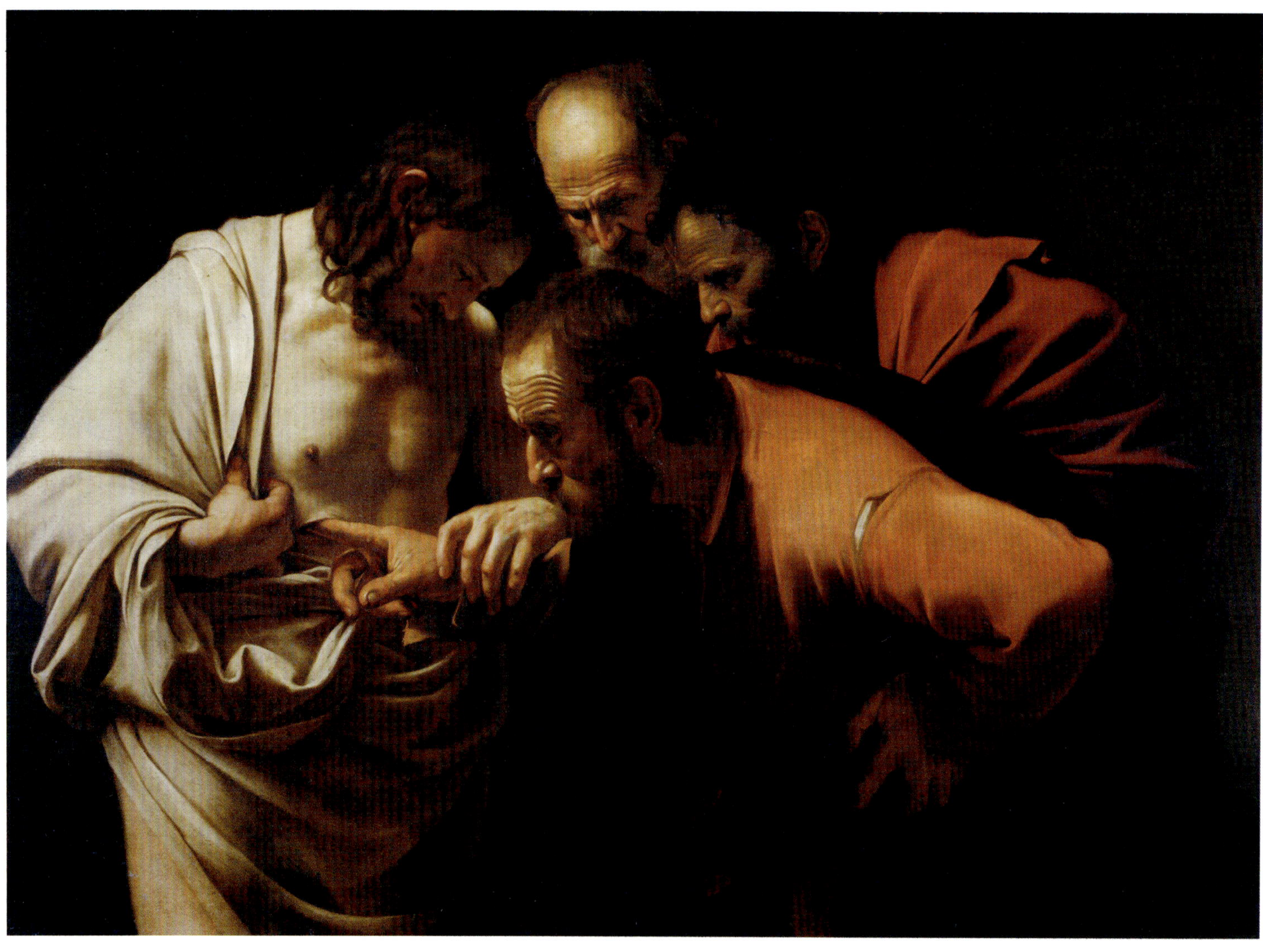

therefore, from those by numerous artists (which can be identified by their frontal position and their gaze turned towards the spectator), and is evidence of an existential participation in the scene of martyrdom.[25]

That this choice is not simply motivated by the desire to display his own image in public, is confirmed by the presence of Caravaggio's self-portraits in sacred works for private patrons. Referring you for this subject to Gianni Papi's essay in this catalogue, it should be noted that in the *Taking of Christ* (1603; cat. 14), the artist plays an active role by raising a lantern to see Christ, a gesture that has been interpreted as "an allegory of Diogenes, who seeks man with a lantern, whence Caravaggio-Diogenes seeks Christ, the Man *par excellence,* amidst darkness and the forces of evil. Thus a Stoic emblem of faith and redemption."[26] The comparison with the Greek philosopher is pertinent because the painter evokes the thinkers of antiquity on several occasions[27]; in any case, he identifies with the Gospel episode opposing his curiosity and docile expression to the swagger of the men at arms and the traitor.

It should be noted in passing that Caravaggio did not portray himself in the *Incredulity of Saint Thomas* (Potsdam, Sanssouci, Bildergalerie; fig. 3), a painting that has been considered

Alessandro Zuccari

a kind of manifesto for his lack of religious belief[28], despite the fact that the Gospel episode ends with the disciple's confession of faith. However, had the painter wished to manifest his "incredulity" in the painting, he would have given Thomas his own physiognomy, as he had done in the *Taking of Christ*; and it would not have been difficult for him to do so, since it was a painting purchased by his greatest collector, the Marchese Vincenzo Giustiniani. Instead, the apostle has the humble appearance of a bewildered commoner who accepts the invitation of the Risen Christ to make the dreadful gesture of inserting his finger into the wound in his side.

Such self- identification by Caravaggio becomes more frequent in the last troubled period of his life. The best known expression of this is the signature "f[ra] Michelangelo" (the "f. makes his membership of the order of Malta explicit), written with the blood of the martyr in the *Beheading of John the Baptist* in Malta [fig. 2; overall fig. 8 on p. 18], the colossal canvas placed on the altar wall of the Knights' Oratory in 1608. Given that the signature is an *unicum*, and the tragic nature of the means chosen for its inscription, it is a declaration of undoubted existential significance, which may sound "as a condemnation, and at the same time a desire for expiation on the part of the fugitive narrowly escaped from the blood-bath of Rome."[29]

Fear, guilt, meditation on death and, above all, a desire for redemption grow in Caravaggio's last works, expressing an inner anxiety that *ad evidentiam* cannot be separated from a longing for salvation. In the *Raising of Lazarus* he turns towards the unnatural light that illuminates the dark cavern [fig. 11 on p. 23][30], as also in The *Martyrdom of Saint Ursula* [cat. 24], which offers us "one last image of the painter looking on, as in the *Taking of Christ* . . . in the act of seeing and witnessing the tragic event."[31] Finally, the Borghese *David with the Head of Goliath* [fig. 4; cat. 19], perhaps painted for Cardinal Scipione Borghese as a pledge to obtain a pardon,

[fig. 4]
David with the Head of Goliath, c. 1606 / 1609, detail, Galleria Borghese, Rome [cat. 19]

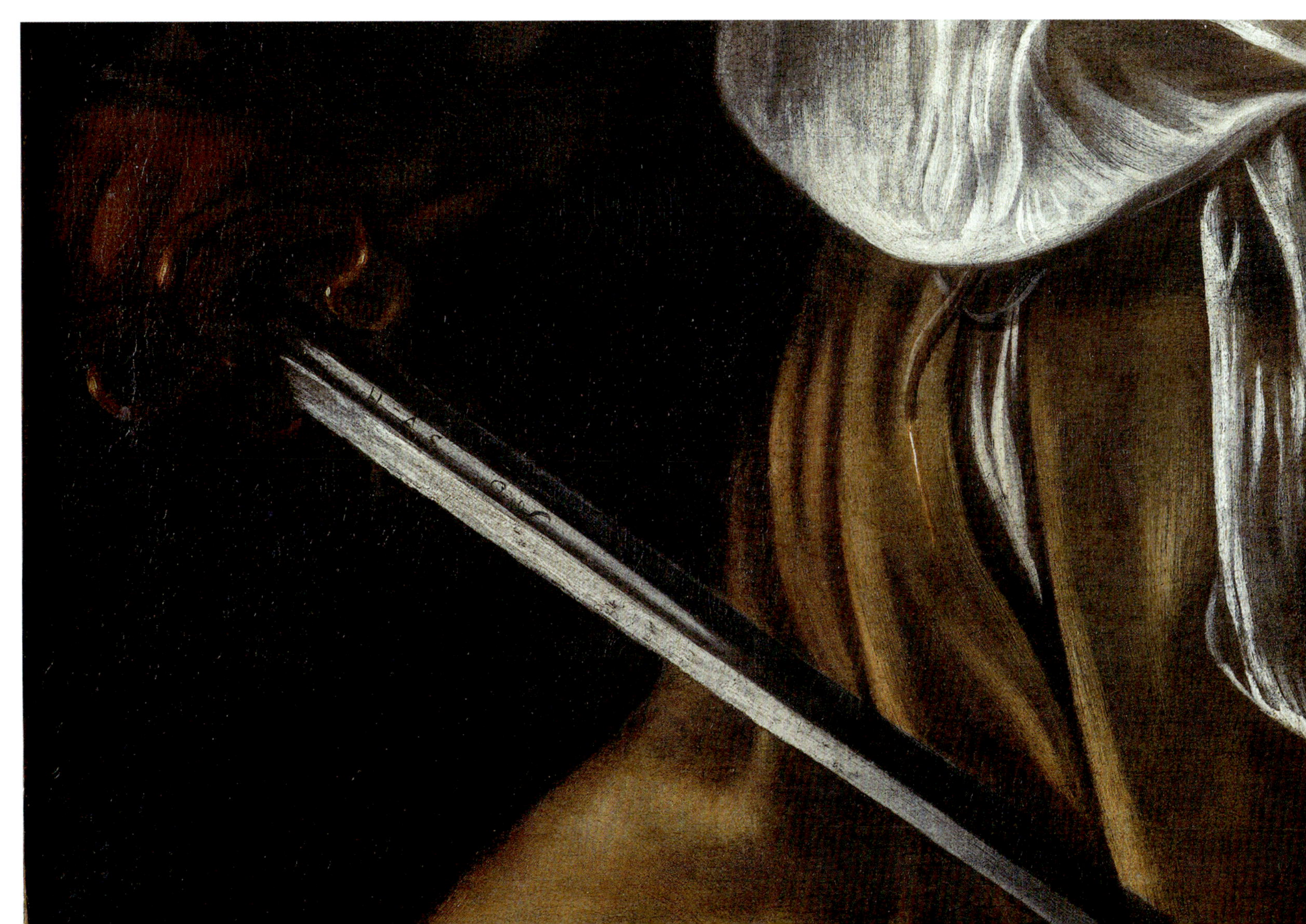

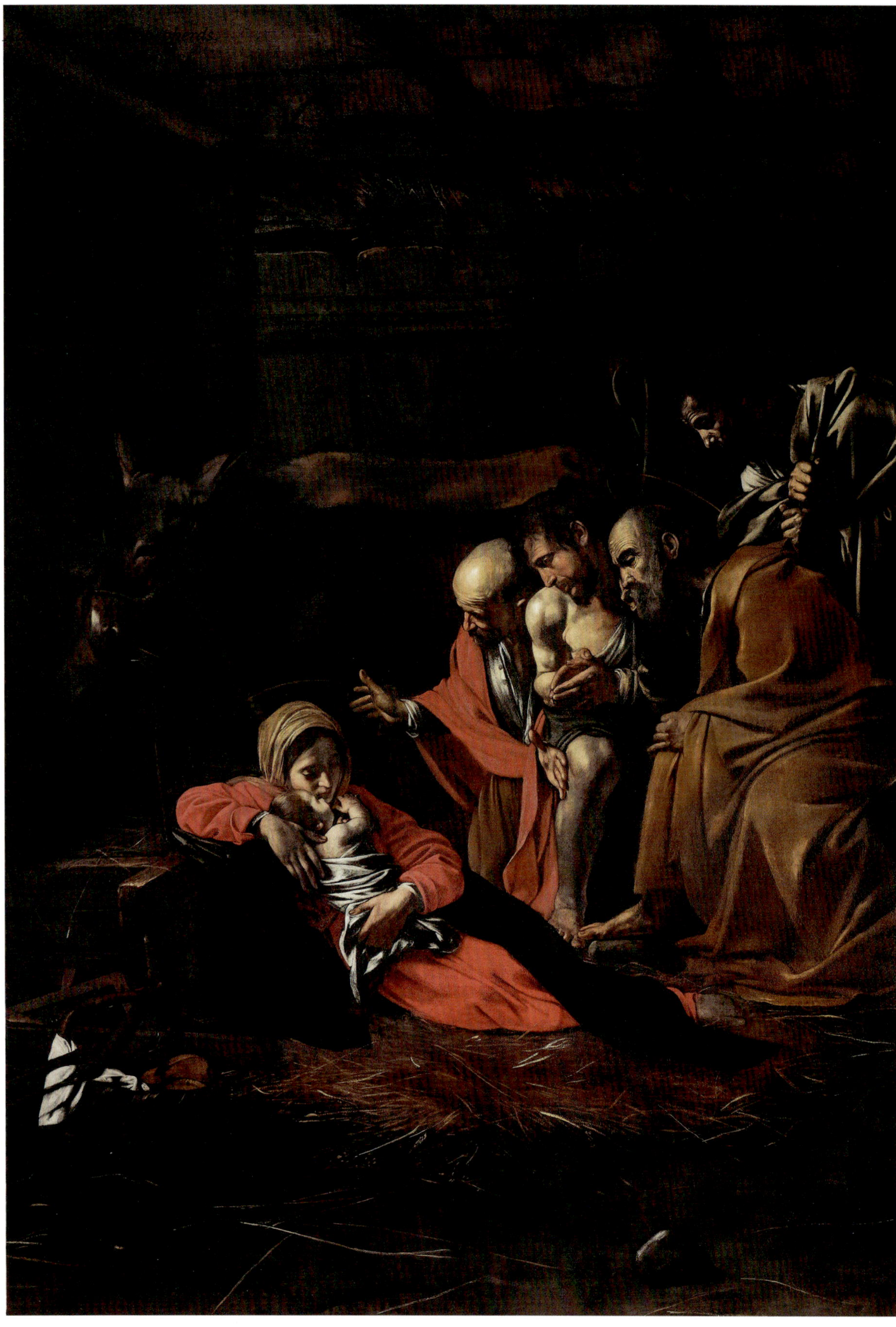

Alessandro Zuccari

in which the young shepherd (a well-known pre-figuration of Christ) turns his pitying gaze on the scarred and severed head of the Philistine who has the painter's features. The deciphering of the acronym (taken from Saint Augustine) by Maurizio Marini is illuminating: "Confirming the humble, anti-heroic, Christological interpretation of David and the self-portrait in Goliath, symbol of the evil one, it is clear that the motto engraved in the shell-moulding of the hilt of the sword [fig. 4], the final instrument of Justice, depends on 'H[humilit]as O[ccidit] S[uperbiam]'."[32] An admission of guilt by the 'proud' murderer, who reinforces his humble request for pardon with a quotation from the Church Fathers, an indication of Caravaggio's degree of erudition, and of his troubled spirituality.

BORROMEO'S "HUMILITAS" AND THE FRANCISCAN SPIRIT

"Humilitas", as is well known, is the motto loved and popularised by Saint Charles Borromeo, the austere and intransigent archbishop of Milan who left a defining mark on the Church and post-Tridentine spirituality, also because of the ascetic rigour of his lifestyle and his sensitivity towards the poor, orphans, widows and the sick (his dedication during the plague of 1576–1577 is famous). It is in the figure of Borromeo and in his reforming activities that the *imprinting* Caravaggio received in Lombardy and the roots of his sacred painting have been identified, in the wake of the scholarship of Friedländer, Argan, Cinotti and especially Calvesi. There is no need for us to return to the results of their research as these are widely known, and also because of the wealth of studies that substantiate them.[33] However, it is worth emphasising, among the elements in his religious paintings, the humble nature of the figures and settings, and the touches of pity represented with that vivid 'realism' that is so admired, and that changed the course of Western painting.

The depiction of commoners, beggars, cripples or pilgrims with bare feet is certainly not an invention of the Lombard master and boasts illustrious precedents; what is innovative, is the principle of truth and the crudeness with which he presents these in altarpieces or in paintings for private collectors. This anti-academic 'maniera' provoked bitter dissent from the most established artists of the time and numerous seventeenth-century critics linked to the "good rules of painting" or the 'Idea of Beauty' ("L'Idea del Bello") of the new Classicism.[34] Despite this, the fascination exerted by his paintings was enormous both for the momentous nature of the new style and the humanity of the subjects depicted. And it is significant that Caravaggio's renewed success occurred in the twentieth century, in a period of heightened social awareness, to explode in 1951 with the Milanese exhibition curated by Roberto Longhi, that led to a public debate that came to see Caravaggio, among other things, as the painter of the proletariat, almost a forerunner of the class struggle.[35] Readings of this kind are understandable because every era will interpret the past with its own categories, and they are induced by the 'modernity' of Caravaggio, whose art is perceived to be akin to the sensibilities of our own time. However, a correct understanding of his work cannot ignore a historical contextualisation: without this, one easily falls into simplifications and clichés, also resulting from an outdated conception of the age of the Counter-Reformation, seen as a monolithic whole, solely reactionary and obscurantist.[36] Studies have now rendered this reading obsolete, shedding light on the complexity of a much more culturally and religiously multifaceted world, making clear that atypical and innovative figures could coexist within a rigid institutional framework (the Accademia dei Lincei, the first scientific academy in Europe, was founded in Rome in 1603),[37] of which Caravaggio himself was an expression. As far as the attitude towards the poor and disinherited

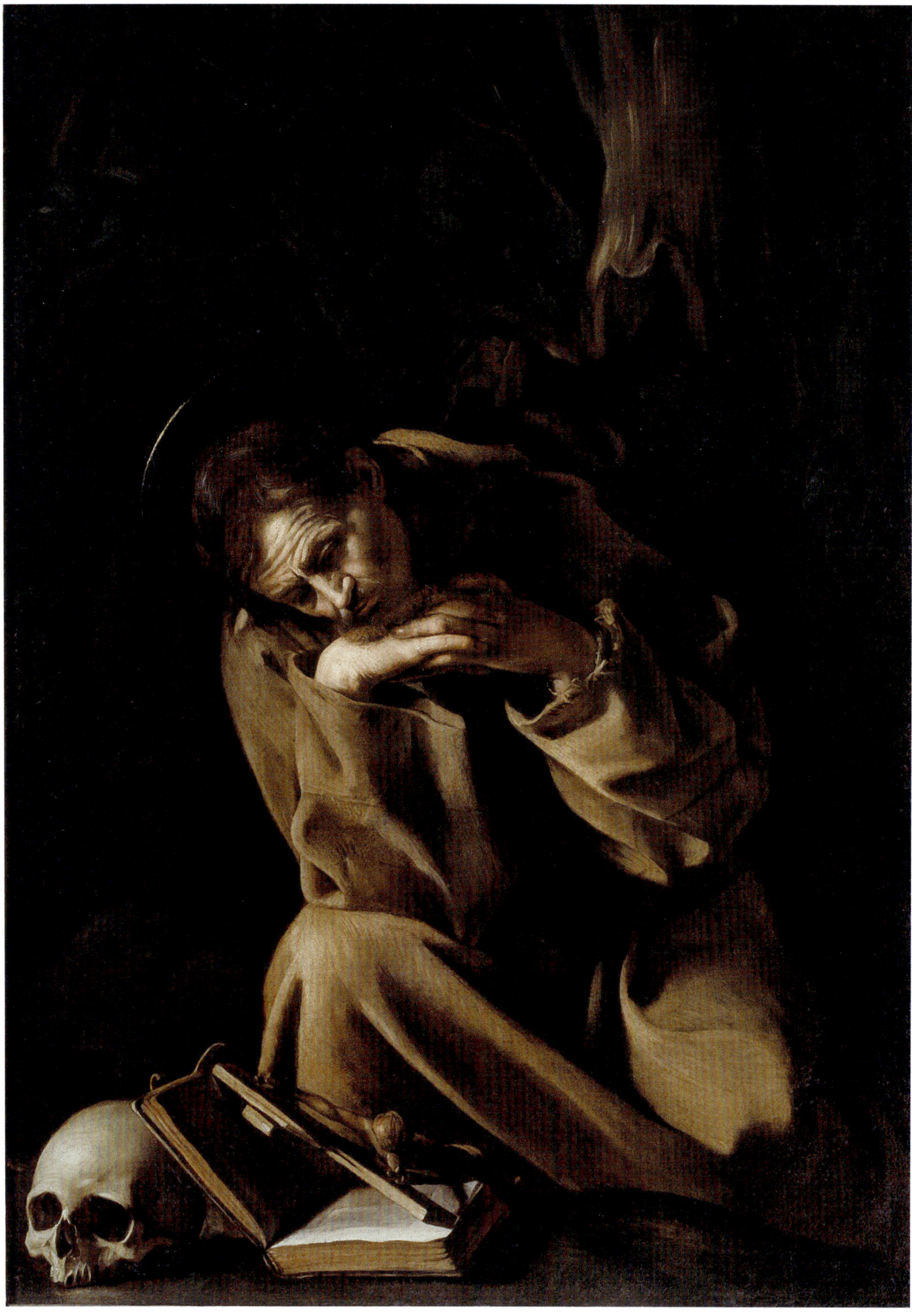

Alessandro Zuccari

is concerned, it cannot be overlooked that in sixteenth-century Italy social awareness and commitment were particularly developed thanks to the presence of enlightened spiritual figures, certain religious orders, and numerous charitable associations, old and new.[38] In characteristic or in updated configurations, the Lombard painter would have been familiar with their inspiration and manifold activities in Lombardy, Rome, Naples and elsewhere.

Evidence of this familiarity is provided by the paintings he executed for a number of Franciscan churches and, in particular, by the *Adoration of the Shepherds* [fig. 5], painted in Naples in 1609 for the Capuchins of Messina (now in the Regional Museum).[39] The poetic, humble status of the figures, the extreme poverty of the setting and the affective atmosphere of the scene correspond to the lifestyle of the Franciscan branch which broke away from the Observants around 1525 to return to the evangelical spirit of its founder. In Messina, for the church of those friars—who had chosen to live in bare cells, with roofs of wood, reeds and mud—Caravaggio painted a miserable hut similar to their own dwellings, as a rule made "as humbly as possible of reeds and lute, or stones and earth."[40] The Capuchins, moreover, had long been disliked and despised because they were suspected of heresy and above all because of their radical poverty, which made them beg, in urban centres and in the countryside, barefoot, with unkempt beards

[fig. 6]
Saint Francis of Assisi in Meditation, c. 1606, Museo Civico "Ala Ponzone", Cremona

[fig. 7]
Saint Francis in Meditation, c. 1606, detail, Gallerie Nazionali di Arte Antica, Palazzo Barberini, Rome [cat. 18]

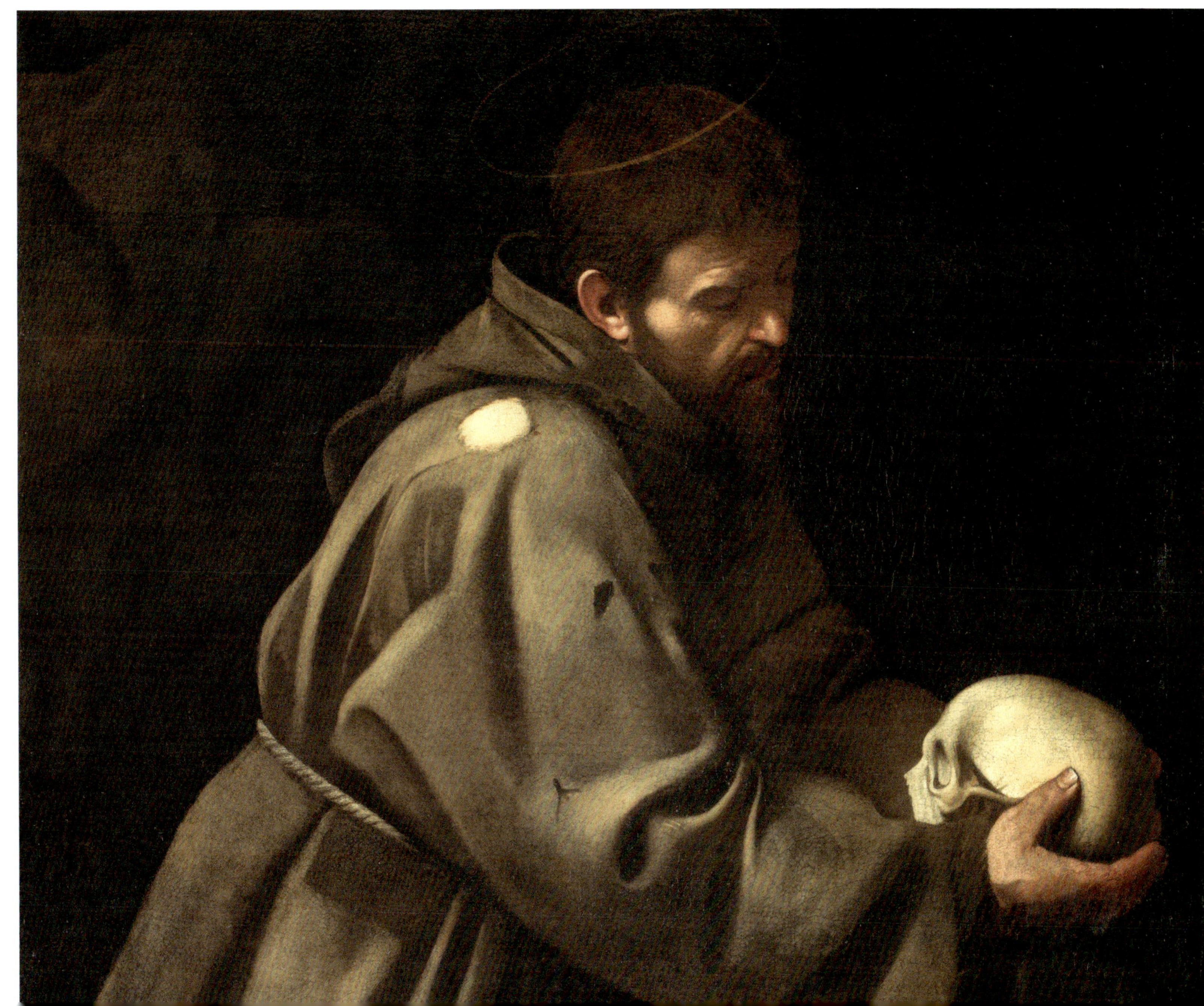

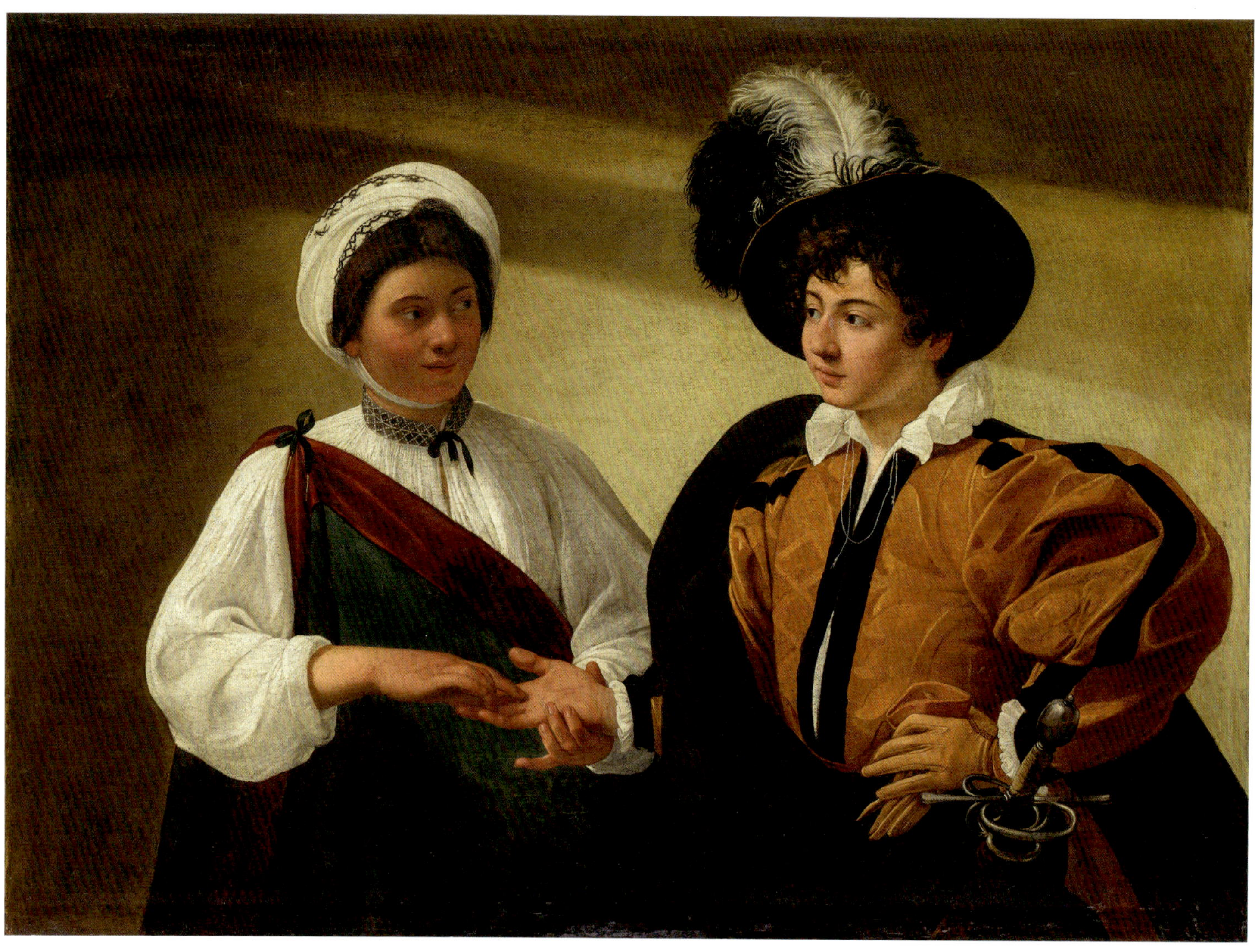

and a patched calf-length habits. Over time, these religious orders succeeded in gaining acceptance thanks to the protection of influential families, in Rome from the Colonna family. And it is important that among these one finds the grandfather and father of Costanza, Marchesa di Caravaggio: Ascanio I, gave the nascent order part of his garden near the palace at Santi Apostoli, and Marcantonio II built the church of Milazzo[41] for them. Perhaps this is also a reason why the painter showed a certain sympathy for their evangelical poverty.

Further indications of Caravaggio's particular attention are provided by the loan of a "Capuchin habit", obtained from his friend Orazio Gentileschi,[42] and by the recurrence in his paintings of the figure of the 'Poverello' of Assisi, who in at least two instances wears the characteristic long-hooded habit. The *Saint Francis of Assisi in Meditation* (Cremona, Museo Civico; fig. 6) painted for Monsignor Benedetto Ala, governor of Rome from 1604 to 1610, and the *Saint Francis in Meditation* (in deposit at Palazzo Barberini; cat. 18) possibly painted in the Colonna fiefs in 1606, are among the most intense and harsh images of the "alter Christus", which present him stigmatised and praying with a skull and crucifix, in ascetic contemplation of death (a typical theme in Capuchin circles).[43] Such

Alessandro Zuccari

empathic and moving expressions demonstrate a personal participation in the subject represented, and a profound understanding of the spirituality of these friars.

THE ACTS OF MERCY

It is well known how the phenomenon of pauperism was a widespread one, and expressed in a variety of different forms, not infrequently connected to aspirations for the reform of social and religious life; among these was the one elicited by Saint Philip Neri, who with a variety of configurations and initiatives proposed a return to the spirit of the Early Church.[44] The reference to the Roman Oratory and its founder in relation to Caravaggio's painting had been proposed by Walter Friedländer, and has been further explored by the author and other scholars who have shown how the circuit of the painter's patrons and collectors was linked to their spiritual and charitable activities, especially those of the Trinità dei Pellegrini, the well-known confraternity that took in a multitude of destitute pilgrims and cared for the convalescent until they were able to be reintegrated into the world of work.[45] Referring to the results achieved in this regard, it is useful to recall how Neri was an atypical figure in the ecclesiastical Rome of the time. His spirit of independence from institutional systems caused him on several occasions not a few difficulties and opposition: the Oratory was suspected of being a secret gathering of heretics, and the accusations focused mainly on meetings held in private, sermons given by laymen, and songs in the vernacular (from which the musical oratorio was born). Neri did not accept paid positions in order to maintain his freedom of action, and went so far as to refuse a cardinalship; in order to approve his congregation—by then influential even at the curia—Gregory XIII was obliged to do so with a special regulation that preserved its originality and—as Paolo Prodi has made clear—he accepted the "anomaly" of its work.[46] Neri was known for his eccentricities, which saw him wearing his habit inside-out, shaving off half his beard and other idiosyncrasies, indicative of his ascetic dissimulation and his biblically-based and frequently voiced conviction: "Vanitas vanitatum. Et omnia vanitas."

Saint Philip Neri's personality is more complex than has at times been presented, and the depth and breadth of his cultural interests, which included wide-ranging humanistic literature and unorthodox texts, has been established[47]. But the element that brings him closer to Caravaggio's figures is precisely his predilection for the dispossessed, for prisoners and those condemned to death, for 'lost' women and even gypsies [fig. 8]. In fact, the 'eccentric' Florentine priest went so far as to oppose the rigorous Pius V and make him release a certain number of gypsies he had had seized in order to send them to the galleys that were to fight the Turks at Lepanto.[48] Therefore, it cannot be denied that there is at least an affinity between Neri's social (and evangelical) sensibility and the subjects depicted by Caravaggio, especially since the Crescenzi, Giustiniani, Mattei, Aldobrandini, Cavalletti, Costa and Massimo families were involved in Neri's circuit, as well as, to varying degrees, cardinals Federico Borromeo, Ferdinando Gonzaga and Francesco Maria del Monte.[49] However, the *Deposition* painted for the Vittrice Chapel in Santa Maria in Vallicella (now in the Pinacoteca Vaticana; fig. 9) demonstrates how Caravaggio was able to assimilate the traits of Oratorian culture and spirituality whilst adhering to the biblical text in the reference to the origins of Christianity, in the emphasis on the gestures of oration (hence the Oratory), in the physicality and care with which the deceased is borne to burial, the last of the "corporal acts" practiced by Saint Philip Neri and his followers.[50]

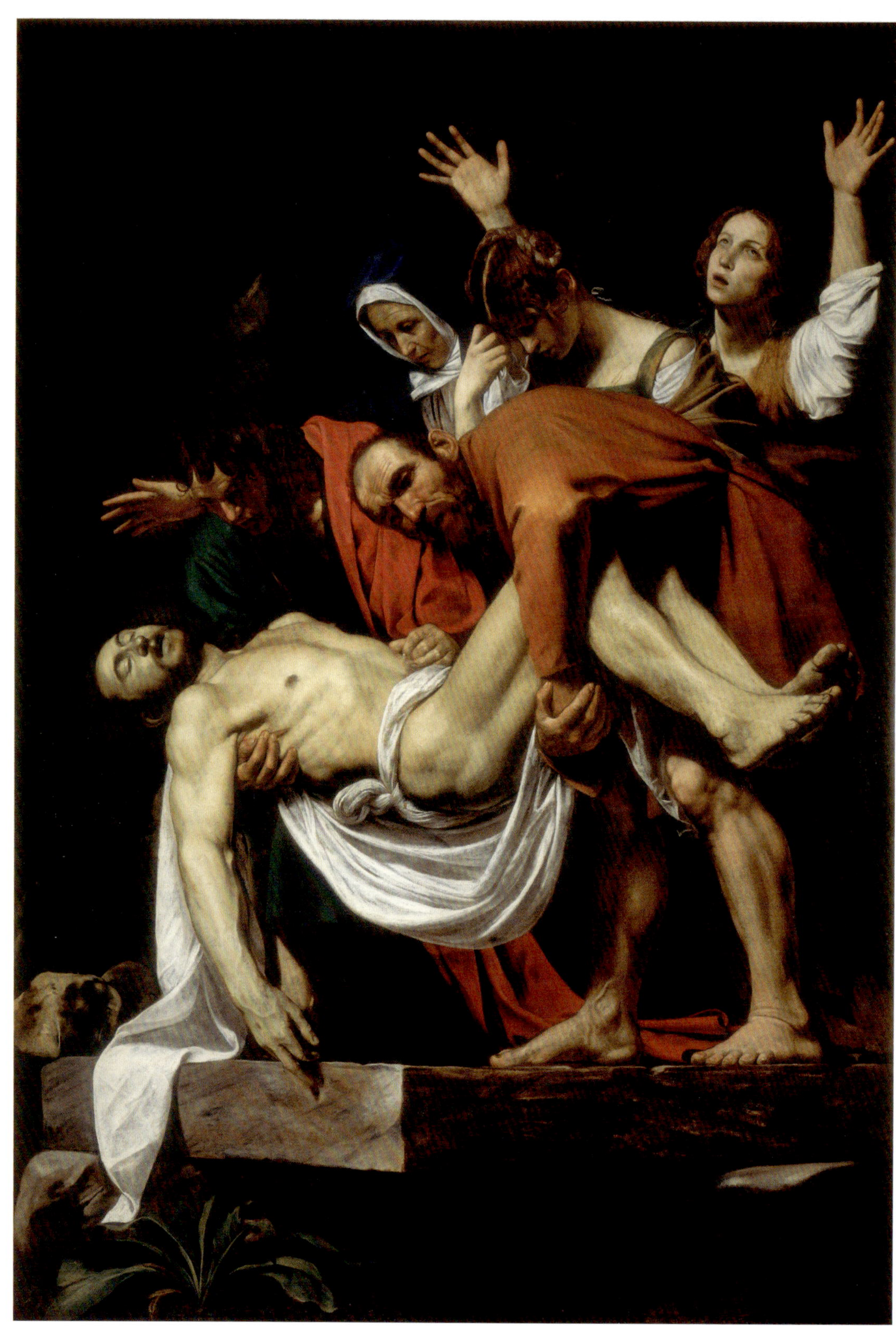

Alessandro Zuccari

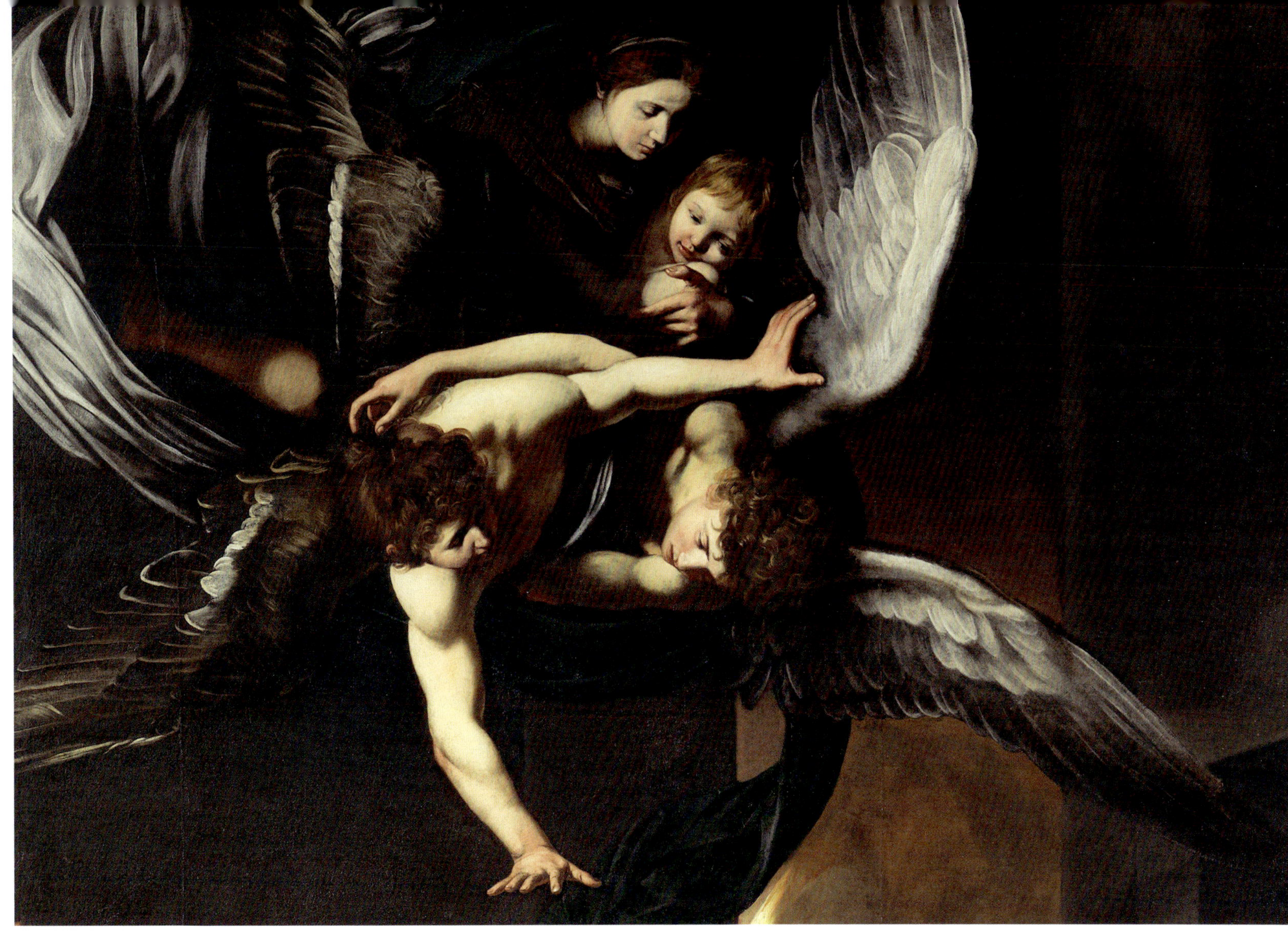

This reference provides a link with the *Seven Acts of Mercy* in the church of Nostra Signora della Misericordia, an altarpiece painted in Naples but infused with similar ideals [fig. 10; overall fig. 2 on p. 63]. It is not possible to retrace the recent gains in our understanding of the social and religious context in which that extraordinary visual synthesis matured, which focused on the figures of Giovan Battista Manso and other cultured personalities related to the illustrious confraternity and its milieu.[51] But it is should be noted how the vivid actualisation of the subject and the theological premises on which it is based are perfectly attuned with the guiding reasons inspiring the Neapolitan Pio Monte, as well as the doctrine of the post-Tridentine Church. That the merciful actions are put forward by Caravaggio in such a sculptural and compelling way rings like an exhortation to their practice, while their close connection with the figure of Mary and the infant Jesus indicates the salvific value attributed to these acts by Catholic theology, which are instead rejected by the Protestants.[52] In fact, the image of the Virgin—who lets fall an approving gaze towards the benefactors and their beneficiaries—plays a central role in the depiction, and is an ingenious reinterpretation of the *Madonna della Misericordia*: the swathes of cloth revolving together with the angels are just such an innovative solution of the iconography of the Marian mantle made famous by Piero della Francesca.[53]

[fig. 10]
Madonna della Misericordia (*Seven Acts of Mercy*), 1606-1607, detail, Church of Pio Monte della Misericordia, Naples

[figs. 11–12]
Madonna dei Pellegrini
or *Madonna di Loreto*,
c. 1604–1605, details,
Church of Sant'Agostino,
Rome

[fig. 13]
Death of the Virgin,
c. 1605–1606, detail,
Musée du Louvre, Paris

As has already emerged, Caravaggio did not follow traditional figurative canons, but imparted new characteristics to his subjects and above all, with the 'partial' nature of his compositions, he placed the human figure at their centre. In essence, he succeeded in transforming his figures into living and eloquent beings, also because—as Bellori observed—"he reinvigorated the colours, and restored blood and incarnation to them."[54] Thus, his iconographic innovations were combined with his stylistic ones, creating a "luminous sculptural" ("plastico luminosa"—Roberto Longhi) formula that gave flesh to the protagonists and body to the objects, the shadows absorbing all that seemed to him of secondary importance. In this way, he brought reality into focus with all its imperfections, provoking the scorn of the old masters and causing uproar over religious works exhibited in public. The discussions surrounding certain of his altarpieces are well-known (dirty feet and a frayed cap in the Madonna dei Pellegrini; figs. 11–12), but these arose from the aesthetic judgements of academicians, or from the reactions of the *'bien pensants'*.

Moreover, the question of the rejected works has been interpreted differently according to documentary evidence: Luigi Spezzaferro's research clarified that only one painting by Caravaggio, the *Death of the Virgin* [fig. 13, overall fig. 10 on p. 134], was actually removed,[55] while "in all other cases it was possible to establish that the alleged rejections were in fact commissions that took a different course than expected."[56] For the altarpiece now in the Louvre, the crude and cruel image of the Madonna, "swollen and with her legs uncovered weighed heavily" (Bellori), as did doubts about the permissibility of depicting the Virgin dead and, perhaps, even the murder committed by the author, who had by then fled Rome. Moreover, the friars of Santa Maria della Scala also rejected the replacement painting by Carlo Saraceni, forcing him to paint a new version.[57] On the other hand, it is now established that Caravaggio's religious paintings are not at variance with

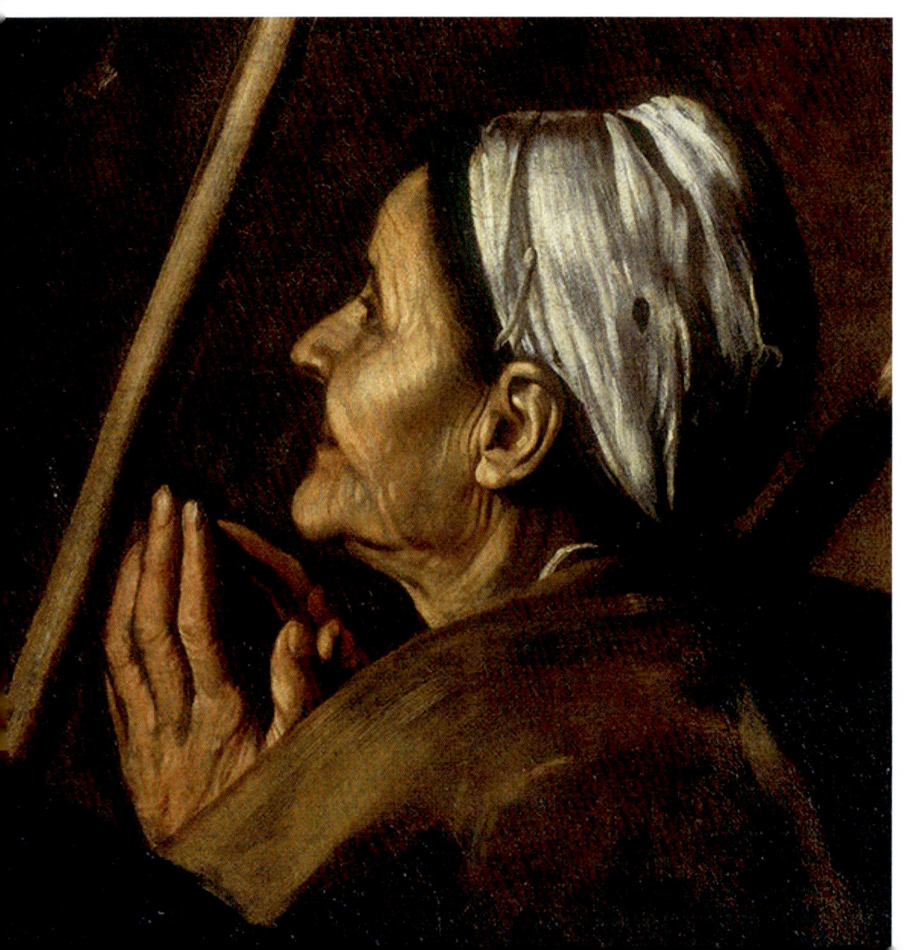

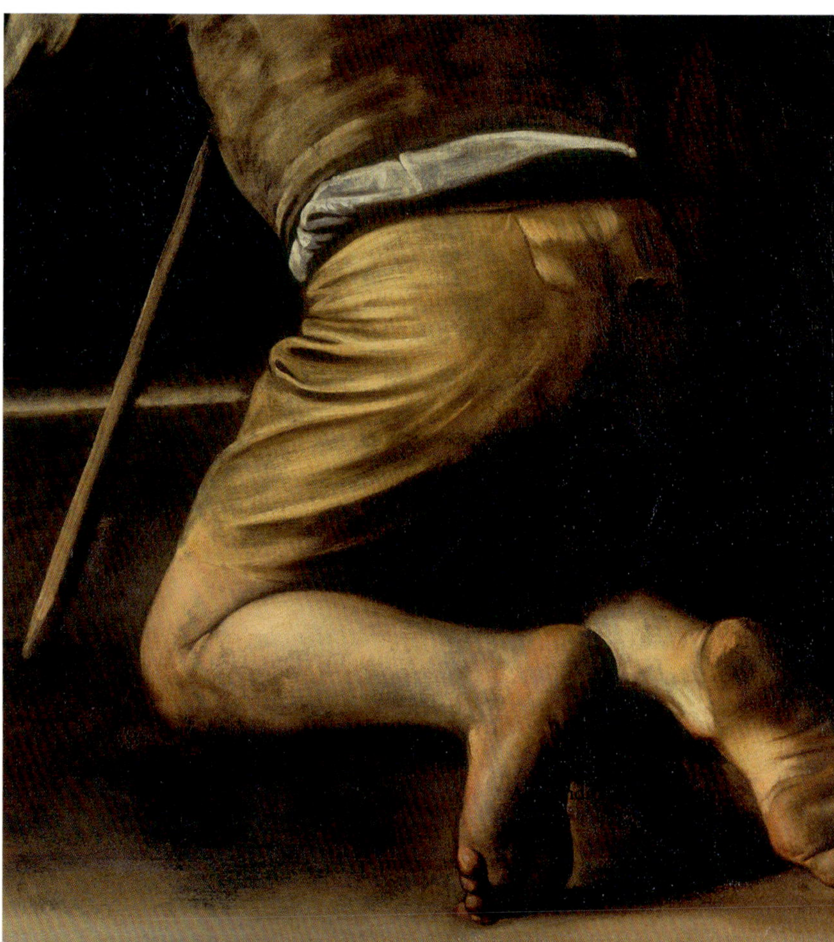

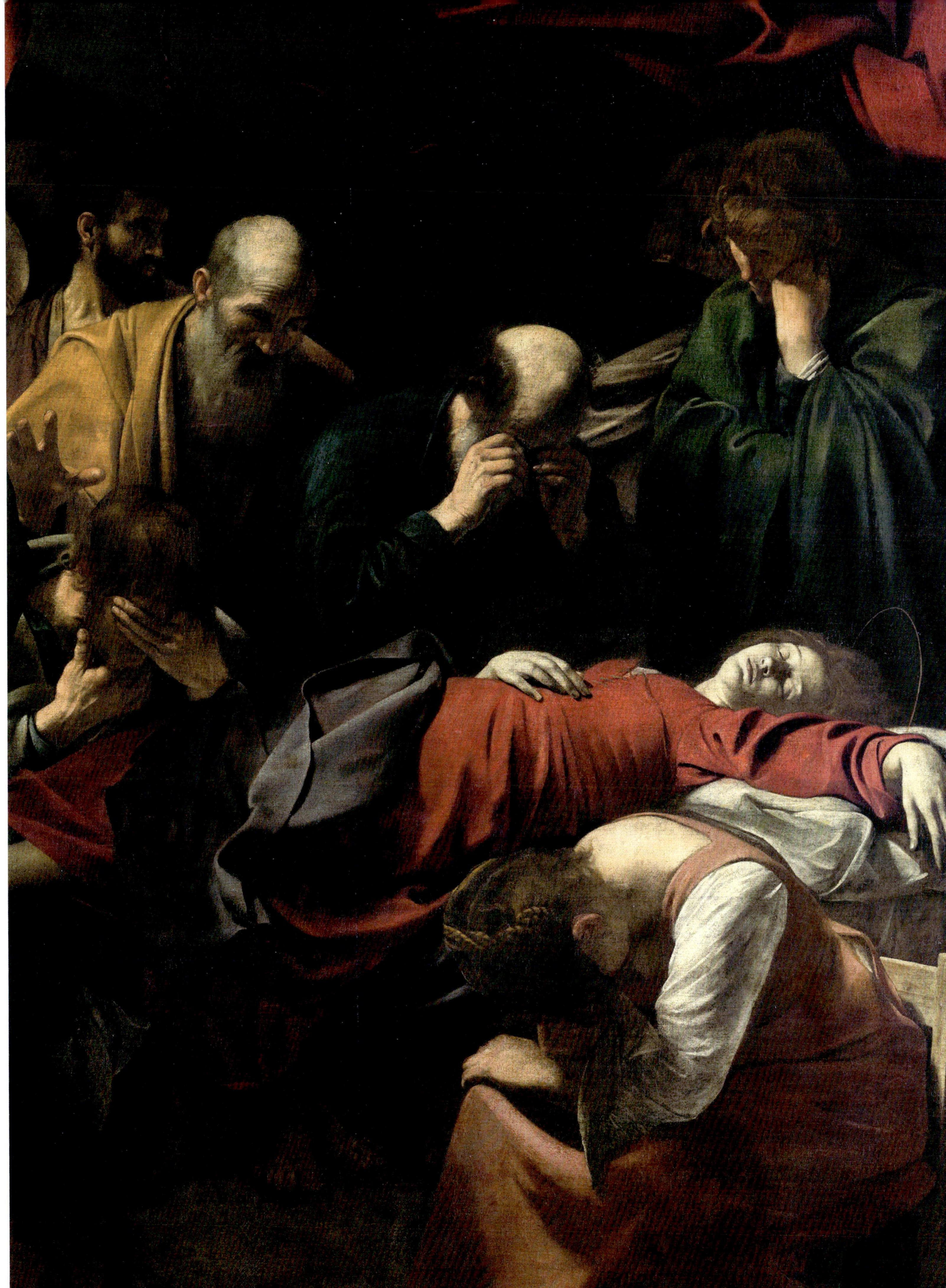

the framework of Catholic theology, but rather break new ground in the subjects represented thanks to the painter's ability to implement the instances of renewal of sacred iconography, in line with the revision of historical and hagiographic data aimed at expunging incorrect and legendary elements.[58] The examples are numerous, and it is not possible to summarise them in a few lines, but they concern both altarpieces and paintings for private collectors.[59]

To give an example of the results produced by Caravaggio's pictorial formula, one may recall an early observation by Lionello Venturi on the *Supper at Emmaus*, painted in 1601 for Ciriaco Mattei (National Gallery, London; fig. 14; overall fig. 6 on p. 14): "Not physical beauty; only moral beauties! It is as though the artist reveals the souls independently of the body that serves as the wrapping. Whence comes that power of the young Christ blessing the bread? Why does it make that outstretched hand tremble? Perhaps never has an Italian artist, as did Caravaggio, put one in the position of not being able to answer."[60] The protagonists in Caravaggio's paintings reveal a soul (serene or tormented) and their beauty is more 'moral' than aesthetic, also because it does not conceal their pathos and fragility. The supernatural figures take on the same features as ordinary people because they manifest the 'incarnation' of the divine in the human, whilst the miserable or suffering appearance of many of the them is no stranger to the evangelical teaching practiced by all those who continued to identify the poor, the sick, the imprisoned or the foreign, with Christ himself: "Truly I tell you, whatever you did for one of the least of these brothers

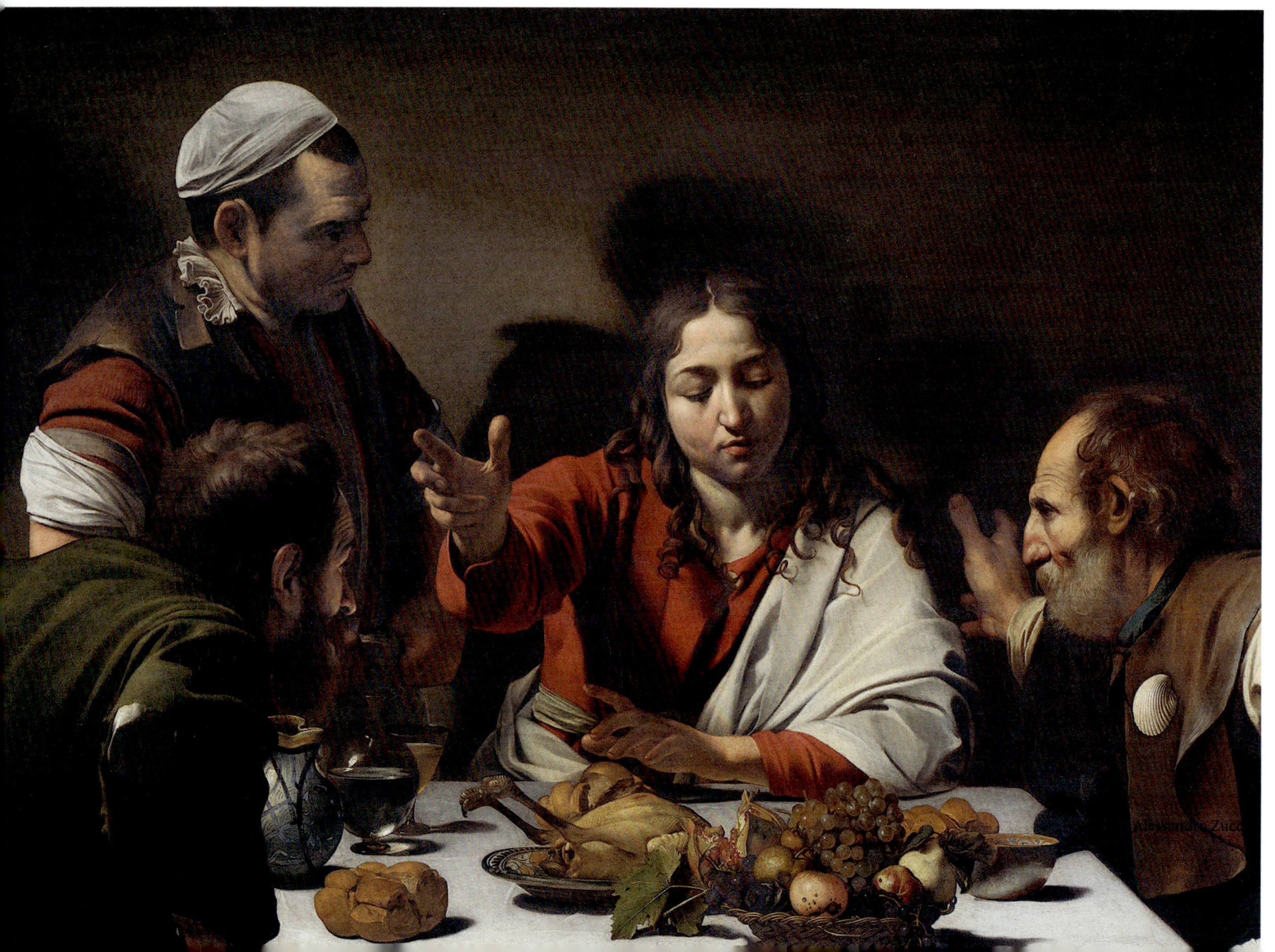

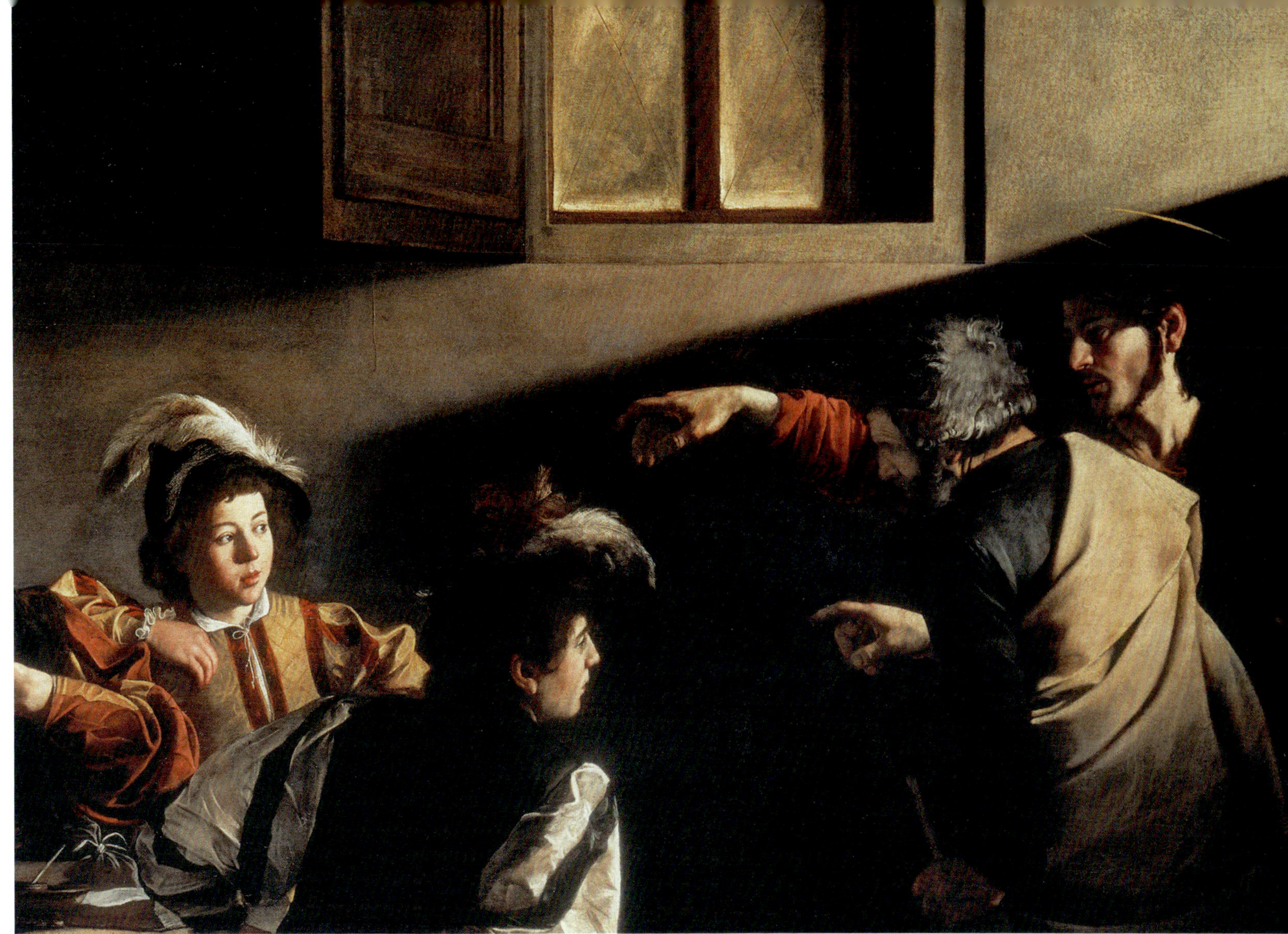

and sisters of mine, you did for me." (Matthew 25:40). This does not mean "presenting Caravaggio's painting as a handbook of edifying fervid exhortations, of post Tridentine purport,"[61] but to identify the profound reasons that inspired it, taking into account the historical context in which the artist lived, and to recognise that he was able to stage the 'drama of human life' with a sensitivity all his own, but certainly not without a singular spirituality.

On the other hand, also the 'unnatural' light[62] that renders those humble and heroic figures pulsating with life derives from his ability to bring together an unprecedented stylistic language with a theological metaphor. One need only recall Calvesi's studies on this subject, and dwell on the *Vocation of Saint Matthew* [fig. 15] to verify this.[63] In the painting in San Luigi dei Francesi, although there is a window in the background, the light irrupts into the darkness of the room from a source 'off-stage', and accompanies the Saviour's gesture as he calls the publican from the tax collector's table. As Argan had sensed, the famous beam of light is both the unifying factor of the composition and the symbol of divine grace: "With Christ and Peter a shaft of light enters: it strikes the figures, it ignites the fabrics, the feathers, the faces in the darkness. It is a beam of physical light, but it is also a ray of grace: reality is revealed and burnt by the sudden irruption."[64] It should

[fig. 15]
Vocation of Saint Matthew,
1599–1600, detail, Church of
San Luigi dei Francesi, Rome

also be noted that the identification between the stylistic and symbolic dimensions of the new luminism is developed by Caravaggio in works with sacred subjects. In fact, the first paintings to have a strong chiaroscuro contrast are the *Saint Catherine of Alexandria* in the Thyssen collection in Madrid [cat. 10] and the *Martha and Mary Magdalene* in the Detroit Institute of Arts; cat. 11) painted in Cardinal del Monte's house around 1598–1599, just before the turning point of the Contarelli Chapel.[65] From that time onwards, this light became the painter's unmistakable signature whilst gradually taking on more frayed, dramatic and darting forms, as for instance in the *Crucifixion of Saint Andrew* in Cleveland [fig. 9 on p. 68], the *Burial of Saint Lucy* in Syracuse or the Borghese *Saint John the Baptist* [cat. 23], and in particular in the *Martyrdom of Saint Ursula* [cat. 24] in which a final ray of hope falls across the tragic scene.[66] One could go on at length, given the variety of sacred subjects in Caravaggio's *corpus*, but ultimately it appears that Caravaggio's sensitivity was inspired by an intense spirituality, clearly *sui generis*, as was his personality. And in order to try to understand it, it is necessary to immerse oneself in his multifaceted and contradictory world, in his restless aspirations, in his moving poetics, making the effort to look at his paintings putting aside, for a moment, the 'lenses' through which we read our own time.

1 Among the numerous studies from the second half of the twentieth century: Friedländer 1955; Argan 1956, pp. 25–41; Venturi 1963; Longhi [1968] 1982; Frommel 1971, pp. 5–52; Röttgen 1974; Zuccari 1981, pp. 76–112; Cinotti 1983; Hibbard 1983; Pacelli, 1984; Calvesi 1990; Bologna [1993] 2006; Gregori 1994; Puglisi 1998; Marini 2001, also the collection of writings by Luigi Spezzaferro in Spezzaferro 2010.

2 For the annotated repertory of documents on Caravaggio and his milieu, see Macioce 2023.

3 See *Caravaggio e i letterati* 2020.

4 See the latest information disclosed in Sorrentino 2024b, pp. 54–73.

5 On Caravaggio's existential condition in his last years, see Calvesi 1987, pp. 13–41.

6 See Calvesi 1986, pp. 7–14.

7 For an updated analysis of the document see Pampalone 2011a, pp. 46–53.

8 See Hardon 2003.

9 On the family members and Merisi's youth in Lombardy, see Berra 2005.

10 See the baptismal certificate traced by Vittorio Pirani in Macioce 2023 (p. 14 doc. 97) with documents on his paternal and maternal families. On the religious instruction received by Caravaggio see Berra 2020, pp. 20–44: p. 20.

11 On the quarrel with his younger brother, see Di Tomasi 2018, pp. 45–65. Before entering Peterzano's workshop, Caravaggio must have completed regular studies as Giovan Battista had done before entering the seminary (see Berra 2005, p. 261).

12 See Macioce 2023, p. 198, doc. 628.

13 See the text by Carducho (1633) in *ibid.*, p. 363. The judgement of the "jealous" painter, who saw in the affirmation of Caravaggio's style "an omen of ruin and the end of painting" comparable to the coming of the Antichrist, is all centred on artistic issues (the damage caused by "this anti-Michelangelo"), interpreted however in a moralising key.

14 See Susinno's biography (1724), in Macioce 2023, p. 404. Moreover, even if Caravaggio's words reported by Susinno were true—on entering the church, to those who offered him holy water "to erase venal sins", the painter is said to have replied: "There is no need, because mine are all mortal"—this sounds like an admission of guilt for the murder and his irascibility, rather than the reaction of an 'unbeliever'.

15 On Caravaggio in Malta, his entry into knighthood and his vicissitudes, see Calvesi 1990, pp. 131–145, 363–370, Macioce 2010a, pp. 96–122; Farrugia Randon 2004; Sciberras, Stone 2006. On Merisi's aspiration to obtain a noble rank see Zuccari 2011, pp. 239–253.

16 On the degree and widespread violence in the society of the time, see Fosi 1985.

17 On the issue of the banishment and the pardon, see Curti 2023, pp. 86–111.

18 See Bologna [1992] 2006, in particular pp. 161–168.

19 Ricci 2021, pp. 13–23.

20 Ibid., pp. 16–18.

21 See also Zuccari 2022b, pp. 197–202 (review of the book by S. Brevaglieri, *Natural desiderio di sapere. Roma barocca tra vecchi e nuovi mondi*, Rome 2019).

22 See Ricci 2021, pp. 14–15, 19–21.

23 Other works referred to in the sources were also mostly of sacred subjects. For a survey of Caravaggio's autograph works see Zuccari 2022a, pp. 332–373. On Caravaggio's self-portraits see Rossi 1996, pp. 316–330.

Alessandro Zuccari

24   Cinotti 1983, p. 531.

25   That Caravaggio turns his eyes towards the saint may have "the same meaning of contemplation full of sorrow and pity" that Buonarroti had conferred on Nicodemus in the *Pietà* in the Florentine cathedral: see Calvesi 1990, p. 281; also Ebert-Schifferer 2019, p. 126.

26   Marini 2001, p. 480.

27   See Lavin 1994, pp. 138–148; Zuccari 2011, pp. 231–235.

28   See Bologna [1992] 2006, in particular pp. XXI–XXIII, 168, 320.

29   Fagiolo dell'Arco 1968, pp. 37–61: p. 50. On the interpretation of the signature in the *Beheading* in Malta, see Calvesi 1990, pp. 41, 367; Treffers 2000, p. 109 ff.

30   See Zuccari 2022a, pp. 306–308. There it is noted that "the motif of the stone placed over the tomb, and therefore over the body of the deceased, also recurs in Saint Augustine's interpretation of the subject of Lazarus: "The dead man under the stone represents the guilty under the law"—and he adds—"'What then does the word of the Lord mean: Take away the stone? It means: Proclaim grace.' This interpretation, despite referring to the Mosaic law, may have evoked something for Caravaggio in relation to his personal story, since the removal of the stone for Augustine has the meaning of proclaiming grace; that grace that in its dual meaning, spiritual and juridical, would have freed him from the condemnation of the law and the unbearable burden of capital punishment" (p. 308).

31   Gregori 2004, pp. 48–55: p. 54. Here Caravaggio has his face "almost grafted onto the same pierced-through body of the saint", almost identifying himself in that condition: Calvesi 1990, pp. 144, 150.

32   The Augustinian text from which the motto comes is in *Enarrationes in Psalmos*, XXXXIII, 4. See Marini 2001, p. 568.

33   These can be found in the most recent monographs on the painter, including those by Giacomo Berra, Francesca Cappelletti, Sybille Ebert Schifferer, Sebastian Schütze and Rossella Vodret.

34   For seventeenth-century criticism see Dell'Acqua 1983, pp. 257–262.

35   On the importance of the Milanese exhibition and the debate that followed, see Aiello 2019.

36   For a reinterpretation of the Tridentine age see Prodi 2010.

37   Among the numerous contributions on pauperism see Pullan 1978, pp. 981–1047; Rosa 1977, pp. 161–179; Politi 1980, pp. 858–864; Rosa 1980, pp. 775–806; *Timore e carità* 1982; Cavallo 1995.

38   See the contributions in *Convegno celebrativo del IV centenario della nascita di Federico Cesi* (Acquasparta, 7–9 October 1985), Accademia Nazionale dei Lincei, Rome 1986; Baldriga 2002.

39   See the new documents attesting to the payment in Naples of the Messina altarpiece, in Sorrentino 2024b.

40   See in particular Zuccari 2011, pp. 121–135. The quotation is taken from the Capuchin *Costituzioni* ratified in 1536. On the early years and the spirituality of the Capuchins, see *Architettura cappuccina* 1995; Gieben 1999, pp. 375–403; *Andare oltre* 2018; Costantini 2022, pp. 125–138; d'Alençon 2024.

41   See Zuccari 2011, pp. 122–124; Margiotta, Travagliato 2013, pp. 91–106. On the early support given to the Capuchins by Vittoria Colonna, see Ranieri 1994, pp. 337–351; Copello 2017, pp. 296–327.

42   See the testimony of Orazio Gentileschi in the well-known "Baglione trial", in Macioce 2023, p. 169, doc. 569.

43   See Calvesi 1990, pp. 331–339; Treffers 2015, pp. 67–88; Zuccari 2023, pp. 76–95.

44   Suffice it to consult Ponnelle, Bordet 1986; Dupront 1932, pp. 219–259; Dupront 1935, pp. 296–307; Frajese 1997, *ad vocem*.

45   See in particular Friedländer 1955, pp. 117–135; Zuccari 1981; Calvesi 1990, pp. 284–287 and *passim*; Pupillo 2001; Treffers 2015, pp. 76–82, 132–134; Zuccari 2011, *passim*.

46   See Prodi 1995, pp. 333–339.

47   See Cassiani 2010; Cassiani 2022, pp. 109–111

48   See Ponnellee, Bordet 1986, pp. 226–227. Neri, the Capuchin Pistoia, the Dominicans Franceschi and Bernardini presented a brief of representations before which Pius V, albeit "with some difficulty", had to yield.

49   See Pupillo 2001, pp. 54–73, also for other figures in contact with Caravaggio and his patrons.

50   See Zuccari 1995, pp. 340–354; Zuccari 2011, pp. 36–101. However, as has been shown, the figurative programme of the chapels and the iconography of the paintings were followed by the Oratorians with both care and skill.

51   See in particular Gazzara 2003, pp. 51–67; Gazzara 2018, pp. 39–67; Gazzara 2019, pp. 60–69.

52   See Zuccari 2022a, pp. 251–273.

53   See Forgione 2021, pp. 25–38: p. 32 ff.

54   See the biography of Bellori 1672, in Macioce 2023, p. 374. On the representation of the body in Caravaggio: Zuccari 2013, pp. 61–71.

55   Spezzaferro 1974b, pp. 125–138; Spezzaferro 1980, pp. 49–64; Spezzaferro 2002, pp. 23–33.

56   Terzaghi 2021a, pp. 9–25: pp. 20–21.

57   On the *Death of the Virgin*, iconography and the "rejections", see Askew 1990.

58   For the question of sacred images in relation to the renewed approach to historiography and hagiography, see the classic Mâle 1984; and among numerous studies, Ditchfield 1995; Zuccari 2012, pp. 445–501.

59   For the sake of brevity, we refer to the writer's specific research, much of which is collected in Zuccari 2011 and Zuccari 2022a.

60   Venturi 1909a, pp. 2–7: p. 6.

61   Bologna [1992] 2006, p. XXII.

62   It has been shown that Caravaggio portrayed his models in natural light, but then modified the effects to emphasise the forms: the shadows in fact do not always coincide with those produced by the light source.

63   See Calvesi 1971, in particular p. 114; Calvesi 1990, pp. 21, 29–39, 44–46, 62–66, 98–99, 209–210, 281–284.

64   Argan 1970, III, p. 277.

65   As Bellori notes, this is the moment in which Caravaggio began "to ingagliardire gli oscuri" (Bellori [1672] 1976, p. 217), that is to create those powerful contrasts of light and shadow that give an unprecedented prominence to the figures and that correspond to the stylistic signature with which the Lombard master's entire oeuvre is now usually identified.

66   On the subject of these paintings and their iconographic peculiarities, see Zuccari 2011, pp. 103–120, 157–161.

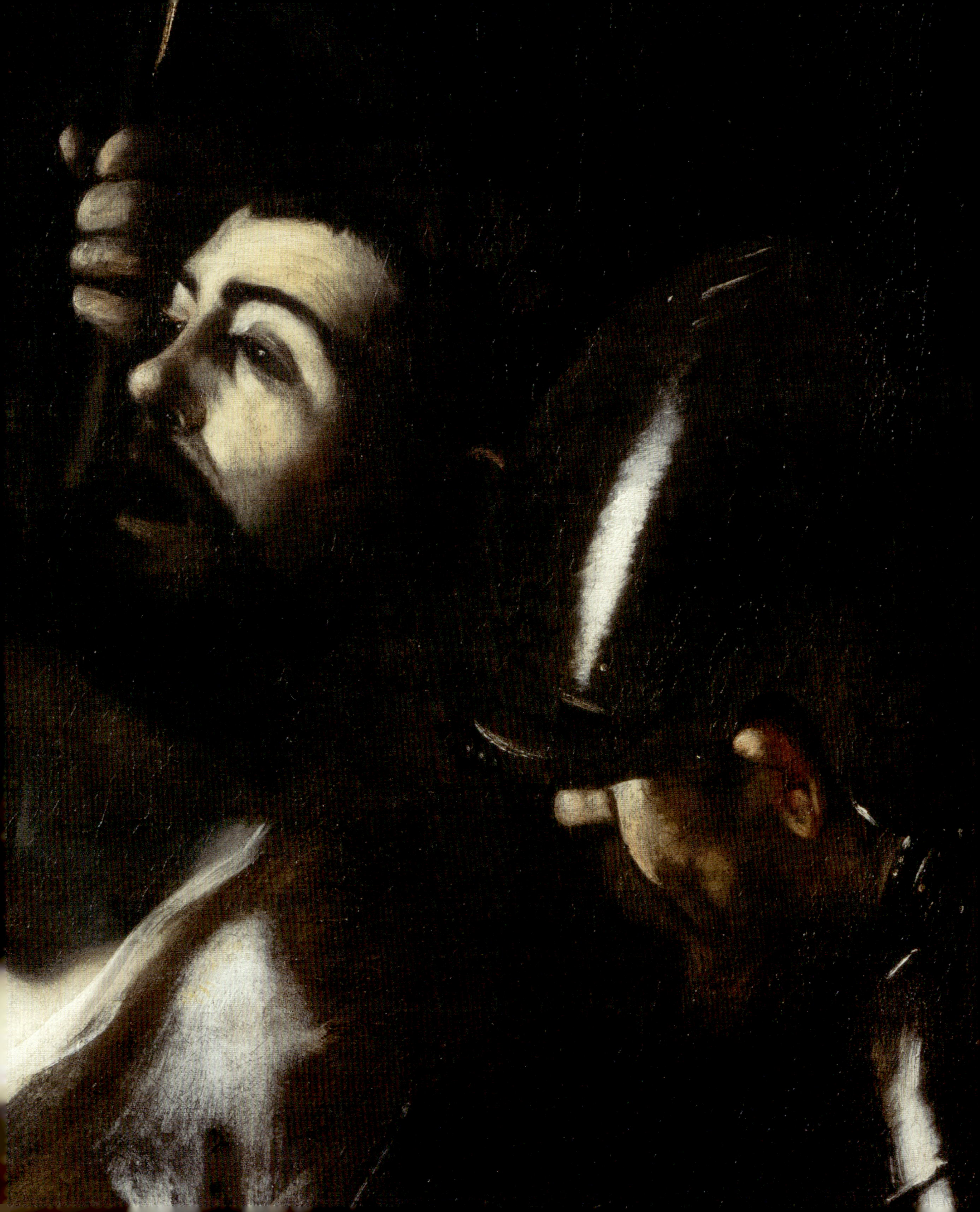

Gianni Papi

NOTES AND PROPOSALS ON CARAVAGGIO'S PORTRAITURE

The documentary traces that have come down to us indicate that many works in the portrait genre were painted by Caravaggio in Rome (and not only). Most of these have not yet re-emerged. Indeed, very few portraits can be attributed to the painter, and even fewer among these are to this day generally agreed to be autograph works. Caravaggio's activity as a portrait painter must have had as sitters, on the one hand figures linked to the papal power, and on the other (most probably the greater part), friends and acquaintances with whom he had established relationships.

Bellori relates a significant piece of information when he reports that Caravaggio in Lombardy (that is before moving to Rome), had mainly painted portraits and that this was his main practice on the professional front.[1] However, to date, no reliable evidence of this production in northern Italy has come down to us, neither in the form of documents, nor as evidence in paintings.[2]

This clarification by the biographer must have had a solid basis of truth because shortly after his arrival in Rome, during the first months in which Caravaggio got by as best he could in order to survive while waiting for things to improve, he frequented the workshops of Lorenzo Carli and Antiveduto Gramatica, and his role in these workshops had been to paint "heads".[3] Along with his activity as a painter of portraits, Caravaggio's naturalism, which eschewed any idealisation of his models and instead faithfully portrayed their physical presence, first of all disseminated many self-portraits within his paintings, and also the clearly identifiable faces of people close to him in his daily life.

As I have just said, the painter very frequently used himself as a model; at first probably, as related by his biographers, because he could not afford to pay the models, but

[fig. 1]
Martyrdom of Saint Ursula, 1610, detail, Collezione Intesa Sanpaolo Gallerie d'Italia, Naples

subsequently his self-representation would continue regardless of these motivations. The painter would depict himself, at times in the role of a principal actor in the scene, at others peripheral to the action, but always somehow emotionally involved. In this approach, completely unprecedented especially when repeated with such insistence, one perceives a very modern artistic demeanour: his presence in the scenes transforms these into personal representations. Caravaggio speaks about himself and the whole image then becomes an interpretation in which he involves himself emotionally in that which he is representing.

The first self-portrait is in the *Sick Bacchus* in the Galleria Borghese [cat. 1]; later, when Caravaggio was already living in Cardinal del Monte's palazzo, we see him again as one of the young men in *The Musicians* [cat. 6], now in the Metropolitan Museum of Art in New York, and it is probably him again in the *Saint Francis of Assisi in Ecstasy* [cat. 8] that belonged to the banker Ottavio Costa, in the Wadsworth Atheneum in Hartford. In the Contarelli *Martyrdom of Saint Matthew*, he is the mysterious figure fleeing to the left [fig. 4 on p. 9], glancing back with a sorrowful gaze at the slaughter taking place. But the most astonishing depiction of himself is certainly in the Casino del Monte (today Boncompagni Ludovisi), where in the ceiling painting executed in oil, Caravaggio depicts himself three times entirely nude in the figures of Pluto, Neptune and Jupiter. Later still we find him again in the figure holding up the lantern in the Mattei *Capture of Christ* [cat. 14], while the most tragic and shocking self-portrait is undoubtedly in the head of Goliath in the Borghese *David* [cat. 19], probably painted in 1606 in Zagarolo, immediately after his flight from Rome. And it is probably at the same time that Caravaggio depicted himself in the suffering *Saint Francis of Assisi in Meditation* in the Museo Civico "Ala Ponzone" in Cremona [fig. 6 on p. 90]. In his later sojourns in Sicily and Naples, the painter again reappears in highly dramatic scenes, when he portrays himself in the figure trying to make room for himself among the heads of the onlookers in the *Raising of Lazarus* in Messina [fig. 11 on p. 23], or finally, in the spectator watching, physically spent (as Caravaggio must have been a few months before the end of his life), the *Martyrdom of Saint Ursula* [fig. 1; cat. 24].

I have dwelt on several occasions on the presence of another model who can officially be identified in the registers. We know—from the diary of Richard Symonds, an English traveller to Rome in 1650[4]—that he posed for the *Amor Vincit Omnia* Giustiniani [fig. 2], now in the Gemäldegalerie in Berlin. This was the very young Francesco Boneri, the apprentice and later a celebrated painter (better known as Cecco del Caravaggio), who seems to have been Caravaggio's companion for some years between 1600 and 1606–1607, and who is documented as living with him in 1605 in the house in Vicolo San Biagio.[5] In this instance also, as with the self-portraits, Caravaggio's personal life, his story, bursts into the scenes that he paints, transforming them into an intimate experience in which the painter's own existence is a key player.

Using Caravaggio's famous Berlin painting as a compass, we see Cecco da Caravaggio growing from image to image.[6] Perhaps he was already the screaming boy faced with the slaughter in the *Martyrdom of Saint Matthew* in San Luigi dei Francesi. He certainly is still the model for the brazen *Saint John* in the Pinacoteca Capitolina [fig. 3], for the angel embracing Jesus in the first version of the *Conversion of Saul* [cat. 13] now in the Odescalchi collection in Rome, for Isaac in the Barberini *Sacrifice of Isaac*, and it is he again, now a young man and fleeing Rome together with Caravaggio in 1606, who offers his likeness to David in the aforementioned *David and Goliath* painted for Scipione Borghese.

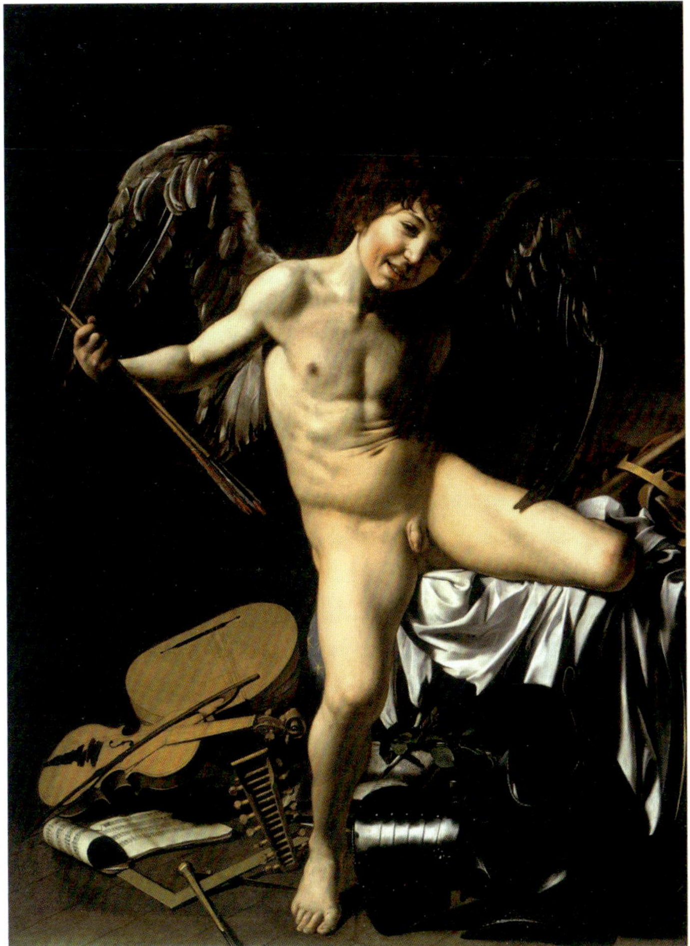

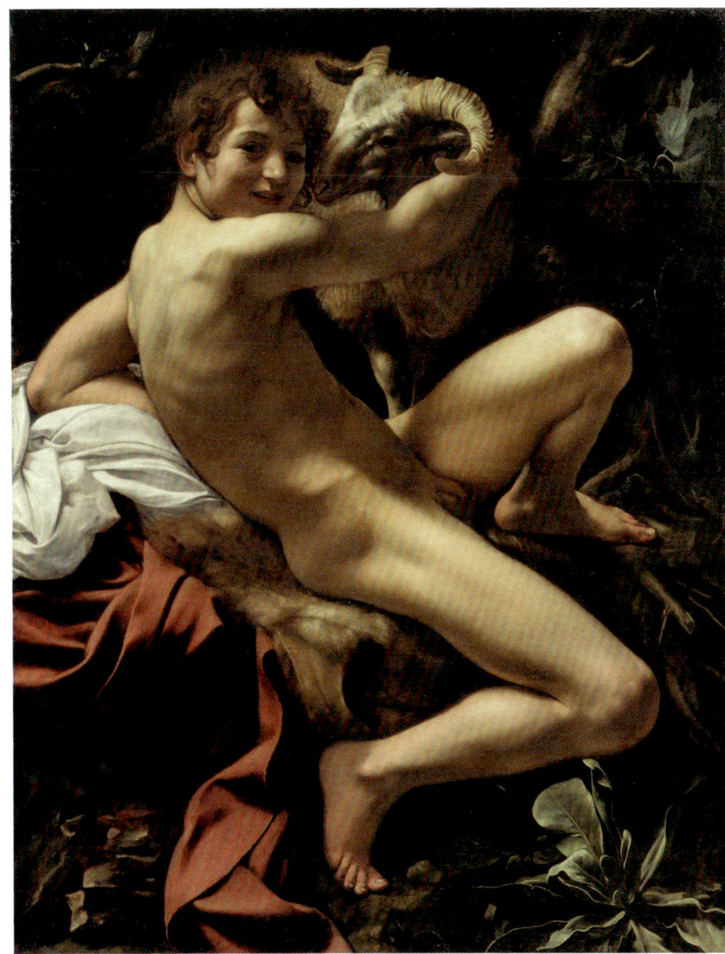

Another easily recognisable model is the elderly man who posed for the figure of Abraham in the Barberini *Sacrifice* in the Uffizi; it is he who interprets Saint Matthew in the second version of *Saint Matthew with the Angel* on the altar of the Contarelli Chapel in San Luigi dei Francesi, and it is he again who plays the main role in the *Crucifixion of Saint Peter* [fig. 5] for the Cerasi chapel in Santa Maria del Popolo, just as it is he who embodies the apostle at the centre of the *Death of the Virgin* today in the Louvre [fig. 10 on p. 134].

Finally, with regard to the recurring models used for the female figures, I refer you to Francesca Curti's essay in this catalogue.

Moving on to discuss the portraiture *stricto sensu*, perhaps the most unanimously accepted portrait by Caravaggio, and also the most solidly documented, was unfortunately destroyed in 1945 in Berlin, in the fire of the Kaiser Friedrich Museum's storerooms: the *Portrait of Fillide Melandroni*[7] [fig. 4], known only through photographs. I have already expressed an opinion on this painting regarding its dating,[8] which can unfortunately only be established on the basis of the surviving photographs. In particular, the beautiful photographic image preserved in the Fondazione Longhi which is very clear even in the smallest details.[9] It suggests that the painting was a youthful work by Caravaggio, probably to be dated 1597, in close proximity to the *Portrait of Maffeo Barberini* as a young man [cat. 3], and works such as the Doria Pamphilj *Magdalene* [fig. 8 on p. 58], the *Lute Player* now

[fig. 2]
Amor Vincit Omnia,
c. 1601, Staatliche Museen,
Gemäldegalerie, Berlin

[fig. 3]
Saint John the Baptist, 1602,
Musei Capitolini – Pinacoteca
Capitolina, Rome

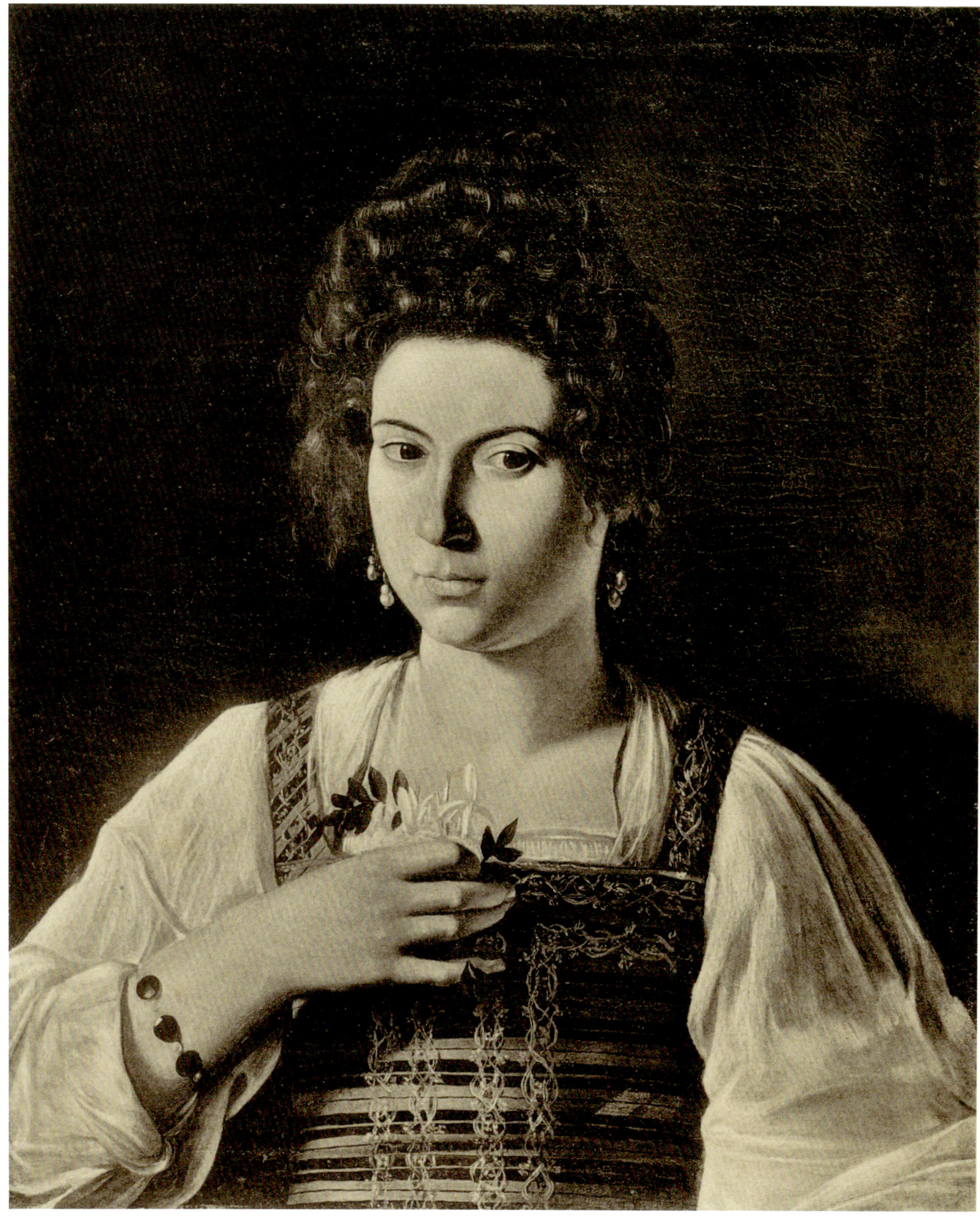

in the Hermitage [fig. 11 a p. 38], and *The Fortune Teller* in the Louvre [fig. 8 on p. 92]. The structure and handling of the sleeves is very close to that of the *Maffeo*, and the still immature crispness of the application of the paint, smooth and precise, is far-removed from the synthetic execution that would progressively characterise the paintings from the Contarelli Chapel onwards.

The inclination to consider the Berlin *Portrait* as a work belonging to Caravaggio's sixteenth-century years (between 1597 and 1598), was most widespread among scholars, at least until the penultimate decade of the last century.[10] Subsequently, it has been re-peatedly affirmed that the painting was commissioned by Fillide's alleged lover, the poet Giulio Strozzi (there is no definitive documentary evidence of this relationship, and none in the sixteenth century), and that the painting was returned to him upon the prostitute's death (1618), bequeathed to him in an earlier testamentary will.[11]

As a result, the date of the work has often been pushed forward; Fiora Bellini has main-tained that Fillide's supposed relationship with Strozzi began between 1603 and 1605; it follows that the work should then be dated to between these dates, if one insists on linking it with this, hypothetical, affective relationship.[12] But these are suppositions,[13] not substantiated by reliable data, while it is certain that Strozzi, on 5 July 1606, was in Venice, where he was born (in 1583) and grew up.[14]

A passage in Fillide's will of 1614 refers to the portrait that was to go to Giulio Strozzi. The probable execution of the work around 1597 excludes, in my opinion, that it was commissioned by Giulio Strozzi, who was at the time in Venice and fourteen years old. It is not impossible that the painting was at the centre of financial dealings between Fillide and Strozzi; on the other hand, relations of this kind between the prostitute and Giulio can be deduced from the guarantee in favour of the poet taken out by Fillide Melandroni's heirs on 19 November 1618.[15]

It seems more likely that it was Fillide herself, or another patron who commis-sioned the portrait from Caravaggio. The latter could have been her current lover, that is Ulisse Masetti, who was the prostitute's lover and her protector from 1597 for about three years.[16] Masetti was in the service of cardinal Benedetto Giustiniani; the Masetti–Giustiniani connection would have its own logic for the painting's transfer into the collec-tion of the cardinal and his brother Vincenzo. But this would imply that the portrait left to Giulio Strozzi was a second portrait of the prostitute, one unknown to us.

In 2010, the Florence exhibition *Caravaggio e caravaggeschi* proposed two important portraits that were attributed to the Lombard painter. For the first, the *Portrait of Maffeo Barberini* as a young man [cat. 3], it was more the case of a recovery, as the work had often been considered autograph in the past, but for over fifty years had no longer been considered part of Caravaggio's œuvre (apart from sporadic attempts that had not been followed through, such as the more than half-hearted attempt by Francesco Petrucci in 2008).[17] The restoration executed for the Florentine exhibition and the scientific analy-ses that were carried out[18] reaffirmed what could already be perceived directly, even be-fore the cleaning. Longhi's negative opinion[19] had weighed down on the work for years, casting it into obscurity for half a century; but from the very first viewing, when the paint-ing was still dirty, there could be no doubt as to its status as an early autograph work by Caravaggio.

The *Portrait of Maffeo Barberini* as a young man is an official portrait, yet the image is devoid of the rigidity of paintings of this genre executed in the late sixteenth century. The movement of surprise that animates the figure at the moment when he seems to be about

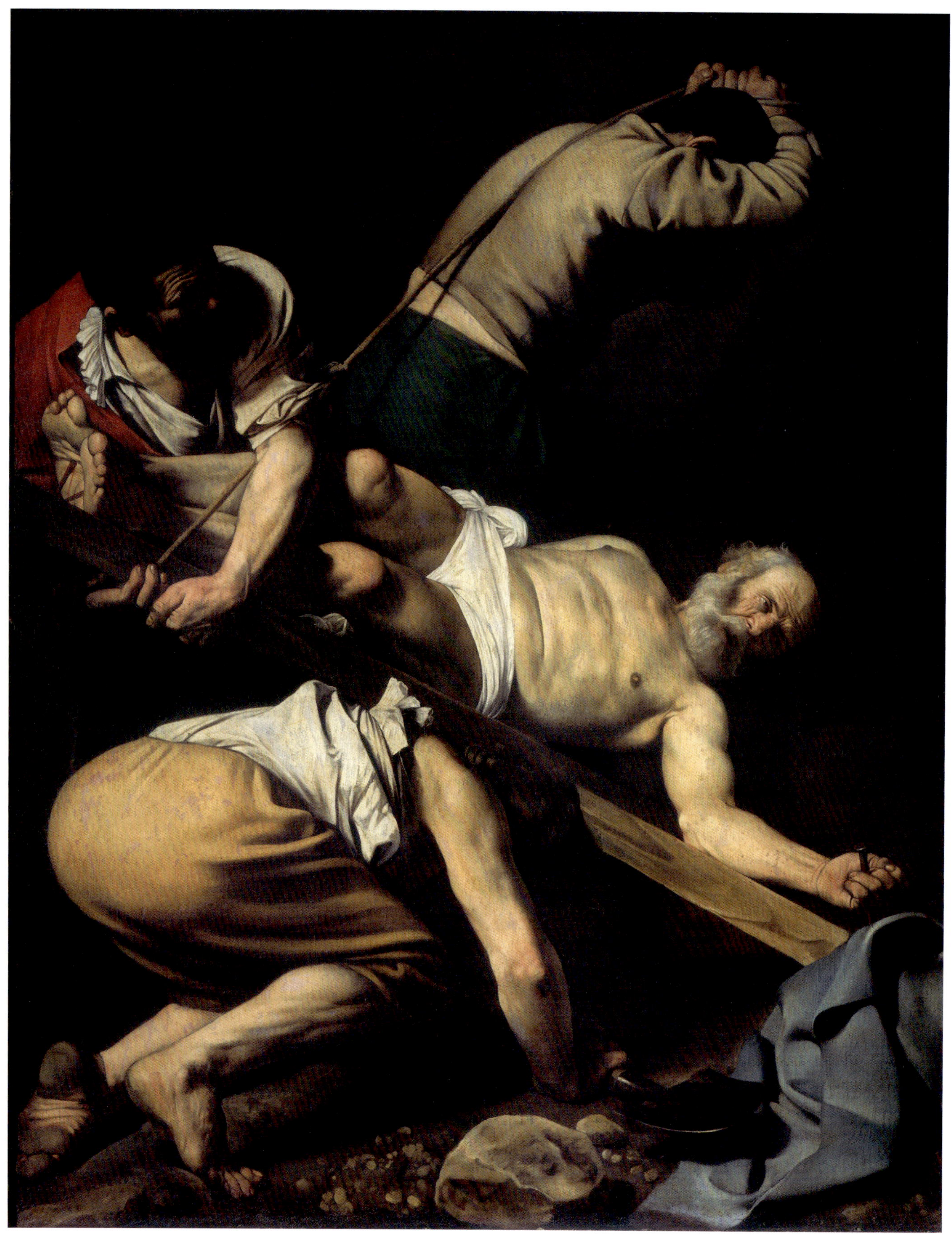

Gianni Papi

to rise up from his chair, as if stimulated by the arrival of the visitor/spectator, has no part of officialdom.

There is a flavour of the under-ripe in the painting, which emerges in the crudity of some elements in the drapery and in the setting of the figure; but in it we already see the unfolding of a powerful, impatient and strong depiction (the hand clutching the armrest of the armchair, the rendering of the face, impenetrable and magnetic, as if an oriental idol).

The admirable insertion of the flowers in the glass vase, the water already a little opaque with the passage of time, probably anticipates by only a few months that in the Giustiniani *Lute Player*, now in the Hermitage in St. Petersburg.

As I have said, this is an early portrait, the dating of which, in my opinion, must precede the *Bacchus* of the Uffizi [fig. 14 on p. 43] and the Giustiniani *Lute Player*. It would therefore have to be placed shortly before or shortly after the painter entered the Del Monte household. In light of the latest discussions on Caravaggio's arrival in Rome, this can be placed in 1597. Next to *Maffeo*, the Barberini Inventories record from 1623[20] the *Portrait of Francesco Barberini* (now in a private collection), which I believe to be an autograph work, and to which I will return with an essay dedicated to it.

Maffeo Barberini as a young man differs from the other portrait (also in a private collection) in which, beginning with Longhi, the same sitter has been identified [cat. 9]. Since the painting re-emerged in 1963, it has been accepted by all scholarship, although it has never been exhibited publicly until the present occasion, when the work can finally be seen in the flesh.[21] The painting has clear characteristics that mark it as an autograph work by Caravaggio. It is a true masterpiece of early seventeenth-century portraiture, with the sitter portrayed in an action even more manifest and tense than that of the first *Maffeo*. He seems to be giving an order with his right hand, and with a penetrating gaze and slight frown, addressing someone outside the scene, with his left hand vigorously clutching a letter which may have just been delivered.

As far as the dating of the second *Maffeo* is concerned, I find that the dates prevalently proposed—the final years of the sixteenth century, starting with Roberto Longhi who placed it in 1595,[22] are not satisfactory. For some time now I have been proposing a more mature dating, in the seventeenth century.[23]

It is probable that this painting can be linked to the four payments received by Caravaggio between 1603 and the beginning of 1604 (for a total of 100 *scudi*) for the execution of "paintings" commissioned by Maffeo Barberini,[24] payments that have often been put in relation with the *Sacrifice of Isaac* now in the Uffizi, which in my opinion should instead be placed at an earlier time, around 1601–1602.[25]

An argument that should not be underestimated concerns the identity of the sitter, whom Longhi, as early as 1963, maintained was Maffeo Barberini. On this identification it may be legitimate to have some doubts, although until proven otherwise it seems wise for the moment to maintain this traditional identification in favour of the Barberini sitter.

One has the impression that it was Longhi's authority that forced, that turned into a certainty, what was evidently only one possibility among others (at least according to what was published in the 1963 article).[26] In the same article, the scholar seems uncertain as to the provenance of the painting; this is also evident from the recent publication of the Longhi-Briganti correspondence, in which, in the letter of 2 July 1963, Longhi explicitly asks Briganti (who would appear to be the true discoverer of the painting) where it came from.[27]

However, it is precisely the payments to the painter between 1603 and the beginning of 1604 referred to above that constitute an important element in establishing the Barberini provenance, given that the physiognomic element, at least in my opinion, is not decisive. The shapes of the faces do not correspond (in the second *Maffeo* it is decidedly rounder), and the strabismus in the former seems to me much attenuated or even non-existent in the latter. However, for its identification as Maffeo, the youthful portrait has on its side the inventory indications that speak of it, as a portrait of the prelate who later became pope, as early as 1623, and then again in 1655 and 1672, while the same cannot be said for the second *Maffeo*.[28] However, one should remember—in order to justify at least in part the non-similarity between the two physiognomies and leave open the possibility that it is really the same personage—Giulio Mancini's passage in which he specifies the characteristics of Caravaggio's portraiture.[29]

The other portrait that staged a come-back at the 2010 exhibition was the so-called *Portrait of Cardinal Baronio*[30] [fig. 6], belonging to the Giovio Collection of portraits in the Uffizi Gallery. The attribution to the Lombard artist had been proposed by John T. Spike in 1995, and subsequently in the 2001 monograph;[31] already in the 1980s moreover, Calvesi, even if only evoking Caravaggio's name, had stressed the quality of the work among the sequence of portraits in the Uffizi collection.[32] In any case, Spike's proposed attribution was not followed up by scholarship.

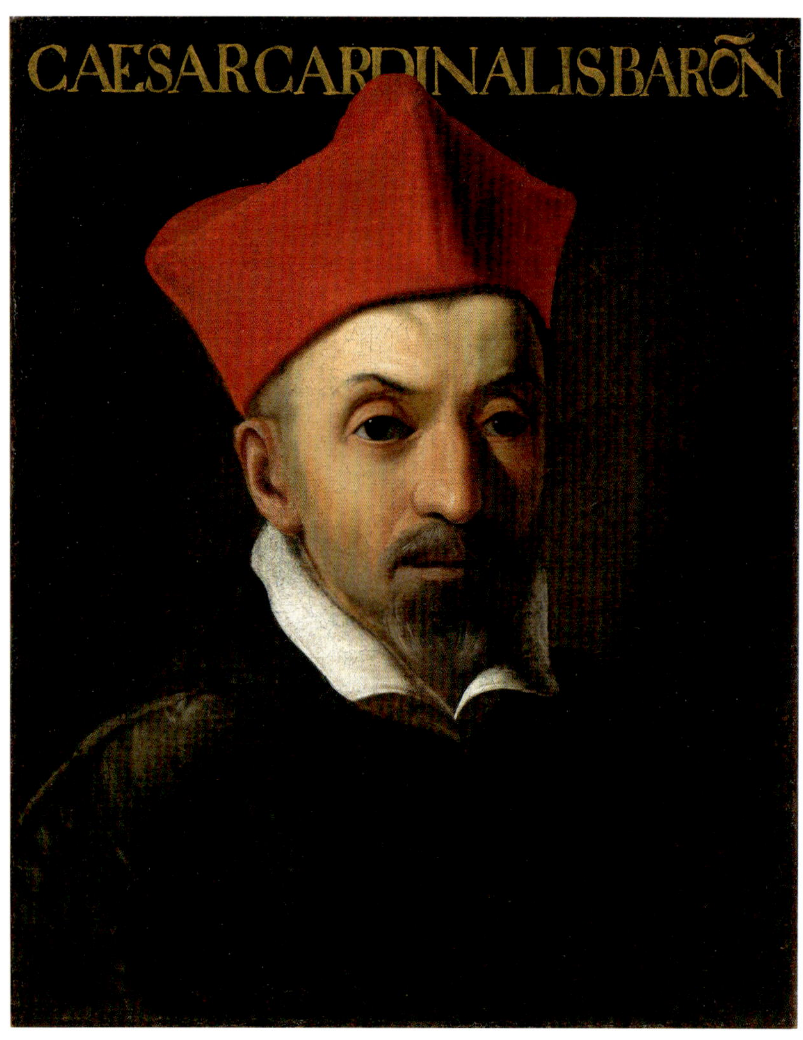

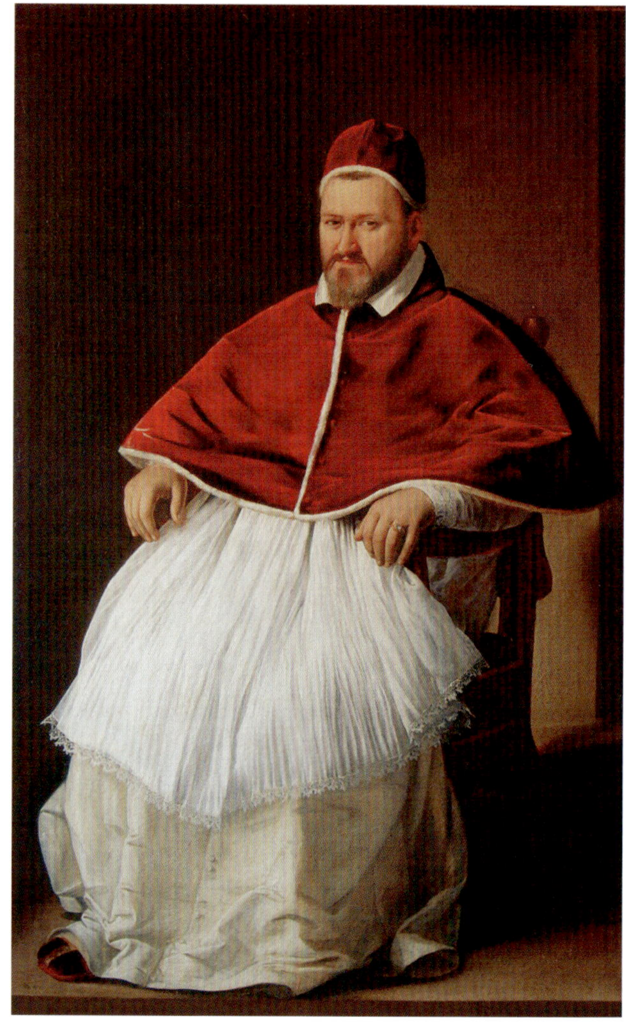

Gianni Papi

The present writer revived the attribution to Caravaggio after the new cleaning carried out for the 2010 exhibition,[33] an operation that highlighted the resplendent quality of the most intact parts, that is the entire lit part of the face, in the midst of which emerges the extraordinary sharpness of the sitter's gaze, the admirable execution of the eye, the eyelids and the arched eyebrow. Also characteristic of Caravaggio is the luminous density of the impasted paint used for the areas of skin, which in the forehead reveals a kind of lump (an element of naturalism uncensored by the painter), while the skin of the chin is shaded by the freshly shaven beard. A crisp, full-bodied vermilion red is used for the cardinal's hat which, in the area in shadow, has lost some of its glazes.

Elena Fumagalli has pointed out to me an important document that has removed all doubt as to how the painting arrived in Florence. It is a letter, dated 14 June 1704, from Antonio Maria Fede to Grand Duke Cosimo III, in which he announces the sending of three paintings received from the Duca di Bracciano; among them is the "Portrait of the famous Cardinal Baronio painted by Caravaggio," which entered the Guardaroba Mediceo on 1 August 1704.

In all likelihood, when the work arrived in Florence at the beginning of the eighteenth century, the earlier inscription was legible identifying the work as the portrait of Cardinal Cesare Baronio (now visible in the X-radiograph), and in order to make it uniform with the other canvases in the Giovio Collection, it was perhaps cut down to adjust its size, the inscription was covered over, and the new one (the one visible today) was added, along the top, as in the others in the series, and with the same script.

However, there is no correspondence with the known and 'official' images of Baronio, that is the 1600 engraving, in Gradoli in the Biblioteca Giovardiana, when the cardinal would have been 62 years old, and the 1602 engraving by Francesco Villamena, which depicts the cardinal at the age of 64 (see also the *Portrait* in the Biblioteca Apostolica Vaticana, which Francesco Petrucci attributes to Villamena himself).[34]

I would be inclined to bring forward by a few years Spike's proposed dating of 1602–1603. I think a date of around 1599–1600 might be the most appropriate, close to or at the same time as the Contarelli canvases. In 1599 Baronio would have been 61 years old; it seems very difficult to believe that the figure in the Uffizi portrait is of such an age.

Who, then, is the cardinal depicted in the painting? Taking into consideration the traces we have of Caravaggio's paintings with portraits of cardinals, in 2010 it seemed to me that that a similarity existed between the face in the Uffizi portrait and that of Benedetto Giustiniani, as conveyed to us by the engraving in the *Galleria Giustiniani*, which may have had as its model Caravaggio's painting recorded in the inventory of Vincenzo Giustiniani's property in 1638.[35] The expression is relatively similar, somewhat frowning, the gaze penetrating; Benedetto Giustiniani in 1599 was 45 years old, an age that seems far more plausible for the figure depicted.[36]

Caravaggio's portrait of Benedetto Giustiniani is painted on a *tela d'imperatore*, recorded in 1638, and has not as yet resurfaced. The canvas soon disappeared (the last time it is recorded with any certainty is in the Giustiniani Inventory of 1667). Taking into consideration that the Uffizi *Portrait* was purchased by Grand Duke Cosimo III in 1704, in the intervening forty years there would therefore have been more than enough time to cut it down, make the changes, and transform it into a *Portrait of Baronio* on a *tela di testa*, which was perhaps a portrait sought after by the Grand Duke.

I also believe Caravaggio's *Portrait of Paul V Borghese* [fig. 7] to be an autograph work, which it was possible for me to examine directly on the occasion of its exhibition at the

Caravaggio a Roma. Una vita dal vero.[37] Already with the naked eye one could discern the presence of pentimenti, incisions and the transparency of the brushstrokes in the underlying *abbozzo* (sketch). All of this, as well as the image, naturally, has conclusively convinced me that this is an autograph work by the painter, evidently executed between 1605 and 1606, probably coinciding with (or shortly after) Camillo Borghese's accession to the papal throne, as Federica Papi's catalogue entry also proposes, opting for a date between August and November 1605.

It is a painting executed with great speed, as is also the case with the other Borghese painting, which is very close to it also chronologically, that is the *Saint Jerome* now in the Borghese Gallery. What is striking is the suspicious and enquiring expression of the new Pope, with his two hands only apparently in repose on the armrests of the armchair, but rather nervously expectant; nor can one remain indifferent to the dramatic, naked setting in the cubic space in which the armchair and the figure are placed, joined together, almost condemned to be one.

Painted at a not dissimilar date is the beautiful Klesch *Portrait of a Gentleman with a Ruff* [fig. 8], which has recently been the focus of a publication of mine.[38] It seems plausible to me that the painting was executed in Rome, between late 1605 and early 1606, and that it may represent the jurist Andrea Ruffetti, who was probably Caravaggio's last host, at whose house Caravaggio painted the *Madonna dei Palafrenieri*. The quality of the Klesch canvas, with the astounding swiftness and confidence of the brushstrokes, is an indication of a very late date within Merisi's Roman career, which precisely coincides with his sojourn in the Ruffetti household. The most palpable similarities are with works painted during the same time period, namely the Borghese *Saint Jerome*, the *Flagellation* in Rouen [fig. 8 on p. 67] and the *Penitent Saint Jerome* in Montserrat.

In the Klesch painting, the brushstrokes, in more than one instance, are not aiming for mimetic results, but allow themselves to be picked out, one by one. One remains awe-struck by the vehemence of the inspiration and the immediacy of the outcome, so much so that one can surmise that Caravaggio may have painted the Klesch *Portrait of a Gentleman with a Ruff* in just two or three days (perhaps as a gesture of gratitude for Ruffetti's hospitality?).

From the time after the Roman period, two *Portraits* have come down to us depicting two important personalities that Caravaggio encountered during his stay in Malta. These are two renowned works that are now unanimously accepted by scholars, the *Portrait of Alof de Wignacourt with a Page* now in the Louvre [fig. 9], and the *Portrait of a Knight of Malta* now in the Galleria Palatina of Palazzo Pitti in Florence[39] [cat. 22]. If the former was certainly painted in Malta, for the latter which, in my opinion, is to be identified as the portrait of Antonio Martelli, the possibility remains that it may belong to Caravaggio's sojourn in Messina, where Martelli held the position of prefect of the Knights of Malta in 1609, during the months in which Merisi was also in the city. Much has been said about the two paintings and perhaps it will suffice here to emphasise the differences with the portraiture of the Roman period. Especially in the beautiful *Portrait* in Florence, as is the case in the Sicilian paintings, the handling of the brush has become feverish, incandescent, synthetic to the utmost degree, to the point of leaving certain parts of the image unfinished (such as the hand holding the rosary, for example). All this increases the essential quality of the depiction, and in no way reduces the sharpness of the physiognomic rendering of the sitter, of his face—with the proud, authoritative gaze of one accustomed to command—looking to the right, beyond the space of the painting.

Gianni Papi

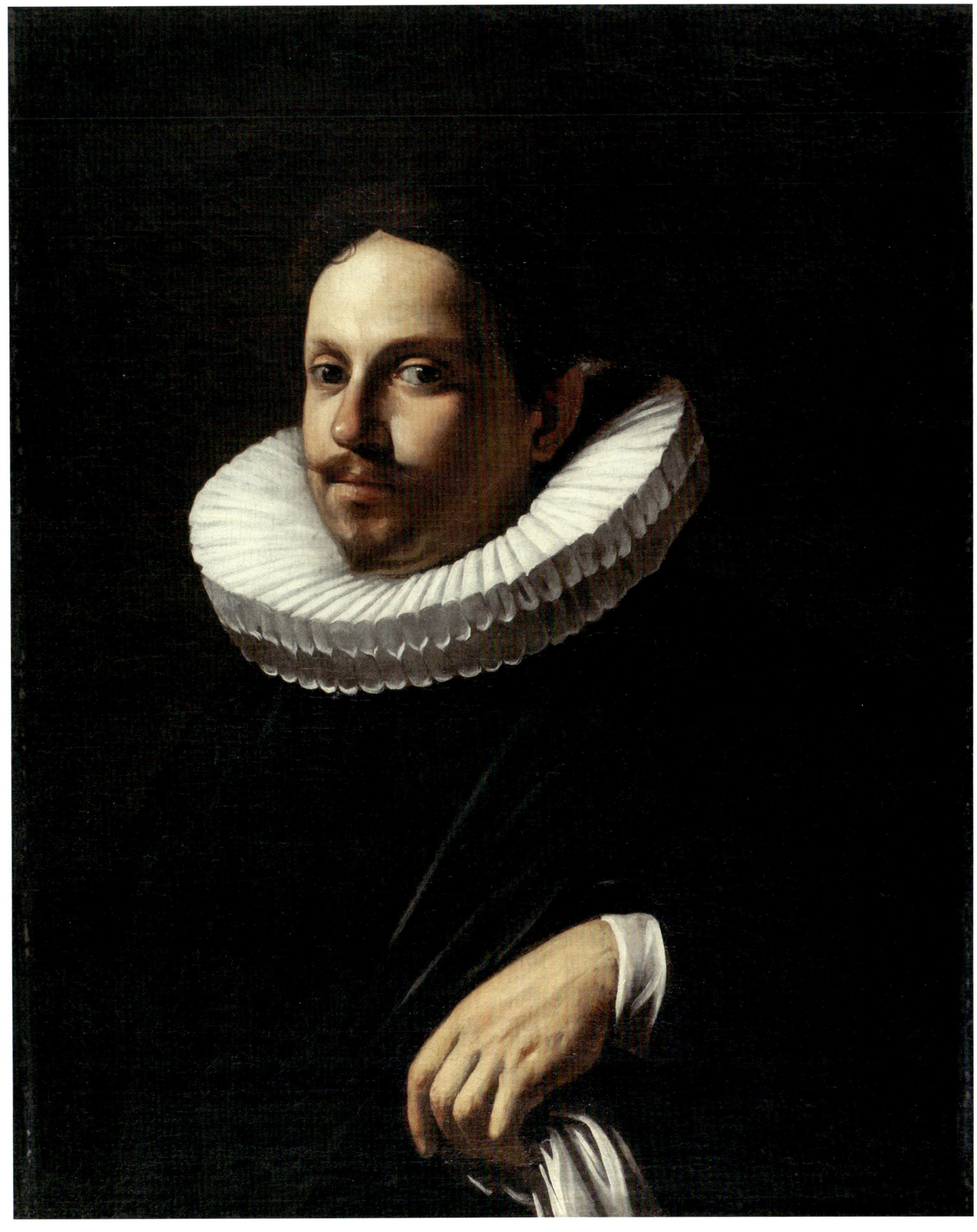

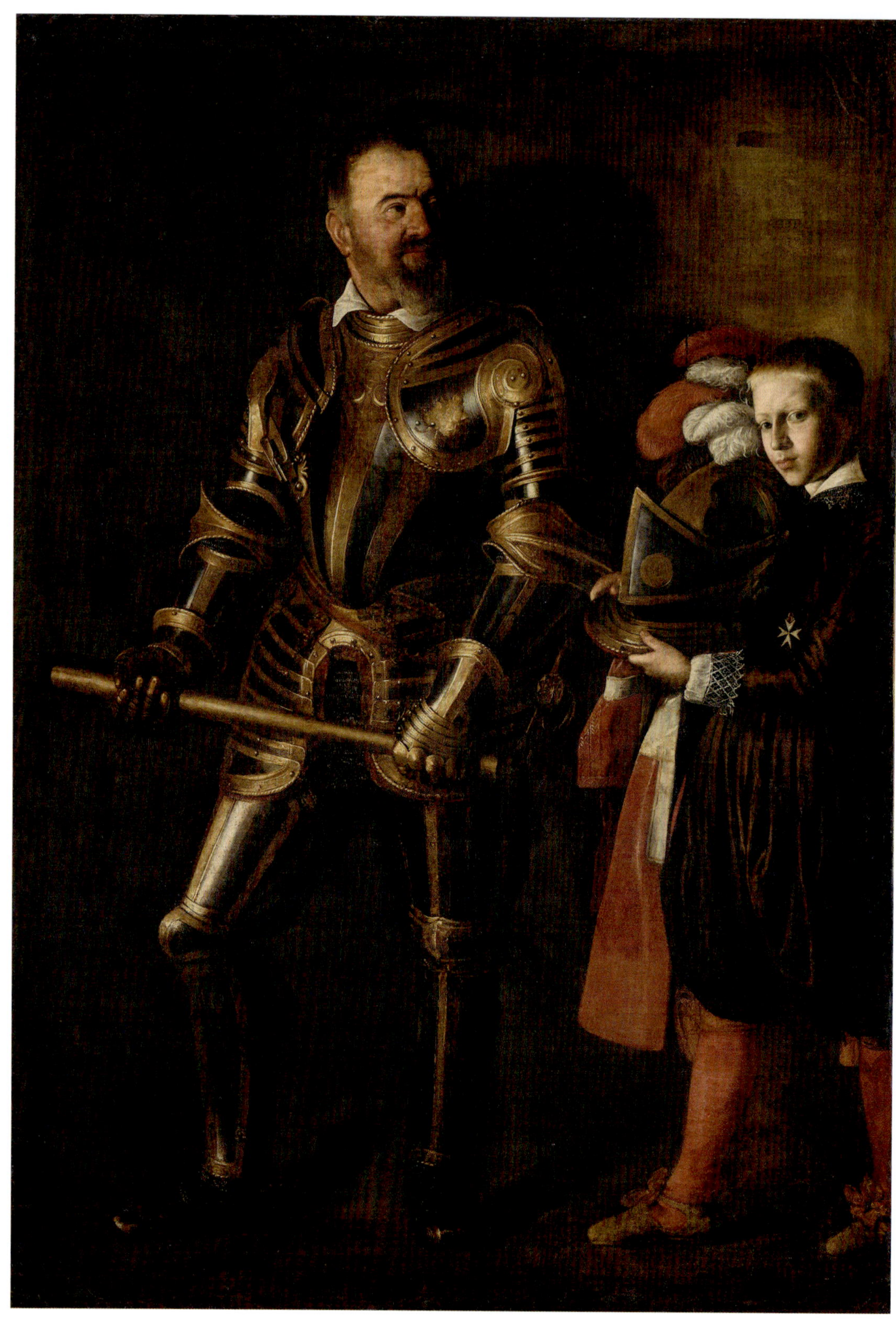

[fig. 9]
*Portrait of Alof de Wignacourt
with a Page*, 1608,
Musée du Louvre, Paris

Gianni Papi

As for the *Portrait of Alof de Wignacourt*, it is widely documented by biographers during Caravaggio's stay in Malta (July 1607–October 1608). In fact, Baglione, Bellori and Susinno[40] speak of it and, except for the opposition of Longhi[41] (stubbornly attached to the idea that Caravaggio would have refused to paint state portraits) and Ferdinando Bologna,[42] the Paris canvas has been accepted by all scholars. Obviously Caravaggio is less able here to paint a personal portrayal, forced as he is to depict the cumbersome armour; he concentrates rather on the figure of the page, on his enquiring and perhaps ambiguous gaze that turns towards the spectator. The paint itself is still quite compact and blended, quite different from that which characterises Martelli's portrait, a clue that in my opinion confirms the fact that the two works were not painted contemporaneously in Malta.

In closing, it may be useful to provide a list of the painter's works that can be considered to be portraits, which remain unidentified and therefore currently missing, and that have been referred to in biographers' accounts, in inventories (at least in the most reliable ones, because they are early or fairly early), and in various documents.

Giulio Mancini in his *Considerazioni* passes on the news of a portrait, painted in the first months of Caravaggio's sojourn in Rome, which depicted an "innkeeper" ("un hoste") with whom "he took refuge" ("si ricoverava").[43] The biographer also mentions the "portrait of a villager" ("villico") that has on occasion been linked to the *Boy with Basket of Fruit* [fig. 2 on p. 160] now in the Galleria Borghese.[44]

The *Portrait of Cardinal Serafino Olivier Razali* of Lyon, who ascended to the cardinal's purple on 9 June 1604, is mentioned in a sonnet by Marzio Milesi with the title *Per lo ritratto del Cardinal Serafino / Fatto da Michel Angiol da Caravaggio*.[45]

A sonnet in Giovambattista Marino's *Galeria* has a portrait of the poet by Caravaggio as its subject: "On the portrait of the author by Michelangelo da Caravaggio."[46] Marino's portrait is also referred to by Bellori: "Caravaggio had painted the portrait of Cavalier Marino."[47]

The Giustiniani Inventory of 1638 lists three portraits that at the moment are missing: "A painting of a Lombard Matron wearing a white veil over her head and an inscription of her name Marsilia Sicca painted on a canvas 2 *palmi* in height and 2 *palmi* in width [of the first manner of Michelangelo da Caravaggio, it is believed]" and "a painting of a half-figure, portrait of a famous courtesan, painted on canvas, unfinished, 4 ½ *palmi* in height. About 3 ½ wide [by Michelangelo da Caravaggio] with its black frame."[48] Also listed was "A painting with the portrait of the Farinaccio Criminalista depicted on a *tela da testa* [by the hand, it is believed, of Michelangelo da Caravaggio],"[49] which has recently been linked (without being followed up) to a painting in a private collection in the United Kingdom.[50]

Costanzo Patrizi's 1624 Inventory records "a painting of the portrait of Bernardino Cesari by the hand of Caravaggio, with a gold frame, twenty-five *scudi*, 25."[51] It should be noted that the Inventory was drawn up by Cavalier d'Arpino, that is Bernardino's brother: the information is probably accurate.

Caterina Campani's will, drawn up in July 1652, contains a "portrait on canvas of Signor Honorio Longo, painted by Michelangelo Merisio da Caravaggio . . . and another portrait of Signora Catherina Campani, testatrix, on another *tela da testa*, its companion, also with a pearwood frame, painted by Michelangelo Merisio da Caravaggio."[52] Caterina Campani was the wife of Onorio Longhi, who was a great friend of Caravaggio. In the will of the couple's son, the architect Martino Longhi, drawn up on 31 July 1656–5 January 1657, in addition to the portraits of his parents, also listed is another canvas painting '*da testa*', depicting "an orator wearing a toga, painting by Caravaggio."[53]

The 1671 Inventory of Cardinal Antonio Barberini mentions the portrait of "a Woman with a Topknot, about 3 *palmi* by the Hand of Caravaggio."[54]

Bellori's *Life* of Caravaggio refers to two portraits of members of the Crescenzi family; that of Monsignor Melchiorre Crescenzi, cleric of the Camera ("Michele painted the portrait of this most learned prelate"), and of his father Virgilio Crescenzi.[55] In the case of Virgilio, it must have been a *post mortem* portrait, as the senior Crescenzi died in 1592, when Caravaggio was not yet in Rome. Finally, a portrait of the baron Crescenzio Crescenzi, brother of Monsignor Melchiorre Crescenzi, appears in Crescenzio's will, drawn up on 14 February 1641. The baron bequeathed both his own portrait and that of Giovambattista Marino (see above) to his nephew Francesco Crescenzi, "ambo facti per manus Caravaggi."[56]

The 1693 Inventory of Palazzo Borghese lists "a painting on canvas of five *palmi* with a portrait of a Prelate seated holding a document in his hand . . . by Michelangelo Caravaggio."[57]

1   Bellori [1672] 2005, p. 179: "He made his way for four or five years making portraits, and then, as he had a troubled and quarrelsome nature, being of a turbid and contentious intellect, he fled Milan because of certain clashes and arrived in Venice."

2   I cannot agree with the attempt, albeit a courageous one, to attribute to Caravaggio a substantial series of portraits datable to the Milanese period, made by Moro 2016.

3   This information can be found among the annotations written by Bellori in the margin of his copy of Giovanni Baglione's *Lives* (1642); see Macioce 2003, p. 318.

4   Wiemers 1986, pp. 59–61.

5   Marini 1981b, pp. 180–183.

6   On Cecco del Caravaggio see Papi 2001, as well as the catalogue *Cecco del Caravaggio* 2023.

7   We know, from the baptismal certificate, that Fillide was born in Siena on 8 January 1581 (Bellini 2009); outwardly, the woman portrayed in the painting formerly in Berlin seems to have been a few years older than a sixteen-year-old girl; however, it is not difficult to imagine that the challenging situations she had already encountered in her life would make a girl mature more quickly; indeed, her hairstyle also, with the 'topknot', would make a girl appear older.

8   Papi 2023a, pp. 36–40; Papi 2024.

9   Photograph no. 101740, p.

10   See the entry in Spike 2010, pp. 104–106 of the CD with the catalogue of paintings, for a summary of opinions regarding the chronology of the portrait. Spike himself dates the painting to 1598.

11   See Corradini 1993, p. 112.

12   Bellini 2009. See in this regard the very recent work by Vodret 2022b, which now seems to place the painting no earlier than 1604. Already in her monograph (Vodret 2021a, pp. 176–177), the scholar placed the work in the seventeenth century (1600–1603). A dating after 1601 has also been proposed by Ebert-Schifferer 2009, pp. 290–291; Ebert-Schifferer 2010a, pp. 59–74. However, Danesi Squarzina 2001, p. 31, had already maintained that, following the discovery of Fillide's will, the work could not be dated before 1603–1605.

13   Even Giulio's presence in 1601, argued by Ebert-Schifferer (see previous footnote), is not certain because in the letter of 14 May referred to by the scholar (see Bigazzi 1977, pp. 209–210) his father Roberto Strozzi asks his cousin Giovanbattista (permanently in Florence, but at the time in Rome) about his son's behaviour. The letter makes no mention of the city where Giulio was to be found, which could also have been Florence.

14   Baroncini, Collarile 2016, p. 22. It is interesting to read the following in the volume by the two musicologists: "He [Giulio Strozzi] completed his early training in Venice under the guidance of an apparently lay master, a certain Doctor Penna, with whom he stayed "a donzena". . . For how long Giulio availed himself of Dr. Penna's teachings is unclear, but from some other new documents that have emerged, it would seem that he remained in Venice until 1606". Indeed, on 5 July of that year, Giulio was a witness at a wedding celebrated in the church of the Redentore. I thank Francesca Curti, who brought the volume in question to my notice, and the important information it contains.

15   Corradini 1993, pp. 120–124.

16   Bassani, Bellini 1994, p. 121.

17   Petrucci 2008, II, p. 294; III, fig. 84.

18   It was the first time after almost sixty years (that is since the Milan exhibition of 1951) that the painting, restored for the occasion by Muriel Vervat, had been exhibited. On the autograph attribution expressed in the 2010 exhibition see Papi 2010, pp. 22–41; K. Christiansen, in *Caravaggio e caravaggeschi* 2010, pp. 100–103.

19   Roberto Longhi had already rejected Caravaggio's authorship (Longhi 1943, pp. 37–38), attributing the painting to the circle of Pulzone. In 1951 the painting was exhibited as an autograph work by Caravaggio at the great Milan exhibition of 1951 (p. 17, no. 10) against Longhi's opinion. In 1963 (Longhi 1963, pp. 3–11) contributed to the definitive exclusion of the portrait from Caravaggio's canonical catalogue. The discovery of

the other *Portrait of Maffeo Barberini* in a private Florentine collection (exhibited here; cat. 9), marked the beginning of the critical eclipse of the painting.

20   Lavin 1975, p. 68, nos. 111–112. The work was exhibited at the exhibition *L'immagine sovrana. Urbano VIII e i Barberini* (see *L'immagine sovrana* 2023, p. 160), with an entry by S. Schütze attributing it to an anonymous painter of the late 16th century.

21   Longhi 1963, pp. 3–11.

22   Ibid. Among the various opinions in favour of a sixteenth-century dating are those of Mia Cinotti, Mina Gregori, Catherine Puglisi and Maurizio Marini (Marini 2001, pp. 424–425, to whom we also refer for earlier opinions) who date the painting to 1598, and more recently that of Francesca Cappelletti (2009, p. 48), to 1599. For a later dating John T. Spike (2010, pp. 220–222) opted instead for 1603.

23   Beginning with Papi 2012, pp. 332–334.

24   Lavin 1967, p. 473; D'Onofrio 1967, pp. 60–61, 429, no. 128. Zuccari 2022a, p. 345 has also recently confirmed a date of 1603–1604.

25   G. Papi, in *Caravaggio e caravaggeschi* 2010, pp. 113–115.

26   In fact, we read there: "It is more than reasonable to admit that it comes from Casa Barberini, that it is a relic of the scandalous cultural catastrophe that swept away the artistic heritage of that family between 1930 and 1935; and not only what was exhibited to the public, but also for all those things piled up in the attics of the palazzo and dispersed almost without any control. This painting will probably have been brought out from there, a little battered and dishevelled," and regarding the identity of the sitter, "no doubt can indeed arise if one compares it with the meticulous effigy, painted a few years earlier in Pulzone's circle [that is the *Portrait of Maffeo Barberini* as a young man]" (Longhi 1963, pp. 3–11).

27   *Giuliano Briganti, Roberto Longhi* 2022, pp. 128–130 ("Is it possible to know where the painting came from?").

28   See Bastogi 2010, p. 348.

29   Mancini [c. 1619–1621] 1956–1957, I, p. 136: "Remembering that in Padua I had seen, at the Porta della Paglia, a painter that makes portraits that are remarkable likenesses ("somigliantissimi") who for the rest was graceless, without skill and design ("disegno"); others who were not so highly skilled, but did not succeed in making likenesses, whose handling of paint and colour ("colorito") was not similar to nature, like Caravaggio ("simile al naturale").

30   G. Papi, in *Caravaggio e caravaggeschi* 2010, pp. 110–112.

31   Spike 1995, pp. 588–590; Spike 2001, entry in the attached CD.

32   Calvesi 1985b, p. 229.

33   G. Papi, in *Caravaggio e caravaggeschi* 2010, pp. 110–112.

34   Petrucci 2008, III, fig. 726. There is no resemblance to Baronio. In the engraving he has a large beard that frames his face up to his ears, a meek and mild gaze in his small eyes, and his nose is very long.

35   The identification with Benedetto Giustiniani has already been proposed by me in *Caravaggio e caravaggeschi* 2010, p. 110–112. For the citation in the Giustiniani Inventory of 1638, see Danesi Squarzina 2003, *Inventari*, I, p. 400.

36   Caravaggio's portrait of Benedetto Giustiniani painted on a *tela d'imperatore*, recorded in 1638, has not yet surfaced. The canvas soon disappeared, as it was no longer present in the second half of the seventeenth century (the last time it is recorded with certainty is in the Giustiniani Inventory of 1667, see Danesi Squarzina 2003, *Inventari*, II, pp. 55, 113).

37   See the exhaustive commentary by Federica Papi (in *Caravaggio a Roma* 2011, pp. 225–228), who cites all the opinions that have historically been expressed relating to the painting, including those, profoundly contrasting, of Matteo Marangoni and Roberto Longhi, the latter altogether resistant to the idea of a Caravaggio portraitist engaged in making likenesses and, as in the case of this work, closely linked to a 'publicising' of power. On the occasion of the publication of the so-called *Portrait of Maffeo Barberini* (Longhi 1963), herewith what the scholar wrote in relation to the *Portrait of Maffeo Barberini* as a young man: "The recovery of the real 'Maffeo Barberini' serves not only to remove from Caravaggio's catalogue the two poor-quality portraits in Florence [one of which is the *Portrait of Maffeo Barberini* as a young man], but also, about ten years later, the portrait of Paul V. To believe, as is still currently the case, that Caravaggio wanted to settle for such a miserable documentary report . . . is not something that testifies in favour of the state of Caravaggio studies."

38   Papi 2023a. We also refer you to this volume for the reasons on the basis of which the identification of the jurist Andrea Ruffetti is made.

39   The *Portrait of a Knight of Malta* was attributed to Caravaggio by Mina Gregori (see Gregori 1974); gradually, after some initial rebuttals, it is now accepted by all scholars.

40   Baglione 1642, p. 138; Bellori [1672] 2005, p. 183; Susinno [1724] 1960, p. 109.

41   Longhi 1968, p. 42.

42   Bologna [1992] 2006, pp. 337–338.

43   Mancini [c. 1619–1621] 1956–1957, I, p. 224.

44   The first to make the connection was Luigi Salerno, in Mancini [c. 1619–1621] 1956–1957, II, p. 112, footnote 885.

45   Fulco 1980, pp. 80, 83, n. 41, 88.

46   Marino [1620] 1979, I.

47   Bellori [1672] 2005, p. 181. Maurizio Marini (2001, pp. 233–242) proposed identifying it with a painting in a private collection depicting a young man. See also Schütze 2009, pp. 262–263, who agrees on both the attribution and the identification of the sitter.

48   Danesi Squarzina 2003, *Inventari*, II, pp. 417, 399.

49   Danesi Squarzina 2003, *Inventari*, I, pp. 421–422.

50   Cardinali *et al.* 2016, pp. 249–283.

51   Pedrocchi 2000, pp. 114–117. Pedrocchi's proposal to identify the painting with a *tela da testa* (43 × 31 cm) still in the Patrizi collection cannot be accepted. It is possible, in my opinion, that its author is Paolo Guidotti.

52   Pugliese, Rigano 1972, pp. 154–155; see also Sickel 2007, p. 112. Onorio Longhi and Catarina Campani were married in May 1601; Sickel hypothesises that the two portraits were executed by Caravaggio for that occasion.

53   Negro, Roio 2017, p. 141.

54   Lavin 1975, p. 293.

55   Bellori [1672] 2005, p. 181.

56   Carderi 1968, pp. 421–423.

57   Della Pergola 1964, p. 460, no. 367.

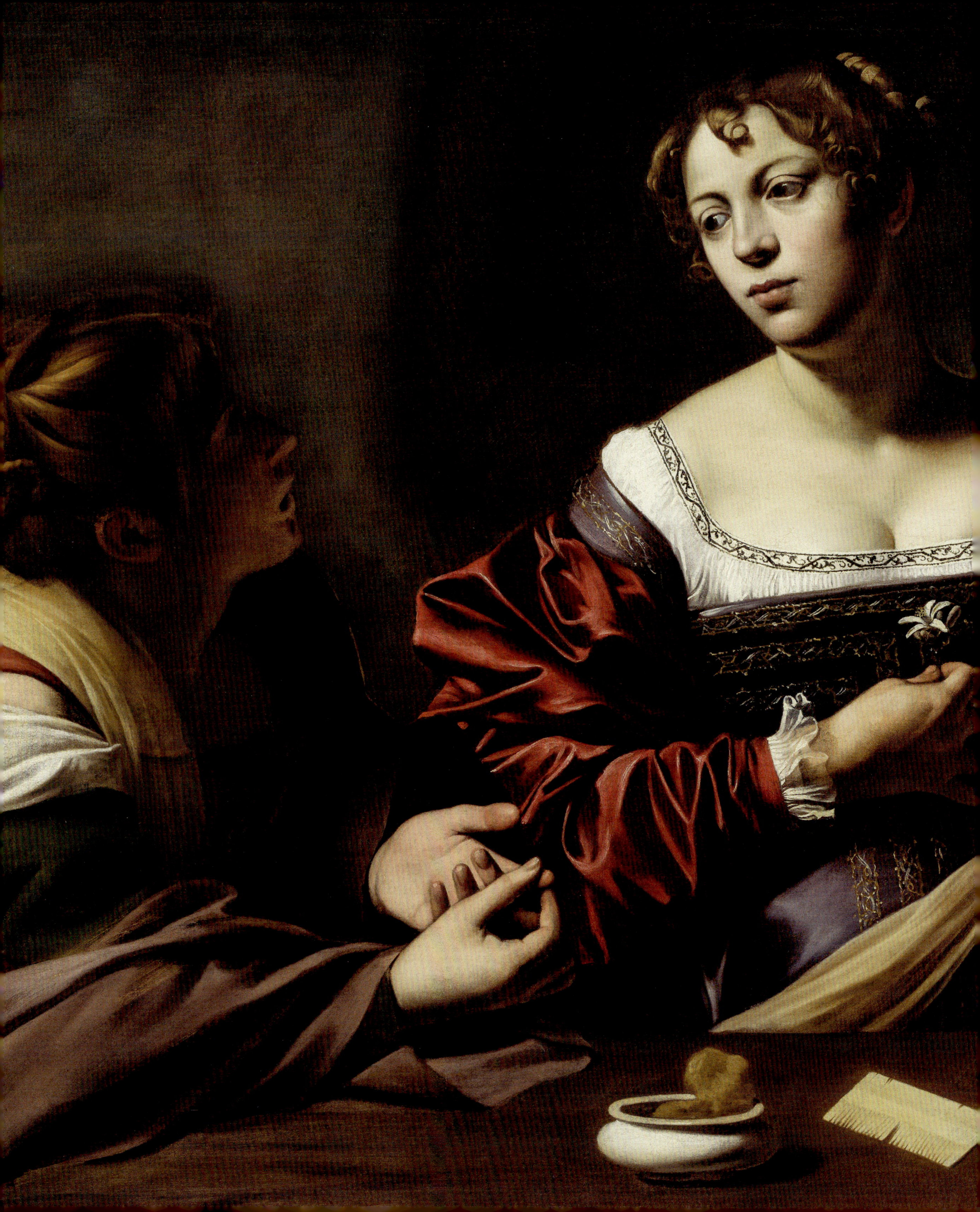

Francesca Curti

THE WOMEN DEPICTED BY CARAVAGGIO IN THE DOCUMENTS OF THE TIME

"AND MICHELANGELO MADE EVERY EFFORT TO HAVE THIS YOUNG WOMAN TO BE THE MODEL FOR THE MOTHER OF GOD."

In the collective imagination, in the adventurous and tragic life of Michelangelo Merisi, a prominent place has always been held by the women the painter frequented and whom the sources report were immortalised in his paintings. There is no doubt that their notoriety contributes to our fascination with the dramatic events suffered by Caravaggio in his personal life. After the rediscovery of the artist at the beginning of the twentieth century, countless works popularising the artist have come into being, from books to documentaries and films, emphasising the most violent and dissolute aspects of his personality, giving us the portrait of a tormented man, a painter "accursed", whose existence was spent in debauchery among brawls and prostitutes. And it is precisely the women who shared his nights of revelry that Caravaggio used as models for his paintings, destined for the most important churches in Rome, in defiance of the bigoted morals of post-Tridentine papal Rome. It is in the wake of this narrative, that in recent years attempts have been made to reconstruct the biographies of the many young women of the populace who had themselves represented as the Virgin or saints, to identify their features in the female faces portrayed in Caravaggio's paintings, and even investigating the kind of relationship they might have had with the painter.

It is difficult in the instance of a figure such as Caravaggio, the events of whose personal life spill over into fiction, to link up the threads of the past with scientific rigour in an attempt to outline the real or at least plausible contexts in which his human and artistic trajectory unfolded; but in order to be able to carry out as objective an analysis as possible of the women with whom he came into contact during his Roman years, it is necessary to reinstate their lives, and that of the painter, into a historical perspective. This means that, first of all, one needs to bear in mind that Caravaggio, although a brilliant artist with

[fig. 1]
Martha and Mary Magdalene,
c. 1598–1599, detail,
Detroit Institute of Arts,
Detroit [cat. 7]

a difficult character, was nevertheless a man of his time and that his intemperance must be understood within the context of a violent society regulated by rigid codes of honour, such as that of late sixteenth-century Rome;[1] in the same way his female frequentations must be framed within the social and cultural dynamics of the historical period in question, which, as far as courtesans are concerned, were regulated by quite different rules and ways of life that cannot be compared to our own, as studies in the field have demonstrated.[2] The artist's relationship with the religious institutions for which he created many of his paintings should also be investigated in a similar manner: it should not be forgotten, in fact, that these works—regarding which the testimonies of some biographers have, in our time, fuelled the reputation of the rebellious genius—were commissioned from him not only because of the undoubted quality of his art, but also and above all thanks to the considerable regard and support he received from the most important prelates and members of the aristocracy of the period, with whom he remained on good terms over time, and from whom he always received protection in case of need.

Secondly, a historical perspective means an approach that is based on documentary and literary sources and their criticism, that is on the evaluation of their different nature and reliability. For this reason, in order to address the subject of the women portrayed and known to Caravaggio, it was deemed necessary to consider only those female figures that are expressly referred to in the documents as having some sort of connection with the artist.[3]

FILLIDE MELANDRONI

The only references testifying to an acquaintance between Fillide Melandroni and Caravaggio are to be found in two documents, one in the courtesan's will drawn up in 1614, in which she declares that she had a portrait of herself painted by Caravaggio in her home for which she makes the provision that it be returned to the Florentine man of letters and apostolic protonotary Giulio Strozzi, her lover at the time, who is to inherit it and to whom it belongs,[4] and the one in the *post mortem* inventory of the Marchese Vincenzo Giustiniani in 1638, which describes a painting "with the portrait of a courtesan called Fillide on a *tela da testa*, with its black frame [by the hand of Michelangelo da Caravaggio]."[5] Of this work, which remained in the family's collection until 1815 when it was acquired, together with the greater part of the collection, by the King of Prussia and then transferred to the Gemäldegalerie des Kaiser-Friedrich-Museum in Berlin, only a few photographic reproductions have survived from the early decades of the twentieth century, as it was lost during the Second World War [fig. 4 on p. 106].[6]

As things stand, apart from the inevitable acquaintance entailed in posing for the painting, despite the research carried out on Fillide Melandroni's life, nothing has emerged that might shed light on the actual nature of her contact with the Lombard painter, apart from the fact that she, as we shall see, frequented figures who moved in the same circles as Caravaggio, such as Ranuccio Tomassoni, then in the service of Cardinal Cinzio Aldobrandini,[7] Ulisse Masetti, Cardinal Vincenzo Giustiniani's accountant, and the man of letters Giulio Strozzi [fig. 2], who was in contact with many members of the Accademia degli Umoristi who were friends of the painter.[8] With regard to the latter, deemed to have commissioned the portrait on the basis of Fillide Melandroni's testamentary request, certain new information that we present here relating to his sojourn in Rome casts doubt on his actual involvement in the execution of the painting, in consequence of which one

Francesca Curti

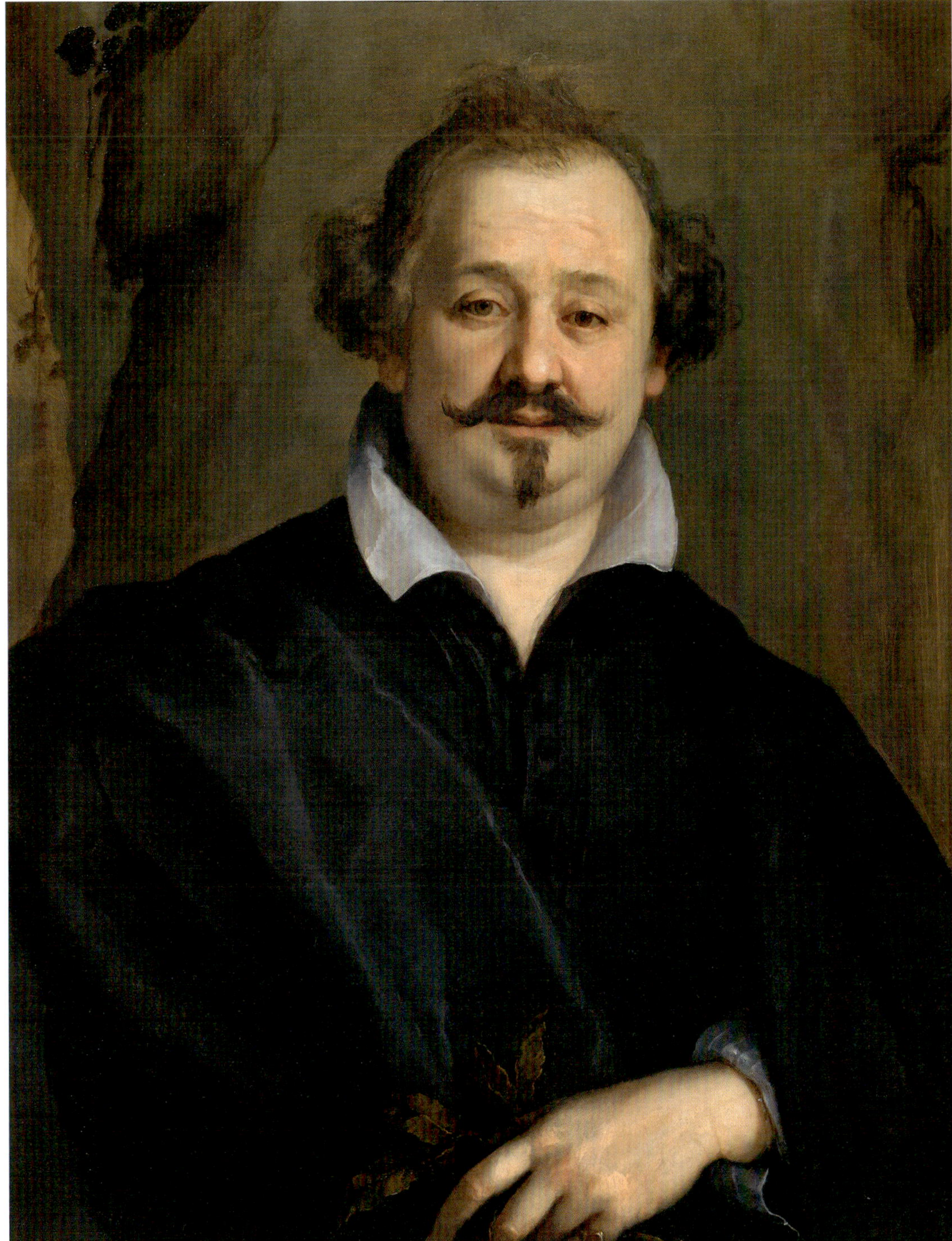

[fig. 2]
Tiberio Tinelli, *Portrait of
the Poet Giulio Strozzi*, 1630,
Galleria degli Uffizi, Florence

is also forced to reflect on its dating, at present set after 1603, the year in which it was thought that Giulio Strozzi might have moved to the papal capital.

We know that Fillide, born in Siena in January 1581, had to come to Rome to work as a prostitute very early on because she was already involved in a brawl with another prostitute named Maria in 1596. Her strong-willed character was clearly manifested in another violent episode in 1600, when she hurled herself with a knife at her rival Prudenzia Zacchia, whom she had caught in bed with Ranuccio Tomassoni, her lover at the time, with the intention of disfiguring her.[9] Her relationship with Ranuccio, the son of a relative of the Farnese, Captain Lucantonio di Terni, is indirectly confirmed in those years by another former lover of Melandroni, Ulisse Masetti, formerly in the service of Cardinal Benedetto Giustiniani in charge of expenditure. One night in July 1601, in fact, the man was stopped by the guards *(sbirri)* as he roamed the streets of the Scrofa district in the company of Fillide. Under questioning, the two initially pretended not to know one other, the one claiming to have gone out at night to bring some accounts that needed checking to Cardinal Giustiniani's steward, the other to have been stopped on her way to the home of a sick aunt living in Campo de' Fiori. Pressed by the judge's questions, they eventually admitted that they had been lovers, and that they were on their way "to Asdrubale's house," where Fillide would remain "to sleep," although they gave different versions as to the end of their relationship. The woman reported that she had stopped having a "carnal relationship" ("havere amicitia carnale") with Masetti about six months earlier, and that at that time she had received a taffeta dress as a gift from him, while the latter stated that he had not frequented her for about two years, having married a year and a half earlier, although confessing to having gone to her house with Ranuccio Tomassoni four months earlier.[10]

From these testimonies it is clear that at the beginning of the seventeenth century, Fillide Melandroni's career, despite her restless character and her youth, was already well underway within the usual path taken by the Roman prostitutes who aspired to achieve a certain economic standard and social 'visibility', understood as a condition that would allow them, if they succeeded in obtaining the protection of a high-ranking clientele, to circumvent the prohibitions imposed on them by the pope, such as, for example, that of riding in a carriage.[11]

She had, in fact, "firm friends" of a good social standing, such as Ranuccio Tomassoni and Ulisse Masetti, that is regular clients who contributed to her upkeep through gifts of furnishings or clothing, or by paying the rent, and others who requested her presence as, for example, the mentioned Asdrubale, not otherwise known; moreover, she also regularly welcomed guests into her home (at the time located in the area where the prostitutes usually lived, in Via del Gambero), who, it should be noted, did not frequent the homes of courtesans only to consummate the sexual act, but also for entertainment. Often, in fact, as would appear in the case of Tomassoni and Masetti, the men did not go alone, but together with friends to sing, play music and cards, to eat and be merry.[12]

A year later, in November 1602, Fillide Melandroni, together with her aunt Pietra, was again the protagonist of another attack, this time against the prostitutes Amabilia Antognetti—known as Pilla—and her sister Maddalena, who had run to her aid.[13] Court records show her to have moved to the area around via del Babuino, where the Stati delle Anime of the parish of Santa Maria del Popolo record her as living, as also the following year, together with her aunt and brother Silvio, in Via Paolina towards Via Margutta, and again in 1605, when she is indicated as the head of a household consisting of her aunt, a child from "S. Spirito", perhaps a foundling that she had taken in, two servants and a girl called Girolama.[14] The presence of two young dependents and of servants leads one to think that Fillide's economic situation had clearly improved. It has been hypothesised that this change in status, which also coincided with a softening of her character as she no longer appears in court documents, could be linked to the beginning of her relationship with Giulio Strozzi, which Fiora Bellini believes was already in place around 1604, when, according to the scholar, the man of letters commissioned the painting from Caravaggio. Silvia Danesi Squarzina shares this view; basing herself on the age of Strozzi, born in 1583, and the beginning of his presumed sojourn in Rome beginning in 1603, she shifted the dating of the painting, previously placed by most scholars around the end of the sixteenth century,[15] to a period between 1603 and 1605.[16] For Sybille Ebert-Schifferer, on the other hand, the portrait was executed after 1601 (any earlier and Strozzi would have been too young), the year in which it was assumed that he was already in the papal capital, his father—Roberto—having written a letter on 14 May to his relative Giovanni Battista Strozzi (a renowned man of letters, resident in Florence, but at that time occasionally in Rome), in which he asked for news of his son's behaviour.[17] Rossella Vodret, after initially proposing a date of around 1600–1603,[18] which she later deemed implausible because of the young man's age and his sojourn in Pisa, where, as hypothesised by Paolo Cecchi, he might have gone between 1602 and 1603 to obtain a degree *in utroque iure*[19]—later proposed a date of 1603–1604.[20] An entirely opposite view is held by Gianni Papi, who recently reaffirmed—for stylistic reasons—a dating of the portrait to the end of the sixteenth century, thus laying aside the hypothesis that it could have been painted for Strozzi, but taking the view, rather, that it was painted at the request of Fillide herself, or for another patron.[21]

Giulio Strozzi's non-involvement in the commissioning of the portrait—as proposed by Papi—may not be entirely without foundation. Although the information relating to Strozzi's sojourn in Pisa to obtain his law degree is reported in a biography of him that dates to 1647[22] and that has subsequently been accepted by all scholars in the field, in fact research carried out on the registers of graduates studying in Pisa in those years, has revealed that his name is not listed.[23] On the other hand, his presence is attested at the University of Padua, where he appears as a witness to the graduation ceremonies of Cristoforo Candido Acquaviva and Carlo, a monk from Rovigo, respectively on 13 August 1601 and 22 March 1603, and is there already recorded as an apostolic protonotary,[24] a post which, given his age, one would have to assume, as the office was venal, had been bought by his father on his behalf, perhaps also thanks the good relations between the Aldobrandini and his relative Giovanni Battista Strozzi.[25] And indeed, Strozzi himself also speaks of a sojourn in the Venetian city, on the occasion of the dedication of his tragedy *Erotilla* to Cardinal Borghese, printed in 1613, stating that he began working there in his times of leisure in Padua.[26] However, neither is Giulio Strozzi's presence attested among the graduates of that university,[27] and the only document relating to his presence in the Venetian city is a marriage contract drawn up in Venice on 5 July 1606 between a wine merchant's daughter and a linen merchant, in which he appears as a witness.[28] One could hypothesise that he arrived in Rome after March 1603 to then leave again for Venice at an unspecified date; however, the serious doubt remains that he may instead have remained in the Veneto until the summer of 1606, before moving definitively to the papal city, where, in that same year, in a house in Via della Croce,[29] he seems to have hosted the poet Giovanni Battista Marino[30] on several occasions.

Even his presumed presence in Rome in 1601, deduced from the letter addressed in May of that year by his father to his uncle who was then in the city, may not be a confirmation, as it cannot be ruled out that Roberto Strozzi was referring to his son's behaviour in another city, perhaps Florence, where Giovanni Battista Strozzi lived on a permanent basis, or perhaps even already Padua, where Giulio is recorded only two months later.[31] And even if he had lived in Rome until the spring of 1601, there can be no doubt that he did not reside there at least for the following three years.

The impossibility of establishing with certainty the arrival of the man of letters in Rome does not, consequently, even allow us to determine when the relationship with Fillide began, a relationship which must have disrupted the young man's life to such an extent that he wanted to marry the courtesan, defying common morality and the wrath of his father, who, according to a directive of 1612, convinced the pope to expel the woman from Rome.[32] On the other hand, we can be fairly certain that this bond lasted until the death of his beloved, which occurred in the papal capital (to which she had returned), on 3 July 1618, the man of letters having agreed to act as guarantor of her inheritance on behalf of her sister-in-law, Felice de Rossi, mother of the designated heirs, Nicola and Giacomo Melandroni, sons of her late brother Silvio, who at the time were minors. Indeed, in the contract stipulated between the two, on 13 July 1618, Giulio Strozzi gave his guarantee that all administrative procedures concerning Fillide's estate would be correctly carried out by Felice, who, for her part, undertook not to sell under any circumstances any of the movable or immovable property belonging to the estate except with the express consent of Strozzi, and to relieve him of any responsibility deriving from the mismanagement of the estate.[33] A month later, under the supervision of the nobleman, Felice, on behalf of the under-age heirs, made a series of investments of a certain financial value, which testify to the economic status attained by the courtesan: on 10 August she purchased assets to the value of 100 *scudi* from a certain Andrea Pagano, to whom, two days later, she sold part of Fillide's assets for the sum of 125 *scudi* and 10 *baiocchi*. This consisted of 287 gold and silver decorated leather hides, which probably adorned the room in which the courtesan received guests, known as the elegant room,[34] to the value of 45.10 *scudi*, and two gold-embroidered silk dresses (one of the precious "ermesino") valued at a total of no less than 63 *scudi*.[35] Finally, on 25 September, again as administrator of the sister-in-law's inheritance, Strozzi granted a loan of 300 *scudi* to Luca Barbirossi, a Florentine, who undertook to repay it within a year.[36] In the autumn, relations between Strozzi and Felice de Rossi began to deteriorate due to the fact that the latter asked the man of letters to return some of Fillide's possessions that were still in his keeping, which probably did not include the portrait, as this had been explicitly declared to be his property in the will. The nobleman refused to hand over these possessions unless the woman first released him from his duties as guarantor. In the end, an agreement must have been reached because, on 16 November, Felice appointed Lorenzo Ratti as guarantor in the place of Strozzi; Ratti in turn guaranteeing to release Giulio[37] from all liability.

On the basis of the new elements presented above, the possibility arises that Strozzi was indeed not involved in the commission of the work, and that the portrait may have been commissioned rather by one of Fillide's "firm friends", Ranuccio Tomassoni or Ulisse Masetti, or by Fillide herself, since, as research on the status of prostitutes in the modern age has demonstrated, the most renowned courtesans liked to have portraits of themselves to keep in their homes.[38] The man of letters may have been involved later, perhaps buying the work from the woman for his collection, but allowing her to keep it in her home for as long as she wished. Indeed Giulio Strozzi, as he himself states in 1627, owned a collection of portraits of which he was very proud,[39] which he began to put together as early as his years in Rome, as testified by his request to Marino for a portrait of himself; a request that the poet granted.[40]

We believe that this kind of reflection is necessary in order to also reconsider the dating of the painting, the style of which should at this point be studied taking into account the

Francesca Curti

possibility that the work was not commissioned by Strozzi. This also in light of the opportunity afforded by this exhibition to study the presumed *Portrait of Maffeo Barberini*, here exhibited to the public for the first time, which would, therefore, have been executed before the *Portrait of Fillide*, if one maintains that the latter portrait was executed in 1603–1604; in my opinion, however, the hypothesis should be explored that the painting, although difficult to judge because it is only known from photographic reproductions, may belong to an earlier phase of Caravaggio's activity, because of its particular Mannerist air, and its densely applied paint.

LENA "WHO IS MICHELANGELO'S WOMAN"

We know of Lena's existence only thanks to a single document; the complaint filed on the evening of 29 July 1605, by Mariano Pasqualoni, the deputy notary of the Tribunale del Vicario, when, still bleeding from the head-wound inflicted by Caravaggio who had attacked him with a sword in Piazza Navona near Palazzo De Cupis, then the residence of the Spanish ambassador, he had run to report the incident to the judge of the Tribunale del Governatore. In the complaint he stated that he had been wounded "because of a woman called Lena, who stands in piazza Navona, past the palazzo, that is the entrance doorway of Signor Sertorio Teofili, and who is Michelangelo's woman"; a few days earlier he had had "words on the Corso" with the painter, and for the same reason.[41] The episode, a fairly rare occurrence, is also recalled in a literary source, *Le vite de pittori, scultori, et architetti che hanno lavorato in Roma* by Giuseppe Passeri, published between 1670–1680, in which the author, in the biography of Guercino, recounts how Caravaggio at the time living in the "Otto Cantoni", had asked one of his neighbours, probably a widow, to let "one of her unmarried daughters, whose features were not unpleasing" pose as a model for the altarpiece of the *Madonna of Loreto* in the church of Sant'Agostino [fig. 3], in exchange for financial compensation, as they were "poor but honest people". Since "this young woman was being courted by a young man who was a notary by profession," who had repeatedly asked her mother for her hand in marriage and had always been refused "being loath to give her daughter [in marriage] to notaries whose damnation (she said) was certain," the latter, offended at having been rejected, realising that the young woman frequently went to the painter's house, reproached her mother for having denied him her daughter and then "giving her as a concubine to a man excommunicated and accursed." The woman, distressed, confided in Caravaggio who, the following day, taking an axe, went in search of the notary and, finding him in Piazza Navona, attacked him in front of the church of San Giacomo degli Spagnoli.[42]

Passeri's account, although romanticised, must have been based on first-hand information, because he retraces the events fairly correctly, giving exact contextual details such as the area where Caravaggio lived at the time, "agli Otto Cantoni", that is in the neighbourhood of the maze of streets close to Vicolo San Biagio (where in 1604 the painter had rented the house of Prudenzia Bruni); the place where the attack took place, in Piazza Navona; and the profession of the victim of the attack. Passeri only differs as to the exact location of the ambush, which Pasqualoni states took place in front of Palazzo De Cupis, the weapon used, and the whereabouts of Lena's residence, which the biographer places near Caravaggio's home, while the notary reported it as located in the southern part of Piazza Navona, more precisely "past the main entrance to the palazzo of Teofilo Sartorio," that is probably in one

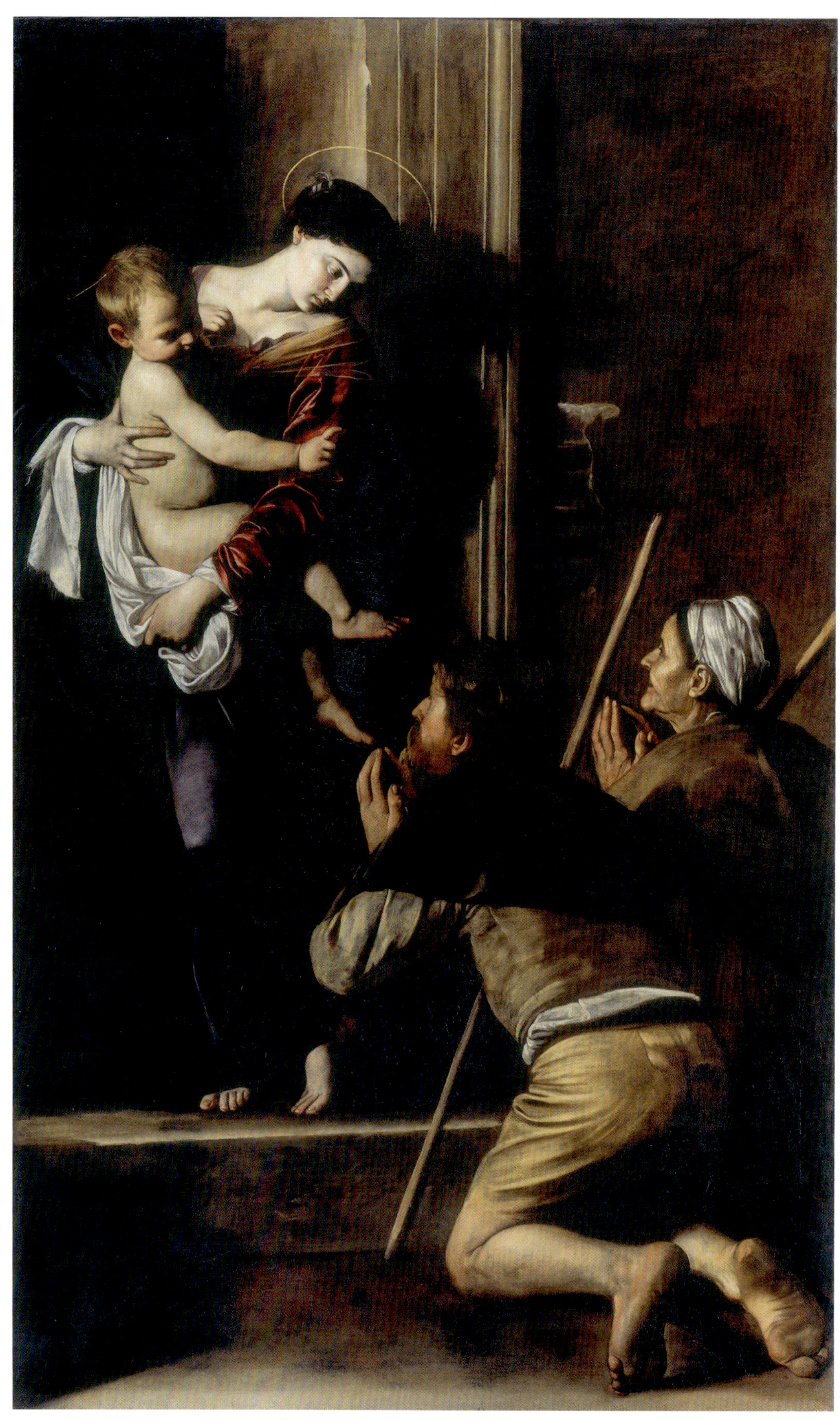

Francesca Curti

of the workshops of the renowned jurisconsult's palazzo, which, in fact, was in the southern part of the piazza, on the side of the church of Sant'Agnese in Agone.[43]

It should be noted that in both accounts Lena is never referred to as a prostitute. Pasqualoni merely refers to her as the painter's woman, while Passeri even describes her as a poor young girl who had agreed to pose for Caravaggio just to make ends meet.

In spite of this, in the 1990s, following a praiseworthy and in-depth search in the archives of the Tribunale Criminale del Governatore that brought to light important information on the eventful everyday life of Fillide Melandroni and her, hitherto unknown, relationship with the man that Caravaggio killed in 1606, Ranuccio Tomassoni, it was thought that one had reached an understanding of the social framework within which the painter's life took place, a framework that also encompassed the consummation of his relationship with the woman with whom the notary Pasqualoni had fallen in love.[44] For this reason, a prostitute called Maddalena Antognetti, on whom some court documents had been found, was identified, due to her name, with the Lena who was "Michelangelo's woman," although Maddalena Antognetti turned out to have almost always lived in the Ortaccio neighbourhood and moved, perhaps around 1603, to the Borgo district, to the home of her lover, the notary Gasparo Albertini.[45]

To corroborate this hypothesis, unsupported by any document attesting to her actual acquaintance with the painter, Caravaggio's name was introduced into the complaint filed on 19 July 1605 by the courtesan against the notary Albertini, who had slashed her face out of jealousy. In the complaint, Maddalena only claimed that her lover had prevented her from frequenting any of her previous clients, among whom Caravaggio was included, although his name did not actually feature.[46]

The presumed identification of Lena with the prostitute Maddalena Antognetti met with immediate success, quickly becaming a certainty, because it contributed in reinforcing the 'romantic' vision of the 'bohemian' painter, of the non-conformist genius whose existence was absorbed in brawls, taverns, brothels and unruly behaviour so dear to our contemporary sensibility.

However, having established the lack of any direct connections in the sources, not only between the Lombard artist and Maddalena Antognetti, but also between the latter and anyone close to Caravaggio,[47] we are obliged to consider the existence of such a relationship unreliable, and induced rather to rethink the whole episode by following the path already taken in the past by Maurizio Marini and don Sandro Corradini,[48] that is of taking as the starting point the only piece of certain information we have on Lena, namely the fact that she probably lived in one of the workshops in the palazzo of the consistorial lawyer Sertorio Teofilo, as related by Mariano Pasqualoni.[49] The notary, in fact, is extremely precise in locating the woman's dwelling, initially explaining that it was after Setorio Teofili's palazzo, and then correcting himself and stating that it was after the palazzo's main entrance, thus in one of the workshops to the side of the entrance.

The building, located on the south side of Piazza Navona, between the house of Teodoro de Rossi and that of Giovanni Battista Pamphilj, behind Piazza Pasquino, and later incorporated into palazzo Doria Pamphilj, was an imposing and austere three-storey edifice onto which opened six workshops[50] [fig. 5]. Research carried out on the tenants revealed an interesting network of relations between people who were friends of Caravaggio and others that the painter might have known, which might explain the possible visits to the palazzo.

This area of Piazza Navona at the time was characterised by the presence of a great number of craftsmen and entrepreneurs: between piazza Pasquino and the surrounding

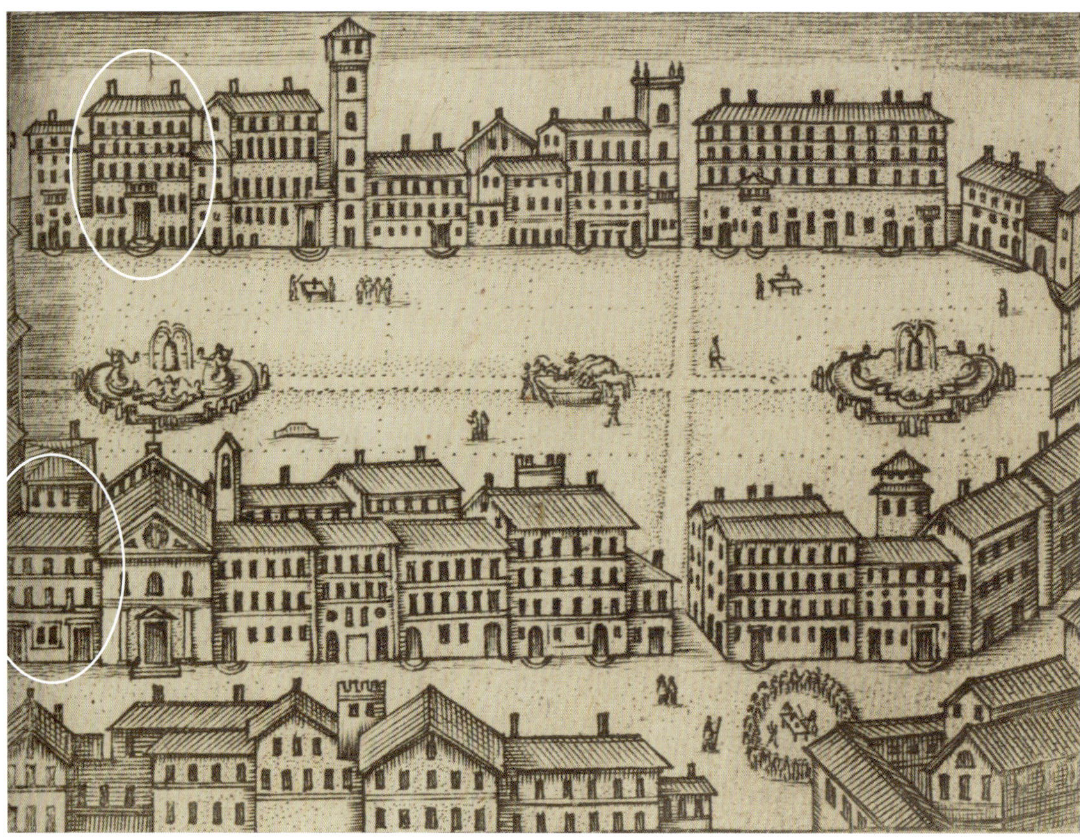

area, in fact, as a result of the presence on the corner with via dell'Anima of the Stamperia camerale, numerous businesses related to publishing and the sale of books had established themselves; a little further on, in the street still known today as the street of the lute-makers, craftsmen of German origin involved in lute-making had settled; in Via dell'Anima there were many carpenters' and coach-makers' workshops, while on the piazza there were as many that sold fabrics and related items, such as "mattress makers" and haberdashers, perhaps also because of the market held every Wednesday.[51] There was also a large Spanish community that gathered around the Spanish embassy and the church of San Giacomo degli Spagnoli.

From the Stati delle Anime of the parish of Sant'Agnese in Agone it emerges that in 1610 (unfortunately, the registers of the previous years have not come down to us) the last shop on the left, facing the palace, was rented out to a Milanese innkeeper, Antonio Arrigoni, who in 1606 had stipulated the lease "ad usum hospitii."[52] The second, in the centre, was inhabited by a second-hand dealer, from Bergamo, who, as can be deduced from his will drawn up on 17 November 1647, more specifically carried out the trade of picture dealer.[53] This activity is also confirmed by two other archival documents, one concerning the purchase, in 1619 of some of the paintings of the inheritance of the Flemish painter Karel Orldrago for his shop, which was still located in Piazza Navona, and the other, the commission to value the paintings in Scipione Ferri's barber shop in 1627.[54] The third workshop, next to the main entrance, was occupied by the haberdasher Giovanni Parisi[55], while the first workshop on the right, immediately after the main entrance, was rented to another haberdasher, Antonio Fugalotti.[56] The last workshop, also on the right, belonged to a singular character, a certain

Francesca Curti

Dionisio Alberti from Padua, identified in studies on the art of healthcare as a notorious "charlatan" who, in order to attract customers to his shop selling medicinal products, had had leaflets printed in which he explained the curative properties of the hippopotamus's tooth;[57] and finally, the one in the centre was rented to a close friend of Caravaggio, the bookseller Ottaviano Gabrielli, who resided there with his wife Lucrezia Angelonga, their son Giovanni Battista and a servant.[58] Unfortunately, it is not known when exactly Gabrielli moved to the premises beneath Palazzo Teofili because some of the documents found indicate that in 1602 he lived "beneath the palazzo del Bonadies in Piazza Navona,"[59] a building which no longer exists that was joined to the church of San Giacomo degli Spagnoli "opposite" Palazzo Torres,[60] where he seems to have remained at least until 1604, because, in a deed of 2 September of that year, he is said to have been domiciled "in regione Sancti Pantaleonis in platea Agonis,"[61] that is in piazza Navona, but on the side, in the area of the church of San Pantaleo, where palazzo Bonadies was located [fig. 4]. However, it is possible that he had soon moved across to Teofili's palazzo, because a payment order found at the Monte di Pietà dated 3 October 1609 records him having moved to the other side of the piazza at least as early as April of that year, having paid the instalment of 17.75 *scudi* to Bernardino Teofili, son of Sertorio who had died in 1607, for the second six months of the rent.[62] The bookseller remained in the shop until his death, which must have occurred before 19 November 1615, when his wife and son Giovanni Battista, referred to as "quondam Ottaviani", rented the workshop formerly inhabited by Alberti.[63]

It is interesting to note that Gabrielli's friendship with Caravaggio seems to have been consolidated at leadt in the very same years in which the painter probably painted the *Madonna of Loreto*, whose face—according to Passeri—reproduces Lena's features, that

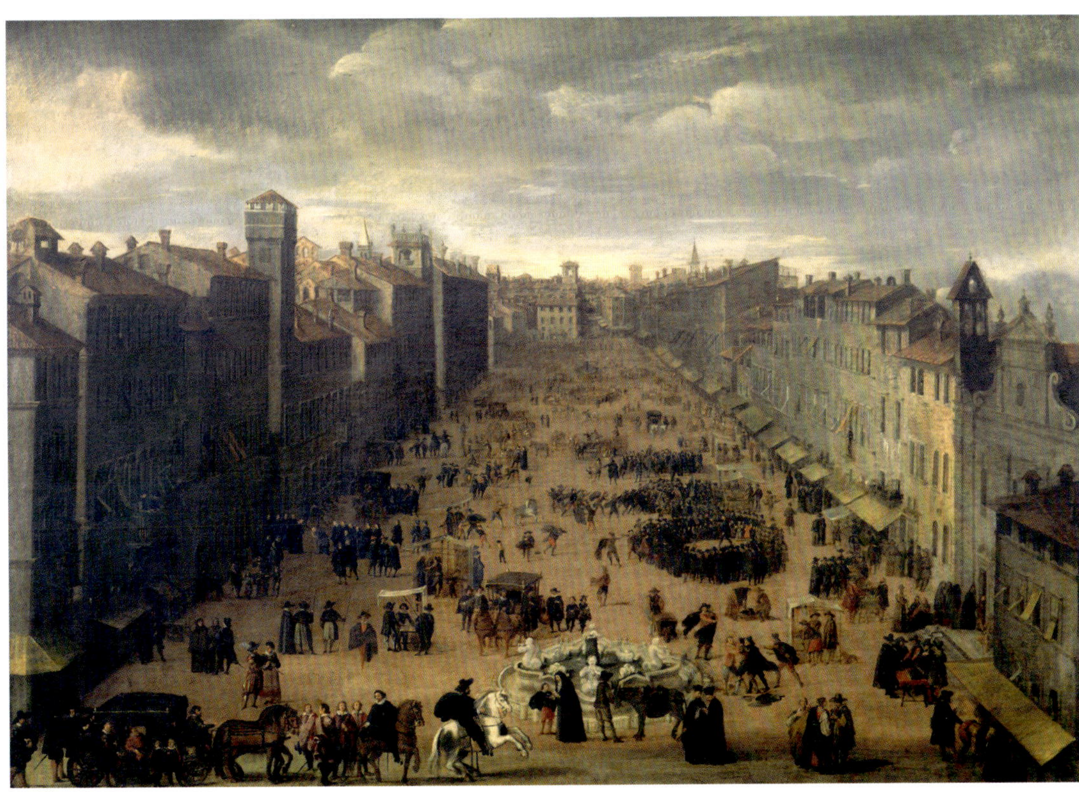

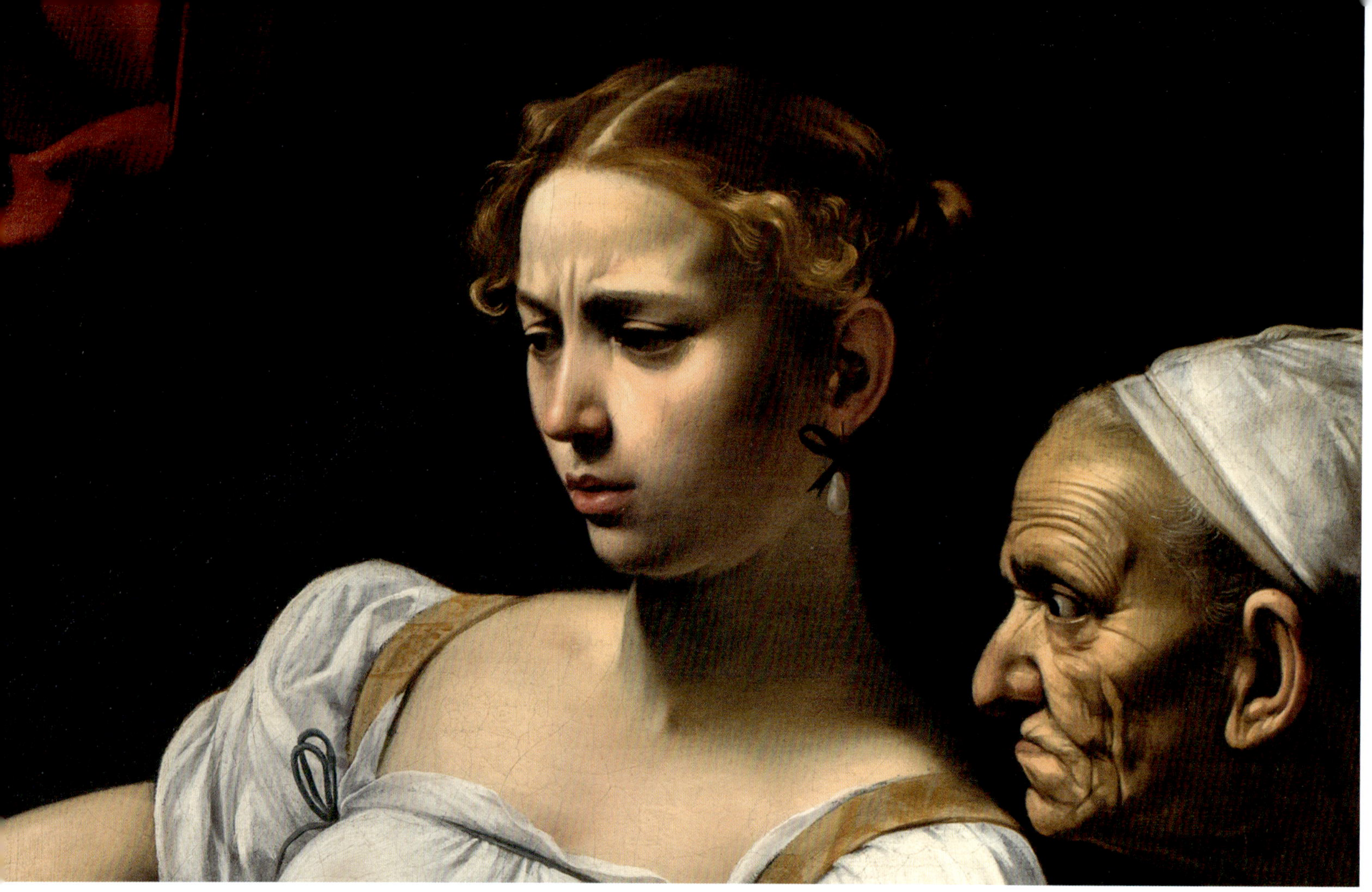

is around 1604–1605.[64] His first appearance in the artist's life is in fact documented on the occasion of Caravaggio's arrest in Via de' Greci on the evening of 19 October 1604 for throwing stones and insulting the patrol policing the streets—the *sbirri*—, when Gabrielli, who was also in the area, was instructed by the painter to run to inform Cardinal del Monte or Olimpia Aldobrandini that he was being arrested. After carrying out the mission, Ottaviano went to the house of the governor of Rome, where Caravaggio had been taken, in order to inform the painter that he had succeeded in alerting his protectors, but he too was taken into custody.[65] Less than a year later, on 19 July 1605, the bookseller, together with Cherubino Alberti, the tailor Girolamo Crocicchia and Prospero Orsi, acted as guarantor for Caravaggio before the Tribunale del Governatore, guaranteeing that the painter would no longer harass Laura and Isabella Della Vecchia, the door to whose house he had defaced the day before.[66]

Caravaggio's familiarity with Gabrielli (who lived in Piazza Navona and who, one might suppose, was acquainted with the artisans of the district[67]), or with other traders living beneath Palazzo Teofili, with whom he may have come into contact, if they were already tenants at the time, such as the innkeeper Arrigoni or the dealer in second-hand goods Poli—both, incidentally, Lombard as was the artist—could have favoured a meeting with Lena who, from what has emerged from the Stati delle Anime, must have had some kind of commercial establishment beneath palazzo Teofili, perhaps a haberdasher's shop, given that over the years several succeeded one another.

Francesca Curti

Ottaviano Gabrielli, however, was not the only tenant in the building who was close to Caravaggio: in one of the palazzo's workshops, in fact, probably from the 1580s and 1590s, also lived for a long time the poet, playwright, writer and painter Giovanni Bricci,[68] father of the "woman-architect" Plautilla, who, as recent studies have shown, was on very close terms with the Cavalier d'Arpino and his workshop collaborators, with whom she shared a common interest in the staging of the so-called "commedia all'improvviso" or "ridiculous" comedy, the forerunner of the commedia dell'arte, to which Bricci dedicated many compositions through-out his life.[69] In a list he drew up of the best actors who had tried their hand at this kind of theatrical comedy, several painters from Cavalier d'Arpino's entourage appear, such as, for example, Matteo Pagani, Flaminio Allegrini and Giovan Angelo Santini known as Toccafondi. That Cavalier d'Arpino was dedicated to this activity is also testified by the founding of a thea-tre in 1608 in his palazzo in Via del Corso, as well as the Accademia degli Uniti.[70]

At an unspecified date, but probably after 1581, the year of Bricci's birth, his father rented the premises in Piazza Navona to carry out his activity as a "mattress-maker". The Teofili family took a liking to Giovanni, so much so that Sertorio wanted him to complete all his studies together with his son Bernardino.[71] He began publishing plays at least as early as 1605, although the first document relating to his connection with Giuseppe Cesari, the Cavalier d'Arpino, dates to 1609, when the latter acted as godfather to his son. However, it is reasonable to think that contact with the painter from Arpino had begun much earlier, and it cannot be ruled out that Bricci had been part of the Cavalier d'Arpino's workshop, where he may have met Caravaggio.[72] On the other hand, confirmation of the hypothesis that the Lombard painter frequented circles close to Bricci, perhaps even after the break with the Cavalier d'Arpino, might come from the presence in the list of actors drawn up by the play-wright, of the Milanese jeweller Francesco Moroni,[73] since 1599 husband of Olimpia Spada,

[fig. 6]
Martha and Mary Magdalene, c. 1598–1599, detail, Detroit Institute of Arts, Detroit [cat. 11]

[fig. 7]
Saint Catherine of Alexandria, c. 1598–1599, detail, Museo Nacional Thyssen-Bornemisza, Madrid [cat. 10]

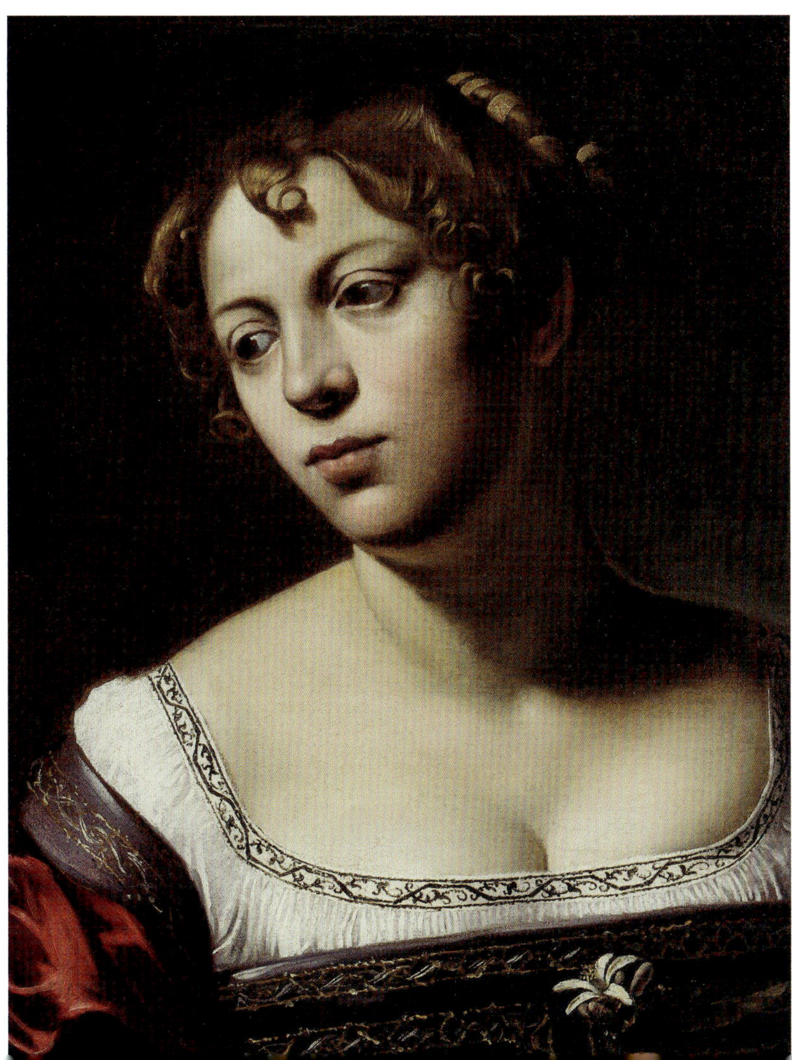

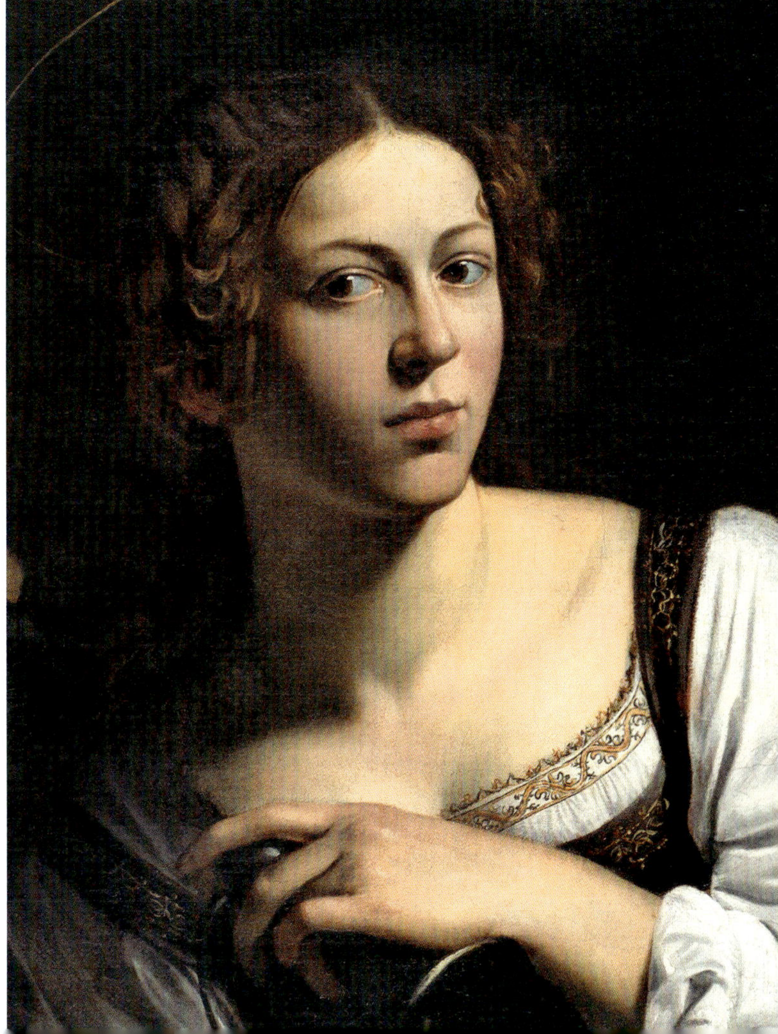

daughter of that Costantino dealer in old paintings ("regattiero di quadri vecchi"), who was one of Caravaggio's closest friends from the time of his arrival in Rome. The information is of some interest because one of the couple's children, Giuseppe, held at his baptism by the Cavaliere himself, clearly had the name of the painter from Arpino imposed upon him by his parents.[74] Such links could, therefore, give weight to the proposed early acquaintance between Bricci and Giuseppe Cesari, and possibly also Caravaggio.

Another painter, Rinaldo Corradini, from Bologna, also belonged to Cavalier d'Arpino's circle of friends. In 1591 he had rented a workshop near the palazzo of Sertorio Teofili, but one located at the back in Piazza Pasquino, perhaps the same workshop where his brother, Annibale, also a painter, died in 1616.[75] During the famous trial endured by the Cavaliere that same year, Corradini claimed to have known the artist from Arpino for over twenty years, to have eaten with him at least "a million times", and to have recently painted a fresco on his behalf at the Campidoglio.[76] Taking into consideration what has emerged regarding the theatrical vocation of the Cavalier d'Arpino's entourage, the painting depicting *Rinaldo Corradini riding a mule* (Cento, Civica Pinacoteca il Guercino), recently reattributed to the hand of Guido Reni, could perhaps also be interpreted as the represention of a scene from a satyrical comedy, evidence maybe that Rinaldo also participated in Cesari's theatrical productions.[77]

Moreover, it should be made known that Gabrielli was also in contact with members of the Corradini family. On 28 May 1604, in fact, Ottaviano Gabrielli bought an entire bookshop from Annibale Corradini's son-in-law, Pietro Paolo De Ferraris, also a bookseller.[78] In the light of what has been reported so far regarding these intricate networks of relations, it is worth mentioning the presence, in 1610, in Annibale Corradini's house, located not far from Piazza Navona near Via della Stufa dei Mellini, of a woman called Maddalena and her daughter Lena, who resided in the painter's apartment as sub-tenants, who at the time lived with his wife, his children Giovanni Battista, Lucrezia and Margherita.[79] The latter, although married to De Ferraris, is registered with her two young children.[80] Apart from the suggestion, which for the moment remains as such, regarding the possibility that this Lena could be Caravaggio's "woman", it should be noted that the name Lena does not appear to be the diminutive of Maddalena—because otherwise one would have to think that she had the same name as her mother—but perhaps rather that of Elena, as suggested on several occasions by don Sandro Corradini.[81]

These deliberations demonstrate that for Lena we can have no certainties, not even as to her actual name, and, on close inspection, one cannot even be sure that she was the Lombard painter's mistress, because, as far as the existence of this relationship is concerned, we only have Pasqualoni's version. If Passeri's words are to be believed, Pasqualoni blinded by jealousy was convinced that the girl frequented Caravaggio's house because she had become his "woman", perhaps not actually aware that she was posing for him as a model, which is why, in his eyes, such a behaviour could only be explained by thinking that the two were intimate. Consequently, it cannot be ruled out that the artist was actually driven to attack Pasqualoni only to defend the girl's honour, which had been sullied by the notary. However, as Passeri's account is a literary source which, as such, reports information gained through hearsay that cannot be verified, and not having any further evidence on the subject other than Pasqualoni's denunciation, also partial, the real reasons for the conflict with the notary as well as the real connection with Lena are destined to remain, for the time being, unsubstantiated.

Francesca Curti

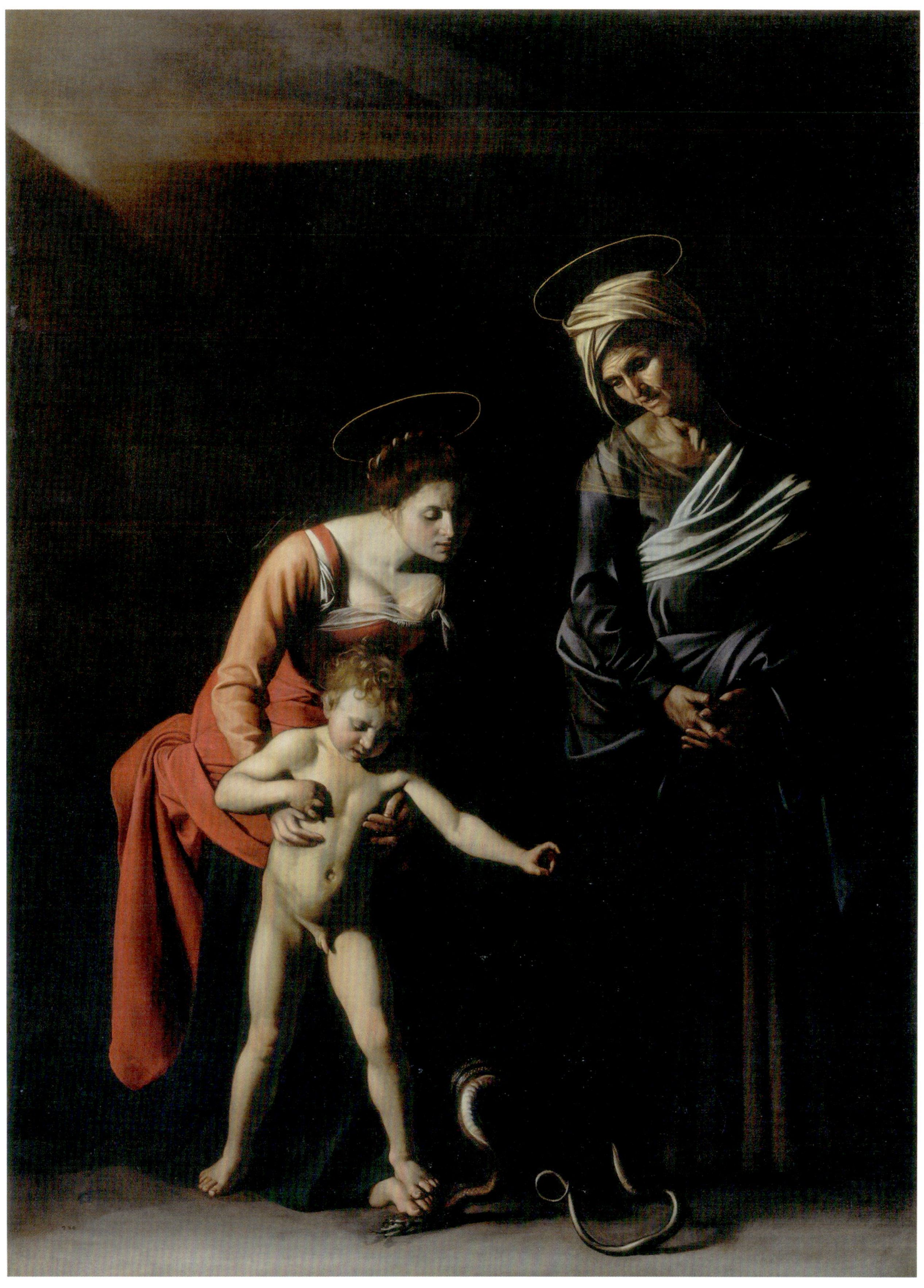

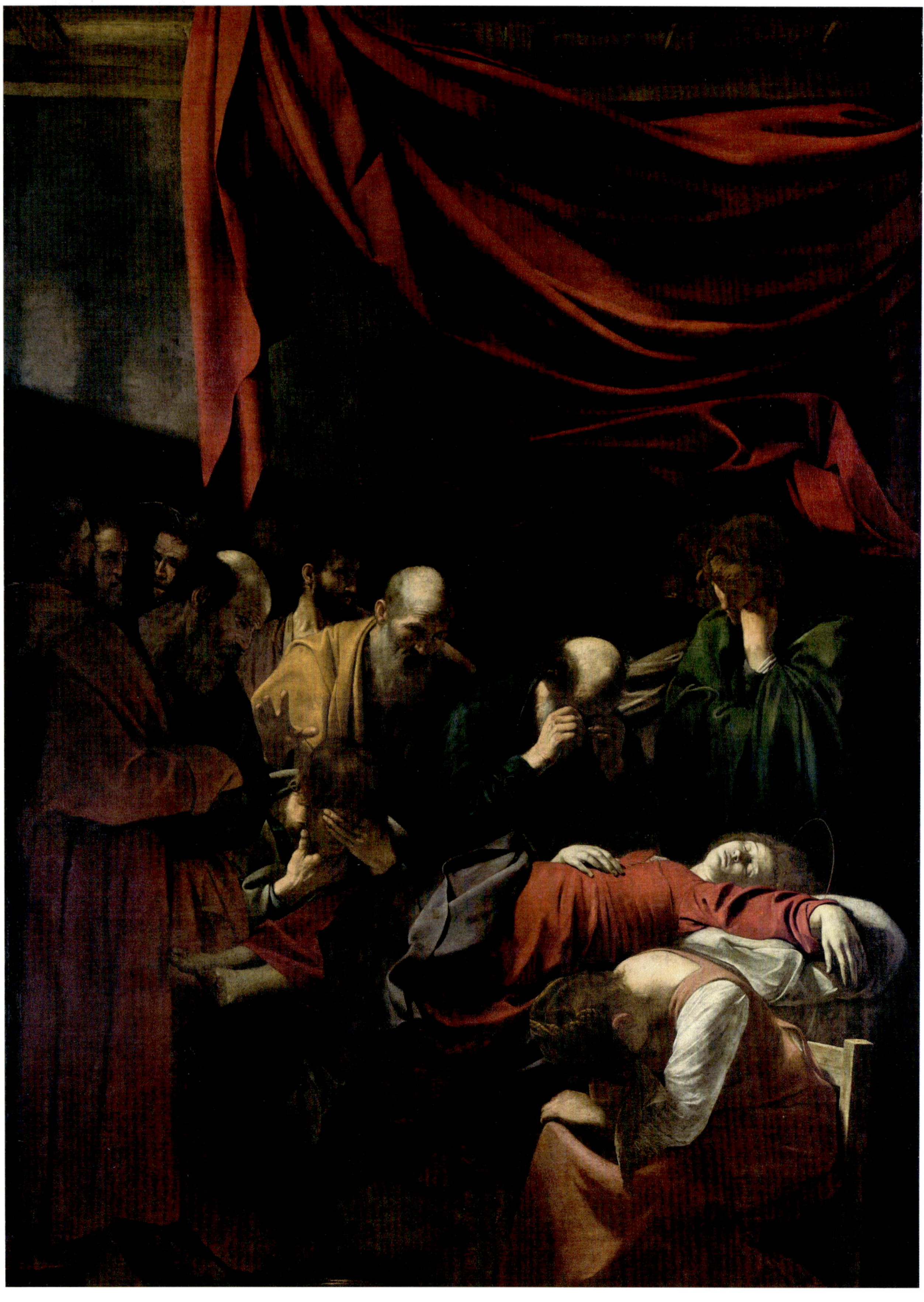

Francesca Curti

Even the figure of the courtesan Menicuccia, to be identified most probably as the Sienese Domenica Calvi,[82] appears only once in documents in relation to Caravaggio, and precisely on the occasion of the painter's arrest for throwing stones and insults on the evening of 19 October 1604, as referred to above, while he was in the company of Ottaviano Gabrielli, of Clement VIII's courier and Cardinal Pietro Aldobrandini, Pietro Paolo Martinelli known as Spaventa, and another person called Aurelio, probably a friend of the bookseller. The sequence of events is not very clear: from the depositions it appears that the four had gone to dine at the Osteria della Torretta,[83] and then had gone on to the prostitutes' quarter in Campo Marzio, probably to go to the home of one of their friends, perhaps Domenica herself, to spend the evening in company, as was common practice at the time, as already observed. While they were in the vicinity of Via dei Greci and Via del Babuino, Martinelli, who was walking ahead of the others, met the corporal of the guard, Francesco Malanno, with whom he struck up a conversation (perhaps to try to distract him?), when suddenly a stone was thrown; it is not specified neither towards whom it was aimed, nor for what reason. Malanno ran in the direction of where the noise originated and saw Caravaggio, who claimed that he was at that moment "conversing with Menicuccia." The corporal, thinking it was the artist who had thrown the stones, arrested him, but not before the latter had managed to ask Gabrielli to run and inform his protectors.[84]

From what has been said so far, Menicuccia, as things stand, seems to be the only woman that one could speculate that Caravaggio 'frequented'. The way he expresses himself towards her, calling her by a pet name, suggests that he knew her; the fact that he had stopped to talk with her, probably in the doorway or at a window—the customary way that prostitutes used to approach the clients with whom they had relationships, and to whom they allowed access to their homes, could denote a certain confidence between the two. In fact, it is worth remembering that the curial courtesans of a certain rank were keen on having a select clientele, whom they generally received in their homes, where they mainly practiced their profession, and, indeed, they were very careful not to associate with men of low social status, such as stable boys or servants, who might have put them in a bad light with other, wealthier friends.[85]

Domenica Calvi undoubtedly belonged to this category of courtesans as she frequented high-ranking figures such as the Modenese nobleman Alessandro Morano, secret secretary to Cardinale d'Este, who in 1600 sent two of his servants for her to bring her to his palazzo;[86] Roberto Capizucchi and Domenico Picchi, scions of the city's nobility; or the abbot Paolo Caetani, who used to dine at her home.[87] She was probably what was known at the time as an "honest courtesan", that is a prostitute who knew how to entertain her guests with conversation, dance and music.[88] Her affluent social situation is evident from the purchases of expensive clothes and furnishings,[89] and above all from the house in which she lived, a dwelling "a centro terrae usque ad c[a]elum,"[90] rented for 70 *scudi* a year, the bedroom which "all furnished with Venetian *brocatello* with its baldaquin, valance, cover, cushions and small table with much other linen,"[91] she sold in its entirety on 9 January 1615, for the considerable sum of 300 *scudi*, to Cassiano del Pozzo, perhaps a client, who probably used it to furnish the house he had rented on his arrival in Rome three years earlier in Via della Croce, the same street where Giulio Strozzi lived, and near to Domenica Calvi.[92] Menicuccia must, therefore, have been a well-known courtesan in the Roman aristocratic circles in which Caravaggio also moved, which is why it would not be surprising if the portrait of "a famous courtesan . . . 4 ½ *palmi* high, about 3 ½ wide" owned by Vincenzo Giustiniani was of her.[93]

[fig. 10]
Death of the Virgin,
c. 1605–1606,
Musée du Louvre, Paris

Finally, for the sake of completeness, it is worth mentioning the two other lost portraits of women that Caravaggio is said to have painted. The first is that of Caterina Campana, married in 1601 to the architect and friend of the painter Onorio Longhi, which, according to her *post mortem* inventory drawn up in 1652, was a pendant to another of her husband by Annibale Carracci, although Caterina also owned a portrait of Onorio painted by Caravaggio. Of the painting, which was part of the woman's inheritance bequeathed to her son Martino Longhi the younger, all traces have been lost, while it has been possible to confirm that the portrait of the architect painted by Caravaggio passed into the ownership of the nobleman Paolo Maccarani, who kept it in his house at least until 1664, when Bellori saw it.[94]

The portrait of Marsilia Sicca, on the other hand, was to be found, together with those of Fillide and of the famous courtesan, in Vincenzo Giustiniani's collection, described as "[74] A painting with the portrait of a Lombard matron with a white veil over her head, and her name inscribed [as] Marsilia Sicca painted on a canvas 2½ *palmi* in height and about 2 wide [in the first manner of Michelangelo da Caravaggio it is thought] without a frame."[95]

The possible identification of the woman with a certain "Marsibilia Secco", wife of the notary Giovanni Battista Gennari who had drawn up some deeds for the Aratori[96] for Caravaggio, is due to Lothar Sickel who, on the basis of the reference to Marsilia's Lombard origins and the fact that the painting belonged to the painter's early days, hypothesised that the work had been executed in Lombardy, while acknowledging his ignorance of the reasons behind its arrival in Rome.[97]

It is difficult to establish with certainty if any or which of the women discussed so far lent themselves to being portrayed by the painter, especially since, as Sybille Ebert-Schifferer has pointed out, Caravaggio was able to adapt his study of nature and his ability to reproduce reality to the expressive demands that each of his paintings imposed.[98] You can therefore certainly argue that in the case of the Detroit *Martha and Mary Magdalene* [fig. 6; cat. 11], the *Saint Catherine of Alexandria* in the Museo Nacional Thyssen-Bornemisza [fig. 7; cat. 10] and the *Judith with the Head of Holophernes* in Palazzo Barberini[99] [fig. 8; cat. 12], the artist used the same ethereal, fair-haired young woman, just as the features of another dark-haired woman with regular features and a deep gaze can be recognized in the *Madonna of Loreto* in the church of Sant'Agostino and in the *Madonna dei Palafrenieri* in the Galleria Borghese [fig. 9]; however, in my opinion, one can go no further in identifying with certainty, for example, Fillide Melandroni as the former model, while on the other hand the possibility of believing Passeri's identification of the second with Lena, is worth considering.[100]

Finally, with regard to the rumour that circulated in relation to the altarpiece of the *Death of the Virgin* (Musée du Louvre, Paris, fig. 10), which, according to Mancini, was removed from the altar "because in the person of the Madonna he had portrayed a courtesan," "some filthy whore from the Ortacci whom he loved" (Domenica Calvi?), "a swollen dead woman" "unconscionably lascivious and lacking all decorum"[101], it seems to me that rather than interpreting the Sienese doctor's words literally, these rumours should be considered as such, that is, just rumours spread to justify the removal from the altar of a painting that probably did not meet the canons of decorum required by the Carmelite fathers, representing the Virgin in all her humanity, caught in death in a dishevelled pose, with her arm abandoned on the pillow and her legs uncovered at spectator height.[102]

Francesca Curti

I am infinitely grateful to Belinda Granata, Orietta Verdi and don Sandro Corradini for their invaluable help, for having offered to check on my behalf many of the archival documents cited in this essay and, in the case of Orietta and don Sandro, for having personally carried out the research, finding important information in the notarial protocols and parish registers that they have allowed me to publish. My sincere thanks also go to Filippo Vignato, official of the Archivio di Stato in Rome, who kindly helped me trace the current shelf-marks of the series of the Tribunale Criminale del Governatore.

1   Blastenbrei 1997, pp. 67–79.
2   Storey 2012 (with previous bibliography).
3   For this reason, the figure of Anna Bianchini was not taken into consideration.
4   Corradini 1993, p. 112; Bellini 2009; for a correct reading of the passage concerning the identification of Fillide in the portrait she possessed, see Vodret 2022a, p. 437.
5   Danesi Squarzina 2003, *Inventari I*, pp. 399–400.
6   Ibid.
7   Macioce 2023, p. 185.
8   On Giulio Strozzi, see Cecchi 2019, *ad vocem*; Baroncini, Collarile 2016, pp. 17–23.
9   Bellini 2009; Ebert-Schiffer (2010, pp. 64–65) has carried out a review of the documents published in Bassani, Bellini 1994, proposing a biography of Fillide based exclusively on the archival records that were actually traceable and correctly reported; Vodret 2022a, p. 433.
10   Archivio di Stato di Roma (henceforth ASR), Tribunale criminale del Governatore (henceforth TCG), Costituti, reg. 540 (now 504), cc. 26*v*–30*r*, the document was found by Bassani, Bellini 1994, p. 72; Bellini 2009; Ebert-Schiffer 2010a, p. 65; Vodret 2022a, pp. 433–434. Contrary to Bassani's hypothesis, Bellini 1994, p. 72, the woman was not on her way to Cardinal Vincenzo Giustiniani, nor to his brother the Marchese as claimed by Bellini 2009.
11   Storey 2012, pp. 95–113.
12   Storey 2012, pp. 203–212.
13   Bellini 2009, pp. 229–232; Bassani 2021, pp. 296–299.
14   Corradini 1993, p. 29, Bellini 2009, pp. 229-232; Bassani 2021, p. 301; Vodret 2022a, pp. 434–435.
15   Hibbard 1983, pp. 47, 284–285; Cinotti 1991, pp. 45, 201; Gregori 1994, p. 147; Puglisi 1998, pp. 131, 398, Marini 2001, pp. 452–453.
16   Danesi Squarzina 2001, p. 31.
17   Ebert-Schiffer 2010a, p. 67. On the letter, see Bigazzi 1977, p. 209, no. 85; Sickel 2007, p. 111, no. 1.
18   Vodret 2021a, pp. 176–177.
19   Cecchi 2019, *ad vocem*.
20   Vodret 2022a, p. 438.
21   Papi 2023b, pp. 39–40.
22   Brusoni 1647, p. 281.
23   Volpi, Ruta, Del Gratta 1979–1980.
24   *Acta graduum academicorum* 1987, pp. 84–85, 272–273.
25   See Rossini 2017, pp. 733–760. As evidence of his good relations with the Aldobrandini, as emerges from another letter from Roberto to Giovanni Battista of 22 September 1601, Giulio would have liked to have a book of the poets of the house of Strozzi reprinted with a dedication to Cardinal Aldobrandini, see Bigazzi 1977, p. 213. The absence of the nobleman from Rome for three years, despite having already been appointed protonotary, leads one to believe that he did not actually perform this role, but that it was rather honorary in nature.
26   Cecchi 2019, *ad vocem*.
27   I would like to thank Dr Remigio Pegoraro of the Centro per la Storia dell'Università di Padova, who kindly carried out the research on the manuscripts in the ancient university archive.
28   Baroncini, Collarile 2016, p. 22, n. 54.
29   The residence in Via della Croce is referred to in a contract for a corporation of 1609, see ASR, Trenta Notai Capitolini (henceforth TNC), ufficio 9, vol. 71, cc. 144*r* and 146*v*.
30   Carminati 2018, p. 101. From an initial check carried out by Giuliana Adorni, a former official of the Archivio di Stato in Rome, to whom I am immensely grateful, Strozzi is not even listed among the graduates of the *Studium Urbis*.
31   According to Rossini (2017, p. 177), Giovanni Battista Strozzi, after living in Rome until 1595-1596, returned there for a period in 1607, the year in which Giulio was certainly already in Rome. A *de visu* verification of the letter of 1601, which I have not been able to carry out, would be necessary to ascertain that the year in which it was written is indeed the one indicated, in order to exclude the possibility that the last figure may have been misread, not least because all the other letters of that year appear to have been sent to Florence (Bigazzi 1977, pp. 210–211).
32   Archivio di Stato, Florence *Mediceo del Principato*, vol. 4028, c. 365bis, see Bassani, Bellini 1994, p. 243. In the original Giulio is indicated as Pietro.
33   ASR, TNC, ufficio 19, vol. 107, cc. 165*r*–*v*, 188*r*.
34   Storey 2012, pp. 192.
35   ASR, TNC, ufficio 7, vol. 89, cc. 47*r*–53*r*. Both the furnishings and the garments are described in the woman's inventory, see Corradini 1993, pp. 117, 119.
36   ASR, TNC, ufficio19, vol. 107, c. 779.
37   Corradini 1993, pp. 116-117; Macioce 2023, p. 308. For Lorenzo Ratti's certificate of guarantee, signed on 19 November 1618, see ASR, TNC, ufficio 19, vol. 107.
38   Storey 2006, p. 35. Support for the hypothesis that it was fashionable for some of the courtesans to have themselves portrayed by painters of a certain renown could perhaps be found in the identification of the presumed true profession of a certain Margherita Rena known as l'Orzarola, known to have been portrayed by Ottavio Leoni in a drawing preserved in the Staatliche Museen Kupferstichkabinett in Berlin, and hitherto believed to be a seller of barley, due to the inscription on the verso of the drawing that defined her as such (see Primarosa 2017, pp. 195, 196, 318), but in the parish registers of Santa Maria del Popolo (Bassani 2021, pp. 269, 274) she is listed as a courtesan. The portrait, besides, is very similar to that of Fillide, both in its pose and in the woman's physiognomy and hairstyle.
39   Ebert-Schiffer 2010a, p. 65.
40   Scaglia 1627, p. 169.
41   Macioce 2023, pp. 199–200.
42   Passeri [1772], pp. 347–349.
43   The biographer also reports information that is not correct regarding Pasqualoni's stay, and the peace, which, according to him, reigned after a few years, see Passeri [1772], p. 349.

44 Bassani, Bellini 1994, pp. 66–68 and *passim*.

45 Bassani 2021, pp. 243, 250–252, 256–257, 266, 272, 274, 297, 300, 302, 352 and *passim*.

46 Ibid., p. 208. Riccardo Bassani made amends for this and other insertions, in Bassani 2021, pp. 352–353, although he continues to consider Maddalena Antognetti the Lena of the Pasqualoni affair, as reiterated in his last book dedicated to the prostitute (Bassani 2021). For a more detailed discussion of the reasons why Bassani's hypotheses are not considered valid, see Curti, Verdi 2022.

47 Excluding the episode of the brawl between Fillide and Maddalena's sister, Amabilia, see Bassani 2021, pp. 132–133, 296–300.

48 Marini 2009, pp. 135–144.

49 Soggiu (2012, pp. 251–253), basing himself on Passeri's account, had proposed identifying Lena with Maddalena Gentile, who lived near Vicolo San Biagio. However, as the biographer's account is a literary source written more than sixty years after the events, and taking into consideration, on the other hand, that the information on Lena's home originates in a source directly involved in the events, such as Pasqualoni, the notary's statement is considered more reliable.

50 On palazzo Teofili and the construction of palazzo Pamphilj, see Leone 2008.

51 Cancellieri 1811; Franchi, Sartori 2001, pp. 19–20, 22–23.

52 Archivio Storico del Vicariato di Roma (henceforth AStVR), *Parrocchia di S. Agnese in Agone, Stati delle Anime*, reg. I (1600–1635), cc. nn.: "The hosteria beneath [the palazzo] of Theofilo, Mastro Antonio from Milan, Antonio his nephew/grandson, Giovanni apprentice 3". The exact topographical location of all the workshops was made possible thanks to the discovery of some rental contracts and the comparison with the inventory drawn up on the death of Bernardino Theofili in 1621 (found by Orietta Verdi, whom I thank for allowing me to use it), in which the workshops and their tenants are described, see ASR, *Ospedale del Ss. Salvatore*, b. 493, Arm. VII, deck III, no. 1, cc. 2r–4v. As can be seen from this list (c. 1v), in 1621, the workshop, still leased to Arrigoni, is indicated as "Workshop that makes the corner with the aforementioned [palazzo] detto Pamfili". For the rental contract for use of the premises as an inn, see ASR, Collegio dei Notaio Capitolini (henceforth CNC), vol. 869, cc. 755r–756r.

53 AStVR, *Parrocchia di S. Agnese in Agone, Stati delle Anime*, reg. I (1600–1635), cc. nn.: "dealer [residing] beneath Theofilo [palazzo], Giovanni Battista dealer from Poli, Clementia his wife, three … are all /boys , and one girl 6". For the will, see ASR, TNC, uff. 6, vol. 760, cc. 641r–642v/675r–676v. The position of this shop and the following one, of the haberdasher Parisi, can be deduced from the fact that in the Stati delle Anime they follow on from that of the innkeeper Arrigoni.

54 Cropper, Panofsky-Soergel 1984, p. 486; Rolfi Ožvald 1998, p. 196, no. 43; Cavazzini 2008, p. 138.

55 AStVR, *Parrocchia di S. Agnese in Agone, Stati delle Anime*, reg. I (1600–1635), cc. nn.: "The haberdasher beneath Il Teofilo, Master Giovanni Parisii, madonna Lucretia his wife, and three apprentices 5". On 20 September 1610, the shop was leased to another haberdasher Cesare Cornaro, see ASR, CNC, vol. 212, cc. 333r–v/344r.

56 AStVR, *Parrocchia di S. Agnese in Agone, Stati delle Anime*, reg. I (1600-1635), cc. nn.: "In the house of master Antonio Fugalotto, haberdasher beneath [palazzo] Teofilo in [Piazza] Navona, Master Antonio above-mentioned, Santa Perini his wife, Valerio Perini, Angelo De Magistri servant, three males and one female … 8". In this instance also, the position of the workshop is deduced from the fact that in the Stati delle Anime the shops on the right precede that of Scipione Cornovaglia, which was located "beneath S. Agnese".

57 AStVR, *Parrocchia di S. Agnese in Agone, Stati delle Anime*, reg. I (1600–1635), cc. nn: "In the house of master Dionisio Alberti beneath the [palazzo] Teofilo, master Dionisio mentioned above, madonna Anastasia, his wife 2". For his activity as a "charlatan", see Micheloni 1977, p. 796. In a deed of 2 March 1613 Alberti, referred to as "Dionisus Albertus patavinus, circulator in Urbe", appears to be the lessee of two workshops located "ad manum dexteram ingrendiendo portae palatii", which were rented out to the famous Veronese printer Pietro Discepoli, who lived in Viterbo, as a result of Dionisio's relinquishing the lease, see ASR, CNC, vol. 212, cc. 185r–186v/201r–v.

58 AStVR, *Parrocchia di S. Agnese in Agone, Stati delle Anime*, reg. I (1600–1635), cc. nn: "In the house of master Ottaviano Gabrielle bookseller, Master Ottaviano referred to above, madonna Angelonga, Giovanni Battista Gabrielli, Pietro Amati 4".

59 We owe the discovery of the document to Bassani, Bellini 1994, p. 120, no. 25, who however replaced the correct indication with another that placed the workshop under palazzo Teofili, to corroborate their hypothesis that Lena did not live in the consistory lawyer's building, but was present there as Gabrielli's guest, in order to escape the notary Pasqualoni, see Soggiu 2011, p. 253, no. 89.

60 For the location of Palazzo Bonadies, see Sickel 2010, p. 246, no. 73.

61 ASR, Notai RCA, vol. 1986, c. 388r ff.

62 ASR, Monte di Pietà, *Libri mastri*, vol. 24, cc. 739r–v.

63 ASR, CNC, vol. 212, cc. 302r. Therefore, what is reported in Bassani 1998 *ad vocem* does not correspond to the truth, neither with regard to Gabrielli's presence after 1605 in the area adjacent to the church of San Tommaso in Parione (the Stati delle Anime of which for the years indicated are missing, see Guercio, Langelotti 1990, p. 103), nor with regard to the affiliation of his son in 1618, the bookseller having already passed away by that date, nor, finally, with regard to the year of his death, which the scholar states was 1635.

64 There is a vast bibliography relating to the painting, therefore we refer you to the latest publications with previous bibliography, see Vodret 2021a, pp. 236–239; Zuccari 2022a, p. 348.

65 Macioce 2023, pp. 187–189.

66 Ibid., p. 199.

67 It should be noted that the wife of the haberdasher Fugalotti, who lived in the shop next to Gabrielli's, could possibly be related to the bookseller because she had the same surname as the latter's mother, Perini, see ASR, Notai RCA, vol. 1986, c. 388r ff.

68 Guerrieri Borsoi 2021, pp. 102–123.

69 Husbands 2013, pp. 93–104; 125–140; Terzaghi 2020a, pp. 79–97.

70 Röttgen 2002, pp. 137–138; Andolina 2020, pp. 13-19; Terzaghi 2020a, p. 87.

71   Bricci continued to frequent the home of the Teofili at least un-
     til the age of fifteen, for at that time he "composed the plays of
     Erminia, of Moses, and others, to the great satisfaction of Lor
     Signori', see Guerrieri Borsoi 2021, p. 120.

72   Terzaghi 2020a, p. 93.

73   Mariti 2013, p. 126: "Francesco Morone, a Milanese jeweller,
     of great presence, played the part of Zanni delightfully; and he
     took great pleasure at Carnival time to mock the *maschere* to
     the great enjoyment of the populace."

74   Curti 2011a, p. 192.

75   In the deed of betrothal of 17 June 1591 between Rinaldo
     Corradini and Girolama Benetti, it is stated that the painter
     lived in Pasquino, see ASR, TNC, uff. 6, vol. 24, cc. 406*r*–*v*.
     For the lease of the workshop/studio beneath Tor Mellina by
     Annibale Corradini in 1607, see ASR, TNC, uff. 9, vol. 64, c. 13*v*.
     For his death, see Calenne 2010, p. 204, no. 32, and *Alla ricerca
     di Ghiongrat* 2011, p. 216.

76   Calenne 2010, p. 204, no. 32.

77   Benati 2022, pp. 30–41. I thank Maria Cristina Terzaghi for
     bringing this painting to my attention.

78   ASR, TNC, uff.15, vol. 36, cc. 219*r*–221*v*/244*r*.

79   *In search of Ghiongrat* 2011, p. 215: although 1601 is given as
     the date of the Stato delle Anime, inspection of the register re-
     vealed that the correct year is in fact 1610, thanks to a series of
     cross-references with other data.

80   One of Margaret's sons would die in the grandfather's house in
     1616, see ibid.

81   Oral communication, and suggested in Marini 2009, p. 140.

82   We owe the identification to Bassani (Bassani, Bellini 1994,
     p. 129) which is based on the discovery of the woman's rental
     contract, drawn up in 1602, for a house in "via Paulina", today
     via del Babuino, in the same place, therefore, where Caravaggio
     claims to have stopped to talk to Menicuccia, see Macioce 2023,
     p. 189. For the deed of the lease see below.

83   In fact, Gabrielli claims to have gone to eat at an osteria at Capo
     le Case with his friend Aurelio, and then to have headed towards
     Via del Babuino to visit Giovanna Borgogna, and once there,
     by chance, to have met up with Caravaggio and Gabrielli, see
     Macioce 2023, pp. 187-188.

84   Macioce 2023, p. 189.

85   Storey 2012, pp. 217–220.

86   Bassani, Bellini 1994, p. 130: ASR, TNC, *Costituti*, reg. 526
     (482), cc. 217*v*–219*r*. It is not true that the person who went to
     get Domenica was the servant of Cardinal d'Este, as stated by
     the scholars.

87   Ibid, p. 131: ASR, TNC, *Costituti*, 551 (now 503), cc. 98*r*–99*v*;
     547 (now 499), cc. 114*v*–115*v*. In August 1601, she was caught
     taking a ride in a carriage escorted by some gentlemen, see
     Bassani, Bellini 1994, p. 128: ASR, TNC, *Relazioni dei birri*,
     reg. 6, cc. nn.; *Costituti*, vol. 540 (504); Storey 2012, p. 108.

88   The courtesan states that she can "strum" and that she in-
     tends to take lessons "from Abbatozzio" (ASR, TNC, *Costitu-
     ti*, reg. 551 (now 503), c. 98*v*, possibly a musician, and not the
     abbot Caetani as reported in Bassani 1994, p. 131, n. 21. On the
     honest courtesan, see Storey 2012, p. 66.

89   Storey 2012, p. 177; Bassani, Bellini 1994, p. 130.

90   ASR, TNC, uff. 19, vol. 56, cc. 881*r*, reported in Bassani, Bellini
     1994, p. 129 and Storey 2012, p. 172.

91   ASR, TNC, uff. 19, vol. 96, cc. 87*r*, cited in Bassani, Bellini 1994
     and in Storey 2012, p. 201.

92   Sparti 1992, p. 42.

93   The hypothesis that identifies Domenica Calvi with the
     Giustiniani portrait had already been proposed by Bassani,
     Bellini 1994, p. 133. For the inventory citation, see Danesi
     Squarzina 2003, *Inventari*, I, p. 399.

94   On the whole matter, see Sickel 2007, p. 112.

95   Danesi Squarzina 2003, *Inventari*, I, p. 417.

96   See Macioce 2023, pp. 79–80.

97   Sickel 2009-2010, p. 26, no. 106.

98   Ebert-Schifferer 2010a, p. 71.

99   It has recently been suggested that the same model may also
     have lent her face for the Virgin in the lost Palermo *Nativity*,
     see Cuppone 2023, pp. 23–24.

100 An endless bibliography exists on the possible identities of the
     women portrayed by Caravaggio, for an overview see Bassani,
     Bellini 1994, *passim*; Cerati 2011, pp. 137–142; Pampalone , in
     Caravaggio a Roma 2011, pp. 188–192; Bellini 2021, pp. 199–
     238; Vodret 2021a, pp. 82–87.

101 Maccherini 1997, pp. 76–78; Mancini [c. 1619–1621] 1956–
     1957, II, p. 224

102 Baglione (1642, p. 138) also states that the painting was re-
     fused on the grounds of decorum. On the painting, see Vodret
     2021a, pp. 240–241; Zuccari 2022a, p. 349 (with previous bib-
     liography). The considerations of F. Gage, *Caravaggio. Reflec-
     tions* 2014, pp. 83-104, in part pp. 96-97, are interesting in this
     regard.

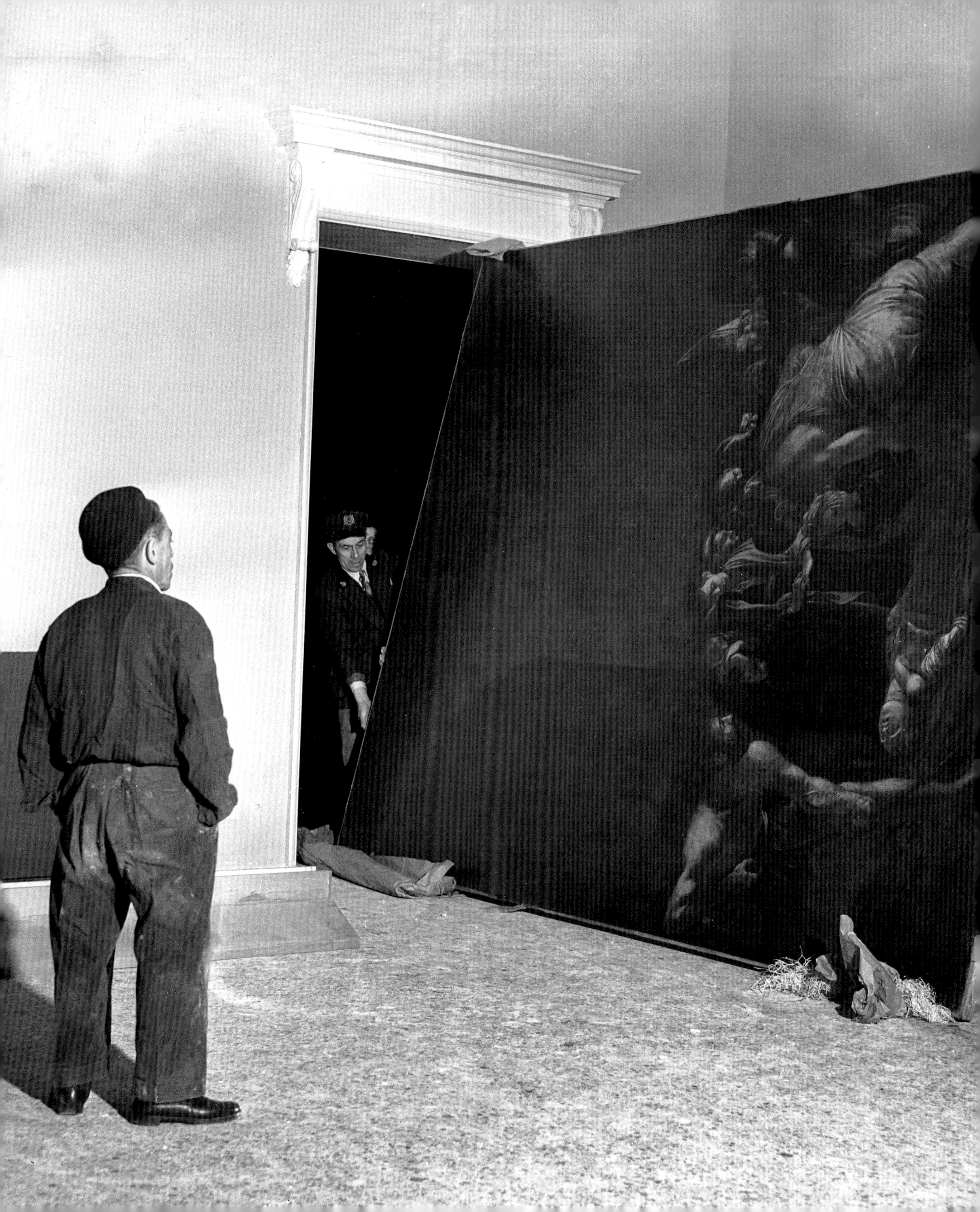

Claudio Strinati

SEVEN MEMORABLE EXHIBITIONS DEDICATED TO CARAVAGGIO

The *Mostra del Caravaggio e dei caravaggeschi* at the Palazzo Reale in Milan (1951), is today credited as a having been some kind of great starting point for the gradual and exciting modern rediscovery of Caravaggio; but in reality, it constituted an up-to-date and critically mature assessment of a whole stream of studies, research and exhibitions that had spanned the entire first half of the twentieth century. The approach that provided the foundations blocks for the magnificent Milanese exhibition reproduced, from a general methodological point of view, that of Hermann Voss's remarkable volume, *Die Malerei des Barock in Rom*, of 1924, the crowning achievement of a type of research that was far in advance for the time, and the validity of which was implicitly reaffirmed in the Milanese exhibition.

Voss, an exceptionally learned and intransigent conservative (he would later be heavily involved with Nazism), had a philosophical approach somewhat tangential to Oswald Spengler's *The Decline of the West* of 1918. Voss divided the book into clear-cut and rigorously organised sections, reinforced by his considerable talent as a connoisseur: Caravaggio and naturalism; Annibale Carracci and the reform of monumental painting; the Roman Baroque in its mature phase; the late Roman Baroque; the Rococo in Rome and the classicist reaction.

An essential part of the section devoted to Caravaggio, the first, is the presence of his Italian and foreign followers—Flemish, German, French.

For Voss *Naturalismus* means "*il naturale*" (the 'real' or 'nature'), in line with seventeenth-century Italian, as used by Baglione and other writers of the time. What exactly was the meaning of this term in the end is not very clear, but Voss confirmed the

[fig.1]
Exhibition installation
at the *Mostra del Caravaggio
e dei caravaggeschi*,
curated by Roberto Longhi
Milan, Palazzo Reale, 1951

traditional reading: painting with the model in scrupulous adherence to the immediate perception of reality. Moreover, it is the contention that Caravaggio himself is said to have declared in his 1603 trial, that a good painter is one who knows how to paint the things of reality well. There are interesting implications to this highly ingenious idea. Because from this it can be deduced that the disciples of a master who paints exclusively from what is 'real', are not disciples in any academic sense of the word because they are in fact disciples of what is itself, 'natural', 'real', which means of nature—not of Caravaggio, but of his model; and indeed it seems that Caravaggio had no pupils in the proper sense of the word.

Thus, in early twentieth-century historiography, which more or less adhered to Voss' theses, an exhibition of Caravaggio *per se* would not have been conceivable, since Caravaggio, by perpetuating in his followers his lesson of the direct approach to nature, would have established, once and for all and with a peremptory break with the past, the only road leading to true art, where 'true' and 'real' are the same thing, and must therefore be expressed in the one and only way, which is the right way.

A conception most certainly pleasing to a haughty conservative like Voss. Caravaggio, in the historical thinking of Voss and his many followers, in the meantime, exists insofar as there are the Caravaggesque painters he created and who nourish his fame and imperishable glory. From then on, 'painting from nature' means painting with Caravaggio's technique and style.

Thus in the 1924 book, Voss, having exhausted the list of certain works by Caravaggio, aligns Carlo Saraceni, Bartolomeo Manfredi, Valentin de Boulogne, Angelo Caroselli, Orazio Gentileschi, Artemisia Gentileschi, Orazio Borgianni, Giovanni Serodine, Giovanni Baglione, Gerard Honthorst, Dirk van Baburen, Wouter Peter Crabeth, Hendrik Terbrugghen, Jan Janssens, Gerard Segers, Lowys (spelled like this) Finson, Theodor Rombouts, Joachim von Sandrart, Simon Vouet, Niccolò (as above) Renieri.

The 1951 exhibition was in perfect alignment with this, but the difficulty of circumscribing the art-historical territory that has Caravaggio as its capital, the Caravaggesque painters as its provinces, and somewhat uncertain borders, already emerged clearly.

In Voss' vision, and that of Longhi almost thirty years later, Caravaggio is unique and inimitable, but he could not stand alone in an exhibition, even if dedicated to him. The Caravaggesque school, from such a historiographical perspective, resembles an orchestra the sole conductor of which is always and only Caravaggio, but the individual musicians are all great instrumentalists worthy of playing under a guide whose authority is undisputed. And they willingly agree to play as he says, and woe betide him who contradicts. Because the great conductor is of necessity an inflexible dictator, without doubt a good one, but not so good when the goal is Art.

Longhi, while broadly in agreement with the critical methodology, to the enhancement of which he himself had contributed so decisively, must have been a little perplexed, aside from those yearnings for primacy which were not, furthermore, solely his own preserve.

Personal facts and institutional factors added up. Coinciding with the middle of the century, Longhi had just launched *Paragone*, and as its director, he assumed Caravaggio-like attitudes, especially in relation to the coeval birth of the journal *Commentari*, organ of the University of Rome. The authors of the articles in *Paragone* had to present themselves as his followers, prior to any other description. It was unthinkable, therefore, to propose an exhibition aimed at a definitive and exhaustive reconstruction of Caravaggio that did not pass through the consecration of the figure of Longhi himself, whose keen achievements could well be compared to the coeval discovery of the oil wells

Claudio Strinati

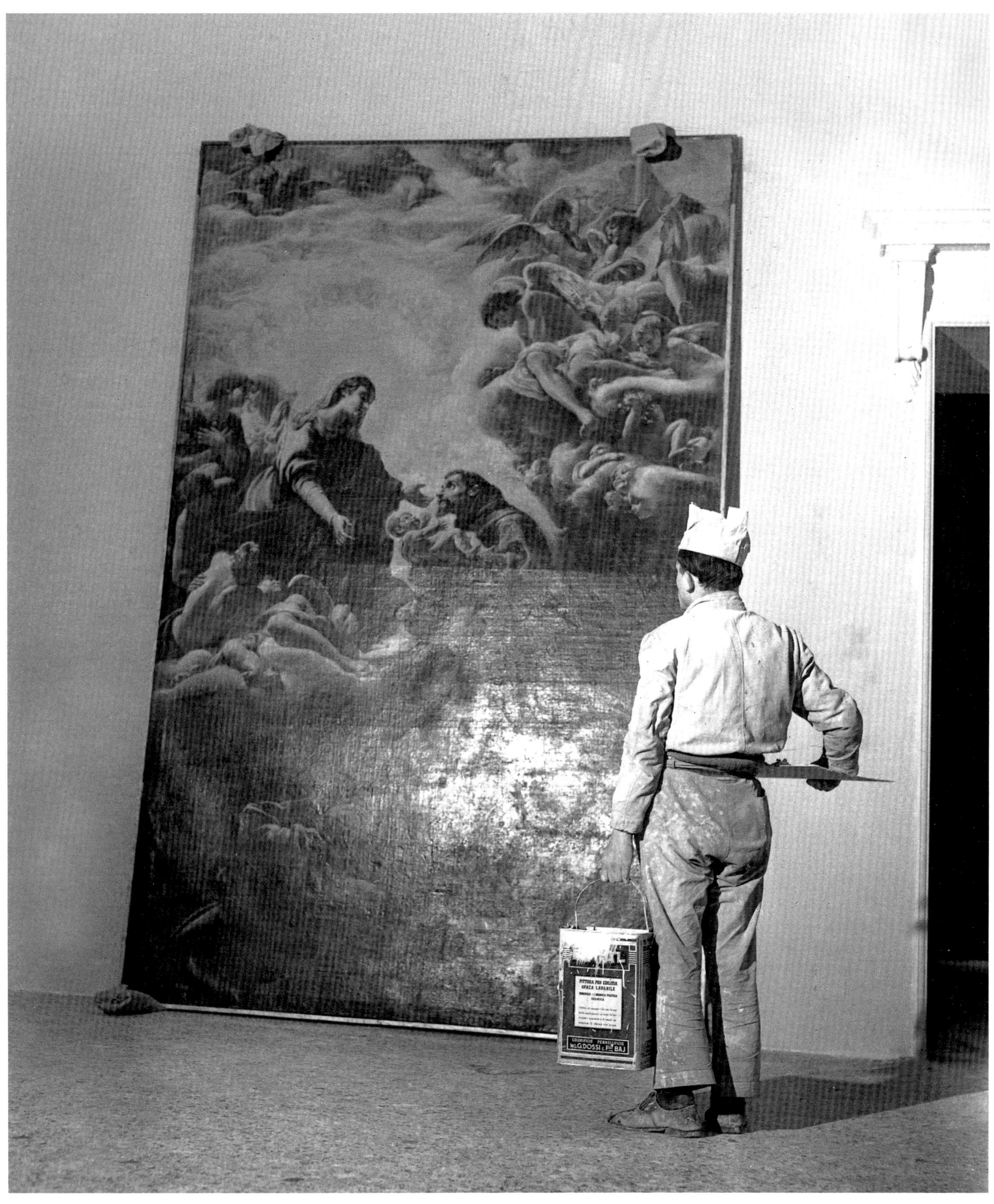

at Cortemaggiore, which turned out to be far less remarkable than expected, but nonetheless a symbol of an Italy endowed with inexhaustible and powerful assets and knowledge. The discovery of the Caravaggesque painters would prove an inexhaustible source, and thus it was. And who should we thank for this latest Italian miracle if not Caravaggio himself, and Longhi his prophet?

In reality, Longhi's more than justified triumphalism requires interpretation, and conceals much. Longhi noted, in conclusion of the formidable introduction to the catalogue published by Sansoni, how the term 'naturalism' had for a long, long time truly been a 'dirty' word: "from Baglione, to Bellori, to Mengs the word itself has been a condemnation that is presumed irrevocable". This was not the case, and Longhi's interpretation lacked philological correctness. But the great scholar's sincere empathy emerged in the conclusions: "I greatly admire the fact that the great Jacob Burckhardt wrote in 1855: '*strictu sensu* modern naturalism begins in the crudest manner with Michelangelo da Caravaggio', that is, that he wrote this in the same year in which Courbet opened the pavilion of his 'Réalisme' at the Exposition Universelle; but I would remind you that *Après-diner à Ornans* was painted in 1849. That is to say, if it has been possible, in the end, to understand Caravaggio and his circle better, this is due to modern painting. It should not be forgotten."

Thus, the 1951 exhibition was transformed from a review into a springboard, and those who had taken the leap from there, have landed seamlessly now in Palazzo Barberini to discover, not without astonishment, that the giant of painting, the master of masters, misunderstood and vilified, idolised and despised, the supreme model of reference in the figurative arts, finally stands alone in an exhibition venue and that the Caravaggio exhibition is truly the Caravaggio exhibition.

From 1951 to the present day, there have been countless and often splendid exhibitions on Caravaggio and his followers (unforgettable, with a catalogue that is still of great relevance today, is the one curated by Richard E. Spear, *Caravaggio and his Followers*, at the Cleveland Museum of Art in 1971), on Caravaggio and his time, on Caravaggio and the Caravaggesque painters of different nationalities, on Caravaggio's 'genius' as a symbol and reflection of an entire epoch, on Caravaggio and Europe, on Caravaggio in relation to the most diverse genres, whether he practiced them or not. And there have been horrendous, fraudulent exhibitions dedicated to Caravaggio in various contexts, in which what were missing were precisely paintings that were by Caravaggio.

Rarely have there been exhibitions on Caravaggio and only Caravaggio; and in a deep sense there is meaning in this. Caravaggio is indeed truly unique and incomparable, but everything about him is shrouded in mystery or at least the seemingly inexplicable. Thus, it has always been thought that the best way to understand him is through what we would today call his 'links'. His style does not seem to have any precedents even though research has extensively identified these, indeed it has identified so many different ones that the most prudent and severe researchers are now calling for the support of concrete objective archival documents that will either encourage or also disprove our hypotheses.

Then there are the existential 'links'. And here documentary research opens up countless hypotheses and deductions. And a staggering amount of clues have emerged that often do not constitute convincing evidence. A similar situation is found with the issue inherent in the iconological and iconographic sphere, as well as in the technical-stylistic one. So that exhibitions dedicated to Caravaggio always seem to be in need of juxtapositions and comparisons, easily found within the Caravaggesque galaxy, which is very diverse but very compact in relation to certain fundamentals.

Claudio Strinati

However, the exhibitions have sharpened the exercise of attribution, both in terms of style and of meaning, confirming how for Caravaggio the precedents may not be very clear, but the followers are almost obvious.

It does not take much to understand whether a painter is Caravaggesque or not. A great deal more to understand who he actually is.

There have been, then, memorable exhibitions which—setting aside the basic misconception of the compulsory label 'Caravaggio and the Caravaggesque painters,' have seriously investigated the core issues. A fine example was *Caravaggio: L'ultimo tempo 1606–1610*, in Naples between 2004 and 2005, with a catalogue by Electa Napoli, edited by Keith Christiansen, Gabriele Finaldi, David Jaffé and Nicola Spinosa in which, through a strict historiographical analysis, only the master's original works were presented, but which also addressed the colossal problem of early copies, replicas, and repeated versions of celebrated prototypes, so relevant to the more general issue of Caravaggism, as was seen immediately afterwards in the interesting and challenging exhibition *Caravaggio: Originale und Kopienim Spiegelder Forschung*, curated by Jürgen Harten and Jean-Hubert Martin under the supervision of Sir Denis Mahon, in Düsseldorf in 2006–2007, the catalogue of which (Hatje Cantz) remains a monument of erudition even if controversial.

In this area of philological fine-tuning in the context of biographical research, and not only, a decisive contribution was made by the exhibition *Caravaggio a Roma: Una vita dal vero*, organised in 2011 by the Archivio di Stato di Roma under the direction of Eugenio Lo Sardo, curated by Michele di Sivo and Orietta Verdi (held immediately after the 2010 exhibition commemorating the fourth centenary of Caravaggio's death at the Scuderie del Quirinale), which gave rise to a new generation of Caravaggio researchers and experts, who in the last fifteen years have literally revolutionised studies, naturally relying on the great repertories and treatises that have accumulated on Caravaggio since the Second World War, among which burns brightly the documentary collection edited—in several editions—by Stefania Macioce.

Meanwhile, exhibitions have been held that have finally focused on Caravaggio's specific characteristics, regardless of followers or predecessors. Among the earliest, one should mention at least the memorable exhibition *La natura morta al tempo di Caravaggio* (catalogue Electa Napoli), held in 1995–1996 in Milan and Rome, for which an array of renowned experts—including Mina Gregori, Luigi Spezzaferro, Alberto Cottino, Elena Fumagalli—carried out a kind of anatomical dissection of the various components of Caravaggio's paintings, identifying a myriad aspects of the so-called naturalism, no longer interpreted in a philosophical or otherwise theoretical key, but specifically technical-expressive.

Technique, of course, is difficult to explain in an exhibition, yet even in this area, there have been critical exhibitions that have made it clear just how indispensable—in the case of Caravaggio—it is to approach the works with precise knowledge regarding the methods of execution and handling of the materials.

A milestone in this regard was the exhibition *Michelangelo Merisi da Caravaggio: Come nascono i capolavori* (Florence and Rome, 1991–1992, Electa catalogue) curated by Mina Gregori, the first perhaps to investigate Caravaggio *iuxta propria principia*, although not free of certain misconceptions that later historiography has duly corrected, but which today puts us in a position to count on a wealth of knowledge (the bibliography in this volume provides exhaustive evidence of this) that has put an end to so many common misconceptions, very harmful where they are still credited, in order to approach the works of such a genius seriously, according to their own nature and principles.

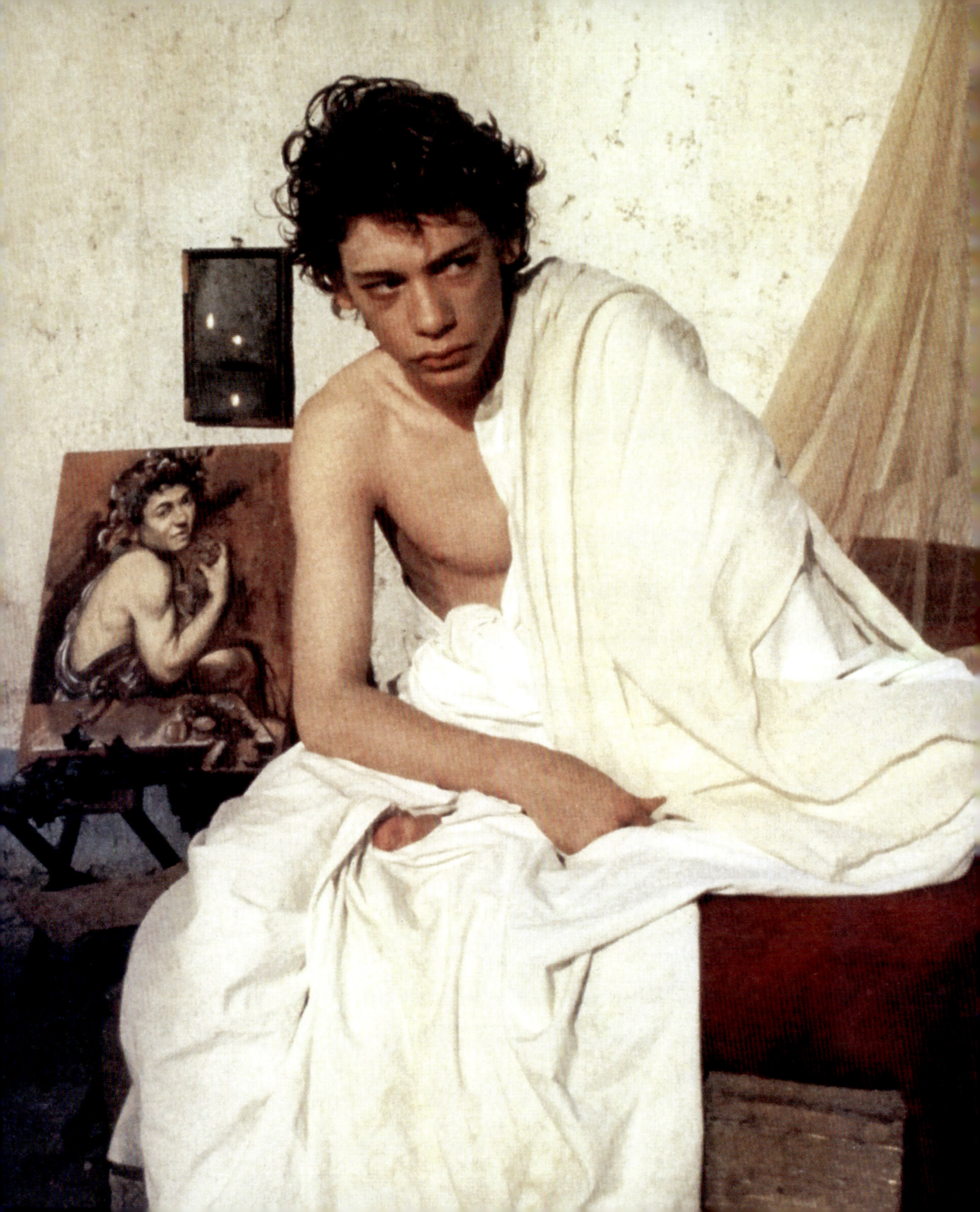

Stefano Causa

1951–2024:
THE AGE
OF CARAVAGGIO

Caravaggio, here is a lesson that never ends. . .[1]
Giovanni Testori

For the past seventy years we have been living the age of Caravaggio. A painter "human and not humanistic,"[2] according to his greatest sponsor, the Piedmontese art historian Roberto Longhi (1890–1970); "true" and "human", as the now more than centenarian Mina Gregori, who has never lost sight of Caravaggio (1571–1610),[3] would have presented him without lexical artifice to an admiring Cristina Terzaghi. If, over a century ago, the focus was on Leonardo da Vinci and his humanist and Renaissance troupe, now, in the century of Galileo and Claudio Monteverdi, the actors of the sacred come together, lit selectively by the spotlight inside dark interiors resembling cleared warehouses. "An intensely theatrical painter, never declamatory", "he ripped apart the balm of sacred subjects as also of academic subjects of mythological origin." That is how an unparalleled devotee of the seventeenth-century cosmos sees Caravaggio.[4]

Because of the repeated in-depth studies and the not always well-advised attributions; because of the recalibration by archival documents as well as the succession of the great number of exhibitions, to finish with this Jubilee exhibition, which has two of the best-equipped art historians in circulation at its helm, it must be admitted that Caravaggio's *œuvre*—some seventy works scattered over twenty-seven locations around the world—is the dominant and compelling subject-matter of studies over the last half-century. Reaching adulthood in the last thirty years of the sixteenth century, but with one foot in the seventeenth, it is Caravaggio who occupies the highest podium.

[fig. 1]
Scene from *Caravaggio*
by Derek Jarman, 1986

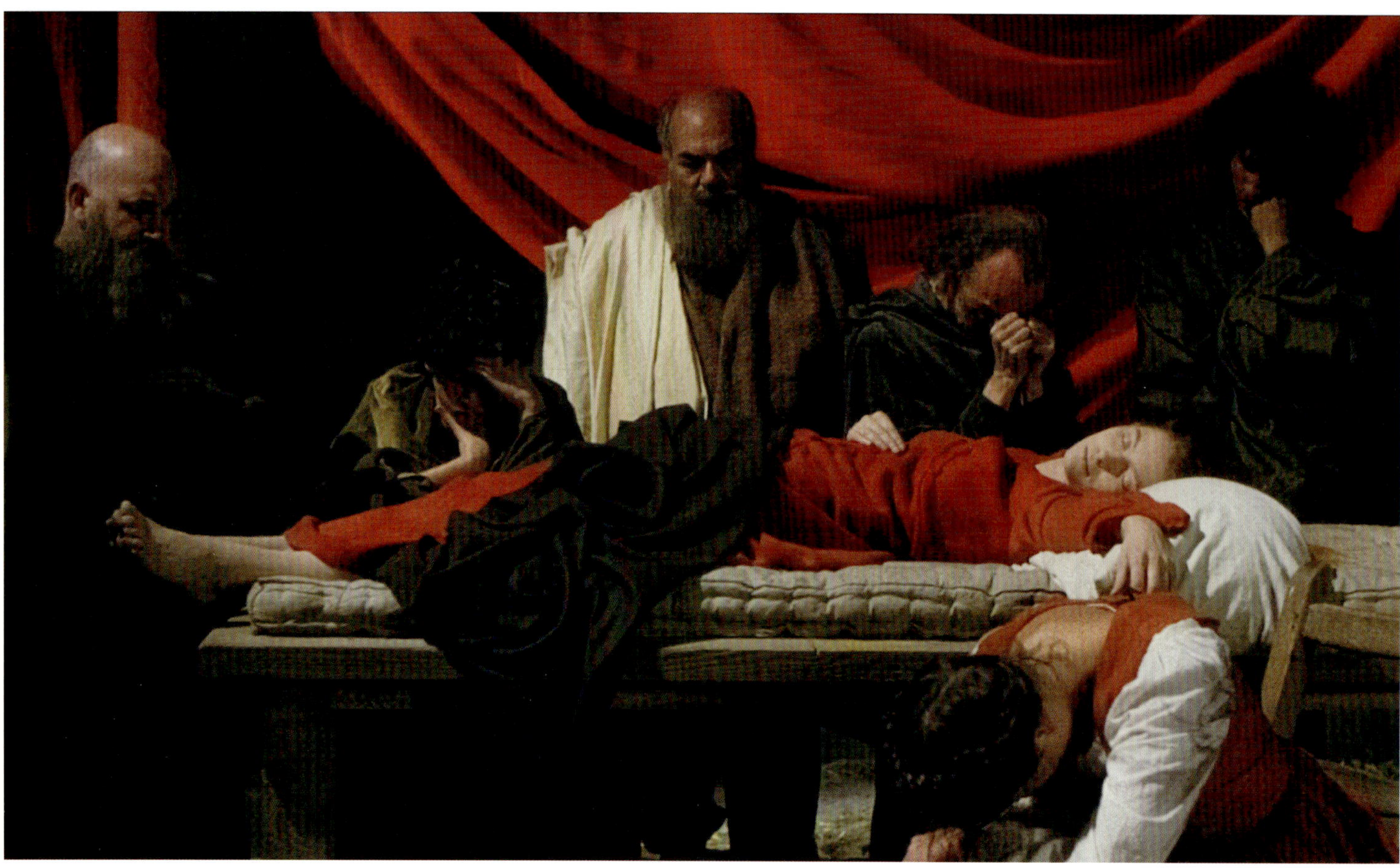

None of the other names in the rosary of 'big' names has been the object of the same degree of enthusiasm that has transformed the Lombard painter, who lost his life on the coast of Lazio in 1610, into an idol placed somewhere between fiction and the comic-strip, attracting a public which, due to its school-day memories, retains an affectionate distance from the network of Italian museums. In the revival of the Caravaggio 'brand', gossip and other biographical fragments (we are dealing here with a textbook cursed artist) will have played their part, but for years we have been watching Caravaggio through the filter of the big screen. Longhi explained this in the 1951 exhibition catalogue: "On film, Caravaggio's images, compared to those of other painters, seem to us to have been shot on real bodies, and not painted ones."[5] An observation that should be placed as a heading to any research on cinema and painting: from Goffredo Alessandrini's *Pittore maledetto* (1941) to Michele Placido's *Ombra di Caravaggio* (2022), via a decisive work, for actual Caravaggio studies, such as the film *Caravaggio* by British director Derek Jarman (1986) [figs. 1-2].

THE TESTING GROUND OF CRITICAL STYLE: THE 'STILCRITICA'

More than other artists, Caravaggio is the ideal (natural) vantage point from which to recount how the art historian's profession has altered over the twentieth century: from pure connoisseur to iconographer, to seeker of documents, to context reconstructor, to

Stefano Causa

investigative scientist. Caravaggio requires both the faculty and the welding together of these skills, as well as constraining unwilling scholars to the upkeep of the tools of their trade. But the demon of naturalism rears its head again when it comes to illustrating the change in the parameters of vision since the first cameras were integrated into smartphones. So many things, too many—and so the Caravaggio 'club' cannot ever be said to be in danger of overcrowding. What remains is the solidity of the two different paths…

"All that I can learn about Caravaggio has been said by Longhi," confessed the director and author Pier Paolo Pasolini, four years after Longhi's death. And from this can be deduced that Caravaggio's success in our country is the sum of Longhi's vision, his literary style and its reception. To confront Caravaggio has meant measuring oneself against the focal points of Longhi's vision, whether to adhere or distance oneself, from his degree thesis at the height of Futurism, to the final edition of the monograph on the painter in 1968 (between the birth of Arte Povera and the Italian echoes of Pop Art). Pursuing Caravaggio presents us with a choice: to adhere to the formal reading of the works or to lay down the lens of the iconologist.

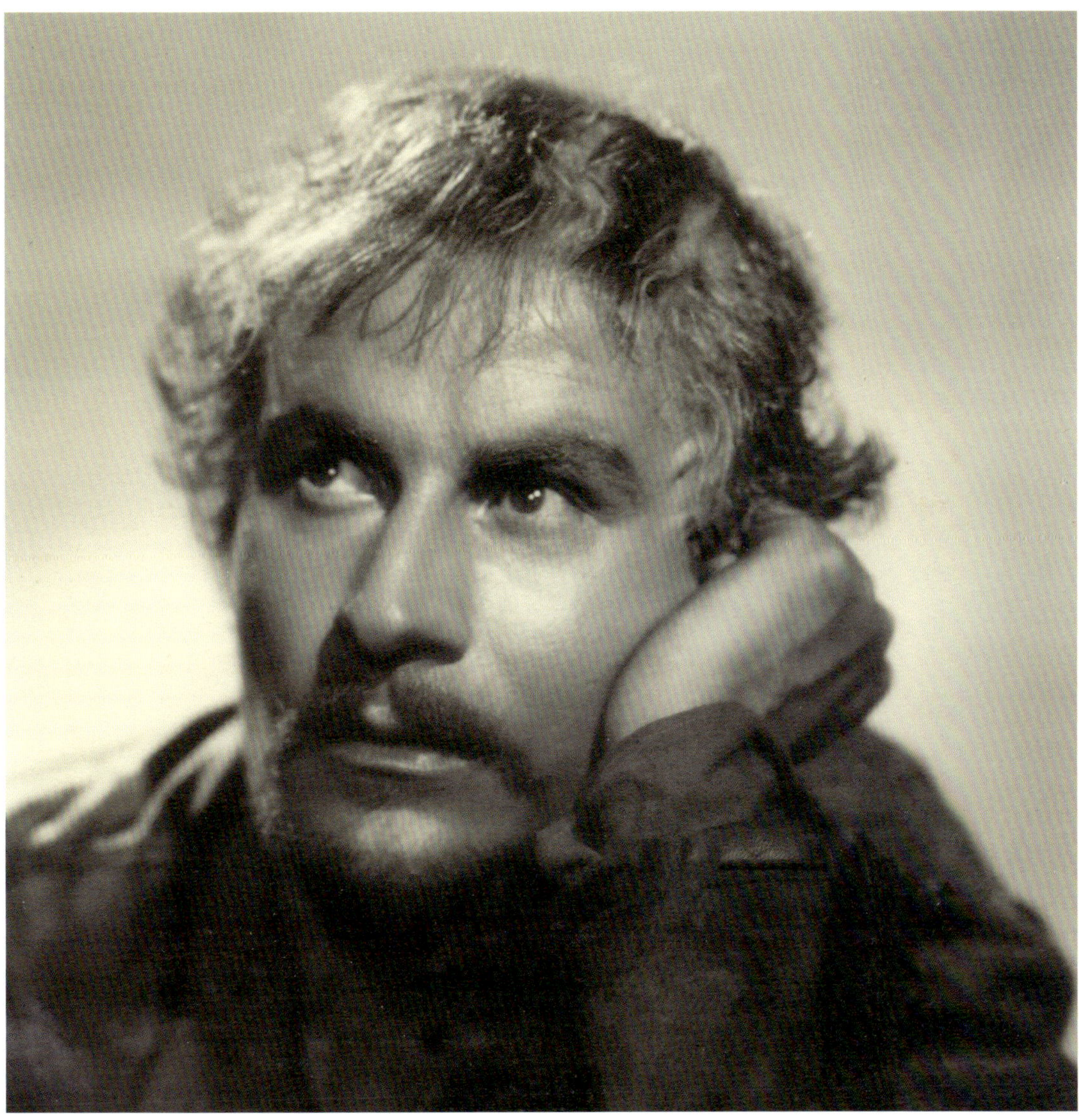

[fig. 3]
Amedeo Nazzari in *Il pittore maledetto* by Goffredo Alessandrini, 1941

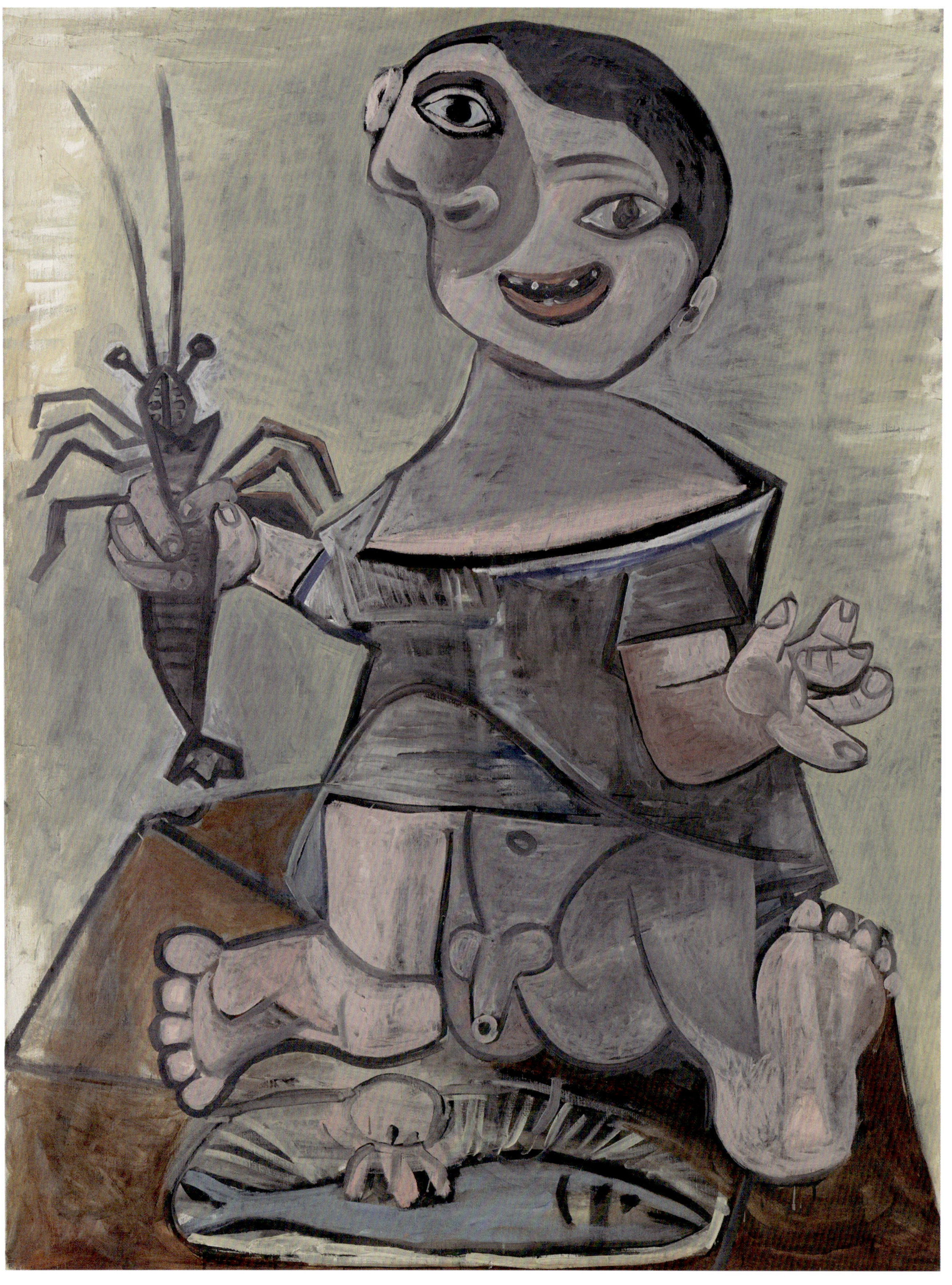

Stefano Causa

But the fact that this is the testing-ground of the critical style—the *"stilcritica"*—, of which Longhi is the highest Italian exponent, can also be deduced from the contributions on still-life painting: one of the most arduous of challenges for the connoisseur, a wall with few footholds up which the most-important members of Longhi's 'workshop' will try ascend.

THE PASSION FOR CARAVAGGIO

Longhi staked all of his cards on Caravaggio, propelling seventeenth-century culture into the preferential lane of painting from reality, beginning with regional areas in artistic ferment (Genoa and, with an element of exaggeration that is still with us, Naples and the Spanish viceroyalty, without counting, in the transition to the Bourbon era, a Caravaggesque fruit that fell into the wrong century, like Traversi). In its version that we term Neo-realism, the passion for Caravaggio dominated the Italy that survived the war. As exclusive as all true passions are, it made no concessions; in 1952, on the occasion of the celebrations for the fifth centenary of his birth, the 'difficulties' of Leonardo belong above all to Longhi's idiosyncratic eye; but Caravaggio has the adherence of everyman.

Two years after the exhibition, at the first Picasso retrospective, again held in Milan (1953), the *Child with Lobster* of 1941 [fig. 4] is nothing less than a cover for The *Boy Bitten by the Lizard* [fig. 13 on p. 41]. But Caravaggio is one of Picasso's best kept secrets.[6]

A LONG OPPRESSION

The emergence of Caravaggio into the limelight in 1951 was the fruit of a long period of oppression. Published at a time when the Fascist regime was in full swing, Longhi's pages on the painter's precursors (1928–1929), and the 'trimmings' of the *Ultimi studi sul Caravaggio e la sua cerchia* of 1943, were but an approach: the latter, a fundamental and in depth mine of an essay, for some represents an apex in Longhi's production.[7] Nor should it be forgotten, descending into the Naples of 1938, that for the Fascist propaganda operation that was the *Exhibition of Neapolitan painting of the 17th-18th-19th centuries* (*Mostra della pittura napoletana dei secoli XVII-XVIII-XIX*,[8] the curtain-raiser was entrusted to Caravaggio, with the *Seven Acts of Mercy* [fig. 2 on p. 63], the *Flagellation* [cat. 21], the Malta *Saint Jerome* [fig. 12 on p. 71] and the *Bacchus* of the Uffizi [fig. 14 on p. 42]). Meanwhile, on the screen, Caravaggio was being enlisted for the genre surrounding the artist's legend. In 1941, Goffredo Alessandrini's *Il pittore maledetto (The Accursed Painter)* in the character of Caravaggio sanctioned the acting skills of an Amedeo Nazzari still only in his early thirties [fig. 3]. An archive photograph shows the director and the set designer Salvo D'Angelo bent over a book with a reproduction of the *Conversion of Saul* from the Cerasi chapel.

MILAN 1951, A WATERSHED EXHIBITION

With the title *Mostra del Caravaggio e dei caravaggeschi* [fig. 5], in the spring of 1951, the Milan exhibition was preparing to welcome visitors; at the same time Luchino Visconti's *Bellissima* and De Sica's *Miracolo a Milano* were being released in the cinemas. It was the opening shot of a renown that would never fail, placing Caravaggio among the few Old Masters known to the general public. Longhi was by now over the age of sixty; the following year he would give the go-ahead, the 'si stampi', to the monograph on Caravaggio (and he would be 78 when, two years before his death, he published a second, expanded edition).[9] If by mid-century there was a great increase in the contributions to the art history journal *Paragone*—which would become a privileged forum for the additions to the corpus of the painter's works—in the catalogue of the Palazzo Reale exhibition of 1951 and, more organically, in the monograph, Longhi's literary style finally unravelled, becoming clearer without losing its standing. No longer was it the time for plays on words, back-flips and daring metaphors. The time had come to break the bread and make oneself understood without misunderstandings: "The public should therefore try to read 'naturally' a painter who has tried to be 'natural', comprehensible; human rather than humanistic; in a word, popular."[10] Here, perhaps, is one of the first instances in which an art-historian calls into play the 'public' and is concerned with the recipient.

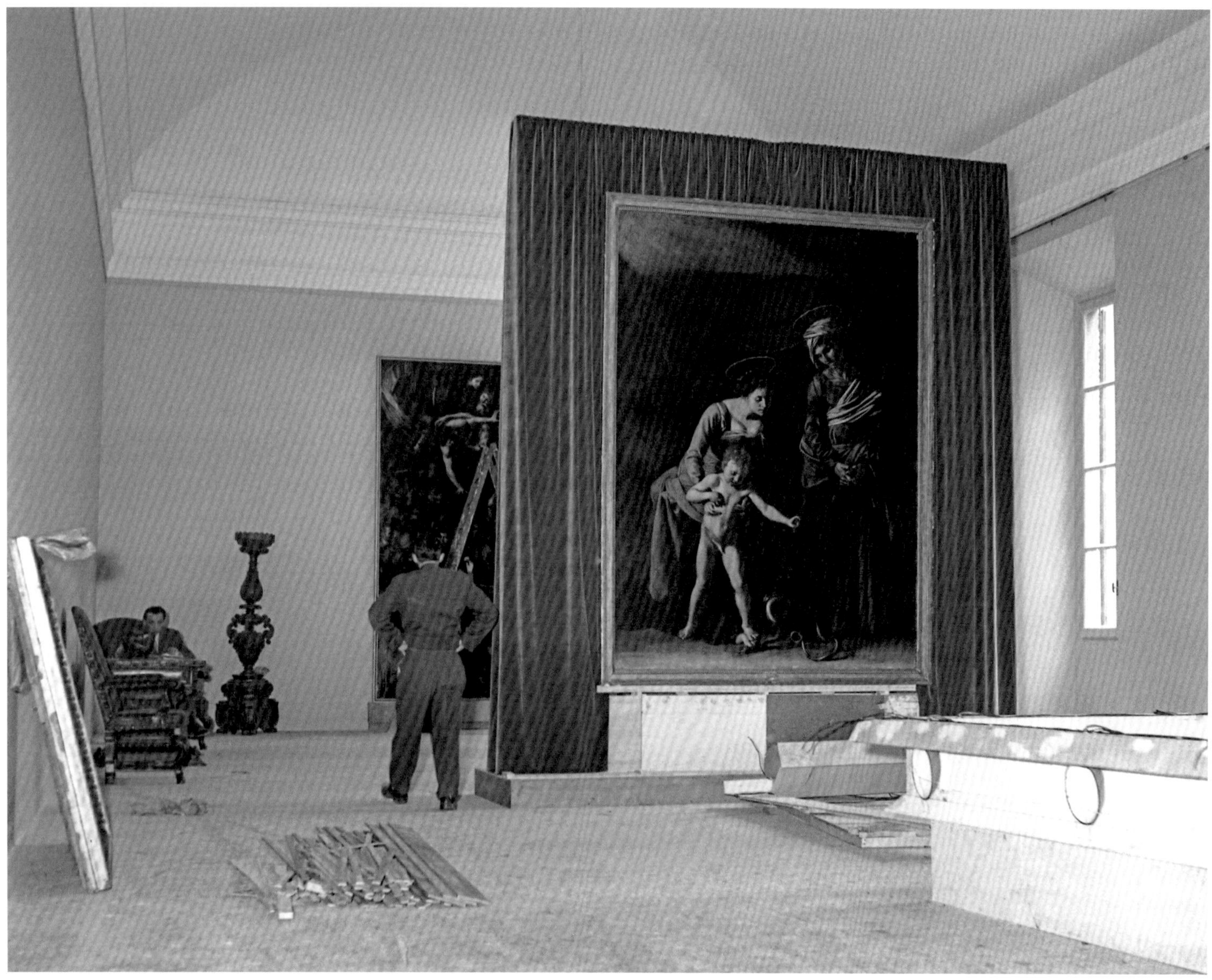

Stefano Causa

The Milanese exploit convinced Longhi of the solidity of forty years of isolated work. The pre-eminence of the painter was also contested by the left. In *La Stampa* in July 1951, the Sicilian writer and critic Elio Vittorini objected that "Caravaggio's realism was born as a reaction to the academicism of the various Italian schools that had come into being, under the strong influence of the works of Raphael . . ., of Michelangelo, and of Titian. But it is not a realism that calls everything into question. Caravaggio does not dare renounce the skilled craftsmanship that academicism had allowed him to gain. Of that academicism, he only rejects the ideal aspirations. Instead, he preserves its skills, its artifice, its thousand cunning technical devices, and it is with a hand gloved in the nuts and bolts of academicism that he strikes within the heart of natural reality."[11]

Meanwhile, Bernard Berenson's pamphlet, *Del Caravaggio, delle sue incongruenze e della sua fama* (1951) had become available; provocative and full of unfamiliar paths, like all misguided books.[12] Having confessed to the difficulty of clarifying the meaning of compositions dominated by the power of a lighting other than that of his beloved Renaissance masters, Berenson casts Caravaggio back among the Venetians, alluding also, bravely for the times, to the painter's homosexuality (the *incongruenze* of the volume's subtitle). Now, if it is not generous to justify these pages as "the fruit of the unpredictable wanderings of an old man's mind"[13], one should also take into account, to hear a different voice, that "the exhibition on Caravaggio was applauded even before its inauguration, and Longhi was able to manipulate it to his own glory and that of his new journal . . . , exploiting the cultural fashion launched by the Italian left. Populist realism favoured the exaltation of Caravaggism as revolutionary 'painting of reality', but it was an interpretation that did not persuade Berenson. He admired Caravaggio's attention to physicality in details and figures, but was disconcerted by the incoherence of certain of his *ensemble* visions; and in his view, Caravaggio was not proposing a revolutionary painting, but merely aspiring to excel, adhering to the lessons of his sixteenth-century predecessors."[14]

MAESTRI DEL COLORE

In the years of the economic boom, the interest of large art publishers is rekindled. In 1966, with Raffaello Causa as their author, two books of the series *Maestri del Colore* (*Masters of Colour*), complete with a spread of full-page images, recounted Caravaggio's chromatic evolution with a fair degree of accuracy for the standards of the time: the light hues of his first works at the end of the sixteenth century, the bold darks at the beginning of the next century, and the abandonment of all the lures of style in his last. His inclusion in the pantheon of the Fratelli Fabbri series lifted the painter out of the field of academic study, and it is from this point that the flirtation began between Caravaggio and the idea of popularisation (did the illustrations to Milo Manara's *La tavolozza e la spada*, in which Caravaggio has the features of Andrea Pazienza, enrich Caravaggio's cause in 2015? Or did a historian such as Simon Shama, who covered Caravaggio on the BBC in 2006, defend it? Or did Placido's film, with Scamarcio as Caravaggio and the director as Cardinal del Monte, attempt to bring the painter to a mainstream audience?).

Only a year after Causa's slim dossiers, the volume in Rizzoli's *Classici dell'Arte* (1967) boasts an introduction by a master such as Renato Guttuso. The title *Antiaccademia*, written as a single word, conveys the idea of the Caravaggio prevailing shortly before the protests of the 'French May'. But it is no less useful in bringing into focus the projects of a painter who, with momentum after the 1951 exhibition, would show a profound understanding of Caravaggio's realism. In that year, Italian television audiences would associate Caravaggio with the face of Gian Maria Volonté in the three-part mini-series directed by Silverio Blasi. Longhi died on 3 June 1970. In the same year, Causa made known the results of the X-radiography of the painting above the altar of the Pio Monte di Misericordia. In studying that monument within a monument with renewed attention, he is one of the few to unravel in it the difficulties of the style of the Master's last paintings: "While taking into account the various cultural and environmental factors, Causa was able to grasp the creative process with greater lucidity, the making of the painting almost *alla prima* (as is indeed Caravaggio's practice)."[15]

CARAVAGGIO ON THE HUNDRED-THOUSAND LIRA NOTES

Anyone who found a 100,000 lire note in their wallet in 1983 would have carried in their pocket the face of Caravaggio drawn by Guglielmo Savini and engraved by Trento Cionini [fig. 6]. Those were the days of Bettino Craxi and Giovanni Goria, Minister of the Treasury. Whoever had changed that banknote into two 50,000 lire notes would have seen Bernini's double-effigy. As for Raphael, he appeared on the 500,000 lire: but are we sure that the ranking should not be corrected today by substituting Caravaggio? Of course, from that decade onwards, it is exhibitions, with their catalogues, that would become the privileged channel for cultural offerings.

Given that titles are the key to the concept of an event, nothing reflects the state of art in the late 1980s more clearly than *L'età di Caravaggio* (*The Age of Caravaggio*) chosen for the Capodimonte exhibition, headed by one who, as did Gregori, rose to the rank of doyenne of Caravaggio studies. Fifteen years after Longhi's death (and thirty-five years after the Milanese exhibition that boasts a title as unequivocal as a gunshot), the model for the title is that for the celebration of the Bourbon age—*Civiltà del '700 a Napoli*, capacious and generic, adopted in the hope of appealing to a more varied audience (1979).

In Naples, in 1985, the museum saw the arrival of Caravaggio's iconic works as well as controversial paintings (above all the *Toothpuller* [fig. 3 a p. 5]), while the list of precursors that Longhi had limited to the Lombard milieu was broadened. It was a crucial exhibition, attacked, at times boorishly, by those on the master's left wing who contested any deviation from Longhi's vision of Caravaggio. But the fruitfulness of the teachings of an authority lies in its questioning. In 1991–1992, Gregori's courage increased twofold with the exhibition *Caravaggio: Come nascono i capolavori*, which made both scholars and the public defer to the evidence that, in the field of Caravaggio studies, the investigations of scientists were an aid to the eye of the connoisseur. Complementing an exhibition that promoted restorers to the role of co-pilots, the bookshelf was enriched with a collection of essays by Ferdinando Bologna (1925–2019). Published in 1992, *L'incredulità del Caravaggio e l'esperienza delle 'cose naturali'* broadened the formalist perspective within which the painter had been cast. The scholar's exceptional display of knowledge of the civilisation of the sixteenth and seventeenth century makes it one of the masterpieces of turn-of-the-century historiography. But it is a fact that the book was nevertheless

Stefano Causa

received with less enthusiasm among art historians: disappointment because of unclear attributions and, perhaps, because of the polemical tone towards an important volume by Maurizio Calvesi, *Le realtà del Caravaggio*, published two years earlier.

BEYOND LONGHI

In her brilliant definition of the *Caravaggio Millenial*, Terzaghi does a good job of conveying the efforts of the last twenty-five years in which—from formal analysis to documentary sources, from scientific investigations to the history of taste—the most varied skills have come together to narrate the painter within the broadest possible opening of the compass, that is to say: no longer only with the tools of Longhi's '*stilcritica*'.[16]

It is enough to consider the volume of work fostered by the curators of this exhibition to confirm the quality and the choral nature of the approach. And it is here that the transition takes place between historians brought up with different rules of engagement. Computer literacy and access to an iconographic material, numerically and qualitatively unthinkable, have altered the physiognomy of the connoisseur, and the meaning of attribution: pre-requisite for the navigation in Caravaggesque waters. The fame of a master is measured by exhibitions in which the standard of their spectacular quality clashes with the difficulty of obtaining loans from museums that do not wish to deprive themselves of the works of one who is, by now, the star of every collection. In the Palazzo Reale exhibition in Milan in 2005, Sgarbi presiding, fourteen originals were seen, including the *Adoration of the Shepherds* from Messina [fig. 5 on p. 88], which a young seventeenth-century scholar linked to a Neapolitan commission, proving—documents in hand—, the connections with the local art-scene, especially with Caracciolo, which others, the present writer included, had already detected in terms of style.[17] But where the Milanese event took on the apparel of a homage to its 1951 precursor, is in the unprecedented solution of disengaging from the exhibition's itinerary an appendix given the title of the "genius of the anonymous artists", reminiscent of Longhi, in which Gianni Papi's unparalleled knowledge of the Caravaggesque field could both be vented and rewarded.[18]

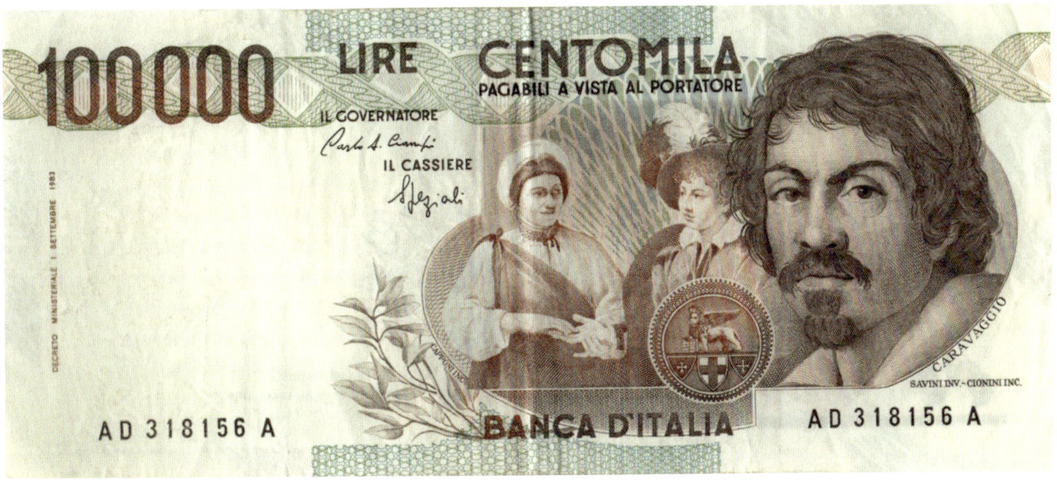

In 2004, the focus on the late works by Caravaggio held at Capodimonte was imprinted in the eyes of many as the last chance to comprehensively embrace one of the fundamental turning points in European culture.[19] Thus, again in Naples, in 2019, the best *Caravaggisti* who had grown up in the 1980s, who were still endowed with what Umberto Eco would call a 'paper-based memory'—*memoria cartacea*,[20] measured themselves against the maestro's finale in the format of an exhibition. Two years later, with the death of Luigi Spezzaferro (2006), seventeenth-century studies lost one of its most comprehensive voices; as well as a vantage point to study the way in which, in the wake of that natural opponent of Longhi who was Giulio Carlo Argan, an approach to Caravaggio matured that complemented the fruits deriving from Longhi's 'workshop'.[21] Rome and Florence: differing cities in which to test Caravaggio. Outside of Italy, but with decisive contacts with the circle of the Biblioteca Hertziana in Rome, Caravaggio is once again the privileged observation point for understanding the progress and openings of the field of art-history.[22]

LATEST NEWS FROM THE EXCAVATIONS

At the end of 2019, we have the eruption of Covid-19, but the Caravaggio project does not come to a stand-still for all that, if we look at the broader surveys that are published.[23] In the midst of the pandemic, between remote lectures and exhibitions that closed a few days after their opening, an *Ecce Homo* [cat. 20] surfaces in Spain, as a good omen, which several scholars under their breath attribute to Caravaggio. A photograph of the painting circulates on WhatsApp, which has long since become a meeting ground for scholars. But it is Terzaghi, who had also intuited the Maestro's hand, who flew to Madrid. And so, arguing the attribution of this impressive trio from the Pérez de Castro Méndez collection, anchoring it to the artist's first Neapolitan sojourn.[24]

Needless to say, the re-emergence of a masterpiece, true or presumed, unleashes a riot of proposals, which are now multiplied by social networks (especially when one intends to challenge the author of the attribution rather than the attribution itself): "Caravaggio is now a national heritage, and is discussed in the same way as the aftermath of the European Football Championship, when everyone becomes a coach."[25] And we speak above all of the late Caravaggio (1606–1610), between Naples, Malta and Sicily.[26]

FAREWELL TO TESTORI (AND LONGHI)

Testori observed: "Caravaggio, here is a lesson that never ends. His way of being direct, of embracing everything, of being ensnared in a flood, and depicting it not remotely, at arm's length, but rather with an absolute and lacerating simplicity."[27] This seems to us the best heading in justification of a new choral work on the Maestro. On the one hand, there are still knots to be untangled, to the point that every effort on Caravaggio presents itself in the manner of a *cantiere,* a work-in progress—as per the title of a recent book.[28] On the other hand, anyone who decides to attempt the ascent, must begin at the beginning, making the journey a new. Authoritative Caravaggio scholars have left us: Spezzaferro, Maurizio Calvesi, Maurizio Marini, Bologna, and even Vincenzo Pacelli.

At the head of them all: Longhi. Now, it is significant that this exhibition falls at the same time as the publication of a re-edition, with a multi-authored commentary, of an anthology of his writings.[29] We must not forget that when it is a matter of adjusting the painting on the wall a little to the left or to the right, what counts at the end of play, is who first nailed the painting to the wall. There is this sense of an unbroken thread, therefore, in the exhibition to the public of the *Portrait of Maffeo Barberini* [cat. 3] from a private collection which, in 1968, in Longhi's *Caravaggio*, peeped out in colour between the *Saint Catherine of Alexandria* [cat. 10] and the *Vocation of Saint Matthew* [fig. 15 on p. 99].

1   Arbasino 2015, p. 470.
2   Longhi [1951] 2024.
3   Causa 2001.
4   Manganelli 2023, pp. 156–157.
5   Longhi [1951] 2024.
6   Causa 2001.
7   Papi, in Longhi [1973] 2024, p. 897.
8   Causa 2013, p. 215.
9   Gregori, Vodret, in *Caravaggio* 2024, pp. 827–829.
10 Longhi [1973] 2024, p. 916.
11 Vittorini [1957] 1999, p. 377.
12 Causa 2001, pp. 58–60.
13 Sewell 2001, p. 38.
14 L. Vertova, in Berenson 1994, p. 7.
15 Causa 2020, pp. 58–59.
16 Terzaghi 2021b.

17 Sorrentino 2024b.
18 Papi 2005.
19 *Caravaggio. L'ultimo tempo* 2004.
20 *Caravaggio Napoli* 2019.
21 Spezzaferro 2010.
22 Schütze 2009; Ebert Schifferer 2009.
23 Vodret 2021a.
24 Terzaghi 2021b, pp. 188–210. But see also Sgarbi 2021.
25 Terzaghi 2021b, p. 196.
26 Less investigated is the sixteenth-century Caravaggio. In 2016, Franco Moro's *Caravaggio sconosciuto* (*The unknown Caravaggio*) tries to open up new scenarios on the master's early period with many unpublished attributions.
27 Arbasino 2015, pp. 470–471.
28 Zuccari 2022a.
29 Longhi [1973] 2024.

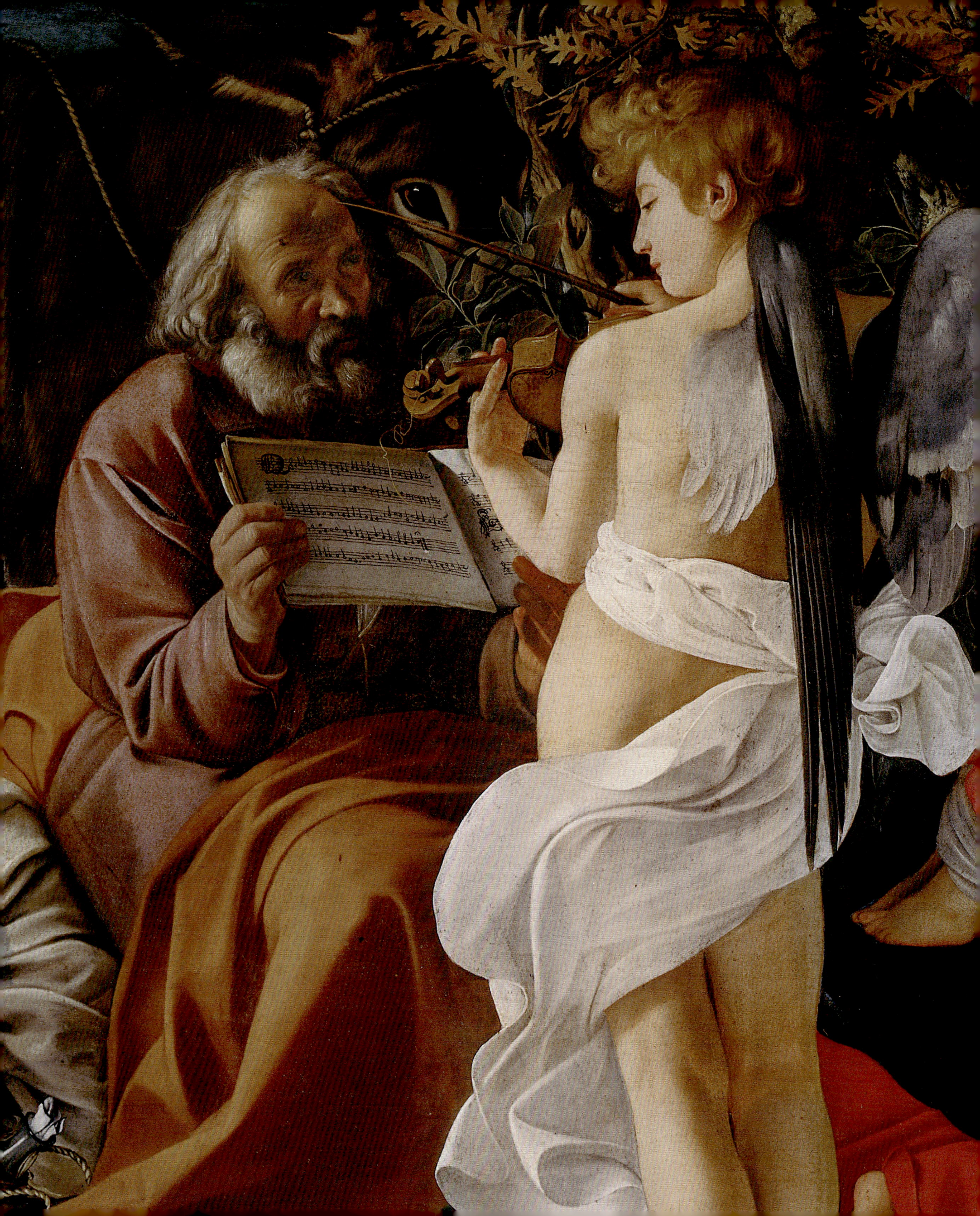

Rossella Vodret

CARAVAGGIO: NOTES ON THE PAINTING TECHNIQUE

The exceptional quality of Caravaggio's style, which enchants and enraptures anyone who approaches his paintings, has long been admired throughout the world; equally extraordinary, however, is his revolutionary way of painting which, in recent years, through the technical investigation of his paintings, has become one of the essential components for a full understanding of the Caravaggio 'phenomenon'.

Technical investigation
The technical investigation of works of art is a methodology born in the nineteenth century, derived from both medical and investigative techniques, based on scientific analyses which, by analogy with medical investigations (such as X-radiography) and the methodologies of forensic investigation (of a chemical-physical kind), provide information that cannot be deduced with the naked eye both in terms of an artist's painting technique, in our case Caravaggio, which is generally as characteristic as handwriting or a signature is for any one of us, as well as on the state of conservation of works of art.

The use of the most advanced technologies makes it possible to explore the 'visible' surface in detail (macrophotography, microphotography, raking light photography), but also to penetrate beneath it (by means of X-rays, infrared and ultraviolet radiation), while chemical-physical analyses allow a study of the pigments (stratigraphy). Through the latter, it is possible to 'see' the layers on which the painter worked, from the ground layers upwards, making it possible to follow all phases of the artist's creative process.

The scientific investigation of paintings, with new information and new elements of evaluation, therefore complements the visual analysis and stylistic study by specialists which remains nevertheless the fundamental element for the knowledge and the correct

[fig. 1]
Rest on the Flight into Egypt, c. 1597, detail, Galleria Doria Pamphilj, Rome. Trust Doria Pamphilj

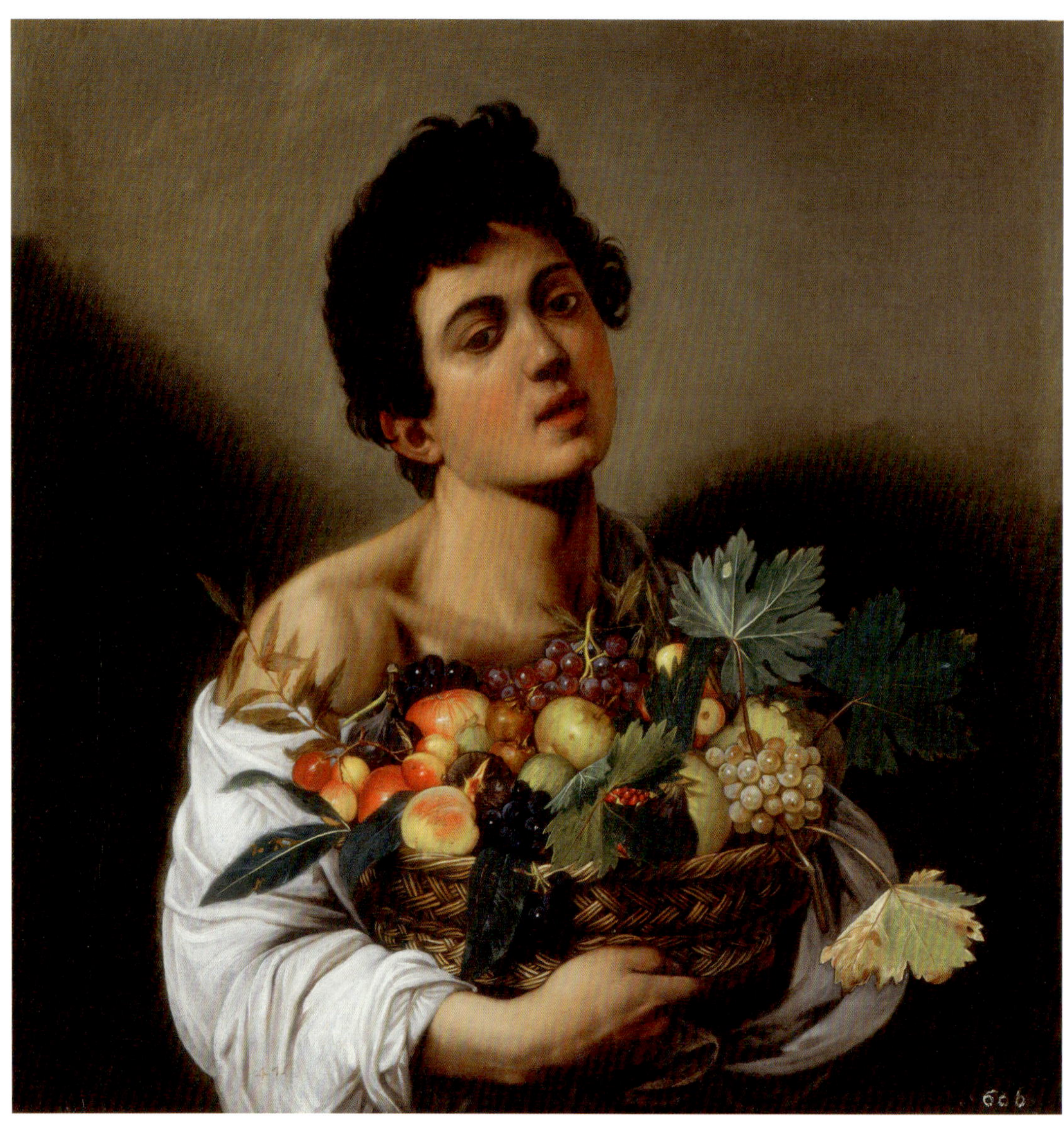

historical-artistic framing of a work of art, which represents the foundation on which we must always base ourselves in order to identify its characteristics. As we shall see, this is a series of precious elements that allow us, in the case of Caravaggio, to better understand the painter's creative process in the execution of his masterpieces.

The scholarship

Four great art historians—Lionello Venturi, Cesare Brandi, Sir Denis Mahon and Giovanni Urbani—were involved in the first radiographic investigations of Caravaggio's work in the Contarelli Chapel in the 1950s. Fundamental studies, which were then taken up, expanded and deepened in the 1980s by other well-known scholars, especially Corrado Maltese, Edoardo Arslan, Mina Gregori and Keith Christiansen, to whom we are obliged for drawing attention to the need to analyse the painter's works from a diagnostic point of view. Mina Gregori, in particular, participated in the 1985 exhibition in New York and Naples and, above all, curated the 1991–1992 exhibition in Florence

Rossella Vodret

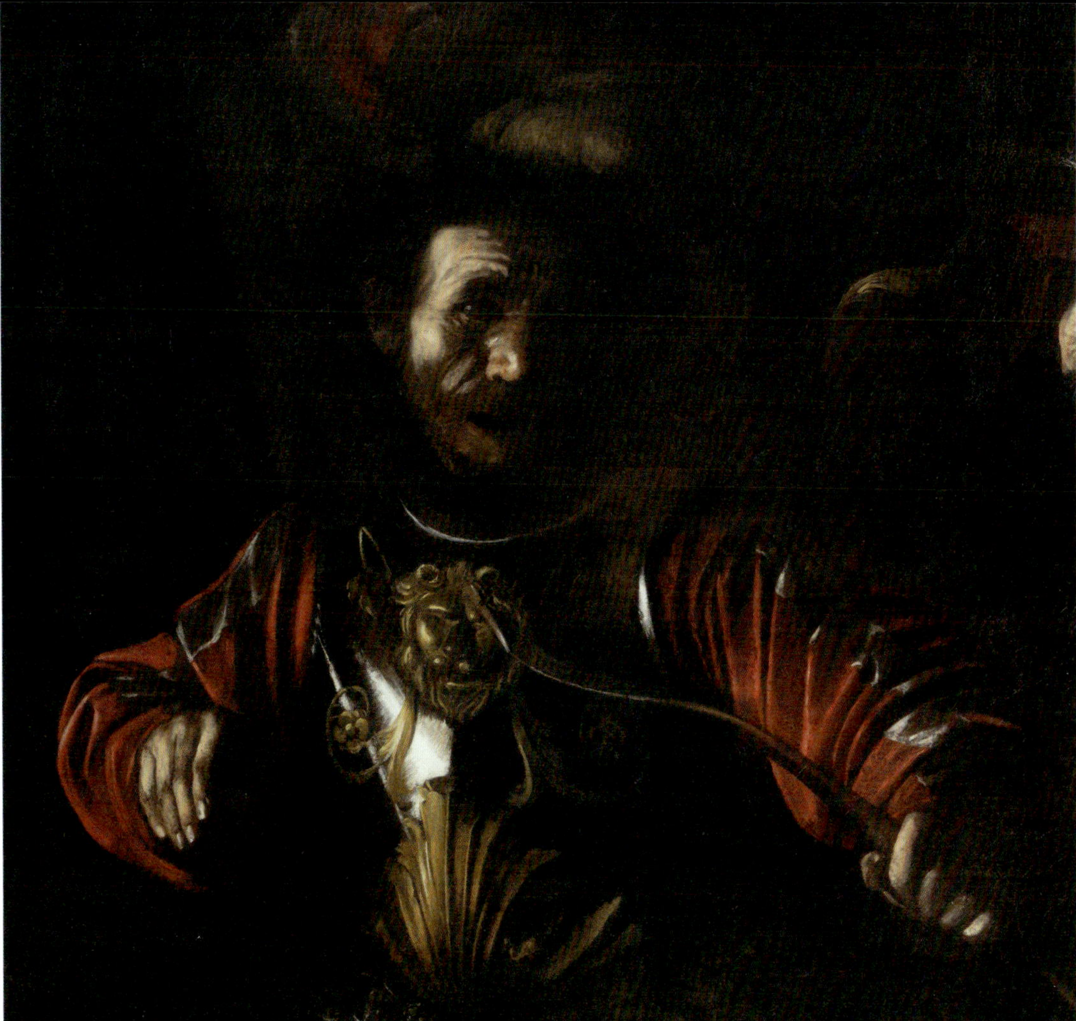

and Rome, two fundamental initiatives that paved the way for studies on Caravaggio's technique in Italy.

From these studies[1] derives the research on Caravaggio's execution technique that has been systematically developed over the last decade, which has essentially taken the form of the scientific diagnostic investigations collected in the two volumes of *Caravaggio. Opere a Roma. Tecnica e stile* of 2016, relating to the twenty-two Roman autograph masterpieces by the great Milanese painter;[2] in the catalogue of the exhibition *Dentro Caravaggio* (Milan, Palazzo Reale, 2017–2018), on the occasion of which new analyses were carried out on a conspicuous part of the twenty-one paintings on display that were lacking in these;[3] and finally, in the monographic volume *Caravaggio 1571–1610*, of 2021.[4] In the latter publication, the art-historical descriptions of the seventy-two paintings by Caravaggio considered to be autograph works were flanked—on the basis of the available documentation—by specific technical-diagnostic notes, drawn up by Claudio Falcucci, which for the first time supplemented and completed, and on a large scale, the interpretation of the painting technique of Caravaggio's works. Thanks to these publications, we now have material on about sixty of Caravaggio's autograph works, of the just over seventy accepted by the greater part of scholarship. A decidedly large sample with which to reliably delineate the essential traits of the development of the great Lombard painter's specific painting technique.

On the basis of the available scientific data, by following the painter through the various stages of execution and thus through the successive 'layers' of which a painting is composed, it is possible to identify certain essential elements that characterise his painting technique over the fourteen years during which Caravaggio's artistic career came to maturity (1596–1610), with an absolutely astonishing evolution as is demonstrated, more effectively than through the use of words, by the comparison between one of his earliest and his last works: the *Boy with a Basket of Fruit*, 1596 (Rome, Galleria Borghese, fig. 2) and the *Martyrdom of Saint Ursula*, 1610 (Collezione Intesa Sanpaolo Gallerie d'Italia, Naples, fig. 3; cat. 24).

THE SUPPORTS

The support mainly employed by Caravaggio is canvas.[5] The only exceptions cited by the sources, of paintings on panel, relate to the two early versions of the two lateral paintings for the Cerasi Chapel in Santa Maria del Popolo, painted on cypress wood, to which we must add the *David with the Head of Goliath* in the Kunsthistorisches Museum in Vienna [fig. 11 on p. 70], on a poplar panel previously used by a Flemish painter.[6] A *unicum* is the work painted in oil on wall depicting *Jove, Neptune and Pluto* [fig. 2 on p. 4] in the *Camerino* of the Casino Boncompagni Ludovisi in Rome.

Recent studies[7] have revealed some interesting data, derived from the analysis of the kinds of the canvas on which the great Lombard artist painted, which may prove useful in dating certain works which are controversial in terms of their date of execution. Although a systematic study of the typology of canvases used by Caravaggio is still in its infancy, we describe below some of the elements that have emerged.

Rome and escape to the Colonna fiefdoms (1596–summer 1606)
The canvases used during the ten 'Roman' years are the most varied: plain-weave canvases, damask-weave and twill[8] canvases, which guaranteed greater stability.

In the early paintings and up to those used in the Contarelli Chapel, the canvases are generally rather closely-woven and of a plain-weave, commonly used in the sixteenth century, usually different from each other, with a density of no less than $8/10 \times 12/13$ threads cm².[9] The only different canvases are those used for *The Fortune Teller* in the Pinacoteca Capitolina (twill weave) [cat. 4], the *Bacchus* [fig. 14 on p. 42] in the Uffizi and the *Rest on the Flight into Egypt* of the Doria Pamphilj Gallery (Flanders, damask-weave linen canvas) [fig. 1; overall fig. 5 on p. 13].[10]

Beginning with the Contarelli canvases (1600) up to the flight from Rome (1606), with rare exceptions, the density of the canvases seems to decrease, and he seems to have preferred the canvases usually referred to as Roman or Lazio canvases ($6/8 \times 9/10$ threads/cm²).[11] In the papal city, there do not seem to have been problems finding canvases, both in terms of size and kind. Even very large paintings, for example for altarpieces, are executed on a single piece of canvas without resorting to seams. For example: the Vatican *Deposition* (before September 1604) [fig. 9 on p. 94], which measures 300×203 cm, is painted on a single piece of plain-weave canvas, while the *Madonna dei Palafrenieri* (1605–1606) [fig. 9 on p. 133], also very large, 292×211 cm, is also executed on a single piece of canvas, but one which has a twill weave.[12]

Rossella Vodret

Thus, the current state of investigations seems to indicate that the canvases used by Caravaggio in Rome, have different characteristics not only in terms of the type of weave, but also in terms of the number of threads in the warp and weft.

The only exceptions are four pairs of works that appear to have been painted on plain-weave canvas, with identical warp and weft characteristics, as if they were painted on canvases from the same bolt. In three cases, the two works in question were painted at the same time or very close together chronologically. These are the two lateral paintings in the Contarelli Chapel (with canvases of 8×8 threads/cm²),[13] the two in the Cerasi Chapel, datable to 1604–1605 (with canvases of 11×7 threads/cm²)[14] and two of the canvases painted at the same time for the Mattei family in 1602[15]: the *Saint John the Baptist* in the Capitoline Museums [fig. 3 on p. 105], and the *Taking of Christ* in Dublin [cat. 14] (in both cases 9×8 threads/cm²).

The fourth case, which is still being studied, relates to *The Musicians* of the Metropolitan Museum (92×118.5 cm) and the *Lute Player* in the Hermitage (94×119 cm) [fig. 11 on p. 38], of very similar measurements, so much so as to suggest that they are pendants, painted on two canvases, with the same thread count of 7×7 threads/cm². Taking into account the measurements, and the prevalent date proposed for both (1597), one would imagine that, as for the works cited above, the two paintings were painted very close together in time, using canvas from the same 'piece' or bolt of linen. One could hypothesise that they were painted when Caravaggio was hosted by Prospero Orsi, as Celio writes in relation to the *Lute Player*[16] (late 1596–early 1597), or at the beginning of his sojourn in Del Monte's household (before July 1597).

To these can be added, surprisingly, the *David with the Head of Goliath* in the Galleria Borghese (so far dated mainly to 1609, fig. 4; cat. 19)[17] and the Brera *Supper at Emmaus* in (datable to 1606; fig. 5; cat. 17), both painted on two canvases with identical characteristics: plain-weave canvas, with a very open weave of 6×6 threads per cm².[18] The identical nature of the weave suggests that the two works [figs. 3 and 4] were probably painted very close together, probably during Caravaggio's flight to the Colonna fiefs (summer 1606).[19]

[fig. 4]
David with the Head of Goliath, c. 1606 / 1609, Galleria Borghese, Rome [cat. 17]

[fig. 5]
Supper at Emmaus, 1606, detail, Pinacoteca di Brera, Milan [cat. 14]

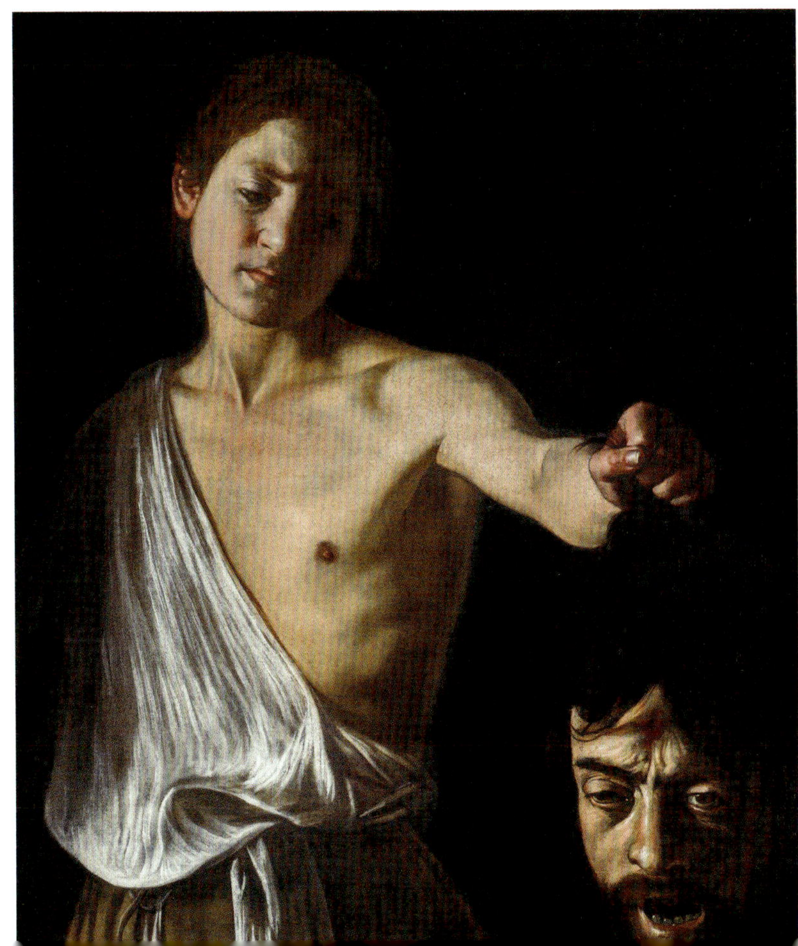

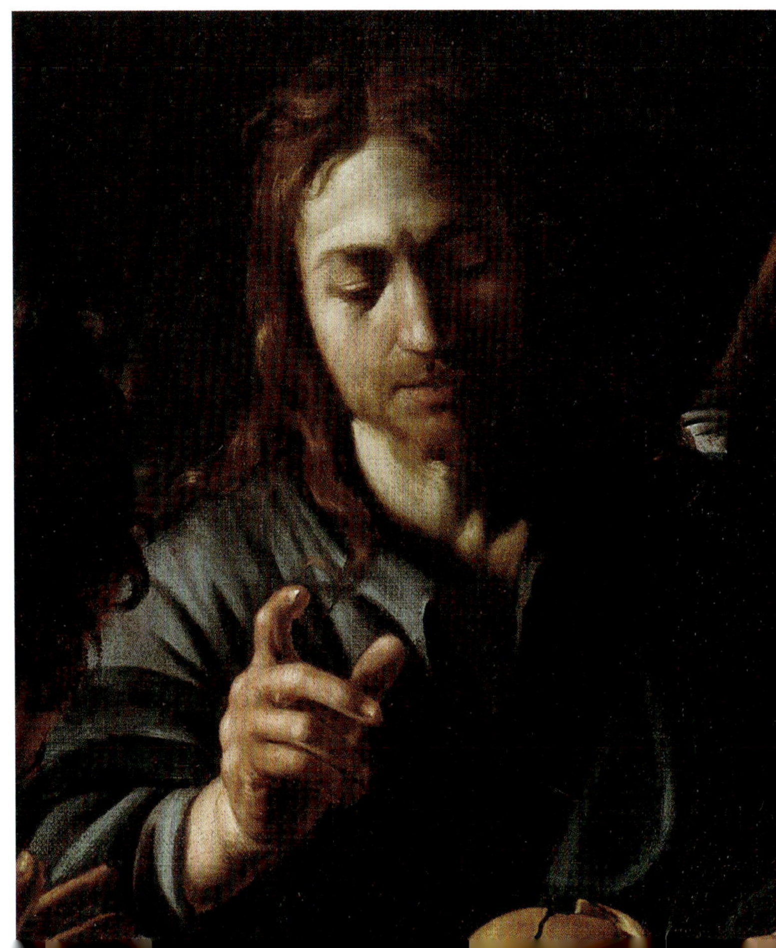

Naples, first sojourn (late September/early October 1606–June 1607)
The canvases seem to differ profoundly from those employed in Rome. In particular, it has emerged that the works painted during this period are all on canvases of a reduced width with a closely woven twill-weave, as if neither wide canvases nor plain-weave canvas were available in the capital of the Viceroyalty. The only support other than twill weave is used for the *Crucifixion of Saint Andrew* (first half 1607), now in Cleveland [fig. 9 on p. 68], painted on a tightly woven damask-weave canvas.

These data suggest that canvases of considerable density were available in Naples but with a limitation on size, as is suggested by the need to sew several canvases together for the larger size. The maximum width of the cloth used is only 122 centimetres for the twill-weave canvas (the width of one of the two pieces of canvas sewn together in the *Seven Acts of Mercy,* fig. 2 on p. 63), and 153 centimetres for the damask-weave (width of the *Crucifixion of Saint Andrew,* painted on a single piece of canvas).[20]

In the *Seven Acts of Mercy*, of 1606 (388.5 × 255.5 cm), Pio Monte di Misericordia, the support consists of three pieces of twill-weave canvas sewn vertically;[21] the *Flagellation,* of 1607 (286 × 213 cm) [cat. 21], Capodimonte, is executed on two pieces of canvas, again twill-weave, joined vertically near the centre.[22]

From this perspective, the analysis of the large canvas of the *Madonna of the Rosary,* datable to 1606 (364.5 × 249.5 cm; Vienna, Kunsthistorisches Museum; fig. 10 on p. 69), is very interesting, as it is made up of three vertical pieces of canvas, also twill-weave, sewn together (like the *Seven Acts of Mercy*).[23] An element that seems to confirm the dating of the large altarpiece to the early Neapolitan period and not, as has been proposed by various scholars on stylistic and technical grounds, to Caravaggio's years in Rome,[24] where he could easily have procured large canvases without being forced to sew together three pieces of canvas.

Malta (June/July 1607–October 1608)
Technical data relating to the supports of the Maltese works are very scarce. In any case, the sojourn in Malta seems to lead to other choices in the selection of the cloth, with a return to the plain-weave canvas, which he would also use in Sicily and during his last sojourn in Naples. The maximum width of the canvases used seems to drop to around one metre, all of a plain-weave, as if neither wider pieces nor canvases with a twill-weave were available on the local market.[25] For the so-called *Martelli Portrait* in Palazzo Pitti in Florence (c. 1608), even though small in size (118.7 × 95.7 cm), it proved necessary to join two together vertically small plain-weave canvases.[26]

Sicily (October 1608–October/November 1609)
Large-size canvases do not seem to have been available here either. The three works today in Sicily, the *Burial of Saint Lucy* [fig. 9 on p. 19], from the end of 1608 (408 × 300 cm), the *Raising of Lazarus* [fig. 11 on p. 23] from the first half of 1609 (380 × 275 cm),[27] and the *Adoration of the Shepherds* [fig. 5 on p. 88] in Messina (314 × 211 cm),[28] probably painted in the summer of 1609, all of considerable size, are not painted on a single large canvas, as were the works in Rome, but all three are painted on several canvases, each about 80-90 centimetres wide, sewn together vertically.[29]

In this regard, it is interesting to note that this is not the case for the *Nativity* in Palermo (268 × 197 cm), which was instead painted on a single large canvas,[30]as were all the Roman works. An element which, together with the stylistic characteristics, constitutes further

Rossella Vodret

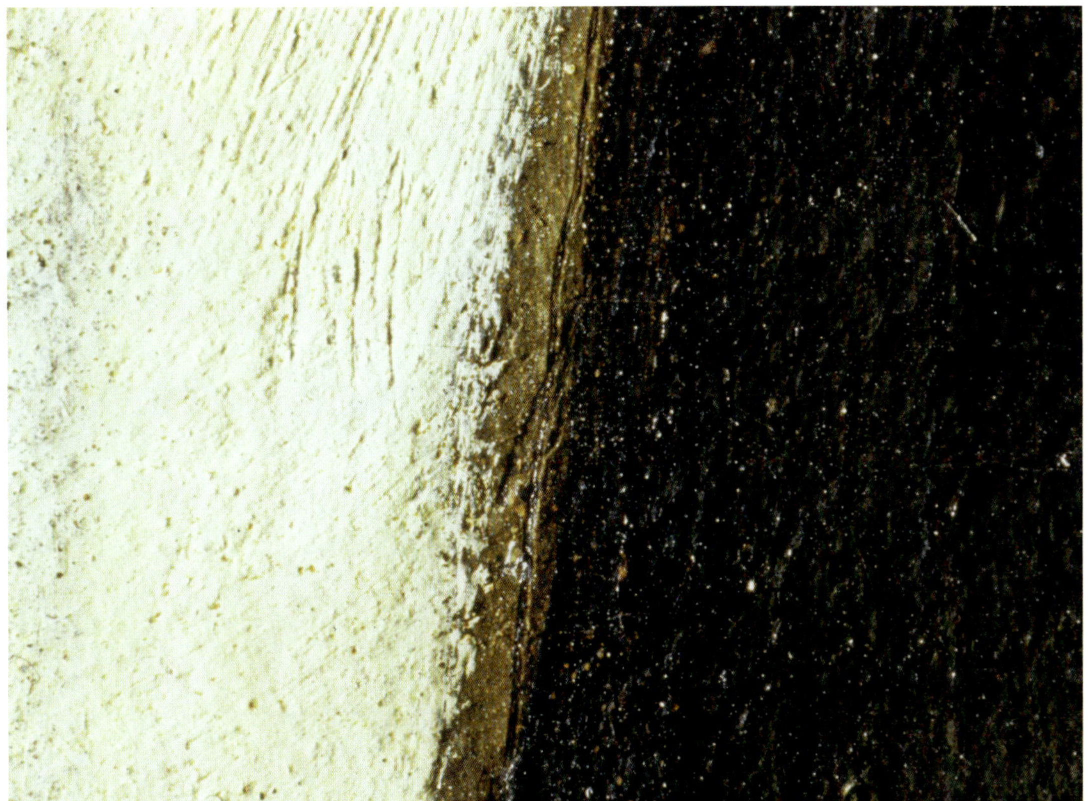

confirmation that the *Nativity* is to be identified with the famous large painting commissioned from Caravaggio in Rome by Fabio de Nutis on 5 April 1600, paid for on 5 November of the same year, and then sent to Sicily. It is therefore not to be dated to Caravaggio's Sicilian period, as was thought, but at the time of his Roman period.[31]

Naples, second sojourn (autumn 1609–June/July 1610)
From the available data, it seems that plain-weave canvases have returned into use, but not in large-size. For the not so large Borghese *Saint John*, in fact, which measures 159 × 124 cm, sent by Diodato Gentile from Naples to Scipione Borghese,[32] two canvases of about 80 centimetres each were sewn together, joined horizontally at the height of the belly of the painted figure.[33]

In the case of the *Martyrdom of Saint Ursula* [cat. 24] on the other hand, painted for the Genoese Marcantonio Doria, a rather large work (156 × 180 cm), only one single piece of canvas was used. It may be, given the importance of the patron, that the canvas came directly from Genoa, at that time a flourishing market in the production of textiles.

THE GROUND

The choice of the type and colour of the ground applied to the support before proceeding to the execution of a painting is of fundamental importance for every painter, especially for the final appearance that it will determine in the work (warm or cold tone, smooth or

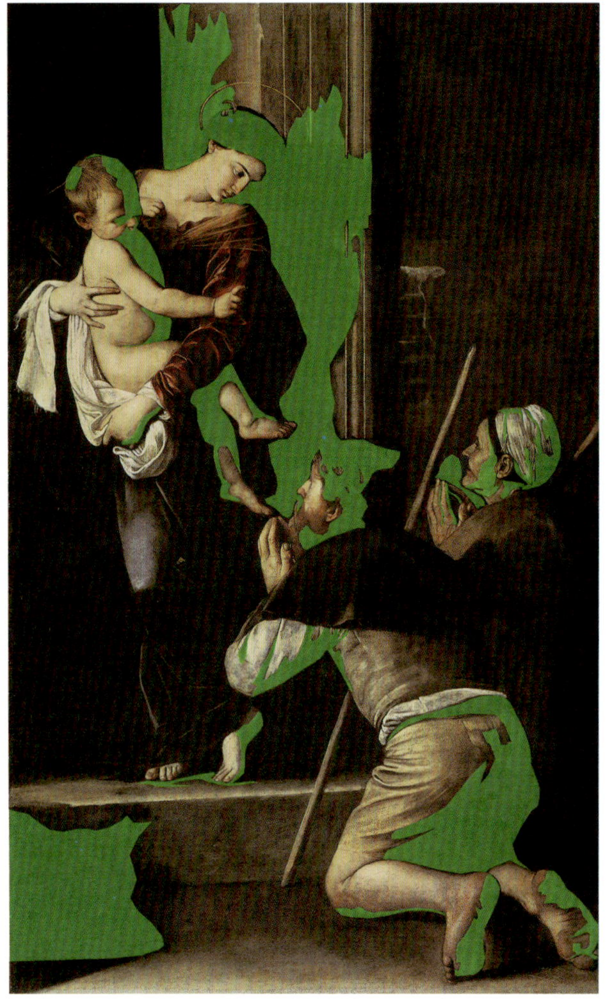

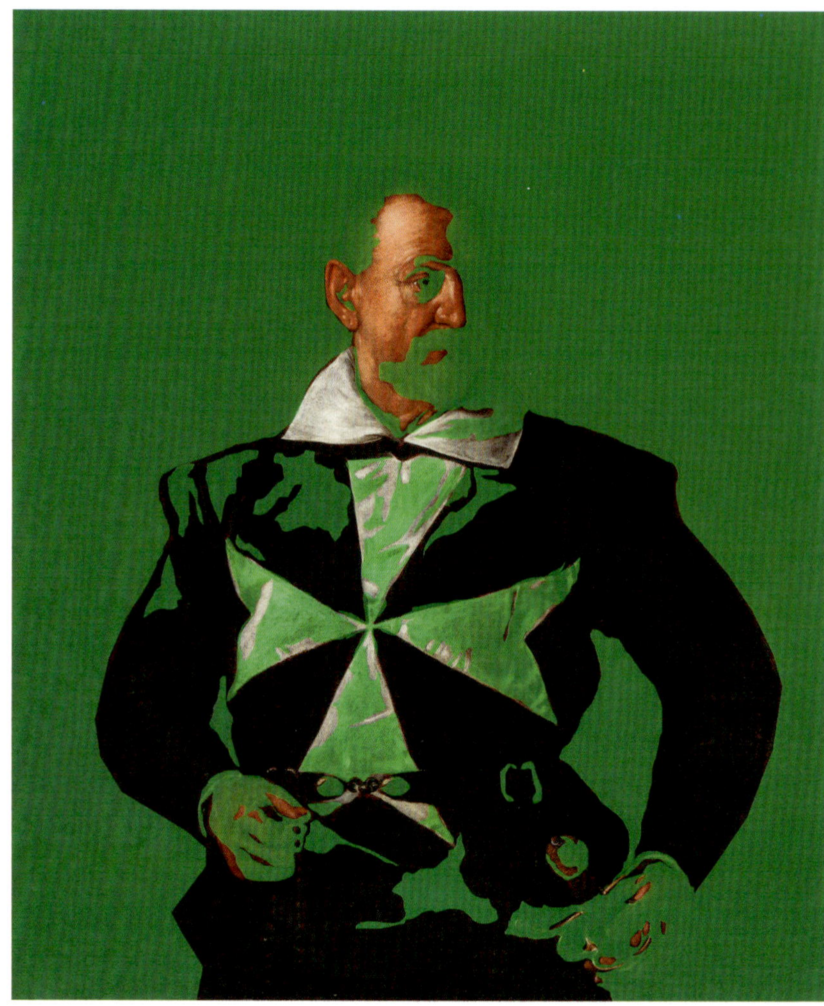

rough paint surface).[34] For Caravaggio, the role of the ground layer plays an even more important role because of the, unscrupulous,—to say the least—use he made of it throughout his painting career, leaving it largely exposed in dark backgrounds, in shadows and in outlines ("profili a risparmio") [fig. 6].

Already in his early works, the tonality of ground is left visible between adjoining paint applications, a starting point for what would become a recurring characteristic in Caravaggio's paintings: the outlines with exposed ground. According to this practice, Caravaggio avoids any overlap between adjacent areas of paint, juxtaposing the paint without the applications touching one another, thus leaving the ground visible as a contour. This technique avoids the necessity of waiting for the paint already applied to dry completely before completing the work. A technical expedient that results in a considerable saving of time.

According to Claudio Falcucci, who has made an in-depth study of the ground layers of Caravaggio's paintings, the painter took the technique of transforming the ground into a true final paint layer to the extreme, avoiding the application of paint layers on top of it, where the colour of the latter corresponded to that of the ground. A practice that was already noticed in 1672 by the biographer Giovan Pietro Bellori who, in relation to the *Beheading of Saint John the Baptist* [fig. 8 on p. 18] in Malta, wrote: "In this work

Rossella Vodret

Caravaggio used all the power of his brush, working at it with such intensity that he let the priming of the canvas show through the half-tones."[35]

It is precisely from this role of the ground that we must start in order to understand the variety of colour in the ground layers with which the Lombard painter prepared his canvases, which to date have escaped any attempts at schematic or logical classification. Even the hypothesis of a distinction between the use of light-coloured grounds in early paintings and dark-coloured ones in later works, is not confirmed in systematic research. If it is true that the use of light-coloured grounds was indeed abandoned before the turn of the century—with the exception of the *Conversion of Saint Paul* [cat. 13] now in the Odescalchi collection[36]—dark grounds of various hues were already widely used by Caravaggio concurrently with light grounds. An example of this are the dark grounds that appear in the New York *Musicians*, the Hermitage *Lute Player* and the two versions of the *Boy Bitten by a Lizard* [fig. 13 on p. 40] in London and Florence (all four dated 1597), painted in the same years as the two early works in the Galleria Borghese (*Boy with a Basket of Fruit* [fig. 2] and the *Sick Bacchus* [cat. 1], painted between 1596 and 1597), which, as others in this period, were painted on a light ground.

The hypothesis of the chronological precedence of light grounds over dark ones is also contradicted by *The Fortune Teller* [cat. 4] in the Pinacoteca Capitolina (c. 1596–1597),[37] painted on a canvas previously used for a *Madonna and Child*, also recently attributed to Caravaggio.[38] From the stratigraphic analysis carried out on the painting it clearly emerged that the *Madonna and Child* beneath *The Fortune Teller* was painted on a dark-brown ground; the composition was then entirely covered with a light-grey ground in order to then paint the overlying *Fortune Teller*.

[fig. 9]
Rest on the Flight into Egypt, c. 1597, Galleria Doria Pamphilj. Trust Doria Pamphilj, Rome, IR reflectography, underdrawing detail

[fig. 10]
Boy with basket of Fruit, c. 1596, Galleria Borghese, Rome, incisions graphics, graphic processing by Emmebi

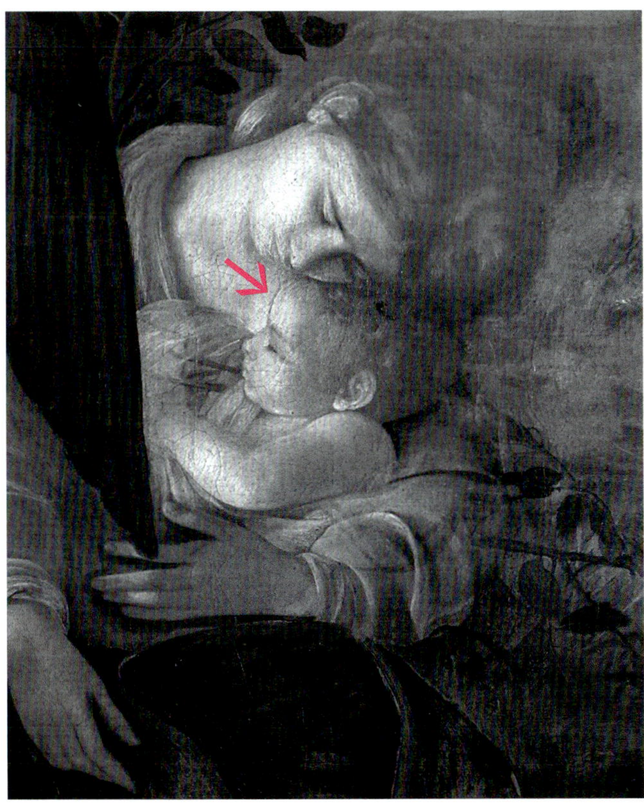

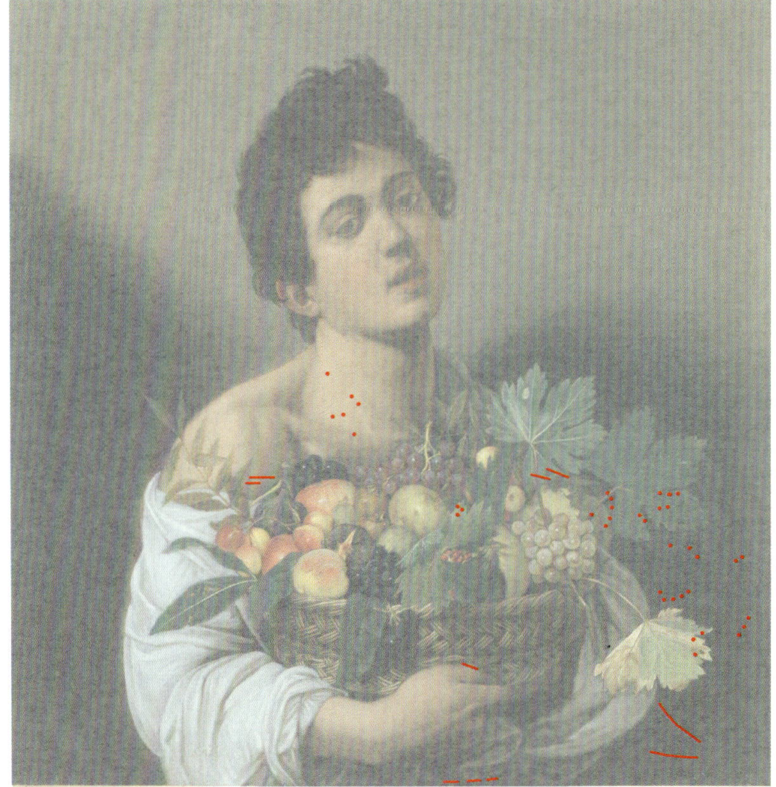

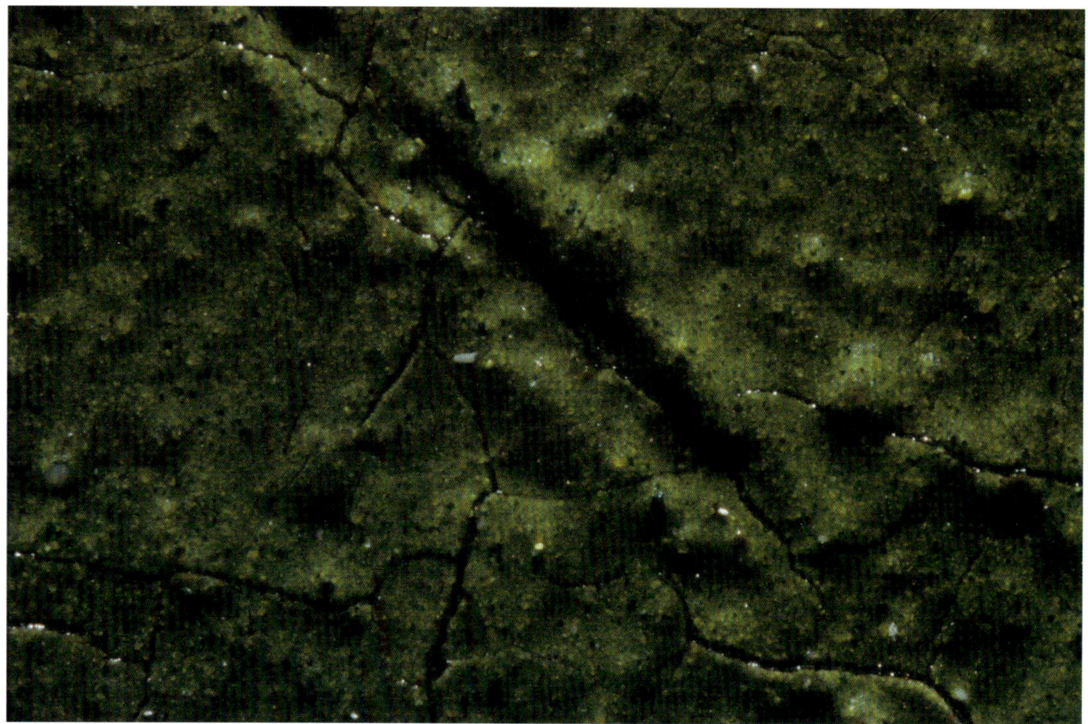

[fig. 11]
Boy with a Basket of Fruit,
c. 1596, detail of an incision,
macrophotography

After the large Contarelli works, one witnesses a diversification in the colour and tonalities of the dark grounds and the number of the ground layers, which is only apparently random. Just to cite a few examples, we pass from the light-brown ground of the *Madonna dei Pellegrini* to the red-brown ground of *Saint John the Baptist* [cat. 16] in the Corsini Gallery, the brown of the *Madonna dei Palafrenieri*, the light-brown of the *Saint Jerome* in the Borghese Gallery, to the almost black of the *Seven Acts of Mercy*, the brownish ground of the Messina canvases, and the brownish-orange of his last work, the *Martyrdom of Saint Ursula*.

This continuous variation in the colour and tonality of the ground can only be interpreted by taking into account the role attributed to it by Caravaggio in relation of his visible use of it 'in reserve'.

The preparation of the canvas is one of the most complex operations in the Lombard painter's work: it must assume exactly the colour, luminosity, brilliance and ability to diffuse light that are instrumental to the effect of the work to be painted. In the initial stages of the planning of a painting, Caravaggio must already have had a clear vision in mind of how to achieve a surface that will remain visible in more or less extensive areas (areas in shadow, contours) while obviously having to relate these to the surrounding painted areas. Hence the Lombard painter's care in the application of the ground, that is, defining its appearance by at times adding a second layer (and sometimes a third), slightly differing from the first if required.

After the two Contarelli canvases and up to Caravaggio's last works, the ground layer takes on an increasingly important role, and in his mature and late works it is left visible or barely glazed over in progressively larger sections. The colour of the ground on the canvas thus enters, with an ever-increasing role, into the palette of colours/hues of his paintings [figs. 7, 8].

Rossella Vodret

THE SETTING-OUT OF THE COMPOSITION: UNDERDRAWING, INCISIONS AND THE SKETCHING-OUT (THE ABBOZZI)

The underdrawing

In contradiction of the established myth that the great Lombard master did not make use of underdrawing, clearly drawn strokes have emerged in the early works, both on the light and the dark grounds, as demonstrated on the one hand by the *Boy with Basket of Fruit* and the *Rest on the Flight into Egypt* , in which the outlines of the flesh tones are carefully drawn [fig. 9], and on the other the *Boy Bitten by a lizard* in the Longhi Foundation and *The Musicians* of New York, in which the face and hands of the former, and parts of the faces and outlines of the garments of the latter are respectively defined with the brush[39].

Caravaggio, therefore, begins to paint following what was the traditional technique of his time: he first applies a ground on the canvas and on this he traces the underdrawing with charcoal or thin dark strokes of the brush. He then proceeds to apply the paint as glazes, that is as layers of colour, and finally adds the shadows.

In his early works short incised strokes also appear, such as those in the *Boy with a Basket of Fruit* (1596) [fig. 10], which roughly outline the space taken up by the basket, but these only begin to play a more extensive role in *The Fortune Teller* in the Capitoline Museums (1597) and, above all, in the *Saint Francis of Assisi in Ecstasy* [cat. 8] in Hartford (c. 1599), where the incisions define the folds of the angel's white drapery.

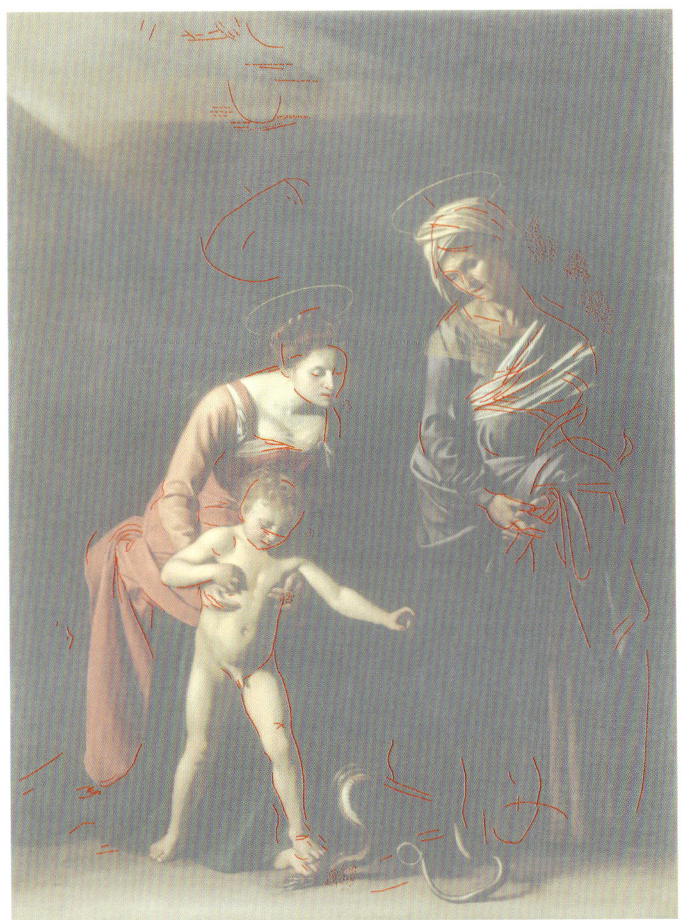

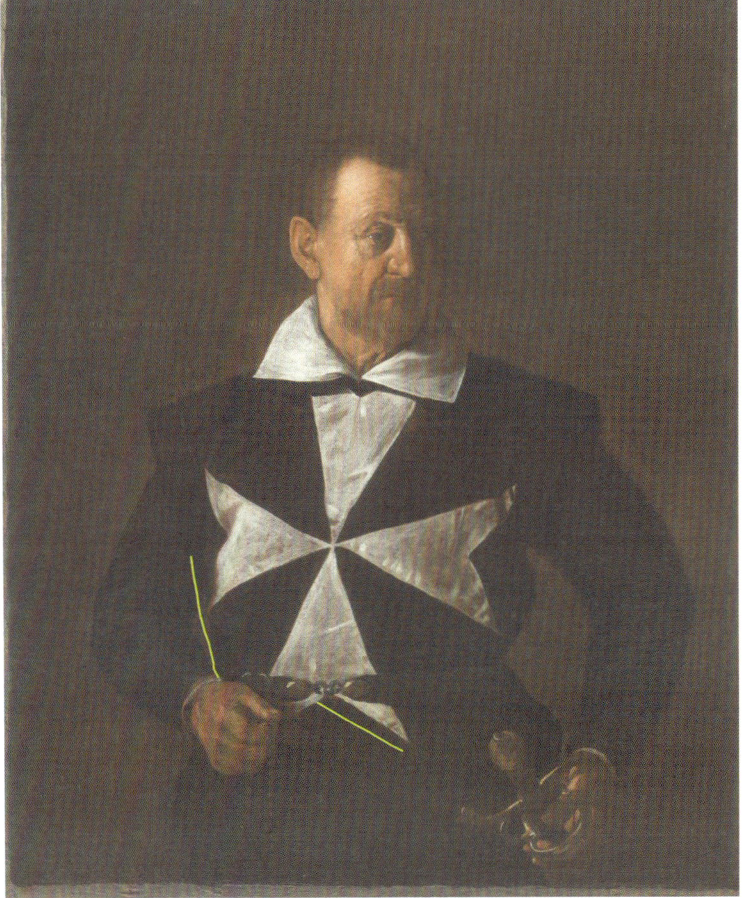

The incisions

The crucial change in the artist's execution technique already occurred to a certain degree in the last years of the sixteenth century, but was perfected above all in 1599–1600, when Caravaggio was commissioned to execute the two canvases for the Contarelli Chapel in San Luigi dei Francesi: his troubled public debut in the Roman art scene, which was hostile to him, and on very large canvases (approx. 320 × 340 cm) to which he was not accustomed.

He was given only one year to complete the work (July 1599–July 1600). Caravaggio was forced to hastily develop a new working method: the ground layer became steadily darker, in various shades of brown, allowing him to add only the light parts and the half-tones, using a basic tonality for the shadows, the background and the outlines with exposed ground. This made for great speed of execution. On the dark ground, however, the traditional practice of drawing was less visible. Thus, in order to quickly set-down the essential parts of the composition, he used a few broad, darker brushstrokes and, above all, incised strokes [fig. 11], made with a pointed tool—perhaps the tip of the handle of the brush—on the more or less freshly applied ground layer and, above all, which would remain visible in the raking light he used to illuminate his models.[40]

The incised lines are of various types and accompany the various stages of the creation of a work. Some are traced on the freshly applied ground, others correspond to the initial sketches (the *abbozzi*); others relate to the application of colour, others, finally, are executed over the already completed painting with an effect defined as 'decorative'.[41]

The function purpose of the incisions seems to vary; the most important function seems to be linked to the need to reposition the models during the various posing sessions necessary for the realisation of the painting, but they may also have been an aid for the setting-up of the composition: the presence of incised lines, the use of which developed above all in the Roman period after 1600, helped the painter to summarily define the size of the figures, the main features, the folds and outlines of the drapery and the transitions from areas in shadow to those in light. The incised lines guarantee the visibility of the graphic reference in raking light even through the initial applications of paint, and become almost invisible on the completed painting.

Having thus delineated the design of the composition, Caravaggio only adds the lights and the half-tones, that is he only paints the parts in light or in half-shadow, leaving the dark ground visible, sometimes glazed, throughout the rest of the painting. Thus, in the parts in shadow and in the background of Caravaggio's paintings there is no paint as such, only the brown ground layer: therefore, he does not paint the figures in their entirety, but only the parts of them reached by the light, the remainder of the figure is 'empty', un-painted, or only sketched in. In this way, the execution of his paintings was extremely fast, a characteristic that his contemporaries also remarked on, and that has been passed down to us by some of his biographers.[42]

A complex technique, therefore, that requires a lucid initial approach and an out of the ordinary creative vision that involves bringing out from the darkness only the lit parts of the figures, and not all the rest, which *a priori* requires clear planning of the final result. The light-coloured brushstrokes, used for example in the flesh tones, are full-bodied and therefore are also those with the greatest relief, while the dark parts—with the ground layer visible or only thinly glazed—are flatter and less perceptible. The work can therefore be executed with greater speed and at the same time the effect is enhanced by our visual perception: that is, what is dark and barely visible remains in the background, what is light emerges with maximum clarity.

Rossella Vodret

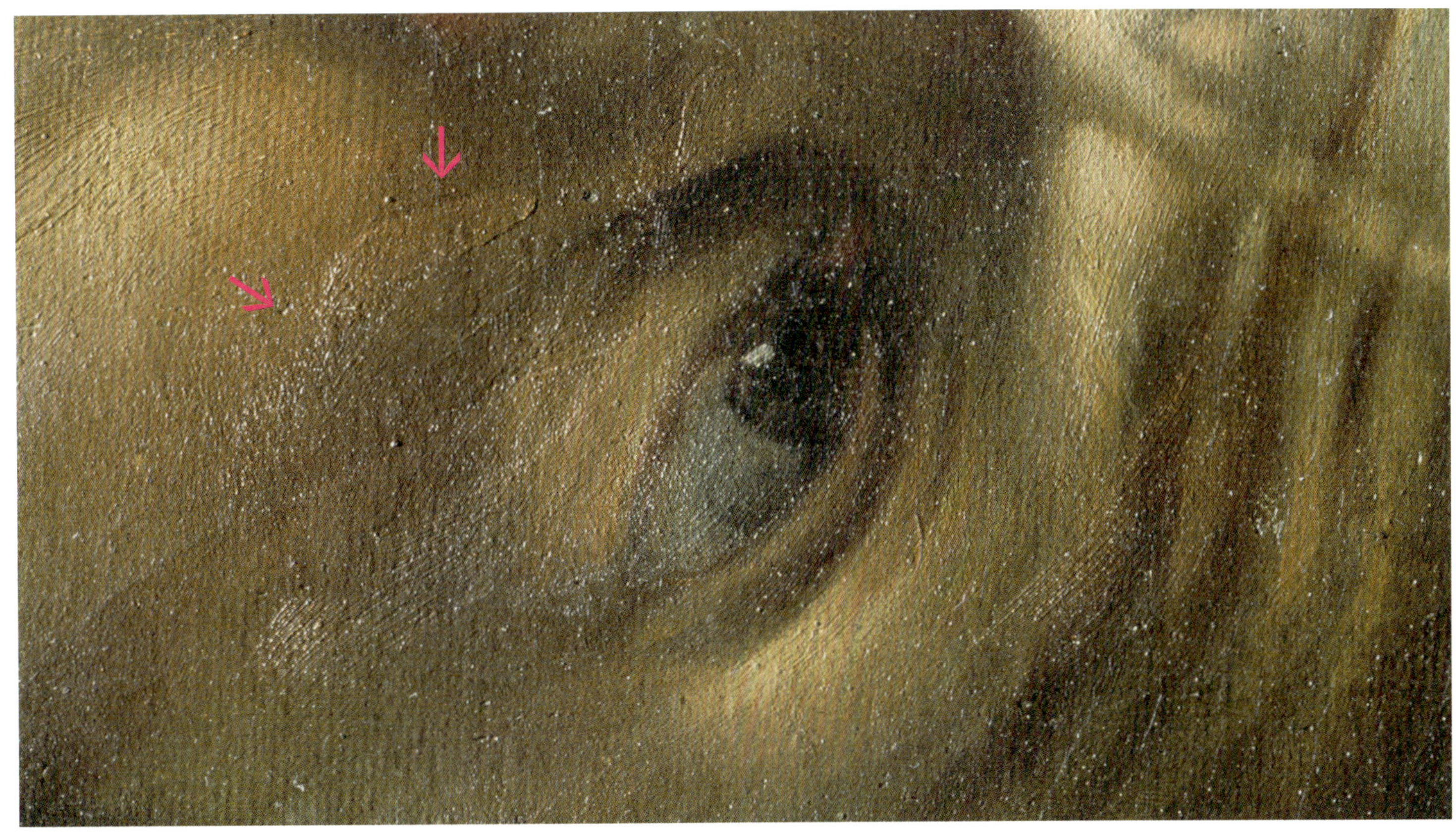

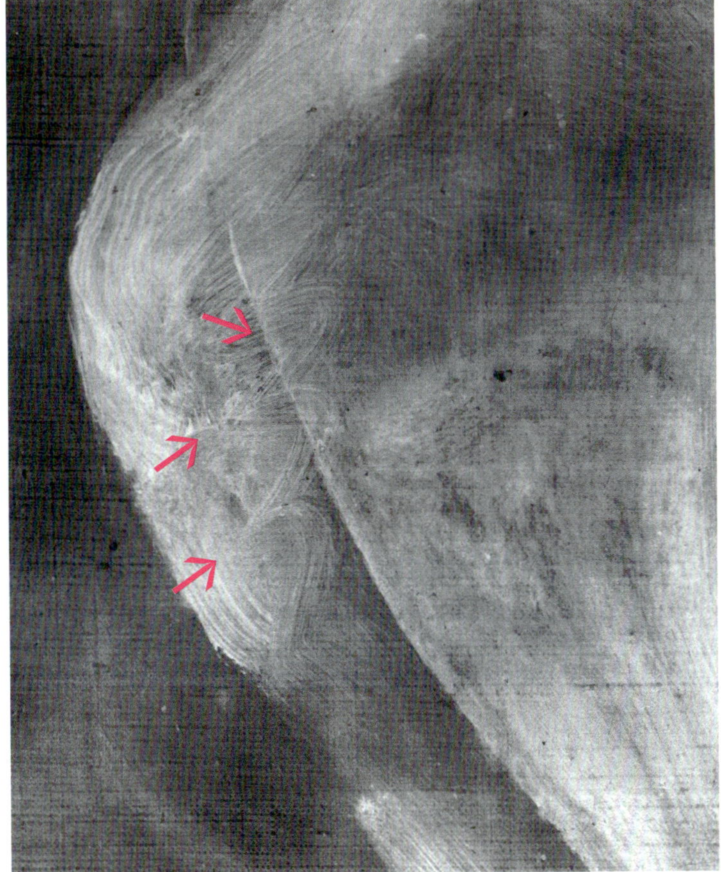

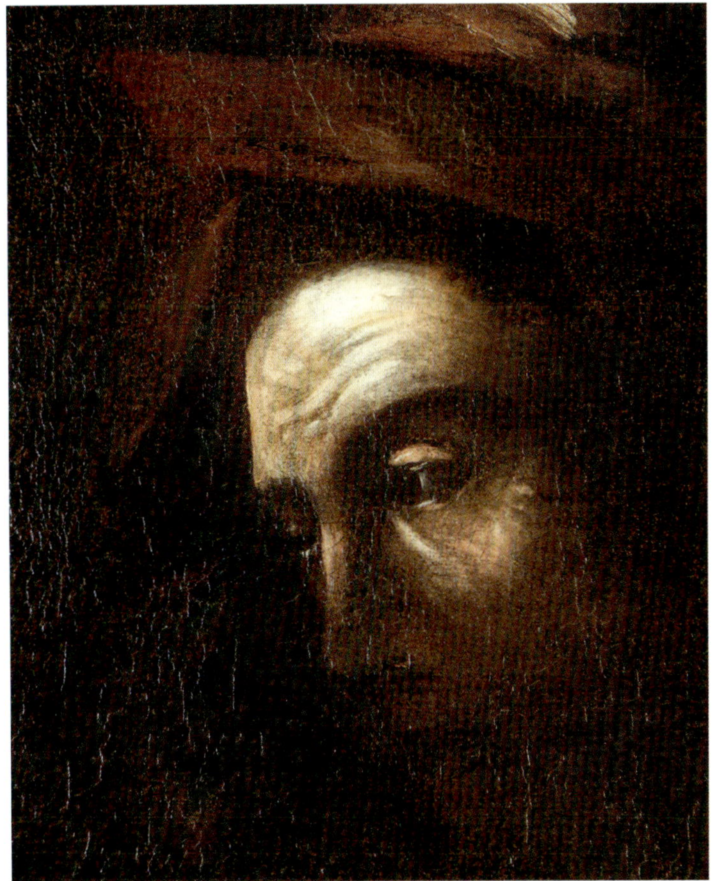

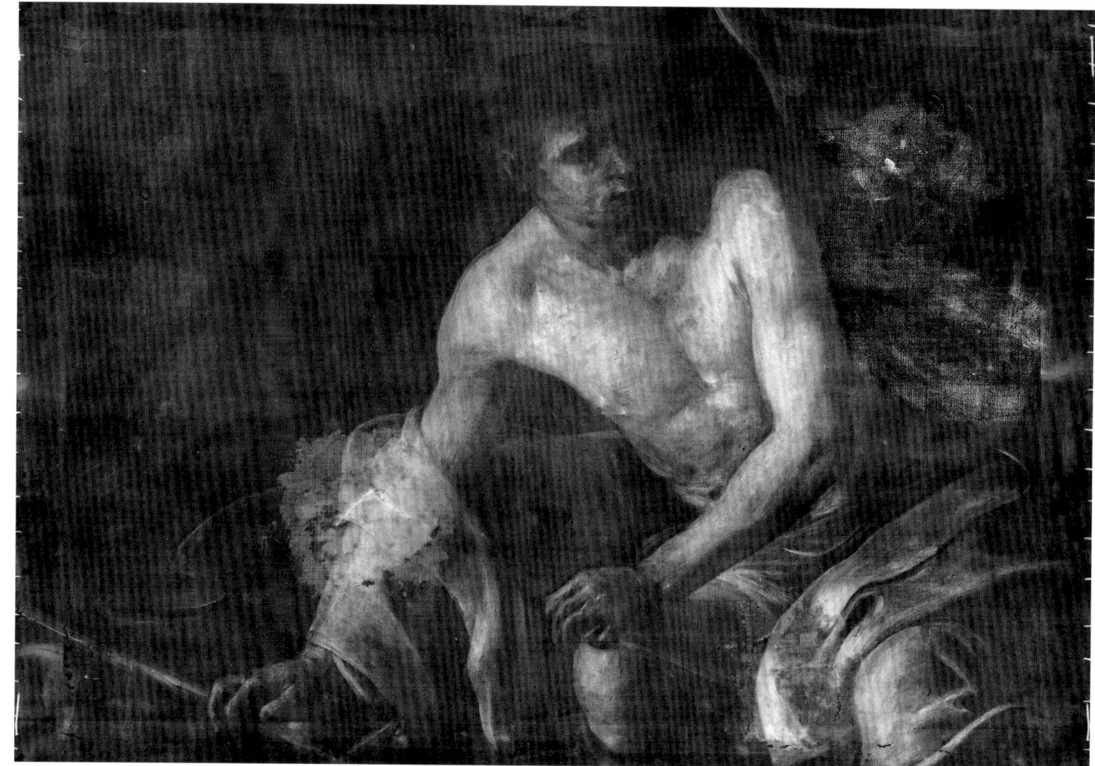

[fig. 17]
Saint John the Baptist, 1604, Gallerie Nazionali di Arte Antica, Galleria Corsini, Rome, X-ray. On the right is visible the clear presence of the lamb, later removed, towards which the Saint turned

From the Contarelli Chapel onwards, up to the flight from Rome in 1606, incisions are a constant in Caravaggio's working method; they are often used as an actual incised drawing, as for example in the *Sacrifice of Isaac* (c. 1603) and the *Madonna dei Palafrenieri* (1605–1606) [fig. 12], both very demanding works.

After his flight from Rome, his use of incisions diminished markedly: the works painted in Naples, Malta and Sicily show a drastic decrease in the use of incised lines [fig. 13; cat. 18]. Curiously enough, their role declined precisely when he left the papal city, almost as if there was some correlation with the working methods he had adopted up until then; as if, for example, after his departure from Rome he was able to paint without the aid of the live model.[43]

The 'abbozzi'

Around 1600, Caravaggio began to systematically use another tool for the setting-up of the composition, the so-called '*abbozzo*', a sketch: usually light in colour [fig. 14],[44] clearly visible on the dark ground. These are executed with rapidly applied, full-bodied brushstrokes of lead white on the ground during the initial phases of a painting; with the *abbozzo* Caravaggio sets down certain details of the composition on which he wants to concentrate the maximum amount of light, brushstrokes that progressively take on various shapes and widths (broad, circular, zig-zag,[45] fig. 15). The use of this kind of sketching seems to have been limited up to the paintings in the Contarelli Chapel, becoming increasingly important from the early seventeenth century onwards. We find *abbozzi* in many paintings such as, for example, in the Barberini *Judith with the Head of Holophernes* (in my opinion of c. 1602, Vodret 2021a) [cat. 12], the *Sacrifice of Isaac* in the Uffizi (probably 1603), the *Madonna dei Pellegrini* (c. 1604–1605), the *Madon-*

Rossella Vodret

na dei Palafrenieri in the Borghese Gallery (1605–1606), the *Saint Jerome* of Montserrat and the Borghese Gallery painting (1605–1606), the *Saint John the Baptist* in the Corsini Gallery (1605–1606), the Borghese *David* (in my opinion dating from 1606). Sometimes these strokes of paint could also be coloured, as well as light, for instance red and brown, in order not to interfere with the tonality of the paint layers that would later be applied to the same area. Coloured *abbozzi* have been found in the ear of Martha in the Detroit *Martha and Mary Magdalene* (1600–1601) [cat. 11] and in the upper part of the ear of the *Saint Francis in Meditation* from Carpineto Romano (1606), as well as in the later *Seven Acts of Mercy* (1606) (for Samson's ear), in the *Adoration of the Shepherds* in Messina (1609) (for the ear, nose and cheekbone of the shepherd closest to the Virgin) and in the *Salome with the Head of the Baptist* in the National Gallery, London (probably 1609, in the woman's joined hands, and in the hand, forearm and right ear of the executioner). This frequent use of sketched strokes in the ears might be explained by their possible role in defining the positioning of the heads.

The full-bodied light, red and brown brushstrokes, or even darker ones in the shaded parts, all seem to be different aspects of the same practice, that of sketching, in alternation with or accompanied by incisions for the setting-out of the composition.

In his final years, Caravaggio's painting practice became increasingly summary, terse and essential with its extreme expression in the magnificent *Martyrdom of Saint Ursula*, of 1610, the year of his death, where darkness now takes over from light and the figures— outlined with just a few sketchy brushstrokes—are literally engulfed by the darkness/ ground [fig. 16] that occupies more than half of the painting's surface, light years away from what is probably his first known work, the *Boy with a Basket of Fruit*, painted only fourteen years earlier [fig. 2, 10].

The 'hidden' images

Another important aspect in the study of Caravaggio's painting technique, which goes beyond the more strictly 'material' aspects dealt with in this essay, is the discovery of a series of 'hidden' images. These are the original compositional ideas set-down by Caravaggio in the initial creative stages and then changed during the course of the work, and now made visible again in X-radiographs. They are exceptional images that allow us to penetrate the painter's creative process and reveal the painter's 'thought-processes' as he proceeded in the creation of his works.

In numerous paintings, the changes are highly significant from a compositional point of view, and have involved the deletion of entire figures and the alteration of their size, as well as the change in position of some of the figures and other elements in the painting. Among the works with the most significant alterations, which are already widely known, apart from the resounding case of the *Martyrdom of Saint Matthew* in the Contarelli Chapel, we can also mention the Doria *Rest in the Flight into Egypt* [fig. 1], the *Calling of Saint Matthew* in the Contarelli Chapel,[46] *Judith with the Head of Holophernes* and *Saint Francis in Meditation* in the Barberini Gallery, *The Sacrifice of Isaac* in the Uffizi, the *Conversion of Saint Paul* in the Cerasi Chapel, *Saint John* [fig. 17], for which we refer you to what has already been published.[47] To these can be added the *Madonna of the Rosary* in Vienna and the *Flagellation* in Capodimonte, both of which were probably modified following specific requests from their commissioners.

Caravaggio therefore, overcame the traditional practice of painting, conceived in successive phases, conceiving the creation of a painting as a single creative act, a powerful synthesis in which the tonality of the ground, the incisions, the *abbozzi*, the application of the paint, all come together to achieve the extraordinary expressive power of his masterpieces.

A technique that Caravaggio did not like to divulge—in fact, he had no pupils and never aimed to have a school—but which attracted an endless series of young painters to Rome from all over Europe who flocked to the papal city in the first two or three decades of the seventeenth century, precisely to learn the secrets of his painting.

1   I would like to thank Giorgio Adamo and Claudio Falcucci for their valuable suggestions and constant help in writing this essay. I would also like to thank Andrés Ubeda de Los Cobos, Valentina Certo and Pietro di Loreto for useful exchanges of ideas. This essay is a summary of what I have written on this same subject in my earlier works, to which I refer in the notes. For greater completeness of data, I have also made use of some recent studies, of a more technical nature, by Claudio Falcucci, which are also cited in the notes. Mahon 1951, pp. 223–234; Arslan 1959, pp. 191–218; Rotondi, Urbani 1966, pp. 1–120; *The Age of Caravaggio* 1985. Extensive technical documentation, mainly in the form of X-radiographs, accompanied the catalogue entries, edited by Mina Gregori, for the Caravaggio paintings displayed in the two exhibitions. Christiansen 1986, pp. 421–445; Gregori, in *Michelangelo Merisi* 1991.

2   *Caravaggio. Opere a Roma* 2016.

3   *Dentro Caravaggio* 2017. For scientific reasons, the individual lenders of the works in the exhibition were asked to carry out the analyses on their works according to the quality standards set by the Istituto Centrale del Restauro. Where this was not possible, Claudio Falcucci's 'studio Mida' was commissioned to carry out the investigations. All new investigations on works in the exhibition that lacked them were carried out thanks to the Fondazione Bracco.

4   Vodret 2021a, with technical entries by C. Falcucci which provide an overview of the technical investigations on Caravaggio's works carried out up to 2021; see also Vodret 2021b; Falcucci 2021; Falcucci 2017; Vodret 2017a. The new technical analyses carried out during 2017 on the works loaned to the exhibition *Dentro Caravaggio*, complemented those carried out between 2009 and 2012 on the twenty-two autograph Roman masterpieces by the great Milanese painter published in 2016 (*Caravaggio. Opere a Roma* 2016). Also worth mentioning are the studies by T.M. Schneider 1987; R. Lapucci, technical entries in *Michelangelo Merisi. Come nascono* 1991 and Lapucci, in *Come dipingeva* 1996. Numerous works have been published since 2000, including those of the ICR (Istituto Centrale del Restauro) and the OPD (Opificio delle Pietre Dure) in Florence. On the history of painting techniques, see also Cardinali 2016, with earlier bibliography.

5   For an in-depth technical study see Falcucci 2017, pp. 305–326.

6   For the paintings in the Cerasi chapel see Falcucci 2008, for the *David with the Head of Goliath* the analysis of the support was carried out by Emmebici of M. Cardinali, M.B. De Ruggieri and C. Falcucci in 2002.

7   Cuppone 2021a, fig.22; Falcucci 2017, pp. 307–308; Falcucci, oral communication during the study day on the occasion of the exhibition *Nono dialogo Brera* 2022; Vodret 2025b in press.

8   In a nutshell: for the different types of canvas weave, that is the way the warp and weft threads are interwoven, in *plain*-weave canvas each warp thread passes alternately over and under successive weft threads, resulting in a uniform fabric. In *twill*-weave, on the other hand, the binding points are arranged diagonally. This is achieved by passing the warp thread alternately once above and once below the weft thread, and by sliding the position of the binding stitches with each warp thread. Twill-weave fabric, which is much stronger, is the one used today for jeans. Damask-weave is generally that found used for Flanders damask tablecloths.

9   This is not the case in the New York *Musicians* and the *Lute Player* from the Hermitage, both with 7×7 thread/cm² canvases) and the Fort Worth *Bari* (8×8 thread/cm²), see below.

10   On this subject see also Seccaroni 2013.

11   The *Sacrifice of Isaac* in the Uffizi (13×20 threads/cm²) and the *Madonna dei Palafrenieri* (12×12 threads/cm²) are both painted on twill-weave canvas.

12   Among the few works of the Roman period painted on supports made up by joining two pieces of canvas, are the enormous lateral paintings of the Contarelli Chapel (322×340 cm) and the *Supper at Emmaus* today in London (141×195.2 cm). In Rome, Caravaggio was able to obtain twill-weave canvas at least 207 centimetres wide (the width of the canvas of the *Madonna dei Palafrenieri*) and plain-weave canvas at least 175 centimetres wide (the width of the canvas of the paintings still today in the Cerasi Chapel).

13   See Falcucci 2021, pp. 166, 170, nos. 21, 22.

14   See ibid., pp. 222–223, nos. 38, 39.

15   See ibid., pp. 198, 202, nos. 31, 32. For the third Mattei canvas, the *Supper at Emmaus* at the National Gallery in London, executed in 1601, earlier than the other two and on two pieces of plain-weave canvas, of similar size, the technical data relating to the number of threads per warp and weft is not available (Falcucci 2021, pp. 194, 196, no. 30).

16   Gandolfi 2021, p. 320. According to Celio, who was personally acquainted with the Lombard painter, Caravaggio was a guest in the house of Prospero Orsi between the last months of 1596 and the beginning of 1597, where he painted a *Lute Player*, perhaps to be identified with the Giustiniani painting now in the Hermitage (Gandolfi 2018).

17   For dating hypotheses for the Borghese *David*, see most recently Vodret 2021a, p. 316, no. 69; Zuccari 2022a, p. 361.

18   See Falcucci 2021, p. 318, no. 69. In the right-hand margin of the canvas of the *David*, a strip of canvas with the same weave but with a density of approximately 9×8 threads/cm² was added before the application of the ground layer; the analysis of the support of the *David with the Head of Goliath* was carried out by

Emmebici of M. Cardinali, M.B. De Ruggieri and C. Falcucci in 2002.

19 Vodret2021a p. 307 and Vodret 2025a in press.

20 See Falcucci 2017, p. 307; Falcucci 2021, p. 284, no. 57.

21 See Falcucci, 2021, p. 276, no. 54.

22 Ibid., p. 282, no. 56.

23 Ibid., p. 272, no. 53.

24 Vodret 2021a, pp. 270–271 and Zuccari 2022a, p. 353, no. 49, with earlier bibliography.

25 It is impossible to investigate the canvas of the Maltese *Annunciation* in Nancy (285 × 205 cm) painted in the spring-summer of 1608, as the original support of this work is no longer verifiable having been completely removed in the nineteenth century and replaced by a new canvas applied to the reverse (Falcucci 2021, p. 298, no. 63).

26 Falcucci 2021, p. 296, no. 62.

27 See ibid., pp. 304, 306, no. 66.

28 According to some recently discovered documents (Sorrentino 2024a; Sorrentino 2024b), a payment of 300 *scudi* for the *Adoration of the Shepherds* (314 × 211 cm) took place in Naples in November 1609, but this, in the current state of studies, does not prove that the work was painted in the capital of the Vice-royalty, but only that Caravaggio was in Naples at the time, and therefore that is where he was paid. The analysis of the original support does not help in the dating; it is made up of three pieces of plain-weave canvas, sewn vertically, and of varying widths (59, 80, 72 cm), substantially similar to those used both in Sicily and in the second Neapolitan sojourn.

29 An effective graphic elaboration of the canvases on which the three Sicilian works are painted is in Cuppone 2021a, fig. 22 (graphic elaboration by M. Cuppone).

30 See Falcucci 2021, p. 184, no. 26.

31 Cuppone 2021a, p. 78-81; Vodret 2021a, p. 184, Zuccari 2022a, p. 340, no. 21: the backdating of the *Nativity* in Palermo to 1600, in the middle of the Roman period, had already been proposed in the 1950s by Edoardo Arslan (Arslan 1951, p. 451), and later articulated by Maurizio Calvesi also with reference to a possible Roman commission (Calvesi 2011, pp. 24–30).

32 Most recently Macioce 2023, pp. 289–290.

33 Falcucci 2021, p. 322, no. 71.

34 For the analysis of the role of the grounds in Caravaggio, I have made use of, and summarised, Falcucci's essay in Falcucci 2017, pp. 308–311, to which we refer for an in-depth discussion of the subject.

35 Bellori [1672] 2005, p. 183.

36 In the Odescalchi *Conversion of Saint Paul* the ground is white, as is commonly found in paintings on panel; see most recently Falcucci 2021, p. 188, no. 27.

37 Falcucci 2021, p. 188, n. 26.

38 Leone 2016; Vodret 2021a, p. 132, no. 9; Zuccari 2022a, p. 335, no. 11.

39 For further discussion see R. Vodret, in *Caravaggio. Opere a Roma* 2016, p. 28 ff; Falcucci 2017, p. 305 ff.

40 Even today, the most suitable tool for investigating the presence of incisions in Caravaggio paintings is in almost all cases observation in raking light. The systematic use of incisions is not only a characteristic of Caravaggio; many painters of his time also made use of them.

41 A classification of the incisions was introduced by Thomas Schneider (Schneider 1987) and Keith Christiansen (Christiansen 1986), then taken up and expanded by Roberta Lapucci in 1991 (Lapucci 1991a, p. 44).

42 The first to make an observation on the speed with which Caravaggio painted his canvases, is Van Mander 1604: "Now, he is a mixture of wheat and chaff; in fact he does not devote himself continually to study, but when he has worked for a couple of weeks, he goes about for a month or two with his broadsword at his side and a servant following, going from one ball game to another, very prone to duelling and brawling, so that it is rare that one can attend him."

43 For hypotheses on the organisation of Caravaggio's studio, also on the basis of what is reported in biographical sources and, in particular, on the way his paintings were lit, see Falcucci 2017, pp. 323–324. On this topic see also Cardinali, De Ruggieri, Falcucci 2005, pp. 50–71; *Caravaggio. La bottega del genio* 2010; Cardinali 2016, I, pp. 52–88; De Ruggieri 2016a. On this subject, it is worth citing what Mancini and Bellori wrote: Mancini [c. 1619–1621] 1956–1957, I, p. 108, writes: "To light with a single beam of light ('lume unito') and that comes from above without reflections, as from a window in a room with the walls painted black."; also from what Bellori [1672] 1976, and 2009, p. 217, one can deduce that he painted in an enclosed room: "He never brought any of his figures out into open sunlight, but found a way of setting them within the dusky air of a closed room, taking light from high up that fell straight down on the main principal part of the body, and leaving the remainder in shadow in order to gain force through the intensity of light and dark." It is also worth mentioning that the inventory of assets seized from the painter on 26 August 1605 (see Macioce 2023, p. 205) included a "mirror shield" ("scudo a specchio"), probably a circular mirror, we do not know whether it was concave (able to produce a concentrated beam of light, like the "lume unito" described by Mancini or Bellori's "light from high up that fell straight down") or convex, like the one depicted in the *Martha and Mary Magdalene* in Detroit. The same inventory of 1605 also includes a "large mirror", which could be useful for reproducing models, lit and reflected in a flat mirror, which would already offer a two-dimensional view of the scene to be reproduced on the canvas.

44 These are light-coloured brushstrokes consisting largely of lead white.

45 It has recently been discovered that Annibale Carracci also used zig-zag strokes of the brush to sketch, similar to Caravaggio's, as revealed by the recent restoration of the Prado *Venus*. I would like to thank Andrés Ubeda de los Cobos, Deputy Director for Conservation and Research at the Prado Museum for this important information (written communication 2023).

46 On the modifications of the *Vocation of Saint Matthew*, we refer you to the recent studies by Moretti 2025 in press and by Vodret 2025c in press.

47 For all the works cited, please refer to the relevant entries published in *Caravaggio. Opere a Roma 2016 passim*, and finally to the technical entries drawn up by C. Falcucci, in Vodret 2021a, *passim*, with earlier bibliography. For an overall discussion on the 'hidden' images see also the essays by Vodret, in *Caravaggio. Opere a Roma* 2016, pp. 36–40; Vodret 2017a, pp. 206–230; Vodret 2021b, pp. 98–100.

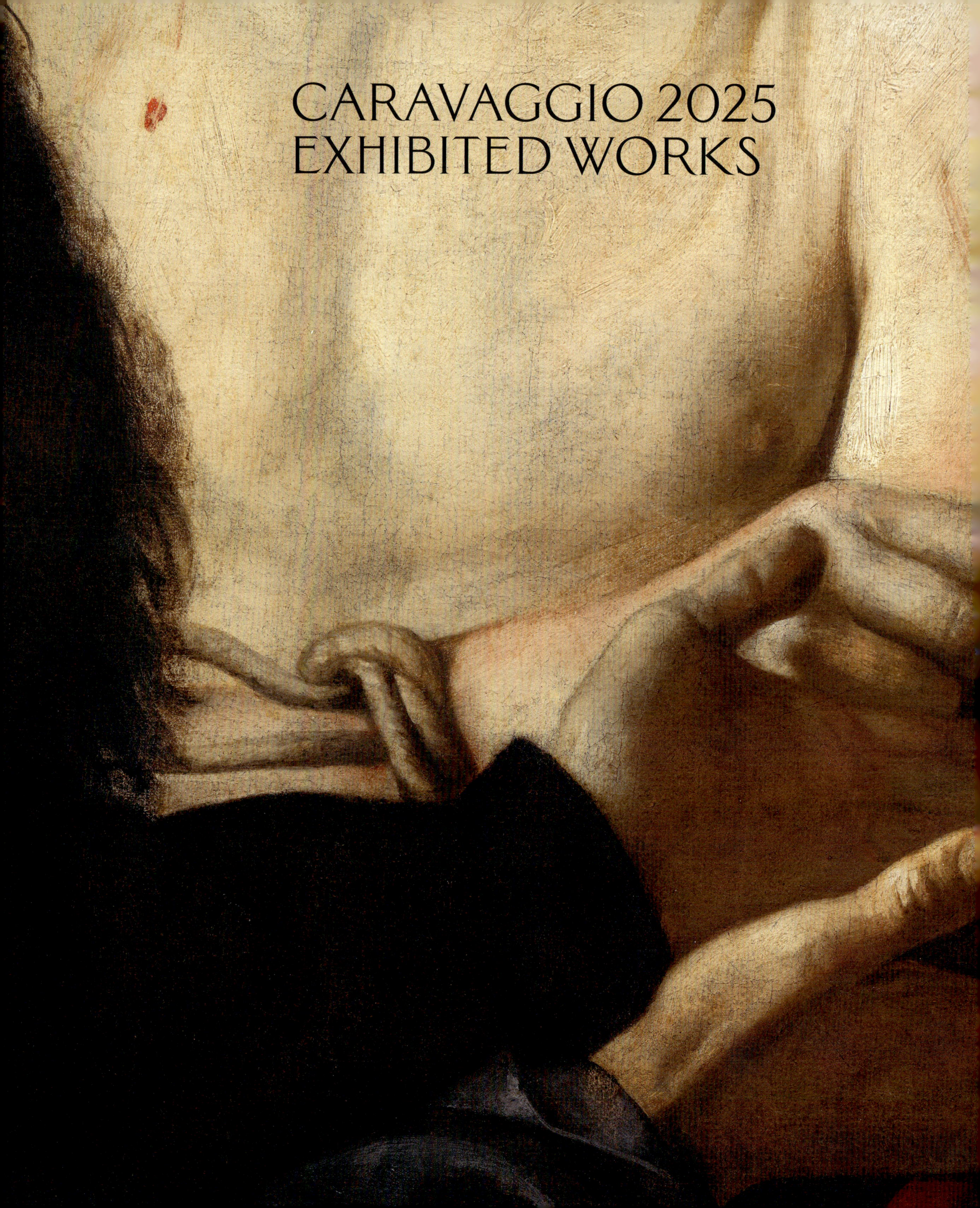
CARAVAGGIO 2025
EXHIBITED WORKS

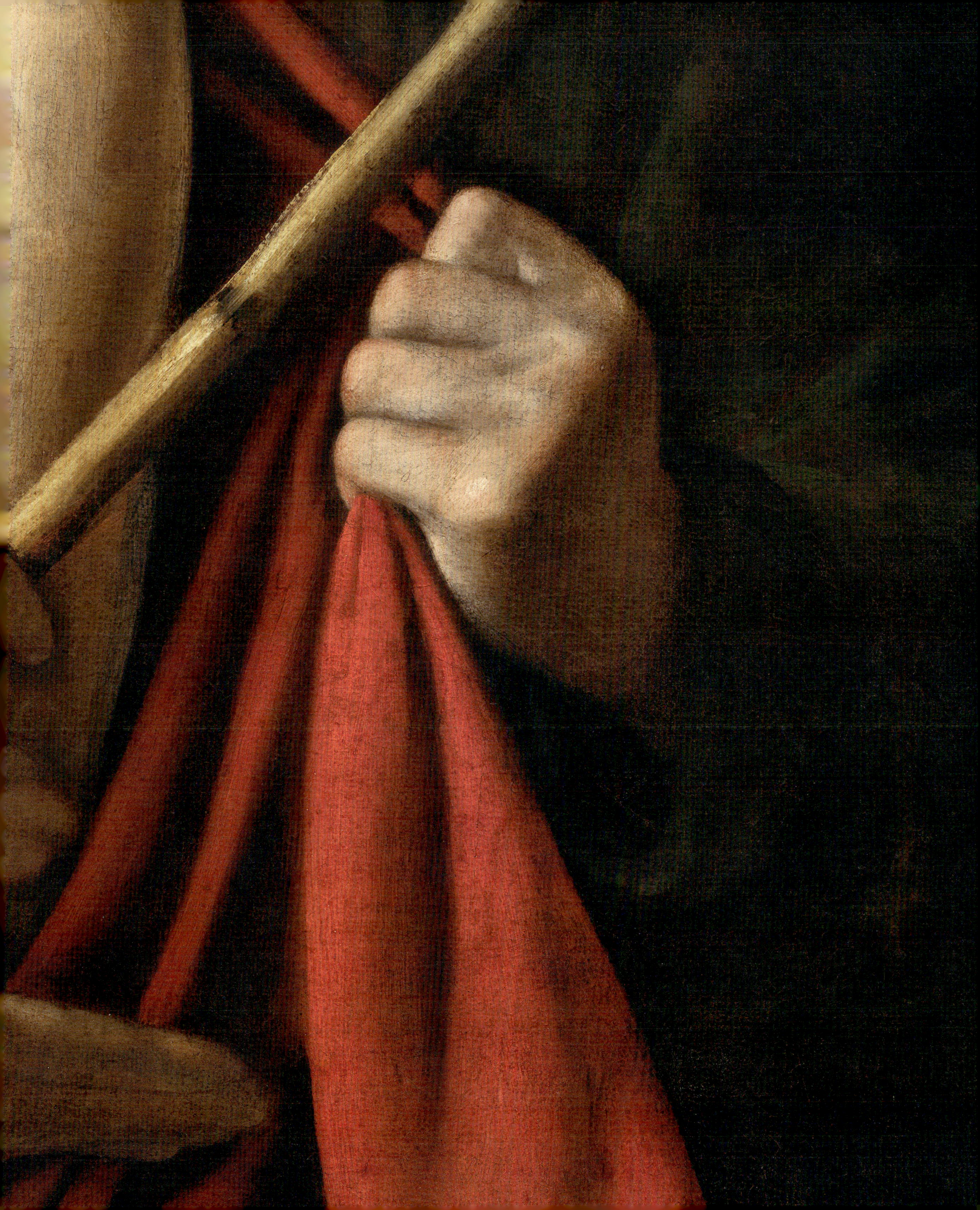

SELF-PORTRAIT AS BACCHUS (SICK BACCHUS)

c. 1595–1596
oil on canvas, 67 × 53 cm
Galleria Borghese, Rome, inv. 534

Provenance: Rome, Giuseppe Cesari known as Cavalier d'Arpino, before 1607; Rome, Cardinal Scipione Borghese 1607.

Bibliography: Mancini [c. 1619–1621] 1956–1957, I, p. 226; Baglione [1642] 2023, p. 401; De Rinaldis 1936, pp. 110, 114, no. 54; Longhi 1927, pp. 301–302; Della Pergola 1959, II, pp. 76–78, n. 112; Calvesi 1971, pp. 98–102; Cinotti 1983, pp. 505–509, no. 52; Herrmann Fiore 1989, pp. 95–134; Calvesi 1990, pp. 12–14, 224–228; Cappelletti 2009, pp. 21–24; Curti 2011a, pp. 167–197; Lemoine 2014, pp. 25–27; Morel 2015, pp. 341–362; Gandolfi, Zuccari 2017, pp. 254-256 Teza 2018, pp. 56–63; Terzaghi 2020c, p. 252, no. VI.3; Hermann Fiore, in Vodret 2021a, II, pp. 44–46.

Identified by Roberto Longhi ([1927] 1967, pp. 301–302) as an autograph work by Caravaggio and referred to by the scholar as the *Sick Bacchus* (*Bacchino malato*), the *Self-portrait as Bacchus* is one of the most representative works of the Lombard artist's entire production. The painting was recorded for the first time in 1607 amongst the paintings confiscated by Paul V from the Cavalier d'Arpino and donated by order of the same pontiff to his nephew Cardinal Scipione Borghese; listed at no. 54, the painting is described in the following terms: "Another small picture with a young man with a garland of ivy around [his head] and grape[s] [on a] vine in his hand, without a frame" (De Rinaldis 1936, pp. 110, 114, no. 54; Della Pergola 1959, II, pp. 76–78, no. 112). Giulio Mancini, who had the opportunity to see the work in the Borghese collection—where it is documented moreover in all subsequent known inventories (Della Pergola 1959, II, pp. 76–78, no. 112)—makes a hand-written note in the margin of Caravaggio's biography, in some respects revealing the history of the painting, before it entered the Cavalier

d'Arpino's collection of works of art: "Among the many [paintings] he made a very beautiful Bacchus and he was beardless [?]. It is with Borghese, it was with [Costantino]" (Mancini [c. 1619–1621] 1956–1957, I, p. 226). According to the testimony of the Sienese doctor, the canvas must have been on sale by the "dealer in old paintings" ("*regattiero de quadri vecchi*") Costantino Spada, who owned the shop near the church of San Luigi dei Francesi (Curti 2011a, pp. 167–197), therefore, reaching the Cavalier d'Arpino before 1607, in circumstances that have as yet to be clarified.

Scholars agree that the work is one of the pictures 'painted from a mirror' ("*ritratti allo specchio*"), paintings referred to by Baglione among the artist's early works ([1642] 2023, p. 401), which also include the *Boy Bitten by a Lizard*, which the Roman biographer recalls was offered for sale by Caravaggio (see Zuccari 2018, pp. 65–74). It has been suggested that, in the same way, the *Bacchus* was also introduced onto the market by the Lombard painter, perhaps together with the *Boy with a Basket of Fruit*, thus entering Scipione Borghese's collection at a later moment in time (Terzaghi, in *Peterzano: allievo di Tiziano* 2020, p. 252, no. VI.3). In view of the recent documentary findings, this remains the most plausible hypothesis, although the absence of early replicas of the work—in contrast with the other Caravaggio *juvenilia*—raises a few issues on the actual circulation on the market of the two Borghese paintings.

The enigmatic nature of the subject, amenable to an allegorical interpretation, has engaged generations of scholars from the beginning of the twentieth century to the present day. Traditionally, the iconography has either been interpreted in a Christological key (Calvesi 1990, pp. 12–14, 224–228; Herrmann Fiore 1989, pp. 95–134) or alternatively as a symbol of inspiration and artistic creation (Morel 2015, pp. 341–362; Lemoine 2014, pp. 25–27). But all scholars are in unanimous agreement that the work represents a self-portrait of the artist in the guise of Bacchus. It is possible that in this choice Caravaggio may have been inspired by Giovanni Paolo Lomazzo's *Self-portrait* (1568); in the painting in the Pinacoteca di Brera the artist proclaims himself as the abbot of the Val di Blenio, crowned with ivy, the classical symbol of divinity.

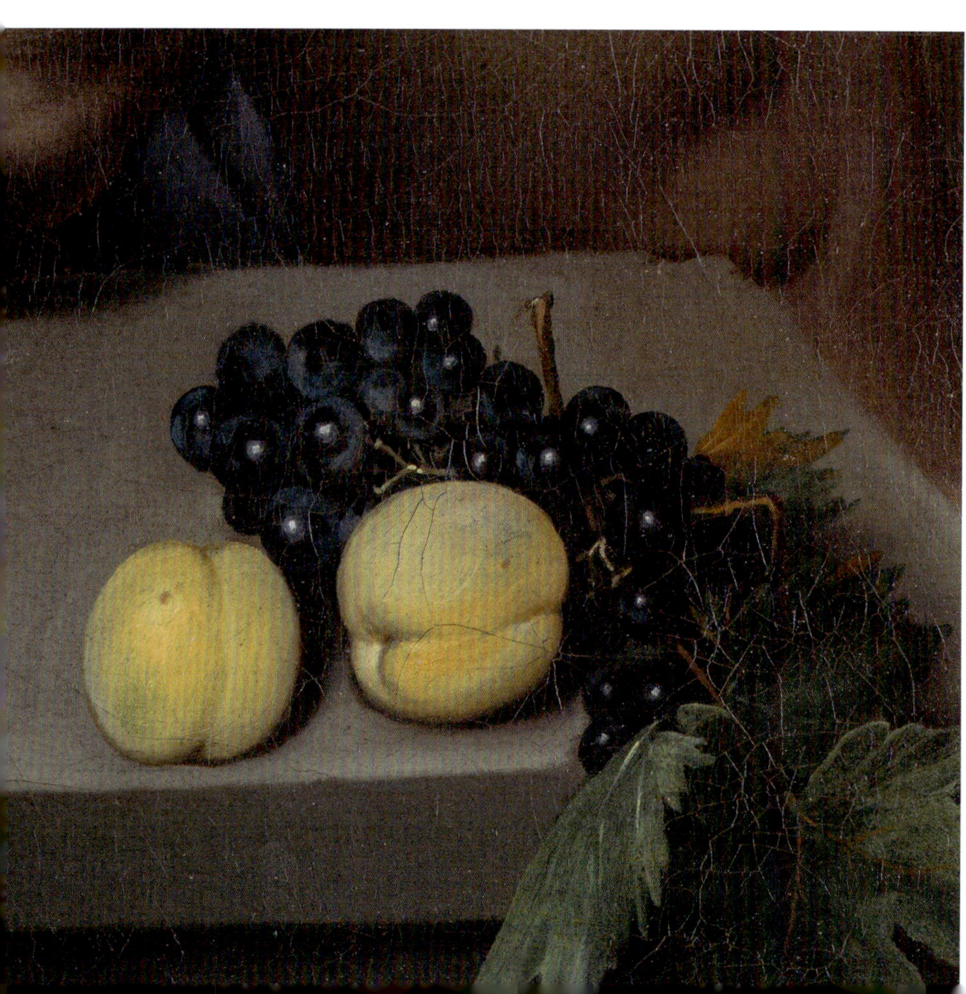

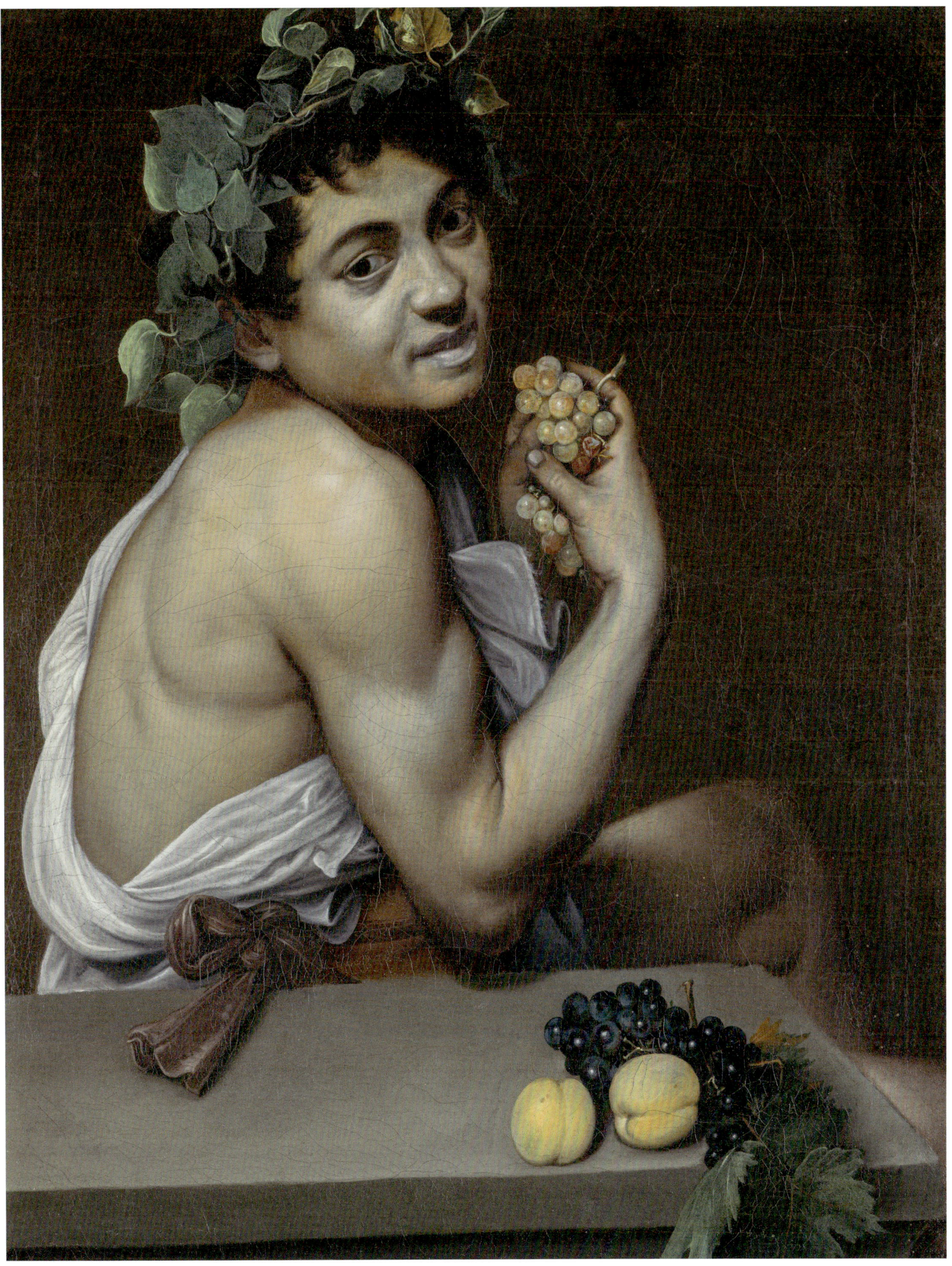

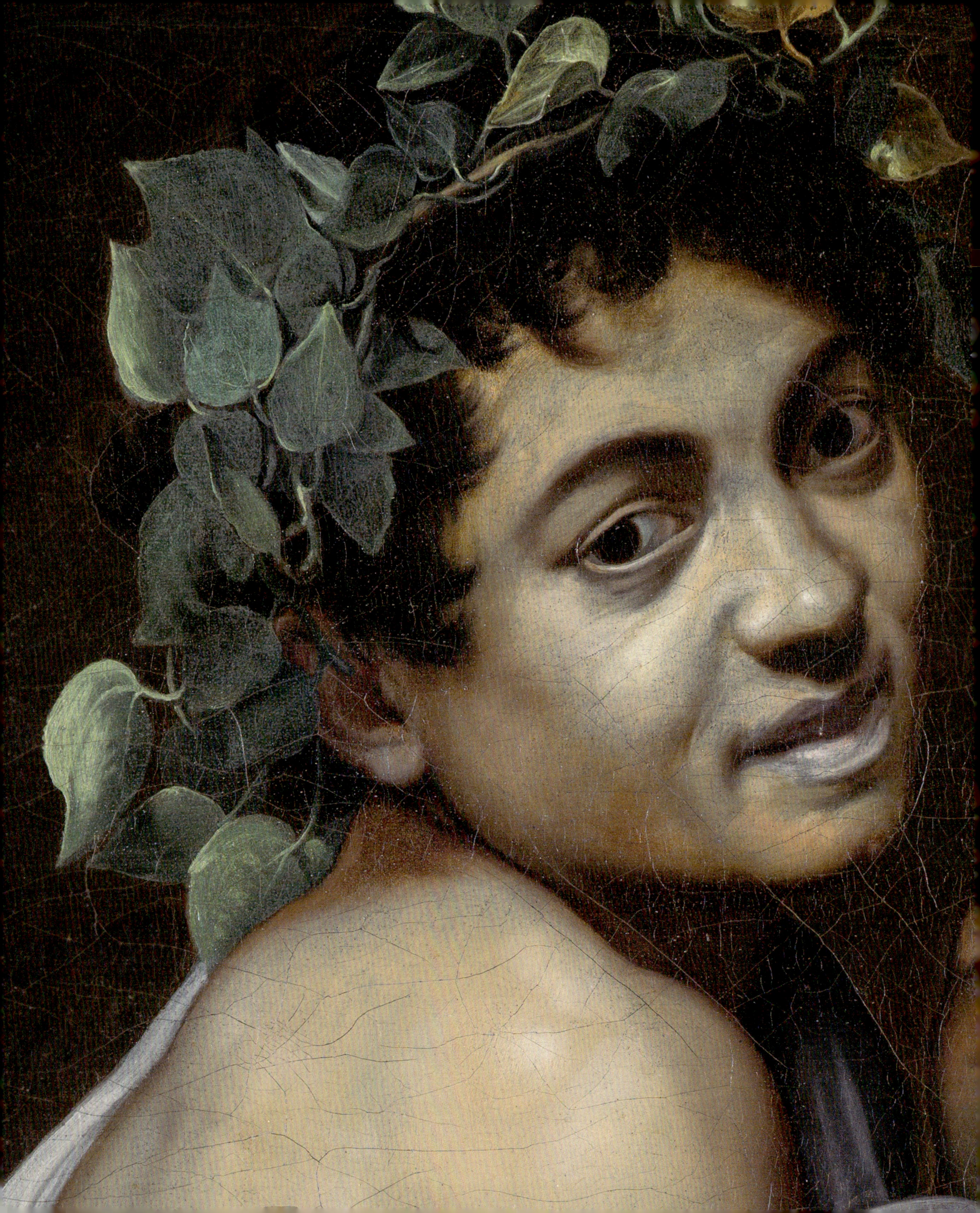

The subject's Bacchic link is also reflected in the gesture of the hand squeezing grapes between the fingers, emblematically depicted in the centre of the composition. The physiognomic component and the melancholic air with which the artist has imbued the work, through the pale and almost unhealthy complexion of *Bacchus*, which has made him famous, can reasonably be considered decisive elements that have contributed innovative elements to the traditional iconography of the god of wine and intoxication.

The evident stylistic similarities with Milanese painting and with the models widespread in the workshop of his master Simone Peterzano (1573–1596)—see for instance the *Study for a Sybil* (Milan, Castello Sforzesco, inv. Au. A 1717/57), a preparatory work for the frescos in the Certosa di Garegnano—have contributed to placing the work at the beginning of Caravaggio's artistic career (Gandolfi, Zuccari 2017, pp. 254–256; Teza 2018, pp. 56–63). The cross-referencing of literary and archival sources, as discussed above, would suggest a date of 1596, before Cardinal Francesco Maria del Monte welcomed him into his palazzo, and after Caravaggio's admission to the Ospedale della Consolazione around 1596. Baglione's observation of a "somewhat dry manner" in the painting, deserves to be taken into consideration, and interpreted as the consequence of a hand that is only beginning its first anatomical and perspectival experimentation. The Borghese *Bacchus* is at the origin of the series of works in which Caravaggio practiced the representation of his own face, probably in front of a mirror, and thus would have been executed not long before before the *Boy with a Basket of Fruit*, the *Boy Bitten by a Lizard*, and the *Bacchus* in the Uffizi (Terzaghi 2020c, p. 252, n. VI.3).

[EG]

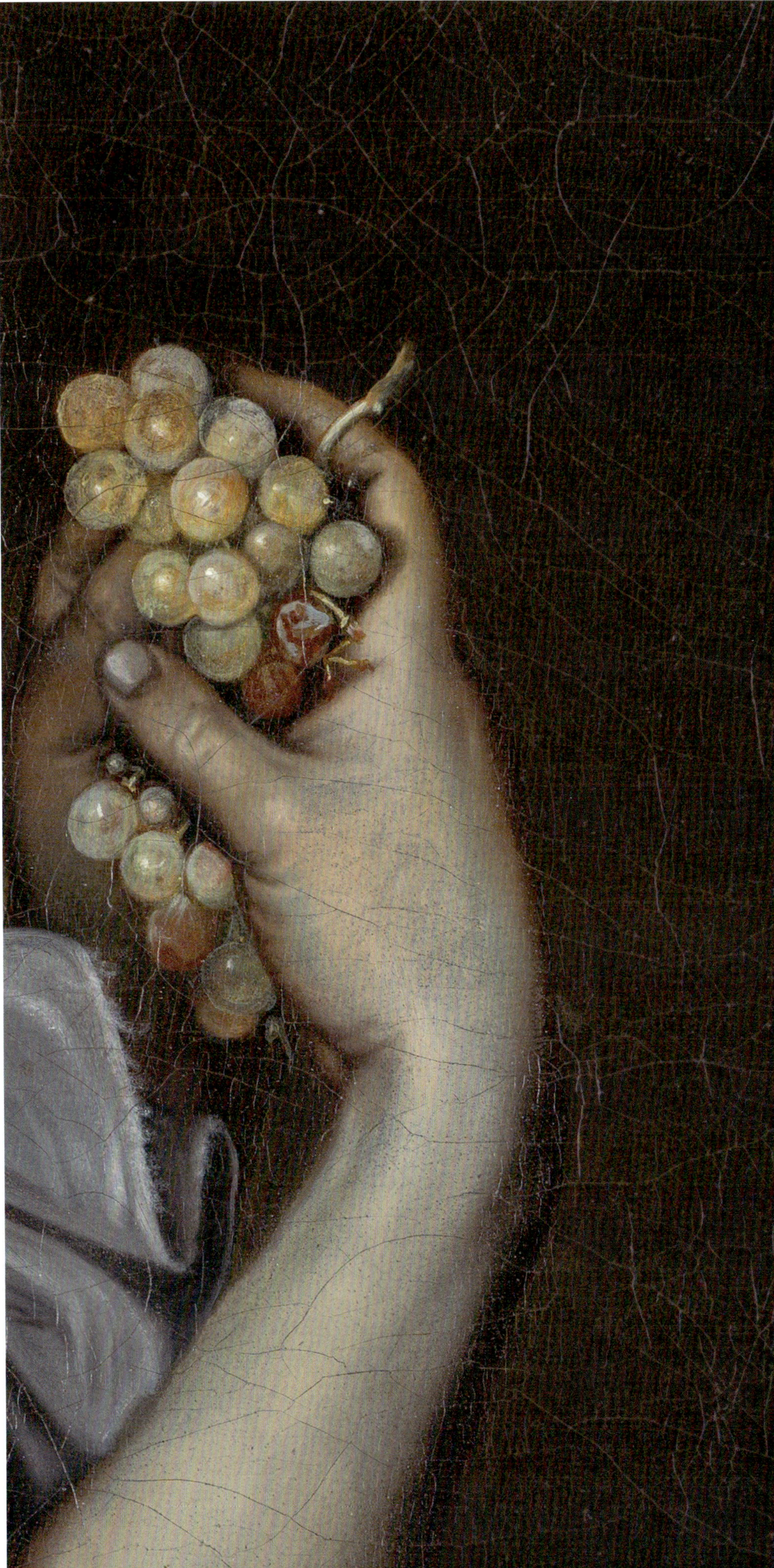

BOY PEELING FRUIT

c. 1595-1596
oil on canvas, 63 × 53 cm
The Royal Collection / H.M. King Charles III, Hampton Court Palace, London

Provenance: Probably acquired by Charles II, but first recorded in the 1688 inventory of James II's works in Whitehall, Windsor Castle, Hampton Court Palace and in the custody of Catherine of Braganza, Somerset House ("By Michel Angelo – A work, representing a boy in a shirt, peeling fruit").

Bibliography: Mancini [c. 1619–1621] 1956–1957, I, p. 224; Collins Baker 1929, p. 20; Friedländer 1953, p. 145; Moir 1976, pp. 103-104; Marini 1979, p. 76; Mahon, in Nicolson 1979, p. 34; Fumagalli 1996, p. 143; Macioce 2003, pp. 241-242; Teza 2013, pp. 11–12, 18, 48–55; Papi 2009, p. 25; Savina 2013, pp. 91–99; Treves 2016, p. 42.

The *Boy Peeling fruit* in Hampton Court is abraded and worn, particularly in the figure of the boy intent on peeling the fruit. Nevertheless, the high quality of the inset of the fruit arranged on the table has led some scholars (Papi 2009, p. 25; Teza 2013, p. 50; Treves 2016, p. 42) to consider this painting as the version that could aspire to be recognised as the original. Numerous non-autograph—contemporary and high-quality—versions of the *Boy Peeling fruit* (or *Mondafrutto*) are in existence, testifying to the success of the subject (see Moir 1976, pp. 103–104; Savina 2013, pp. 91–99).

The early history of the painting remains shrouded in mystery until its inclusion in James II's inventory of 1688. In this inventory, the work is attributed to "Michael Angelo" (Caravaggio); however, by the mid-nineteenth century, it was erroneously ascribed to Bartolomé Esteban Murillo. This attribution may have been influenced by the presence of a similar, non-autograph, version that once belonged to Sir Joshua Reynolds, also incorrectly attributed to Murillo. This version is now in the Ishizuka collection (Savina 2013, p. 94; Treves 2016, p. 42).

The *Boy Peeling fruit* is commonly numbered among the earliest works attributed to Caravaggio, along with the *Sick Bacchus* [cat. 1], the latter long considered by scholarship to be the first work he produced. As reported by Mancini in his *Considerazioni*, the *Boy Peeling fruit* was painted during the artist's first sojourn in Rome, when he was a guest of the prelate Monsignor Pandolfo Pucci, a native of Recanati. during which time Caravaggio painted some "devotional copies" ("*copie di devotione*") and several paintings. In the same house, but not commissioned by the prelate, but intended rather for sale, the artist painted "a boy crying because he has been bitten by a lizard" and "a boy peeling a pear [or an apple] with a knife" (Mancini [c. 1619–1621] 1956–1957, I, p. 224).

A "boy at a table with an apple in his hand" is referred to in the records of the repossession of Cavalier d'Arpino's collection in 1607. This citation had led some scholars to suggest that the original work had passed into Cardinal Scipione Borghese's collection. This hypothesis was laid aside thanks to the identification in Scipione Borghese's inventory of a painting with a similar subject-matter attributed to Sodoma, now lost (Fumagalli 1996, p. 143).

It is possible, on the other hand, that the original was part of Cesare Crispolti's collection. In a letter of August 1608 addressed to Cardinal Scipione Borghese, the governor of Perugia, Lorenzo Sarego, refers in fact to a painting by Caravaggio in Crispolti's testamentary bequest of a youth, painted at half-length, in the act of peeling a peach (Fumagalli 1994, pp. 113–114; Macioce 2003, pp. 241–242). However, as Teza rightly observes (Teza 2013, p. 11), it is difficult to establish whether this was an original or a copy.

Cesare Crispolti was *Principe* of the Accademia degli Insensati in Perugia, an illustrious institution that brought together figures of great cultural importance, united by their adherence to a poetics of truth reinterpreted in a symbolic key. Members of the Academy included prominent personalities such as Maffeo Barberini, Gaspare Murtola and Aurelio Orsi, brother of Prospero Orsi, the latter a close friend of Caravaggio. These ties played a significant role in Caravaggio's early Roman years (Teza 2013, pp. 41–42).

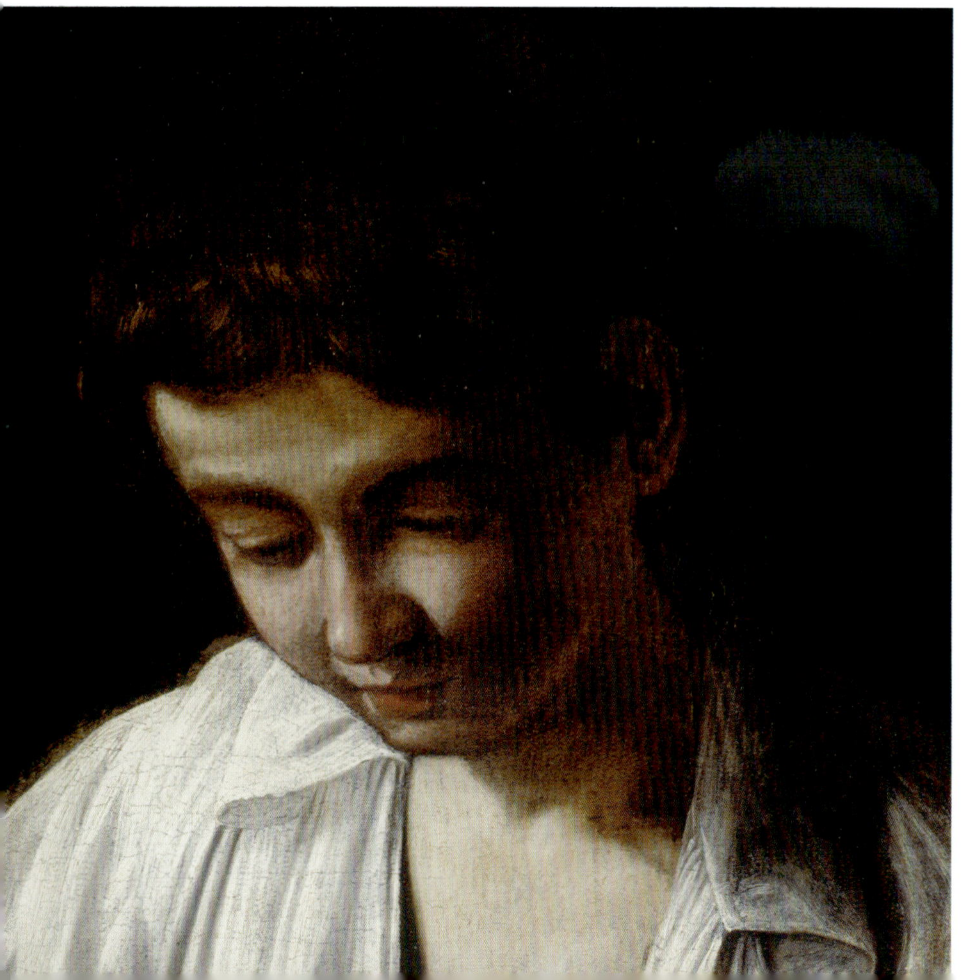

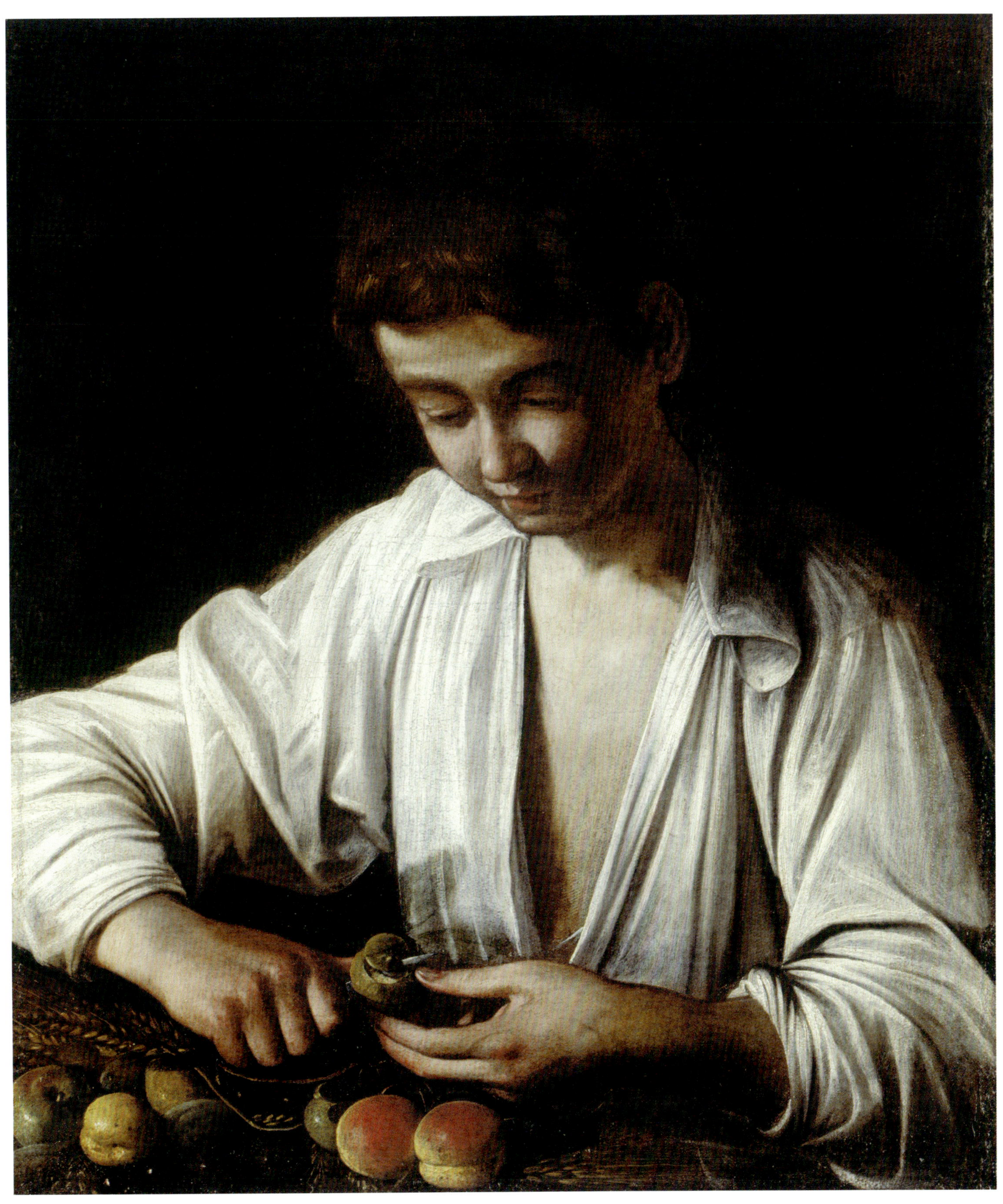

Scholars have for a long time debated the nature of the fruit that the young man depicted in the painting is peeling. This element, not clearly identifiable in early biographical sources, has been the subject of discussion in order to understand whether the work concealed an allegorical meaning. In the catalogue of Hampton Court paintings of 1929, the hypothesis was put forward that the fruit could be a nectarine, a theory later taken up by Friedländer (Collins Baker 1929, p. 20; Friedländer 1953, p. 145). Maurizio Marini suggested instead that it was a bitter orange, a *merangolo* (Marini 1979, p. 76), while Denis Mahon proposed that it was a bergamot (Mahon, in Nicolson 1979, p. 34), each identification being attributed a different symbolic meaning.

In 2013, Laura Teza identified the fruit as a *Citrus auranti folia neapolitanum*, that is the Naples limoncello: a small, ovoid fruit with a greenish skin, the juice of which was traditionally given to children for intestinal hygiene. The *Boy Peeling fruit* could thus be interpreted as a figurative emblem reflecting the most authoritative pedagogical principles of the time, in harmony with the precepts expressed in Giovanni della Casa's *Galateo*. The latter evokes values such as cleanliness, hygiene and temperance, symbolically represented by the lemon that the young man is about to consume (Teza 2013, pp. 60–70).

Crispolti was particularly open to such subjects, so much so that in 1604 he wrote a pedagogical treatise, *L'idea dello scolare che versa negli studi, affine di prendere il grado del dottorato* (*The idea of the school-boy poring over his studies, so as to take a doctoral degree*) (Teza 2013, p. 66). Therefore, the uncertainty surrounding the authenticity of the work in his possession, in light of the proliferation of copies, does not preclude the possibility that the *Boy Peeling fruit* fits coherently into the pedagogical project he had conceived. Through the foundation of his Academy, Crispolti aimed to promote a symbolic reading of reality, reinterpreting the canons of the representation from life (*dal vero*), and harmonising them with the educational and moral values of his time.

[GM]

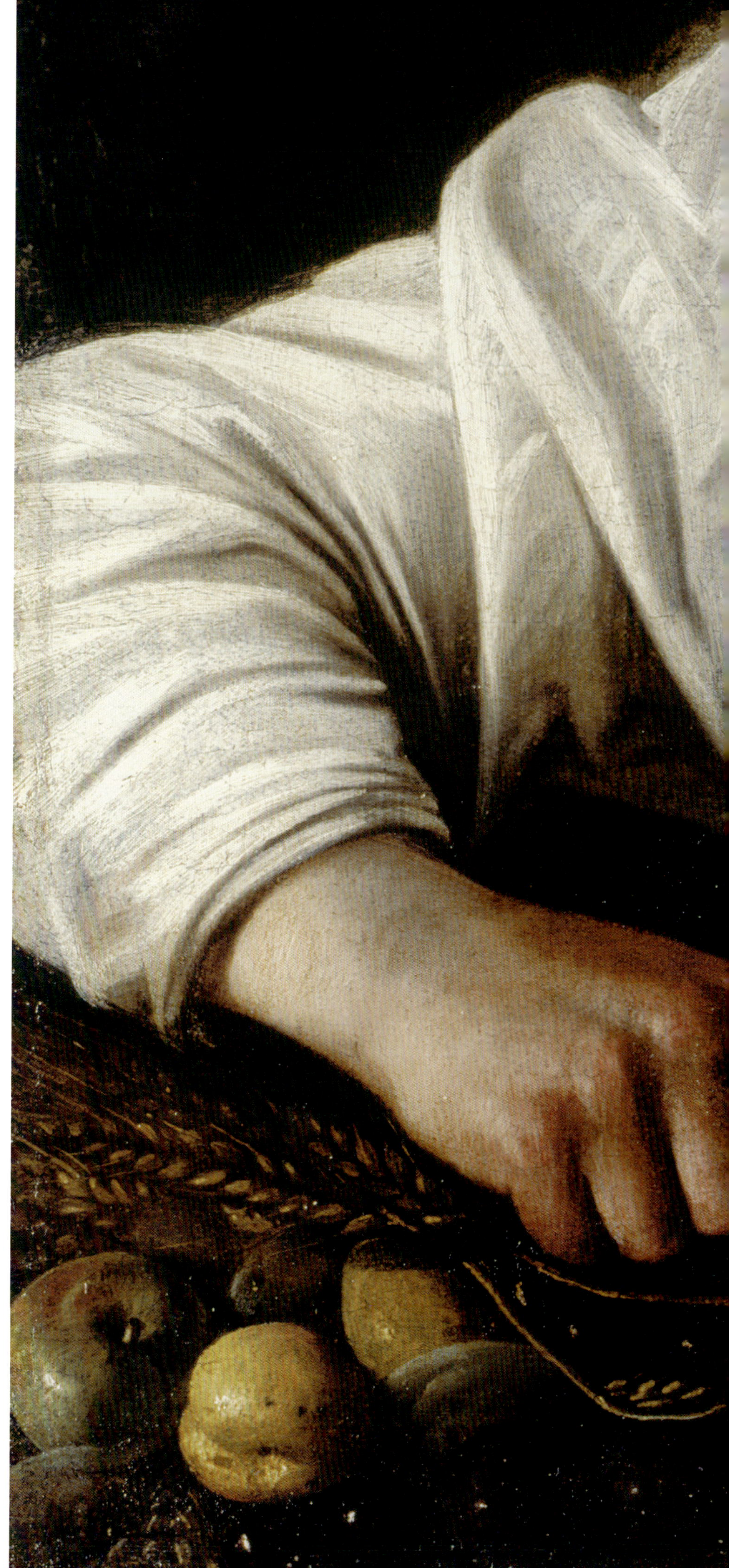

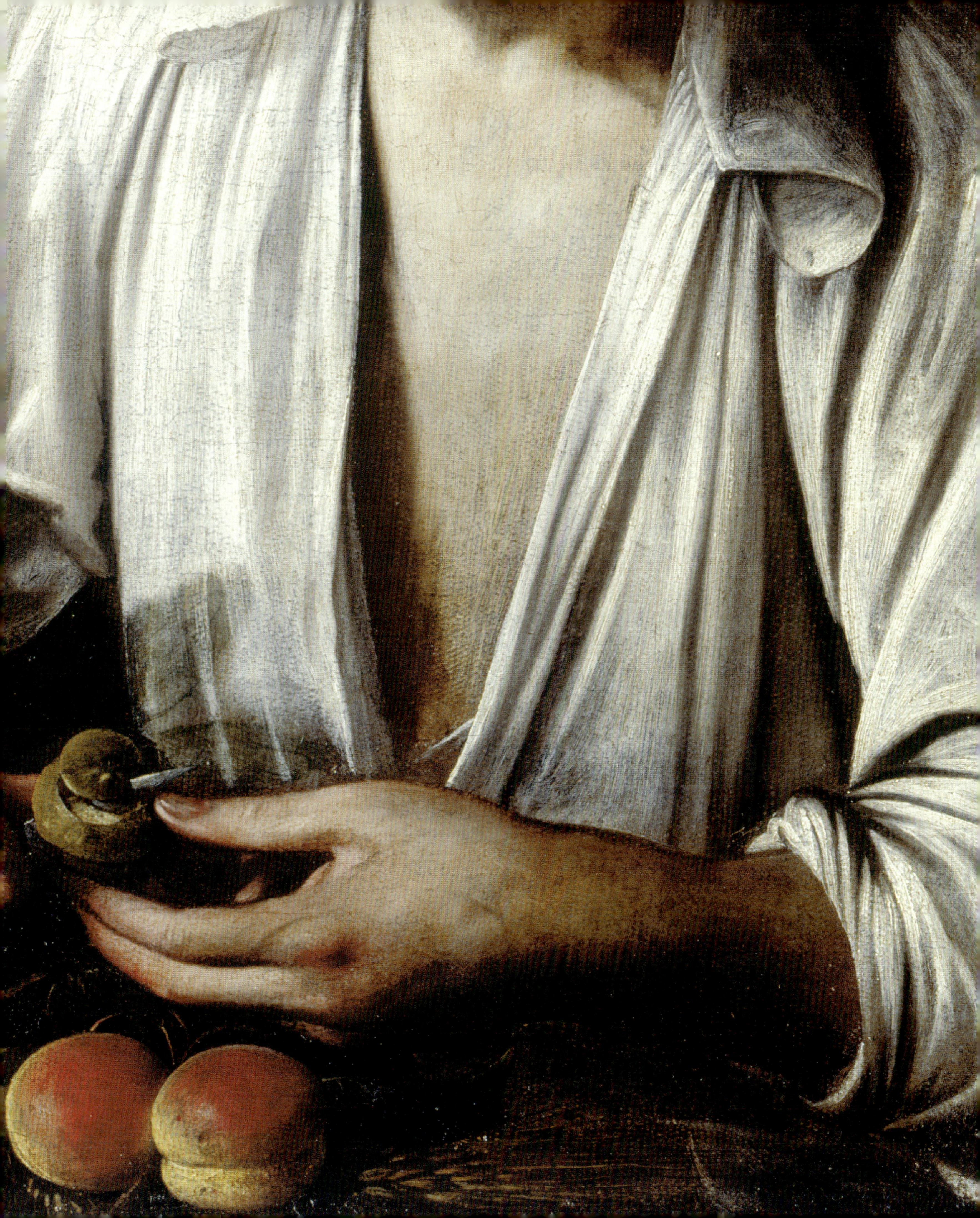

PORTRAIT OF MONSIGNOR MAFFEO BARBERINI AS PROTONOTARY APOSTOLIC

ATTRIBUTED

c. 1595
oil on canvas, 122 × 95 cm
Private collection, Florence

Provenance: From 1911 to the present owners, from the estate of Anna Barberini Colonna, since 1858 wife of Tommaso Corsini (attributed to Caravaggio); inventories of the Barberini estate: 1853 (attributed to Scipione Pulzone); 1844 (attributed to Scipione Pulzone); 1655, inventory of Maffeo Barberini (the Younger), Rome, Palazzo in Via delle Quattro Fontane (without attribution); 1648, inventory of Taddeo Barberini, Rome, Palazzo in Via delle Quattro Fontane (without attribution); 1623?, inventory of Maffeo Barberini (the Elder) , Rome, Palazzo in Via delle Quattro Fontane (without attribution); 1608?, Maffeo Barnerini's inventory, Rome, Palazzo Salviati (without attribution).

Bibliography: *Mostra del ritratto* 1911, p. 218, cat. 4; Venturi 1912, pp. 1–2; Voss 1925, pp. 446, 689; Longhi [1943] 1999, p. 31; Longhi 1951a, p. 17; Longhi 1963, p. 281; D'Onofrio 1967, pp. 17, 60–63; Cinotti 1983, pp. 437–38; Previtali 1985, p. 76; Bona Castellotti 1998, p. 59; Marini 2005, p. 423; Schütze 2007, pp. 153, 230; Christiansen, in *Caravaggio e caravaggeschi* 2010, pp. 100–103; Papi 2010, pp. 23–25; Papi 2014b, pp. 66–70; Schütze, in *L'immagine sovrana* 2023, pp. 158–159, 160–161.

Chosen to represent Scipione Pulzone's skill in the *Mostra del ritratto italiano* (*Italian Portrait Exhibition*) in 1911 (*Mostra del ritratto* 1911, p. 218, cat. 4), the painting was displayed together with the *Portrait of Francesco Barberini*, Maffeo's uncle, also attributed to Pulzone, with the indication of the common provenance from the Corsini collection, to which the paintings were bequeathed by the Barberini themselves. Indeed, in 1858, Anna Barberini Colonna, one of the last descendants, married Tommaso Corsini and moved to Florence. Soon after the exhibition, Lionello Venturi chose to publish only the *Maffeo* as a work by Caravaggio: "At a period in his life when he was just beginning to reduce chromatic variety to the effects of light and shade." (Venturi 1912, pp. 1–2). At a later date, Voss (1925, pp. 446, 689), would attribute also the *Portrait of Monsignor Francesco Barberini* to Caravaggio, insisting on the common provenance, location and attribution of the canvases. Roberto Longhi's opposition was fierce (Longhi [1943] 1999, p. 31); while agreeing with Voss on the common authorship, Longhi stated that their: "Author is to be sought among the followers of Pulzone, not uncommon in Rome, in the genre, for example, of the Pietro Fachetti whose life is recounted in Baglione". Nevertheless, the canvas under examination was exhibited at the Palazzo Reale in Milan in 1951 (Longhi 1951a, p. 17) as an autograph work by the Lombard master, despite the fact that the catalogue entry repeated Longhi's contrary opinion, while the *Portrait of Francesco Barberini* was passed over in silence. The lack of success of the attribution of the painting to Caravaggio seems to have been consolidated a decade later by the publication, again by Longhi (1963), at the suggestion of Giuliano Briganti, of a new portrait: *Il vero "Maffeo Barberini" del Caravaggio* [cat. 9], a title that speaks for itself. Scholars for the most part aligned themselves with Longhi's opinion, despite the impossibility of direct contact with the work housed in a private collection (Cinotti 1983, pp. 437–438), while the other *Maffeo*, the one under discussion, went out of the picture. The first to suggest a possible reconsideration of the affair was Previtali (1985, p. 76), followed by Marco Bona Castellotti (1998, p. 59), and finally, more extensively, Petrucci (2008, II, pp. 292–297). The decisive rehabilitation of the painting as an autograph work by Caravaggio occurred in 2010 at the

Mostra di Caravaggio e dei caravaggeschi a Firenze (Christiansen, in *Caravaggio e caravaggeschi* 2010, pp. 100–103; Papi 2010, pp. 23–25), a view that was subsequently reiterated on several occasions, until the very recent exhibition in these same rooms where the *Maffeo* was displayed as a work by Caravaggio, while the *Francesco* was generally considered the work of a Roman artist (Schütze, in *L'immagine sovrana* 2023, pp. 158–159, 160–161).

The provenance of the portrait from the Barberini collection is perfectly traceable. The work in fact came to the Corsini family in Florence through the marriage of Anna Barberini Colonna, eldest daughter of Carlo and Giuliana Falconeri, with Tommaso Corsini in 1858 (Christiansen, in *Caravaggio e caravaggeschi* 2010, p. 100). In the inventory of the gentlewoman's possessions drawn up in 1911, the work is described as coming from the Barberini collection, together with the *Francesco*, with the attribution to a "Caravaggio", the memory of whose real name, however, had been lost: "142 Portrait of Bishop Maffeo Barberini, later Urban VIII. Lecchi Giovan Battista known as Caravaggio Height m. 1.22 × 0.92 L 6000" and further on: "144 Portrait of Monsignor Francesco Barberini, uncle of Urban VIII. Idem [Lecchi Giovan Battista known as Caravaggio] Height 1.22 m. × 0.92 L 8000" (Archivio Corsini, Florence, Stanza 6.a, armadio 4.o., unnumbered file. Present in the Getty Provenance Index site with the incorrect identification of the artist as "Giovanni Battista Gariboldi", the citation was already present in Christiansen (in *Caravaggio e caravaggeschi* 2010, p. 100). Going backwards, the two paintings are recorded in the 1853 and 1844 inventories of the Barberini's possessions as the work of Scipione Pulzone (Christiansen, in *Caravaggio e caravaggeschi* 2010, p. 100), with the attribution and identification of the sitters with which they were included in the 1911 exhibition, which not surprisingly was mounted in Florence by a team of Florentine scholars including Ugo Ojetti and Carlo Gamba, evidently up to date with the Corsini collection. One is surprised, however, that the posthumous inventory of Anna Barberini Colonna Corsini, drawn up after 11 July 1911, when the exhibition was coming to an end, did not refer to the attribution with which the canvas was displayed on that important occasion.

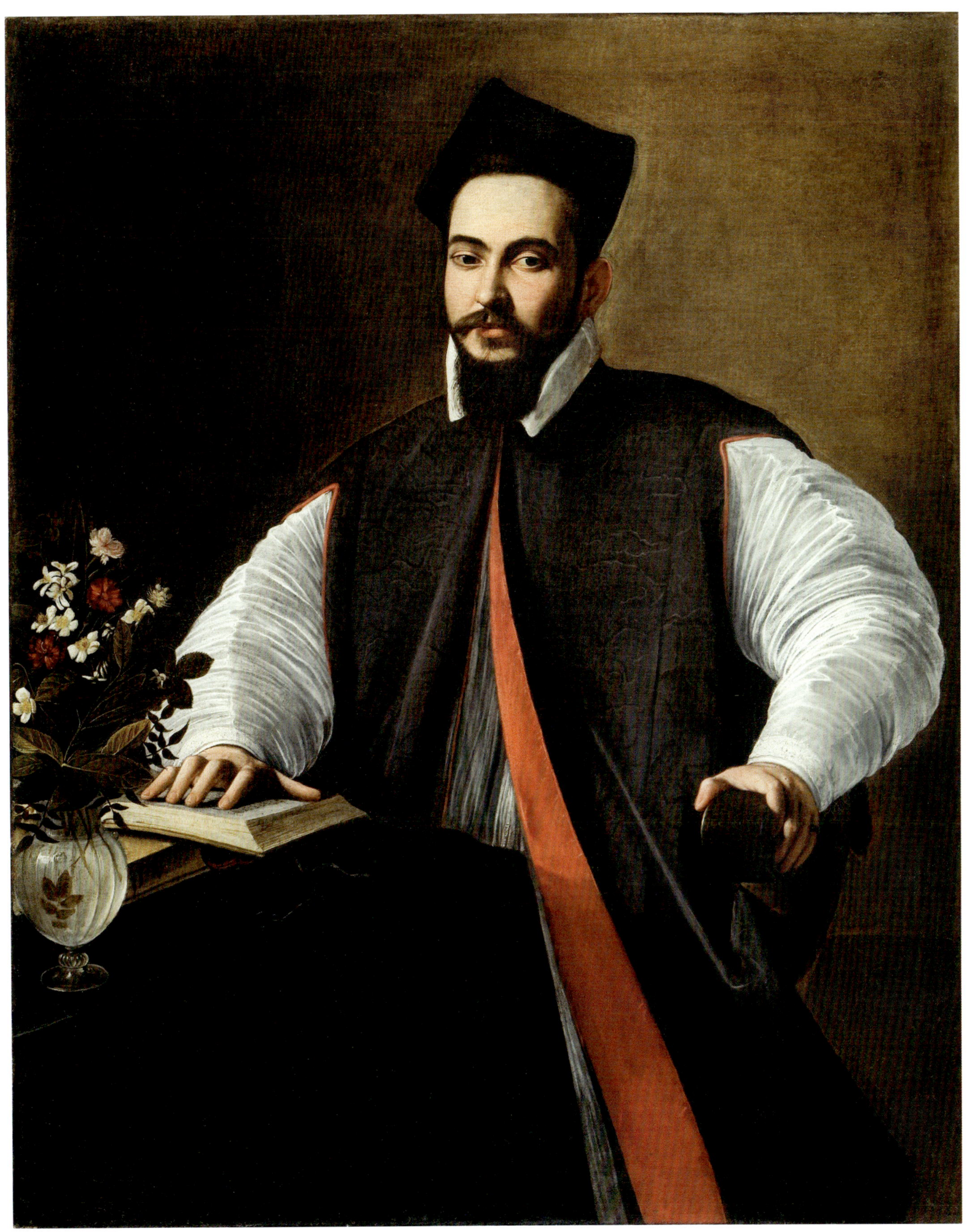

[cat. 3] PORTRAIT OF MONSIGNOR MAFFEO BARBERINI AS PROTONOTARY APOSTOLIC

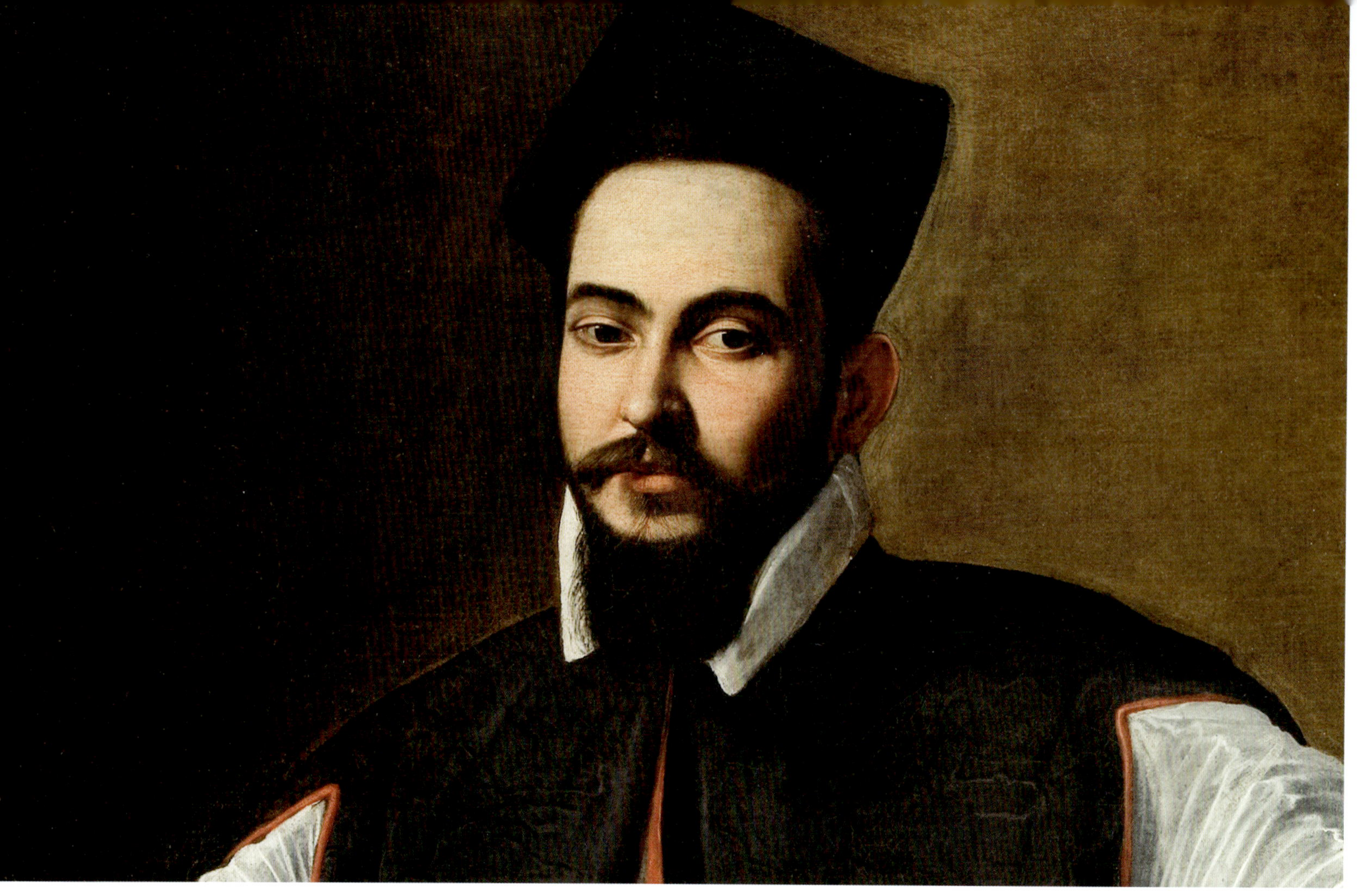

Although not always contiguous, both the *Portrait of Maffeo Barberini* and that of *Francesco* are referred to in the Barberini inventories, identifiable by their similar dimensions and the same black wood frames. In particular, the 1655 inventory perfectly describes the canvas in the palazzo in Via delle Quattro Fontane: "A painting with a Portrait of a Prelate, with a carafe with flowers in it with an open book, with his hand on it, a beech-wood frame tinted black, six and a quarter *palmi* high and five wide" (Lavin 1975, p. 281, no. 351; Christiansen 2010, p. 100), and to this listed entry, I would add that in the same palazzo there was also: "A Painting with a Portrait of an Old Prelate, Who Sits with a brief in his hand, called Francesco Barberino, with a beech-wood frame tinted black, six and a quarter *palmi* high and five wide" (Lavin 1975, p. 382, no. 379). The two portraits were at the time housed together in the palazzo in Via delle Quattro Fontane, whereas a few years earlier in 1648 they were listed in Taddeo Barberini's collection but in two different locations: in the palazzo in Via dei Giubbonari, "A portrait painting on canvas of Monsig[nor] Francesco Barberino with a black frame about 6 *palmi* high about 4 *palmi* wide", and in the palazzo at the Quattro Fontane, "A portrait

painting of Pope Urban the Eighth when he was prelate, six and a half *palmi* high and five *palmi* wide with a black frame" (Lavin 1975, pp. 193, 209–210). Finally, in the most complete inventory of Maffeo Barberini, drawn up in 1623,—when he ascended to the papal throne with the name of Urban VIII—, is recorded: "A portrait of S[igno]r C[ardinal] Barb[erini] when he was Chierico di Cam[er]a with a black frame," and immediately following, "Portrait of Mons[igno]r franc[esc]o Barberino without a Frame" (Lavin 1975, p. 68, nos. 111–112). In fact, the oldest inventory of Maffeo Barberini's possessions of 1608 (he was then resident in Palazzo Salviati), documents how the illustrious prelate possessed two portraits with his likeness: "Two Portraits of His Illustrious Lordship," which Lavin 1967 believes refers to the portrait under examination, and to the one in the private collection [cat. 9].

Thanks to the liberality of Francesco Barberini the Elder, who protected his nephew's career from the outset, on 24 October 1593, Maffeo took up the post of protonotary apostolic granted him by his uncle. The future Urban VIII, however, was only appointed Chierico di Camera (Cleric of the Apostolic Camera) in March 1597. The description of the painting of

Maffeo Barberini is not therefore a perfect fit for the painting under examination. However, the robes with the black cassock and ruby threading worn by Maffeo, common to both protonotaries apostolic and Chierici di Camera, make it difficult to make the distinction. Indeed, even in the other *Maffeo* [cat. 9] the ruby lining of the mantelletta can be glimpsed beneath the robes, painted with refined skill. Although caution in identifying the painting is mandatory, D'Onofrio (1967) reasonably observed that of all the portraits of Maffeo Barberini referred to in that inventory, the one described is the only one that could be identified with our painting.

It is, in any case, evident how the painting is in perfect dialogue with the *Portrait of Francesco Barberini*, which displays, in addition to the same format, the same setting and the same robe with the ruby threading clearly in view, signifying precisely that the two prelates shared the same office. Leaving aside all the proposed attributions, it seems likely therefore that the works were linked in the minds of their patrons, even though each might have taken a separate path within the vast Barberini collection. In relation to this, Marini (1974, p. 132; 1987, p. 415) and Schütze (2007, p. 153; 2009, p. 256) even thought to link the paintings to the payment of 10 *scudi* by Maffeo Barberini on 3 July 1604 to the Florentine painter Nicodemo Francucci, a pupil of Passignano: "For the overall price of two portraits that he has painted for me" (D'Onofrio 1967, p. 62). This opinion was decisively refuted by Christiansen (2010, p. 102) from a stylistic point of view, and—in my opinion—also risky in terms of the interpretation of the documentary source.

From his youth, Maffeo Barberini nurtured a special passion for the arts and for culture. In particular, at the end of the seventeenth century his connection with the Accademia degli Insensati in Perugia is well known, where personalities from Caravaggio's circle served, including Aurelio Orsi, brother of the painter Prospero, and Cesare Crispolti, who owned a version of the *Boy Peeling Fruit* [cat. 2]. Maffeo was, in any case, in direct contact with Caravaggio between May 1603 and January 1604, when he paid him for a painting, generally identified with the *Sacrifice of Isaac* in the Uffizi (D'Onofrio 1967, p. 62, note 26), which some scholars refer on the other hand to the other *Maffeo Barberini* (cat. 9; Papi 2010; Christiansen, in *Caravaggio e caravaggeschi* 2010). The prelate's devotion to the art of Caravaggio is also acknowledged by Mancini ([1619–1621] 1956–1957, I, p. 227): "He made portraits for Barberino", and by Bellori ([1672] 1976, p. 224), who however speaks of these in the singular. There is no doubt that the strength and power of the other *Maffeo Barberini* [cat. 9], which is undoubtedly by the hand of Caravaggio, compel one to reflect more deeply on this painting, which assuredly displays a taste for naturalism in the detail of the

hand vigorously grasping the chair, in the still-life, and above all in the dramatic chiaroscuro of the prelate's face, but also displays some weaknesses, for example, in the heavy handling of the robes, not simple to justify in comparison with the other painting. It is difficult for the moment to resolve the question; however, I believe that the suggestion that the two paintings were executed at a great distance in time, one in Caravaggio's early days, the other in 1604, cannot be considered decisive, as the *Maffeo Barberini* in the private collection is, in my opinion, a luminous example of Caravaggio's transition from his *juvenilia* to the tragic manner of the Contarelli Chapel, both in terms of the chromatic choice of the background, where one can see the remarkable transition from the lighter tonality on the right to the darker one on the left, and the extraordinarily eloquent gesture of the hand. The qualitative difference between the young prelate's face and his robes, which seems to me evident in the portrait under examination, and is shared by the *Portrait of Francesco Barberini*, might rather suggest that the canvases belonged to the serial production of the workshops in which Caravaggio had also participated in his early days in Rome, a moment that would not be too far removed from the *terminus post quem* of the autumn of 1593, set by the aforementioned succession of posts held by the young Maffeo Barberini.
[MCT]

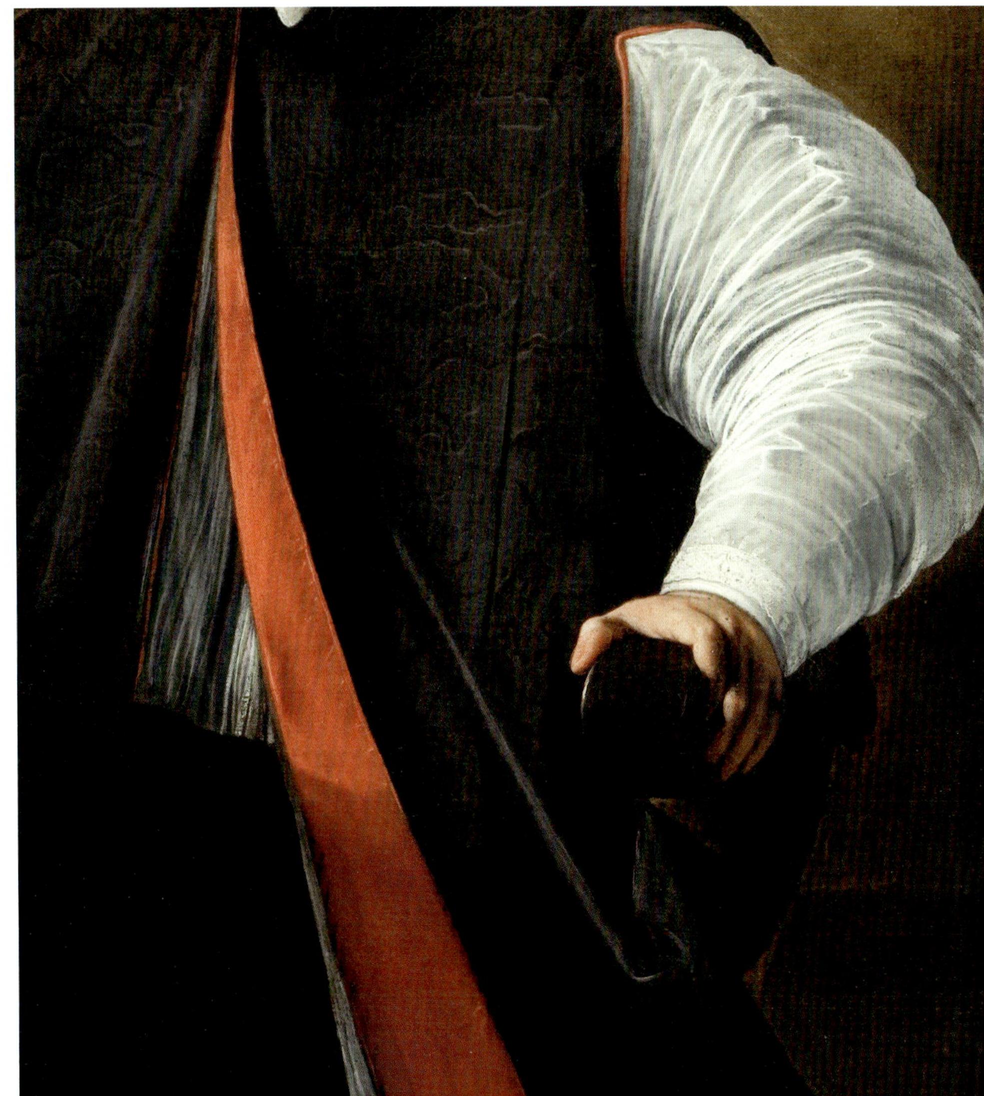

THE FORTUNE TELLER

c. 1596–1597
oil on canvas, 115 × 150 cm
Musei Capitolini – Pinacoteca
Capitolina, Rome

Provenance: Cardinal Francesco
Maria del Monte (1549-1626), Rome,
1627; acquired by Cardinal Carlo
Emanuele Pio (1578-1641), Rome,
1628; by succession to the heirs; heirs
of Pio da Carpi until 1749; acquired
by Pope Benedict XIV for the
Pinacoteca Capitolina in 1750.

Bibliography: Mancini [c. 1619–
1621] 1956–1957, I, pp. 109, 140,
224; Baglione [1642] 2023 p. 402;
Battisti 1955, p. 182; Frommel 1971,
p. 31; Kirwin, 1971, p. 55; Cuzin 1977,
p. 11; Christiansen 1988, pp. 26–27;
Mahon 1988, p. 21; Tittoni Monti
1989, p. 180; Cappelletti, Testa
1990c, pp. 77–80; Cinotti 1991, p. 3;
Gregori, in *Michelangelo Merisi da
Caravaggio. Come nascono* 1991,
pp. 86–90; Sickel 2003a, p. 223;
Loire 2006, pp. 64–70; Curti 2011b,
pp. 65–76; Leone 2016, pp. 192–200;
Vodret, in *Dentro Caravaggio* 2017,
pp. 207–209; Vodret 2018, p. 81;
Vodret 2021a, p. 132.

The Fortune Teller in the Musei Capitolini is unanimously recognised by scholarship as an original work by Caravaggio. It differs from a second version, also painted by him, which is smaller in size (99 × 131 cm), and is now in the Louvre. The presence of the Parisian canvas is attested in the collection of Girolamo Vittrice as early as 1609 (Sickel 2003a, p. 223). It later entered the Pamphilj collection and was presented to Louis XIV in 1665 (Loire 2006, pp. 64–70).

The version in the Musei Capitolini comes from the collection of Cardinal Francesco Maria del Monte. Confirmation of this origin is corroborated by the discovery, on the back of the painting, of the Del Monte seal that emerged during the re-lining carried out during the 1986 restoration (Tittoni Monti 1989, p. 180). This seal is accompanied by the inscription "Pio I 9343". A similar seal was also found on *The Cardsharps* in the Kimbell Museum in Fort Worth [cat. 5], also from the same collection (Mahon 1988, p. 21; Christiansen 1988, pp. 26–27).

The first documentary evidence of this work is found in Cardinal del Monte's posthumous inventory, drawn up in 1627, in which it is described as "Gypsy by Caravaggio five *palmi* in size with a black frame" (Frommel 1971, p. 31). The following year, in 1628, the painting was sold at auction together with other important works, including the Capitoline *Saint John the Baptist*, for a total value of 240 *scudi* (Kirwin 1971, p. 55). Acquired by Cardinal Carlo Emanuele Pio, it appears in the inventory of the Pio da Carpi collection in 1641 (Cappelletti, Testa 1990c, pp. 77-80); later, the collection passed into the hands of his brother Ascanio, and then to his eldest son Carlo (ibid.). The work is also present in the 1724 inventory with an attribution to Caravaggio, although the catalogue edited by Trevisani in 1740 omits the name of the author. Caravaggio's authorship was definitively confirmed in the 1749 inventory compiled by Giovanni Paolo Panini, on the occasion of the sale to Benedetto XIV Lambertini for the establishment of the Pinacoteca Capitolina (Battisti 1955, p. 182).

Although the Capitoline version is now unanimously accepted as an autograph work, its dating, closely linked to the interpretation of documentary sources, continues to be the object of debate,

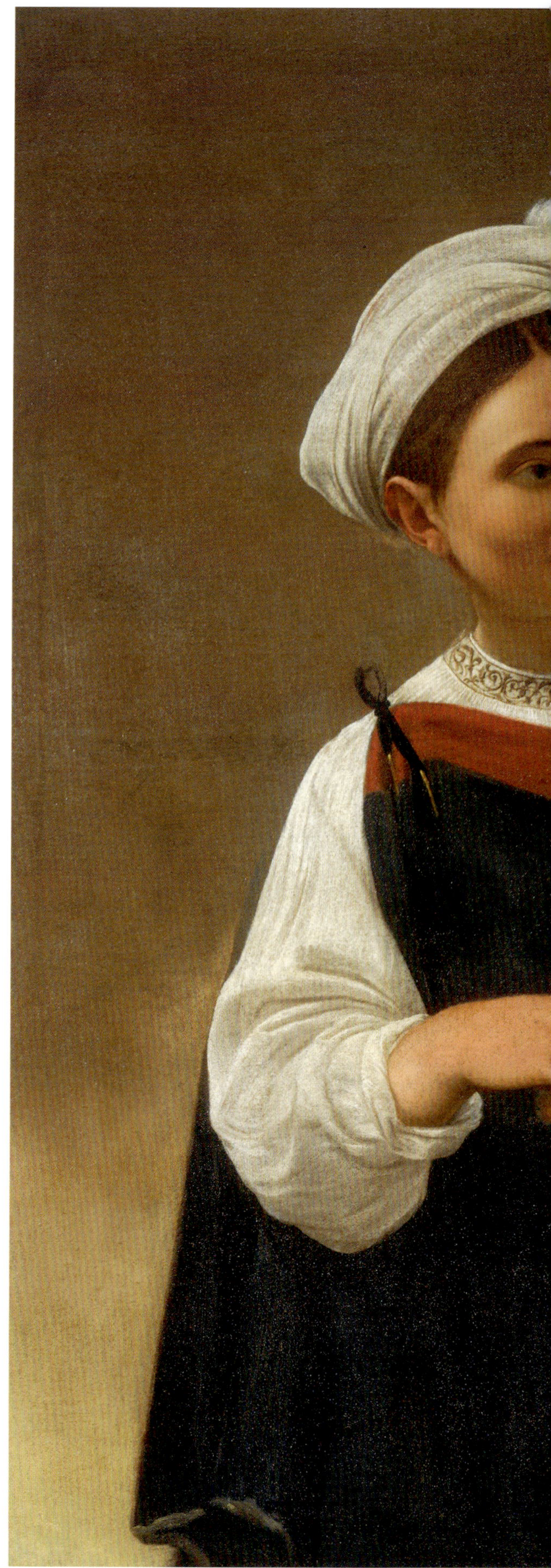

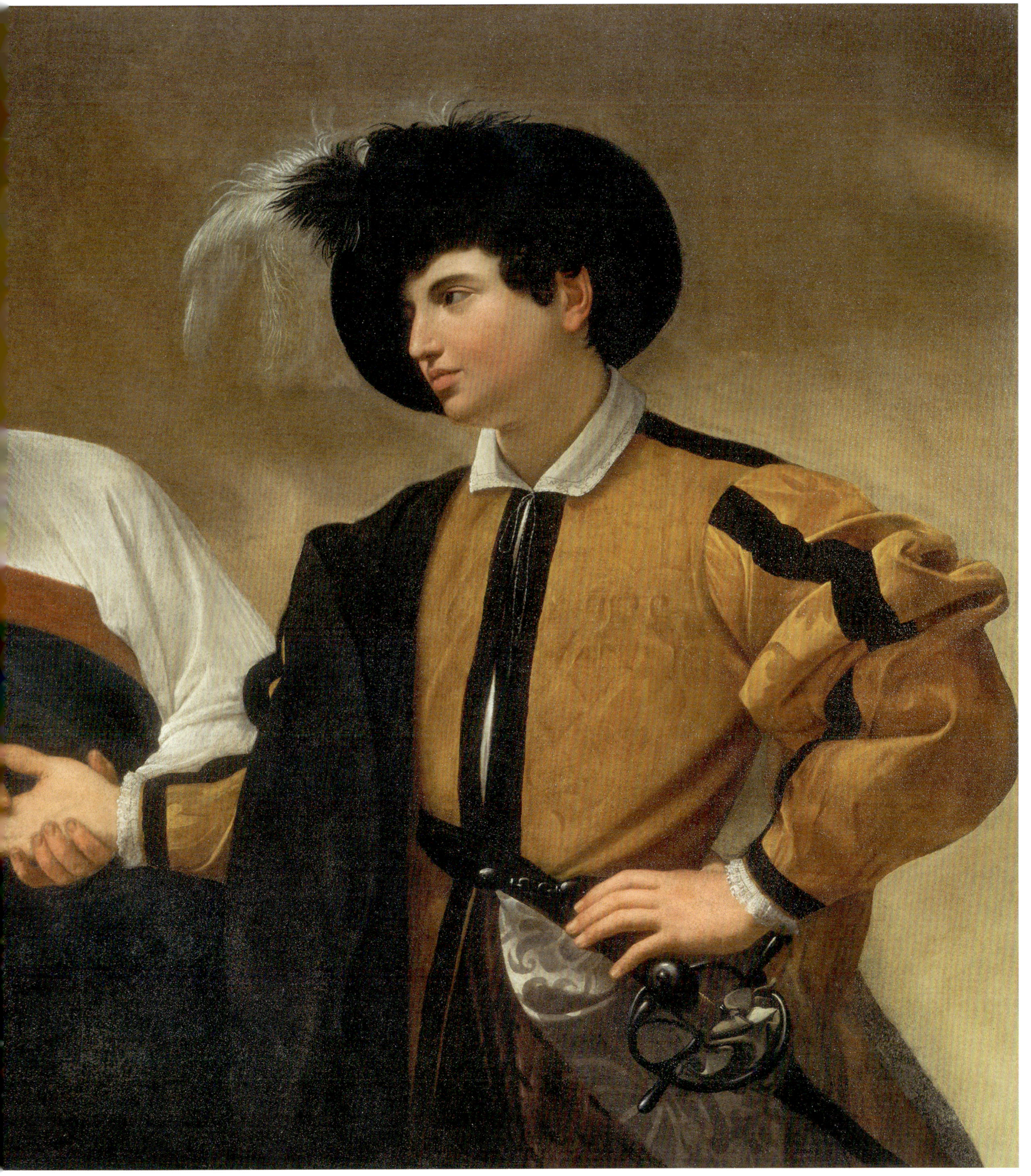

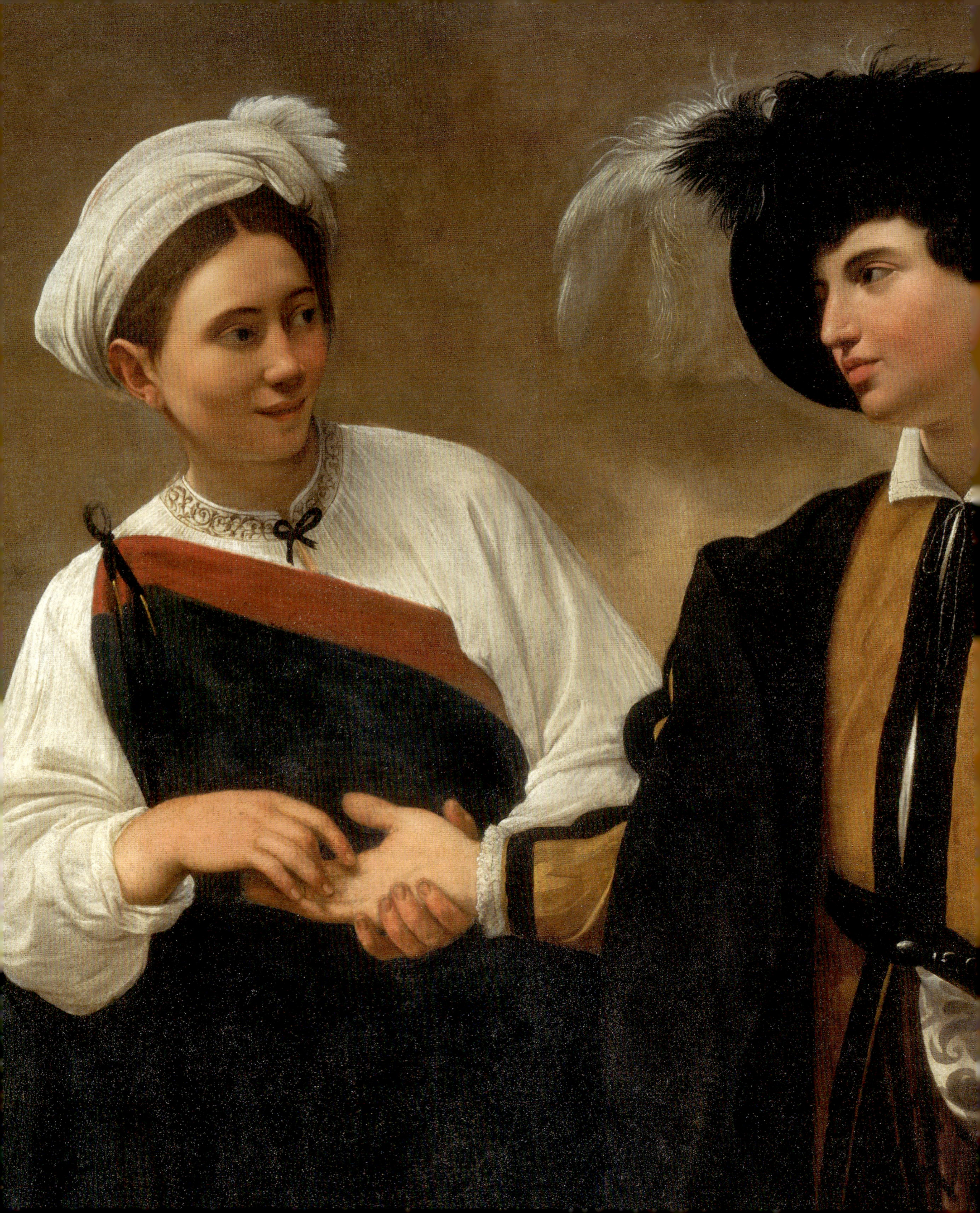

especially in relation to the version in the Louvre. Rossella Vodret (2017a, pp. 201-236: pp. 207-209; 2018, p. 81; 2021a, p. 132) places the execution of the Louvre painting before that of the Capitoline version, relying on the indications provided by Giovanni Baglione, who in 1625 included the work among those painted for Cardinal del Monte: "He portrayed [in] a beautifully coloured [painting a] Gypsy, telling the fortune of a young man" (Baglione [1642] 2023 p. 402. English translation adapted from Friedländer [1955] 1976, p. 234).

A number of scholars are of a different opinion, considering the Louvre version later than the one in the Musei Capitolini (Cinotti 1991, p. 31; Gregori, in *Michelangelo Merisi da Caravaggio. Come nascono* 1992, pp. 86–90). This latter hypothesis is based on the testimony of the Sienese physician Giulio Mancini ([c. 1619–1621] 1956–1957, I, pp. 140, 224. English translation in Friedländer 1955 1976, p. 255), who, in his *Considerazioni*, reports that Caravaggio painted "a gypsy telling a young man's fortune" during his time with Fantino Petrignani and the Cavalier d'Arpino.

In the same text, albeit in a separate section, Mancini states that he saw *The Fortune Teller* in Alessandro Vittrice's house, presumably referring to the version now in the Louvre (Mancini [c. 1619–1621] 1956–1957, I, p. 109). This statement has divided scholars: some maintain that Mancini is still referring to the same version, that is the Vittrice one, while others speculate that he is referring to two separate versions.

In 1977, on the occasion of an exhibition dedicated to the Parisian painting curated by Jean-Pierre Cuzin, the presence of a Madonna at prayer was detected beneath the painted surface of the Capitoline version, for which the scholar drew parallels with the *Coronation of the Virgin* in Santa Maria della Vallicella in Rome, painted by the Cavalier d'Arpino between 1592 and 1615 (Cuzin 1977, p. 11).

More recently, Leone (2016, pp. 192-200) has explained that the image underlying the Capitoline painting should not be interpreted as a Virgin at prayer, but rather as a Virgin adoring the sleeping Child. The scholar has also suggested a possible connection with the iconography of a work described in the inventory of Lorenzo Carli's workshop, drawn up on 10 April 1597, shortly after his death. This document, discovered by Francesca Curti (2011b, pp. 65–76), refers to "the image of the Madonna with her son sleeping on a pillow and Saint John, Saint Iseppe and Saint Isabella," thus offering a useful element for the dating of the work.

The Fortune Teller depicts a gypsy woman in the act of reading the hand of a young man, while with a furtive gesture she pulls the ring from his finger. The subject, imbued with a moral meaning relating to the subject of deception and guile, enjoyed a resounding success among Caravaggesque followers. The composition, characterised by a dramatic use of narrative gestures, seems to draw inspiration from the theatrical representations of the "zingaresche", a dramatic genre very popular in seventeenth-century Italy (see the entry for *The Cardsharps*; cat. 5).

[GM]

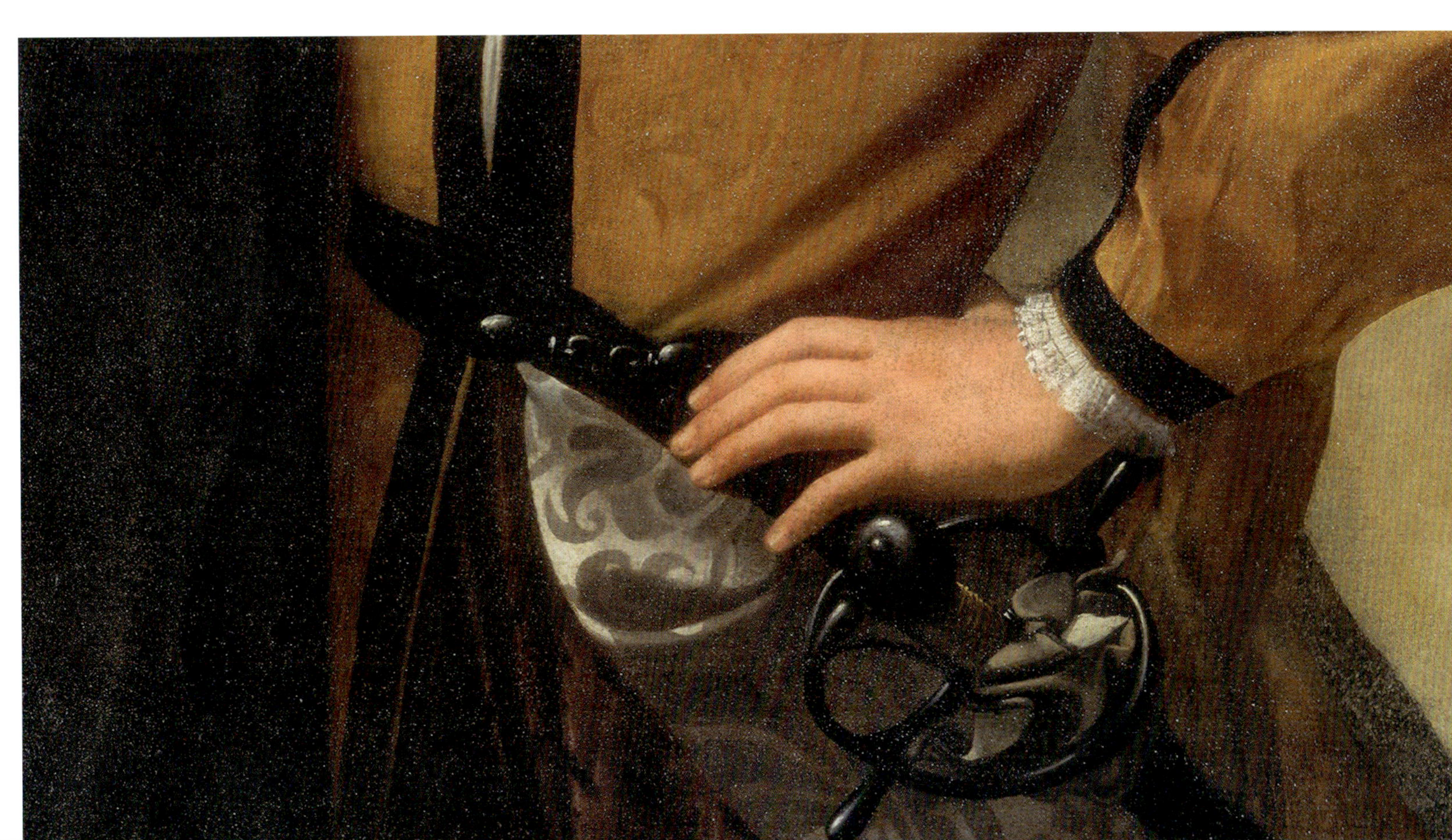

THE CARDSHARPS

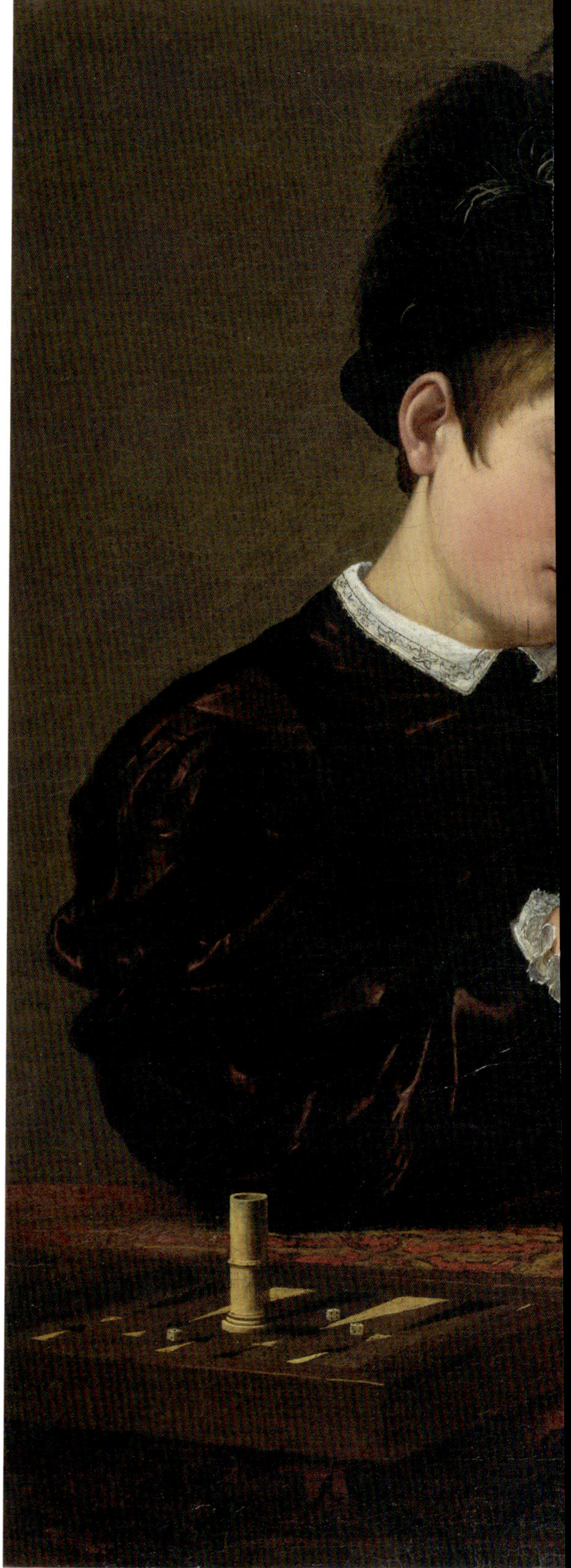

c. 1596–1597
oil on canvas, 94.2 × 130.9 cm
Kimbell Art Museum, Fort Worth
(TX), inv. AP 1987.06

Provenance: Cardinal Francesco Maria
Bourbon del Monte (1549–1626),
Palazzo Madama, Rome, 1627;
inherited by his nephew, Alessandro
del Monte, Bishop of Gubbio (d. 1628);
acquired in 1628 by Cardinal Antonio
Barberini (1607–1671), Palazzo
Barberini alle Quattro Fontane and
Palazzo ai Giubbonari, Rome; by
descent to his nephew, don Maffeo
Barberini, Prince of Palestrina
(1631–1685), Palazzo Barberini,
Rome; by descent to his son, don
Urbano Barberini, prince of Palestrina
(1664–1722), Palazzo Barberini,
Rome; by descent to his brother,
cardinal Francesco Barberini, prince
of Palestrina (1662–1738), Palazzo
Barberini, Rome; by inheritance to
his niece, donna Cornelia Costanza
Barberini (d. 1797) and her husband,
Don Giulio Cesare Colonna di Sciarra
(1705–1787), Palazzo Barberini, Rome;
assigned in 1812 to their nephew,
Don Maffeo Barberini Colonna di
Sciarra, 7th Prince of Carbognano
(1796–1849), Palazzo Sciarra, Rome;
by descent to their son, Don Maffeo
Barberini Colonna di Sciarra, 8th Prince
of Carbognano (1850–1925), Palazzo
Sciarra, Rome, and Paris, until about
1895; purchased by the Kimbell Art
Foundation, Fort Worth, in 1987.

Bibliography: Bellori [1672] 2005,
p. 180; Vicchi 1889, pp. 43–44;
Venturi 1950, pp. 41–42; Mahon 1951,
pp. 229, note 67, 234; Frommel 1971,
p. 25; Kirwin 1971, pp. 54–55; Lavin
1975, p. 167; Moir 1976, pp. 104–107;
Christiansen 1988, pp. 26–27; Mahon
1988, notes 53 and 61; Gregori 1991a,
p. 102; Langdon 2001, pp. 44–52;
Macioce 2003, pp. 286–288; Marini
2005, pp. 402–403; Gregori 2008,
p. 30; Terzaghi 2007, pp. 27–30;
Savina 2013, pp. 111–120; Terzaghi
2010a, p. 43; Terzaghi 2020a, pp. 93–
94; Vodret 2021a, pp. 128, 130.

With the title "Il giuoco" ("The game") in ancient sources, the painting is attested by Bellori (Bellori [1672] 2005, p. 180) as being one of the first works by Caravaggio acquired by Cardinal del Monte and kept in his palazzo di Ripetta, together with *The Fortune Teller* [cat. 4] and other paintings by the artist (Gregori 2008, p. 30).

The first documentary references to the painting in question date back to the inventory of the cardinal's estate, drawn up on 21 February 1627 (Frommel 1971, p. 25). Following the auction of the assets of the estate in 1628 (Kirwin 1971, pp. 54–55), the painting was acquired by Cardinal Antonio Barberini, together with other famous works such as the *Lute Player* and the *Saint Catherine*. The acquisition is accurately detailed in the Barberini inventories from 1644 to 1812 (Lavin 1975, p. 167). Following a hereditary succession, the work became part of the prestigious Colonna di Sciarra collections.

At the end of the nineteenth century, the painting was transferred to Paris by Maffeo Barberini Colonna di Sciarra to be sold. In 1895 the painting was still in the French capital, the subject of negotiations both with the National Gallery in London and the Duke Agénor de Gramont. The negotiations did not lead to any final outcome, and knowledge of the painting's whereabouts was subsequently lost (Mahon 1988, notes 53 and 61).

In 1950, Lionello Venturi, in a statement destined to prove highly controversial, identified a copy of the painting found in New York as the original (Venturi 1950, pp. 41–42, figs. 67–69, plates XXII–XXIV). This position contradicted the evidence regarding the provenance of the Sciarra Colonna canvas, the image of which was known thanks to Leone Vicchi's volume dedicated to the collection (Vicchi 1889, pp. 43–44, plate IX) and the photographic documentation produced by the Parisian firm Braun, Clément & Compagnie (neg. 43210, 35 × 45.5 cm). The hypothesis put forward by Venturi was promptly challenged by Denis Mahon, who emphasised the importance of the provenance and the extraordinary quality of the Sciarra Colonna painting reproduced by the Braun photograph (Mahon 1951, pp. 229, note 67, 234).

In 1986 the original work re-emerged in Zurich and, thanks to the expertise of scholars Mina

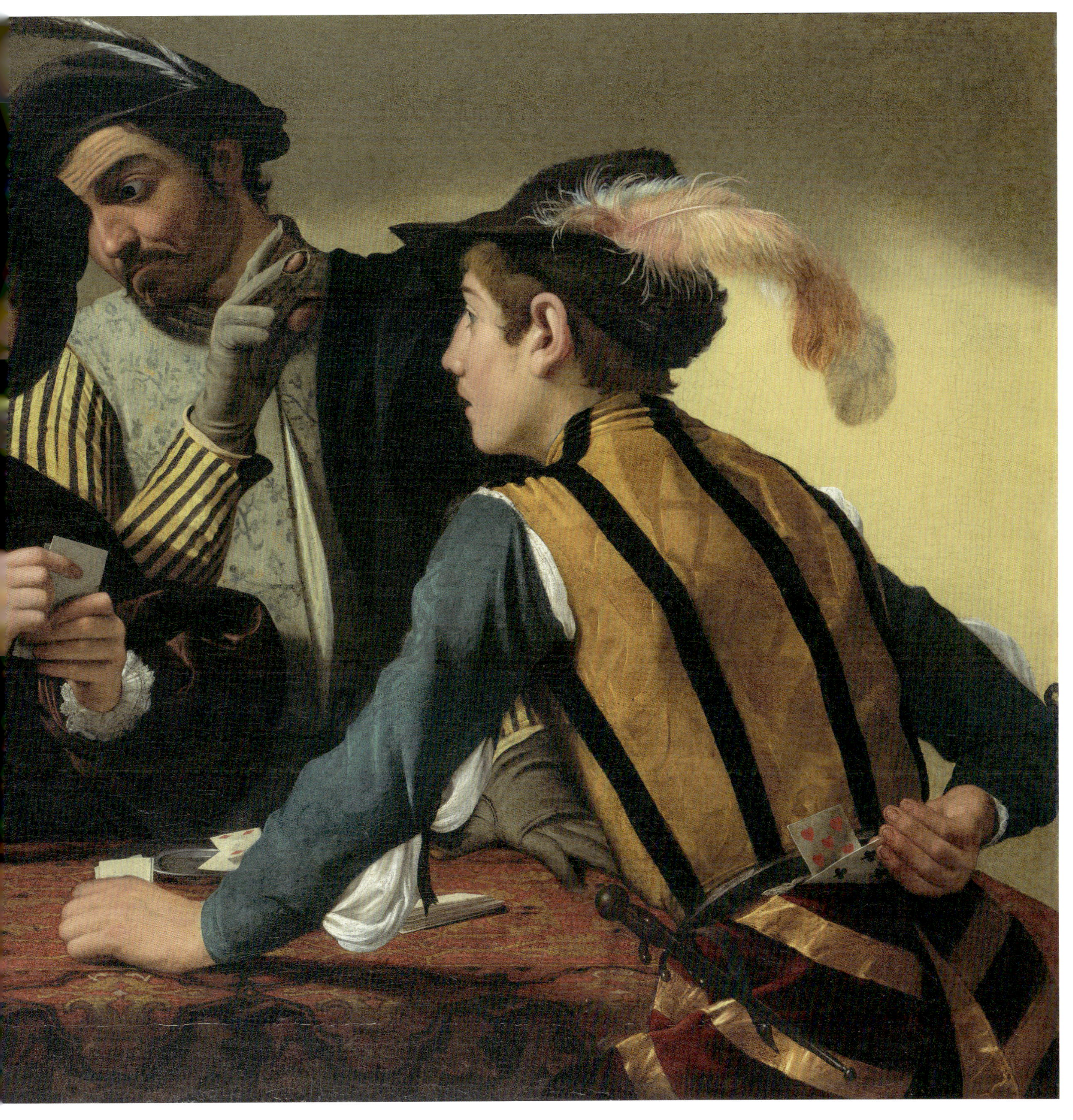

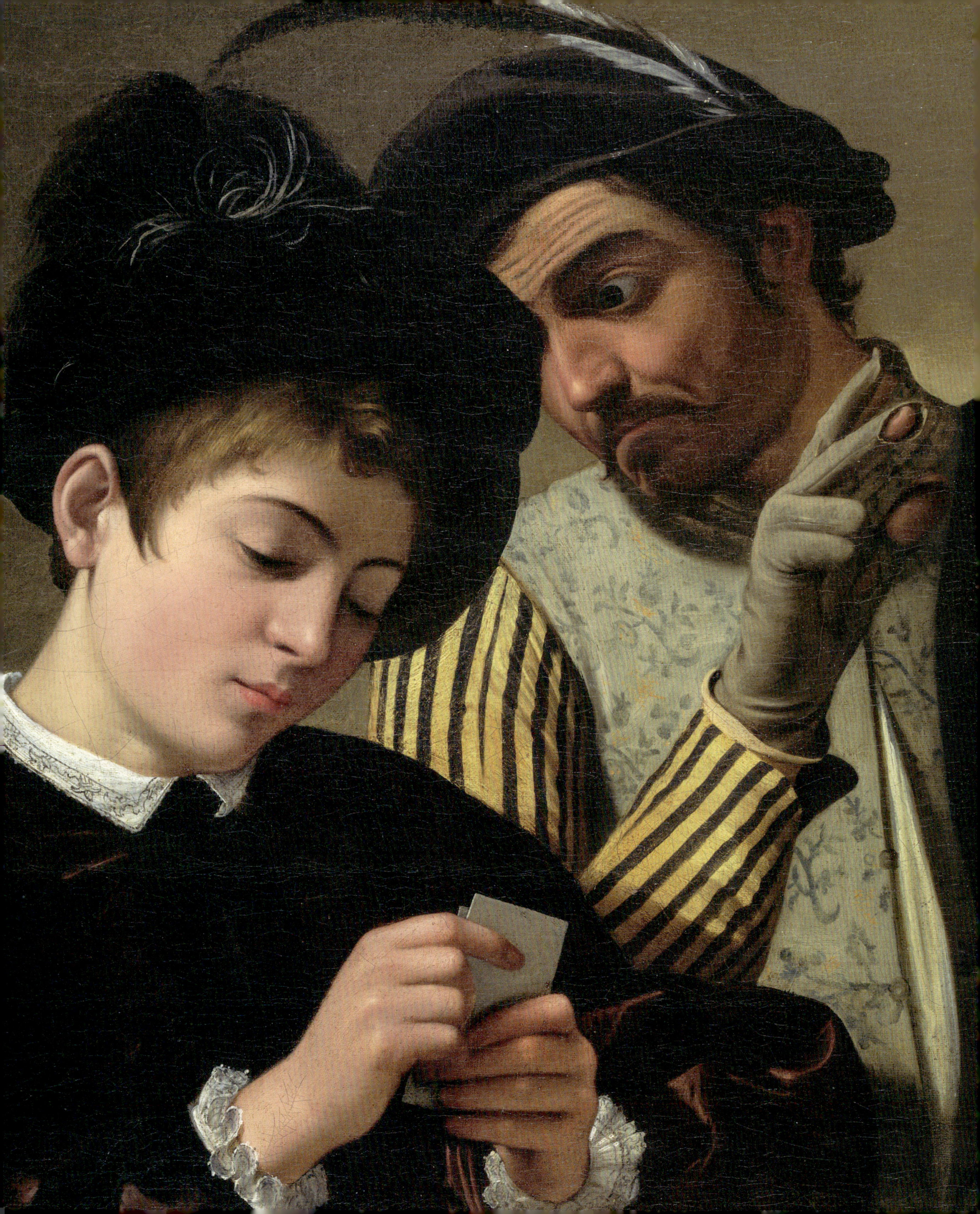

Gregori and Richard Pillsbury, it was recognised as an authentic creation by the artist (Mahon 1988) and the following year, in 1987, the painting was acquired by the museum.

The Cardsharps was an immediate success, as attested by Mancini as early as 1621: " many [copies] were made" (Macioce 2003, pp. 286–288). To date, over thirty versions are known (Moir 1976, pp. 104–107; Savina 2013, pp. 111–120), some of them of high quality. These have not only complicated the identification of the original held in the Kimbell Art Museum, but have also led Mina Gregori to propose as autograph the version previously belonging to Denis Mahon, now in the Ashmolean Museum in Oxford. However, this attribution has not been accepted by Maria Cristina Terzaghi and Rossella Vodret (Terzaghi 2010a, p. 43; Vodret 2021a, p. 128).

From an iconographic point of view, both *The Cardsharps* and *The Fortune Teller*—once exhibited in the same room and presented in black frames (Terzaghi 2010a, p. 43)—are inspired by the theatrical representations of the *zingaresche*, in which naïve youth is deceived by malice and cunning (Gregori 1991a, p. 102; Marini 2005, pp. 102–107). 102; Marini 2005, pp. 402–403; Langdon 2001, pp. 44–52; Terzaghi 2007, pp. 27–30; Terzaghi 2010a, p. 43 and Terzaghi 2020a, pp. 93–94). Scholars agree in placing both paintings as early works, prior to the artist's relationship with Cardinal del Monte. This chronological attribution is supported both by Bellori's observations (Bellori [1672] 2005, p. 180) and by stylistic characteristics such as the light hues of the palette and softer painting technique, both hallmarks of the artist's early production. In *The Cardsharps* are also present numerous incisions, particularly evident in the decorative elements, and a grey ground layer consistent with the works executed by the painter in his youth (Christiansen 1988, pp. 26–27; Vodret 2021a, p. 130).

[GM]

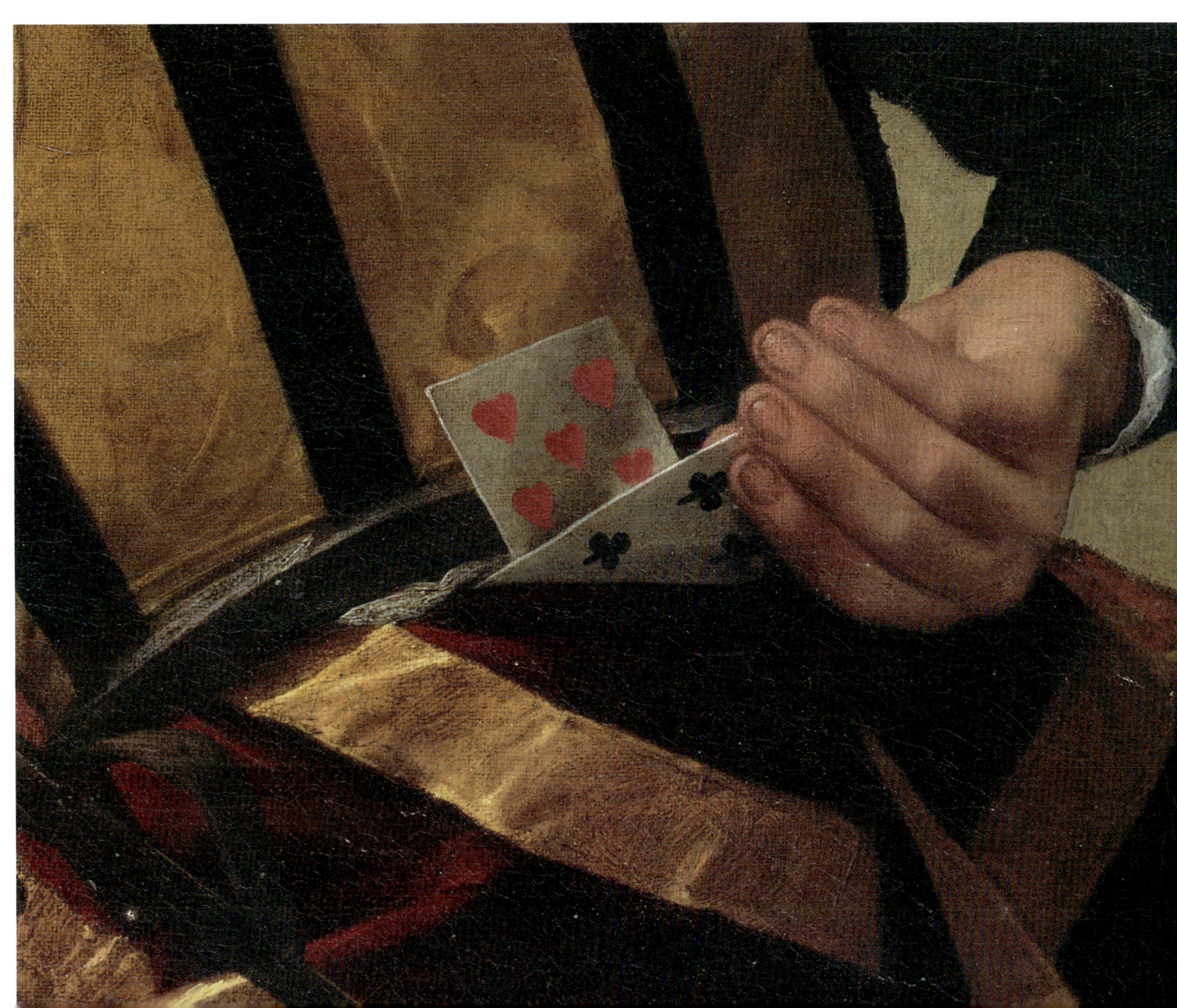

THE MUSICIANS

1597

oil on canvas, 92.1 × 118.4 cm
The Metropolitan Museum of Art,
New York (NY), Rogers Fund, 1952,
inv. 52.81

Provenance: in the inventory of
the possessions of the late Cardinal
del Monte (†27 August 1626), the
original painting was listed on 28
February 1627 as "a Concert by the
hand of Michelangelo da Caravaggio
with a black frame, about five *palmi*
[in size]", located "in the first room
of the new apartment" in Palazzo
Avogrado a Ripetta, after its long
sojourn in Palazzo Madama. After
the cardinal's death, the "painting
of Youths singing" was acquired in
May 1628 by Monsignor Prospero
Fagnani, who bought it either for
himself or as a 'front-man' for the
young cardinal Antonio Barberini,
who, according to a Roman "notice"
of 15 July 1634, then donated
it—before 8 July of that year—to
Maréchal Charles de Blanchefort,
Marquis de Créquy, Ambassador
Extraordinary of the King of France
Louis XIII to the Holy See, who
was resident in Rome from 7 June
1633 to July 1634. The painting
was secured onto a wood panel
with hot glue to better endure the
difficult transport to Paris—an
operation that compromised the
support of the painting, altered the
colours and caused the progressive
fragmentation of the paint layers
in many areas of the work. It was
recorded in 1638 in the inventory
of the Créquy collection as "a
concert by Caravaggio painted on
wood [panel]" with a gilded frame,
with the inscription in gold leaf in
capital letters affixed to the lower
left of the painting "michelang. da
carava|gio". The painting then passed
into Cardinal Richelieu's collection
and was inventoried in 1643 as "a
Concert of music the first work by
Caravaggio" and then later assigned
to the Duchesse d'Aiguillon and
listed in her inventory of 1675, still

In all likelihood the painting is the first work expressly commissioned from the young Caravaggio
by Cardinal Francesco Maria del Monte, his first
patron, in whose collection it is recorded for the
first time in 1627, on the occasion of the *post mortem* inventory of the prelate's possessions. In this
respect, Baglione ([1642] 1995, p. 136: "he painted
for the cardinal a concert of young men portrayed
from life in half-length figure") and Bellori ([1672]
2005, p. 216: "for this lord he painted a concert
of young men portrayed from life in half-length
figures") are in absolute agreement. The first evidence of Caravaggio as "Cardinal De Monte's
painter" dates to the spring of 1597, on the occasion of the interrogations of 10–12 July in relation
to the attack by unknown persons on the musician
Angelo Tanconi; and this is the date around which
The Musicians must have been executed, its composition still close—in terms of style and iconography—to the Veneto-Lombard background of the
artist, whose features are moreover identifiable in
the cornett player in the background.

Naturally, the musical content is fundamental to
the understanding of the work, which its troubled
conservation history has, however, contributed
to obscure. It is only recently that the incomplete
notation of the music partbook held by the singer seen from the back, which has in the past been
variously and imaginatively deciphered, has finally
been identified—also thanks to a comparison made
with a later copy in which the musical excerpts are
better preserved—with the *incipit* of "Ben può di
sua ruina", a composition from the *First book of
madrigals for six voices* (*Primo libro de madrigali a
sei voci*) by the Neapolitan Pompeo Stabile, printed
in Venice in 1585 (D'Alessandro 2018); more precisely, it is the musical setting of the second part of
Iacopo Sannazaro's sonnet, "Icarus fell here, these
waves do know it" ("Icaro cadde qui, queste onde il
sanno"), included in the *editio princeps* of the Neapolitan poet's *Sonnetti et canzoni*, published post-
humously in 1530. Graduating in civil and canon
law at the University of Pisa, Stabile was organist at
the Santa Casa dell'Annunziata in Naples in 1582–
1583, and later, between 1587 and 1590, in the service of Cardinal Alessandro Peretti Montalto
The meaning of the madrigal lends a moralising tone to the subject of the painting, previous

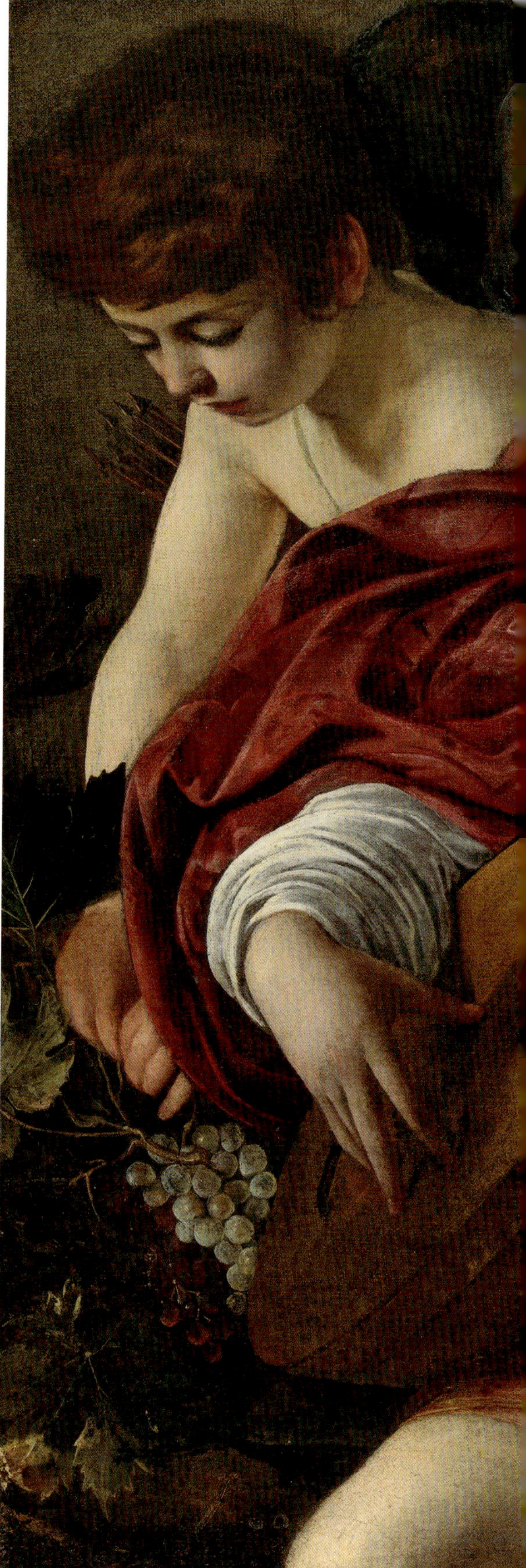

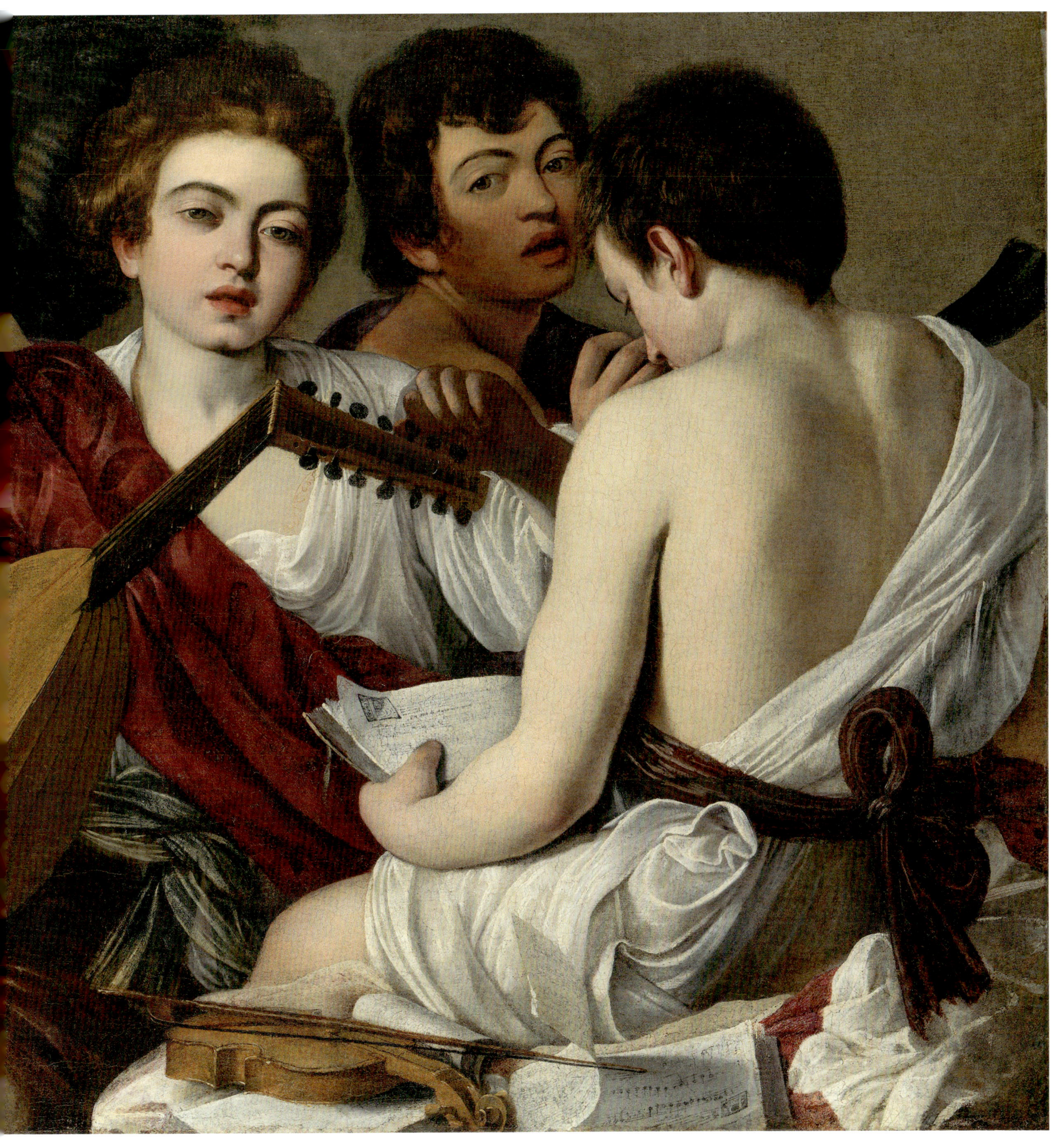

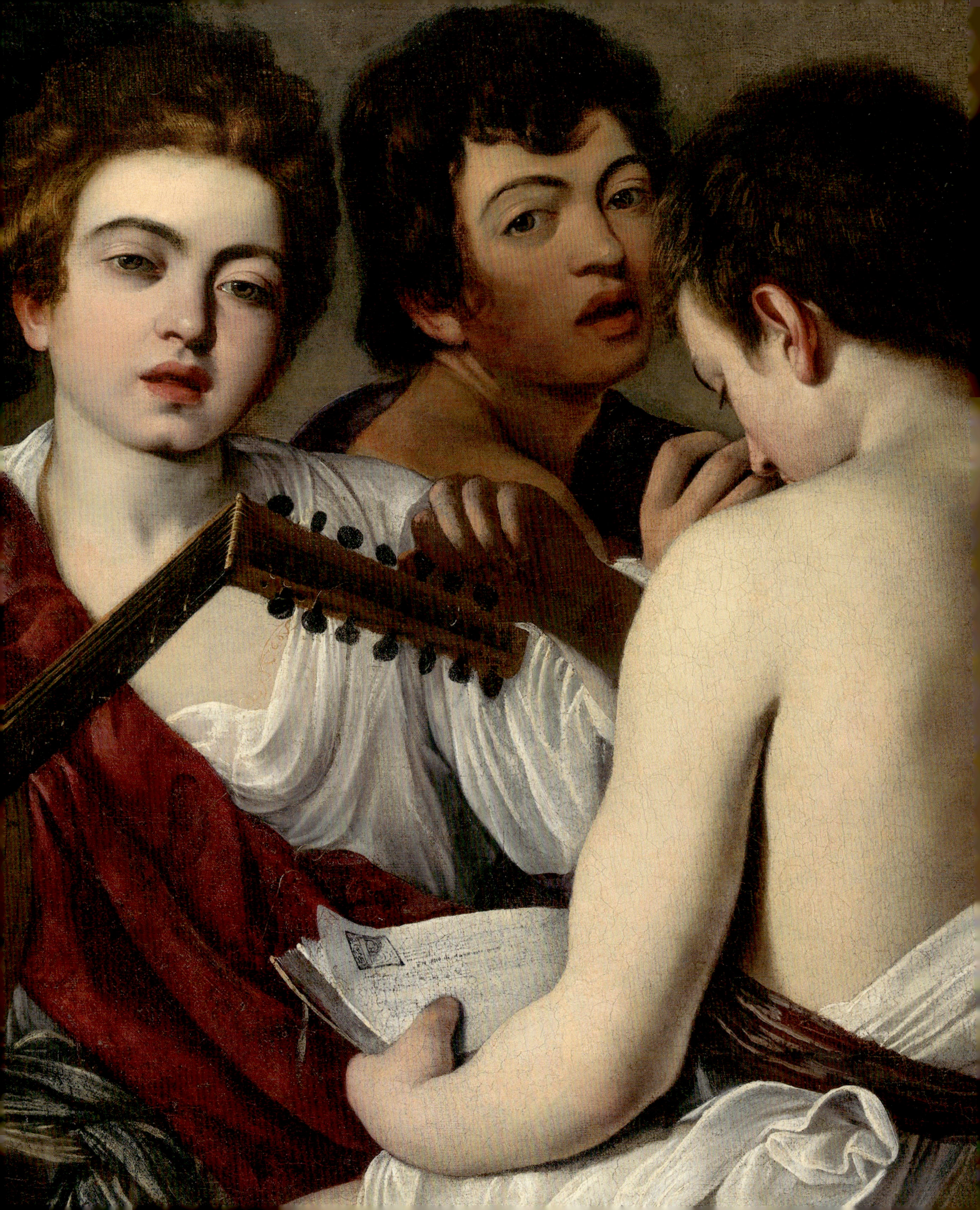

interpretations mainly emphasising the homoerotic allusions: the reference to the myth of Icarus should be read as a warning of the dangers of excess and the importance of moderation, a reminder that fits well with del Monte's humanistic culture. The parable of Icarus, a metaphor for the striving towards knowledge and the danger of *hybris*, reflects the intellectual aspirations of Neo-Platonism, counselling the need to elevate the soul by purifying it of the passions. As in *The Cardsharps* [cat. 5] and *The Fortune Teller*, however, the *caveat* was destined to go unheeded.

Although a work not commissioned nor acquired by Cardinal del Monte, but one that can be linked to the cultural influence of del Monte because of its strong religious allusions, in the *Rest during the Flight into Egypt* (Rome, Galleria Doria Pamphilj; fig. 5 on p. 13) Caravaggio uses instead the motet by the Franco-Flemish composer Noël Baulduin *Quam pulchra es et quam decora* (1519, but in the painting appearing in the version of 1526), played in the highest register voice by the angel-violinist as a lullaby for the infant Jesus. The text of the motet is taken from the *Song of Songs* (7:6), a dialogue between bridegroom and bride, who in the Catholic tradition are Christ and his Church. Although one hypothesis links the work to the Roman milieu of Saint Philip Neri, and to Cardinal Pietro Aldobrandini as the patron (Trinchieri Camiz, Ziino 1983, pp. 79-82), the *Rest*, painted over thin strokes of drawing on a damask linen from Flanders with a geometric patterned weave—similar to the canvas used for the *Bacchus* in the Uffizi and the *Crucifixion of Saint Andrew* in Cleveland [fig. 9 on p. 68]—with its highly elaborate iconology and refined musical reference "seems, in its formal characteristics, as in its intellectual allusions, to be a painting entirely in line with Del Monte" (Cappelletti 2017, p. 40).

The *Lives* of Baglione (1642) refer that after *The Musicians*, Caravaggio had painted, again for Cardinal del Monte, "also a young man playing the lute, who seemed alive, and the whole true [to life], with a carafe of flowers full of water, in which the reflection of a window could be seen perfectly…". The description refers—the reflection in the glass and other minor differences aside—to the *Lute-player* (or rather, more correctly a singer with lute) in the Hermitage [fig. 11 on p. 38], which belonged to the Marchese Vincenzo Giustiniani and is unanimously considered an autograph work (a problematic copy with the "reflection" present, formerly belonging to the Dukes of Beaufort in Badminton House, is now in a private collection in London). In this painting, the young singer—probably the Spanish castrato Pedro Montoya, a singer in the pontifical Sistine Chapel from February 1592 to September 1600 and a protégé of del Monte—is the same model as the singer-lute-player portrayed in the foreground of *The Musicians*. In the St. Petersburg painting, the presumed Montoya is captured while singing, to the accompaniment of a six-course lute, the madrigal *Voi sapete ch'io v'amo anzi v'adoro* (You know that I love you, rather I adore you) contained in the first edition (1539) of the *First Book of Madrigals* for four voices by Jacques Arcadelt, a composer favoured by Marchese Giustiniani; more precisely, Caravaggio fixes the moment in which the singer is pronouncing precisely the declaration "v'amo"—I love you—, which ends on the C-major chord of the four voices as performed on the lute (D'Alessandro 2017, pp. 57-61).

Cardinal del Monte possessed a variant of the *Lute-player/Singer with lute*, sold at his death (†1626) by his heirs to Cardinal Antonio Barberini, for which we have two testimonies: one, until 2013 was on loan to the Metropolitan Museum from the Wildenstein collection, generally considered at least in part autograph; the other, in the Salini collection in Paris, is believed to be a copy. In this variant, the same model for the singer accompanies himself on a more 'modern' seven-course lute, similar to the instrument in *The Musicians* and played by the same performer, but with a different musical 'still-life' and two other madrigals, which can be ascribed to the composers Francesco Layolle and Jacquet Berchem and are included in Arcadelt's 1539 collection of madrigals referred to above. The absence of the textual *incipits* of the two madrigals below the musical staff is, however, unusual in an autograph work by Caravaggio with vocal music present. Therefore, as early as 1976, Alfred Moir identified the painting with the copy made by Carlo Magnone in 1642 at the request of Cardinal Barberini, along with that of *The Cardsharps*, while more recently the name of Prospero Orsi, Merisi's inseparable friend, has also been put forward.
[DAD]

described as "canvas glued to panel". After its time in France from at least 1638 to 1675, and the eighteenth-century documentary void—with the exception of a poorly researched sale in Amsterdam on 20 April 1700 of 'Eenstuk van musikantenna Michel Angelo Caravaggio'—the subsequent nineteenth-century transfers of the work are lost in Great Britain between two London Christie's auctions (1815 and 1834), confused with the events surrounding the copy used for its restoration in 1982-1983 (Christie's auction of 1839). In the twentieth century, the painting resurfaced, acquired by David Burns of Fernacre, Whitehaven, Cumberland (his son gives an account), who had made several purchases in 1920-1930 at the Whitehaven Castle auction (Earl of Lonsdale's collection) and at various auctions in Edinburgh; the painting was resold by his widow at the end of World War II or shortly afterwards to a dealer (J. Cookson, Kendal), until its rediscovery in 1951 by David Carritt in the collection of William Glossop Thwaytes of Maulds Meaburn, near Penrith. Finally, it was purchased at a Christie's auction in London through the Rogers Fund, arriving in the Metropolitan Museum of Art in New York in 1952, after Denis Mahon had published the painting earlier that year.

Bibliography: Cinotti 1983, pp. 476–479, no. 38; Trinchieri Camiz, Ziino 1983, p. 71, footnote 18; Slim 1985, pp. 241–242; Lapucci 1991b, pp. 114–123; Marini 2005, pp. 395–398, n. 16; D'Alessandro 2017, pp. 49–65; Terzaghi 2017, pp. 15–47; D'Alessandro 2018, and see the website https://www.metmuseum.org/art/collection/search/435844.

NARCISSUS

1597-1598?
oil on canvas, 113.3 × 94 cm
Gallerie Nazionali di Arte Antica,
Palazzo Barberini, Rome, inv. 1569

Provenance: 1913, Milan, Paolo
D'Ancona collection (probably from
the Laudadio della Ripa collection);
1914, Vasily Khvoshinsky gift.

Bibliography: Longhi 1916, pp. 258;
Mahon 1951, p. 234; Venturi 1951,
p. 41; Voss 1951, p. 168; Friedländer
1955, p. 139; Longhi 1956, pp. 181,
264; Wagner 1958, pp. 84–85, 91,
203 notes 373–376; Arslan 1959,
pp. 201–202, 214 note 41; Moir 1961,
pp. 3–14; Salerno 1970, pp. 235, 241;
Posner 1971, pp. 323 note 46; Spear
1971, p. 78; Damisch 1976, pp. 109–
146; Marsicola 1979; Nicolson 1979,
p. 31; Cinotti 1983, I, pp. 518–519;
Gregori, in *The Age of Caravaggio*
1985, pp. 265–268; Papi 1986, pp.
24–25; Bann 1989, pp. 127–156;
Gregori 1989, p. 145 note 45; Marini
1989, pp. 442–443; Vodret 1989,
pp. 222–225; Posèq 1991, pp. 21-31;
Bologna 1992, pp. 349–350; Papi, in
*Michelangelo Merisi da Caravaggio.
Come nascono* 1991, pp. 359–368;
Raabe 1996, pp. 56–59; Vodret 1996,
pp. 167–183; Bal 1999, pp. 231–261;
Papi 2003, pp.155–160; Maccherini,
in *Siena e Roma* 2005, pp. 403–406;
Bann 2009, pp. 343–355; Schütze
2009, pp. 75–77; Vodret 2009, pp.
242–247; Fried 2010, pp. 134–139;
Spike 2010, pp. 370–373; Koering
2014, pp. 95–108; Careri 2017,
pp. 66–72; Papi 2018b, pp. 217–232;
Schütze 2019, pp. 46–55; Berger
2020, pp. 612–639; Hodde 2022.

By a kind of specular fate of both the painting and its subject, the history of the *Narcissus* in the Gallerie Nazionali is one of difficult and uncertain identifications, if not of constant misconceptions. An elusive work, that indeed eluded, as far as is known, the attention of both contemporary and modern observers, at least until 1913, when Roberto Longhi in Milan, in the home of his colleague Paolo D'Ancona, believed that he had recognised a youthful creation by Caravaggio. Little or nothing could be established of its earlier history, since the hypothesis of its provenance from Liguria—where a *Narcissus* ascribed to Caravaggio is referred to in certain inventories between the seventeenth and nineteenth centuries—remains uncertain. The painting was then purchased by the Russian diplomat Vasiliy Khvoschinsky, a collector and art lover, who then donated it to the Regia Galleria di Palazzo Corsini.

What continues to powerfully strike anyone looking at the painting today, as it did then, is without a doubt the extraordinary *inventio*, unusual from a compositional and also a conceptual perspective. The unfortunate lover is entirely immersed in the disturbing contemplation of his own simulacrum—"ears and eyes", wrote Philostratus (2010, p. 46)—indifferent to the presence of the viewer, who remains excluded from the closed circle of the image. But just as the reflection in the water is the external agent for an objectifying act of consciousness, the point of view of the observer, precisely because extrinsic as that of the voyeur, is the only perspective from which the drama of the as yet unrecognised 'doubling' can be grasped. The Barberini painting then looms up as a reflection on the visual and psychological implications of that catoptric obsession that seems no less congenial to modern sensibility than it was to seventeenth-century culture; on the "double deception" that "deludes and taunts" both the viewer *in* the painting and the viewer *of* the painting, as Marino had suggested, precisely in relation to a *Narcissus* in a picture (Marino 1629, p. 6).

Indeed, *Narcissus* remains elusive far beyond the didactic requirements of the catalogue label, in terms of its own visual structure. Beginning with what it represents: "Mythology in modern dress," as defined by Longhi (1956, pp. 181), and yet, despite the omission of any contextual detail that explicitly refers to the sources, that tacit link remains unassailable, so much so as to make the painting almost a visual archetype, of which the ancient texts are no more than an ekphrastic illustration (Bann 1989, p. 133), as though the painter had wanted to

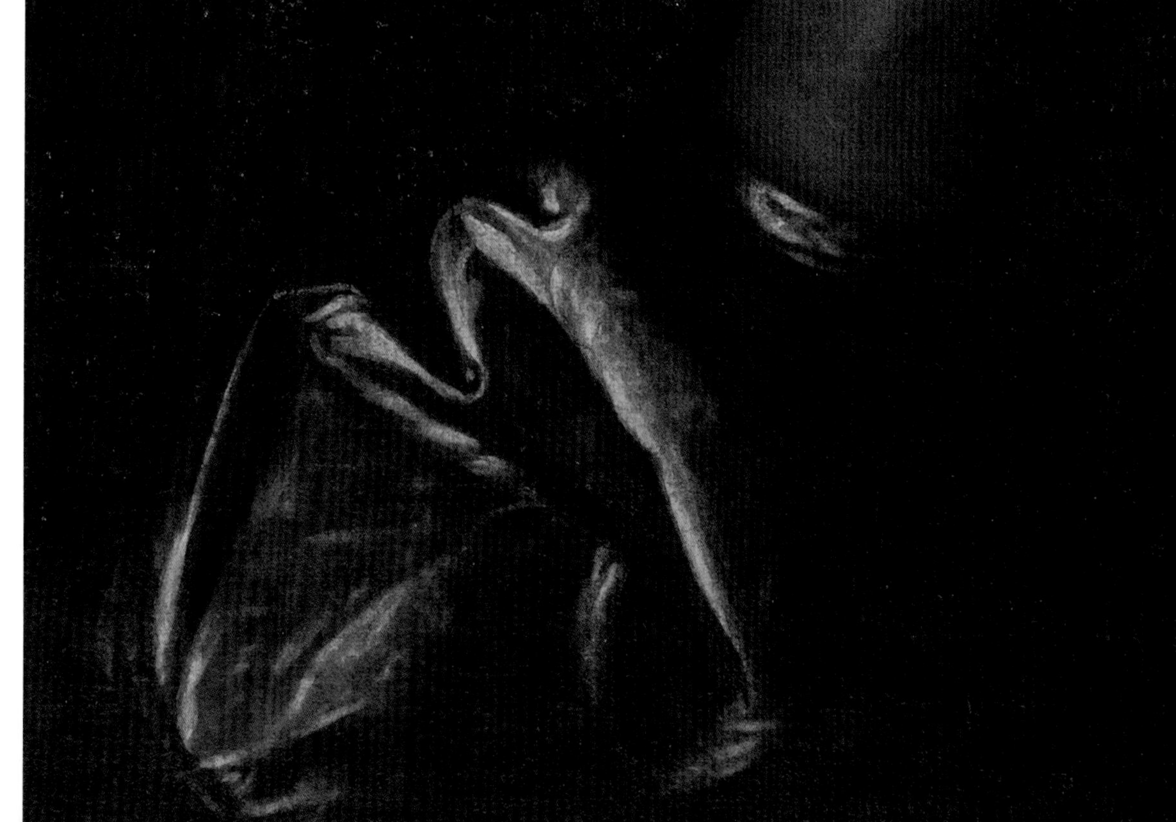

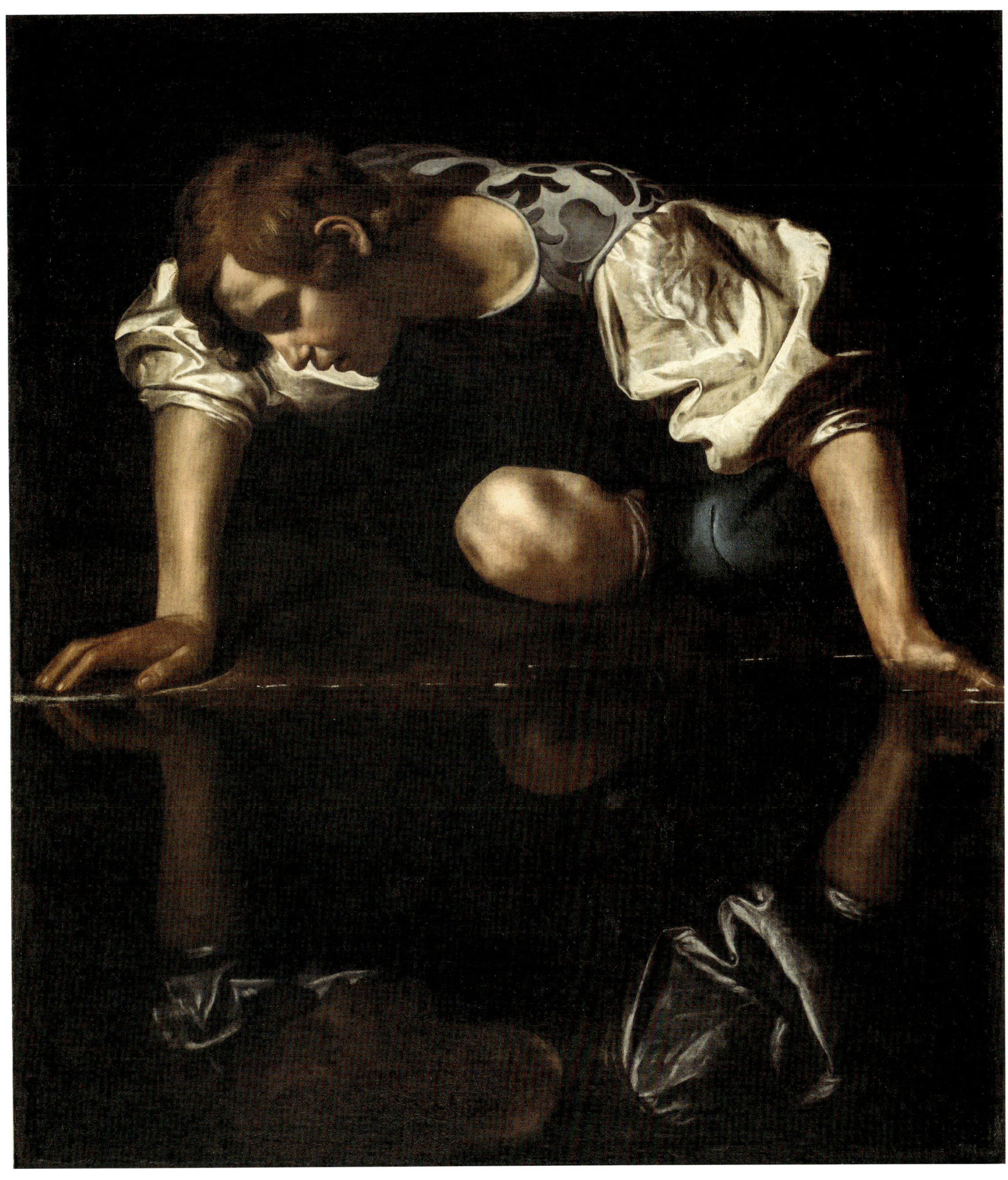

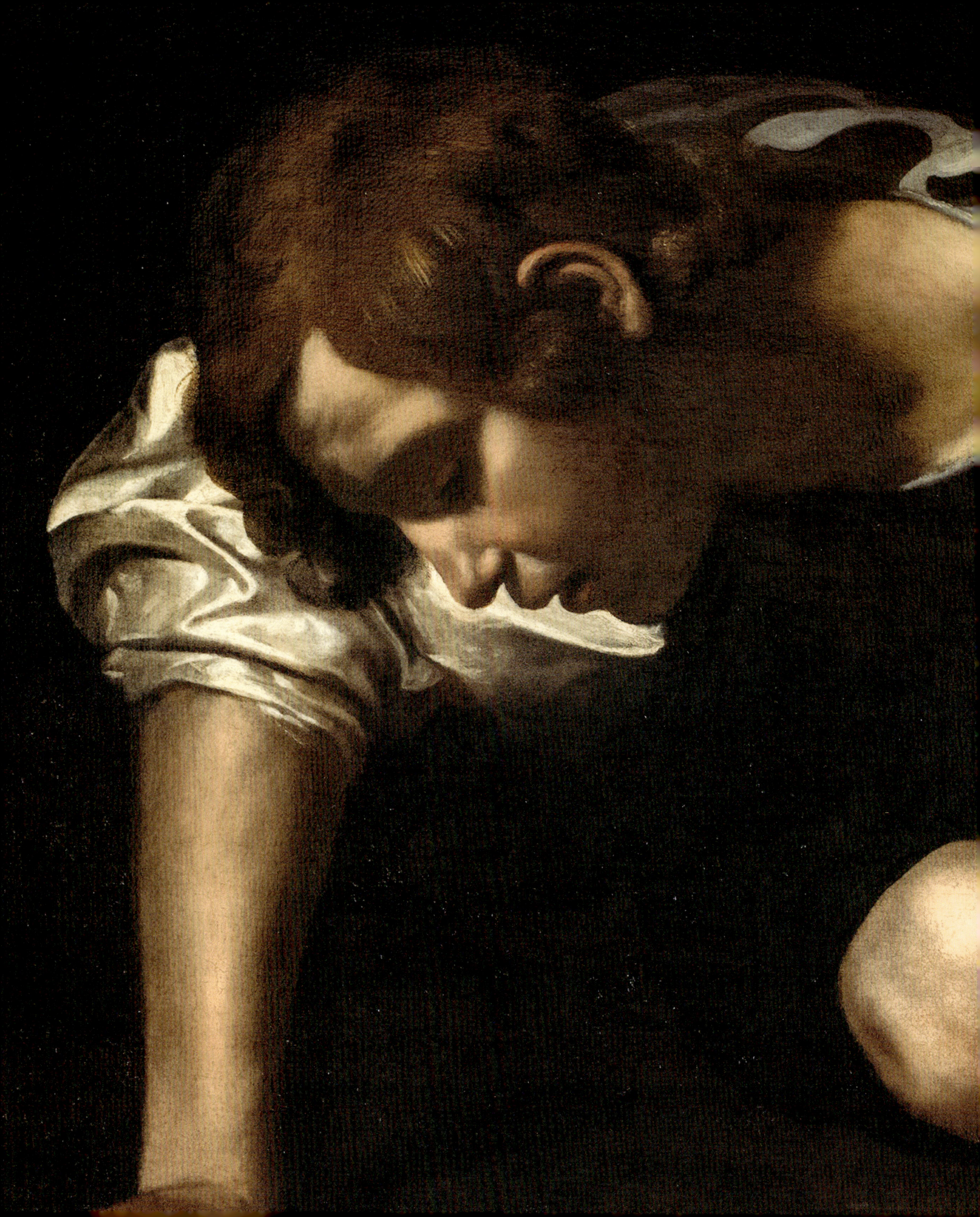

evoke, rather than the figure in Ovid or Philostratus, the Narcissus that is (in) any young man, which could be present in any one of us.

"Painter and painting," Narcissus does not contemplate himself in a *speculum veritatis*, and rather than an exercise in perfectly specular mimesis, the painting can perhaps be considered more a speculation on the limits of mimetic perfection, of that which is attributed to a model of art that is as mechanical as it is ideal, if not mythical. It would not have escaped the notice, not even of Caravaggio—who swore that he wanted to "imitate natural things well"—that such a function cannot be reduced to producing mere copies of reality; if this were the case, as Descartes would say so well, "there would be no distinction between object and image" (Descartes 1824, p. 39). And one would end up viewing Caravaggio's naturalism as naively as Narcissus. Not even Caravaggio and his followers could be satisfied with the pure model of the mirror, unless they understood it as *speculum videns*, "seeing" rather than "blind", as Giordano Bruno warned in *De compositione imaginum* (1889, p. 119). The mirror of painting may well be imperfect, unfaithful, even unnatural, but perhaps precisely for this reason it can make us reflect all the more.

For more than a century now, rivers of ink have been spilled on the subject of whether the painting is an autograph work, an issue debated since its discovery. In the wake of Longhi, many scholars, including Pevsner, Cinotti, Marini, Berenson, Wagner, Spike, Fried, Careri, and Schütze, have ascribed the painting to the *corpus* of works by Caravaggio, believing that only a painter of his calibre could have created such a sophisticated iconography, unique of its kind, and dating it towards the end of the sixteenth century, shortly before the Contarelli Chapel canvases. One of the most strenuous defenders of the autograph status of the work is also Rossella Vodret, who bases her conviction not only on certain stylistic affinities with, in particular, the Pamphilj *Magdalene*, but also on the results that emerged from the diagnostic analyses carried out when the painting was restored in 1996. In fact, not only were a number of *pentimenti* found, but also some technical evidence constituting points of contact with Caravaggio's *modus operandi*, including the absence of under-drawing, the sketched construction of the figures through *abbozzi*, the practice of leaving the ground visible, as well as the progressive overlapping of the applications of paint.

Other scholars, however, have questioned or denied Caravaggio's authorship of the *Narcissus*: while Voss, Salerno, Spear and Nicolson included it among the doubtful works in Caravaggio's catalogue, Venturi, Friedländer, Moir, Arslan, Posner and Frommel have argued for its clear exclusion.

Among the various attributional proposals formulated over the years, the name of Spadarino stands out: the hypothesis, first put forward by Brandi in 1974 (never published, but recalled by Marsicola), and forcefully re-proposed on several occasions by Gianni Papi, is the one that has of late gained the greatest consensus among experts, including Gregori, Bologna and Montanari. Papi believes that the *Narcissus* should be dated to around the first half of the fifth decade of the seventeenth century, emphasising not only the stylistic similarities with Galli's works, in particular with *The Baptism of Constantine* in Colle Val d'Elsa, but also the differences in the execution of the painting with respect to the manner in which the paint is applied, and with Caravaggio's "dramatic, tormented and severe expressiveness."

[MDM]

SAINT FRANCIS OF ASSISI IN ECSTASY

c. 1597–1598
oil on canvas, 93.98 × 129.54 cm
Wadsworth Atheneum Museum of Art, The Ella Gallup Sumner and Mary Catlin Sumner Collection Fund, Hartford (CT), inv. 1943.222

Provenance: Rome, Ottavio Costa, until 1639, and by descent to his heirs until 1833; Rome, Arciconfraternità degli Operai della Divina Pietà, until 1875 (?); Malta, private collection; Alexandria, private collection, until 1925; Trieste, Guido Grioni, until 1938; New York, Arnold Seligmann, Rey & Co., until 1943.

Bibliography: Cinotti 1983, pp. 440–442, no. 19; Gregori, in *The Age of Caravaggio* 1985, pp. 21–27, cat. 68; Spike 2010, CD-ROM, pp. 45-52, cat. 8; Vodret 2021a, pp. 148–151, cat. 14a.

Unknown artist (after Caravaggio), *Saint Francis of Assisi in Ecstasy*, before 1607, Galleria d'Arte Antica, Musei del Castello, Udine

The subject depicts a swooning Saint Francis of Assisi supported by an angel after receiving the stigmata; on the left, in the background, immersed in darkness, one catches a glimpse of Brother Leo dozing and a group of shepherds. This last unusual detail, together with the focus on the wound to Francis' side—the only visible wound—is a reference to the more detailed narration of the event found in the anonymous *Considerations on the stigmata* (see *Fonti francescane* [1977] 2004, pp. 1250–1251; see Treffers 1988, p. 158). However, no text relates an angelic intervention after the impression of the stigmata, produced—according to the sources—by the vision of a crucified man in the figure of a seraphim. In Caravaggio's interpretation, focused on the inner dimension of Francis' experience, the scene is evidently modelled on the agony of Christ in the Garden of Gethsemane, which includes, in the passage in the gospel according to Saint Luke (22:43–44), precisely the appearance of a consoling angel. In all likelihood, the introduction of the latter motif into Franciscan iconography, steeped as it was in post-Tridentine spirituality and destined for an immediate success in the Roman context, has at its origin precisely the Hartford painting (see Askew 1969, pp. 284–294).

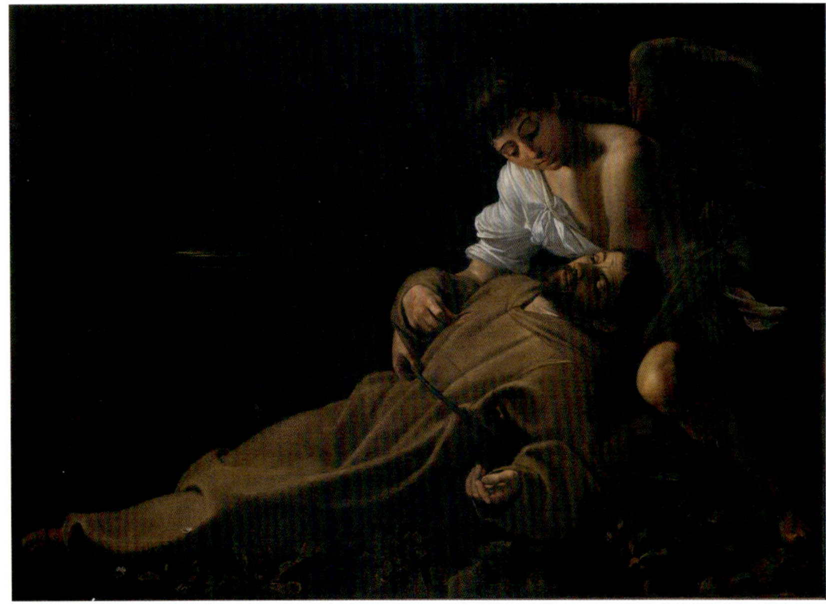

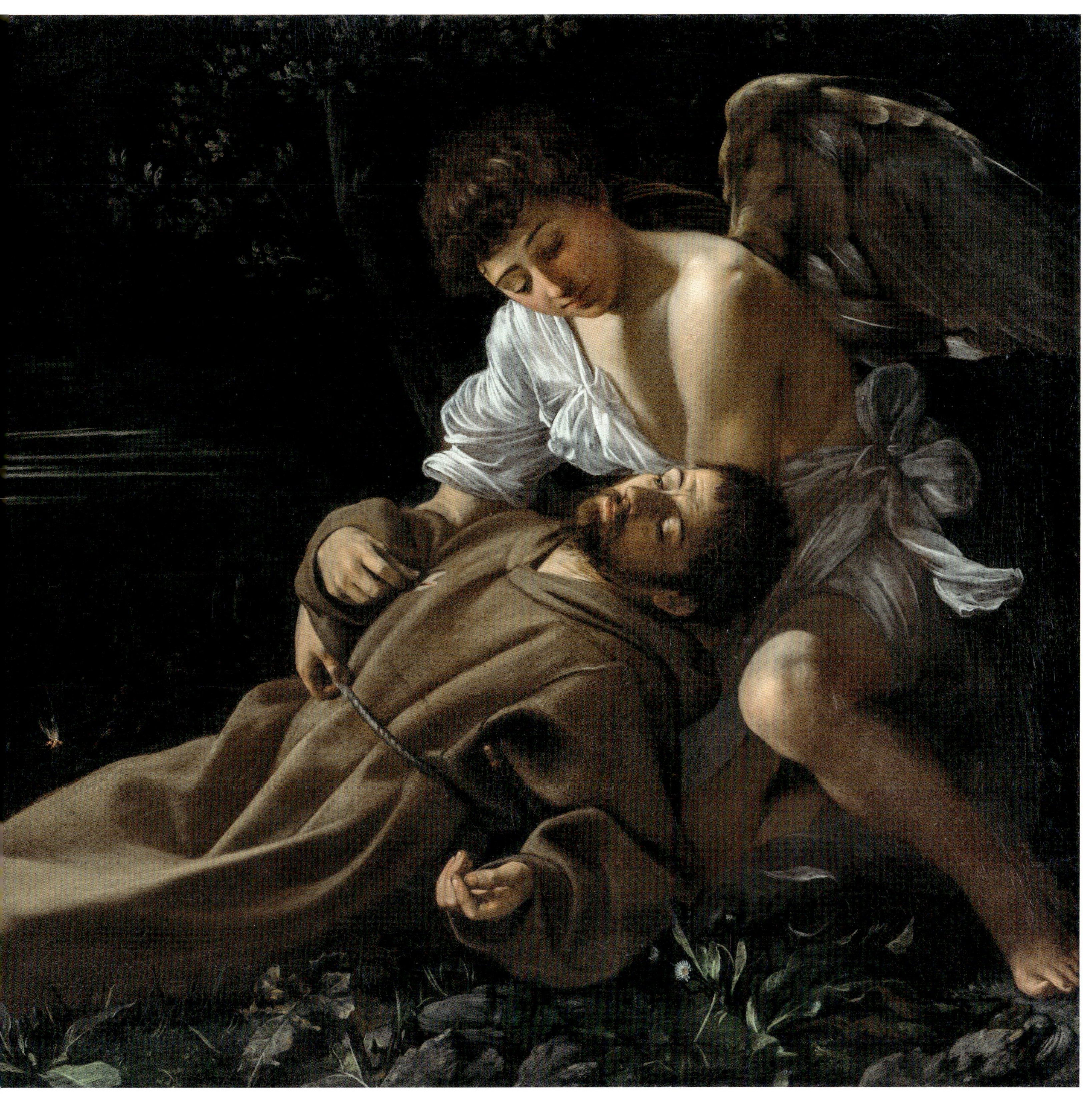

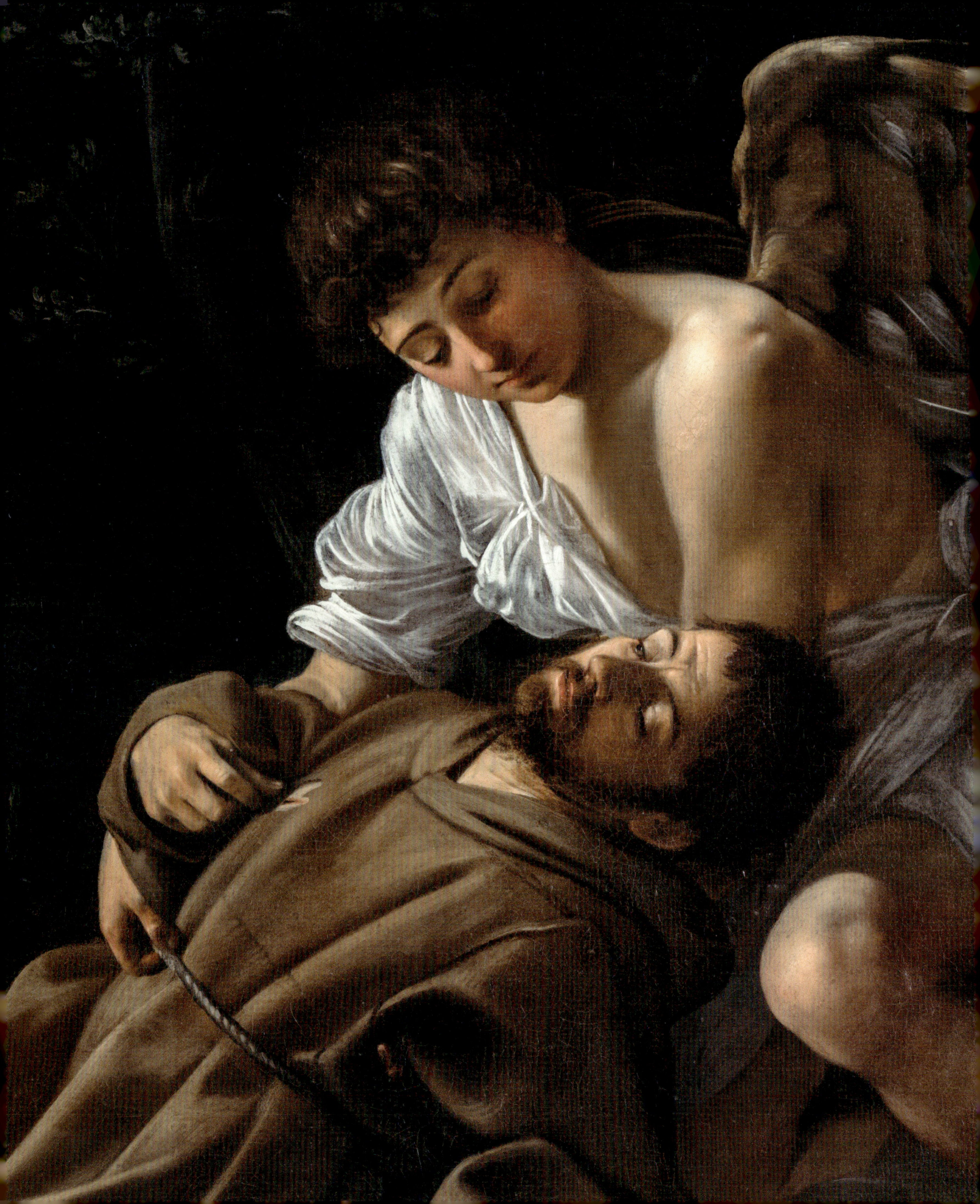

After Luigi Spezzaferro's initial breakthroughs (1974a), the complex collecting history of the work has been definitively clarified by the research of Josepha Costa Restagno (2004b, *ad indicem*) and Maria Cristina Terzaghi (2007, in particular pp. 273–274, 300–302): unknown to ancient literature, the painting is to be identified as the "painting of Saint Francis made [by] Caravaggio" recorded in Rome in 1639 in the *post mortem* inventory of the possessions of the Ligurian banker Ottavio Costa, an early admirer of the artist; at the same time, the *Saint Francis*, the traces of which can be followed without interruption until 1846, is in all probability the first of the works requested from Caravaggio by Costa, who also commissioned—as we know—the *Judith and Holophernes* in Palazzo Barberini [cat. 12] and the *Saint John the Baptist in the Wilderness* in the Nelson Atkins Museum in Kansas City [cat. 15].

Caravaggio's authorship of the *Saint Francis*, which is no longer disputed today, was first put forward by Matteo Marangoni (1929), when the painting was in the Grioni collection in Trieste; the composition was, however, already known through an excellent copy, although this was in a poor state of conservation at the time, in the Galleria d'arte antica in the castle in Udine (inv. 45; considered to be an original by Tancred Borenius (1925, p. 26, note), who identified it at least until 1894 in the church of San Giacomo in Fagagna, and also by Adolfo Venturi (1928), who illustrated it in what was by then already its current location, to which it had been moved in 1912 for safekeeping (G. Bergamini, in *Galleria d'arte antica* 2002, p. 152, no. 99). The opinions of Borenius and Venturi, together with the negative judgement expressed by Roberto Longhi (1928, p. 30, footnote 2) on both the Udine version and also—initially, and on the basis of a photograph alone—on Marangoni's proposed attribution, enabled the painting to be exported from Italy in 1938 (D'Anza 2014, pp. 88–91, and—after passing through the antiquarian market—its arrival in 1943 at the Wadsworth Atheneum, becoming the first work by Caravaggio to enter a US public collection (see Zafran 2017, pp. 35–37).

Current scholarship is in agreement that the Hartford *Saint Francis* is a masterpiece, executed by the artist towards the end of the sixteenth century, perhaps the earliest among those with a sacred subject, in any case pre-dating the Contarelli cycle. The feeling for nature that pervades its conception, similar to that found in the *Rest on the Flight into Egypt* in the Galleria Doria Pamphilj [fig. 5 on p. 13], is directly connected to the painter's Venetian-Lombard cultural background. Already Robert Oertel (1938, p. 230), in line with an interpretation that would subsequently be widely developed in scholarship, highlighted the particu-

lar resonance of this melancholic nocturne with the works of Giovan Girolamo Savoldo, to the point of hypothesising its execution even before Caravaggio's departure for Rome.

Among the various copies of the Hartford prototype known to date (for a list, see Moir 1976, pp. 83–84, cat. 3, and Cinotti 1983, p. 440), the Udine replica stands out, as observed above, and its status as an authentic work has been periodically put forward, especially at a local level (see for instance Gasparrini, in *Meraviglie del Barocco* 2010, pp. 150–151, cat. 10; Tiozzo 2015). The importance of this version lies first and foremost in its documented link with the original, which is at the basis of the attributional misunderstandings that have surrounded it: it was in fact donated by Costa himself as a token of friendship to Ruggiero Tritonio of Udine, commendatory abbot of Pinerolo and secretary to Cardinal Peretti Montalto, before finding its way to the church of Fagagna in 1852 through a bequest from one of Tritonio's heirs, the Count Giacomo Fistulario. In Tritonio's will of 1607, the work is registered as "Divi Francisci signum a Caravaggio … pictum" and in fact the previous year Costa, seriously ill, had reserved in his will for Tritonio, as the first of his two executors, the choice of a "quadrum S[anc] ti Francisci" or, alternatively, "S[anc]tae Marthae et Magdalenae", both works without specification as to their author. Nonetheless, the Udine version, even after the restoration carried out by Lucio Zambon between 2020 and 2021, and despite the presence of a significant variant such as the stigmata on the saint's hands, remains inferior in quality to the Hartford *Saint Francis*; and thus Costa, once he recovered, must have delivered to his friend— according to a practice that was not unusual for the collector (Terzaghi 2009, p. 93)—nothing more than a copy of the precious autograph work in his possession.

[GPO]

PORTRAIT OF MAFFEO BARBERINI

c. 1598–1599
oil on canvas, 124 × 90 cm
Private collection

Provenance: Untraceable before its reappearance in Rome in 1963.

Bibliography: Mancini [c. 1619–1621] 1956–1957, p. 227; Bellori [1672] 1976, p. 224; Longhi 1963, pp. 3–11; plates 1-3; Lavin 1967, pp. 470–473; D'Onofrio 1967, pp. 61–63; Lavin 1975, I, p. 65, n. 33; pp. 68, 111; Longhi [1968] 1982, p. 51, fig. 23; Marini 2001, ill. p. 191, pp. 424–425, cat. 31; Cinotti 1983, pp. 437–438, cat. 17, 597; Gregori 1994, p. 148, cat. 27; Spike 2001, entry in enclosed CD; Whitfield 2001, fig. 53, p. 144; Fumaroli 2007, p. 1, fig. 1; Cappelletti 2009, pp. 41, 48; Schütze 2009, pp. 35, 78, 255, cat. 21; Christiansen, in *Caravaggio e caravaggeschi* 2010, p. 102; Papi 2010, pp. 24–25, fig. 1; Ebert-Schifferer 2012, pp. 164–165, fig. 117; Papi 2012, p. 332; Christiansen 2014, pp. 49–55, fig. 3.8; Papi 2014a, pp. 65-74, figs. 4, 11; Puglisi 2014, pp. 108–109; Papi 2018b, p. 125, fig. 6; Schütze 2020, pp. 253–255; Laureati, in *Giuliano Briganti, Roberto Longhi* 2021, pp. 126–130, nos. 24-25; Vodret 2021a, pp. 152–153, cat. 15; Zuccari 2022a, p. 345, cat. 33; Cappelletti, in *Caravaggio e come cercarlo* 2024, pp. 12–13, fig. 8; Papi 2023a, pp. 8–12, fig. 2; pp. 44–47, fig. 7; Macioce 2023, pp. 426–27.

The work depicts Maffeo Barberini (1568–1644), future pope Urban VIII and great patron of the arts, in his early thirties, when he was a cleric of the Apostolic Chamber. The first account we have of portraits painted by Caravaggio for the Barberini family is Giulio Mancini's account according to which Caravaggio "made portraits for Barbarino" (1619–1621). This information is taken up by Giovan Pietro Bellori (1672) who expressly refers to two works: "For Cardinal Maffeo Barberini, in addition to the portrait, he painted the *Sacrifice of Abraham*" (Florence, Galleria degli Uffizi). We can identify the painting, albeit with an element of doubt, in the early inventories of Maffeo Barberini: in the one dated 1608 as one of the "Two portraits of his most Illustrious Lordship" (Lavin 1975, no. 33, p. 65), and in the subsequent one dated 1623, compiled at the time of his election to the papacy, in the "portrait of Signor Cardinal Barberino when he was Chierico di Camera (Cleric of the Apostolic Chamber), with a black frame" (Lavin 1975, no. 111, p. 68). The painting was published by Roberto Longhi in "Paragone" in 1963 (*Il vero 'Maffeo Barberini' del Caravaggio*) in which it was presented as a cornerstone of Caravaggio's portraiture. According to his hypothesis, the painting must have remained in the Barberini collection for centuries, reaching the antiquarian market following the dispersion of the collection in the twentieth century. From the recent publication of the Longhi-Briganti correspondence, we know that the work had been discovered shortly before by Giuliano Briganti, who transferred the right of publication to the master (Laureati, in *Giuliano Briganti, Roberto Longhi* 2021). In around 1962, the painting underwent a significant restoration by Amleto De Santis (former collaborator of Mario Modestini at the Studio d'Arte Palma in Rome). Federico Zeri also accepted the attribution to Caravaggio (University of Bologna, Federico Zeri Photographic Archive), as is clear from the photograph which on its reverse indicates its provenance from the Sestieri studio; this is probably a reference to Carlo Sestieri, a member of the antiquarian dynasty to which Ettore, art historian and curator of the Galleria Barberini, also belonged. After Longhi's discovery, the painting was unanimously accepted by scholarship as an autograph work by Caravaggio (Cinotti, Gregori, Vodret, Cappelletti, Zuccari, Schütze, Christiansen, Papi, Ebert-Schifferer, Whitfield).

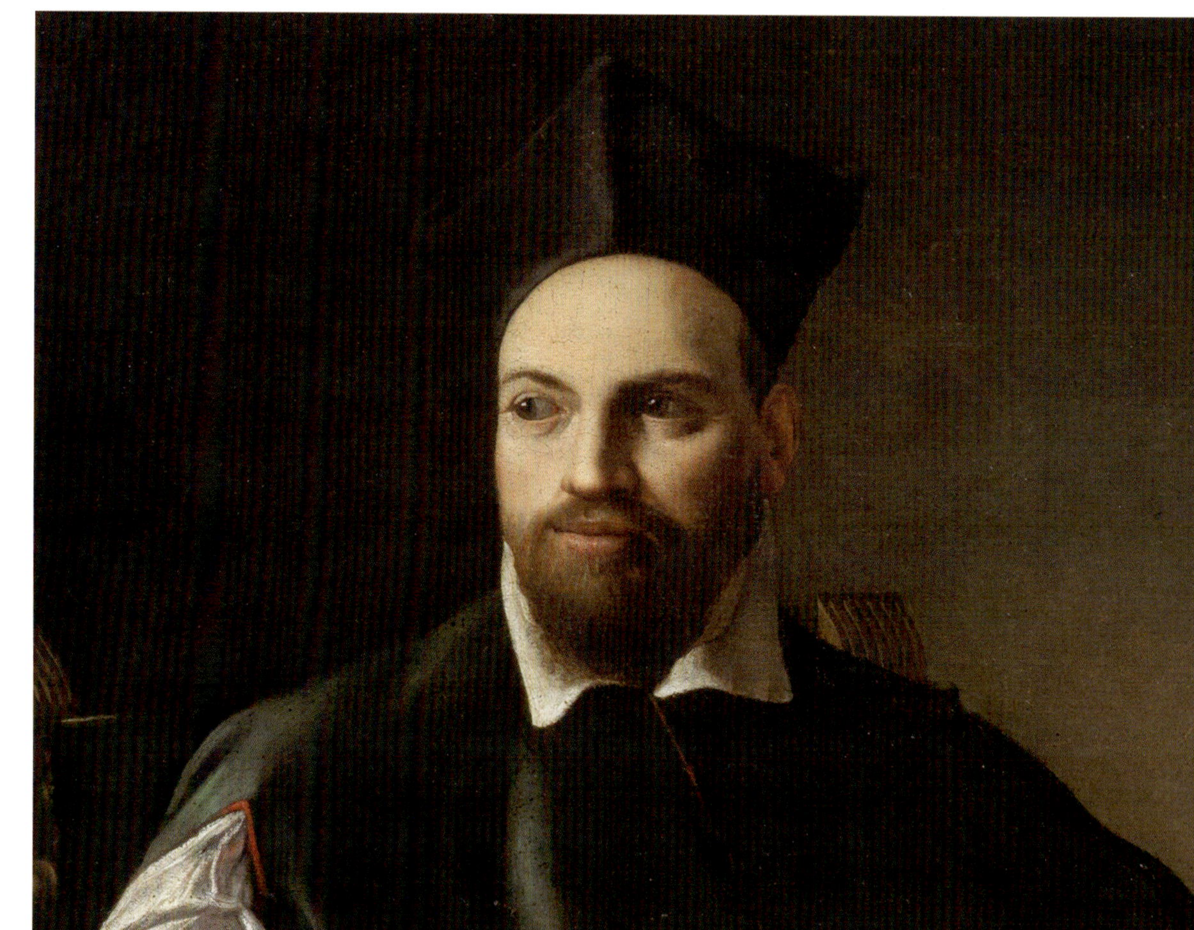

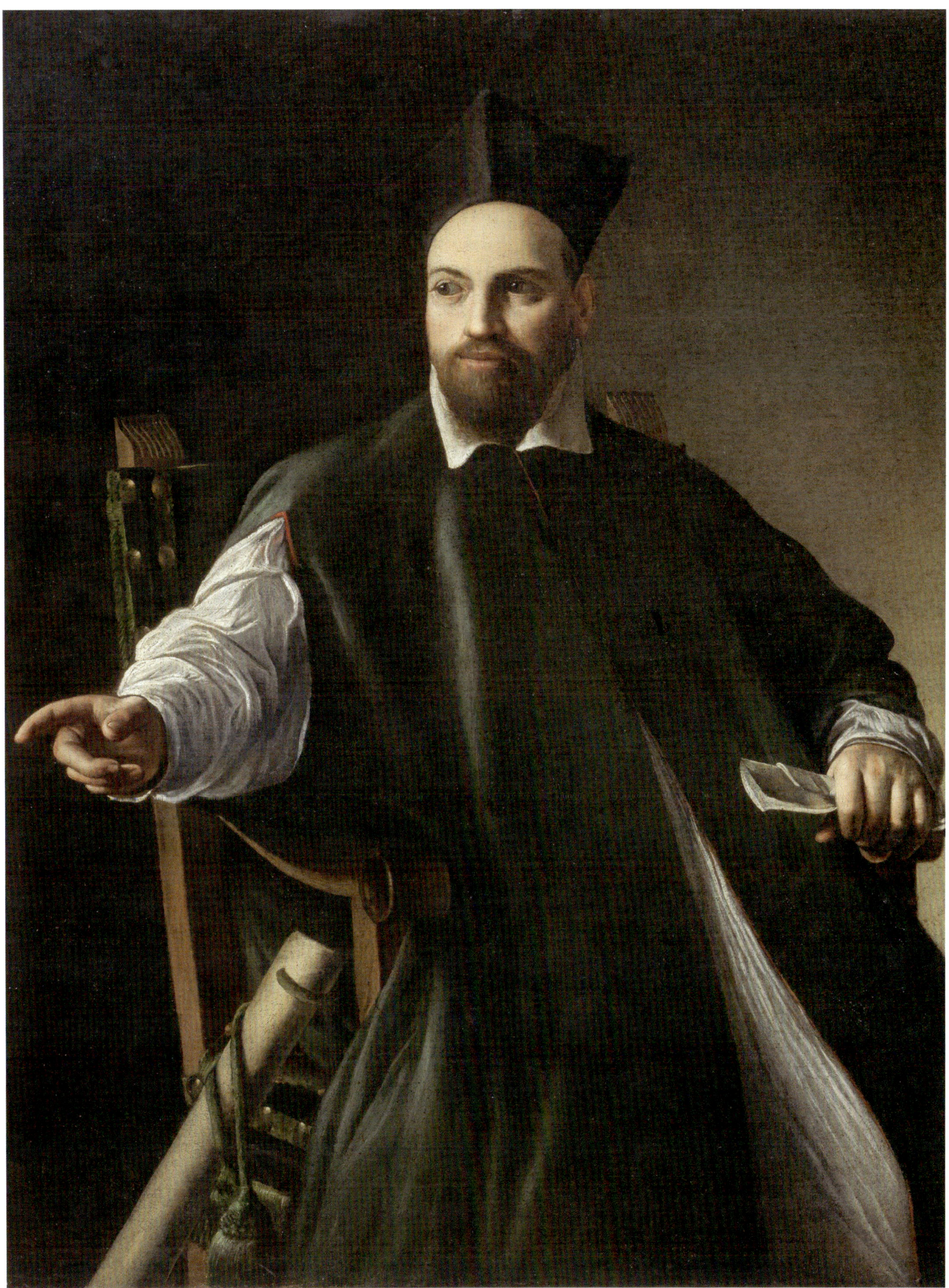

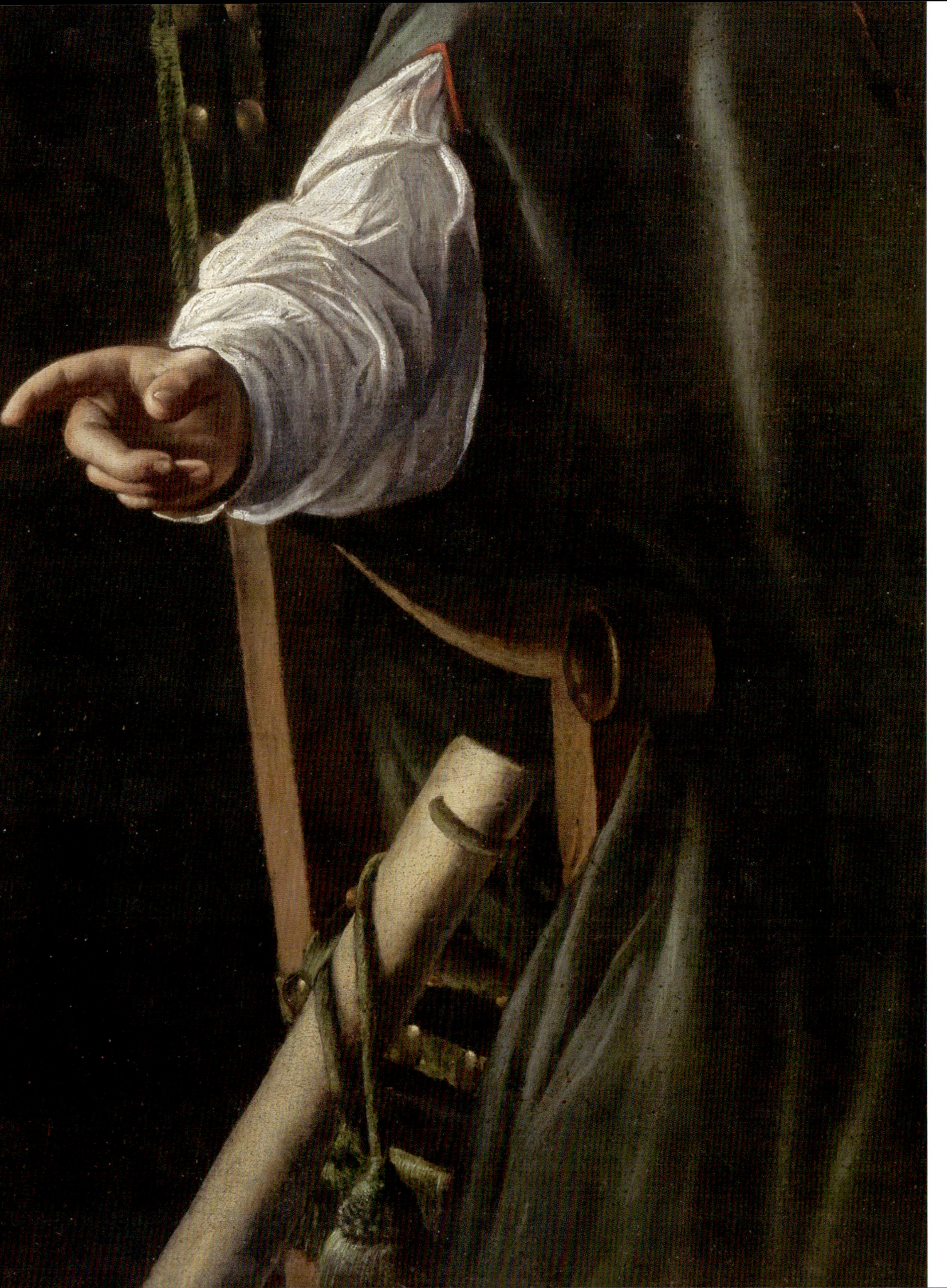

Most scholars consider the work datable to around 1598–1599 and link the commission to the appointment of Maffeo Barberini as a cleric of the Apostolic Chamber (March 1597), a key step in the *cursus honorum* towards the cardinalship (in particular Cappelletti, Vodret, Schütze). This is the moment in which he began "to ingagliardire gli oscuri", an effective phrase coined by Bellori to indicate the paintings with powerful contrasts of light and shadow, the master's stylistic signature. Another hypothesis is that the occasion is connected to his appointment in 1602 as papal commissioner for the reclamation of Lake Trasimeno. That this office represented an important moment in the prelate's career is demonstrated *ex post* by the choice to depict the episode in a tapestry from the series on the life of Urban VIII, executed from a cartoon by Antonio Gherardi in 1665 (Rome, Gallerie Nazionali di Arte Antica), in which the painter seems to have been inspired for his portrayal of Maffeo Barberini as a young man by Caravaggio's painting, both in terms of his face and his vestments, and for the decisive gesture of his right arm. According to other hypotheses, the portrait should be postponed to 1603 (Papi, Christiansen, Zuccari, Ebert-Schifferer). The painting would have been commissioned from Caravaggio by the cultured and ambitious Maffeo Barberini, on the occasion of his prestigious appointment as apostolic ambassador to Paris, at the court of Henri IV, in October 1601 as extraordinary nuncio, and in November 1604 as ordinary ambassador. It is to this portrait therefore that could refer the four payments received by Caravaggio between 20 May and July 1603 with the balance on 8 January 1604 (100 *scudi* in total) for the execution of "paintings" commissioned by Maffeo Barberini, the subject of which is not specified, but traditionally identified with the *Sacrifice of Isaac* in the Uffizi Gallery.

The painting fills a considerable gap, as for Caravaggio the practice of portraiture during his Roman period was anything but insignificant; however, almost all of these works have been lost or destroyed. In the portrait, the cleric wears black clerical biretta and a *soprana* or prelatic *pallium* lined with red fabric, that is an overcoat with hanging sleeves, of which he wears the left one, while the right one is left hanging behind his back, and an underlying sleeved tunic of white cloth with very fine folds (*rocchetto* or *tunica manuleata*). The whole, clothing and accessories, are appropriate to the status of cleric of the Apostolic Chamber. The figure is presented in a three-quarter view and turning, illuminated by a beam of light from the left, seated in an armchair set at an angle; it emerges with great power out of the bare surroundings of the room. Caravaggio isolates a fragment of reality to give psychological depth to the sitter. Without superfluous detail, he brings out the hands, the gaze, the scroll, the folded letter. The impatience of his gaze and the action of the hand that pierces the space "with the right hand turning, in mid-air" (Longhi 1963) compose a narrative made up of gestures and glances. The figure, enveloped in the *soprana*, of which we catch a glimpse of a pocket, energetically clasps a letter with his left hand, which stands out against the light background, while perhaps he dictates a reply to a secretary outside of the scene. In the foreground is a scroll of documents, a perspectival guide to the pyramidal composition in which the figure is placed, his presence magnetic and monumental, yet devoid of all rhetoric. If the cultural sources of the work can be traced back to the Renaissance portraiture of the Veneto-Lombardy, from Savoldo to Moroni, the patron, an intellectual from the highest social sphere, is caught in a private moment, with a naturalism and psychological insight that are completely unprecedented. With just a few confident strokes of the brush, Caravaggio delivers to us "the modern portrait" (Longhi 1963). The fall of light irradiates the skin, smooth and dazzling, especially on the forehead where thickly impasted paint places the right eye as the area of maximum incidence. On the light-coloured eyes, marked by a slight squint, the painter has left visible a thin outline of the ground and then applied to the iris a small but substantial dollop of lead white to establish the reflected light and add intensity to his gaze. The palette of pigments is basic: lead white and earth pigments for the flesh (without vermilion), different copper-based pigments for the vestments and the armchair, vermilion for the red outlines, lead-tin yellow for the studs, brown earth pigments for the ground visible through the thinnest paint-layers of the white sleeves. The nuances play-out in a symphony of grey-greens, modulated in highly original harmonies: the grey vestment with its bluish highlights and the shimmering golden green of the velvet of the armchair and the tassels of the scroll in the foreground.

[PN]

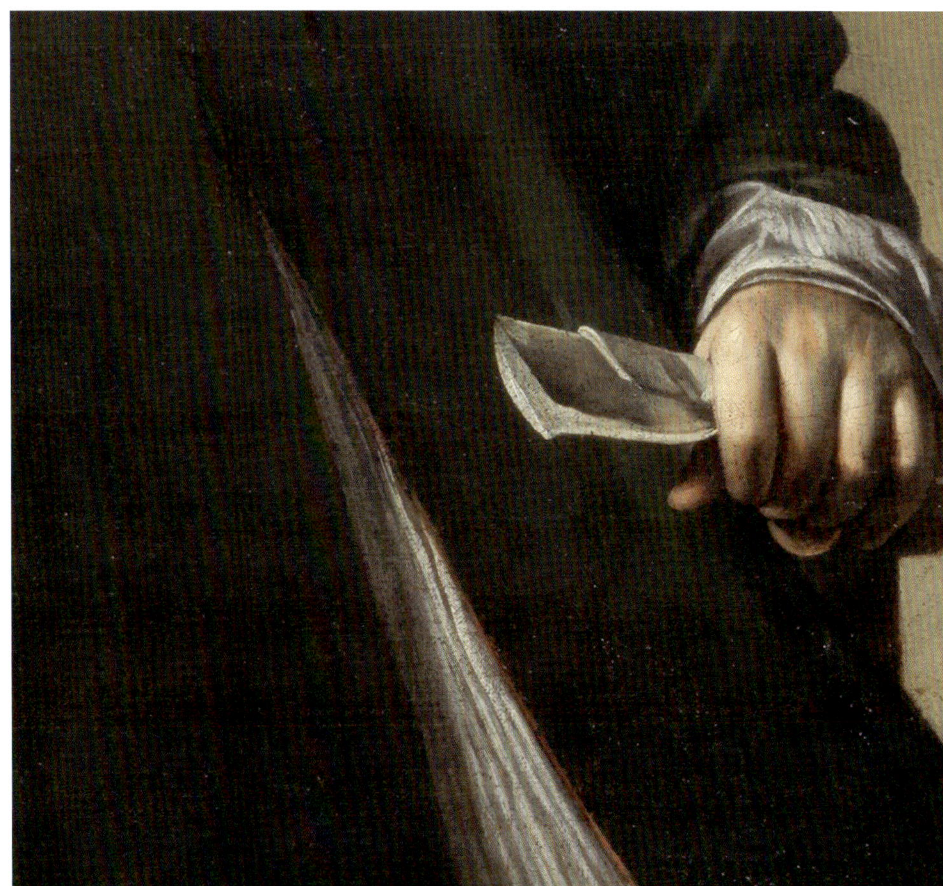

SAINT CATHERINE OF ALEXANDRIA

c. 1598–1599
oil on canvas, 173 × 133 cm
Museo Nacional Thyssen-
Bornemisza, Madrid,
inv. 81 (1934.37)

Provenance: Cardinal Francesco
Maria del Monte, Rome, 1627; by
descent to Uguccione del Monte,
later to his brother, Alessandro del
Monte, Rome, 1628; from whom it
was acquired by Cardinal Antonio
Barberini, Rome, 1628; Prince
Maffeo Barberini (1631–1685),
Rome; Prince Urbano Barberini
(1664–1722); listed in 1817 by
Vincenzo Camuccini in the Barberini
collection (no. 12); acquired by Baron
Heinrich Thyssen in 1935 (Villa
Favorita in Castagnola, Lugano),
transferred to the Museo Thyssen-
Bornemisza in Madrid in 1992.

Bibliography: Bellori [1672] 2009,
pp. 216–217; Mariotti 1892, p. 127;
Longhi 1916, pp. 264-265; Voss 1923,
pp. 80–81; Longhi 1943, pp. 10–11;
Mahon 1951, pp. 228, no. 55; Longhi
1951c, pp. 10–18; Frommel 1971, pp.
53–56; Kirwin 1971, pp. 54–55; Lavin
1975, pp. 167, 296; Marini 2001,
p. 420; Zuccari 2009, pp. 188-189;
Ebert-Schifferer 2010b, p. 92; Vodret
2021a, p. 180.

The *Saint Catherine of Alexandria*, commissioned by Cardinal del Monte, marks a stylistic turning point in the artist's career, as noted by Bellori, who distinguishes it from his early production (Bellori [1672] 2009, pp. 216–217). The saint shared a name with the cardinal's mother and was therefore considered her patron saint. As evidence of this devotion, the inventory of his possessions reveals the presence of four additional paintings depicting Saint Catherine (Kirwin 1971, p. 53; Marini 2001, p. 420).

The 'F. 12' placed in the lower right-hand corner of the painting corresponds to the number in the Barberini inventory drawn up by Vincenzo Camuccini in 1817, with which the work is identified (Mariotti 1892, p. 127). The painting appears in the inventory of the assets of the Del Monte bequest, drawn up on 28 February 1627, in which it is described as a "Saint Catherine of the Wheel, the work of Michel Agnolo da Caravaggio with a frame decorated with gilding, seven *palmi*" (Frommel 1971, pp. 53–56). In the inventory of the sale of the estate, dated 7 May 1628, the work is referred to together with the painting of *The Cardsharps* (Kirwin 1971, pp. 54–55). Although the name of the buyer is not explicitly stated, one can reasonably assume, as for *The Cardsharps*, that the buyer was Cardinal Antonio Barberini. This hypothesis is confirmed by the presence of both paintings in the Barberini inventory of 1644, and the subsequent inventory of 1671 (Lavin 1975, pp. 167, 296).

In 1916, Roberto Longhi attributed the work to Orazio Gentileschi, bringing it to the attention of scholars (Longhi 1916, pp. 264–265). In 1922 Marangoni cautiously put forward an attribution to Caravaggio, later confirmed by studies by Voss 1923, pp. 80–81) and by Longhi himself (Longhi 1943, pp. 10–11), who revised his initial judgement. Following the dissolution of the entailment that saddled the Barberini collection, the painting was acquired by Baron Thyssen-Bornemisza in 1935 and transferred to the Villa Favorita in Castagnola (Lugano). Only in 1992 did the work reach its current home (Museo Nacional Thyssen-Bornemisza, Madrid).

Bellori was the first to identify in the *Saint Catherine of Alexandria* a crucial moment in the stylistic evolution of Caravaggio's painting: "For this lord [Cardinal del Monte] he painted . . . Saint Catherine on her knees leaning against the wheel; the latter two [the *Lute Player* and *Saint Catherine*] are also in the same chambers [of Cardinal Antonio Barberini], but they display deeper colouring, for Michele was already beginning to fortify the dark tones" (Bellori [1672] 2005, p. 180)

Bellori's analysis placed the *Saint Catherine of Alexandria* at the moment of transition from Caravaggio's youthful phase, characterised by luminous, limpid paint, to a new creative period marked by the more dramatic use of *chiaroscuro*. Light, from being a secondary element in the

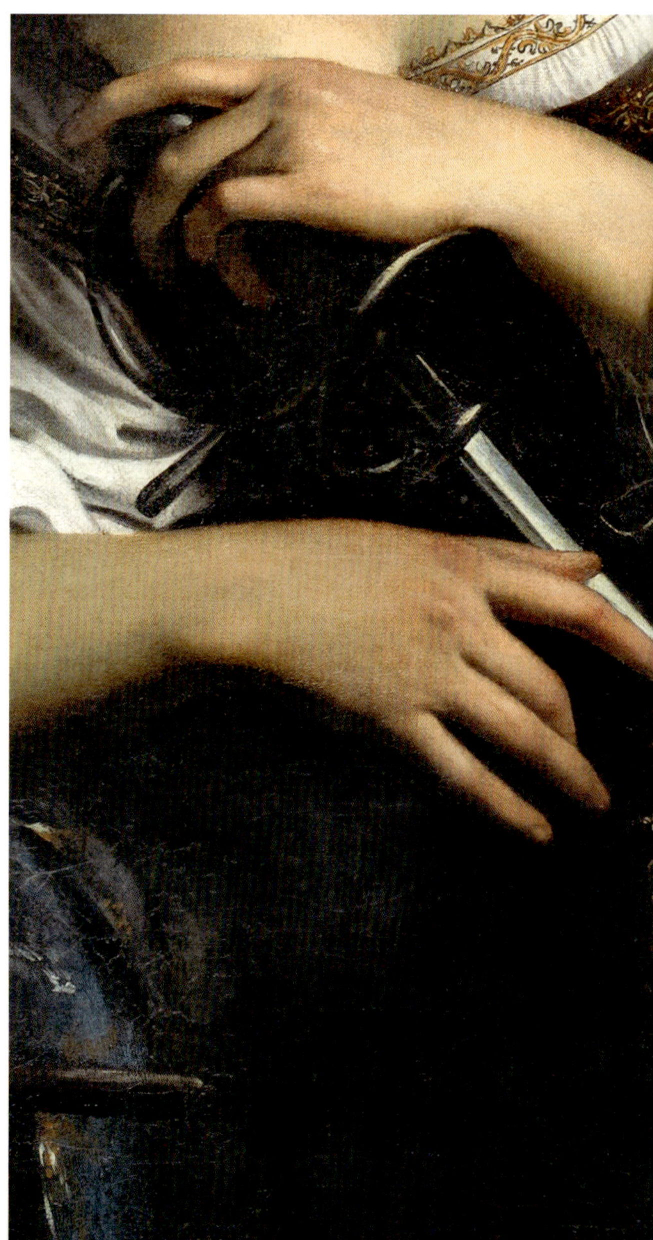

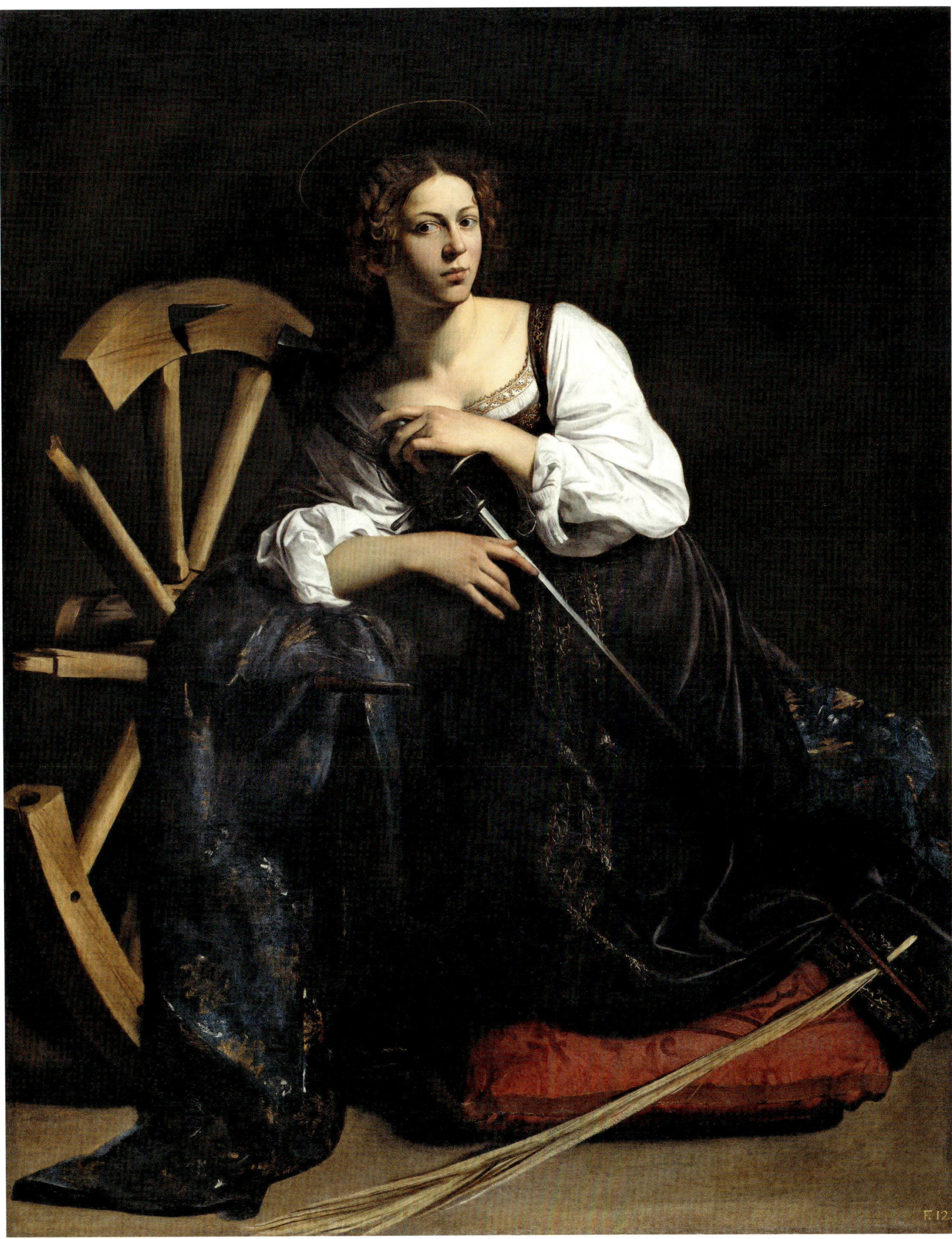
F. 12.

composition, takes on a central role, structuring space and defining volumes. Although Caravaggio had earlier experimented with soft light and a use of light designed to bring out the background, in this work he achieves full mastery of this element, employing light not only to give shape to objects, but also to place them in a precise location in space. Several scholars (Voss 1923, p. 81; Mahon 1951, p. 228, no. 55) have identified the Sienese courtesan Fillide Melandroni as the model who posed for the *Saint Catherine*. Although there are doubts as to the validity of this hypothesis (see Curti, in this catalogue), the same female figure has also been correctly identified in other works by Caravaggio, such as the *Martha and Mary Magdalene* (Longhi 1943, pp. 10–11; cat. 11) and *Judith with the Head of Holophernes* (Longhi 1951c, pp. 10–18; cat. 12).

The iconography of Saint Catherine is made manifest by the regally majestic figure, characterised by a refined elegance. The saint, kneeling on a damask cushion—an element of great value which, together with the lapis lazuli blue mantle decorated in gold, underlines her elevated status—turns her back to the toothed breaking-wheel, split by the divine thunderbolt. The blood-soaked sword, the true instrument of her martyrdom, is delicately held in her hands. At her feet, the palm, the icono-graphic attribute of martyrdom, is represented diagonally, invading real space.

As pointed out by Zuccari (2009, pp. 188–189), the Catholic Reformation, with its objective of purging the *Martyrologium Romanum* of historically inaccurate elements, deeply affected the iconography of Saint Catherine of Alexandria. A decree of 1593 imposed a revision on depictions of the saint, dictating that the wheel, an instrument of torture, be relegated to a secondary position, as it was not the ultimate cause of martyrdom. In line with the new theological directives, images painted after the Council of Trent portrayed the saint kneeling, praying, or in the act of offering her neck to the executioner. Caravaggio, in his interpretation, adhering to these precepts, introduces a significant innovation, placing the wheel on the left, but behind the saint, in accordance with the directive, and highlighting the sword, the true instrument of martyrdom, giving it a central position in the image. This choice emphasises the crucial role of the beheading in the saint's sacrifice and, as noted by Ebert-Schifferer (2010b, p. 92), marks a fundamental shift in the iconographic evolution, from the wheel to the sword.

[GM]

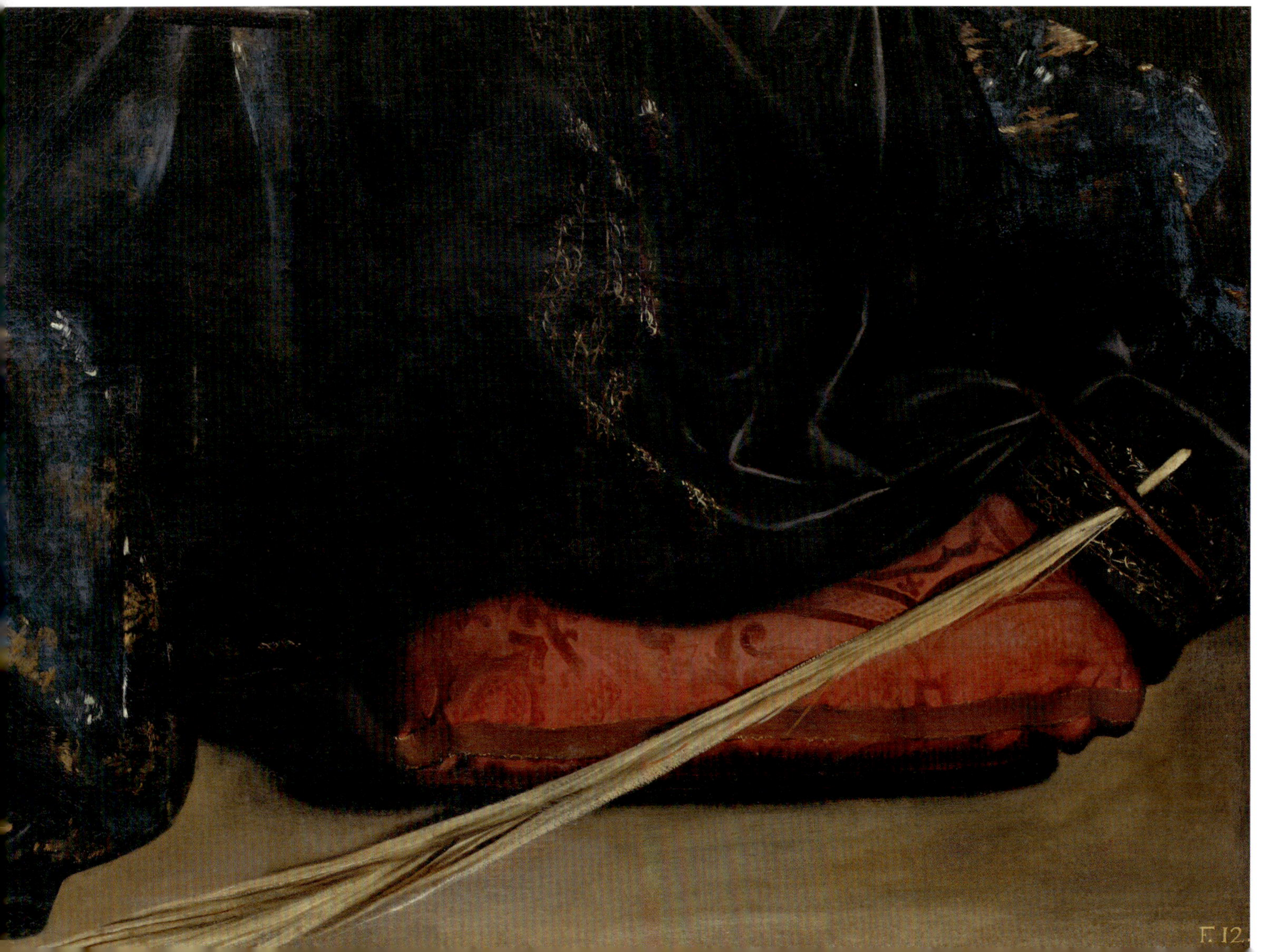

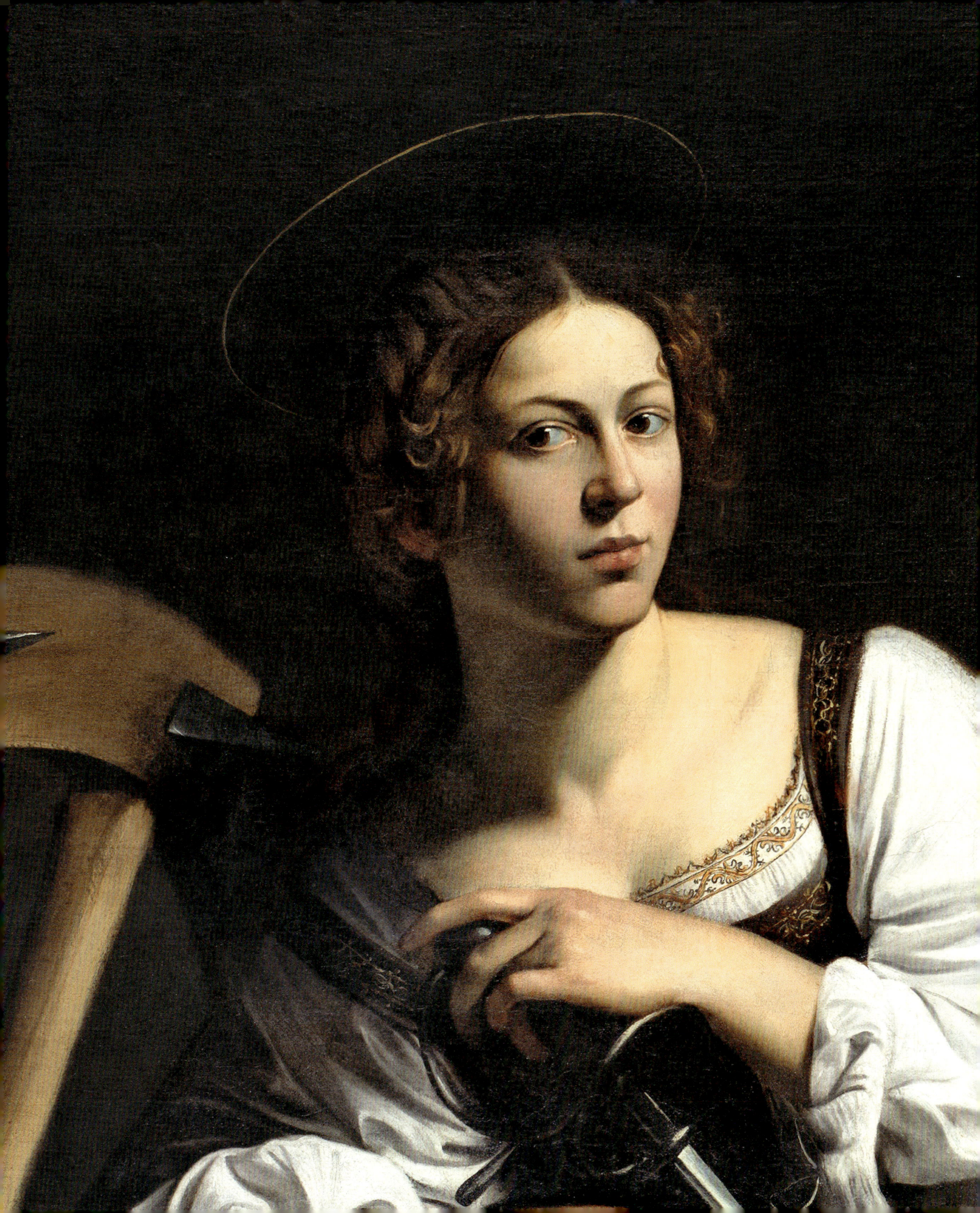

MARTHA AND MARY MAGDALENE

c. 1598–1599
oil on canvas, 100 × 134.5 cm
Detroit Institute of Arts, Detroit (MI). Gift of the Kresge Foundation and Mrs. Edsel B. Ford, inv. 73.268

Provenance: Arezzo, Panzani Family Collection; 1897, legally exported through Milan customs; between 1904 and 1909, acquired by Indalecio Gómez, Argentine ambassador in Berlin (Paris, France); by descent, Carlos Gómez de Alzaga collection, Indalecio's grandson (Salta province and later Buenos Aires, Argentina); 1971, sold at auction (Christie's, 25 June 1971, lot 21, London, England); bought by Ambassador Carlos Gómez de Alzaga; in 1973 acquired by the Detroit Institute of Arts (Detroit, Michigan, USA).

Bibliography: Longhi 1943, p. 11; Cummings 1974, pp. 563–564; Spezzaferro 1974a, pp. 586–593; Moir 1976, pp. 107–109; Cinotti 1983, p. 426; Gregori 1985a, p. 250; Calvesi 1990, p. 207–210; Cappelletti, Testa 1990b, p. 241; Marini, Corradini 1993 pp. 162–169; Testa 2002, pp. 131–133; Terzaghi 2007, pp. 343–410; Macioce 2010b, p. 173; Vodret 2021a, p. 178.

The painting depicting *Martha and Mary Magdalene* is not mentioned by early biographers, although the composition must have enjoyed a certain notoriety at the time, as attested by the large number of contemporary copies and reinterpretations (Moir 1976, pp. 107–109).

In 1943, Roberto Longhi was the first to attribute the composition to Caravaggio, publishing two non-autograph copies (Longhi 1943, p. 11).

The work, according to the nineteenth-century inscriptions on the reverse of the canvas, came from the Panzani family, originally from Arezzo. It was exported from Milan in 1897 to be sold and, between 1904 and 1909, bought in Paris by Indalecio Gómez, minister of the imperial court in Berlin. In 1909, Gómez moved the painting to Buenos Aires, where it remained until 1965.

On 25 June 1971 Carlos Gómez-Alzaga, the owner's grandson, tried to sell the painting at auction at Christie's in London. The work, presented as an original by Caravaggio with a catalogue entry by David Carrit, the representative of the London auction house, remained unsold. Only in 1973, thanks to the definitive attribution put forward by Cummings, who also clarified the iconography (Cummings 1974, pp. 563–564), was the painting acquired by the Detroit Institute of Arts. Currently housed in the museum, it is unanimously accepted by scholarship as an autograph work by the Lombard painter.

The early provenance of the painting is still a matter of considerable debate: initially, on the basis of Ottavio Costa's first will drawn up on 6 August 1606, later amended on several occasions as the banker died in 1639 (Terzaghi 2007, pp. 370–371), scholars postulated a link between the painting and the Costa collection (Spezzaferro 1974a, pp. 586–593). However, neither in the Costa nor the Herrera inventories is the canvas that corresponds in subject matter ever explicitly attributed to Caravaggio, nor is it ever referred to again (Terzaghi 2007, pp. 343–410). On the other hand, Laura Testa (2002, p. 133) has suggested that the work came from the Aldobrandini collection.

Olimpia Aldobrandini's involvement in Caravaggio's judicial affair, documented in 1604 (Macioce 2010b, p. 173), and her deep devotion to Mary Magdalene (Testa 2002, pp. 131–133) seem to

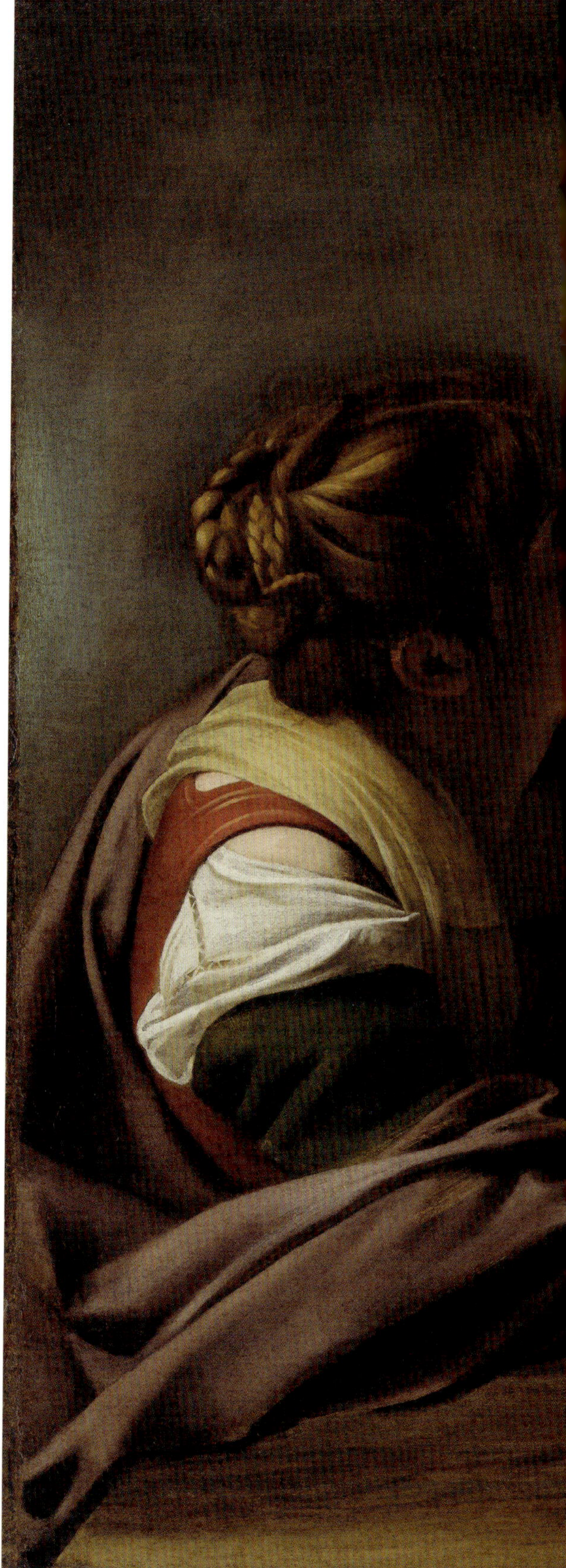

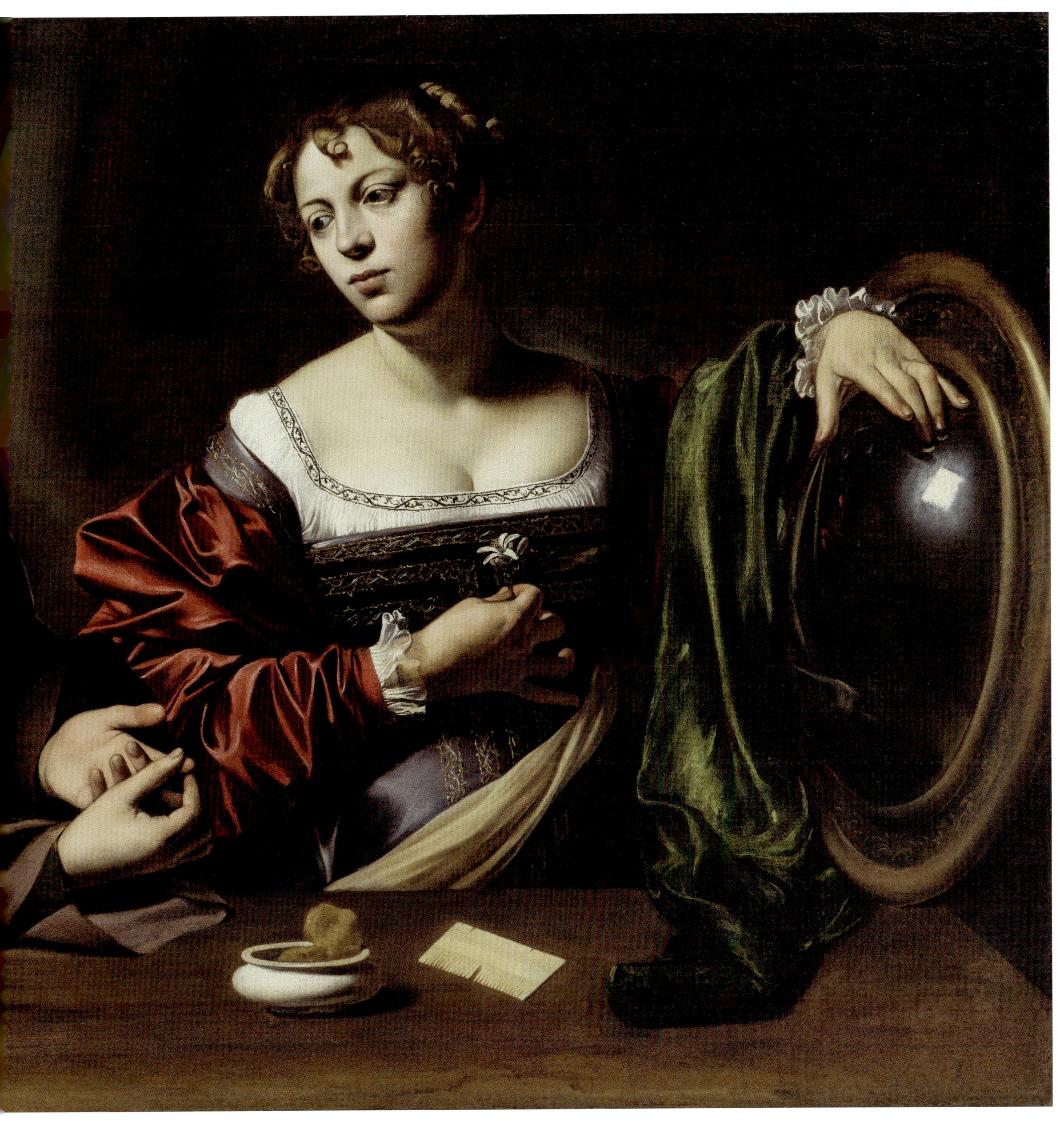

support the hypothesis of a direct commission by Olimpia herself. In confirmation of this, the inventory of Olimpia Aldobrandini's possessions drawn up in 1606 records "a painting of Saint Martha and Mary Magdalene, as she converts her, with frame[s] set with gold" (Cappelletti, Testa 1990b, p. 241).
The work is referred to again in the inventories of 1611, described as: "a painting of Saint Martha and Magdalene with black frame[s], with gold and stars". The same description is found in documents prior to 1615, as well as in the inventories of 1626 and 1634. Furthermore, a note dated July 1638, entitled "Paintings taken from Monte Magnanapoli by order of the Signor Cardinale and brought to the Palazzo del Corso to H[is].E[xcellency].", drawn

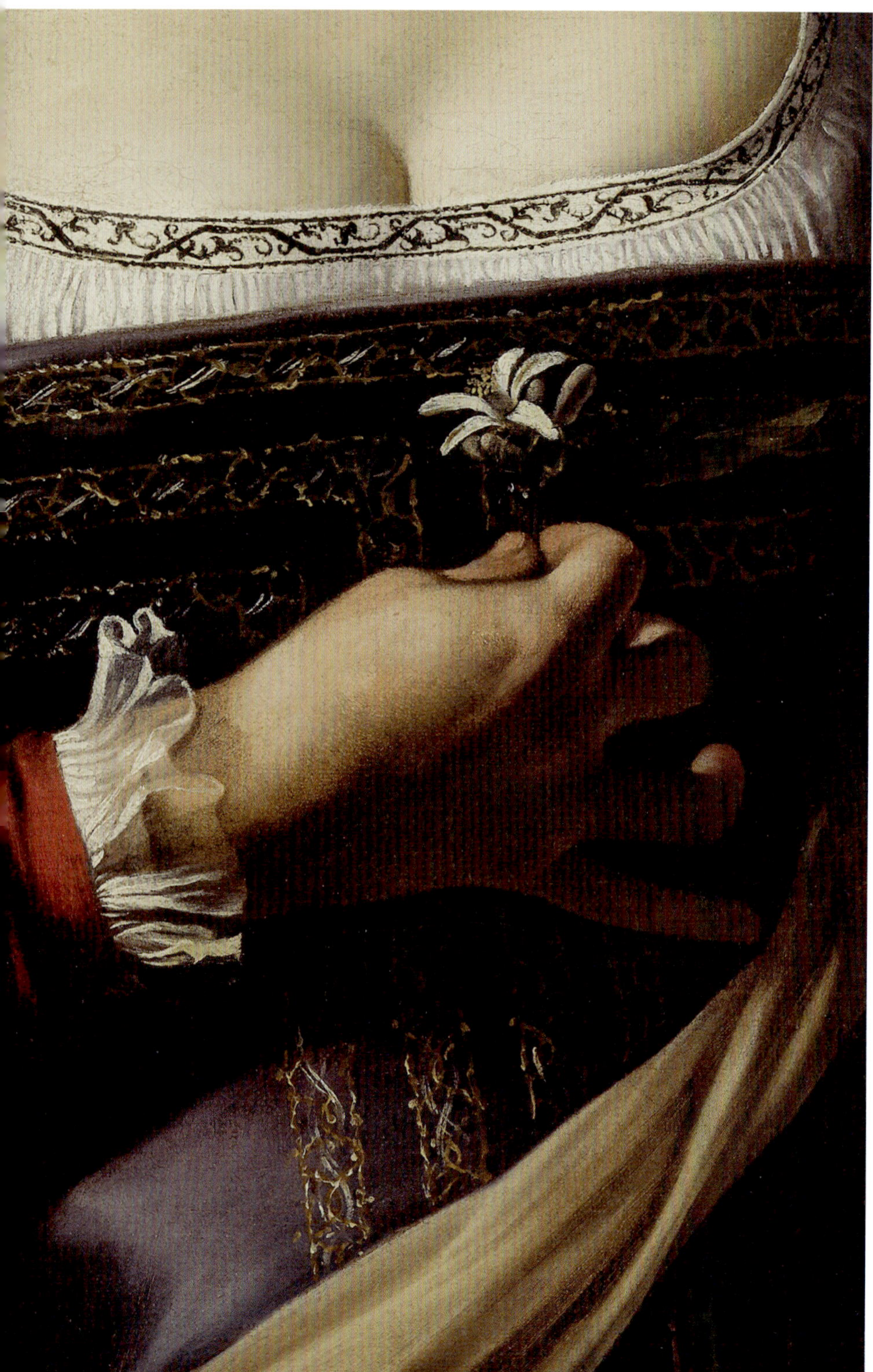

up for Cardinal Ippolito Aldobrandini, Olimpia's son and heir, attributes the canvas with greater certainty to Caravaggio. The painting, again associated with the same frame, is described as: "A landscape format ("*bislongo*") with a Magdalene and Martha, holding a flower, with a black frame ornamented with gold by Caravaggio." The work is also documented as present in the villa of Monte Magnanapoli in the inventories of 1646, 1662, 1682 and 1769, remaining in the Aldobrandini picture gallery until at least the 1890s (Testa 2002, p. 132).
In the depiction, Martha seems to radiate a divine light that illuminates the face of Mary Magdalene, caught in a moment of deep reflection. The contrast between Martha's severity and Mary Magdalene's delicate beauty highlights the inner drama of the conversion, sealed by the symbols of the mystic marriage: the orange blossom and the gold ring. These elements recall, according to Calvesi's interpretation, the figure of the Bride in the *Song of Songs* (Cummings 1974, pp. 563–564; Calvesi 1990, pp. 207–210).
Belonging to the genre of '*vanitas*' paintings, the work displays a clear stylistic debt to Titian, especially in the richness and sumptuous quality of Mary Magdalene's dress (Gregori 1985a, p. 250). Iconographic sources include a *Mary Magdalene* attributed to Leonardo and recorded in the collections of Cardinal del Monte, which Caravaggio may have seen. This painting, according to scholars, may correspond to one of the examples in the Sciarra collection representing *Modesty and Vanity* and attributed to Luini (Cinotti 1983, p. 426). The detail of the round convex mirror might resemble the so-called *scudo a specchio* (mirror shield) that was used by Caravaggio as part of his artistic practice, and is documented in the inventory of his possessions of 1605, which also lists a second, larger, mirror (Marini, Corradini 1993, pp. 162–169).
The work shows remarkable affinities with the *Saint Catherine of Alexandria* [cat. 10] in the Museo Nacional Thyssen-Bornemisza in Madrid, and with the *Judith with the Head of Holophernes* in Palazzo Barberini in Rome [cat. 12], with the same model as used in both the latter paintings, traditionally identified as the famous Sienese courtesan Fillide Melandroni (see Francesca Curti's essay on the subject in this catalogue).
[GM]

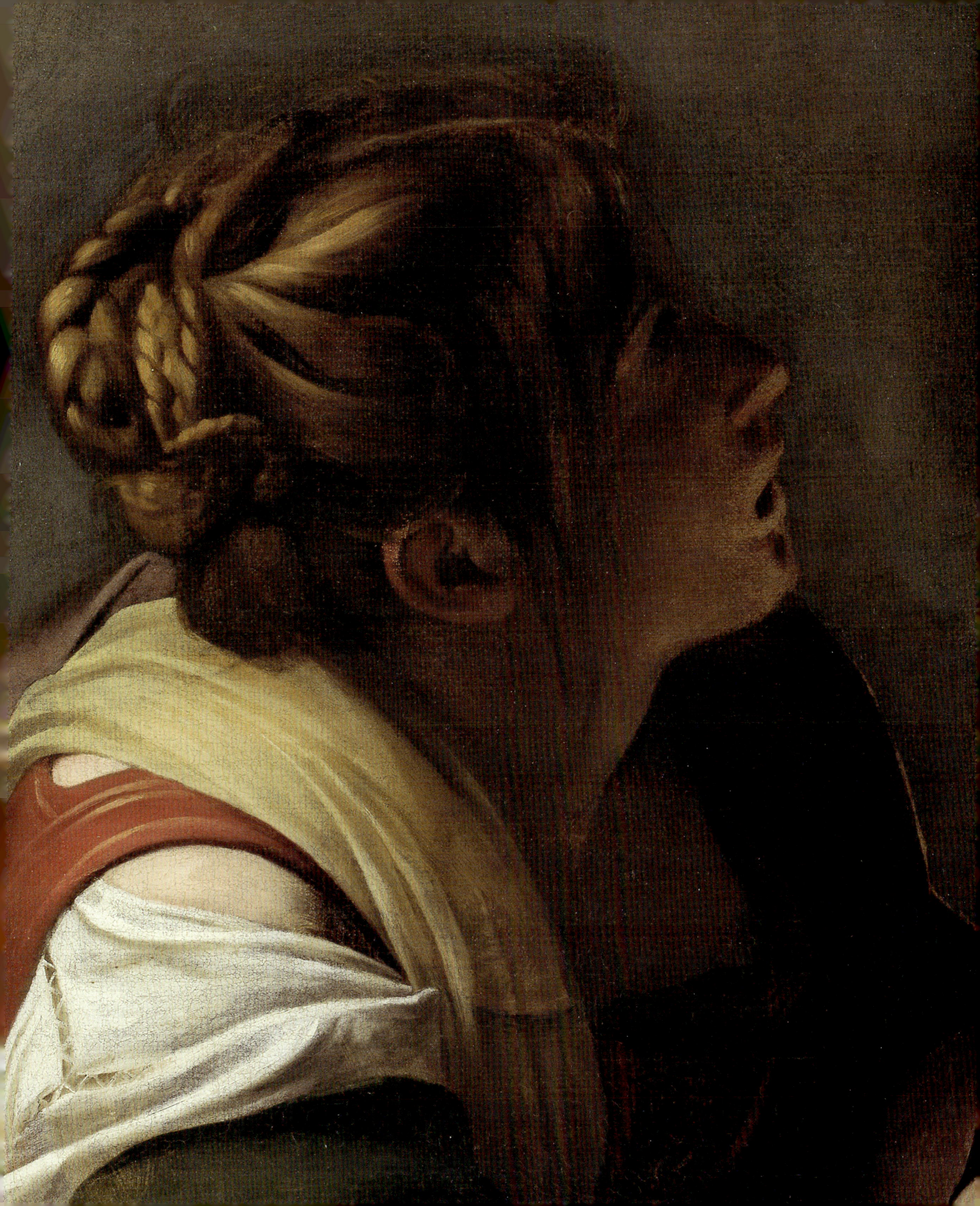

JUDITH BEHEADING HOLOPHERNES

c. 1599–1600
oil on canvas, 145 × 195cm
Gallerie Nazionali di Arte Antica,
Palazzo Barberini, Rome, inv. 2533

Inscriptions: on the back, on the
original canvas, inscribed with a
brush, in capital letters about 10
cm high "C.O.C."; on the back of the
frame, "D'Orazio"; "36'".

Provenance: Ottavio Costa's
collection, Rome, up to 1639; by
inheritance to his daughter-in-
law Maria Cattaneo Costa, Rome,
1688; by inheritance to Monsignor
Guido Del Palagio, Rome, 1732; by
inheritance to Monsignor Carlo
Origo, Rome, 1792; by inheritance
to Giuseppe Origo, Rome 1834; by
inheritance to the Congregazione
degli Operai della Divina Pietà,
Rome, 1834–1846, number
36 (visible on the frame of the
painting); by inheritance to Cavaliere
Antonio de' Cinque, Rome 1854;
by inheritance to Ferdinando De'
Cinque Quintili, Rome, 1873; by
inheritance to Matilde de' Cinque
Quintili, Rome, 1887; by inheritance
to her daughter Paolina Giannuzzi
Savelli, Rome; by inheritance to
her son Vincenzo Coppi, Rome; by
purchase for the Italian State, 1971.

Bibliography: Baglione 1642, p. 138;
Longhi [1951] 2000; Safarik 1972,
pp. 26–30; Cinotti 1983, pp. 515-517;
Gregori, in *The Age of Caravaggio
| Caravaggio e il suo tempo* 1985,
p. 256; Christiansen 1986; Gregori, in
*Michelangelo Merisi da Caravaggio.
Come nascono* 1991, pp. 188–192;
Vodret 1999; Costa Restagno 2004a;
Costa Restagno 2004b; Marini 2005,
pp. 424–426; Terzaghi 2007, pp.
144–147; Papi 2016a, pp. 56-63;
Papi 2016b, pp. 8-18; Vodret 2017b,
pp. 88-91; Terzaghi, in *Caravage à
Rome* 2018, pp. 85–86; *Caravaggio
e Artemisia* 2021; Terzaghi 2021a;
Terzaghi 2021b; Vodret 2021a,
pp. 204–206.

In a veritable *coup de théâtre*, the canvas appeared
in all its splendour on 7 July 1951 at the exhibition
organised by Roberto Longhi at the Palazzo Reale
in Milan, which had been extended by two months
specifically to exhibit the masterpiece. Pico Cellini,
who had restored the painting many years earlier as
a work by Orazio Gentileschi (a reference not coinci-
dentally inscribed on the back of the frame), after visiting the Milan exhibition realised that the work, "an
extremely dirty painting, but one that makes a huge
impression on me" (Terzaghi 2021c, p. 48), could be
by Caravaggio. Without delay, the restorer submit-
ted the attribution to the judgement of Longhi who
confirmed the authorship, dedicating an article to
the painting in *Paragone* (Longhi 1951c). Vincenzo
Coppi, who was the owner of the painting at the time
and who sold the canvas to the Italian State twenty
years later in 1971 for two hundred and fifty million
lire, had inherited the painting from his maternal
grandmother, Matilde de' Cinque Quintili, whose
grandfather, the knight Antonio de' Cinque Quintili,
had bought the work from the Congregazione degli
Operai della Divina Pietà in Rome in 1854. The painting had come to the Congregation as the final step in
a series of changes of ownership through inheritance
from the wealthy banker Ottavio Costa, originally
from Albenga, at the head of one of the most active
banks in Roman finance, together with his Span-
ish-born partner Juan Enríquez de Herrera (Costa
Restagno 2004a; Terzaghi 2007; Terzaghi 2022a).
Among the early sources, the painting and its first
owner are referred to by Giovanni Baglione: "For
the signor Costi he painted a Judith cutting off the
head of Holophernes" (Baglione 1642, p. 138. English translation from Wittkower [1955] 1976, p. 235).
Longhi, who believed that the painting under consideration here was the one cited by the biographer, also
knew of a second early reference to a *Judith* by Caravaggio for sale in Naples in 1607, made known by the
correspondence between the Flemish painter Frans
Pourbus who had been sent to Naples by Vincenzo
I Gonzaga and the Mantuan court (Baschet 1868,
p. 448). Doubts as to the origin of the painting remained in the subsequent literature, so much so that
Safarik (1972, pp. 24–30) drew up an extensive list of
possible documentary references to which the work
could be linked, until Spezzaferro (1974a) published
the documents relating to the estate of Ottavio Costa,

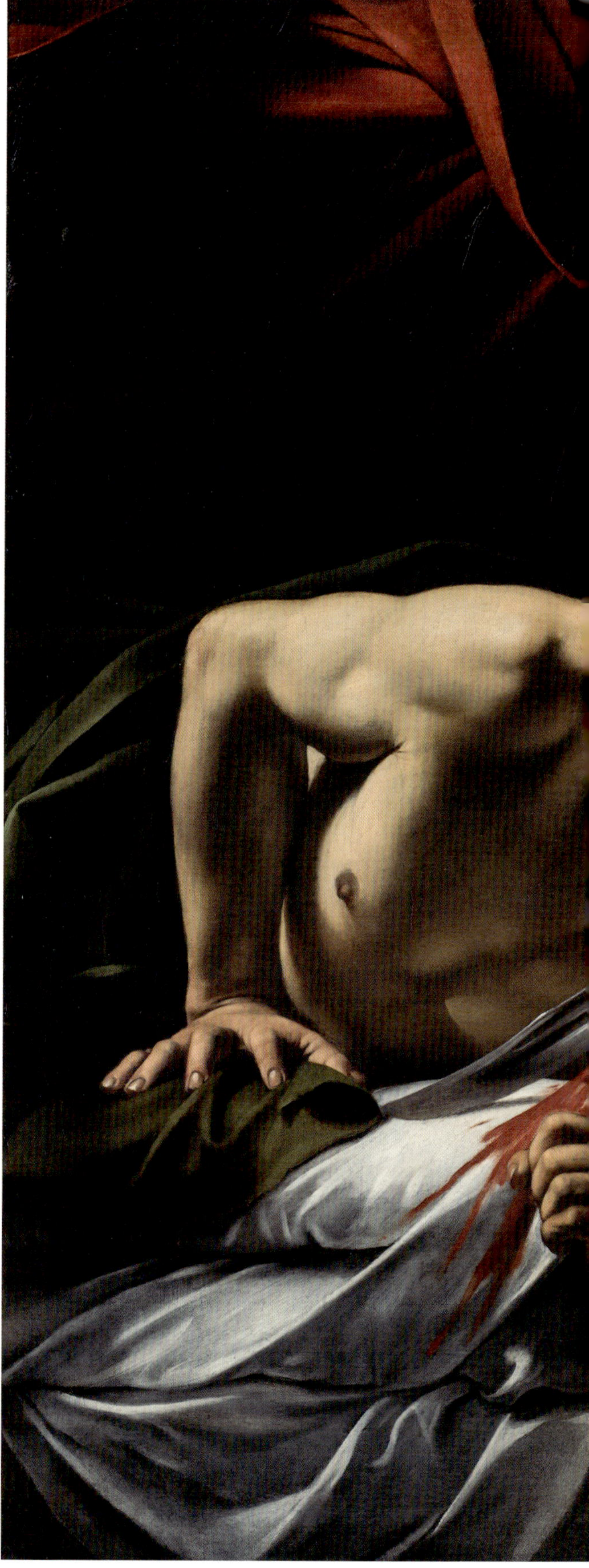

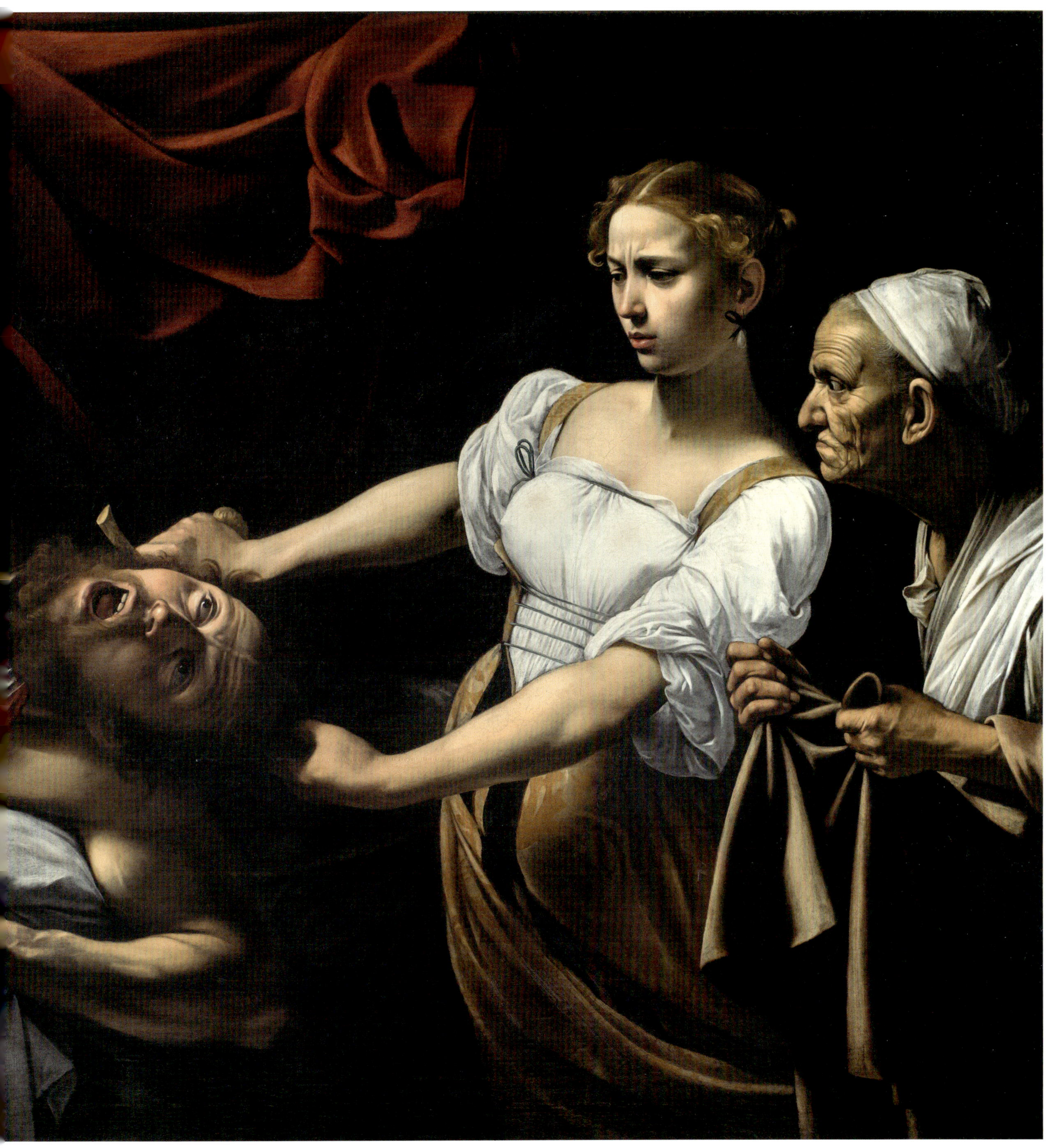

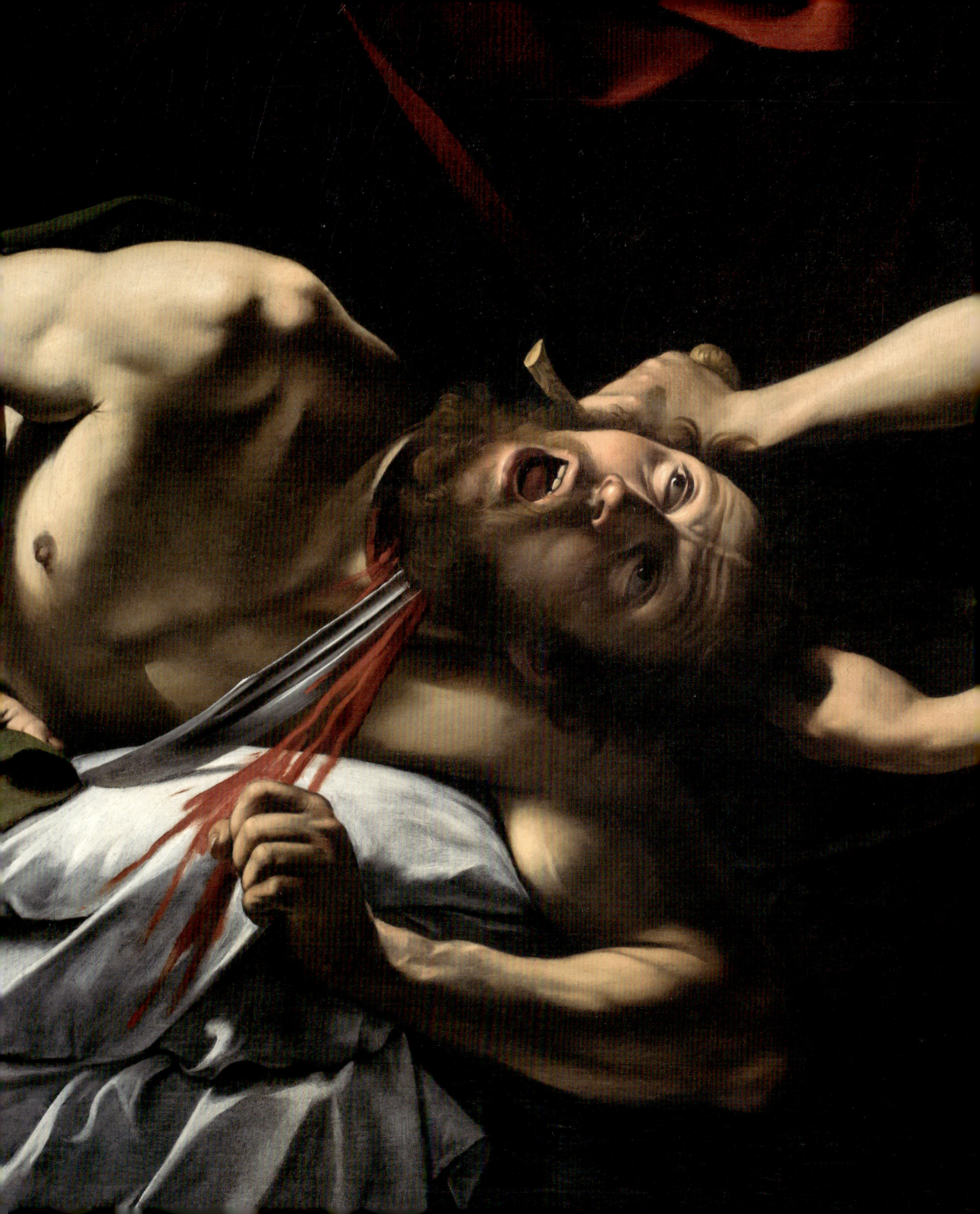

who died in Rome in 1639, having drawn up at least three wills. In the last two, of 1632 and 1639, the banker explicitly forbade the transfer of all his works by Caravaggio, and particularly the *Judith*, which he considered to be his most precious, to the extent that it was displayed in the collection covered by a silk drape. The painting followed Ottavio Costa to his homes in Rome: the Palazzo Gaddi-Bandini (today Via del Banco di Santo Spirito 41), the Palazzo in Piazza Fiammetta and finally the Palazzo Pichi between Via del Paradiso and Palazzo Massimi. Evidence of the work's importance to its owner is the monogram "C.O.C." found on the original canvas, inscribed with a brush, and correctly resolved as: "Comites Octavius Costa" (Vodret 1999; Costa Restagno 2004a, p. 430). Costa was a true and impassioned enthusiast of the paintings of Caravaggio, whom he knew and rewarded with commissions from the artist's Roman beginnings. For Ottavio Costa Caravaggio executed his first religious painting, the *Saint Francis of Assisi in Ecstasy* in Hartford [cat. 8] and the beautiful *Saint John the Baptist* (Kansas City, Nelson-Atkins Museum; cat. 15). Although the banker had made provision for the paintings to be transferred to Liguria after his death, his heirs disregarded his wishes, and the works, including the *Judith*, remained in Rome until the nineteenth century. Nevertheless, Costa's jealousy over his paintings was such that he always forbade their reproduction, thus there are no early copies of the painting, only a nineteenth-century drawing from which an engraving plate was made (Rome, Istituto Nazionale per la grafica, inv. D-CL806) by Giacomo Maria Conca (Rome, 1787-1852). However, the extraordinary novelty of the painting worked its way into Roman painting in the first and second decade of the seventeenth century, as is documented by the beautiful work by Giuseppe Vermiglio (London, Klesch Collection; Dominioni, in *Caravaggio and Artemisia* 2021, p. 117), and an extraordinarily fascinating *Judith* that has been attributed to Caravaggio himself, perhaps with the help of a collaborator, discovered in Toulouse (*Caravaggio. Judith and Holofernes* 2019), of which a reduced-size early replica exists that is attributed to Louis Finson (Naples, Gallerie d'Italia).

The relationship between the banker and Caravaggio is also documented by a receipt from the Herrera & Costa bank that attests to an advance payment made by Ottavio Costa on 21 May 1602 to Caravaggio himself: "For a picture that I am painting for him" (Terzaghi 2007, p. 298). As the painting referred to in the receipt is not specified, scholars have been divided on the interpretation of the document between those who have linked it to the *Saint John the Baptist* (Terzaghi 2007, pp. 298-299) and those who instead believed it to be the *Judith* (Papi 2016a and Papi 2016b; followed by Cuppone 2016 and Vodret 2017b).

Caravaggio interprets as a violent assassination the crucial moment in the story of the biblical heroine Judith, who, in order to save her people from the siege of the Assyrian general Holophernes, seduces the warrior with a stratagem, only to behead him in his intoxicated slumber; an extraordinary innovation compared to the sixteenth-century pictorial tradition, which had attempted to sublimate the story by recounting the moment after the killing. Judith, beautiful in her ochre-coloured robes with the feather-weight shirt that barely masks her breasts, her auburn hair and the pearls in her ears, seems oblivious of her seductive power and totally engrossed in her divine task. Effort and concentration can be read on her furrowed brow, while, true to the biblical text, a silent prayer hovers on her lips: "Give me strength today, O Lord God of Israel!" (Judith 13:7–8). The beauty of the heroine is exalted by the contrast represented by the grizzled head of the old maid-servant who looks out horrified on the right-hand side of the scene, ready to gather up the general's head in her sack. However, the real protagonist of the scene is Holophernes' agonised scream, in which one can read, as if its watermark, Caravaggio's thoughts, who in this drama questions himself on the exact moment of the passage from life to death.

Longhi was the first to evoke in relation to this painting the tragic episode of the end of the noblewoman Beatrice Cenci, executed in 1599 when only eighteen for having been the instigator of the murder of her violent father who had segregated her far from Rome with her stepmother. It is now clear that Caravaggio could not have been unaware of this fact; the chronology also fits in singularly well with another painting that can be compared to the work here studied, that is the Ludovisi wall-painting, where the painter's self-portrait as Neptune with his mouth wide-open fits in remarkably with the depiction of Holophernes in our painting (Terzaghi 2021c, p. 59). Here, moreover, in the role of Judith, is the same model (whether or not the Sienese courtesan Fillide Melandroni) who also appears in the Thyssen *Saint Catherine* [cat. 10] and in the *Martha and Mary Magdalene* [cat. 11]. I therefore believe it is difficult to disengage the painting and place it too far from the dates of these works, around 1598-1599. Furthermore, as the payment made in 1602 referred to above was 'on account', we should imagine the balance to have been paid later, and hence the work referred to would at the earliest have been painted in the summer of 1602, when Caravaggio had already demonstrated his spatial skill, which in the *Judith*, where all the figures are depicted on the same plane, does not yet seem so evolved. Be that as it may, the work constitutes Caravaggio's first striking meditation on violence and fate, inaugurating the tragic style that would accompany him to the end.

[MCT]

THE CONVERSION OF SAUL

1600–1601
oil on cypress panel,
237 × 189 cm
Nicoletta Odescalchi collection,
Rome

Provenance: Tiberio Cerasi, 1600;
Cardinal Giacomo Sannesio, 1646;
Juan Alfonso Enriquez de Cabrera,
1647; Agostino Airolo; Francesco
Maria Balbi, inventory 1701;
Odescalchi Balbi di Roma, c. 1950.

Bibliography: Mancini [c. 1619–1621]
1956–1957, I, p. 225; Baglione [1642]
2023 p. 405; Mahon 1951, pp. 226–
227; Cinotti 1983, pp. 540–542;
Spezzaferro, Mignosi Tantillo 2001,
pp. 108–124; Boccardo, in *Capolavori
da scoprire* 2006, p. 87; Vodret 2009;
Buranelli 2010, pp. 106–115; Granata
2016, p. 304.

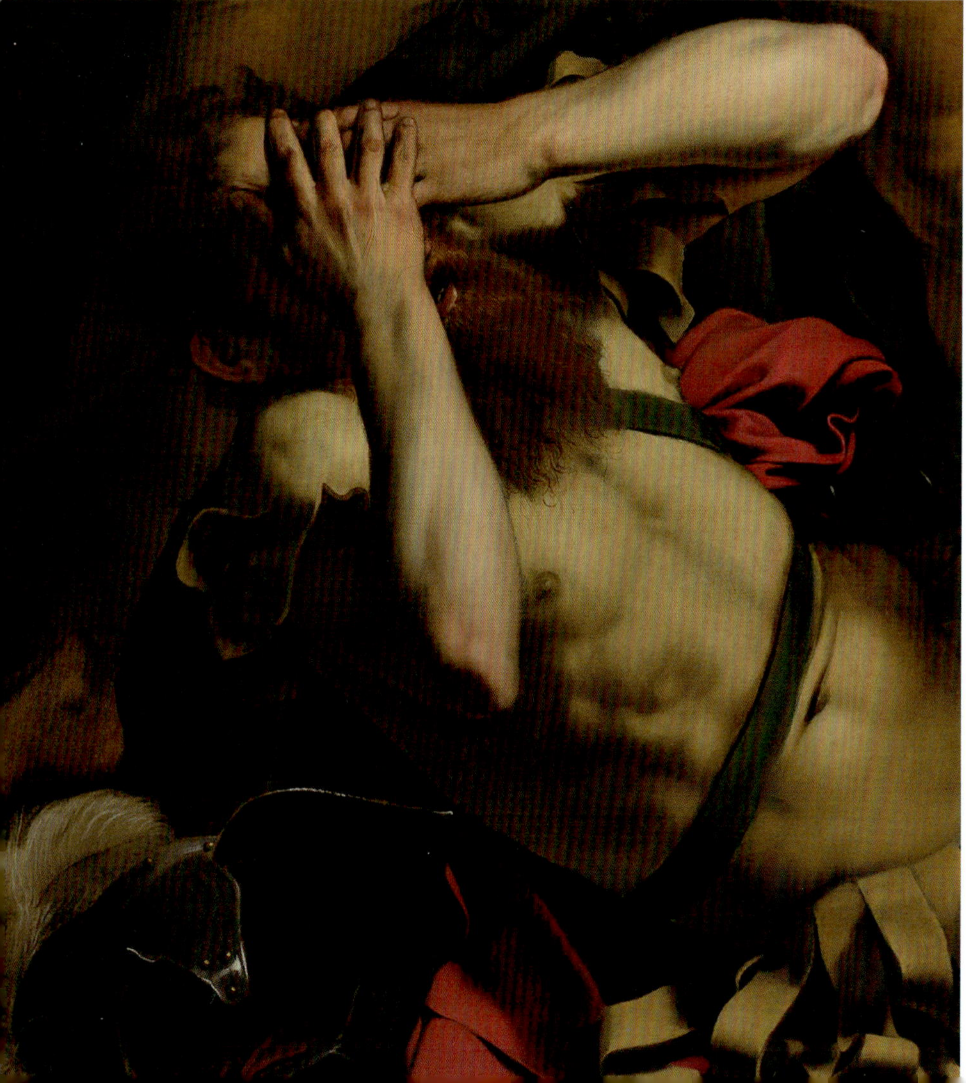

"In the Madonna del Popolo on the right-hand of side of the main altar, on the side walls of the chapel of the Signori Cerasi, are by his hand the Crucifixion of Saint Peter and, opposite it, is the Conversion of Saint Paul. These pictures were first worked in another manner; but because they did not please the patron, they were taken by Cardinal Sannesio; and Caravaggio then painted the two pictures which one now sees there—in oil, because he used no other medium; Luck and Fame, so to speak, carried him through." Thus Giovanni Baglione ([1642] 2023, p. 405; English translation in Wittkower [1955] 1976 p. 235, slightly amended) presents the question of the execution of the paintings for the Cerasi Chapel in two stages. The contract between the banker Tiberio Cerasi and Michelangelo Merisi da Caravaggio, dated 24 September 1600 (Mahon 1951, pp. 226–227), envisaged the execution of two panel paintings for the family chapel in Santa Maria del Popolo in Rome. The agreed fee was 400 *scudi*, to be paid within eight months of the signing of the contract. However, the payment to Caravaggio was not made until 10 November 1601, with a deduction of 100 *scudi*. The affair, as reported by Baglione and also by Giulio Mancini, was rather complex. Initially, Caravaggio painted two panels that for reasons that are still to be clarified were removed from the chapel and perhaps never delivered. The death of Monsignor Cerasi on the night between 2 and 3 May 1601 led to the passing of the inheritance to the bretheren of the Ospedale della Consolazione, causing a delay in the payment to Caravaggio (Buranelli 2010; Granata 2016, p. 304). The painter probably kept the two paintings in his studio in Rome for almost four years. In the meantime, he had to paint a second version of the works, this time on canvas, which were then placed in the Cerasi Chapel that had been restored and modified in the early years of the century (Bernardini 2001). In May 1605, a carpenter named Mastro Bartolomeo was paid to put the canvases in position in the chapel designed by the architect Carlo Maderno (Spezzaferro, Mignosi Tantillo 2001, p. 111, n. 9). Baglione writes that the two paintings "did not please" the patron; however, this statement has been questioned, both because Cerasi died prematurely and did not have the opportunity to judge the works, and also because of the alteration of the spaces within the chapel probably imposed a different arrangement of the lateral works (Vodret 2009).

The path followed by the two panels, in the collection of Cardinal Sannesio until 1646, was long and fragmented. In 1647, they arrived in Madrid where they appear in the inventory of Juan Alfonso Enrìquez de Cabrera, the ninth Almirante of Castile. Upon his death, the collection was dismembered and sold, probably leading to the separation of the two works. The *Conversion of Saul* was bought by the Genoese nobleman Agostino Airolo, and then passed to his brother-in-law Francesco Maria Balbi, appearing in his inventory of 1701 (Boccardo, in *Capolavori da scoprire* 2006, p. 87). In the course of the 1950s, it passed through inheritance from the Balbi family to the Odescalchi Balbi family of Rome, and then arrived, again through maternal inheritance (through princess Vittoria Odescalchi Balbi di Piovera), to the current owner. The subject is narrated in the Acts of the Apostles

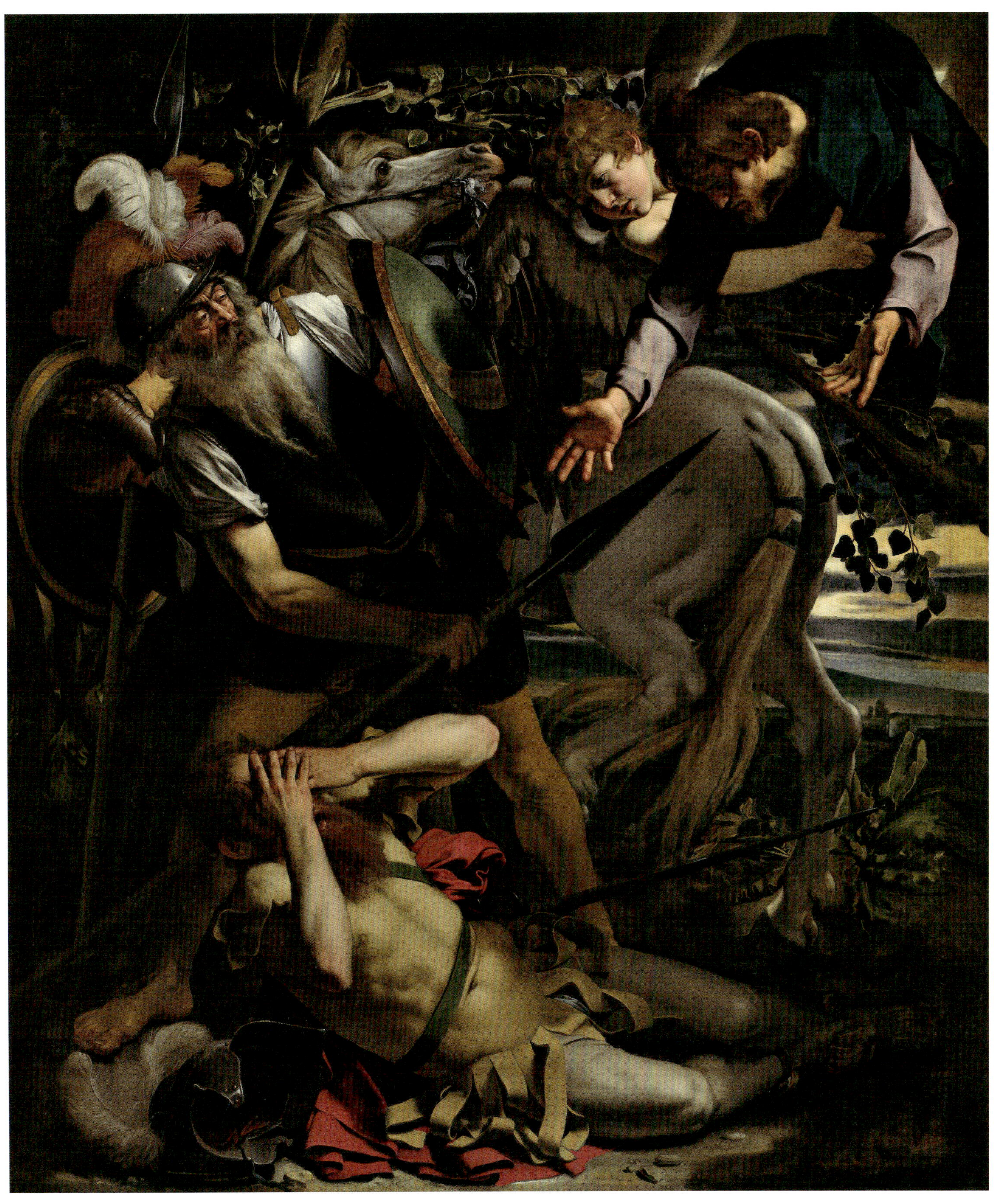

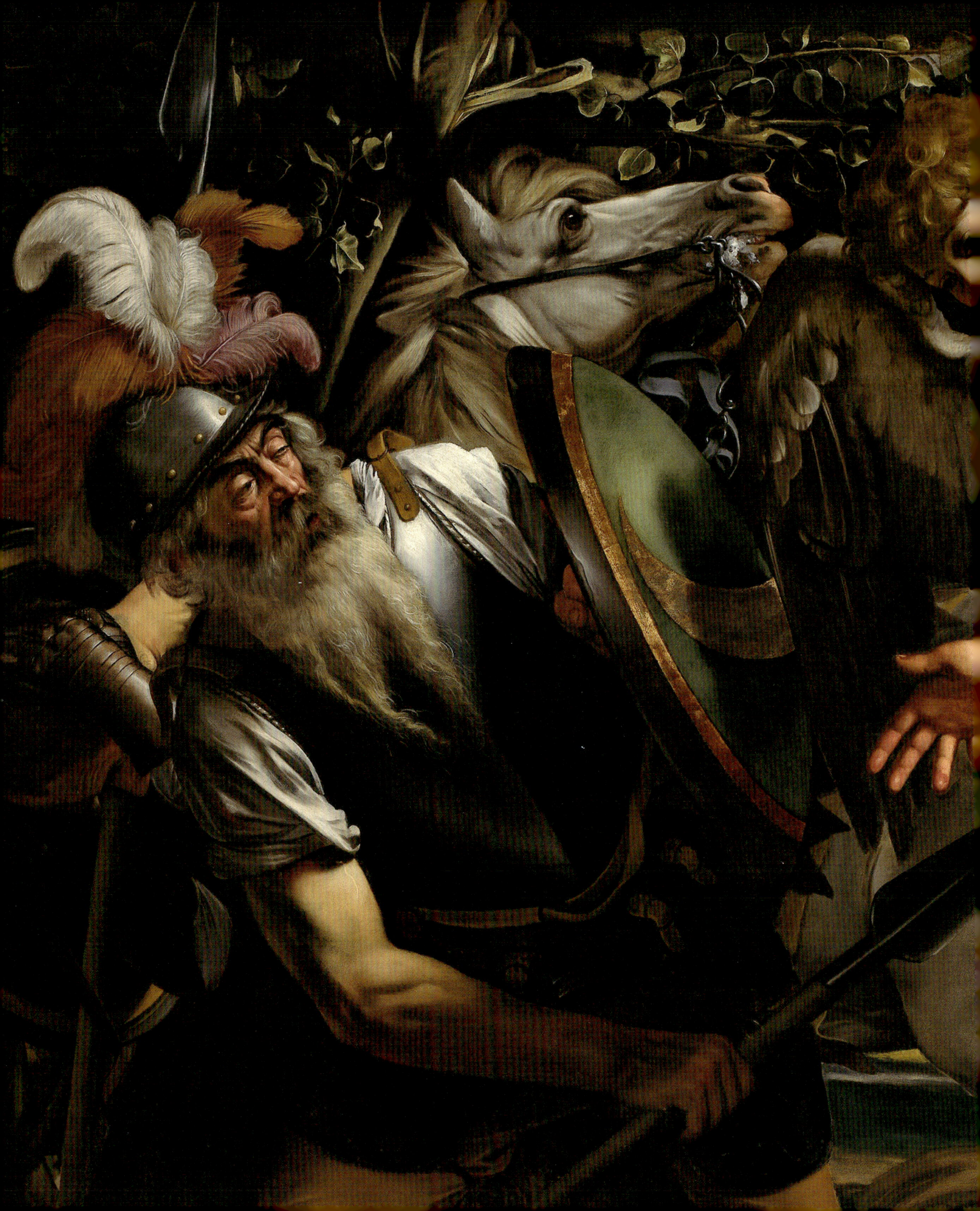

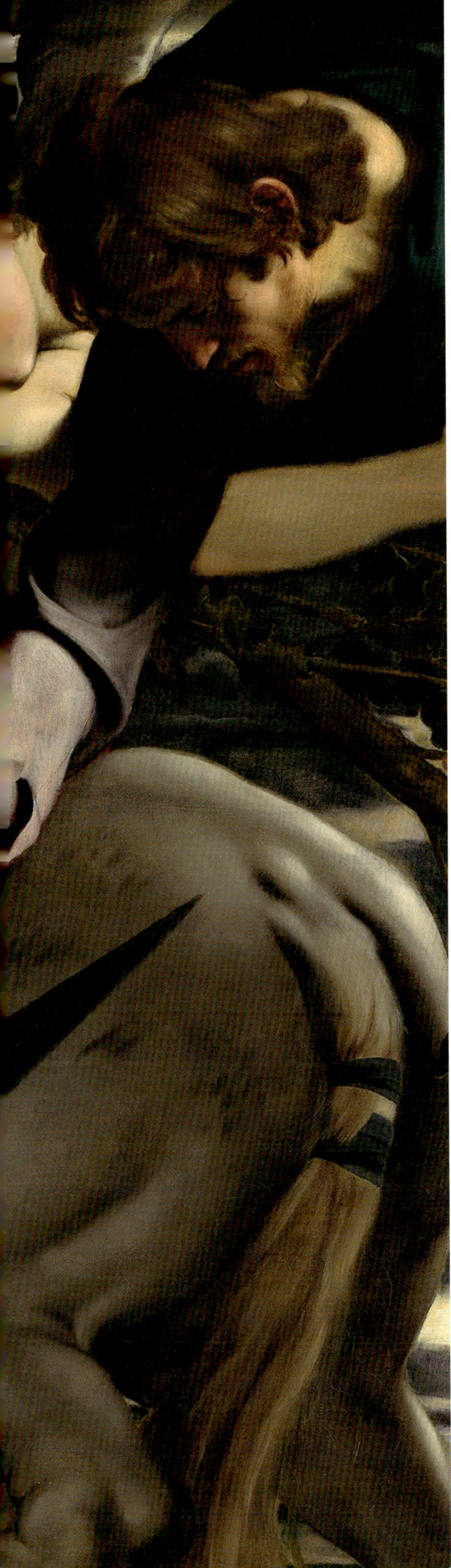

(IX,1-8 and XXII,6-12): Saul of Tarsus, persecutor of the Christians, while on his way to Damascus is suddenly converted by Jesus, who manifests himself through a blinding light. His companions hear the voice but see no one (IX,7), or, according to the other version of the Acts, they see the light but do not hear the voice. Caravaggio had two iconographic options: either the canonical depiction in which Christ does not appear physically, but as a light that provokes Saul's reaction, or the one adopted for example by Michelangelo in the Cappella Paolina in the Vatican palace, in which he descends from the clouds, releasing a thunderbolt. Caravaggio chooses to show Jesus, but with a fundamental difference. Whereas in sixteenth-century works the divine and human spheres remain separate, in this work Christ, supported by an angel, bursts with overwhelming force into natural reality. According to Cinotti (1983), this depiction of Christ, so intense and so physical, may have been the reason why the work was not initially accepted. It is not a detached celestial apparition, but an event that takes place in the earthly world.

The links with the sixteenth-century tradition and with Caravaggio's works before 1600 also emerge in the use of a golden light that pervades the scene, and in its chromatic richness, with warm, dense and deep hues. The palette is extensive and bright, with passages that include blue and purple in Christ's robes, while metallic gold and red characterise the figure of Saul on the ground. Moreover, the green of the shield is reminiscent of the colour of the 'background' of the *Medusa* now in the Uffizi; the opening of the landscape on the right, wonderful in its synthetic representation of sky and earth, is also a very rare occurrence in Caravaggio's works. The Odescalchi *Conversion* is an extraordinary masterpiece, of deliberation and experimentation, in which Caravaggio's reflection on sacred drama and the intensity of the gestures and expressions of his subjects continues.

[GB]

TAKING
OF CHRIST

1603
oil on canvas, 135.5 × 169.5 cm
National Gallery of Ireland, Dublin

Provenance: Ciriaco Mattei, Rome, 1602; by descent to the Mattei heirs; sold by Duca Giuseppe Mattei to William Hamilton Nisbet on 27 January 1802; by descent at Biel House (near Edinburgh), to Mrs Mary Georgiana Constance Nisbet Hamilton Ogilvy (d. 1920); auction at Dowell's, Edinburgh, 25 June 1921, lot 30, purchased by John Kent Richardson (a.k.a. Kemp) for 8 guineas; auction at Dowell's, Edinburgh, 3 May 1922, lot 480, purchased by the Hon. Major Charles Noel for 5 guineas; purchased by Marie Lea-Wilson at an unknown date; donated by her to the Jesuit Community, Leeson Street, Dublin, c. 1930; on permanent loan to the National Gallery of Ireland in 1993 from the Jesuit Community, Leeson Street, Dublin.

Bibliography: Celio [1620–1624] 1638, p. 134; Bellori [1672] 2005 p. 182; Longhi 1943, pp. 13–14; Longhi 1951a, no. 55; Longhi 1969, pp. 59–62; Moir 1976, pp. 109–110; Marini 1981a, p. 368; Cappelletti, Testa 1990a, pp. 4–7; Cappelletti, Testa 1990b, pp. 234–244; Benedetti 1993, pp. 731–741; Herrmann-Fiore 1995, pp. 24–27; Benedetti 2010, p. 133; Wilson 2009, p. 691; Flynn 2011, p. 529; Savina 2013, pp. 139–141; Papi, Sframeli 2019; Vodret 2021a, p. 202.

The *Taking of Christ* in the National Gallery, Dublin was identified as an autograph work by Caravaggio in 1990 by Sergio Benedetti (Benedetti 1993, pp. 731–741) and is the third painting executed for Ciriaco Mattei (Cappelletti, Testa 1990b, pp. 234–244). In 1943 Roberto Longhi identified in a canvas in a private collection—today known as the ex-Sannini painting—an early copy of the Caravaggio original, highlighting its close correspondence with Bellori's description (Longhi 1943, pp. 13–14) and, in 1951, included it in the monographic exhibition dedicated to the Lombard artist as a replica of a lost original (Longhi 1951a, no. 55). Numerous non-autograph versions have been identified since the 1951 exhibition, subsequently catalogued by Moir (Moir 1976, pp. 109–110) and Savina (Savina 2013, pp. 139–141); to these has recently been added a further copy, in the Gallerie degli Uffizi (Papi, Sframeli 2019).

The earliest documents relating to the *Taking of Christ* in the Mattei collection are to be found in Gaspare Celio, who, in his work written between 1620 and 1624, laconically mentions it (Celio [1620–1624] 1638, p. 134). 134), but it is Giovan Pietro Bellori who provides a more detailed and vivid description of the painting: "Judas has his hand on the Master's shoulder, after the kiss; at the same time a soldier in full armour reaches out his ironclad arm and hand towards the breast of the Lord, who stands still, patient and meek, with his hands intertwined before him, while at the back Saint John flees with outstretched arms. He imitated the rusty armour of that soldier, whose head and face are covered by a helmet, while his profile emerges slightly; and behind him a lantern is raised, with two other heads of armed men following." (Bellori [1672] 2005 p.182

In 1990, Francesca Cappelletti and Laura Testa discovered the payment that attests to the commissioning of the work from Caravaggio in January 1603 by Ciriaco Mattei (Cappelletti, Testa 1990b, pp. 234–244).

Upon Ciriaco Mattei's death, the work passed to his son Giovanni Battista, as testified by the inventories of 1616 and 1624. It was later donated to his cousin, the abbot Paolo Mattei. In 1626, commissioned by Asdrubale Mattei, Paolo's father, the painter Giovanni di Attilio made a copy of the original painting. Benedetti has proposed identifying this copy with the one currently housed in the Museum of

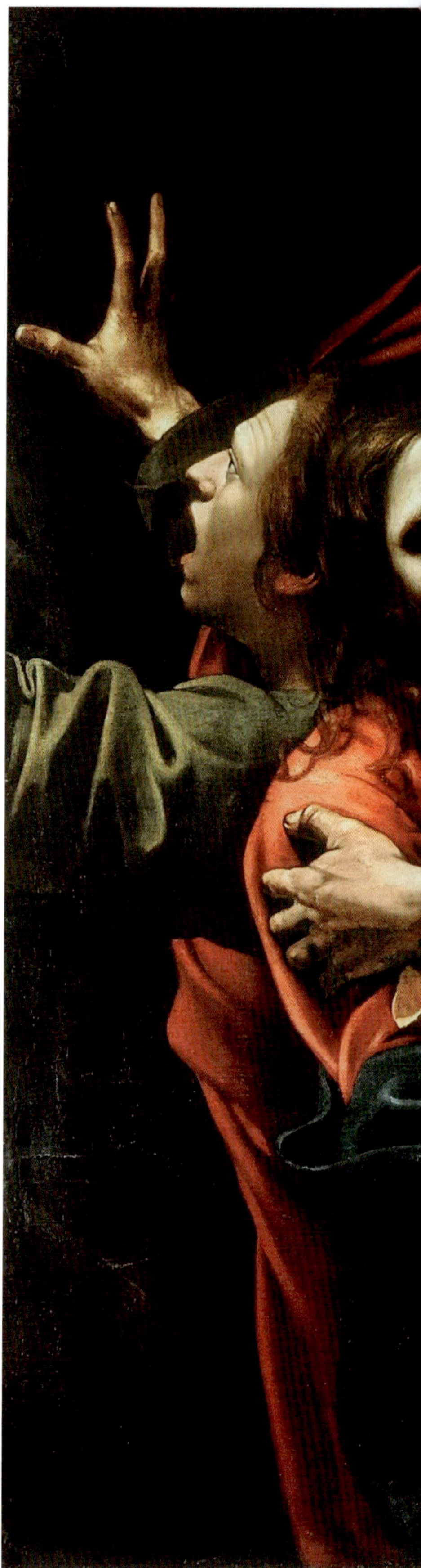

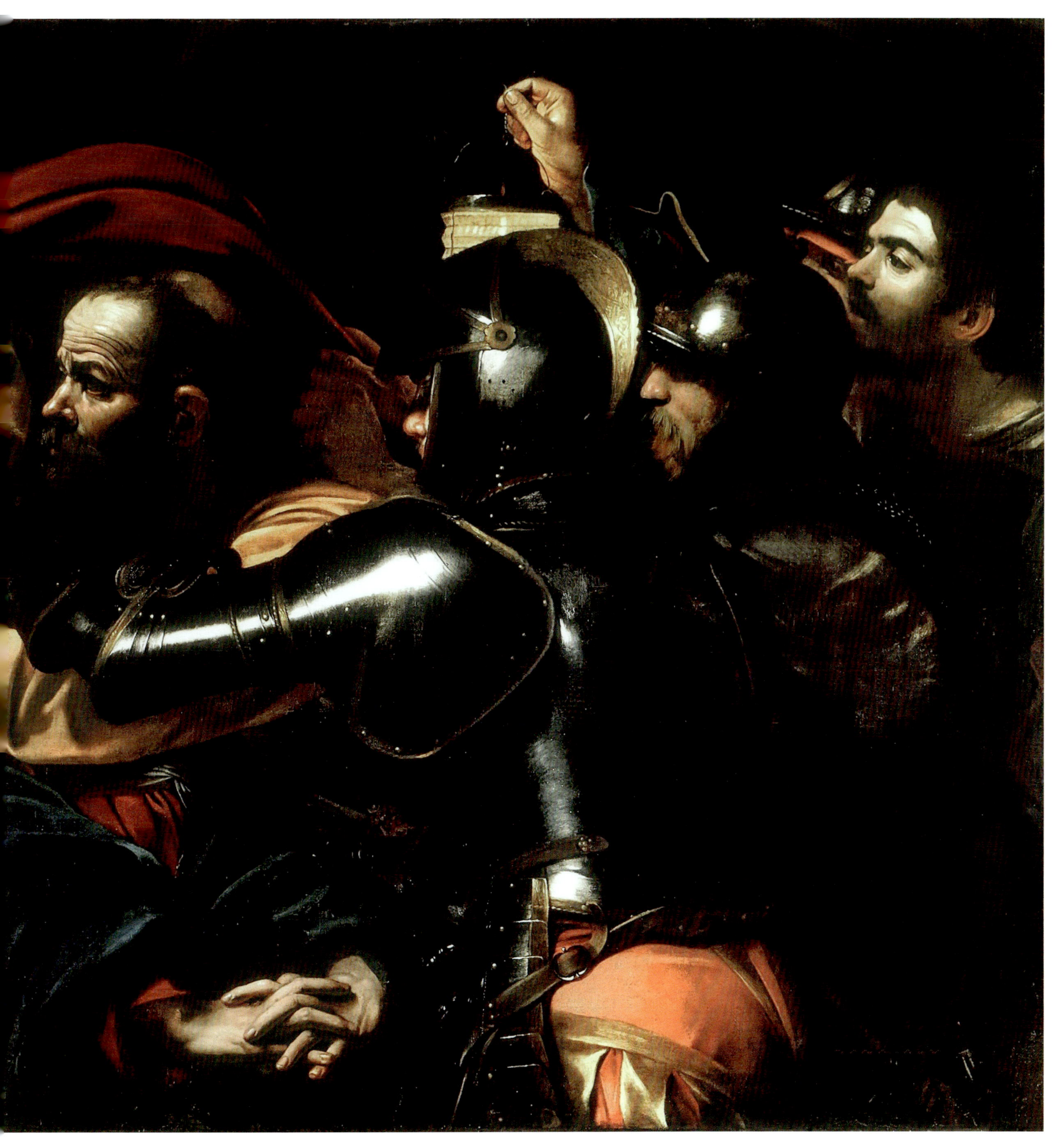

Western and Eastern Art in Odessa (Benedetti 2010, p. 133). However, this identification remains uncertain as the first documentary evidence of the Odessa painting only dates back to 1870.

The original remained for a long time in the family's palazzo in Santa Caterina de' Funari, as documented by inventories that continued to attribute it to Caravaggio from 1638 onwards (Cappelletti, Testa 1990a, pp. 4–7). In 1793, however, it was erroneously attributed to Gherardo delle Notti and, in 1802, was purchased by the Scotsman Hamilton Nisbet (Benedetti 1993, pp. 731–741). In 1921, the work was sold at auction by Dowell's in Edinburgh for only 8 guineas to the antiquarian John Kent Richardson (Wilson 2009, p. 691). The following year, the same auction house sold it to the Honourable Major Charles Noel for 5 guineas (Flynn 2011, p. 529). Later, the painting was bought by the Irish widow Marie Lea-Wilson, who donated it to the Jesuit House of St. Ignatius in Dublin in 1930, and in 1993 it was deposited permanently in the National Gallery of Ireland in Dublin.

In the work, Caravaggio offers a complex and articulated representation of the event as recounted in the Gospels, constructed through a composition that lends itself to multiple levels of interpretation. The reddish-brown ground of the work is left visible in some of the contours and the painting is characterised by its confident brushstrokes and the limited use of incisions (Vodret 2021a, p. 202). The narrative focus is on Judas' kiss, a symbolic gesture that sanctions the betrayal and designates Christ as the recipient of the capture. In the background, Saint John is depicted as he frantically flees, while a soldier tries to hold him back by grabbing his cloak, in a clear reference to the account in the Gospel of Mark (14.51–52), in which it is narrated that the young man abandons his cloak to continue running naked. On the far right, scholars have identified a possible self-portrait of Caravaggio, associated with the figure of Diogenes, interpreted as a symbol of man in search of God (Marini 1981a, p. 368). From an iconographic point of view, although the *invenzione* is entirely original, Caravaggio seems to have taken some elements from Dürer's print depicting the same subject (Herrmann-Fiore 1995, pp. 24–27), and from Moretto's *Martyrdom of Saint Peter of Verona*, in particular for the figure of the fleeing Saint John, similar to the figure in the background of the latter painting (Benedetti 1993, p. 737).

Caravaggio's the *Taking of Christ* was of such importance that it was not only copied numerous times, but also reinterpreted by some of his followers, including Bartolomeo Manfredi and Dirck van Baburen.

[GM]

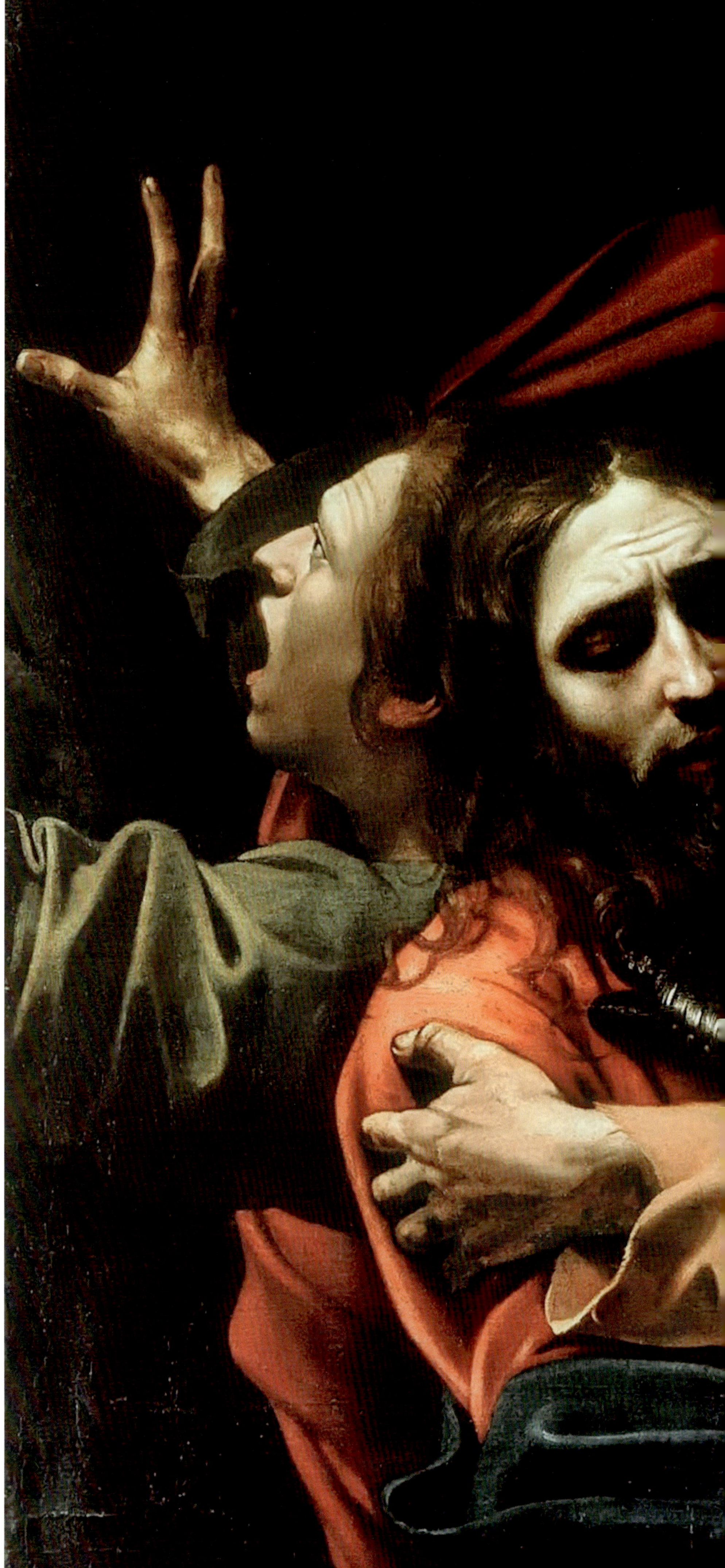

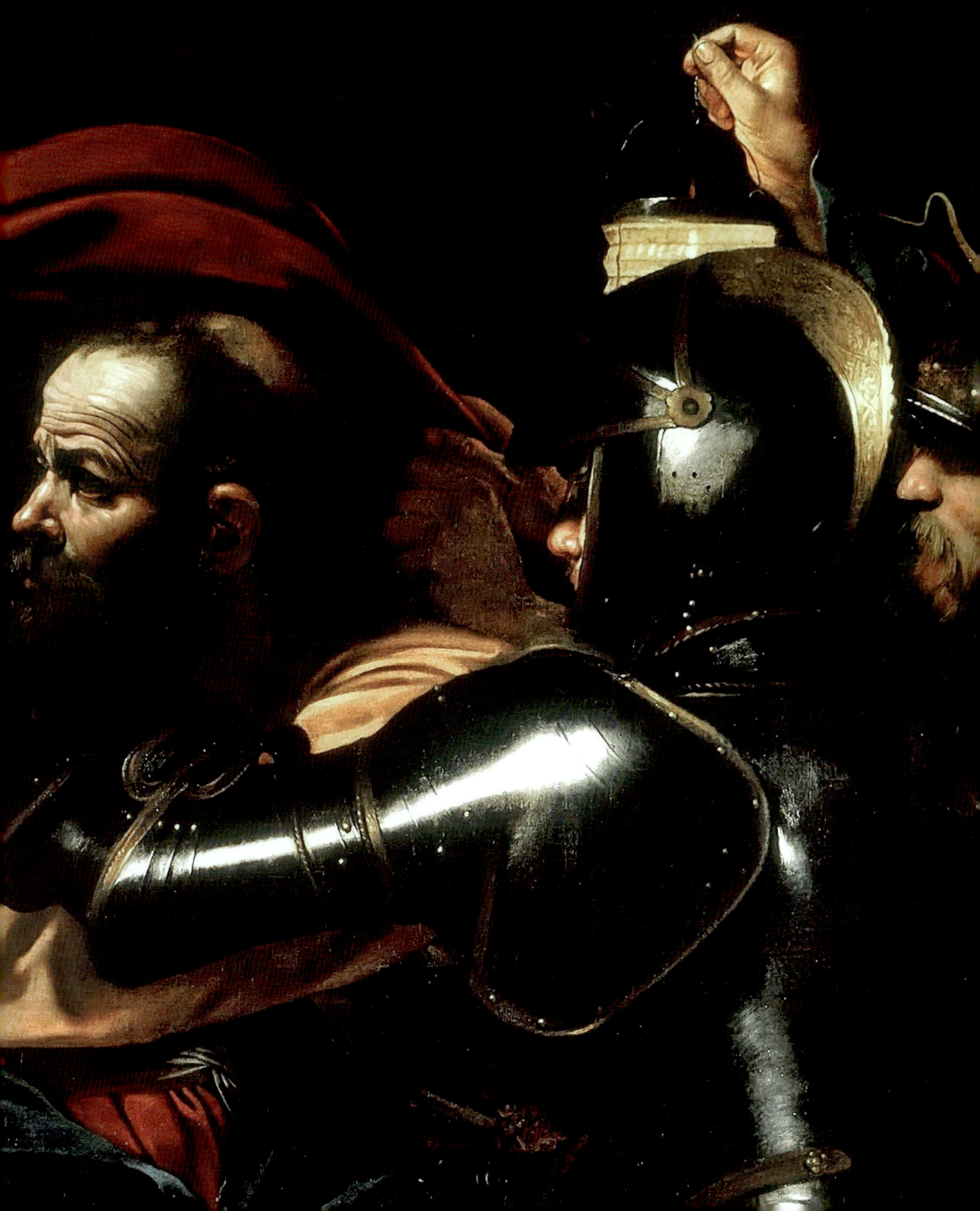

SAINT JOHN THE BAPTIST IN THE WILDERNESS

c. 1602–1604
oil on canvas, 172.72 × 132.08 cm
The Nelson-Atkins Museum of Art,
Kansas City, Missouri. Purchase:
William Rockhill Nelson Trust,
Kansas City (MO), 52-25

Provenance: Commissioned by
Ottavio Costa (1554–1639), Rome;
by descent to his son Benedetto
Costa (1603–1659), Rome, and
thence by inheritance through the
Del Palagio and Origo families to
Giuseppe Origo (d. 1833), Rome;
bequeathed by the latter to the
Congregazione degli Operai della
Divina Pietà, Rome, to which the
painting belonged until 1854 (unsold
at auction 26 March 1846, lot 23);
purchased by Marchese cav. Antonio
De Cinque, Rome, on 9 January
1854; Monte di Pietà, Rome, from
1857 until its sale on 28 December
1875, lot 1175; Rosina, Lady Clifford
Constable (c. 1831–1908), Rome,
probably after 1901; by inheritance
to her great-grandson, Lieutenant
Colonel Walter George Raleigh

The depiction of *Saint John the Baptist in the Wilderness*, imposing in its monumentality, departs from traditional iconography omitting the lamb and presenting the saint immersed in deep meditation. The position of the subject, his back bent and legs splayed, has suggested references both to Michelangelo—in particular to the prophets *Isaiah and Jeremiah* in the Sistine Chapel (Marini 2005, pp. 483–485)—and to works of antiquity such as the *Torso Belvedere* and the *Laocoon* (Gregori 1985b, pp. 300–303; Zeri 1998, p. 33). The rendering of the anatomy is further defined through incisions that mark the contours and details, while the ground of the painting consists of two layers of dark brown (Vodret, in *Dentro Caravaggio* 2017, pp. 114–117; Vodret 2021a, pp. 226–227).

The painting in the Nelson-Atkins Museum of Art in Kansas City was attributed to Caravaggio by Roberto Longhi in 1943 (Longhi 1943, pp. 14–15). However, the composition was known since 1927 thanks to a copy that Longhi himself published and subsequently exhibited in the famous 1951 exhibition on the Lombard master (Longhi 1951a, p. 41). This copy is currently housed in the Museo di Capodimonte in Naples.

A further version of the painting, not by the hand of the master, was discovered in 1962 (Torre 1962, p. 9) in the church of Sant'Alessandro in Conscente, Liguria, and is now in the Museo Diocesano in Albenga. Patrick Matthiesen and Stephen Pepper (Matthiesen, Pepper 1970, p. 456) identified the banker Ottavio Costa (1554–1639) as the commissioner of the Ligurian canvas. However, it was Richard Spear (Spear 1971, pp. 11, 75–76) who linked the Albenga canvas to the Kansas City original, emphasising its provenance from the Costa collection.

A decisive contribution for the reconstruction of the painting's history was provided by Maria Cristina Terzaghi, who identified among the papers of the Herrera & Costa bank a receipt of payment dated 21 May 1602, made out by Caravaggio to Ottavio Costa (Terzaghi 2007, pp. 297–298; Terzaghi 2016b, pp. 11–15). Although the document does not specify the subject of the painting, the advance payment of 20 *scudi* has allowed the scholar to propose a dating of the work to around 1602–1603.

Other scholars (Papi 2016b, pp. 8–18; Cuppone 2016, p. 80; Vodret 2017a and Vodret 2021a,

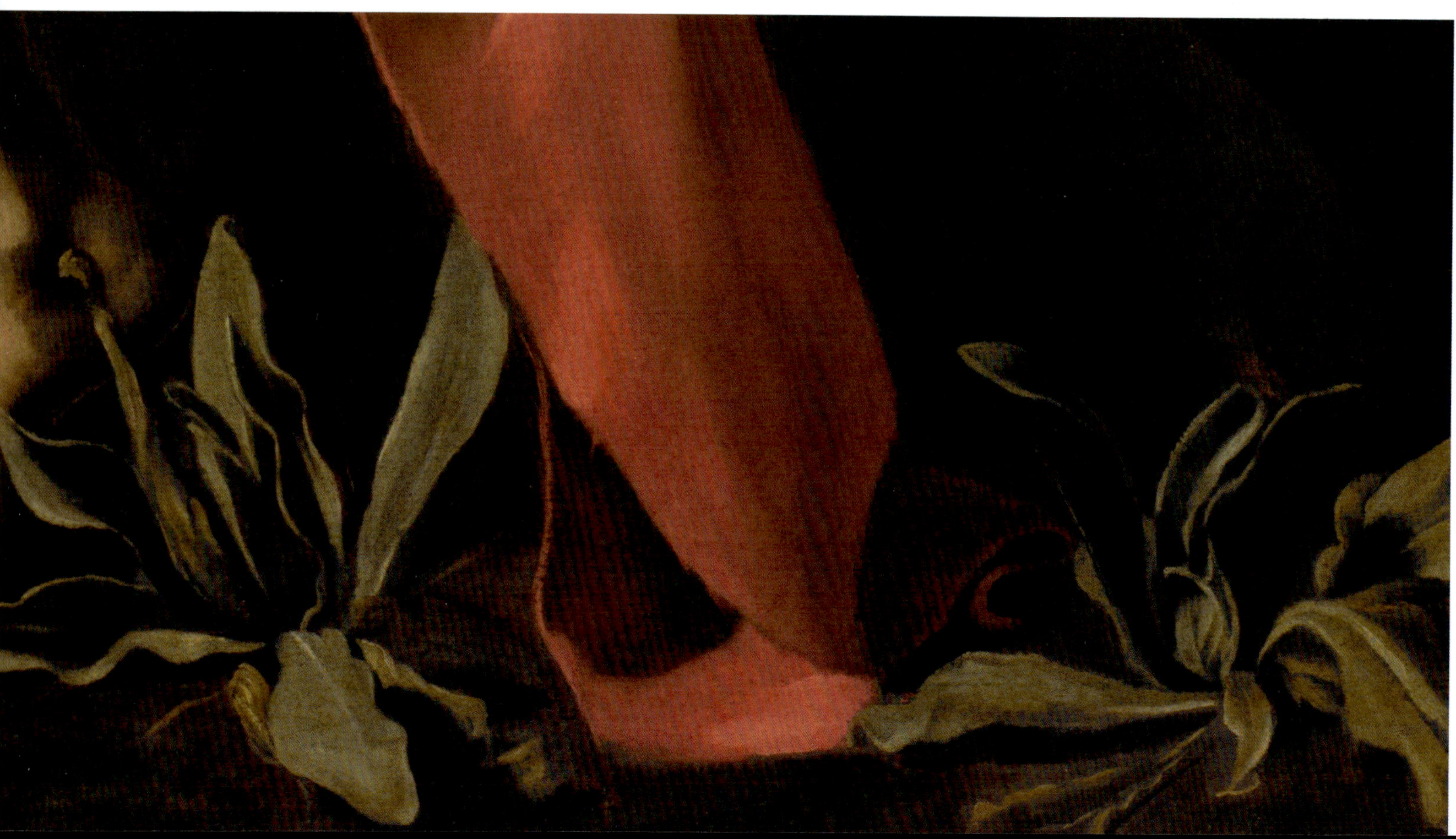

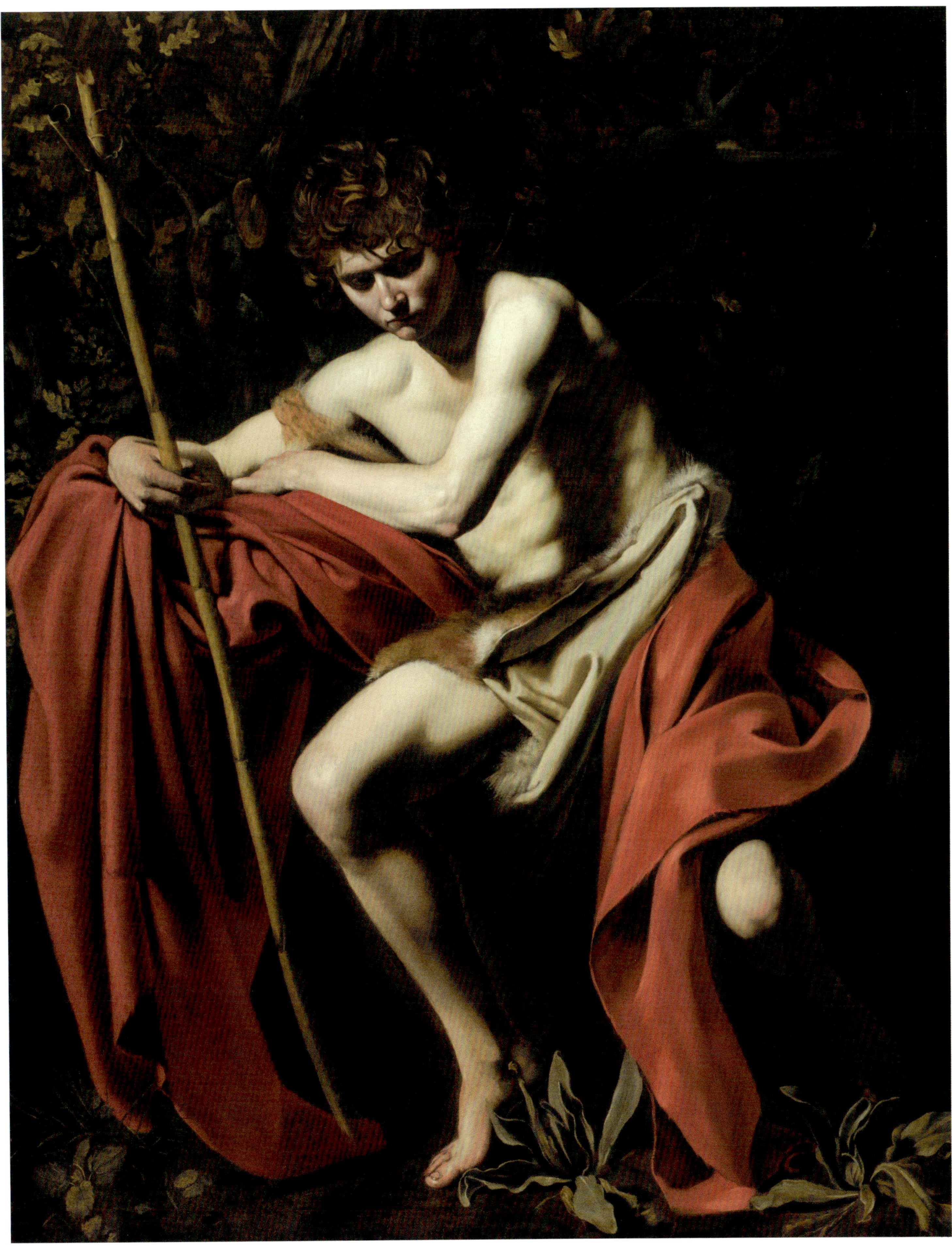

Chichester-Constable (1863–1942), Burton Constable, Yorkshire, by 1910; by descent to his son, General Raleigh Charles Joseph Chichester-Constable (1890–1963), Burton Constable, Yorkshire; by the latter sold to Edward Speelman; since 15 January 1951 jointly owned by Edward Speelman & Sons, Thomas Agnew & Sons, Vitale Bloch and Volterra (each owning a quarter share in the painting); purchased from Thomas Agnew & Sons Ltd., London, by the Nelson-Atkins Museum of Art, Kansas City, on 8 August 1952.

Bibliography: Longhi 1943, pp. 14–15; Longhi 1951a, p. 41; Gregori 1985b, pp. 300–303; Torre 1962, p. 9; Matthiesen, Pepper 1970, p. 456; Spear 1971, pp. 11, 75–76; Spezzaferro 1975, pp. 103–118; Zeri 1998, p. 33; Marini 2005, pp. 483–485; Terzaghi 2007, pp. 297–298; Terzaghi 2016b, pp. 11–15; Papi 2016, pp. 8–18; Cuppone 2016, p. 80; Vodret, in *Dentro Caravaggio* 2017, pp. 114–117; Vodret 2021a, pp. 226–227.

p. 226), however, suggest a date of 1604–1605, putting forward the hypothesis that the documented payment refers to *Judith and Holophernes* in Palazzo Barberini [cat. 12], another work painted by Caravaggio for Ottavio Costa, together with Hartford's *Saint Francis of Assisi in Ecstasy* [cat. 8].

Historical sources relating to the Conscente Oratory allow us to state that the copy of the painting was made after 1603, since this was the date of the papal bull by which Clement VIII sanctioned the new dedication of the parish church to Saint Alexander and the transformation of the earlier one into an oratory dedicated to Saint John the Baptist. Ottavio Costa and his brothers were entrusted with the decoration of both buildings. The painting must therefore have already been in the oratory in 1606, the year of its consecration, as attested by the plaque still present on the façade (Terzaghi 2007, pp. 297–298; Terzaghi 2016b, pp. 11–15).

It is probable that Costa, after acquiring the painting, decided to keep the original in his Roman residence, allocating a copy for the altar of the Ligurian oratory (Terzaghi 2007, pp. 297–298; Terzaghi 2016b, pp. 11–15). This hypothesis is corroborated by Luigi Spezzaferro's evidence that emphasises the strong link between Costa and Caravaggio's works, to the extent that in his will he forbade their sale by his heirs (Spezzaferro 1975, pp. 103–118).

The original work belonged to the Costa family until 1857, when it was inventoried in the Galleria del Sacro Monte di Pietà in Rome. It was subsequently sold at auction in 1875 and entered the collection of Lady Rosina Clifford Constable. Upon her death in 1908, the painting was acquired by the London antiquarian Edward Speelman & Sons, who exhibited it at the Royal Academy. Finally, in 1952, the Nelson-Atkins Museum of Art acquired it from Thomas Agnew & Sons, transferring it to the United States.

[GM]

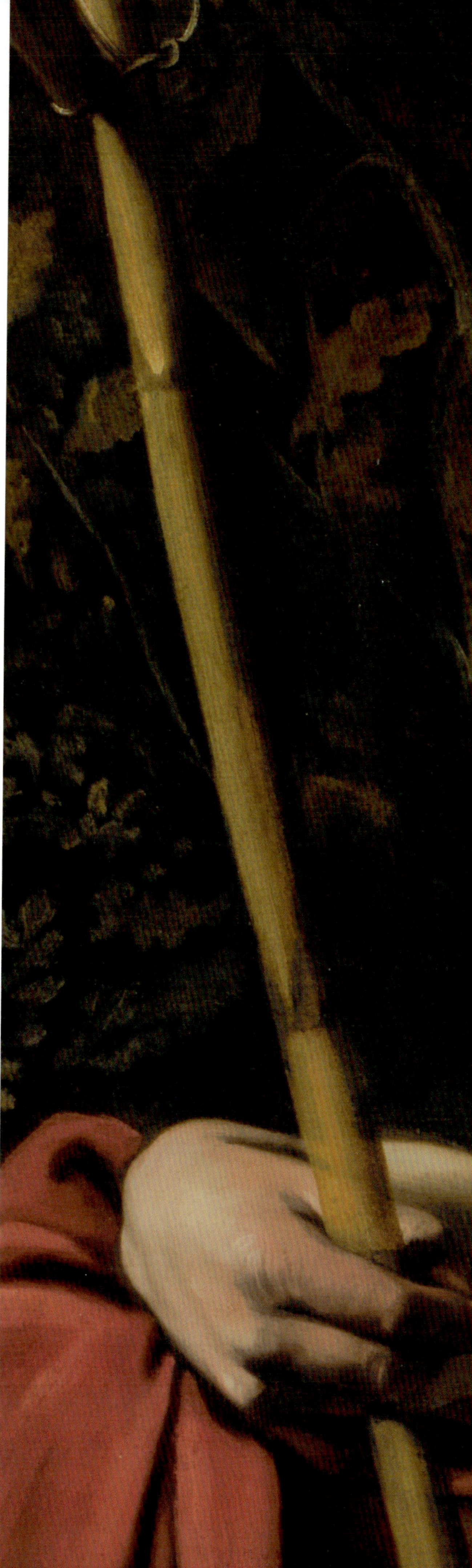

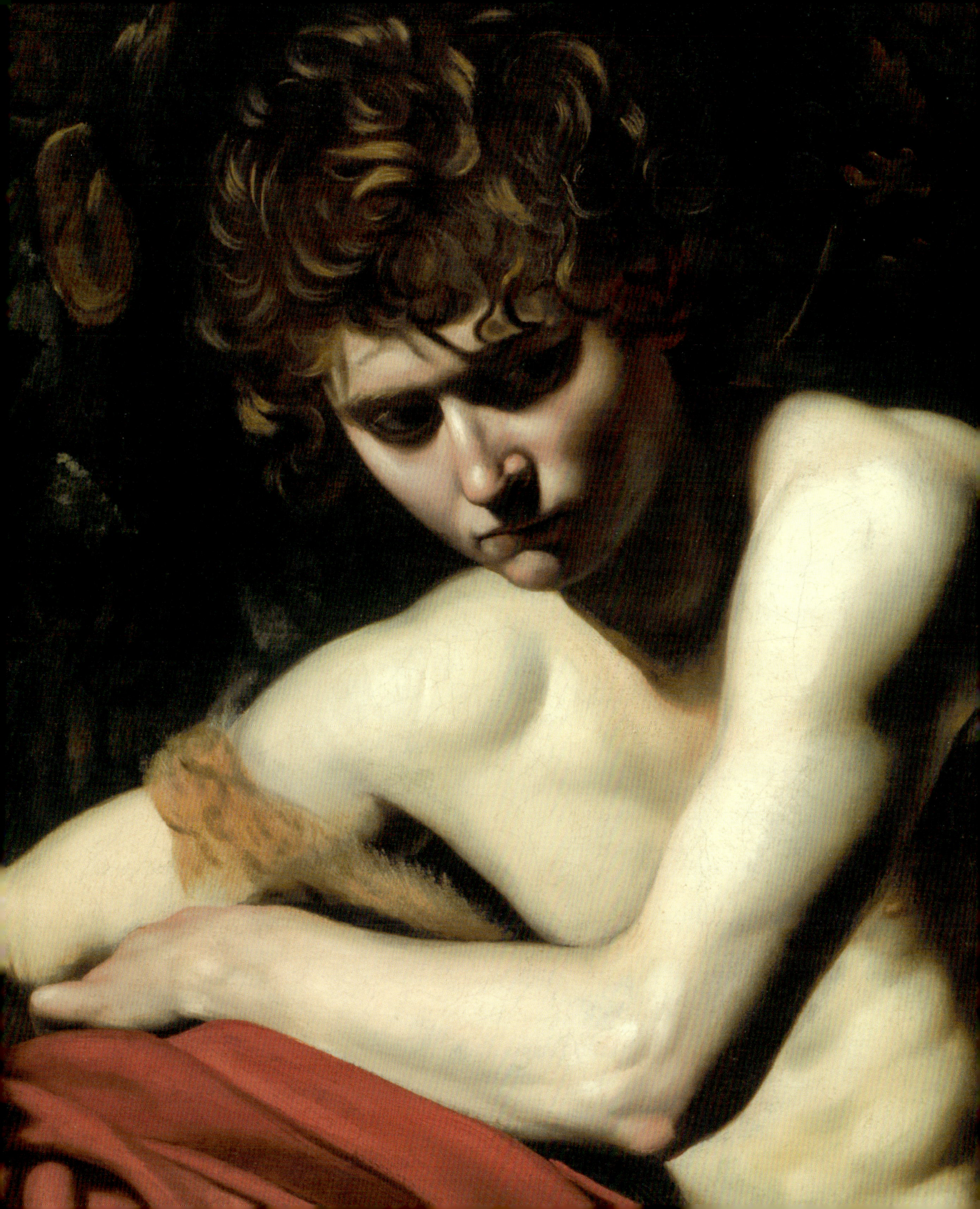

SAINT JOHN
THE BAPTIST

c. 1604–1605
oil on canvas, 97 × 131 cm
Gallerie Nazionali di Arte Antica,
Galleria Corsini, Rome, inv. 433

Provenance: 1784, Rome, Palazzo
Corsini alla Lungara, where it
remained until the Corsini collection
was donated to the Italian State in
1883.

Bibliography: Longhi 1927, p. 31;
Longhi 1943, p. 14; Longhi 1951a,
p. 32; Longhi [1952] 1999, p. 184;
Mahon 1952, p. 19; Marini 1974,
p. 411; Cinotti 1983, pp. 517–518;
Gregori 1991b, pp. 262–268; Alloisi
1998, pp. 64–66; Marini 2001,
pp. 503–504; Pacelli, in *Caravaggio*
2010, pp. 158–167; Leone 2015,
pp. 18–31; Vodret 2015, pp. 33–43;
Negro 2016, pp. 522–524; De
Ruggieri 2016b, pp. 526–528; Papi
2016c, p. 30; Di Monte 2017, pp. 124-
-131; Vodret 2021a, p. 230.

The painting depicts Saint John the Baptist, a subject that Caravaggio painted several times during
his career [cats. 15, 23]. The saint is depicted in
the desert as a young adolescent, according to an
iconography which had become widespread since
the sixteenth century, particularly in the Tuscan
region. The artist has in this instance, however,
chosen an unusual landscape format, the figure
framed, close-up, in the foreground, and together
with some of the details, such as the cross of reeds
for example, seems even to protrude from the figurative space.

The naked body of the young man dominates the
scene, its forms defined by the light that invests them
so that they emerge out of the background. This is
a characteristic element of Caravaggio's figurative
language, which in his works with a religious subject
is also charged with clear symbolic value. Suffice it
to cite, in the case of the Baptist, the words intoned
by Zachariah at the birth of the saint: "Through the
tenderness and mercy of our God, the rising sun will
come to us from heaven to shine on those living in
darkness and in the shadow of death, to guide our
feet into the path of peace." (Luke 1:78-79). John
is covered with a white loincloth and an ample red
cloak that—as is often the case in Caravaggio—constitutes the dominant colour in the painting, while
the customary camel-skin referred to in the sources
is absent (Mark 3,4). Studied with particular care
is the young man's pose, inspired by the classical
model of the *Wounded Gaul* (*Galata ferito*), today
in Naples, but in Rome in the seventeeth century,
or the *Dying Gaul* (*Galata morente*) in the Musei
Capitolini, documented from 1623, the date of discovery is, however, not precisely known (Alloisi
1998, pp. 64–66; Leone 2015, pp. 27–28). The tor-
sion of the face and the position of the arms suggest a
sudden movement, as if the saint had awakened from
his meditation to then "appear[ed] publicly to Israel" (Luke 1:80) by grasping the reed cross placed, not
by chance, next to the bowl which would be used for
the baptism, and that so struck Longhi ([1952] 1999,
p. 184) that he compared it to Velázquez. Moreover,
the stones and dry trunk in the background—as well
as denoting the hermitage of the saint—also clearly
allude to the Baptist's baptismal sermon (Di Monte
2017): "I tell you that out of these stones God can
raise up children for Abraham. The axe is already at

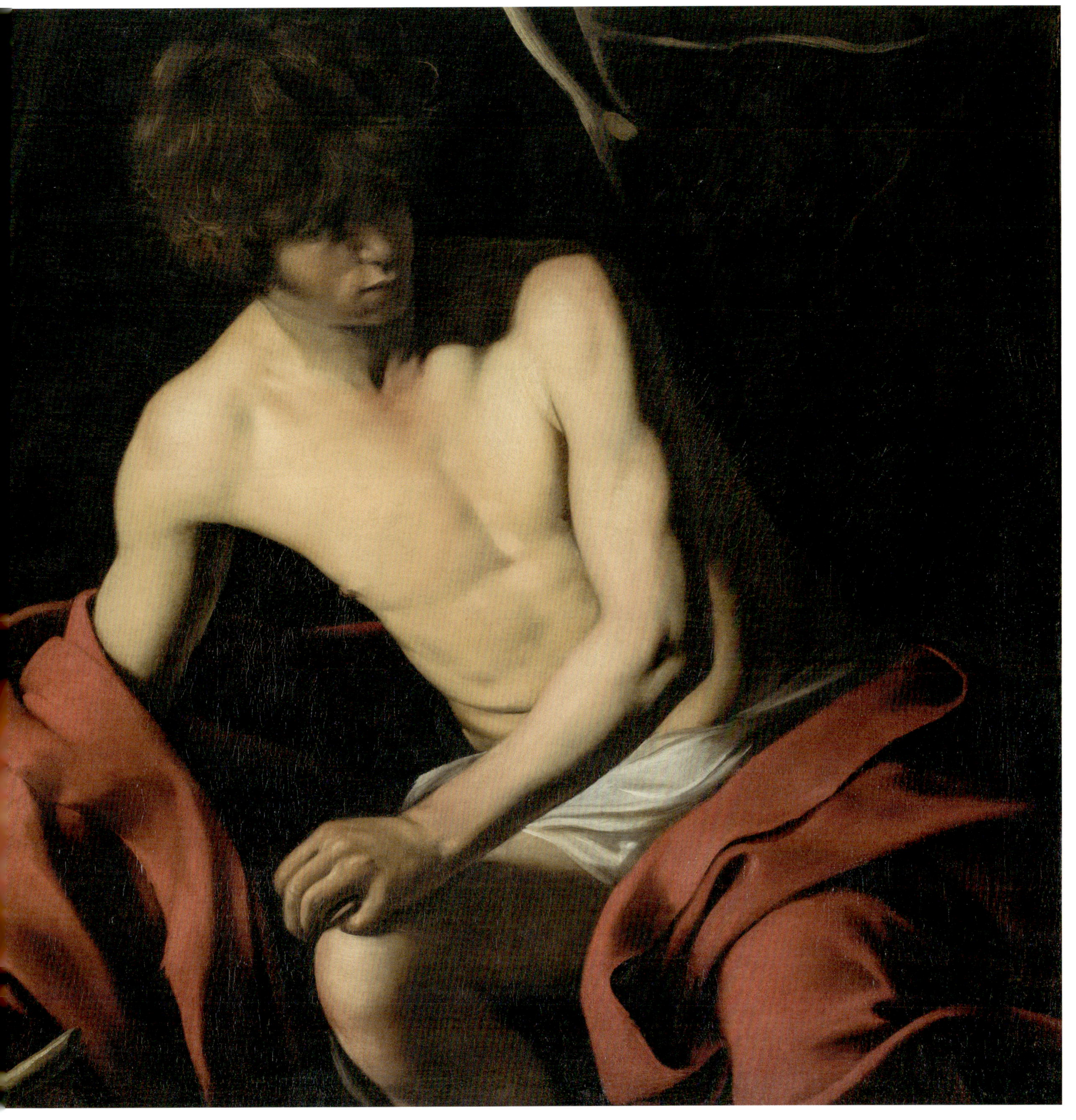

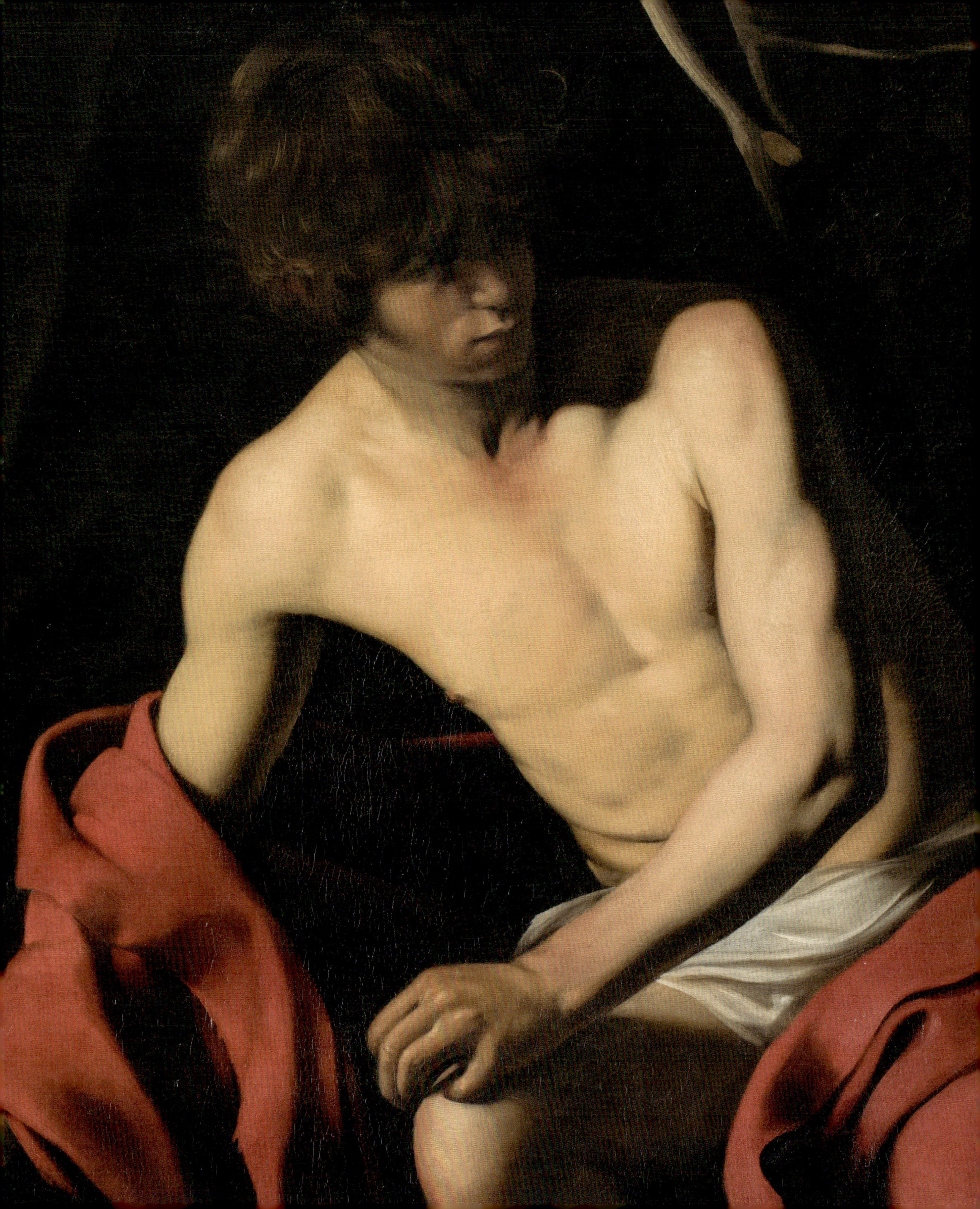

the root of the trees, and every tree that does not produce good fruit will be cut down and thrown into the fire." (Matthew 3:9-10).

Recent diagnostic investigations carried out on the painting (2001, 2009) revealed the presence of the lamb in the upper right-hand corner, later removed by Caravaggio, and confirmed the relocation of the cane cross originally held in the left hand (Vodret 2015, pp. 37–40; De Ruggieri 2016b, pp. 526–528). The earliest known reference to the work dates to the 1784 inventory of the Corsini collection, in which a "St. John the Baptist, style of Caravaggio" is listed as located in the gallery of the prince Bartolomeo Corsini's (1729–1792) apartment on the second floor of the palazzo in Via della Lungara (Borsellino 2017, II, p. 325). The proposal to identify it with the *Saint. John the Baptist* referred to in Caterina Campani's will of 1652 (Marini 1974, p. 411; Gregori 1991b) is not, as yet, supported by any documentary evidence, as is also the case with the hypothesis (Alloisi 1998) that it entered the Corsini collection in 1758 on the occasion of the marriage of the prince Bartolomeo Corsini (1729–1792) to Maria Felice Barberini Colonna (1737–1817).

In the early nineteenth century, the painting was moved to the piano nobile of Palazzo Corsini, together with the principle works in the collection. Restored by Pietro Palmaroli (1810–1812) and Filippo Gagliardi (1825–1827, see Cosma 2016, pp. 24–26; Borsellino 2017, II, p. 93), it remained there with the attribution to Caravaggio until the donation of the collection to the Italian state in 1883. Havin been downgraded to an "unknown fol-

lower of Caravaggio" (Marini 2001, p. 503), it was attributed to the painter by Longhi (1927, p. 31; 1943 p. 14) and progressively accepted by scholarship as an autograph work by the artist (for a summary of the different positions: Gregori 1991b; Leone 2015). More contentious is the chronology of the painting, dated by some scholars to 1606, towards the end of his sojourn in Rome (among others: Alloisi 1998; Marini 2001; Pacelli 2010; Negro 2016), while other scholars give it an earlier date in relation to the *Saint John the Baptist* in Kansas City, the dating of which , however, oscillates between 1602-1603 and 1605 (see cat. 15). Thus, for example, Papi (2016c, p. 30) and Vodret (2021a) date the Corsini canvas to 1605–1606, whereas a date of around 1602-1604 had earlier been proposed by Mahon (1952, p. 19) or Cinotti (1983). The Corsini painting presents numerous points of contact in both style and composition with the American work, in addition to probably using the same boy as a model. The compositional procedure is also very similar with fine strokes of under-drawing, rapidly executed incisions and light-coloured *abbozzi* on the brown ground (Vodret 2015; Vodret 2021a). A greater speed of execution in the rendering of the flesh tones and in the definition of the outlying objects, however, suggest a slightly later dating, as already hypothesised by Gregori (1991b).

A seventeenthth century copy of the painting is known today in the Nationalmuseum in Stockholm (inv. NM 15, 98 × 136 cm).

[AC]

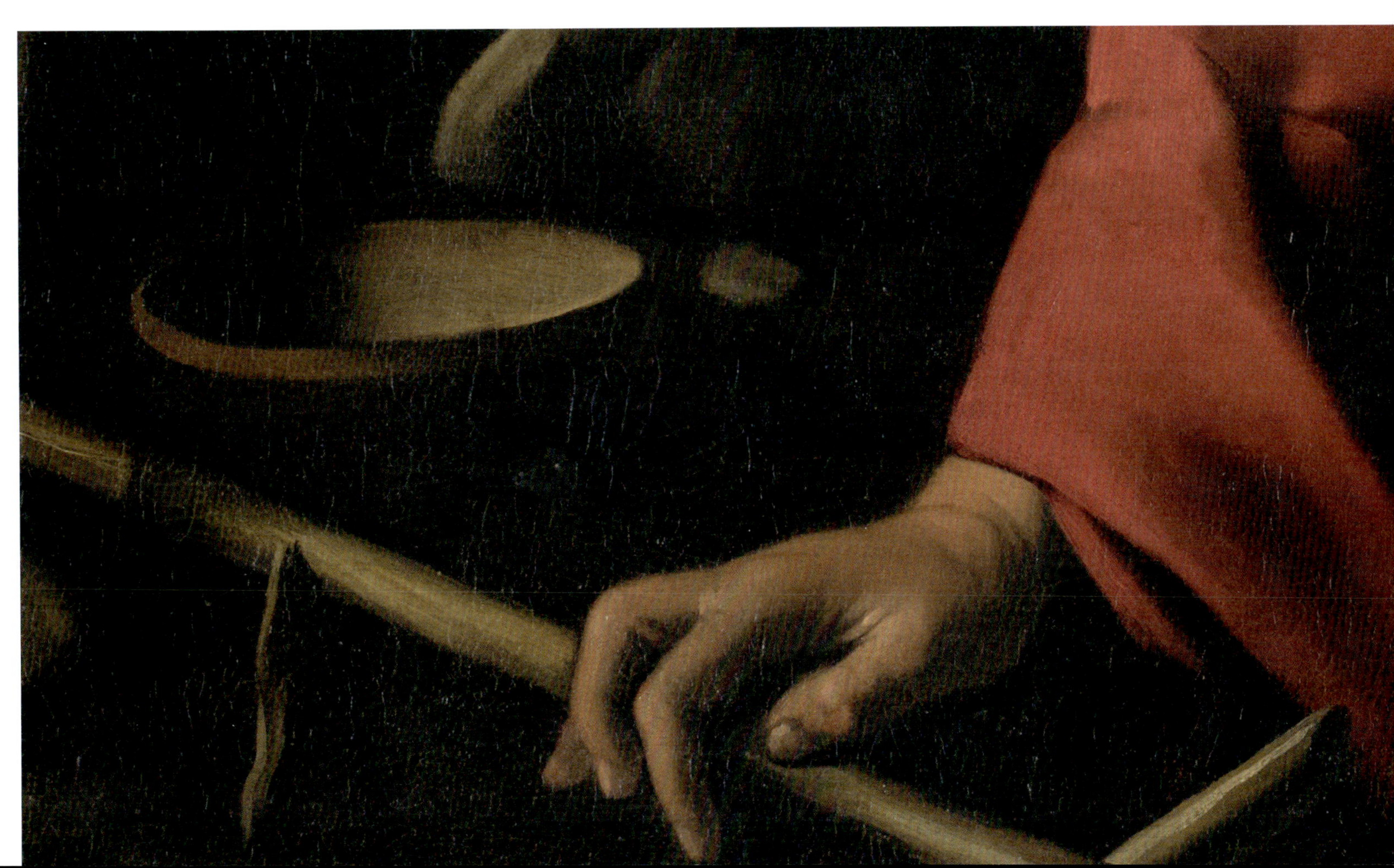

SUPPER AT EMMAUS

1606
oil on canvas, 141 × 175 cm
Pinacoteca di Brera, Milan, inv. 2296

Provenance: Rome, Costanzo Patrizi, 1624; Patrizi Collection (*Patrizi Inventory* 1654; *Patrizi Inventory* 1689; *Patrizi Inventory* 1814, see Pedrocchi 2000, p. 118); Marchese Patrizio Patrizi Collection; Purchase by the Amici di Brera, 1939.

Bibliography: Mancini [c. 1619–1621] 1956–1957, p. 225; Bellori 1672, pp. 223, 225, 231; Venturi 1912, pp. 1–18; Marangoni 1922-1923, pp. 217–229; Voss 1925; Pevsner 1928; Longhi 1951a; Cinotti 1983, pp. 462–463; Gregori 1985, *The Age of Caravaggio | Caravaggio e il suo tempo*, pp. 306–310, n. 87; Marini 2001, pp. 278–279, pp. 505–507, n. 75; Bandera 2009, pp. 120–124; Gregori 2009, pp. 29–38; Papi 2020; *Nono dialogo Brera* 2022.

Supper at Emmaus, 1602,
The National Gallery, London

The painting depicts the moment when the disciples recognise Jesus when, after his death and resurrection, he once more appears and blesses the bread (Luke 24:13–32). According to the Gospel account, in fact, in the days following the crucifixion, two acolytes had set out on their way, encountering another pilgrim on the road. Only once they had arrived in the village of Emmaus did they suddenly realise, observing him in *fractione panis*, that they had travelled all the way with the risen Christ, and were sitting at table with him.

In the centre of the painting, Jesus, with his head tilted slightly to one side and his gaze lowered towards the bread, is the focus of the composition; with the compressed power of his gesture he triggers the reactions of the two seated figures, struck by the miraculous revelation. Caravaggio effectively conceals the face of the disciple on the left, whose silhouette is used to suggest the depth of the planes and to concentrate the light within the scene. Juxtaposed at the other end of the table is the other disciple in profile, his forehead furrowed and his dark hands gripping the edges of the table. Standing, the innkeeper and the elderly woman provide an emotional counterbalance: the dynamism of the surprise is flanked

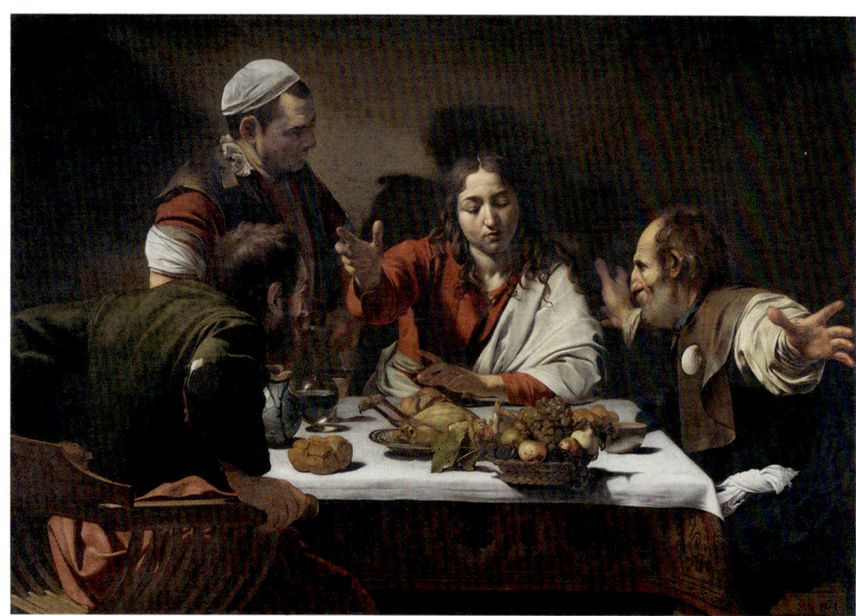

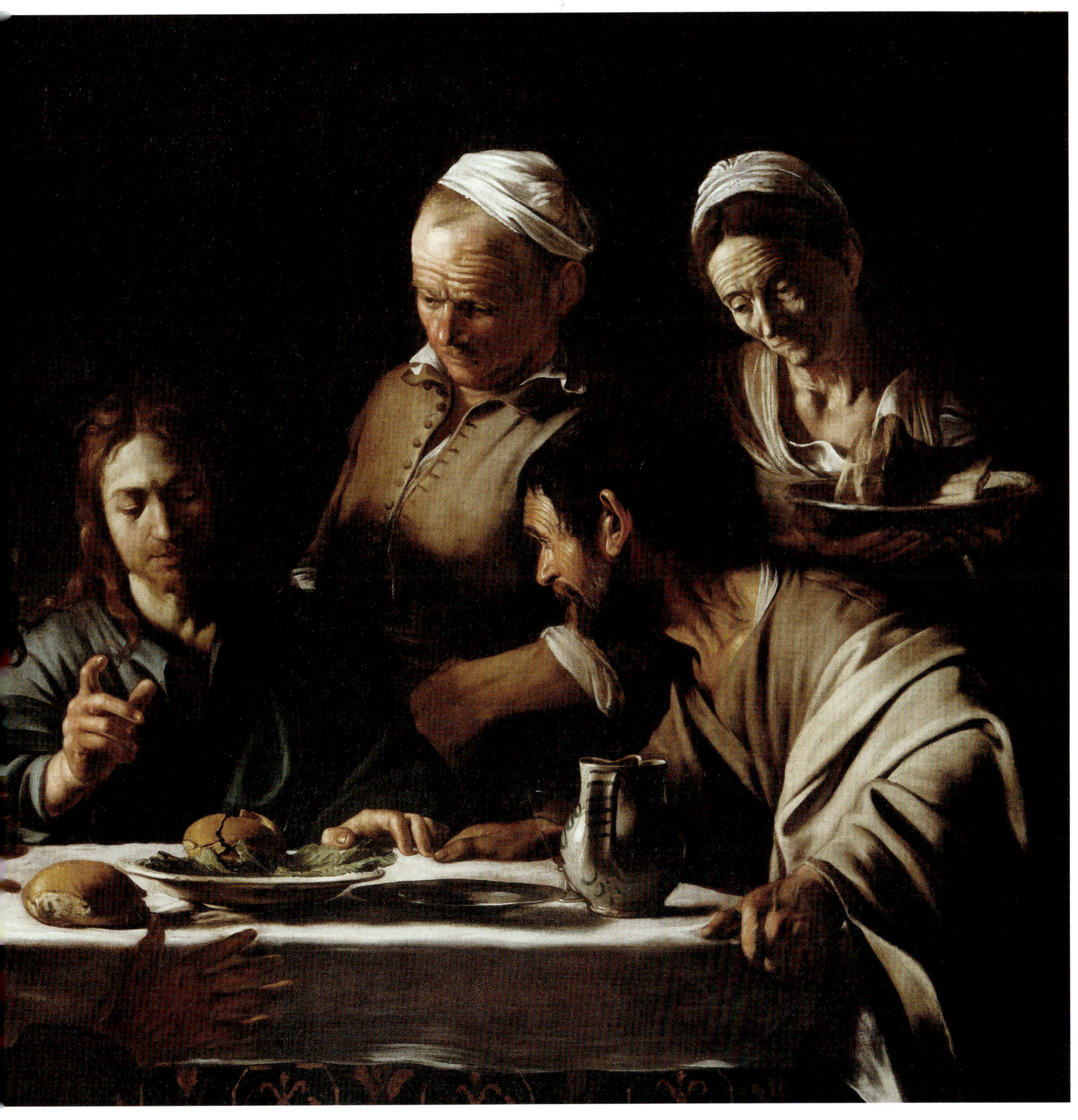

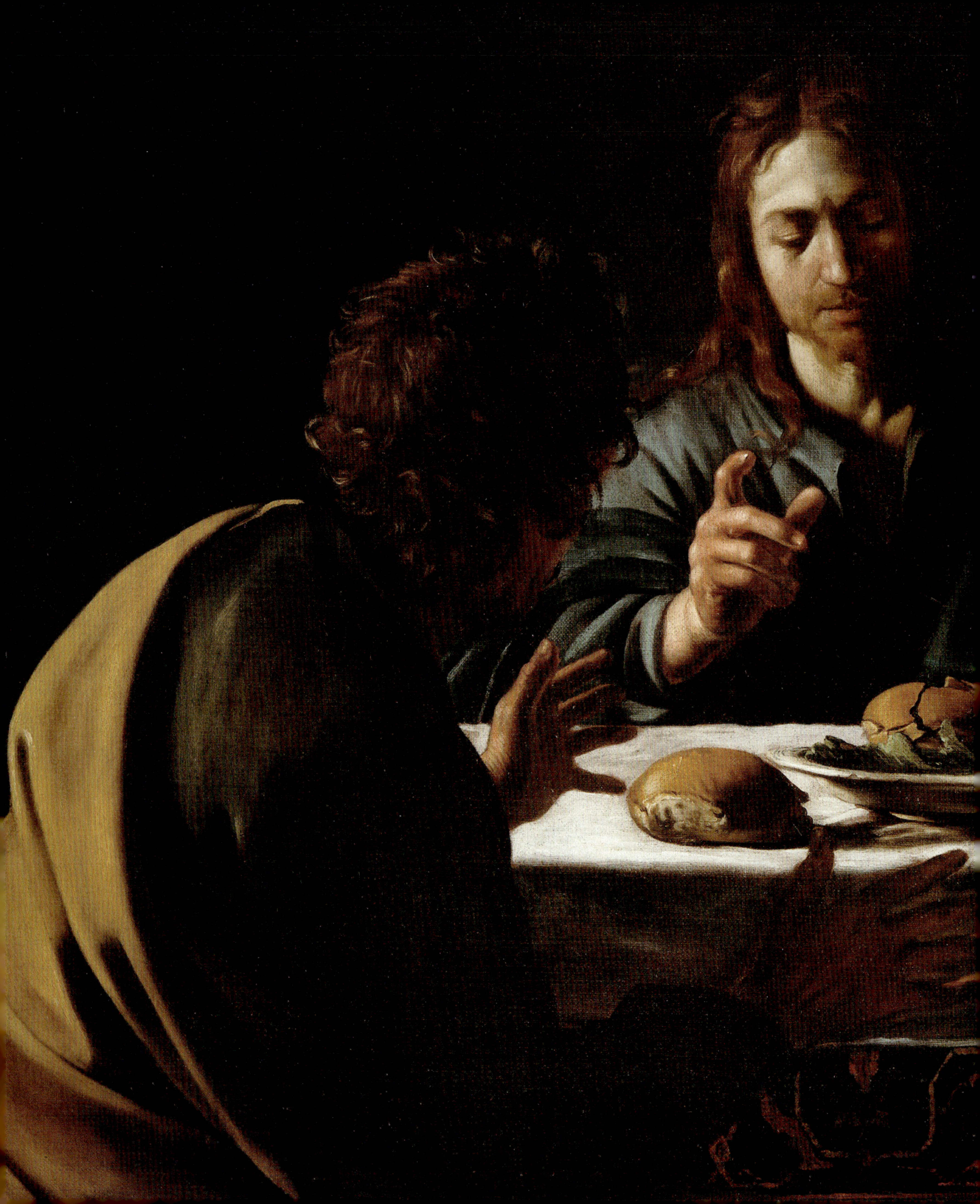

by the immobility of their astonished observation, lacking all understanding of the event. Retaining the energy within the bodies, expressing the emotions of the characters in a restrained manner, imbuing their poses with a measure of sorrow, Caravaggio chooses to move within a register of expressive sobriety, underlined by the use of earthy colours. In this work the painter displays his concentrated and reflective aspect, not the bold and clamourous. The tonalities he employs are dulled, and the shadows thereby softened, a result also achieved by the removal of a further descriptive element in the upper left-hand corner, where we now see a brown colour. Radiographic investigations indeed revealed that the first composition probably included a window (Bandera 2009).

The work was executed around 1606, between Caravaggio's flight from Rome and his arrival in Naples, according to evidence in Giulio Mancini's *Considerazioni sulla pittura*, which links the painting precisely to the tragic events of May 1606, when the painter, having killed Ranuccio Tomassoni, was forced to flee Rome, heading south and finding refuge in the Colonna family feuds. According to Mancini, in fact, "… he had to flee from Rome; he stopped first at Zagarola, where he was hidden by the Prince. There he painted a Magdalene and Christ going to Emmaus which was bought by Costa in Rome" (Mancini [c. 1619–1621] 1956, p. 225. English translation in Friedländer [1955] 1976, p. 257). Giovan Pietro Bellori offers more numerous clues and references regarding the *Supper at Emmaus*, indeed on the different versions of the subject painted by Caravaggio. There is no doubt that he is referring to the *Supper at Emmaus* now in the Pinacoteca di Brera when, in the list of Roman gentlemen who vied for the pleasure of Caravaggio's brush, after the *Ecce Homo* for the Massimi family, the execution of which is dated to 1605, Bellori proceeds to state that "… for the Marchese Patrizi [he painted] the Supper at Emmaus, in which there is a Christ in the middle blessing the bread, and one of the apostles, sitting down, opens his arms as he recognises him, while the other braces his hands on the table and gazes at him in wonder: at the back there is the innkeeper with his cap on his head, and an old woman bringing food" (English translation Bellori [1672] 2005, p. 182). Furthermore, even when narrating the artist's flight from Rome, Bellori gives an account of the paintings executed in the Colonna fiefs: "Fleeing from Rome, penniless and hunted, he took refuge in Zagarolo under the protection of the Duke don Marzio Colonna, and there he painted the picture of Christ at Emmaus between the two apostles and another half-length figure of the Magdalen" (English translation Bellori 1672 [2005], pp. 182–183).

The history of the painting seems less tortuous than that of other Caravaggio masterpieces: it is referred to in Monsignor Costanzo Patrizi's inventory, compiled by the Cavalier d'Arpino on 27 February 1624, and remained in the family's possession until its purchase in 1939 by the Amici di Brera.

Recently, however, different hypotheses have been put forward as to the identification of the 1606 *Emmaus*, based in part on the ambiguity of Giulio Mancini's reference (Papi 2020). Already in the past, some scholars had envisioned the existence of an original work by Caravaggio depicting a *Road to Emmaus*, at times identified as the painting now at Hampton Court (Cinotti 1983; Marini 1974; Marini 2001; see Papi 2020 for a review of the bibliography). Without now going into the discussion on the autograph status of the English painting, it should be noted that, in other instances, a *Supper at Emmaus* has been more generically described as a "Christ going to Emmaus", a definition that later proved—unequivocally—to be a *Supper*. For example, Baglione, in relation to the paintings Caravaggio painted for Ciriaco Mattei, speaks of "a Saint John the Baptist, and when Our Lord went to Emaus" and in this case, by virtue of the very precise documents relating to the payment from Ciriaco Mattei to Caravaggio, it is possible to confirm that the painting Baglione was referring to was without a doubt a *Supper*, the one paid for in 1602 and described in the proof of payment as a "Christ at the table with the disciples of Emmaus," depicted in *fractione panis*, while breaking bread (Cappelletti, Testa 1994).

At this point it is worth returning one last time to Bellori and the paintings of Emmaus depicting the moment of the supper, because the writer is the first to connect the Patrizi work—now in the Brera, after having referred to it and explicitly described it—to the one that in his day was in the Borghese collection, probably originally in the Mattei collection, and now in London, in the National Gallery, describing it as "rather different" (Bellori 1672, p. 223). The comparison established by Bellori has been so successful in the scholarly literature as to become almost inescapable: the London painting shows the young, beardless Christ and the two disciples with their expansive, incisive gestures. With its bright luminous contrasts, with the emphasis on the table where the basket full of fruit gleams, the painting formerly in the Borghese collection presents the painter at his most daring and resolute—in Rome, between the opening of the Contarelli chapel in San Luigi dei Francesi and the commission for the Cerasi chapel in Santa Maria del Popolo, at a time when he was all the rage, the bold and audacious Lombard; in 1606, after the murder and the escape, times were fast changing.

[FC]

SAINT FRANCIS IN MEDITATION

c. 1606
oil on canvas, 113.3 × 94 cm
Gallerie Nazionali di Arte Antica,
Palazzo Barberini, Rome, inv. 5130,
property of Fondo Edifici di Culto,
Ministry of the Interior

Provenance: on deposit
from Carpineto Romano,
church of San Francesco.

Bibliography: Brugnoli 1968, pp. 11–
15; Zuccari 1990, pp. 175-199; Marini
2001, p. 564; Vodret, in *Caravaggio.
Works in Rome* 2016, II, pp. 624–
626; Berra 2018c, pp. 117–125 (with
previous bibliography); Vodret
2021a, pp. 261–265; Primarosa, in
Orazio Gentileschi 2023, pp. 144–
145.

An oblique beam of light breaks through the penumbra of the refuge illuminating the right-hand side of Francis's face, leaving his bust, the stigmatised hand, and the left side of his face partially in shadow. The saint, absorbed in prayer and in devout meditation on the transience of all earthly things, turns his attention away from the crucifix to concentrate on the skull, an attribute of the penitent hermit. The bareness of the composition accentuates the gravity of the mystical reflection of the "poverello di Assisi", which can be linked to the *imitatio Christi*.

The intense contrast in the lighting and the close-up framing of the composition emphasise the heavy folds of the rough and threadbare wool habit that the saint had made "himself, reproducing the image of the cross to ward off all the devil's seductions; he had made it so coarse as to crucify the flesh and all its vices and sins, and so poor and rough as to make it impossible for it to be envied." (*Fonti francescane* [1977] 2004, 356–357).

The painting comes from the church of San Pietro in Carpineto Romano, founded around 1609 by Cardinal Pietro Aldobrandini, nephew of Pope Clement VIII. It was probably this family, who had acquired the fief of Carpineto in 1597 from the Counts of Segni and Valmontone, who commissioned the painting around 1606. The style of the work, moreover, is in accord with Caravaggio's production of this period, and the biographical events occurring at this time also incline towards this hypothesis. In the summer of 1606, in fact, the painter had taken refuge in the Colonna family's feuds south of Rome (biographers refer to Palestrina, Zagarolo and Paliano, all close to Carpineto) to escape the death penalty hanging over him following the murder of Ranuccio Tomassoni on 28 May of that year.

Since 1968, when the painting was made known by Maria Vittoria Brugnoli, it has been linked to the best of its many copies: the one in the Capuchin church of Santa Maria della Concezione in Rome, which until then had been considered to be the original. It was in fact Giulio Cantalamessa, back in 1908, who was the first to attribute the latter painting to Caravaggio, linking it to the events of the 1603 trial and to Orazio Gentileschi's loan of a Capuchin friar's habit to Caravaggio.

The condition of the Palazzo Barberini painting, which has reached us today with its paint layers much thinned and abraded, contributes to confirming its authorship, one which has not been unanimously accepted by scholarship. The work, however, displays a greater precision in the rendering of certain details (from the depiction of the cord, to that of the tears and patches of the habit), as well as the presence of several pentiments not present in the various known versions; these are to be found in the hand holding the skull—initially conceived in a slightly different position—and, above all, in the hood of the saint's habit. The latter was initially painted pointed, as found in the Capuchin habit, and was later adapted to that found in the habits worn by the reformed Friars Minor. This alteration in the shape of the hood, which is also visible to the naked eye, should perhaps be interpreted as an *ex-post* correction brought about by the work's former location: a church assigned to the Friars Minor, which was initially entrusted to the Capuchin order.
[YP]

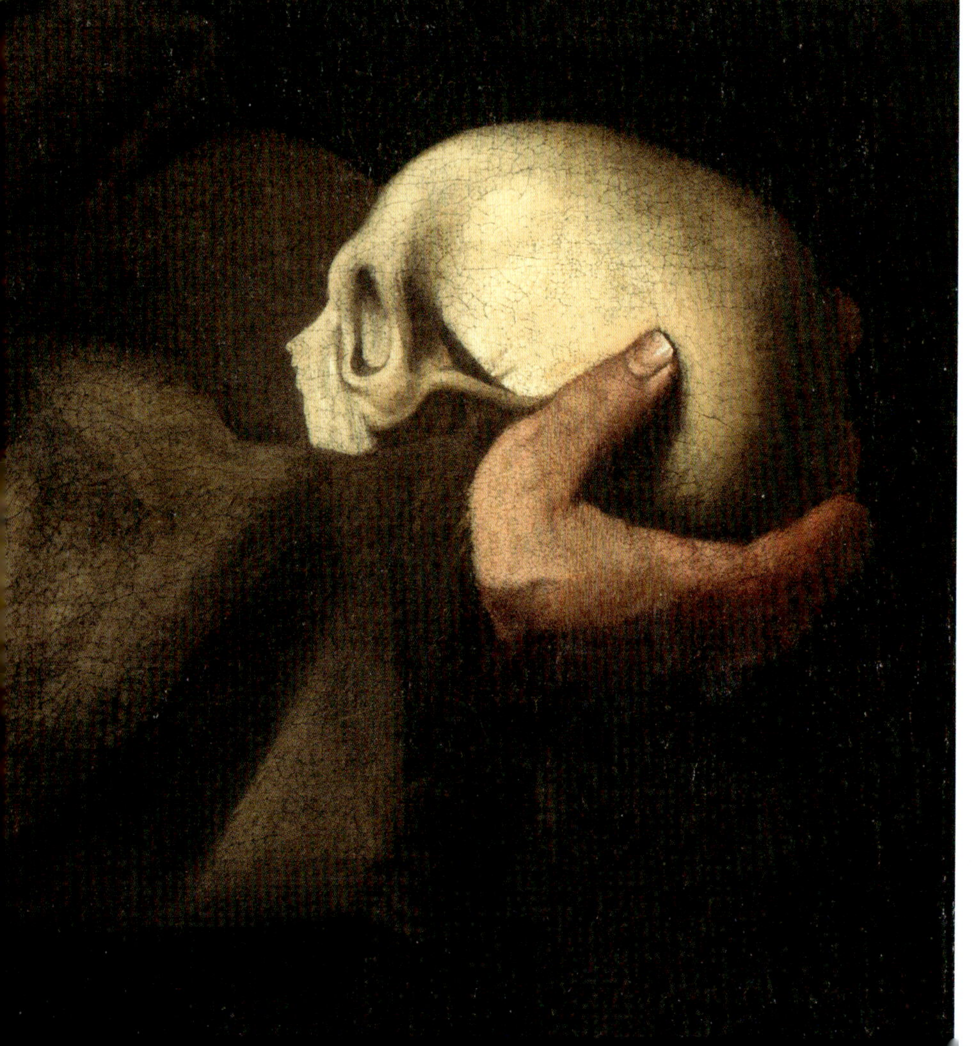

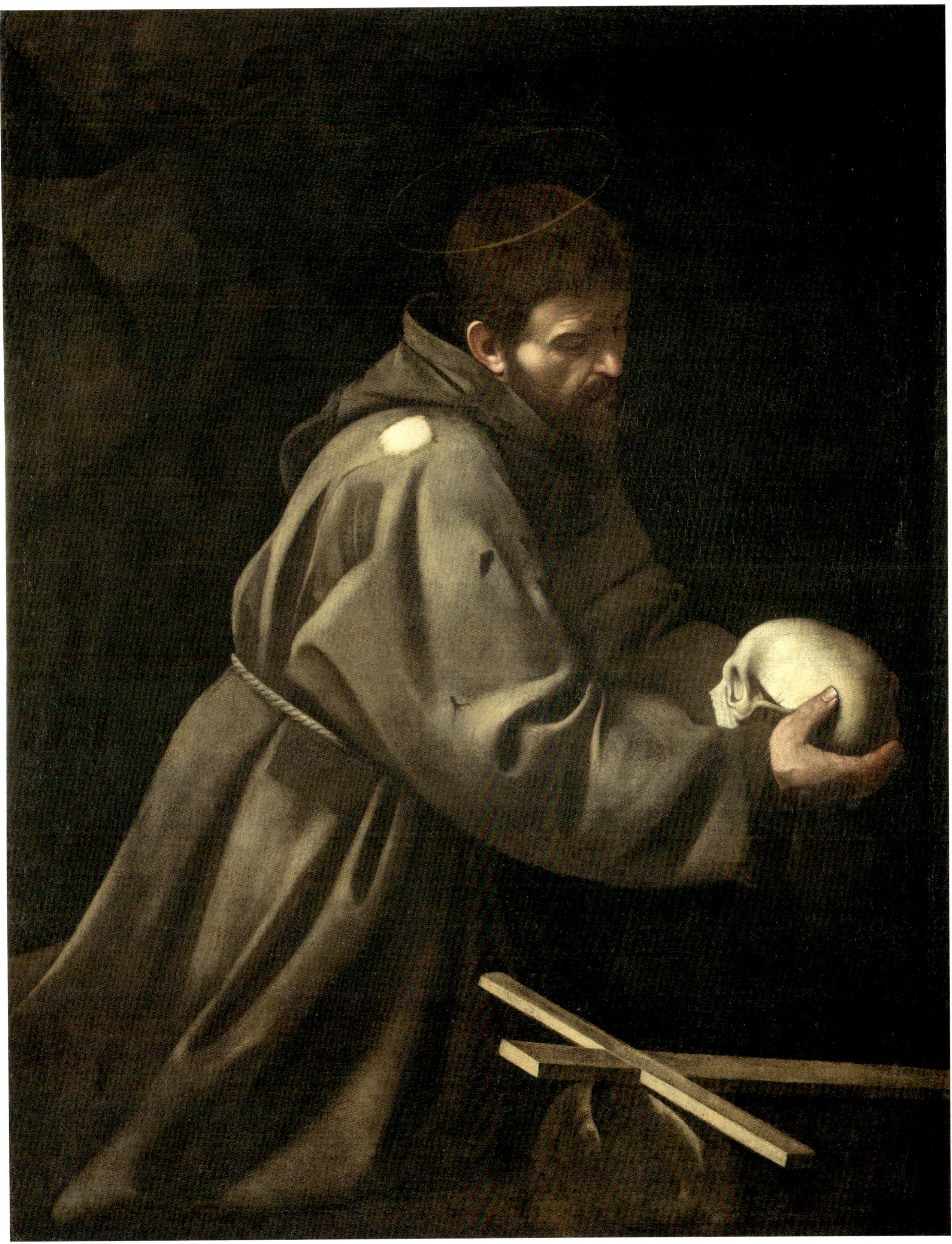

DAVID WITH THE HEAD OF GOLIATH

c. 1606 / 1609
oil on canvas, 125 × 101 cm
Galleria Borghese, Rome, inv. 455

Provenance: Rome, Cardinal Scipione Borghese 1613.

Bibliography: Francucci [1613] 1647, ms. Archivio Apostolico Vaticano, Borgh. 184, 1613, canto III, stanze 182–188, cc. 54*v*–56*r*; Manilli 1650, p. 67; Bellori [1672] 1976, p. 224; Venturi 1893, p. 209; Longhi 1951d, p. 25; Wagner 1958, pp. 13, 108, 121–124, 127, 138, 140, 168, 213, 228, 230–233; Longhi 1959, pp. 25, 30–32; Macrae 1964, pp. 412–416; Causa 1966, nos. 154–155; Moir 1976, pp. 103, 134 no. 225; Pacelli 1977, pp. 819–829; Cinotti 1983, IV, I, 1983, pp. 502–505, no. 51; Calvesi 1985a, pp. 80–85; Marini 1987, pp. 554–556; Christiansen, in *A Caravaggio rediscovered* 1990, p. 52, no. 88; Calvesi 1990, pp. 143–144, 148, 382–383; Papi, in *Michelangelo Merisi da Caravaggio. Come nascono* 1991, pp. 282–289, n. 16; Pacelli 1994, pp. 135, 139, 145, 150, 155–158; Cappelletti 2009, pp. 201, 242; Terzaghi 2010c, pp. 68, 69; Zuccari 2011, pp. 250–251; Terzaghi 2019, pp. 53–56; Vodret 2021a, pp. 316–318, n. 69; Cappelletti 2022, pp. 16–22; Iommelli, in *Nono dialogo Brera* 2022, pp. 116–121; Papi 2023b, pp. 17–19, 92-93, no. 2.

The *David with the Head of Goliath* is undoubtedly one of the most meaningful and most discussed works in Caravaggio scholarship. The painting was referred to for the first time in 1613 by Scipione Francucci, in his verses dedicated to the masterpieces collected by Cardinal Scipione Borghese. The poem does indeed mention Caravaggio by name, although the description lingers on such aspects as the fur, which raises some questions as to the identification of the work (Cappelletti 2022, p. 19). Dating from the same year is a receipt for a payment made by the cardinal to the cabinet-maker Annibale Durante for the installation of some frames, including one for a "painting with the head of the Giant" of "h[eight] 5 and 4 p[*almi*]", measurements which are, broadly speaking, equivalent to those of the painting by the Lombard master (Iommelli, in *Nono dialogo Brera* 2022, p. 118). This is followed by the indisputable description of the work by Iacomo Manilli in his guidebook of the villa published in 1650, which, in addition to describing its location inside the *Casino* Borghese, is also the first source to report that, in the face of the giant, Caravaggio "had wanted to portray himself, and in David . . . his 'Caravaggino'"(Manilli 1650, p. 67). In the figure of the young shepherd, scholars have attempted to discern a figure who was a close contemporary to Caravaggio, with an inclination towards Cecco del Caravaggio, an identification expressed and argued by Gianni Papi (Papi 2023b). Widely confirmed in all the inventories of the collection known to date, the attribution reported in Manilli's text is also found in eighteenth-century guides and in the 1833 lists of trustees. Shared by Giovanni Piancastelli (1891) the attribution was also re-proposed by Adolfo Venturi (1893), and has found favour with all subsequent scholarship, its autograph status never doubted. According to Giovanni Pietro Bellori, Caravaggio painted: "for the same Cardinal [Scipione Borghese] he painted Saint Jerome . . . and another half-length figure, of David holding Goliath's head (which is a portrait of himself) by the hair and gripping his sword: he represented him as a youth exposed with one shoulder out of his shirt, painted with very deep shadows and background, which he would use to lend force to his figures and compositions" (Bellori [1672] 1976, p. 224; Bellori [1672] 2005, p. 182, slightly adapt-

ed). In light of the biographer's words, the canvas should be dated between 1605 and 1606, with a suggested date for its execution around the last months of Merisi's sojourn in Rome, close to that of the *Madonna dei Palafrenieri*. Initially, this dating was shared by Roberto Longhi (1951d, p. 25), who however, a few years later, postponed it to the beginning of the painter's second Neapolitan period, between September and October 1609 (Longhi 1959). The scholar in fact noted some stylistic and compositional similarities with the *Salome with the Head of Saint John the Baptist*, in the National Gallery in London. The new hypothesis on the chronology of the painting was favourably received by most scholars, although not unanimously (see, Causa 1966, nos. 154–155; Moir 1976, pp. 103, 134 n. 225; Pacelli 1977, pp. 819–829; Pacelli 1994, pp. 135, 139, 145, 150, 155–158). Maurizio Calvesi (1985, pp. 80–85), dating the painting to the end of 1609, was the first to interpret the Borghese painting as a gift from Caravaggio that Scipione Borghese delivered to Pope Paul V, in an attempt by the artist to obtain the pontiff's pardon following his conviction for the murder of Ranuccio Tomassoni. The same scholar offered a Christological interpretation of the image, also by virtue of the Augustinian motto—"H.AS O S"—present on the blade of the sword held by the young David interpreted as "H[umilit] AS O[ccidit] S[uperbiam]" (Calvesi 1990, pp. 382–383). Different hypotheses were put forward by Wagner (1958, p. 213), who interpreted the inscription as the painter's monogram: "M. A. C. O." as in "M[ichaeli] A[ngeli] C[aravaggio] O[pus]"), and by Macrae (1964, pp. 412–416), who believed that the inscription was nothing more than the armourer's mark (see also Zuccari 2011, pp. 239–253). Marini identified it as a representation of verse 57 of the Book of Samuel (I,57), in which David, having gained access to Saul's tent (visible in the upper left part of the painting), displays the giant's head, still dripping with blood; but David's unusual, compassionate, almost repentant gaze as he holds his arm raised as in Lysippos' *Apoxyomenos* (Marini 1987, pp. 554–555), imbues the traditional biblical iconography of the triumph of good over evil with a sense of melancholy and deep compassion.
It is in any case now generally agreed that the painting dates to the painter's second sojourn in Naples

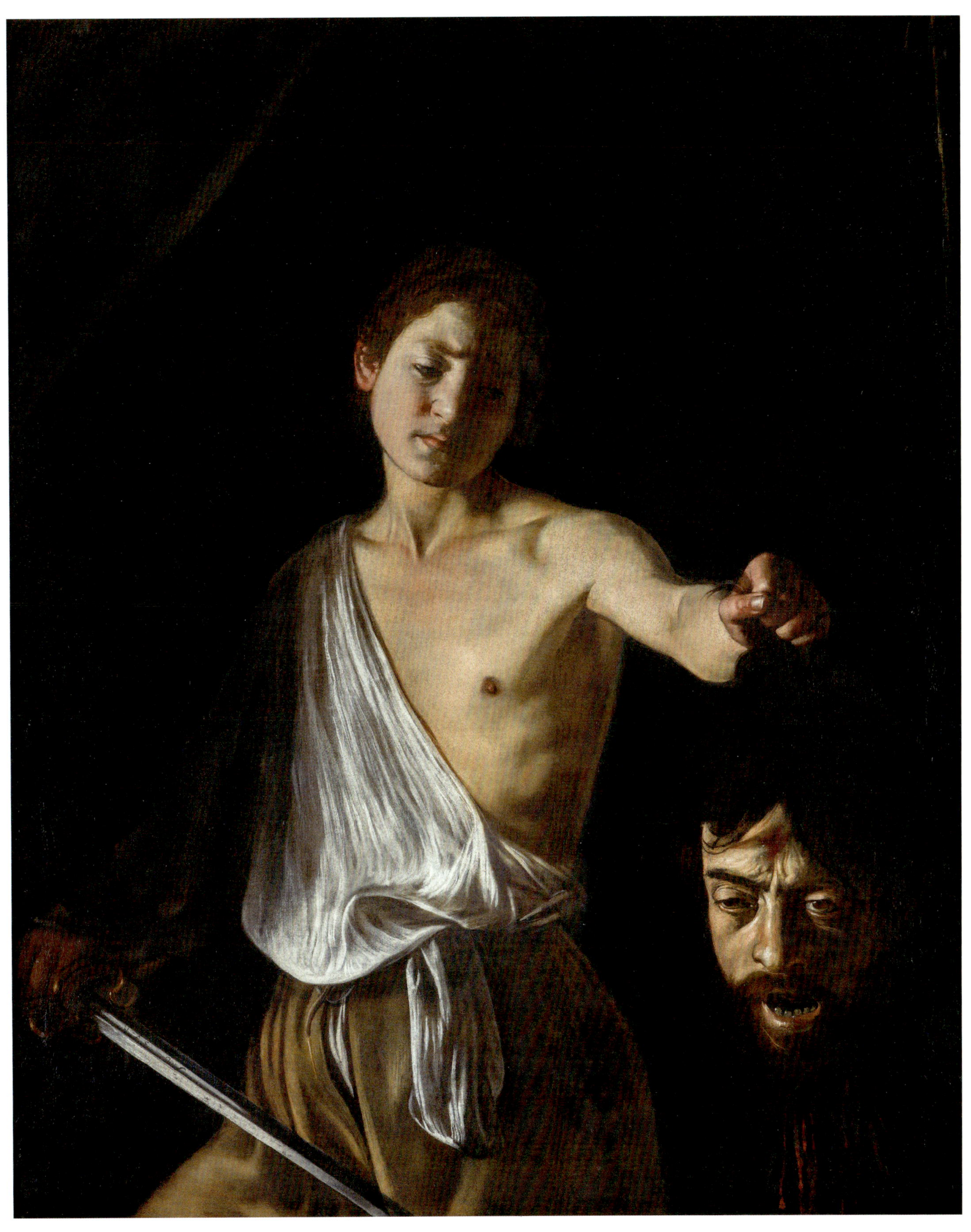

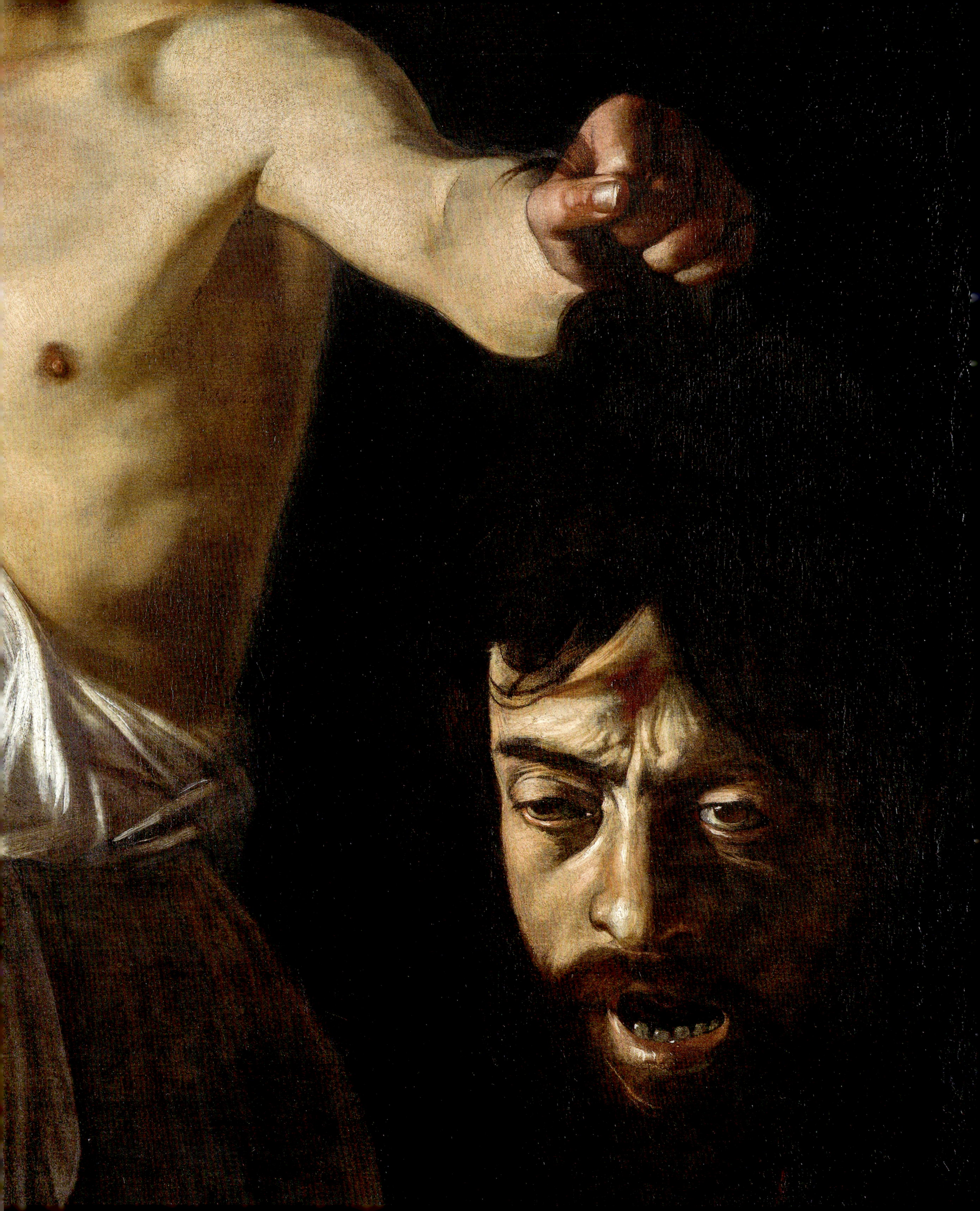

(Terzaghi 2019, pp. 53–56), in particular because of the thin and rapid application of the paint, the urgency with which the forms were traced, the limited palette and, finally, the treatment of light. All of these elements are to be found in Caravaggio's late works, first and foremost in the *Martyrdom of Saint Ursula* in the Palazzo Zevallos in Naples. In this regard, however, one should not underestimate the part played by the condition of the painting, the paint layer of which has been much abraded and thinned by the various restorations that the painting has undergone over time; a condition that may perhaps have favoured the moving forward of the proposed date of execution to the last year of the painter's life. For these reasons, and also taking into account the results of the diagnostic investigations that revealed not only the presence of some incisions, but also of a ground similar to that present in Caravaggio's works painted between 1606 and 1607, the debate on the date of the work remains open. To anticipate its execution, to the period between the end of the first Roman sojourn and the first months of that in Naples, as also suggested by Keith Christiansen (in *A Caravaggio Rediscovered* 1990, p. 52, n. 88), Gianni Papi (in *Michelangelo Merisi da Caravaggio. Come nasco-*

no 1991, pp. 284–285) and Francesca Cappelletti (2009, pp. 201, 242; 2022, p. 25), would reinforce the hypothesis that the painting is to be related to the death sentence and the consequent wish for a pardon from Paul V, as Caravaggio's self-portrait with the severed head of Goliath would suggest.

As far as the events surrounding the painting before its arrival in the Borghese collection, it is important to mention a passage through Naples of a *David* by Merisi. The commission by the viceroy of Naples and count of Lemos, Pedro Fernández de Castro, at the beginning of the second decade of the seventeenth century, of two copies to be made of a *David* by Caravaggio (Pacelli 1977, pp. 819–829; Pacelli 1994, pp. 155–158), by the artist Baldassarre Aloisi, better known as Galanino (Terzaghi 2010c, pp. 68–69), would in fact document the presence of the painting in the city of Naples at least until 1610 (Vodret 2021a, pp. 316–318, n. 69). Although scholars are in general agreement that the Borghese painting was the model for Galanino's replica, even if it cannot be ruled out that the model might have been the painting now in Vienna, the time and manner of the arrival of our work in Rome, have yet to be fully clarified.

[EG]

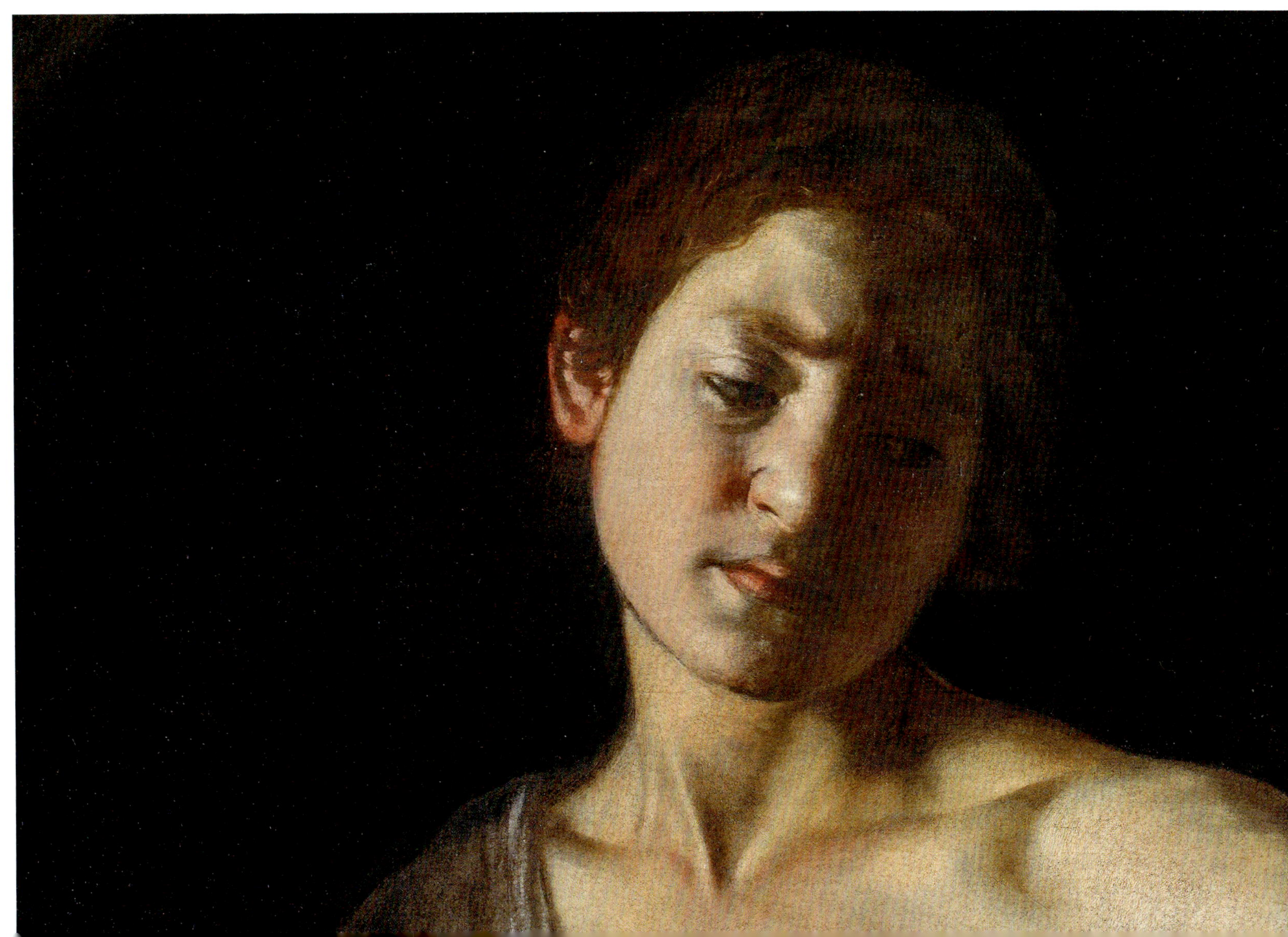

ECCE HOMO

c. 1606–1607 / c. 1609
oil on canvas, 111 × 85 cm
Icon Trust

Provenance: to the present owners by purchase from Diego, Mercedes and Antonio Pérez de Castro Méndez; by inheritance from the descendants of Mariano Pèrez de Castro, Madrid 1849; Évaristo Pérez de Castro, Madrid, 1844; by exchange from the Academia di San Fernando, Madrid 1821; collection of Manuel Godoy, Madrid 1816; Spanish Royal Collection, Charles IV, Madrid, Real Casa de Campo; Spanish Royal Collection, Charles IV, Madrid, private apartments 1701–1702; Spanish Royal Collection, Philip IV, Madrid, Alcázar, inventory 1666, no. 410; Garcia Avellaneda y Haro II Count of Castrillo, Viceroy of Naples, Naples 1657; Juan de Lezcano, Naples 1631 (?).

Bibliography: Sgarbi 2021; Terzaghi 2021b; Zuccari 2022c, pp. 325-329; *Caravaggio. L'*Ecce Homo *svelato* 2023.

Only very recently added to Caravaggio's catalogue, this moving *Ecce Homo* has a very short history of scholarship. Four years ago the canvas passed through the Madrid antiquarian market (Ansorena, Subasta 8 April 2021, lot 229) with the generic reference to the circle of Jusepe de Ribera. Immediately identified by the market and by some art historians as a work of exceptional importance in the output of the great Lombard master (for an account of these reports, see Terzaghi 2021b), the work was then the subject of an 'instant book' (Sgarbi 2021) and indipendently, of a publication in a scientific journal that was able to fully reconstruct the provenance of the painting (Terzaghi 2021b). A subsequent volume then confirmed the autograph status of the work, providing accounts of the masterly restoration (Cipriani 2023), the scientific analysis (Falcucci 2023), and the placing of the work within the master's career (Christiansen 2023; Papi 2023c; Porzio 2023; Terzaghi 2023b).

The painting can be traced in the collection of Garcia Avellaneda y Haro, second Count of Castrillo (1588–1670), Viceroy of Naples from 1653 to 1659, when he returned to Spain. A prominent personality at the court of Philip IV, the Count had always distinguished himself for his interest in the arts. He was in fact one of the leading figures in the construction and decoration of the Palacio del Buen Retiro and, which is of great interest, between 1634 and 1637 had his own family chapel in the church of San Jerónimo de Espeja in Sora designed by the Italian architect Giovan Battista Crescenzi. The connection with Crescenzi, a decisive figure in the events surrounding Caravaggism in Rome, leads one to believe that the aristocrat had already heard of Caravaggio in Spain, and that in Naples he had set out on the trail of the master's works. In his time in Italy, the Count put together a rich collection of valuable paintings (Bartolomé 1994), while research in the Neapolitan archives clearly reveals his function as an intermediary for the purchase of works of art for Philip IV in the city's marketplace (Terzaghi 2023b, p. 26). In 1657, on the occasion of the departure from Naples of his wife, Countess Maria de Avellaneda, an inventory of Castrillo's possessions was drawn up, in which two works by Caravaggio appear: *Salome with the Head of the Baptist*, identifiable with the beautiful canvas now in the Palacio Real in Madrid

(Bartolomé 1994; Milicua 2005; Terzaghi 2016a) and a painting described as: "Mas otro quadro de un Heccehomo de zinco palmos con marco de evano con un soldado y Pilatosque le enseña al Pueblo es original de m° Miçael Angel Caravacho" (Bartolomé 1994, p. 25), to be identified precisely with our *Ecce Homo* (Terzaghi 2021b, p. 26). It is more difficult to establish the paths taken by the work on its way to the Viceroy, and whether it could be the painting owned by another Spanish gentleman, Juan de Lezcano, former secretary to the diplomat, Count Francisco Ruiz de Castro (1579–1637), ambassador to Rome and Viceroy of Palermo, brother of the Viceroy of Naples Fernando de Castro. The *post mortem* inventory of Lezcano, drawn up in Naples in 1631, includes a painting with a description that fits perfectly: "Un eccehomo con Pilato que lo muestra al pueblo y un sayonque le viste de detras la veste porpurea," with the exceptionally high valuation of eight hundred ducats (Vannugli 2009, pp. 360-361), the dimensions of which are compatible with those of the painting under examination (Terzaghi 2021b, pp. 201–202). It is therefore not improbable that upon Lezcano's death the work could have passed either by purchase or as a diplomatic gift to the vice-royal collections.

What is more difficult to establish is the placing of the painting within the master's career. Bellori ([1672] 2005, p. 182) speaks of an *Ecce Homo* painted by Caravaggio "for the signori Massimi," that is during his Roman years. A series of documents that have been exhaustively studied attest to the history of this intricate commission (summarised by Curti 2021; Terzaghi 2021b, pp. 202–206; Terzaghi 2023b, pp. 19–25), which, however, does not seem to be able to be linked to the *Ecce Homo* under discussion (Terzaghi 2023b, pp. 19–25). Whilst the authorship of the painting has been unanimously accepted, the issue of dating the work is therefore much more of a debated issue: some think it could be a work executed between Rome and Naples (Papi 2023c, pp. 54–58; Christiansen 2023, pp. 125–128), others believe it was executed between the time spent in the Lazio fief of the Colonna and the early Neapolitan period (Terzaghi 2021b, pp. 206–207; Terzaghi 2023b, pp. 29–30), and then there are those who, on the basis of the resonance with the Sicilian works, believe it to be

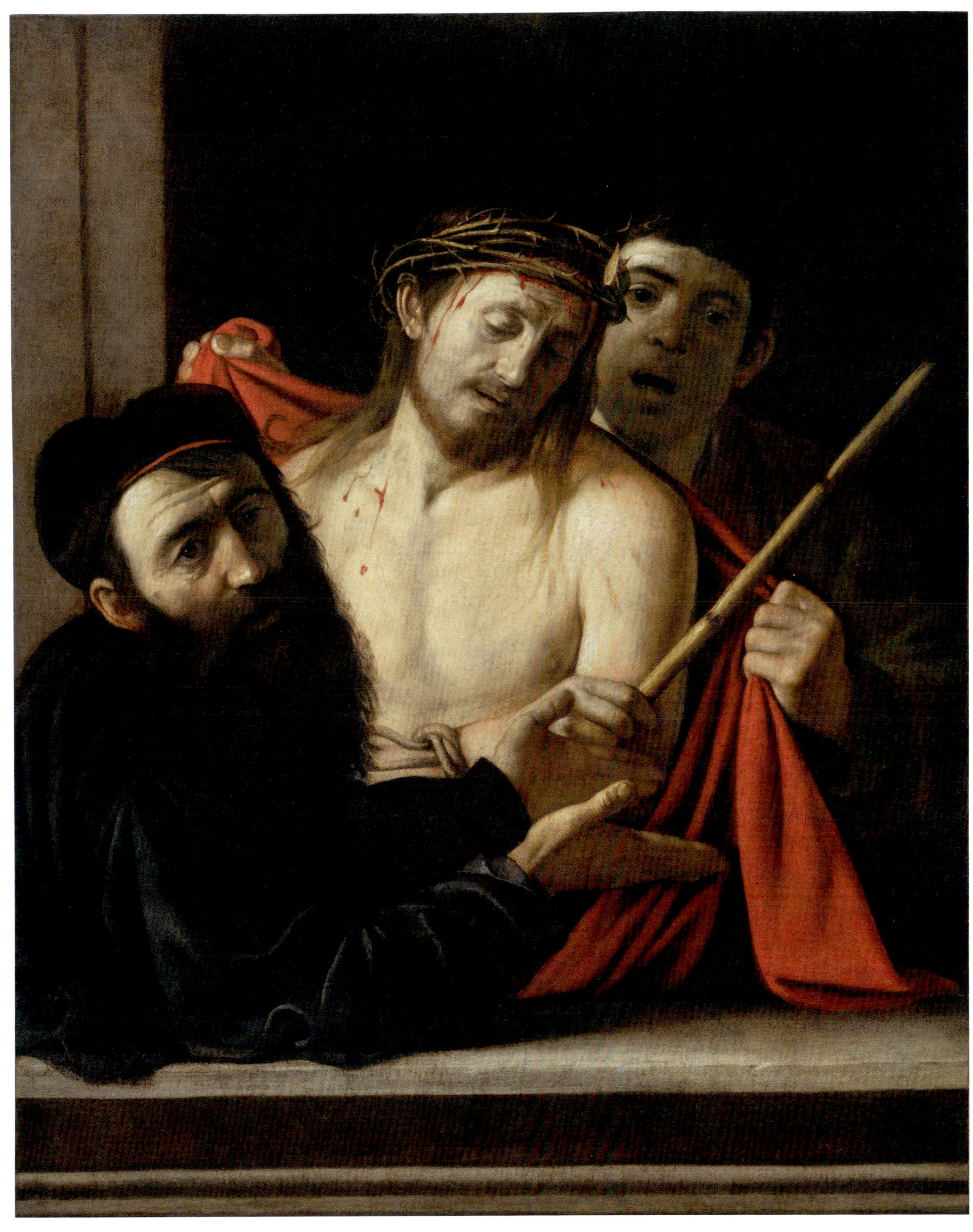

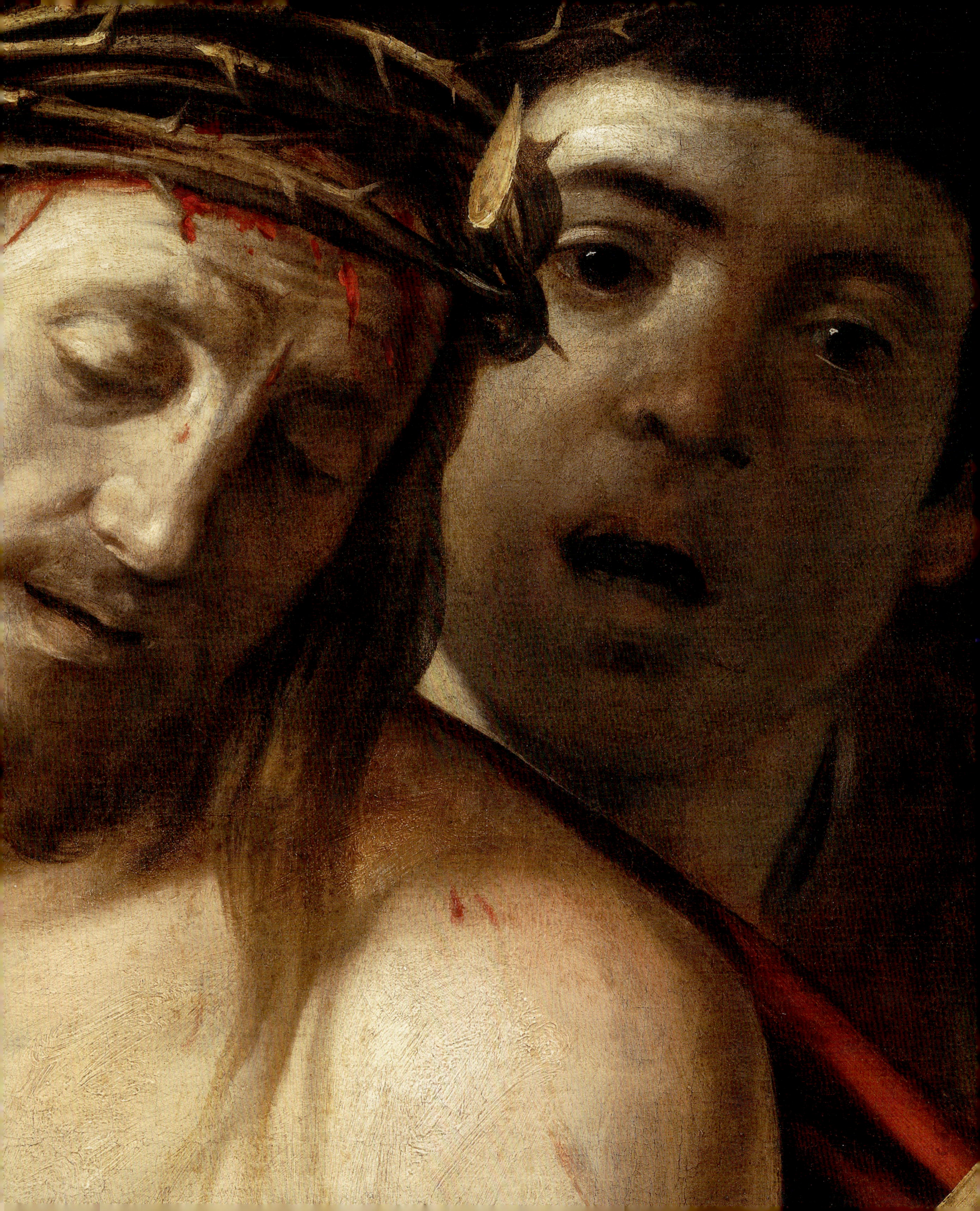

a work painted in the last stretch of the master's life (Porzio, 2023, pp. 101–102 and Porzio in this volume).

Three early copies of the painting are known to date, one of which was already known to Roberto Longhi who on the basis of it intuited the possibility of a lost original (Longhi [1954] 2000, p. 126, fig. 69b). Their location is, however, not relevant for dating purposes (Terzaghi 2021b, pp. 192–194), but is important evidence of the painting's success. It is also possible to identify an echo of the *Ecce Homo* in the works of the Neapolitan artists of Caravaggio's circle, in particular in Battistello Caracciolo and his *Madonna della Stella*, dated 1608, in my opinion a possible *terminus ante quem* for the execution of the canvas.

The painting is characterised by a tight compositional setting, with the figures at three-quarter length, scaled according to different degrees of depth in space, in an admirable cinematographic *fading*. In the foreground, Pilate almost protrudes from the narrative space, leaning out from the balcony; in the centre, a sorrowful, tender Christ, his body marked by the scourge, and on his head which drips with blood, a tangled crown of thorns; behind him stands the extraordinary figure of a young torturer, his mouth wide open in an almost theatrical expression as he reveals and at the same time unveils the figure of Jesus with the dark red cloak. We are faced with the sentencing of the righteous, emphasised by the chromatic difference between the luminous body of Christ, and the entirely earthy hues of the other figures struggling with the shadows. It is precisely the figure of Jesus that reveals some extraordinary iconographic details: first of all, the conspicuously cut branch of the crown of thorns that in Caravaggio's imagery becomes almost flame-like; this has a legacy of illustrious examples, first and foremost Correggio (Berra 2021a). But even more astonishing is the figure of Christ himself, which turns out to have been strongly inspired by an *Ecce Homo* by Giampietrino, closely followed in a panel by a Milanese artist of the second half of the sixteenth century (Nîmes, Musée des Beaux-Arts) that has all the air of being by the same Peterzano who was Caravaggio's master, in which the figure of the Man of Sorrows is worshipped by the donor portrayed in the foreground (Terzaghi 2023b, pp. 31–42). Called to measure himself against one of the crucial moments of the Passion, Caravaggio has used models for the figures of the earthly characters, but when faced with the Divine, the suffering of God made Man, he has preferred to draw inspiration from an image dear to him, that he must have seen painted many times by the best Milanese artists and, evidently for him, perfection wore that face. This is the first time that we can document the absence of a model in the artist's career, and this makes the discovery of this masterpiece even more precious.

[MCT]

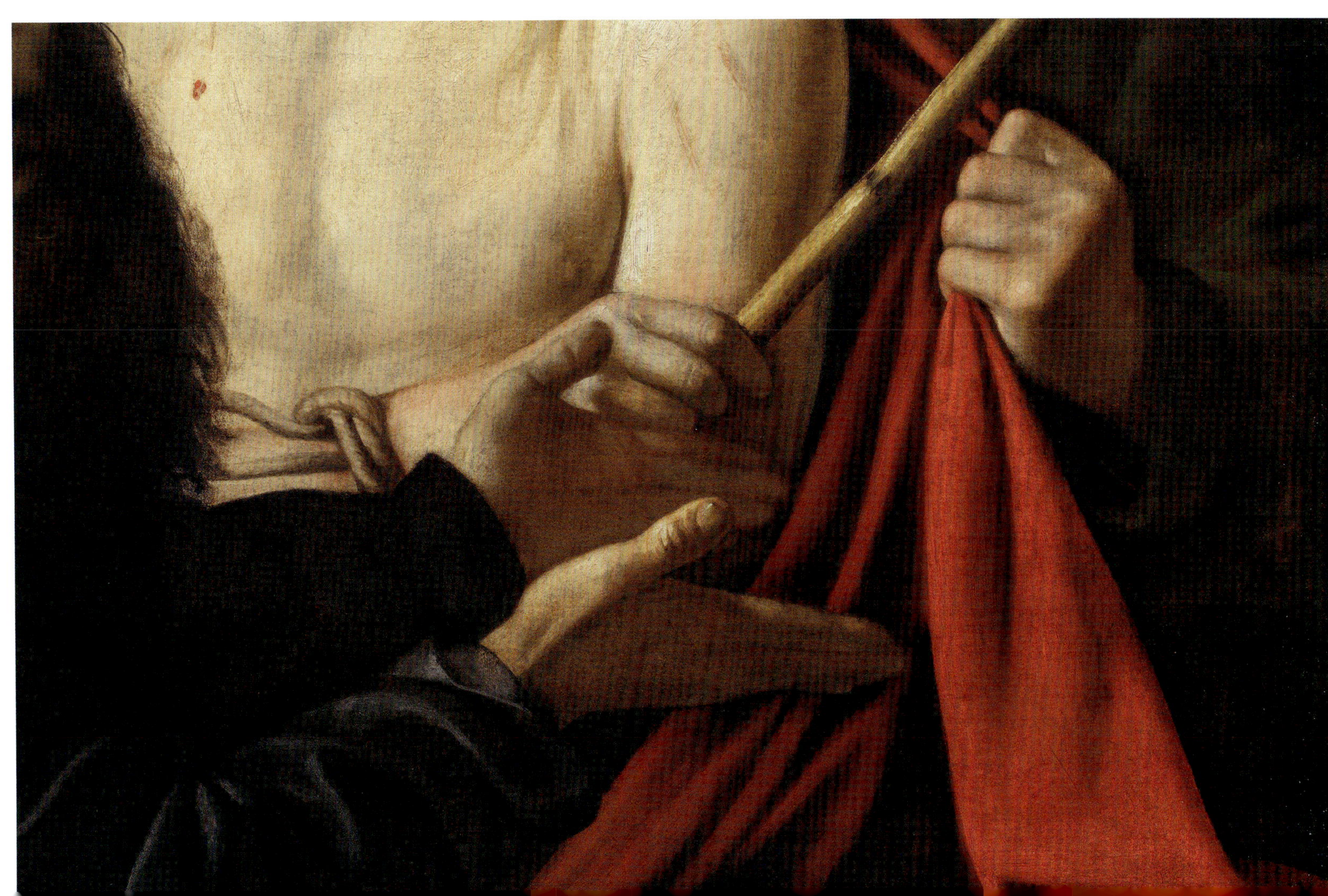

FLAGELLATION OF CHRIST

1607
oil on canvas, 286 × 213 cm
Museo e Real Bosco di Capodimonte,
Naples. Property of the Fondo
Edifici di Culto of the Ministry
of the Interior

Provenance: Naples, Basilica of
San Domenico Maggiore, until 1972.

Bibliography: Cinotti 1983, pp. 468–
471, cat. 35; *La* Flagellazione *di
Caravaggio* 1999; Marini 2005,
pp. 529–532, cat. 86; Spike 2010,
pp. 301–306, cat. 54; *Caravaggio
at Donnaregina* 2024.

With the notable exception of Giovan Pietro Bellori ([1672] 2018, pp. 40–43), the earliest chapter of the historical fortune of the painting is limited almost exclusively to Neapolitan sources. It is referred to for the first time, but in a manuscript text, by the scholar Carlo De Lellis ([c. 1654–1688], II, p. 368) as present over the altar of the first chapel to the left of the entrance of San Domenico Maggiore, at the time under the patronage of the De Franchis (Di Franco, Franchi) family, Marchesi di Taviano and dukes of Ascoli and of Longano; the altarpiece must have been placed in this location around 1652, the year in which the chapel, after prolonged extension and renovation work, was dedicated to the Flagellation of the Lord (Pacelli 1977, p. 824). In 1675, the painting was replaced by a statue in wood by Pietro Ceraso—the so-called "Madonna di zi' Andrea", after the donor, the Dominican Andrea D'Auria from Sanseverino (ibid., pp. 824–825)—and then moved first to the left wall of the chapel (Celano 1692, III, p. 121) and shortly afterwards to the opposite wall (Parrino 1700, I, p. 191; Sigismondo 1788–1789, II, 1788, p. 17). In the course of the nineteenth century, the *Flagellation* underwent further and not always clear-cut changes in location within the church (for a review of the evidence from the guides, see Pacelli 1977, pp. 823–825), until it ended up in the Chapel of the Rosary, the first to the left of the apse, where it remained until December 1972, when it was moved for safe-keeping to Capodimonte, in the end taking on—in the installation completed in 1998—a focal role in the itinerary of the museum's display. In 2018, in the context of the radical reorganisation of the museum, the batten surrounding the canvas, which helped to visually isolate the work in room 78 on the second floor, was replaced by a late seventeenth-century style massive carved frame with phytomorphic motifs.

In the local literature, the *Flagellation* has always enjoyed the highest regard, beginning with De Lellis himself ("the most beautiful work that this illustrious painter has ever made"); and even Bernardo De Dominici ([1742–1743] 2017, II, pp. 970–971), despite his anti-naturalist prejudice, could not but record its astonishing innovations and the exceptional impression it exercised on the city's artistic milieu. However, it was only thanks to the results of the 1928 restoration that the work re-entered modern Caravaggio scholarship, which has by and large placed its execution in the master's first Neapolitan sojourn, on the basis also of a chronological interpretation of Bellori's account ([1672] 2005, p. 183): "Then he [Caravaggio] made his way to Naples, in which city he found employment at once, for his style and reputation were already known there. He received commissions for the Flagellation of Christ at the column in the chapel of the signori De Franchis in the church of San Domenico Maggiore …").

By contrast, beginning with Roberto Longhi (1959, pp. 28–29), an alternative and, all things considered, a minority of scholars have argued in favour of a late date, specifically because of the typological similarities with the *Salome* in the National Gallery in London, generally identified with the "half-length figure of Herodias" that Caravaggio, on his return to Naples, is said to have presented to Grand Master Alof de Wignacourt in an attempt at reconciliation (for an alternative proposal, see my essay in the catalogue, pp. 66–67).

The first and more credible hypothesis, supported by the luminous turning of the volumes and the compact quality of the paint, has found solid confirmation in the documentation of the old Neapolitan public banks (Pacelli 1977, p. 820). In fact, on 11 May 1607, a payment on account was made to the painter by Tommaso de Franchis for a work, the subject of which was unspecified; a work which it seems can precisely be identified with the *Flagellation* of San Domenico Maggiore, not only because of the identity of the client, but also because of the large sum involved, 250 ducats (of which 150 had already been received in cash), to which must be added—in all likelihood—an additional 40 ducats and 9 *grana* on 28 May. However, what the documentary evidence has not clarified is neither the history of the painting up to the first— late—reference to it, the reconstruction of which must take into account both the different layout of the earlier De Franchis chapel, located behind the present one, and incorporated into it in the 1730s, and the silence of writers prior to De Lellis; nor, above all, has it exhausted the debate surrounding the chronology. The conspicuous number of *pentimenti* and modifications brought to light by

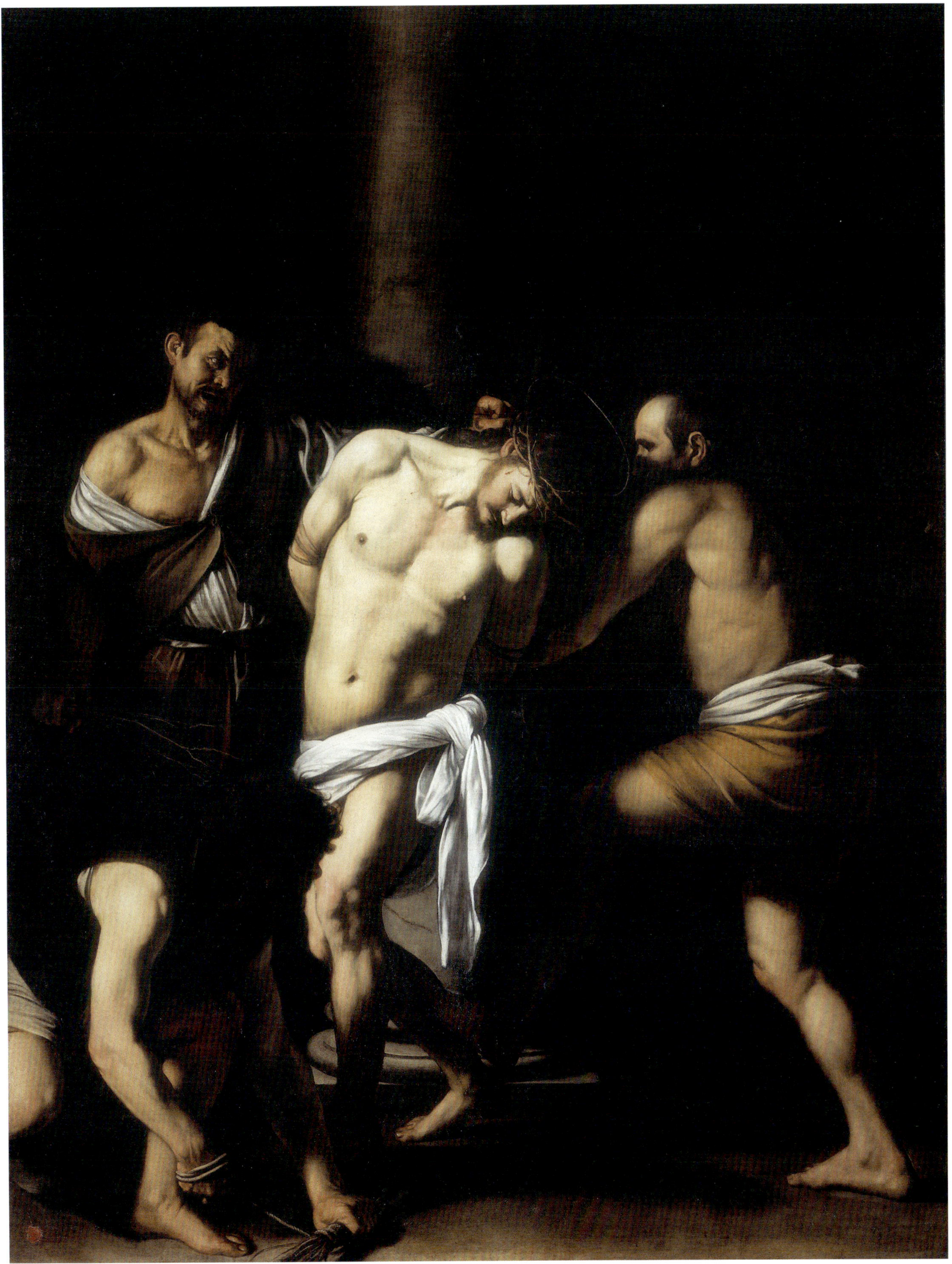

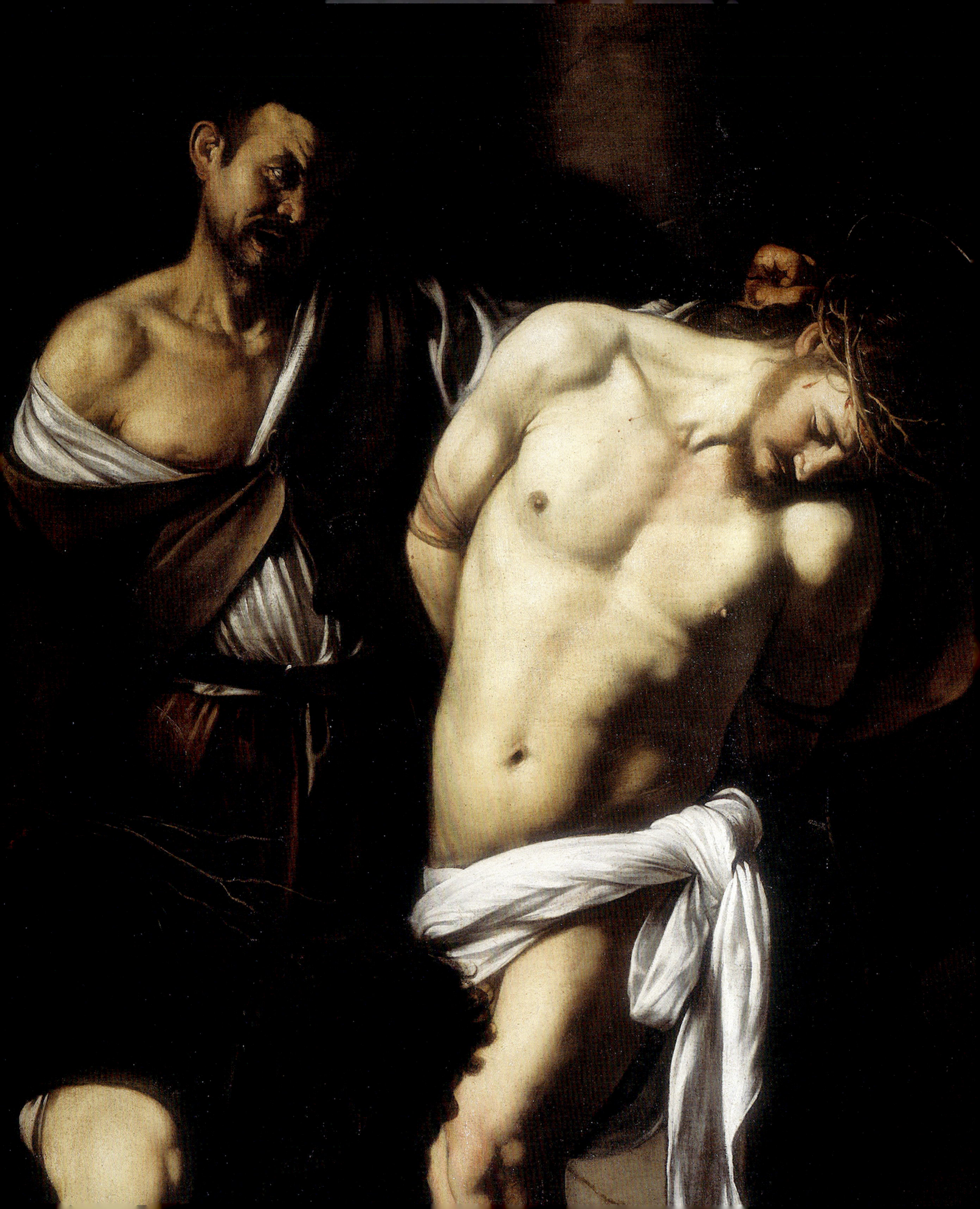

the diagnostic investigations carried out on the *Flagellation*—notable, in particular, is the elimination in the final version of the figure of a bystander, revealed by radiographic examinations in 1983, and variously interpreted as the portrait of De Franchis (Pacelli, Brejon de Lavergnée 1985, pp. 213–215), as Saint Francis (Marini 2005, p. 532), or indeed as a self-portrait (Pagano 1999, p. 20)—prompted first Mina Gregori (in *Painting in Naples* 1982, p. 125) and then, more forcefully, Ferdinando Bologna ([1992] 2006, p. 336, no. 74) to believe that Caravaggio completed the work upon his return to Naples after the Sicilian parenthesis. In support of this thesis, which in truth is not very credible, Bologna insisted in particular on the similarities between the figure of the torturer on the right, and that of the grave-digger on the same side of the painting in the *Burial of Saint Lucy* in Syracuse.

Putting aside the chronological disputes, we are left with the extraordinary figurative depth of this masterpiece, in which the allusions to classical statuary—see for instance in the thug in the lower left, the reference to the so-called "Scythian knife-grinder" (Longhi 1952, tav. XLII])—and to the artist's Veneto-Lombard background (among the possible models have been suggestively evoked Sebastiano del Piombo's *Flagellation* in San Pietro in Montorio [Berenson 1950, p. 38] and Romanino's version of the subject on the *recto* of the banner in the Metropolitan Museum in New York [inv. 1989.86; Christiansen 1996, pp. 27–28]) merge into a living, real, and tangible image. The

same iconography, which appears traditional, is in reality revitalised by the superimposition, to the episode of the flagellation, of the subsequent scene of the Ecce Homo, brought to mind by the marked display of the body of Christ and by the crown of thorns, which—in contrast to the letter of the Gospel (see John. 19:1–5)—already encircles his bowed head as a sign of submissiveness (this singular detail had already been noted in Pagano 1999, p. 20). This is an unprecedented symbolic artifice, with the power to transform the historical fact into an encounter between human reality and the transcendental dimension, demonstrating—once again—how profound and subtle is the question of the representation of the sacred in Caravaggio.

An anonymous early replica of the *Flagellation* is to be found in the basilica of San Domenico Maggiore (G. Porzio, in *Caravaggio nel patrimonio* 2017, p. 58), at times placed in relation, but without concrete evidence, to the work referred to in the church of the Trinità degli Spagnoli by De Dominici ([1742–1743] 2017, II, p. 971, and III, pp. 262–263), who attributed it doubtfully to either Battistello Caracciolo or to Andrea Vaccaro, and by Onofrio Giannone ([c. 1771–1773] 1941, p. 125), who opted for an attribution to Vaccaro. Because of an oversight, this copy has been reproduced in place of the original work in some of the most reliable monographs on the Lombard master (Hibbard 1985, p. 222, fig. 145; Bologna [1992] 2006, plate 54).

[GPO]

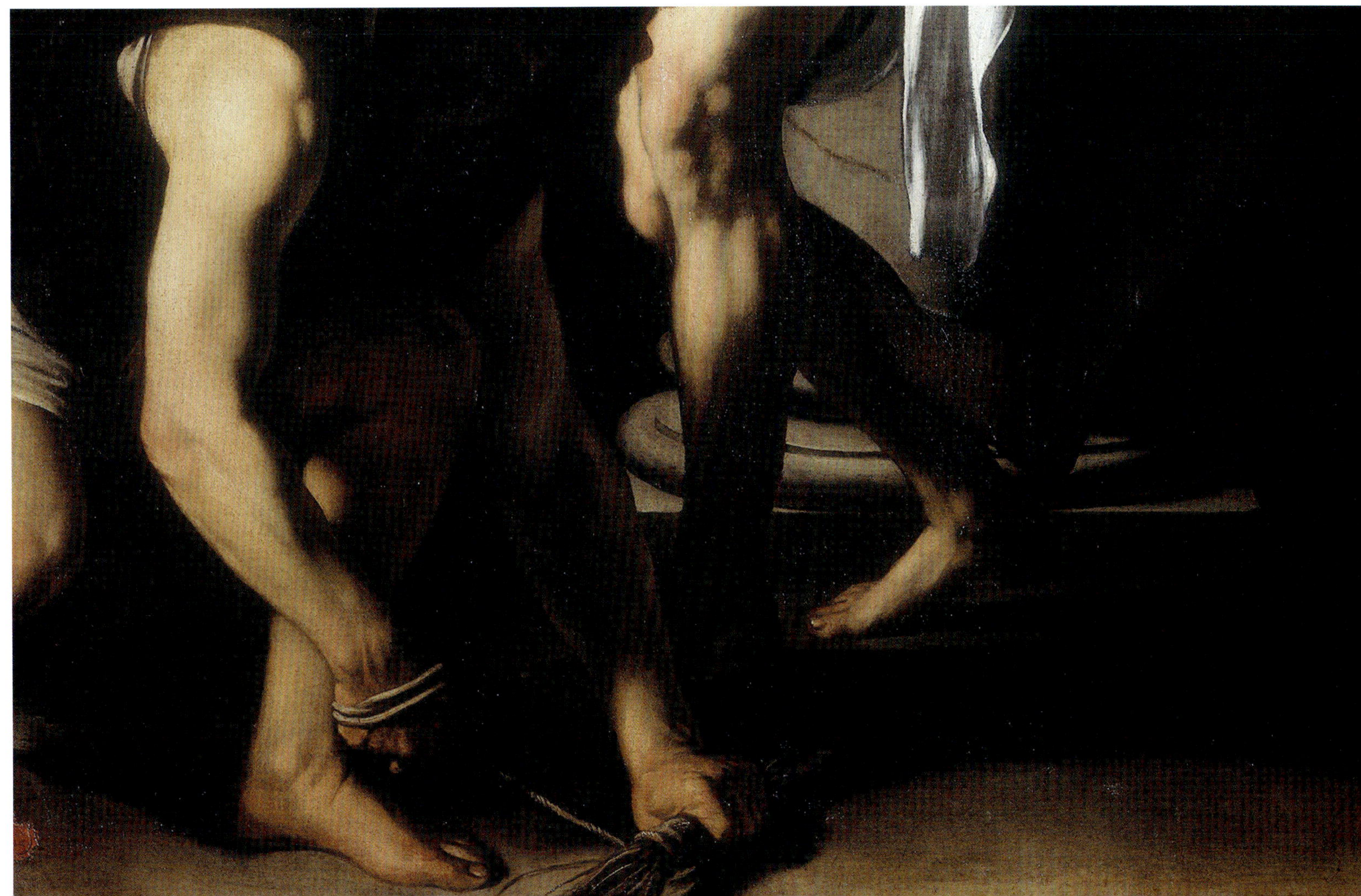

PORTRAIT OF A KNIGHT OF MALTA

1608–1609
oil on canvas, 118.5 × 95.5 cm
Gallerie degli Uffizi, Palazzo Pitti,
Galleria Palatina, Florence

Provenance: 1609 property of
Antonio Martelli; 1666–1670
Florence, Guardaroba Medicea.
Later in Florence.

Bibliography: Borea 1970, pp. 38–39;
Gregori 1974, pp. 594–603; Gregori
1975, pp. 27–60; Cinotti 1983,
pp. 434–435; Gregori, in *The Age
of Caravaggio | Caravaggio e il suo
tempo* 1985, pp. 332-334; Gregori, in
Michelangelo Merisi 1991, pp. 318–
323; Chiarini 1989, pp. 15–16; Gash
1997, pp. 156–160; Gregori, in
*Michelangelo Merisi da Caravaggio.
Come nascono* 1997, pp. 124–128;
Marini 2001, p. 546; Sciberras, Stone,
in *Caravaggio. L'ultimo tempo* 2004,
pp. 119–121; Fabbri 2005, pp. LXV-
LXXI; Cappelletti 2009, pp. 205–
206; Schütze 2009, p. 211; Gregori,
in *Caravaggio e caravaggeschi* 2010,
pp. 119–121; Vodret 2021a, p. 296.

The painting is unanimously accepted as an autograph work by Caravaggio and assigned to his late Maltese or Sicilian production. It was Mina Gregori who first put forward the painter's name in an interview with *La Nazione* in 1966. For four years the canvas was not mentioned, until it was displayed, restored, in the 1970 Caravaggio exhibition (Borea 1970, p. 125), as by the hand of an unknown painter from the circle of Manfredi. Gregori's attribution, correctly cited in the catalogue entry, met with the approval of numerous scholars (from Salerno to Marini, Schleier to Volpe, and Pérez Sànchez); finally, in 1974, the scholar published the painting with the new, important authorship and presented it at the Caravaggio conference held in Bergamo that year (Gregori 1974, pp. 594–603; Gregori 1975, pp. 33–40). Subsequently, the work has been exhibited on several occasions, and its autograph status was before long established without opposition. The identity of the sitter depicted, on the other hand, has proven more divisive. Gregori was the first to identify it as a non-institutional, decidedly more informal portrait of the Grand Master of the Order of Malta, Alof de Wignacourt [fig. 9 on p. 114], on the basis of similarities in the iconography of the figure, deriving from the two prototypes executed by the artist (the first now in Paris, Louvre, the second documented by a copy in Rabat, Malta, in the College of the Canons of the Grotto di San Paolo) and recalled by Bellori ([1672] 2005, p. 183: "He portrayed him standing in armor and seated without armor, in his Grand Master's habit." This identification initially met with considerable support, but doubts arose with Marco Chiarini's intervention in 1989 (pp. 15–16); the scholar retrieved a citation in an entry in the Medici Guardaroba from the years 1666-1670, relating to a portrait of the knight of Malta Marc'Antonio Martelli, which the scholar linked to the painting under examination, also taking into consideration the similar dimensions. The hypothesis did not become established, but contributed to making the identification with Wignacourt more doubtful: indeed, in 1991 Gregori preferred to give the title simply as *Portrait of a Knight of Malta*. More recently, however, the scholar has reiterated her *penchant* for Wignacourt (M. Gregori, in *Caravaggio e caravaggeschi* 2010, pp. 119–121). In 1997, John Gash relaunched Martelli's identikit: the scholar in fact recovered documents that revealed the knight's presence in Malta in 1607 and up to April 1608. Caravaggio could

therefore easily have portrayed him during his sojourn on the island, and the painting may have arrived in Florence following Martelli's return to his native city in the autumn of 1609. In that same year, the knight was in Messina, from whence he would in fact have left for Florence. Subsequently, the opinions of scholars were divided between those who identified Martelli as the sitter, and those who identified the knight with Wignacourt. Those who opposed the Martelli hypothesis appealed to the fact that Martelli, at the time he was portrayed, would have been about 74 years old, whereas the character appears to be younger. This seems to me to be an argument lacking substance, taking into account on the one hand Caravaggio's freedom as a painter of portraits, and on the other hand the vitality of the Florentine knight who in 1617, at the age of 83 (!), was invested with the role of General of the Medici Artillery (Fabbri 2005, p. LXVII).

For my part, I lean towards the identification with Martelli (with however a due margin of doubt), but above all I think that the work may have been executed in Messina where the knight held the role of prior of the Knights of Malta from 1 November 1608 to the end of September 1609. It is no coincidence in my opinion that more or less in the same months Caravaggio lived undisturbed in the Sicilian city, probably under the protection of Martelli, while shortly after his return to Naples (perhaps in the same September 1609), he suffered the revenge of the Maltese with the attack in the Cerriglio tavern.

The outstanding quality of the *Portrait*, is its construction with a rapid, crisp applications of paint, not heeding that certain parts such as the hands are simply sketched-out, which investigates the expression of the face with very rapid, almost non-mimetic brushstrokes; this seems to me to have no close relationship with the execution of the works painted in Malta, which in which the paint is handled much more compactly. The *Portrait* seems to me to be closer to the Messina masterpiece of the *Raising of Lazarus* (Messina, Museo Regionale; fig. 11 on p. 23) and the *Cavadenti* [fig. 3 on p. 5], perhaps also executed for Martelli and, as in the case of the *Portrait* (Fabbri 2005, pp. LXXI–LXXII), arriving with Martelli in Florence in the autumn of 1609 (on 13 November Martelli is documented with certainty in the Medici capital, see Fabbri 2005, p. LXXI).

[GP]

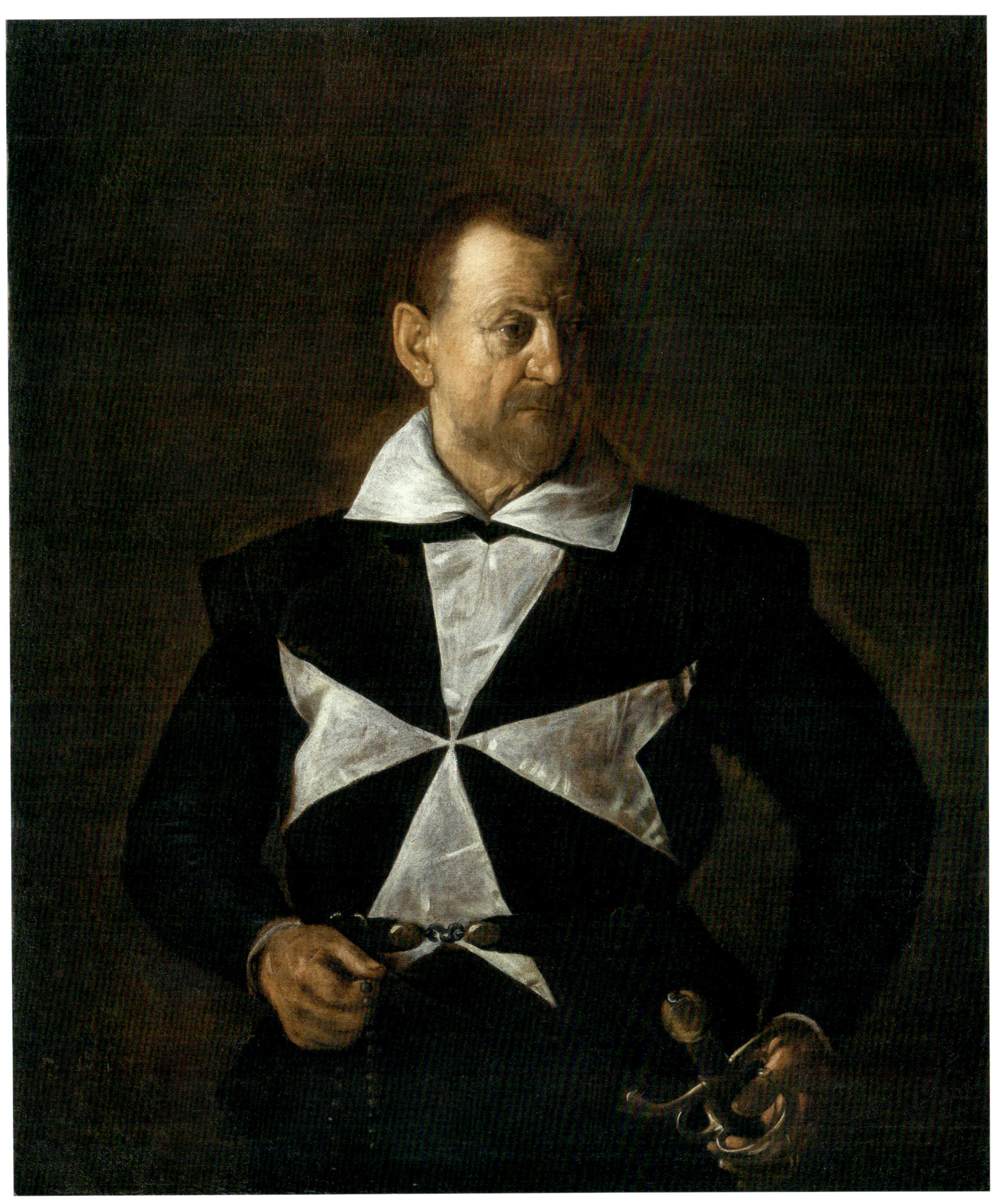

SAINT JOHN THE BAPTIST

c. 1610
oil on canvas, 152 × 125 cm
Galleria Borghese, Rome, inv. 267

Provenance: Rome, Palazzo Borghese (1613); Rome, Galleria Borghese.

Bibliography: Francucci [1613] 1647; Baglione 1642, p. 139; Bellori 1672, pp. 201–215; Vasi 1794, p. 396; Venturi 1909b, pp. 39–41; De Rinaldis, 1948, p. 59; Cinotti 1991, pp. 181, 227; Papi, Lapucci, in *Michelangelo Merisi da Caravaggio. Come nascono* 1991, pp. 348–355; Pacelli 1994, pp. 119–141, in part. pp. 127–128; Spike 2001, pp. 295–299; Puglisi 2003, p. 411; Coliva 2004, pp. 148–149; Lippo 2005, pp. 174–175; Nappi 2007–2008, p. 384; Forgione, in *Caravaggio tra arte* 2012, p. 409, no. A64; Treffers 2013, pp. 243–268; Treffers 2015, pp. 50-63; Schütze 2017, pp. 443–445; Cosmi 2019, pp. 216-217; Vodret 2021a, pp. 322–323; Zuccari 2022a, p. 362; Curti 2023, pp. 97–100; Papa 2023, pp. 111–121; Scanu, in *Caravaggio e come cercarlo* 2024, p. 48; Zappulli 2024, pp. 110–112.

The painting was executed by Caravaggio in 1610; together with two other canvases depicting *Saint John*, a *Magdalene*, and perhaps other paintings also, it had been on board the felucca that in the summer of that year brought the painter first from Naples to Palo, and then to Porto Ercole, on a journey that had as its objectives, Caravaggio had hoped, the establishment of peace with the Tomassoni family, the request for a pardon from the pope, and perhaps a momentary pause in Tuscany while awaiting a definitive return to Rome. The paintings were destined for Cardinal Scipione Borghese, to whom the artist had promised them in order to further the granting of the papal pardon. Events, as we know, did not turn out as expected, and Caravaggio died, according to his biographers Baglione (1642, p. 139) and Bellori (1672, p. 211), on the beach at Porto Ercole, after his release following an arrest, as he watched the boat sail away with the paintings listed above on board, with the exception of the Borghese *Saint John the Baptist*, which remained in what was then the Stato dei Presìdi. The work—unlike the other three which, according to the apostolic nuncio Deodato Gentile, in a series of letters sent to Paul V's nephew (Pacelli 1991, pp. 167–175), were brought back to the Neapolitan city by sailors and delivered to the Marchesa Costanza Colonna, with whom the painter had been living before his departure—was the only painting the artist had managed to disembark before his arrest, which, as recently conjectured by this writer, may have taken place in the Tuscan port and not in Palo, as reported by Gentile. Indeed, as has been made clear, the other paintings were later seized by the Tribunale della Vicaria of Naples, which had opened legal proceedings in relation to Caravaggio's inheritance at the request of the Prior of the Knights of Malta in Naples, Vincenzo Carafa, convinced that the painter still belonged to the Order; this work, together with other objects belonging to the artist, remained in Porto Ercole, until probably the end of August, with the auditor of the Stato dei Presìdi, Diego Roca de Borja, who had carried out the inventory of Caravaggio's possessions (Curti 2023, pp. 97–100). It must have been around this time, in fact, that the work was sent to Naples by order of the Viceroy, the Count of Lemos, Fernando de Castro,

who, at the request of Cardinal Borghese, had sent a letter to Roca on 19 August asking for its immediate return. The *Saint John*, which had arrived soon afterwards in the Neapolitan city, was still in the house of the Viceroy (who also had it copied) on 10 December 1610, when the nuncio wrote to Cardinal Borghese to say that although the work was with the Count of Lemos, it was to be considered as confiscated by the Tribunale, which could not authorise its release because an administrator for the estate had not yet been elected, despite the fact that the nuncio had paid the Vicaria the sum of 300 ducats, a sum established on the basis of an evaluation by the painter Fabrizio Santafede (Nappi 2007–2008, p. 384; Curti 2023, pp. 98–99). The affair would seem to have been resolved in the summer of 1611, because on 26 August, the nuncio informed the cardinal that he had finally succeeded in shipping the painting to Rome wrapped in a taffeta cloth (Zappulli 2024, p. 111). After receiving the painting, the cardinal decided to hang it in the Palazzo di Ripetta, where it is referred to in 1613 in a poem that Scipione Francucci ([1613] 1647, canto IV, st. 266–268) dedicated to his collection. With the amount paid by Gentile in December 1612, the court had, in the meantime, settled the painter's debts to the regular clerics of the church of Santi Apostoli and San Paolo Maggiore (Zappulli 2024, pp. 111–112).

The *Saint John the Baptist*, which is to be considered among Caravaggio's last works in view of the diffuse light in the painting, and the restricted palette of brown and burnt-earth tonalities, has been the object of various iconological interpretations due to the fact that the subject departs from the canonical representations of the Baptist, as his usual attributes—such as the lamb, the reed cross and the scroll with the inscription *Agnus Dei*—are not present. The proposed interpretations agree that these anomalies can be traced to the painter's desire to represent the saint as a forerunner of Christ—Papa (2023, pp. 111–121) identifies the shepherd as Phrixus—, superimposing over the figure of the Baptist that of the Christ of the Passion, and over the *Agnus Dei* the ram of the good shepherd (Kimura 2015, pp. 284–304).
[FCU]

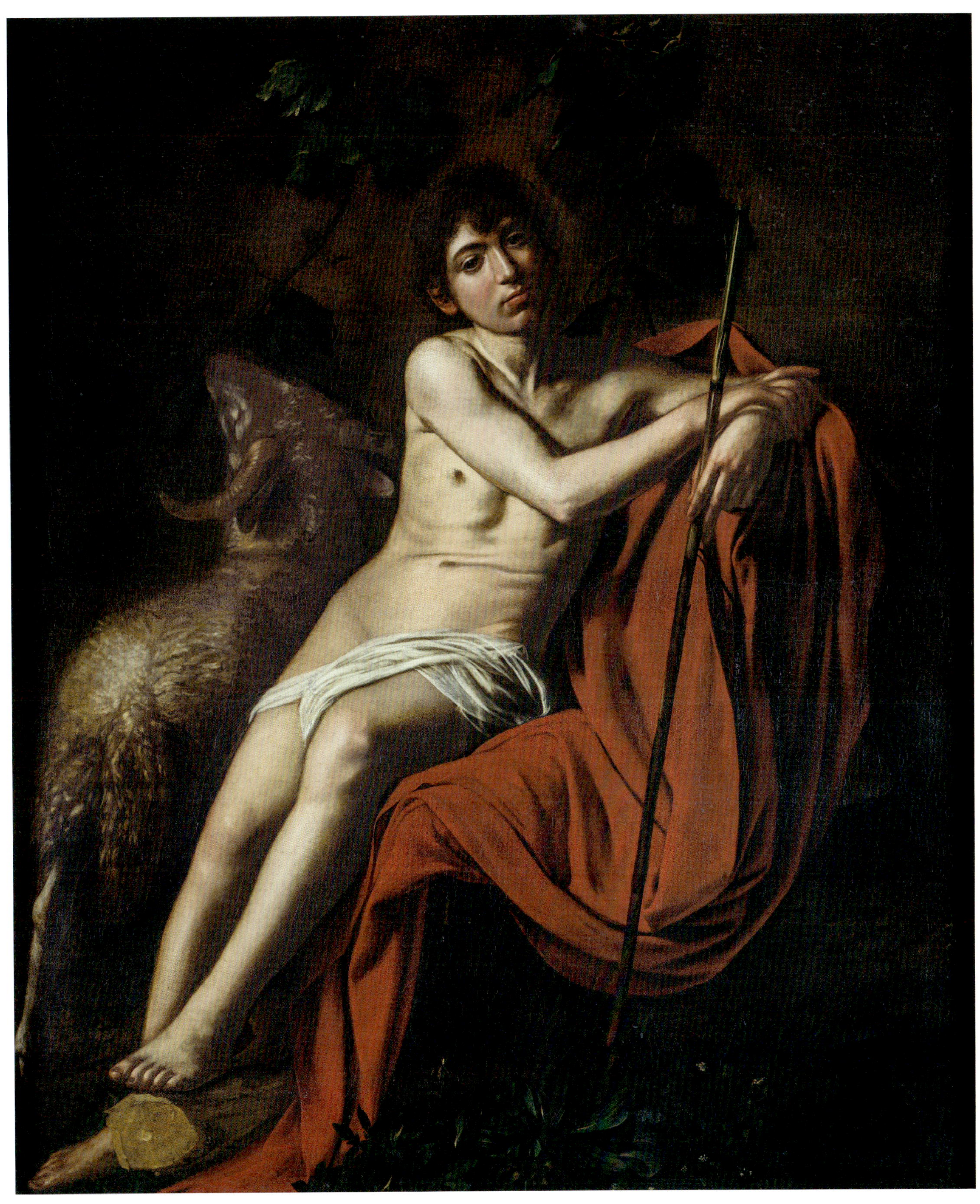

MARTYRDOM OF SAINT URSULA

1610
oil on canvas, 143 × 180 cm
Collezione Intesa Sanpaolo
Gallerie d'Italia - Naples

Provenance: Marco Antonio Doria, Genoa; from 1651, entailed to the heirs of Marco Antonio Doria, Genoa; from 1832, Doria D'Angri family, Naples and then Eboli; from the early decades of the twentieth century, Romano Avezzano family, Eboli; from 1972, Banca Commerciale Italiana (later merged with Intesa Sanpaolo).

Bibliography: Gregori 1975; Pacelli, Bologna 1980, pp. 24–45; Cinotti 1983, pp. 203–641; Delfino 1985; Pacelli 1985; Storchi 1998; Giantomassi, Zari 2004; Gregori 2004, p. 50; Pagano 2004; Fatigati 2005; Schütze 2009; Spike 2010; Denunzio 2014; Porzio 2014; Boccardo 2017; Denunzio 2017; Morandotti 2017; *L'ultimo Caravaggio* 2017; Christiansen 2019; Sorrentino 2024b; Whitlum Cooper 2024.

"I was thinking of sending you the painting of Saint Orzola this week, but to ensure that it was sent well dried, I placed it yesterday in the sun, which caused the varnish to regenerate rather than to dry more quickly, as Caravaggio had applied it very thickly; I want to go back to the afore-mentioned Caravaggio to ask his opinion on what to do to prevent it from spoiling. S[igno]r Dam[iano]o saw it, and was amazed, as were all the others who have seen it" (ASNa, Archivio Doria d'Angri, part II, fascio 290, fols. 9–10, in Pacelli, Bologna 1980).

Although they are so well known, it is worth recalling these few lines from the letter addressed to Marco Antonio Doria by his correspondent in Naples, Lanfranco Massa. Although concise, on the occasion of the finding of the document in 1980, they made it possible to ascertain the authorship, chronology, commissioning and iconography of the painting, as well as to learn of its early conservation history, a circumstance that is highly unusual in art historiography. In subsequent investigations, the same archive yielded extensive documentation in relation to the painting's ownership up to its inclusion in the collections of the Banca Commerciale Italiana in 1972.

Prior to the discovery of this documentary material, Mina Gregori had reinstated the painting as a work by Caravaggio (Gregori 1975), an attribution that did not meet with much success, but would allow the scholar to claim that "it is to connoisseurship, yet to be eradicated . . ., and ahead of the documents, that goes the merit of having restored the work's right to life" (Gregori 2004, p. 50). In the aforementioned letter, dated 11 May 1610, Massa, who was from Ventimiglia and was Caravaggio's intermediary also for other Genoese patrons (Sorrentino 2024b), informs Doria that he had received a painting of Saint Ursula from Caravaggio but could not send it to Genoa before remedying the damage caused by careless exposure to the sun to have it dry it more speedily, once he has sought the artist's advice if not intervention. Sent a few weeks later, the canvas reached Genoa on 18 June and remained there until 1832 when, following complex hereditary vicissitudes, it returned to Naples. It is here, while all memory of its author and its subject was lost, that it remained, in the palazzo Doria d'Angri, before being transferred, at an unspecified date to the family residence in Eboli. The building was later sold, together with all its contents, to the

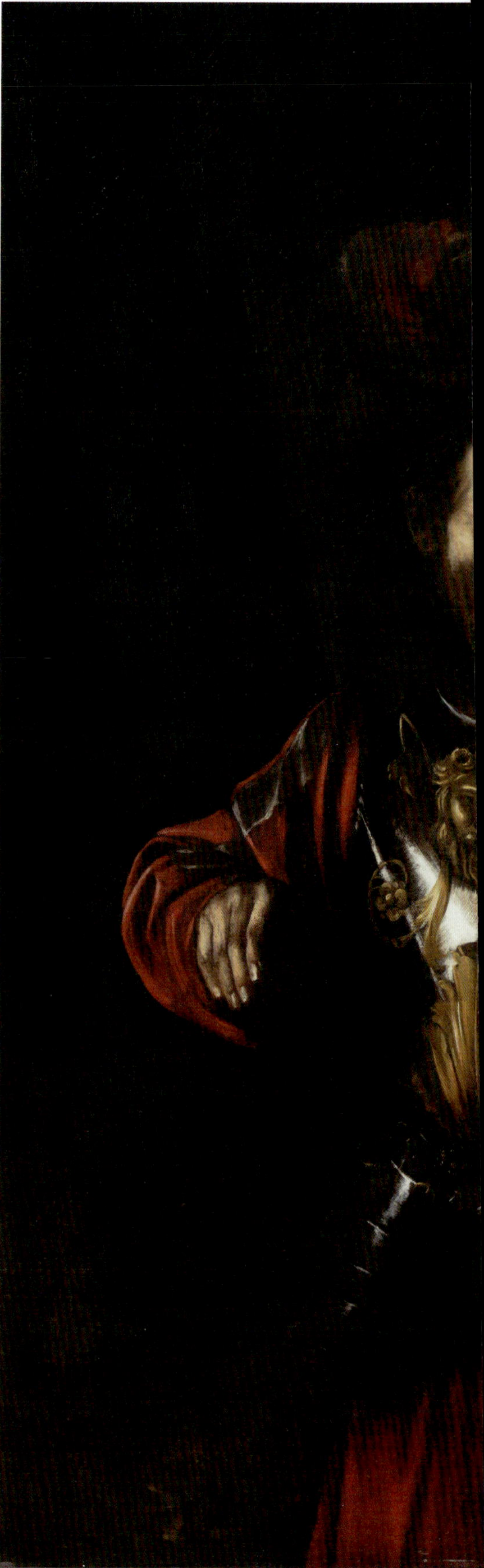

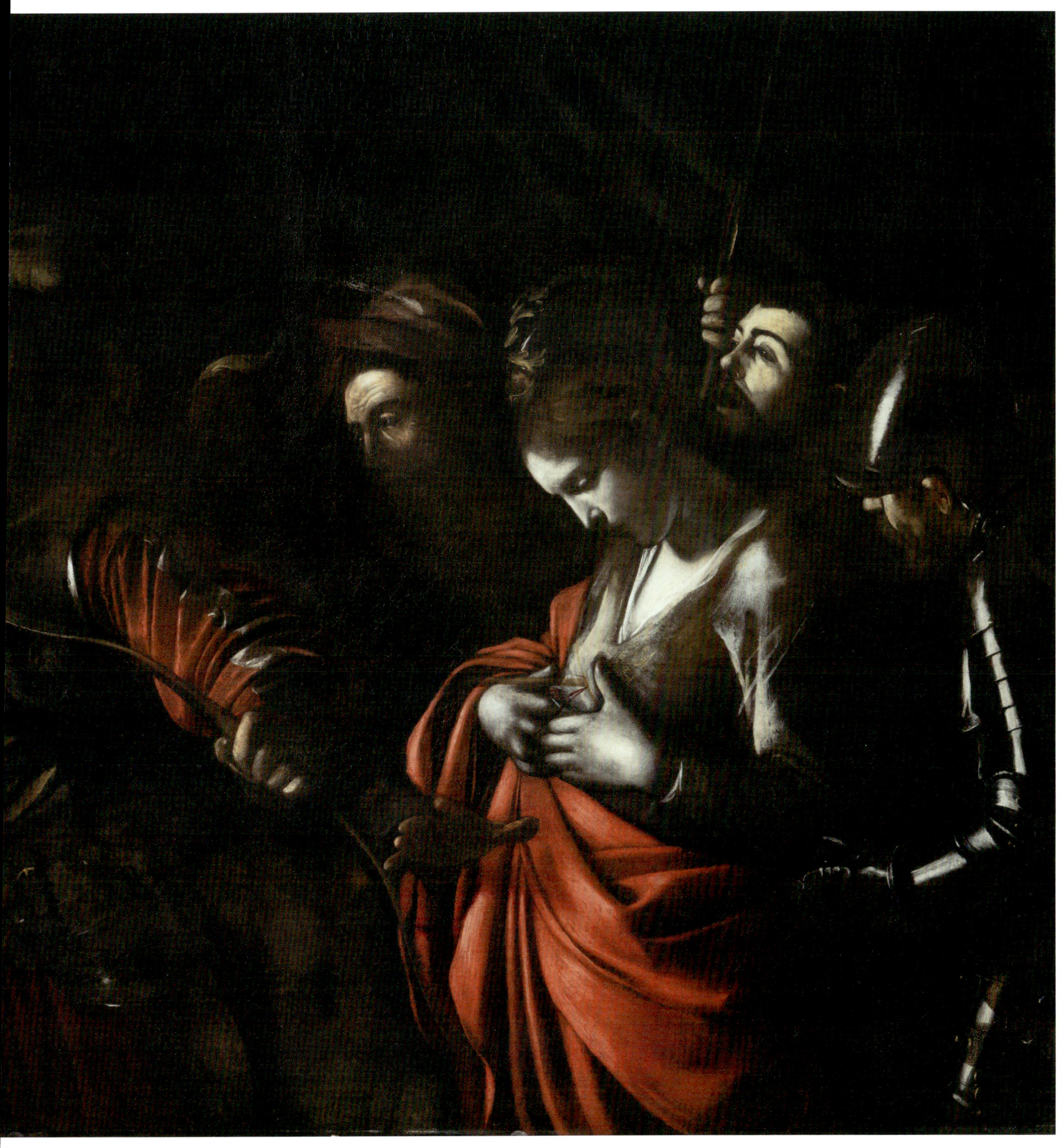

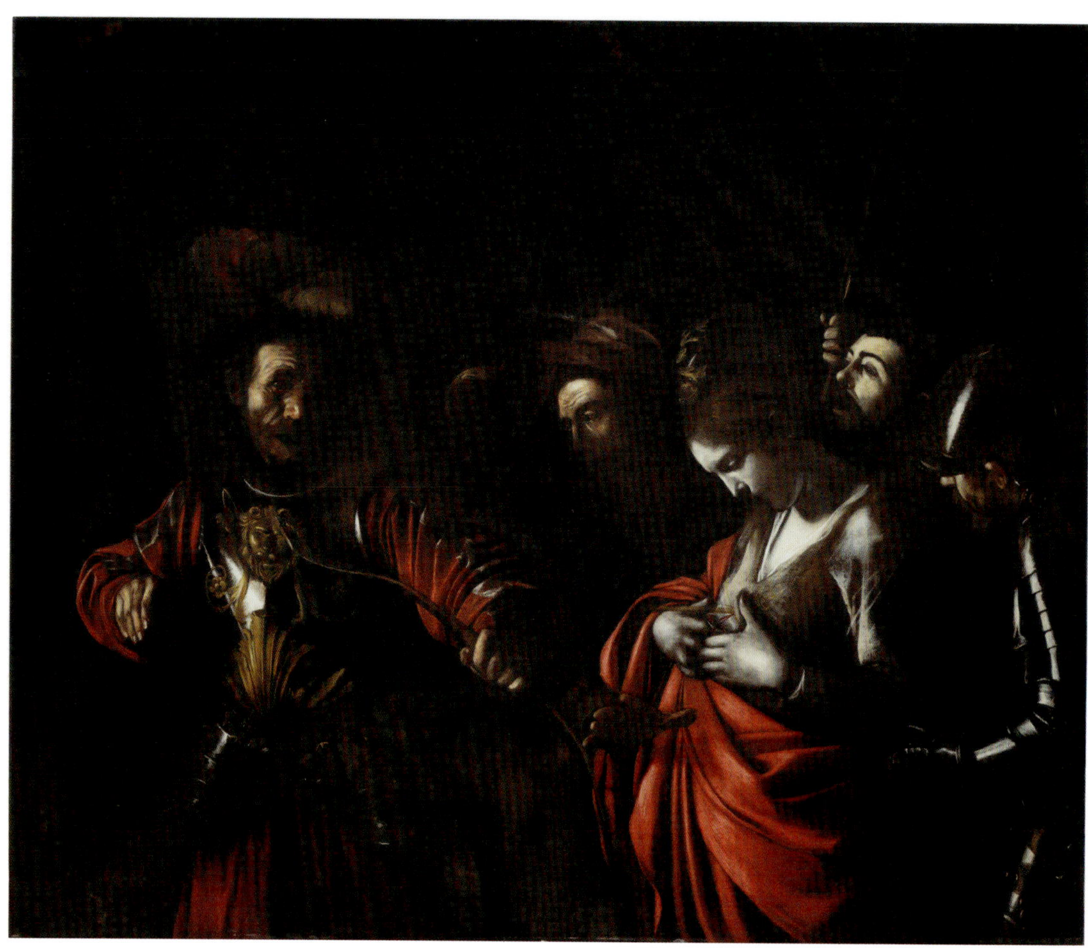

Romano Avezzano barons, from whom the Banca Commerciale Italiana finally purchased the painting as a work by Mattia Preti, depicting an allegorical subject.

The painting's difficult conservation history is also is well documented (Pagano 2004) up to the most recent restoration work. In particular, the treatment carried out in 2004 restored better legibility, allowing for a more detailed understanding of the painting technique and revealing compositional details that one can no longer perceive today (Giantomassi, Zari 2004), the most important of which relate to the outline of two heads, one immediately above the head of Ursula, the other between the archer and the man with the hat behind him. To the latter, it was always thought, belonged the hand—reconstructed during the same restoration—that is outstretched towards the spectator, which in fact could perhaps belong rather to the neighbouring figure that has been missing until now, but which has re-emerged more clearly during the conservation work carried out for this exhibition. The investigations carried out on this occasion also provided more details on the support which consists of two pieces of canvas; the smaller of the two, 13 cm high and stitched horizontally at the top of

the painting, was added at a later date, increasing the size of painting either for aesthetic reasons or for the requirements of display. To ensure the enjoyment of the work in its original format it was decided—then as now—that the added strip at the top should be concealed from sight, by covering it with the frame. The conservation treatment carried out for this exhibition (by Laura Cibrario and Fabiola Jatta, with the scientific support of Maria Beatrice De Ruggieri, Marco Positano, Claudio Seccaroni, under the supervision and direction of the Soprintendenza Archeologia, Belle Arti e Paesaggio per il Comune di Napoli with Alessio Cuccaro and Tina D'Alconzo e Barbara Balbi), guided by new and innovative diagnostic findings, has brought to light further details that enrich the composition. If the addition dates to only a few decades after the execution of the Saint Ursula, as the most recent investigations seem to confirm, the decision to complete the composition with these elements must have been guided by details that were less compromised and therefore more legible than they are today (Christiansen 2019). However, it should be observed that the scene, through iconographic tradition particularly crowded (and we have seen how this was partly so in Caravaggio's intentions), generally had an outdoor setting, in some cases near an encampment tent, the folds of which can be glimpsed in the background together with the spear shafts.

The commissioner of the work is a figure well-known to scholarship: Marco Antonio Doria, second son of the doge Agostino Doria, who managed the family business in the viceroyalty of Naples (Boccardo 2017). His position in the ranks of the local aristocracy had been consolidated through his marriage to Isabella di Carlo della Tolfa, widow of Agostino Grimaldi, prince of Salerno and duke of Eboli, but above all with the purchase in 1612 of the fief of Angri and with the recognition, in 1636, of the princely title that accompanied it. This transaction ensured the name of Doria d'Angri for his descendants, as well as the lasting entrenchment of the dynasty in the viceroyalty (Storchi 1998), which circumstance, as observed above, was at the origin of the painting's return to Naples, bound by the entail that Marco Antonio had himself established (Pacelli 1985; Pagano 2004). Doria's affection for Livia Grimaldi, the daughter of Isabella della Tolfa by her first marriage who on becoming a nun had taken the name of Ursula in the Neapolitan monastery of the Trinità delle Monache, as well as the woman's discomfort as testified by a number of letters (Denunzio 2014), may have been behind the choice of subject for the painting. Livia's choice of the name Orsola (Ursula) for her monastic life is perhaps linked to the fame that Sister Orsola Benincasa enjoyed in Naples at the time, a portrait of whom is documented in the estate of Niccolò Doria, son of Marco Antonio. It should also be noted that a Neapolitan church was named after Sant'Orsola, and that Caravaggio is likely to have been familiar with it, as it was adjacent and connected to the residence of the princes Carafa di Stigliano, today Palazzo Cellamare, where Caravaggio spent his last Neapolitan days, and where he may have painted the *Martyrdom of Saint Ursula* (Denunzio 2017).

While waiting for the damaging effects of the sun to be remedied, the painting was seen by those who frequented Massa's home, and provoked a certain astonishment. Caravaggio's original compositional solution—if one compares it to the more widespread iconographic tradition that saw Ursula's martyrdom accompanied by that of her numerous virgin companions—lies in his depiction, to the exclusion of all else, of the moment in which the saint in Cologne, on her return from a pilgrimage to Rome, is pierced by the arrow shot by the king of the Huns to whom she has refused her hand in marriage, having consecrated herself to God. In accordance with Caravaggio's late manner (which has been explored in some detail in two of the latest exhibitions in which the painting has participated, circumscribed in eloquent dialogue at the Metropolitan Museum in New York with the *Denial of Saint Peter* [fig. 12 on p. 23], and at the National Gallery in London, with the *Salome with the Head of Saint John the Baptist* [fig. 6 on p. 66];

Christiansen 2019, Whitlum Cooper 2024), the narrative is focused on the most dramatic moment of the story, in the instant in which the violent deed has just occurred, the deep obscurity barely pierced by the oblique fall of light. The drama is made actual, as though a common violent episode, thanks to the contemporary dress and armour, and the self-portrait of the painter immediately behind the young martyr with whom he shares the same funereal pallor, almost an omen of their common destiny. The scene is rendered even more ghostly by the means of expression reduced to a bare essential: broad areas of the ground are left exposed, and the palette to a few tonalities with rapidly applied sketched brushstrokes, albeit more detailed than in other works issuing from his brush in these months, perhaps out of greater regard for the prestige of the client (Whitlum Cooper 2024, p. 20).

The weeks that elapsed between the delivery and the shipment of the painting may have been used by Massa to have a copy painted (Delfino 1985), probably also transferred to Liguria, in the context of the controversy between Marco Antonio Doria and his descendants and Massa's heirs (Denunzio 2014). If in Naples the local artistic milieu seems to have been influenced, even if only on the surface, by the powerful innovations introduced in Caravaggio's composition—as testified by Giovanni Bernardino Azzolino's interpretations of it (Porzio 2014), in Genoa, the presence of the painting "was met with almost complete silence" (Morandotti 2017), and the almost ecstatic depictions of the same subject by painters such as Bernardo Strozzi and Giulio Cesare Procaccini, who also frequented the house of Marco Antonio Doria, appear to have been completely deaf to Caravaggio's dramatic "cry".

[AED]

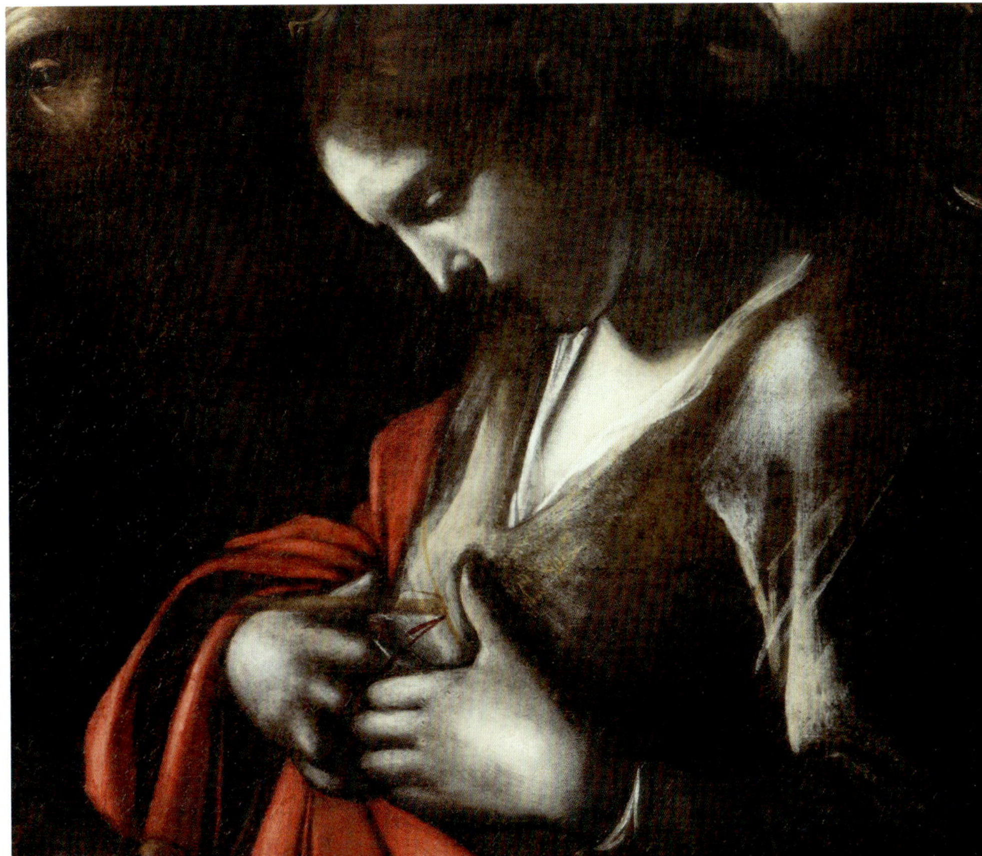

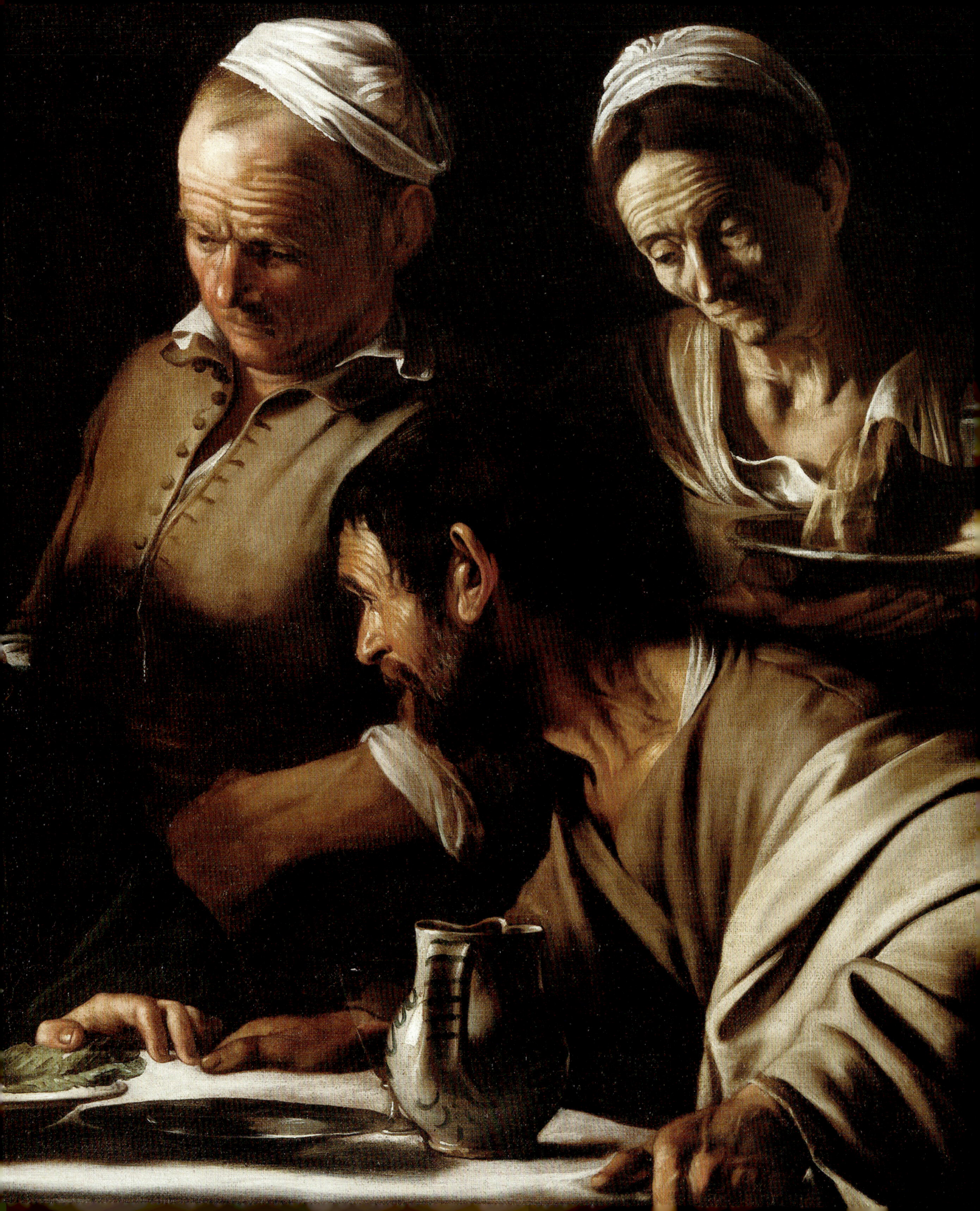

BIBLIOGRAPHY

1604
Van Mander 1604
K. van Mander, *Het Schilder-Boeck*, Harlem 1604.

1616
Comite 1616
O. Comite, *La notte overo il nascimento di Christo*, Naples 1616.

1627
Scaglia 1627
G. Scaglia, *Lettere del Caval. Marino. Graui, argute, e facete. Non più stampate...*, Venice 1627.

1629
Marino 1629
G. B. Marino, *La Galeria*, Venice 1629.

1630
Bolvito before 1630
F. Bolvito, *Notitia della Casa di Santi Apostoli . . .*, ms., before 1630, Biblioteca Nazionale di Napoli "Vittorio Emanuele III", Fondo San Martino, ms. 521.

1638
Carducho 1638
V. Carducho, *Dialogos de la pintura: su defensa, origen, esse[n]cia, definicion, modos y diferencias*, Madrid 1638.

Celio [1620–1624] 1638
G. Celio, *Memoria dell'habito di Christo. Delli nomi dell'artefici delle pitture, che sono in alcune chiese, facciate, e palazzi di Roma fatta dal Signor Gaspare Celio* (c. 1620–1624), Naples 1638.

1642
Baglione 1642
G. Baglione, *Le vite de' pittori scultori et architetti. Dal Pontificato di Gregorio XIII fino a tutto quello d'Urbano Ottavo*, Rome 1642.

1647
Brusoni 1647
G. Brusoni, *Le glorie de gli Incogniti o vero Gli huomini illustri dell'Accademia de' signori Incogniti*, Venice 1647.

Francucci [1613] 1647
S. Francucci, *La Galleria dell'Illustrissimo e Reverendissimo Signor Scipione Cardinale Borghese cantata in versi* [1613], Arezzo 1647, Canto IV, St. 266–268.

1650
Manilli 1650
I. Manilli, *Villa Borghese fuori di Porta Pinciana*, Rome 1650.

1654–1688
De Lellis c. 1654–1688
C. De Lellis, *Aggiunta alla* Napoli sacra *dell'Engenio*, ms. c. 1654–1688, Biblioteca Nazionale di Napoli "Vittorio Emanuele III", X B 20–24.

1672
Bellori 1672
G. P. Bellori, *Le Vite de' pittori, scultori et architetti moderni*, Rome 1672.

1674
Scaramuccia 1674
L. P. Scaramuccia, *Le finezze de' pennelli italiani ammirate e studiate da Girupeno sotto la scorta e disciplina del genio di Raffaello d'Urbino*, Pavia 1674.

1675
Giustiniani 1675
M. Giustiniani, *Lettere memorabili dell'abbate Michele Giustiniani*, Rome 1675.

Sandrart 1675
J. von Sandrart, *L'Academia todesca della architectura, scultura & pittura. Oder Teutsche Academie der edlen Bau-, Bild- und Mahlerey-Künste*, Nurenberg 1675; annotated edition by Th. Kirchner *et al.* :http://www.sandrart.net.

1688
Malvasia 1688
C. C. Malvasia, *Felsina pittrice. Vite de pittori Bolognesi*, Bologna 1688.

1692
Celano 1692
C. Celano, *Notitie del bello, dell'antico, e del curioso della città di Napoli . . . divise in diece giornate . . .*, Naples 1692.

1700
Parrino 1700
D. A. Parrino, *Napoli città nobilissima, antica e fedelissima . . .*, Naples 1700.

1703–1715
Dal Pozzo 1703–1715
B. Dal Pozzo, *Historia della sacra religione militare di S. Giovanni gerosolimitano detta di Malta*, Verona 1703–1715.

1756
Cochin 1756
Ch.-N. Cochin, *Voyage pittoresque d'Italie, ou recueil de notes sur les ouvrages de peinture et de sculpture, qu'on voit dans les principales villes d'Italie*, Paris 1756.

1772
Passeri 1772
G. Passeri, *Vite de' pittori, scultori ed architetti che hanno lavorato in Roma*, Rome 1772.

1788–1789
Sigismondo 1788–1789
G. Sigismondo, *Descrizione della città di Napoli e suoi borghi*, Naples 1788–1789.

1794
Vasi 1794
M. Vasi, *Itinerario della pittura*, Rome 1794.

1811
Cancellieri 1811
F. Cancellieri, *Il mercato, il lago dell'acqua vergine ed il palazzo panfiliano nel Circo Agonale detto volgarmente Piazza Navona*, Rome 1811.

1824
Descartes 1824
R. Descartes, *La dioptrique*, in *Œuvres*, edited by V. Cousin, V, Paris 1824.

1868
Baschet 1868
A. Baschet, "François Porbus. Peintre de portraits à la cour de Mantoue," in *Gazette des Beaux-Arts*, XXV, 1868, 5, pp. 438–456.

1885
Faraglia 1885
N. F. Faraglia, "Notizie di alcuni artisti che lavorarono nella chiesa di S. Martino e nel Tesoro di S. Gennaro," in *Archivio storico per le province napoletane* X, 1885, pp. 455–461.

1886
Bredius, Roever 1886
A. Bredius, N. de Roever, "Pieter Lastman en François Venant," in *Oud Holland* IV, 1886, pp. 1–23.

1889
Bruno 1889
G. Bruno, *De compositione imaginum liber*, in *Opera latine conscripta*, edited by F. Tocco and H. Vitelli, II, III, Florence 1889.

Vicchi 1889
L. Vicchi, *Dieci quadri della galleria Sciarra*, Rome 1889.

1892
Mariotti 1892
F. Mariotti, *La legislazione delle belle arti*, 1892.

1906
Saccà 1906
V. Saccà, "Michelangelo da Caravaggio pittore. Studi e ricerche," in *Archivio Storico Messinese* VII, I–II, 1906, pp. 40–69.

1909
Baedeker 1909
K. Baedeker, *Central Italy and Rome*, London–New York 1909.

Venturi 1909a
L. Venturi, "Il 1609 e la pittura italiana," in *Nuova Antologia di Lettere, Scienze ed Arti* CXLIV, 16 December 1909, pp. 2–7.

Venturi 1909b
L. Venturi, "Note sulla Galleria Borghese," in *L'Arte* XII, 1909, pp. 31–50.

1911
***Mostra del ritratto* 1911**
Mostra del ritratto italiano: dalla fine del sec. XVI all'anno 1861, exhibition catalogue (Florence, Palazzo Vecchio, March–July 1911), Florence 1911.

1912
Venturi 1912
L. Venturi, "Opere inedite di Michelangelo da Caravaggio," in *Bollettino d'arte del Ministero della Pubblica Istruzione*, VI, 1, 1912, pp. 1–18.

1916
Longhi 1916
R. Longhi, *Gentileschi, padre e figlia*, in *L'Arte* XLX, 19, 1916, pp. 245–314.

1920
Orbaan 1920
J. A. F. Orbaan, *Documenti sul barocco in Roma*, Rome 1920.

1922
Fry 1922
R. Fry, "Settecentismo," in *The Burlington Magazine for Connoisseurs* XLI, 235, 1922, pp. 158–169.

1922–1923
Marangoni 1922–1923
M. Marangoni, "Nota sul Caravaggio alla mostra del Sei e Settecento," in *Bollettino d'Arte*, II, 5, 1922–1923, pp. 217–229.

1923
Voss 1923
H. Voss, "Caravaggio's Frühzeit: BeiträgezurKritik seiner Werke und seiner Entwicklung," in *Jahrbuch der Preuszischen Kunstsammlungen* XLIV, 1923, pp. 73–98.

1925
Borenius 1925
T. Borenius, "An Early Caravaggio Re-discovered," in *Apollo* II, 7, 1925, pp. 23–26.

Voss 1925
H. Voss, *Die Malerei des Barock in Rom*, Berlin 1925.

1927
Longhi 1927
R. Longhi, "Precisazioni nelle gallerie italiane: I. R. Galleria Borghese; Michelangelo da Caravaggio," in *Vita Artistica* II, 1927, pp. 28–35.

1928
Longhi 1928
R. Longhi, "Quesiti caravaggeschi," in *Pinacotheca* I, 1, 1928, pp. 17–33.

Pevsner 1928
N. Pevsner, *Barockmalerei in den romanischen Ländern*, I, Wildpark–Potsdam 1928.

Venturi 1928
A. Venturi, "Un quadro ignorato di Michelangelo da Caravaggio," in *L'Arte* XXXI, 1928, pp. 58–59.

1929
Collins Baker 1929
C. H. Collins Baker, *Catalogue of the Pictures at Hampton Court*, Glasgow 1929.

Marangoni 1929
M. Marangoni, "An Unpublished Caravaggio in Trieste," in *International Studio* XCIV, 389, 1929, pp. 34–35, 106.

1932
Dupront 1932
A. Dupront, "Autour de saint Filippo Neri: de l'optimisme chrétien," in *Mélanges d'archéologie et d'histoire* 49, 1932, pp. 219–259.

1934
Passeri [1772] 1934
Giovan Battista Passeri, *Vite dei pittori, scultori e architetti che hanno lavorato in Roma, morti dal 1641 al 1673* [Rome 1772], edited by J. Hess, Leipzig–Vienna 1934.

1935
Dupront 1935
A. Dupront, "D'un "Humanisme chrétien" en Italie à la fin du XVIᵉ siècle," in *Revue Historique* 175, 1935, pp. 296–307.

1936
De Rinaldis 1936
A. De Rinaldis, "Documenti per la storia della R. Galleria Borghese in Roma: I. le opere d'arte sequestrate al Cavalier d'Arpino," in *Archivi* III, 1936, pp. 110–118.

1938
Oertel 1938
R. Oertel, "Neapolitanische Malerei des 17.–19. Jahunderts" (review in *La mostra della pittura napoletana dei secoli XVII–XVIII–IX*, Napoli 1938), in *Pantheon* XXII, pp. 225–232.

1941
Giannone [c. 1771–1773] 1941
O. Giannone, *Giunte sulle vite de' pittori napoletani* [ms. c. 1771–1773], formerly Naples, Museo civico Gaetano Filangieri principe di Satriano, edited by O. Morisani, Naples 1941.

1943
Longhi 1943
R. Longhi, "Ultimi studi su Caravaggio e la sua cerchia," in *Proporzioni* I, 1943, pp. 5–63.

1948
De Rinaldis 1948
A. De Rinaldis, *Catalogo della Galleria Borghese*, Rome 1948.

1950
Berenson 1950
B. Berenson, *Del Caravaggio, delle sue incongruenze e della sua fama*, edited by L. Vertova, Florence 1950.

Venturi 1950
L. Venturi, "Il Baro di Caravaggio ritrovato," in *Commentari* I, January–March 1950, pp. 41–42.

1951
Arslan 1951
E. Arslan, "Appunto su Caravaggio," in *Aut Aut* I, 5, 1951, pp. 444–451.

Berenson 1951
B. Berenson, *Del Caravaggio delle sue incongruenze e della sua fama*, Florence 1951.

Longhi 1951a
R. Longhi, *Caravaggio e i Caravaggeschi*, exhibition catalogue (Milan, Palazzo Reale, April–June 1951), Florence 1951.

Longhi 1951b
R. Longhi, "Michelangelo Merisi (il "Caravaggio"). Regesto", in Longhi 1951a, pp. 5–12.

Longhi 1951c
R. Longhi, "La 'Giuditta' nel percorso del Caravaggio," in *Paragone* II, 19, 1951, pp. 10–18; in R. Longhi, *Studi caravaggeschi*, II, Florence, 2000, pp. 79–85.

Longhi 1951d
R. Longhi, "Sui margini caravaggeschi," in *Paragone* XXI, 2, 1951, pp. 20–34.

Mahon 1951
D. Mahon, "Egregius in Urbe Pictor: Caravaggio Revised," in *The Burlington Magazine* XCIII, 580, 1951, pp. 223–234.

Venturi 1951
L. Venturi, *Il Caravaggio*, Novara, 1951.

Voss 1951
H. Voss, "Ein unbekanntes Frühwerk Caravaggios," in *Die Kunst und das schöne Heim* 49, 1951, pp. 410–412.

1952
Longhi 1952
R. Longhi, *Il Caravaggio*, Milan 1952.

Mahon 1952
D. Mahon, "Addenda to Caravaggio," in *The Burlington Magazine* XCIV, 586, 1952, pp. 2–23.

1953
Berenson 1953
B. Berenson, *Caravaggio: His Incongruity and His Fame*, London 1953.

Gombrich 1953
E. H. Gombrich, "Review of R. Hinks and B. Berenson on Caravaggio," in *The Listener* 50, 1953, p. 1134.

1954
Longhi [1954] 2000
R. Longhi, "L''Ecce Homo' del Caravaggio a Genova," in *Paragone* V, 51, 1954, pp. 3–14; riedition in R. Longhi, *Studi Caravaggeschi*, II, Florence 2000, pp. 121–129.

1955
Battisti 1955
E. Battisti, "Alcuni documenti su opere del Caravaggio," in *Commentari* 6, July–September, 1955, pp. 173–183.

Friedländer 1955
W. Friedländer, *Caravaggio Studies*, Princeton 1955.

1956
Argan 1956
G. C. Argan, "Il "Realismo" nella poetica del Caravaggio," in *Scritti di storia dell'arte in onore di Lionello Venturi*, Rome 1956, II, pp. 25–41.

Longhi 1956
R. Longhi, *Studi caravaggeschi,* I (1943–1968), Turin 1956.

1956–1957
Mancini [c. 1619–1621] 1956–1957
G. Mancini, *Considerazioni sulla pittura* [ms. c. 1619–1621], critical edition edited by A. Marucchi, with commentary by L. Salerno, 2 vols., Rome 1956–1957.

1958
Aristotle 1958
Aristotle, *On Poetry and Style*, translated and edited by G. M. A. Grube, Indianapolis–Cambridge 1958.

Wagner 1958
H. Wagner, *Michelangelo da Caravaggio*, Bern 1958.

1959
Arslan 1959
E. Arslan, "Nota caravaggesca," in *Arte Antica e Moderna* II, 6, 1959, pp. 191–218.

Della Pergola 1959
P. Della Pergola, *Galleria Borghese: i dipinti*, Rome 1959.

Longhi 1959
R. Longhi, "Un'opera estrema del Caravaggio," in *Paragone. Arte* IX, 111, 1959, pp. 21–32.

1960
Susinno [1724] 1960
F. Susinno, *Le vite de' pittori messinesi e di altri che fiorirono in Messina* [ms. 1724], edited by V. Martinelli, Florence 1960.

1961
Moir 1961
A. Moir, "The 'Boy with a flute' by Bartolomeo Manfredi," in *Bulletin of the Art Division* 13, 1961, pp. 3–14.

1962
Torre 1962
S. Torre, "Abbiamo trovato un quadro. È un Caravaggio?," in *Il Giornale d'Italia* LXI, 9–10, 1962, p. 9.

1963
Haskell 1963
F. Haskell, *Patrons and Painters. A Study in the Relations Between Italian Art and Society in the Age of the Baroque,* New York 1963.

Longhi 1963
R. Longhi, "Il vero 'Maffeo Barberini' del Caravaggio," in *Paragone* XIV, 165, 1963, pp. 3–11.

Venturi 1963
L. Venturi, *Il Caravaggio*, Novara 1963.

1964
Della Pergola 1964
P. Della Pergola, "L'Inventario Borghese del 1693," in *Arte antica e moderna* 28, 1964, pp. 219–230, 460.

Macrae 1964
D. Macrae, "Observations on the Sword in Caravaggio," in *The Burlington Magazine,* CVI, 738, 1964, pp. 412–416.

1965
Röttgen 1965
H. Röttgen, "Die Stellung der Contarelli-Kapelle in Caravaggios Werk," in *Zeitschrift für Kunstgeschichte* 28, 1–2, 1965, pp. 47–68.

1966
Causa 1966
R. Causa, *Caravaggio* (I Maestri del colore, 154–155), Milan 1966.

Rotondi, Urbani 1966
P. Rotondi, G. Urbani, "Il restauro delle tele del Caravaggio in S. Luigi dei Francesi a Roma," in *Bollettino dell'Istituto Centrale del Restauro*, 17, 1966, pp. 1–120.

1967
D'Onofrio 1967
C. D'Onofrio, *Roma vista da Roma*, Rome 1967.

Guttuso, Ottino Della Chiesa 1967
R. Guttuso, A. Ottino Della Chiesa, *L'opera completa del Caravaggio* (Classici dell'arte Rizzoli), Milan 1967.

Lavin 1967
M.A. Lavin, "Caravaggio Documents from the Barberini Archive," in *The Burlington Magazine* CIX, 773, 1967, pp. 470–473.

1968
Brugnoli 1968
M. V. Brugnoli, "Un 'San Francesco' da attribuire al Caravaggio e la sua copia," in *Bollettino d'arte* LIII, 1, 1968, pp. 11–15.

Carderi 1968
B. Carderi, "Caravaggio in Abruzzo?," in *Abruzzo*,VI, 2–3, 1968, pp. 421–423.

Longhi 1968
R. Longhi, *Caravaggio,* Rome 1968.

Fagiolo dell'Arco 1968
M. Fagiolo dell'Arco, "Le 'Opere di misericordia', contributo alla poetica del Caravaggio," in *L'Arte* 1, 1968, pp. 37–61.

Longhi 1968
R. Longhi, *Caravaggio*, Rome 1968.

1969
Askew 1969
P. Askew, "The Angelic Consolation of St. Francis of Assisi in Post-Tridentine Italian Painting," in *Journal of the Warburg and Courtauld Institutes*, 32 (1969), pp. 280–306.

Fagiolo dell'Arco 1969
M. Fagiolo dell'Arco, *Le* Opere di misericordia. *Contributo alla poetica del Caravaggio*, Milan 1969.

Longhi 1969
R. Longhi, "'Giovanni della Voltolina' a Palazzo Mattei," in *Paragone* 20, 233, 1969, pp. 59–62.

1970
Argan 1970
G. C. Argan, *Storia dell'arte italiana*, 3 vols., Florence 1970.

Borea 1970
E. Borea, *Caravaggio e caravaggeschi nelle Gallerie di Firenze*, exhibition catalogue (Florence, Palazzo Pitti, summer 1970), Florence 1970.

Matthiesen, Pepper 1970
P. Matthiesen, S. Pepper, *Guido Reni. An Early Masterpiece Discovered in Liguria*, in *Apollo* XCI, 1970, p. 456.

Salerno 1970
L. Salerno, "Caravaggio e i caravaggeschi," in *Storia dell'arte* 7–8, 1970, pp. 234–248.

1971
Calvesi 1971
M. Calvesi, "Caravaggio o la ricerca della salvazione," in *Storia dell'arte* 9–10, 1971, pp. 93–141.

D'Andrea 1971
G. F. D'Andrea, "Il Caravaggio morì veramente nel 1610?," in *Il Rievocatore* XXII, 4–6, pp. 1–5.

Frommel 1971
C. L. Frommel, "Caravaggios Frühwerk und der Kardinal Francesco Maria del Monte," in *Storia dell'arte* 9–10, January–June 1971, pp. 5–52.

Kirwin 1971
C. W. Kirwin, "Addenda to Cardinal Francesco Maria del Monte's Inventory. The Date of the Sale of Various Notable Paintings," in *Storia dell'arte* 9–10, January–June 1971, pp. 53–56.

Posner 1971
D. Posner, "Caravaggio's Homo-Erotic Early Works," in *The Art Quarterly* 34, 1971, pp. 301–324.

Spear 1971
R. E. Spear, *Caravaggio and His Followers,* exhibition catalogue (Cleveland Museum of Art, 27 October 1971–2 January 1972), Cleveland 1971, pp. 11, 75–76.

1972
Longhi [1935] 1972
R. Longhi, "I pittori della realtà in Francia, ovvero i Caravaggeschi francesi del Seicento," in *L'Italia letteraria* 19 January 1935, reprinted in *Paragone* 269, 1972, pp. 3–18.

Pugliese, Rigano 1972
A. Pugliese, S. Rigano, *Martino Lunghi il giovane architetto*, Rome 1972.

Safarik 1972
E. A. Safarik, "Giuditta taglia la testa ad Oloferne," in *Acquisti della Galleria Nazionale d'Arte Antica 1970–72,* Rome 1972, pp. 24–30.

1973
Scherliess 1973
V. Scherliess, "Zu Caravaggios Musica," in *Mitteilungen des Kunsthistorischen Institutes in Florenz* XVII, 1973/1, pp. 141–148.

1974
Cummings 1974
F. J. Cummings, "Detroit's 'Conversion of the Magdalen' (The Alzaga Caravaggio)," in *The Burlington Magazine* CXVI, 859, 1974, pp. 563–564, 572–578.

Gregori 1974
M. Gregori, "A New Painting and Some Observations on Caravaggio's Journey to Malta," in *The Burlington Magazine* CXVI, 859, October 1974, pp. 594–603.

Marini 1974
M. Marini, *Io, Michelangelo da Caravaggio*, Rome 1974

Röttgen 1974
H. Röttgen, *Il Caravaggio. Ricerche e interpretazioni*, Rome 1974.

Spezzaferro 1974a
L. Spezzaferro, "The Documentary Findings: Ottavio Costa as a Patron of Caravaggio," in *The Burlington Magazine* CXVI, 859, 1974, pp. 579–586.

Spezzaferro 1974b
L. Spezzaferro, "La pala dei Palafrenieri," in *Atti del Colloquio sul tema Caravaggio e i Caravaggeschi*, Rome 1974, pp. 125–138.

1975
Gregori 1975
M. Gregori, "Significato delle mostre caravaggesche dal 1951 ad oggi," in *Novità sul Caravaggio* 1975, pp. 27–60.

Lavin 1975
M. A. Lavin, *Seventh-Century Barberini Documents and Inventories of Art*, New York 1975.

***Novità sul Caravaggio* 1975**
Novità sul Caravaggio: saggi e contributi, Proceedings of the international conference of Caravaggio studies in Bergamo, edited by M. Cinotti, Cinisello Balsamo 1975.

Prohaska 1975
W. Prohaska, "Carlo Sellitto," in *The Burlington Magazine* CXVII, 862, January 1975, pp. 3–11.

Spezzaferro 1975
L. Spezzaferro, "Ottavio Costa e Caravaggio. Certezze e problemi," in *Novità sul Caravaggio* 1975, pp. 103–118.

1976
Bellori [1672] 1976
G. P. Bellori, *Le vite de' pittori scultori e architetti moderni* [Roma 1672], edited by E. Borea, Turin 1976.

Damisch 1976
H. Damisch, "D'un Narcisse l'autre", in *Narcisses. Nouvelle Revue de Psychanalyse* 13, 1976, pp. 109–146.

Friedländer [1955] 1976
W. Friedländer *Caravaggio Studies*, Princeton University Press 1976.

Moir 1976
A. Moir, *Caravaggio and His Copyists*, New York 1976.

Zeri 1976
F. Zeri, "Sull'esecuzione di 'nature morte' nella bottega del Cavalier d'Arpino e sulla presenza ivi del giovane Caravaggio," in *Diari di lavoro 2*, Turin 1976, pp. 92–103; riedited in F. Zeri, *Giorno per giorno nella pittura*, Turin 1998, pp. 21–27.

1977
Bigazzi 1977
I. Bigazzi, *Il palazzo non finito*, Bologna 1977.

Cuzin 1977
J. P. Cuzin, *La diseuse de bonne aventure de Caravage*, exhibition catalogue (Paris, Musée du Louvre, Pavillon de Flore, 10 June–31 August), edited by J.-P. Cuzin, Paris 1977.

Micheloni 1977
P. Micheloni, *Il mondo dei denti e la sua storia. Dall'epoca gota al Seicento*, Rome 1977.

Pacelli 1977
V. Pacelli, "New documents concerning Caravaggio in Naples," in *The Burlington Magazine* CXIX, 897, 1977, pp. 819–829.

Rosa 1977
M. Rosa, "Nota critica," in J. P. Gutton, *La società e i poveri*, Milan 1977, pp. 161–179.

1978
Pullan 1978
B. Pullan, "Poveri mendicanti e vagabondi (sec. XIV–XVII)," in *Storia d'Italia*, Annali, I, *Dal feudalesimo al capitalismo*, edited by R. Romano and C. Vivanti, Turin 1978, pp. 981–1047.

1979
Marini 1979
M. Marini, *"Michael Angelus Caravaggio Romanus". Rassegna degli studi e proposte*, Rome 1979.

Marino [1620] 1979
G. B. Marino, *La Galeria... Distinta in Pittura, e Scultura* [Venezia 1620], edited by M. Pieri, 2 vols., Padua 1979.

Marsicola 1979
C. Marsicola, "Note allo Spadarino," in *Prospettiva* XVI, January 1979, pp. 45–52.

Nicolson 1979
B. Nicolson, *The International Caravaggesque Movement. Lists of Pictures by Caravaggio and his Followers throughout Europe from 1590 to 1650,* Oxford 1979.

1979–1980
Volpi, Ruta, Del Gratta, 1979–1980
G. Volpi, L. Ruta, R. Del Gratta, *Acta graduum Academiae pisanae*, Pisa 1979–1980.

1980
Fulco 1980
G. Fulco, "'Ammirate l'altissimo pittore': Caravaggio nelle rime inedite di Marzio Milesi," in *Ricerche di storia dell'arte* 10, 1980, pp. 65–89.

Pacelli, Bologna 1980
V. Pacelli, F. Bologna, "Caravaggio, 1610: la 'Sant'Orsola confitta dal Tiranno' per Marcantonio Doria," in *Prospettiva* 23, October 1980, pp. 24–45.

Politi 1980
G. Politi, "Poveri e potenti," in *Studi Storici* 4, October–December 1980, pp. 855–864.

Rosa 1980
M. Rosa, "Chiesa, idee sui poveri e assistenza in Italia dal Cinque al

Settecento," in *Società e Storia* 10, 1980, pp. 775–806.

Spezzaferro 1980
L. Spezzaferro, "Caravaggio rifiutato? 1. Il problema della prima versione del San Matteo," in *Ricerche di Storia dell'arte* 10, 1980, pp. 49–66.

1981
Giustiniani [c. 1620–1630] 1981
V. Giustiniani, *Discorso sopra la pittura* (c. 1620–1630), in *Discorsi sulle arti e sui mestieri*, edited by A. Banti, Florence 1981.

Marini 1981a
M. Marini, "Caravaggio e il naturalismo internazionale," in *Storia dell'arte italiana*, 6.1 *Cinquecento e Seicento*, Turin 1981.

Marini 1981b
M. Marini, "Un'estrema residenza e un ignoto aiuto del Caravaggio in Roma," in *Antologia di Belle Arti* 19–20, 1981, pp. 180–183.

Zuccari 1981
A. Zuccari, "La politica culturale dell'Oratorio Romano nella seconda metà del Cinquecento," in *Storia dell'arte* 41, 1981, pp. 76–112.

1982
Galasso 1982
G. Galasso, *Napoli spagnola dopo Masaniello. Politica, cultura, società*, Florence 1982.

Longhi [1952] 1982
R. Longhi, *Il Caravaggio* (Milan 1952), edited by G. Previtali, Rome 1982.

Longhi [1968] 1982
R. Longhi, *Caravaggio* (Rome 1968), new edition, edited by G. Previtali, Rome 1982.

***Painting in Naples* 1982**
Painting in Naples 1606–1705. From Caravaggio to Giordano, exhibition catalogue (London, Royal Academy of Arts, 2 October–12 December 1982), edited by C. Whitfield and J. Martineau, London 1982.

***Timore e carità* 1982**
Timore e carità. I poveri nell'Italia Moderna, proceedings of the conference "Pauperismo e assistenza negli antichi stati italiani" (Cremona, 28–30 March 1980), edited by G. Politi, M. Rosa, F. Della Peruta, Cremona 1982.

1983
Cinotti 1983
M. Cinotti, "Michelangelo Merisi detto il Caravaggio. Tutte le opere," critical essay by G.A. Dell'Acqua, in *I pittori bergamaschi dal XIII al XIX secolo. Il Seicento*, I, Bergamo 1983, pp. 203–641.

Dell'Acqua 1983
G.A. Dell'Acqua, "Caravaggio. La critica," in M. Cinotti, *Michelangelo Merisi detto il Caravaggio. Tutte le opere*, in *I pittori bergamaschi dal XIII al XIX secolo. Il Seicento*, Bergamo 1983, pp. 257–287.

Hibbard 1983
H. Hibbard, *Caravaggio*, London 1983.

Trinchieri Camiz, Ziino 1983
F. Trinchieri Camiz, A. Ziino, "Caravaggio: aspetti musicali e committenza," in *Studi musicali* XII, 1, 1983, pp. 67–90.

1984
Cropper, Panofsky-Soergel 1984
E. Cropper, G. Panofsky-Soergel, "New Elsheimer Inventories from the Seventeenth Century," in *The Burlington Magazine* CXXVI, 977, 1984, pp. 473–488.

Delfino 1984
A. Delfino, *Documenti sulla chiesa e il monastero dei Santi Apostoli di Napoli*, in *Ricerche sul '600 napoletano. Saggi vari in memoria di Raffaello Causa*, Milan 1984, pp. 154–156.

Mâle 1984
E. Mâle, *L'arte religiosa nel '600: Italia, Francia, Spagna, Fiandra*, Milan 1984.

Pacelli 1984
V. Pacelli, *Caravaggio. Le Sette Opere di Misericordia*, Naples 1984.

Zuccari 1984
A. Zuccari, *Arte e committenza nella Roma di Caravaggio*, Rome 1984.

1985
***The Age of Caravaggio | Caravaggio e il suo tempo* 1985**
The Age of Caravaggio | Caravaggio e il suo tempo, exhibition catalogue (New York, The Metropolitan Museum of Art, 5 February–14 April 1985, Naples, Museo Nazionale di Capodimonte, 14 May–30 June 1985), edited by M. Gregori, L. Salerno, R. Spear, New York–Milan 1985.

Calvesi 1985a
M. Calvesi, "Le realtà del Caravaggio. Prima parte (Vicende)," in *Storia dell'arte* 53, 1985, pp. 51–85.

Calvesi 1985b
M. Calvesi, "Le realtà del Caravaggio. Seconda parte (I dipinti)," in *Storia dell'arte* 55, 1985, pp. 227–287.

Delfino 1985
A. Delfino, "Documenti inediti per alcuni pittori napoletani del '600 e l'inventario dei beni lasciati da Lanfranco Massa, con una sua breve biografia (tratti dall'Archivio Storico del Banco di Napoli e dall'Archivio di Stato di Napoli)," in *Ricerche sul '600 napoletano* 4, 1985, pp. 89–105.

Fosi 1985
I. Fosi, *La società violenta: il banditismo nello Stato pontificio nella seconda metà del Cinquecento*, Rome 1985.

Gregori 1985a
M. Gregori, "The Conversion of the Magdalene," in *The Age of Caravaggio | Caravaggio e il suo tempo* 1985, pp. 250–255.

Gregori 1985b
M. Gregori, "Saint John the Baptist," in *The Age of Caravaggio | Caravaggio e il suo tempo* 1985, pp. 300–303.

Gregori 1985c
M. Gregori, *Caravaggio oggi*, in *The Age of Caravaggio | Caravaggio e il suo tempo* 1985, pp. 28–47.

Hibbard 1985
H. Hibbard, *Caravaggio*, New York 1985.

Pacelli 1985
V. Pacelli, "Il testamento di Marcantonio Doria: un avvio per la migliore conoscenza dei rapporti artistici fra Napoli e Genova," in *Ricerche sul '600 napoletano* 4, 1985, pp. 77–87.

Pacelli, Brejon de Lavergnée 1985
V. Pacelli, A. Brejon de Lavergnée, "L'eclisse del committente? congetture su un ritratto nella Flagellazione di Caravaggio rivelato dalla radiografia," in *Paragone. Arte* XXXVI, 419–423, 1985, pp. 209–218.

Previtali 1985
G. Previtali, "Caravaggio e il suo tempo: New York, Naples 1985," in *Prospettiva* 41, 1985, pp. 68–80.

Slim 1985
H. C. Slim, "Musical Inscriptions in Paintings by Caravaggio and his Followers," in *Music and Context: Essays for John M. Ward*, a cura di A. Dhu Shapiro, Cambridge (Mass.) 1985, pp. 241–263, updated reprint in H.C. Slim, *Painting Music in the Sixteenth Century. Essays in Iconography*, Aldershot 2002, n. VIII, pp. 241–263.

1986
Calvesi 1986
M. Calvesi, "Caravaggio," in *Art e Dossier* 1, 1986, pp. 7–14.

Christiansen 1986
K. Christiansen, "Caravaggio and 'L'esempio davanti al naturale'," in *The Art Bulletin* LXVIII, 3, 1986, pp. 421–445.

***Convegno celebrativo* 1986**
Convegno celebrativo del IV centenario della nascita di Federico Cesi, Proceedings of the Lincei Conferences (Acquasparta, 7–9 October 1985), Accademia Nazionale dei Lincei, Rome 1986.

Papi 1986
G. Papi, "Una precisazione biografica e alcune integrazioni al catalogo dello Spadarino," in *Paragone* XXXVII, 435, 1986, pp. 24–25.

Ponnelle, Bordet 1986
L. Ponnelle, L. Bordet, *San Filippo Neri e la Società Romana del suo tempo (1515–1595)*, Florence 1986.

Wiemers 1986
M. Wiemers, "Caravaggio's 'Amore Vincitore' im Urteil eines Romfahrers um 1650," in *Pantheon* XLIV, 1986, pp. 59–61.

1987
***Acta graduum academicorum* 1987**
Acta graduum academicorum gymnasii Patavini, edited by F. Zen Benetti, Padua 1987.

Calvesi 1987
M. Calvesi, "Nascita e morte del Caravaggio," in *L'ultimo Caravaggio e la cultura artistica a Napoli in Sicilia e a Malta*, edited by M. Calvesi, Syracuse 1987, pp. 13–41.

Marini 1987
M. Marini, *Michelangelo Merisi da Caravaggio "Pictor Praestantissimus". La tragica esistenza, la raffinata cultura, il mondo sanguigno del primo Seicento nell'iter pittorico completo di uno dei massimi rivoluzionari dell'arte di tutti i tempi*, Rome 1987.

Restaino 1987
C. Restaino, "Giovan Vincenzo Forlì, 'pittore di prima classe nei suoi tempi'," in *Prospettiva* 48, January 1987, pp. 33–51.

Schneider 1987
T. M. Schneider, "La 'maniera' e il processo pittorico del Caravaggio," in *L'ultimo Caravaggio e la cultura artistica a Napoli, in Sicilia e a Malta*, proceedings of the conference (Syracuse, Centro Internazionale di studi sul Barocco in Sicilia, 1–30 April 1985), edited by M. Calvesi, Syracuse 1987, pp. 117–138.

1988
Christiansen 1988
K. Christiansen, "Technical Report on *The Cardsharps*," in *The Burlington Magazine* CXXX, 1018, 1988 pp. 26–27.

Mahon 1988
D. Mahon, "Fresh Light on Caravaggio's Earliest Period: His *Cardsharps* Recovered," in *The Burlington Magazine* CXXX, 1018, 1988, pp. 10–25.

Treffers 1988
B. Treffers, "Il Francesco Hartford del Caravaggio e la spiritualità francescana alla fine del XVI secolo," in *Mitteilungen des Kunsthistorisches Institutes in Florenz* XXXII, 1988, pp. 145–172.

Trinchieri Camiz 1988
F. Trinchieri Camiz, "The Castrato Singer. From Informal to Formal Portraiture," in *Artibus et Historiae* IX, 2, 18, 1988, pp. 171–186.

1989
Bann 1989
S. Bann, *The True Vine. On Visual Representation and the Western Tradition*, Cambridge 1989, pp. 127–156.

Caravaggio. Nuove riflessioni 1989
Caravaggio. Nuove riflessioni, edited by D. Bernini, Rome 1989 (Quaderni di Palazzo Venezia, 6).

Chiarini 1989
M. Chiarini, "La probabile identità del 'Cavaliere di Malta' di Pitti," in *Antichità Viva* XXVIII, 4, 1989, pp. 15–16.

Gregori 1989
M. Gregori, "Il *Sacrificio di Isacco*: un inedito e considerazioni su una fase savoldesca del Caravaggio," in *Artibus et Historiae* X, 20, 1989, pp. 99–142.

Herrmann-Fiore 1989
K. Herrmann-Fiore, "Il *Bacco malato* autoritratto del Caravaggio ed altre figure bacchiche degli artisti," in *Caravaggio. Nuove riflessioni* 1989, pp. 95–134.

Marini 1989
M. Marini, *Michelangelo da Caravaggio pictor praestantissimus*, Rome 1989.

Tittoni Monti 1989
M. E. Tittoni Monti, "La *Buona ventura* del Caravaggio: note e precisazioni in margine al restauro," in *Caravaggio. Nuove riflessioni* 1989, pp. 179–184.

Trinchieri Camiz 1989
F. Trinchieri Camiz, "La 'Musica' nei quadri del Caravaggio," in *Caravaggio. Nuove riflessioni* 1989, pp. 198–221.

Vodret 1989
R. Vodret, "Brevi note al *Narciso*," in *Caravaggio. Nuove riflessioni* 1989, pp. 222–225.

1990
A Caravaggio Rediscovered 1990
A Caravaggio Rediscovered. 'The Lute Player', New York 1990, exhibition catalogue (New York, 9 February–22 April 1990), edited by K. Christiansen, New York 1990.

Askew 1990
P. Askew, *Caravaggio's* Death of the Virgin, Princeton 1990.

Calvesi 1990
M. Calvesi, *Le realtà del Caravaggio*, Turin 1990.

Cappelletti, Testa 1990a
F. Cappelletti, L. Testa, "E per me pagate a Michelangelo Caravaggio. Nuove date per i dipinti Mattei," in *Art e Dossier* V, 42, 1990, pp. 4–7.

Cappelletti, Testa 1990b
F. Cappelletti, L. Testa, "I quadri di Caravaggio nella collezione Mattei. I nuovi documenti e i riscontri con le fonti," in *Storia dell'arte* 69, 1990, pp. 234–244.

Cappelletti, Testa 1990c
F. Cappelletti, L. Testa, "Ricerche documentarie sul 'San Giovanni Battista' dei Musei Capitolini e sul 'San Giovanni Battista' della Galleria Doria Pamphilj," in *Identificazione di un Caravaggio*, edited by G. Correale, Venice 1990, pp. 75–84.

Guercio, Langellotti 1990
M. Guercio, A. Langellotti, *Le scritture parrocchiali di Roma e del territorio vicariale (Fonti per la storia della popolazione)*, Rome 1990.

Trinchieri Camiz 1990
F. Trinchieri Camiz, "Death and Rebirth in Caravaggio's *Martyrdom of Saint Matthew*," in *Artibus et Historiae* 11, 22, 1990, pp. 89–105.

Zuccari 1990
A. Zuccari, "San Felice e i luoghi d'arte cappuccini. Dal convento di San Bonaventura ai tuguri dipinti dal Caravaggio," in *San Felice da Cantalice. I suoi tempi, il culto e la diocesi di Cittaducale dalle origini alla canonizzazione del santo*, proceedings of the conference (Rieti, Cittaducale, Cantalice, 28–30 September 1987), edited by G. Maceroni, A.M. Tassi, Rieti 1990, pp. 175–223.

1991
Cinotti 1991
M. Cinotti, *Caravaggio. La vita e l'opera*, Bergamo 1991.

Cropper 1991
E. Cropper, *The Petrifying Art. Marino's Poetry and Caravaggio*, in *The Metropolitan Museum Journal* 26, 1991, pp. 193–212.

Gregori 1991a
M. Gregori, "Bari," in *Michelangelo Merisi da Caravaggio. Come nascono* 1991, pp. 96–102.

Gregori 1991b
M. Gregori, "Saint John the Baptist," in *Michelangelo Merisi da Caravaggio. Come nascono* 1991, pp. 262–268.

Lapucci 1991a
R. Lapucci, "La tecnica del Caravaggio: materiali e metodi," in *Michelangelo Merisi da Caravaggio. Come nascono* 1991, pp. 31–51.

Lapucci 1991b
R. Lapucci, "Musica di alcuni giovani," in *Michelangelo Merisi da Caravaggio. Come nascono* 1991, pp. 114–123.

Leone de Castris 1991
P. Leone de Castris, *Pittura del Cinquecento a Napoli. 1573–1606 l'ultima maniera*, Naples 1991.

Michelangelo Merisi 1991
Michelangelo Merisi da Caravaggio. Come nascono i capolavori, exhibition catalogue (Florence, Palazzo Pitti, Galleria Palatina, Sala Bianca, 12 December 1991–15 March 1992; Rome, Palazzo Ruspoli, Fondazione Memmo, 26 March–24 May 1992), edited by M. Gregori, Florence 1991.

Pacelli 1991
V. Pacelli, "La morte del Caravaggio e alcuni suoi dipinti da documenti inediti," in *Studi di Storia dell'Arte* II, 1991, pp. 167–175.

Papi 1991
G. Papi, "Musica di alcuni giovani," in *Michelangelo Merisi da Caravaggio. Come nascono* 1991, pp. 110–114.

Posèq 1991
A. Posèq, "The Allegorical Content of Caravaggio's *Narcissus*," in *Source* 10, 3, 1991, pp. 21–31.

Trinchieri Camiz 1991
F. Trinchieri Camiz, "Music and Painting in Cardinal del Monte's Household," in *Metropolitan Museum Journal* 26, 1991, pp. 213–226.

1992
Bologna 1992
F. Bologna, *L'incredulità del Caravaggio*, Turin 1992.

Sparti 1992
D.L. Sparti, *Le collezioni Dal Pozzo. Storia di una famiglia e del suo museo nella Roma seicentesca*, Modena 1992.

1993
Benedetti 1993
S. Benedetti, "Caravaggio's 'Taking of Christ'. A Masterpiece Rediscovered," in *The Burlington Magazine* CXXXV, 1088, 1993, pp. 731–741.

Corradini 1993
S. Corradini, *Caravaggio. Materiali per un processo*, Rome 1993.

Marini, Corradini 1993
M. Marini, S. Corradini, "Inventarium omnium et singulorum bonorum mobilium di Michelangelo da Caravaggio 'pittore'," in *Artibus et Historiae* XIV, 28, 1993, pp. 161–176.

Pacelli 1993
V. Pacelli, *Caravaggio. Le 'Sette opere di misericordia'*, 2nd edition, Salerno 1993.

1994
Bartolomé 1994
B. Bartolomé, "El conde de Castrillo y susinteresesartísticos," in *Boletín del Museo del Prado* 33, 1994, pp. 15–28.

Bassani, Bellini 1994
R. Bassani, F. Bellini, *Caravaggio assassino. La carriera di un "valenthuomo" fazioso nella Roma della Controriforma*, Rome 1994.

Berenson 1994
B. Berenson, *Caravaggio*, edited by L. Vertova, Milan 1994.

Cappelletti, Testa 1994
F. Cappelletti, L. Testa, *Il trattenimento dei Virtuosi: le collezioni seicentesche di quadri nei palazzi Mattei di Roma*, Rome 1994.

Fumagalli 1994
E. Fumagalli, "Precoci citazioni di opere del Caravaggio in alcuni documenti inediti," in *Paragone* 535–537, 1994, pp. 101–116.

Gregori 1994
M. Gregori, *Caravaggio*, Milan 1994.

Lavin 1994
I. Lavin, *Passato e presente nella storia dell'arte*, Turin 1994.

Pacelli 1994
V. Pacelli, *L'ultimo Caravaggio: dalla Maddalena a mezza figura ai due san Giovanni (1606–1610)*, Todi 1994.

Ranieri 1994
C. Ranieri, "'Si san Francesco fu eretico li suoi imitatori son luterani'. Vittoria Colonna e la riforma dei Cappuccini," in *Ludovico da Fossombrone e l'Ordine dei Cappuccini*, proceedings of the conference (Fossombrone, 1993), edited by V. Criscuolo, Rome 1994, pp. 337–351.

1995
***Architettura cappuccina* 1995**
Architettura cappuccina, edited by L. Mocatti and S. Chistè, Trento 1995.

Baglione [1642] 1995
G. Baglione, *Le vite de' pittori, scultori et architetti. Dal Pontificato di Gregorio XIII del 1572. In fino a' tempi di Papa Urbano Ottavo nel 1642* (Rome 1642), facsimile incomplete critical edition, edited by J. Hess and H. Röttgen, 3 vols., Vatican City 1995.

Cavallo 1995
S. Cavallo, *Charity and Power in Early Modern Italy*, Cambridge University Press 1995.

Ditchfield 1995
S. Ditchfield, *Liturgy, Sanctity, and History in Tridentine Italy*, Cambridge 1995.

Herrmann-Fiore 1995
K. Herrmann-Fiore, "Caravaggio's 'Taking of Christ' and Dürer's Woodcut of 1509," in *The Burlington Magazine* CXXXVII, 1102, 1995, pp. 24–27.

Lemoine 1995
A. Lemoine, "Caravage, Cavalier d'Arpin, Guido Reni et la confrérie romaine de la SS. Trinità dei Pellegrini," in *Storia dell'arte* 85, 1995, pp. 416–429.

Prodi 1995
P. Prodi, "San Filippo Neri: un'anomalia nella Roma della Controriforma?," in *Filippo Neri nella Roma della Controriforma*, proceedings of the study conference (Rome, 2 December 1994), in *Storia dell'arte* 85, 1995, pp. 333–339.

Spike 1995
J. T. Spike, "Un ritratto del cardinale Baronio agli Uffizi di Firenze. Problemi di attribuzione e di restauro," in *La regola e la fama. San Filippo Neri nell'arte*, exhibition catalogue (Rome, Palazzo Venezia, October–December 1995), Milan 1995, pp. 588–590.

Zuccari 1995
A. Zuccari, "Cultura e predicazione nelle immagini dell'Oratorio," in *Filippo Neri e la Roma della Controriforma*, proceedings of the study conference (Rome, Oratorio del Borromini, 2 December 1994), *Storia dell'arte* 85, 1995, pp. 340–354.

1996
Cannatà, Röttgen 1996
R. Cannatà, H. Röttgen, "Un quadro per la SS. Trinità dei Pellegrini affidato a Caravaggio, ma eseguito dal Cavalier d'Arpino," in *Michelangelo Merisi* 1996, pp. 80–93.

Christiansen 1996
K. Christiansen, *Thoughts on the Lombard training of Caravaggio*, in *Come dipingeva* 1996, pp. 7–28.

***Come dipingeva* 1996**
Come dipingeva il Caravaggio, Proceedings of the study day (Florence, Aula Magna dell'Università degli Studi, 28 January 1982), edited by M. Gregori with the collaboration of E. Acanfora, R. Lapucci, G. Papi, Milan 1996.

Fumagalli 1996
E. Fumagalli, "Precoci citazioni di opere del Caravaggio in alcuni documenti inediti," in *Come dipingeva* 1996, pp. 143–150.

***Michelangelo Merisi* 1996**
Michelangelo Merisi da Caravaggio. La vita e le opere attraverso i documenti, proceedings of the international conference (Rome, Vicolo Valdina Complex, Palazzo Giustiniani, 5–6 October 1995) edited by S. Macioce, Rome 1996.

Raabe 1996
R. Raabe, *Der Imaginierte Betrachter. Studien zu Caravaggios römischem Werk*, Hildesheim 1996.

Rossi 1996
S. Rossi, "Peccato e redenzione negli autoritratti del Caravaggio," in *Michelangelo Merisi* 1996, pp. 316–330.

Vodret 1996
R. Vodret, "Il restauro del *Narciso*", in *Michelangelo Merisi* 1996, pp. 167–183.

1997
Blastenbrei 1997
P. Blastenbrei, "I romani tra violenza e giustizia nel tardo Cinquecento," in *Tribunali, giustizia e società nella Roma del Cinquecento*, monographic issue of *Roma moderna e contemporanea*, 1, 1997, pp. 67–79.

Frajese 1997
V. Frajese, *Filippo Neri, santo*, in *Dizionario Biografico degli Italiani*, 47, Rome 1997, *ad vocem*.

Gash 1997
J. Gash, "The Identity of Caravaggio's *Knight of Malta*," in *The Burlington Magazine* CXXXIX, 1128, March 1997, pp. 156–160.

Maccherini 1997
M. Maccherini, "Caravaggio nel carteggio familiari di Giulio Mancini," in *Prospettiva* 86, April 1997, pp. 71–92.

***Michelangelo Merisi* 1997**
Michelangelo Merisi da Caravaggio e i suoi primi seguaci, exhibition catalogue (Salonica, Kivernio, 16 April–15 June 1997), edited by M. Gregori, Florence 1997.

Pegazzano 1997
D. Pegazzano, "Documenti per Tommaso Salini," in *Paragone* 571–573, 1997, pp. 131–146.

Spear 1997
R. E. Spear, *The "Divine" Guido. Religion, Sex, Money and Art in the World of Guido Reni*, New Haven–London 1997.

Stone 1997
D. M. Stone, "In Praise of Caravaggio's Sleeping Cupid. New Documents for Francesco dell'Antella in Malta and Florence," in *Melita Historica* 12, 2, 1997, pp. 165–177.

1998
Alloisi 1998
S. Alloisi, "San Giovanni Battista," in *Caravaggio and his Italian followers from the collections of the Galleria Nazionale d'Arte Antica di Roma*, exhibition catalogue (Hartford, Wadsworth Atheneum, 23 April–26 July 1998), edited by C. Strinati, R. Vodret Adamo, E. Zafran, Venice 1998, pp. 64–66.

Bassani 1998
R. Bassani, *Ottaviano Gabrielli*, in *Dizionario Biografico degli Italiani*, vol. 51, *ad indicem*.

Bona Castellotti 1998
M. Bona Castellotti, *Il paradosso di Caravaggio*, Milan 1998.

Cappelletti 1998
F. Cappelletti, "Una nota di beni e qualche aggiunta alla storia della collezione Aldobrandini," in *Storia dell'arte* 93–94, 1998, pp. 341–347.

Cavazzini 1998
P. Cavazzini, *Palazzo Lancellotti ai Coronari. Cantiere di Agostino Tassi*, Rome 1998.

Corradini, Marini 1998
S. Corradini, M. Marini, "The Earliest Account of Caravaggio in Rome," in *The Burlington Magazine* CXL, 1138, 1998, pp. 25–28.

Pegazzano 1998
D. Pegazzano, "Documenti per Tommaso Salini," in *Paragone. Arte* XLVIII, 15–16, 1998, pp. 131–146.

Puglisi 1998
C. Puglisi, *Michelangelo Merisi da Caravaggio*, London 1998.

Rolfi Ožvald 1998
S. Rolfi Ožvald, "Un aromatario senese e la chiesa di Santa Caterina a via Giulia: riflessioni intorno alla committenza e al collezionismo di artigiani e piccoli imprenditori nella Roma del primo Seicento," in *Roma moderna e contemporanea* 5, 1997 (1998), pp. 185–207.

Storchi 1998
M. L. Storchi, "Formazione e organizzazione di un archivio gentilizio. L'Archivio Doria d'Angri tra XV e XX secolo," in *Per la storia del Mezzogiorno medievale e moderno. Studi in memoria di Iole Mazzoleni*, Naples 1998, pp. 547–588.

Testa 1998
L. Testa, "Novità su Carlo Saraceni: la committenza Aldobrandini e la prima attività romana," in *Dialoghi di storia dell'arte* 7, 1998, pp. 130–137.

Zeri 1998
F. Zeri, *Caravaggio. La vocazione di San Matteo* (Cento Dipinti; 2), Milan 1998.

Bal 1999
M. Bal, *Quoting Caravaggio. Contemporary Art, Preposterous History*, Chicago–London 1999, pp. 231–261.

***Caravaggio e i suoi* 1999**
Caravaggio e i suoi. Percorsi caravaggeschi in Palazzo Barberini, exhibition catalogue (Rome, Palazzo Barberini, 18 February–9 May 1999), edited by C. Strinati and R. Vodret, Naples 1999.

***La* Flagellazione *di Caravaggio* 1999**
La Flagellazione di Caravaggio. Il restauro, edited by D. M. Pagano, Naples 1999.

Gieben 1999
S. Gieben, "La cultura materiale dei cappuccini nel primo secolo (1525–1619)," in *Clavis Scientiae*, edited by V. Criscuolo, Rome 1999, pp. 375–403.

Longhi [1952] 1999
R. Longhi, *Il Caravaggio* (Milan 1952), in R. Longhi, *Studi Caravaggeschi, 1943-1968*, Milan 1999, vol. I, pp. 159–225.

Pagano 1999
D. M. Pagano, "Il dipinto," in *La Flagellazione di Caravaggio* 1999, pp. 11–28.

Vittorini [1957] 1999
E. Vittorini, *Diario pubblico. Autobiografia di un militante della cultura* (1957), ed. cons. Milano 1999.

Vodret 1999
R. Vodret, "Caravaggio. *Judith cortando la cabeza de Holofernes*, datossobre la restauracíon," in *Caravaggio*, exhibition catalogue (Madrid, Museo Nacional del Prado, 21 September–21 November 1999; Bilbao, Museo des Bellas Artes de Bilbao, 29 November 1999–23 January 2000), edited by C. Strinati and R. Vodret, Milan 1999, pp. 74–77.

2000
Causa 2000
S. Causa, *Battistello Caracciolo. L'opera completa*, Naples 2000.

***Giuseppe Vermiglio* 2000**
Giuseppe Vermiglio un pittore caravaggesco tra Roma e la Lombardia, exhibition catalogue (Campione d'Italia, Galleria Civica, 10 September–3 December 2000), edited by D. Pescarmona, Milan 2000.

Guerrieri Borsoi 2000
M.B. Guerrieri Borsoi, *Palazzo Besso: la dimora dai Rustici ai Paravicini e gli affreschi di Tarquinio Ligustri*, Rome 2000.

Haskell 2000
F. Haskell, *Mecenati e pittori. L'arte e la società italiane nell'età barocca*, Turin 2000.

Pedrocchi 2000
A.M. Pedrocchi, *Le Stanze del Tesoriere. La Quadreria Patrizi: cultura senese nella storia del collezionismo romano del Seicento*, Milan 2000.

Treffers 2000
B. Treffers, *Caravaggio nel sangue del Battista*, Rome 2000.

2001
Causa 2001
S. Causa, *Il sale nella ferita. Antico e moderno nell'officina di Longhi*, Naples 2001.

Cirinei 2001
A. Cirinei, "Conflitti artistici, rivalità cardinalizie e patronage a Roma fra Cinque e Seicento. Il caso del processo criminale contro il Cavalier d'Arpino," in *La nobiltà romana in età moderna*, edited by M.A. Visceglia, Rome 2001, pp. 255–305.

Cropper 2001
E. Cropper, "Life on the Edge: Artemisia Gentileschi, Famous Woman Painter," in K. Christiansen, J. Mann, *Orazio and Artemisia Gentileschi*, exhibition catalogue (New York, The Metropolitan Museum, 14 February–12 May 2002), New York 2001, pp. 262–280.

Danesi Squarzina 2001
S. Danesi Squarzina, "La collezione Giustiniani. Benedetto, Vincenzo, Andrea nostri contemporanei," in *Caravaggio e i Giustiniani. Toccar con mano una collezione del Seicento*, exhibition catalogue (Rome, Palazzo Giustiniani, 25 January–15 May 20001; Berlin, Altes Museum, 15 June–9 September 2001), edited by S. Danesi Squarzina, Milan 2001, pp. 17–45.

Franchi, Sartori 2001
S. Franchi, O. Sartori, *Le botteghe d'arte e la topografia storico–urbanistica di una zona di Roma dalla fine del XVI secolo ad oggi. Edifici, botteghe, artigiani nella zona di piazza Pasquino, sede storica dei librai*, Rome 2001.

Langdon 2001
H. Langdon, *Caravaggio. Una vita*, Palermo 2001.

Marini 2001
M. Marini, *Caravaggio, "pictor praestantissimus": l'iter artistico completo di uno dei massimi rivoluzionari dell'arte di tutti i tempi*, 3rd updated edition, Rome 2001.

Nicolai 2001
F. Nicolai, "Percorso di Tarquinio Ligustri pittore viterbese," in *Studi romani* XLIX, 3–4, 2001, pp. 376–390.

Papi 2001
G. Papi, *Cecco del Caravaggio*, Soncino 2001.

Pupillo 2001
M. Pupillo, *La SS. Trinità dei Pellegrini di Roma. Artisti e committenti al tempo di Caravaggio*, Rome 2001.

Sewell 2001
B. Sewell, "Guarda, guarda: Caravaggio!," in *Il Giornale dell'arte* 196, February 2001, p. 38.

Sickel 2001
L. Sickel, "Künstlerrivalität im SchattenderPeterskuppel: Giuseppe Cesari d'Arpino und das Attentat auf Cristoforo Roncalli," in *Marburger Jahrbuch für Kunstwissenschaft* XXVIII, 2001, pp. 158–189.

Spezzaferro, Mignosi Tantillo 2001
L. Spezzaferro, A. Mignosi Tantillo, "Appendice documentaria," in M. G. Bernardini, *Caravaggio, Carracci, Maderno. La Cappella Cerasi in Santa Maria del Popolo a Roma*, Cinisello Balsamo 2001, pp. 108–124.

Spike 2001
J. T. Spike, *Caravaggio*, New York–London 2001.

Strunck 2001
C. Strunck, "L'"humor peccante" di Vincenzo Giustiniani: l'innovativa presentazione dell'antico nelle due gallerie di palazzo Giustiniani a Roma (1630-1830 circa)," in *Toccar con mano una collezione del Seicento Caravaggio e i Giustiniani*, Milan 2001, pp. 105-114.

Whitfield 2001
C. Whitfield, "Ritrattistica: dal 'ritratto semplice' alla Ressemblance Parlante," in *Il genio di Roma, 1592–1623*, exhibition catalogue (London, Royal Academy of Arts, 20 January–16 April 2001; Rome, Palazzo Venezia, 10 May–31 July 2001), edited by B. L. Brown, Milan 2001, pp. 140–172.

2002

Baldriga 2002
I. Baldriga, *L'occhio della lince. I primi lincei tra arte, scienza e collezionismo (1603–1630)*, Rome 2002.

***Caravaggio nel IV centenario* 2002**
Caravaggio nel IV centenario della Cappella Contarelli, proceedings of the international study conference (Rome, 24–26 May 2001), edited by C. Volpi, Città di Castello 2002.

***Galleria d'arte antica* 2002**
La Galleria d'arte antica dei Civici musei di Udine, I: *Dipinti dal XIV alla metà del XVII secolo*, edited by G. Bergamini, Vicenza 2002.

Pacelli 2002
V. Pacelli, *L'ultimo Caravaggio 1606–1610. Il giallo della morte: omicidio di Stato?*, Todi 2002.

Röttgen 2002
H. Röttgen, *Il Cavalier Giuseppe Cesari d'Arpino. Un grande pittore nello splendore della fama e nell'inconsistenza della fortuna*, Rome 2002.

Spezzaferro 2002
L. Spezzaferro, "Caravaggio accettato: dal rifiuto al mercato," in *Caravaggio nel IV centenario* 2002, pp. 23–33.

Testa 2002
L. Testa, "'… In ogni modo domatina uscimo': Caravaggio e gli Aldobrandini," in *Caravaggio nel IV centenario* 2002, pp. 129–154.

2003

Danesi Squarzina 2003
S. Danesi Squarzina, *La collezione Giustiniani*, 3 vols., Turin 2003.

Gazzara 2003
L. Gazzara, "Una lettura interpretativa sulla fondazione del Pio Monte della Misericordia in relazione alla sua committenza artistica," in *Napoli nobilissima* IV, 1–2, January–April 2003, pp. 51–67.

Hardon 2003
J. A. Hardon, *The History of Eucharistic Adoration. Development of Doctrine in the Catholic Church*, Oak Lawn (IL) 2003.

Macioce 2003
S. Macioce, *Michelangelo Merisi da Caravaggio. Fonti e documenti 1532–1724*, Rome 2003.

Papi 2003
G. Papi, *Spadarino*, Soncino 2003.

Puglisi 2003
C. Puglisi, *Caravaggio*, London 2003.

Sickel 2003a
L. Sickel, *Caravaggios Rom Annäherungen an eindissonantes Milieu*, Berlin 2003.

Sickel 2003b
L. Sickel, "Un affresco inedito di Tarquinio Ligustri. La 'prospettiva' nella galleria del palazzo Massimo alle Colonne," in *Bollettino d'arte* LXXXVII, 120, 2003, pp. 93–98.

2004

***Caravaggio. L'ultimo tempo* 2004**
Caravaggio. L'ultimo tempo 1606–1610 exhibition catalogue (Naples, Museo di Capodimonte, 23 October 2004–23 January 2005), edited by N. Spinosa, Naples–Rome 2004.

Christiansen 2004
K. Christiansen, "Becoming Artemisia: Afterthoughts on the Gentileschi Exhibition," in *Metropolitan Museum Journal* 39, 2004, pp. 10, 101–126.

Costa Restagno 2004a
J. Costa Restagno, "Ottavio Costa (1554–1639)," in *L'età di Rubens*, exhibition catalogue (Genoa, Palazzo Ducale, 20 March–11 July 2004), edited by P. Boccardo, Milan 2004, pp. 424–430.

Costa Restagno 2004b
J. Costa Restagno, *Ottavio Costa (1554 1639) le sue case e i suoi quadri. Ricerche d'archivio*, Bordighera–Albenga 2004.

Denunzio 2004
A.E. Denunzio, "Aggiunte e qualche ipotesi per i soggiorni napoletani di Caravaggio," *Caravaggio. L'ultimo tempo* 2004, pp. 48–51.

Farrugia Randon 2004
P. Farrugia Randon, *Caravaggio Knight of Malta*, Malta 2004.

***Fonti francescane* [1977] 2004**
Fonti francescane [1977], new edition, edited by E. Caroli, Padua 2004.

Giantomassi, Zari 2004
C. Giantomassi, D. Zari, "L'intervento," in *L'ultimo Caravaggio* 2004, pp. 101–106.

Gregori 2004
M. Gregori, "Una cronistoria e qualche dichiarazione di metodo a proposito del *Martirio di sant'Orsola*," in *L'ultimo Caravaggio* 2004, pp. 48–55.

Pagano 2004
D.M. Pagano, "La storia conservativa", in *L'ultimo Caravaggio* 2004, pp. 91–99.

***L'ultimo Caravaggio* 2004**
L'ultimo Caravaggio. Il Martirio di sant'Orsola *restaurato*, catalogue of the exhibition (Rome, Galleria Borghese, 21 May – 29 June 2004; Milan, Pinacoteca Ambrosiana, 2 July – 29 August 2004; Vicenza, Gallerie di Palazzo Leoni Montanari, 3 September – 10 October 2004), Milan 2004.

2005

Bellori [1672] 2005
G. P. Bellori *The Lives of the Modern Painters, Sculptors and Architects*, a new translation and critical edition (A. Sedgwick Wohl, H. Wohl, T. Montanari); *Life of Michelangelo da Caravaggio,* pp.179–189 Cambridge 2005.

Berra 2005
G. Berra, *Il giovane Caravaggio in Lombardia. Ricerche documentarie sui Merisi, gli Aratori e i marchesi di Caravaggio*, Florence 2005.

***Caravaggio e l'Europa* 2005**
Caravaggio e l'Europa. Il movimento caravaggesco internazionale da Caravaggio a Mattia Preti, exhibition catalogue (Milan, Palazzo Reale, 15 October 2005–6 February 2006), Milan 2005.

Cardinali, De Ruggieri, Falcucci 2005
M. Cardinali, M. B. De Ruggieri, C. Falcucci, "Incisions in Caravaggio's Working Process, from the Illumination of the Subject to the Depiction of Shadows: A Revolution Without Heirs?," in *Technologische Studien Kunsthistorisches Museum* 2, 2005, pp. 50–71.

Fabbri 2005
M.C. Fabbri, "Agli albori del collezionismo caravaggesco presso la corte medicea. Ipotesi e nuove considerazioni," in *Luce e ombra. Caravaggismo e naturalismo nella pittura toscana del Seicento*, exhibition catalogue (Pontedera, Centro per l'arte Otello Cirri, Museo Piaggio 'Giovanni Alberto Agnelli', 18 March–12 June 2005), edited by P. Carofano, Pisa 2005, pp. LXI–LXXVII.

Fatigati 2005
G. Fatigati, "Dell'agnizione di un dipinto di Caravaggio," in *Interventi sulla "Questione Meridionale"*, edited by F. Abbate, Rome 2005, pp. 159–170.

Maccherini 2005
M. Maccherini, "Michelangelo Merisi da Caravaggio. 6.3 La Musica," in *Siena e Roma. Raffaello, Caravaggio e i protagonisti di un legame antico*, exhibition catalogue (Siena, Santa Maria della Scala – Palazzo Squarcialupi, 25 November 2005–5 March 2006), edited by B. Santi and C. Strinati, Siena 2005, pp. 406–407.

Marini 2005
M. Marini, *Caravaggio "pictor praestantissimus". L'iter artistico completo di uno dei massimi rivoluzionari dell'arte di tutti i tempi"*, 4th edition, Rome 2005.

Milicua 2005
J. Milicua, "Caravaggio. Salomé con la cabeza de San Juan Bautista," in *Caravaggio y la pinturarealista europea*, exhibition catalogue (Barcelona, Museu Nacional d'Art de Catalunya, 10 October 2005–15 January 2006), edited by J. Milicua and M. M. Cuyás, Barcelona 2005, pp. 80–85.

Papi 2005
G. Papi, *Il genio degli anonimi: maestri caravaggeschi a Roma e a Napoli*, Milan 2005.

***Siena e Roma* 2005**
Siena e Roma. Raffaello, Caravaggio e i protagonisti di un legame antico, exhibition catalogue (Siena, Santa Maria della Scala – Palazzo Squarcialupi, 25 November 2005–5 March 2006), edited by B. Santi and C. Strinati, Siena 2005.

Trinchieri Camiz 2005
F. Trinchieri Camiz, "'Cantare con una voce sopra un strumento': il 'Sonatore di liuto' del cardinal del Monte e il suo contesto musicale," in Marini 2005, pp. 384–386.

2006

Berenson [1951] 2006
B Berenson, *Del Caravaggio delle sue incongruenze e della sua fama (Milano 1951)*, edited by L. Vertova, Milano 2006.

Bologna [1992] 2006
F. Bologna, *L'incredulità del Caravaggio e l'esperienza delle "cose naturali"* (1992), 2nd expanded edition, Turin 2006.

Capolavori da scoprire 2006
Capolavori da scoprire. Odescalchi, Pallavicini, edited by G. Lepri, Milan 2006.

Falcucci 2006
C. Falcucci, "La tecnica esecutiva," in *Il Caravaggio Odescalchi. Le due versioni della Conversione di San Paolo a confronto*, exhibition catalogue (Rome, Santa Maria del Popolo, 20–27 November 2006), edited by R. Vodret, Milan 2006, pp. 39–46.

Loire 2006
S. Loire, *Florence, Gênes, Lombardie, Naples, Rome et Venise*, Paris 2006.

Rovetta 2006
A. Rovetta, "Gli appunti del cardinale: note inedite di Federico Borromeo per il *Musaeum*," in *Annali di critica d'arte* II, 2, 2006, pp. 105–142.

Sciberras, Stone 2006
K. Sciberras, D. Stone, *Caravaggio Art, Knighthood, and Malta*, Malta 2006.

Storey 2006
T. Storey, "Oggetti e legami nella casa delle cortigiane: erotismo e distinzione sociale nella Roma barocca," in *Genesis* V, 1, 2006, pp. 21–40.

2007

Brookes 2007
A. Brookes, "Richard Symonds's account of his visit to Rome in 1649–1651," in *The Volume of the Walpole Society* 69, 2007, pp. 1–183.

D'Alessandro 2007
D. A. D'Alessandro, "Per una biografia di don Pietro Paolo Stella C.R., alias Scipione Stella," in S. Stella, *Inni a cinque voci. Napoli 1610*, edited by F. Colusso and D.A. D'Alessandro, Lucca 2007, pp. XI–LIV.

Fumaroli 2007
M. Fumaroli, "Le 'siècle' d'Urbain VIII," in *I Barberini e la cultura europea del Seicento*, proceedings of the international conference (Rome, Palazzo Barberini, 7–11 December 2004), edited by L. Mochi Onori, S. Schütze, F. Solinas, Rome 2007, pp. 1–14.

Iacopo da Varazze [before 1264] 2007
Iacopo da Varazze, *Legenda aurea* [ms., before 1264], critical edition with commentary by G. P. Maggioni, Italian translation co-ordinated by F. Stella, Florence 2007.

Nicolai 2007
F. Nicolai, "Novità su Tarquinio Ligustri," in *Bollettino d'arte* XCII, 140, 2007, pp. 97–108.

Schütze 2007
S. Schütze, *Kardinal Maffeo Barberini, späterPapst Urban VIII., und die Entstehung des römischen Hochbarock*, Munich 2007.

Sciberras 2007
K. Sciberras, "Caravaggio, the Confraternita Della Misericordia and the Original Context of the Oratory of the Decollato in Valletta," in *The Burlington Magazine* CXLIX, 1256, 2007, pp. 759–766.

Sickel 2007
L. Sickel, "Caravaggio e Andrea Ruffetti: la cornice storica di un ritratto sconosciuto," in *Caravaggio e il suo ambiente. Ricerche e interpretazioni*, edited by S. Ebert-Schifferer, J. Kliemann, V. von Rosen, L. Sickel, Cinisello Balsamo 2007, pp. 111–117.

Terzaghi 2007
M. C. Terzaghi, *Caravaggio, Annibale Carracci, Guido Reni tra le ricevute del Banco Herrera & Costa*, Rome 2007.

2007–2008

Nappi 2007–2008
E. Nappi, "Documenti inediti per la storia dell'arte a Napoli per i secoli XVI–XVII dalle scritture dell'Archivio di Stato Fondo Banchieri Antichi (A.S.N.B.A.) e dell'Archivio Storico dell'Istituto Banco di Napoli – Fondazione (A.S.B.N.)," in *Quaderni dell'Archivio Storico*, 2007–2008, pp. 361–401.

2008

Casanova 2008
D. Casanova, Fluent ad eum omnes gentes. *Il Monte delle Sette opere della misericordia di Napoli nel Seicento*, Bologna 2008.

Cavazzini 2008
P. Cavazzini, *Painting as Business in Early Seventeenth–century Rome*, University Park, Penn., 2008.

Falcucci 2008
C. Falcucci, "La tecnica esecutiva e la genesi della Conversione Odescalchi attraverso le indagini diagnostiche," in *Caravaggio a Milano. La Conversione di Saulo*, exhibition catalogue (Milan, Palazzo Marino, 16 November–14 December 2008), Milan 2008, pp. 71–101.

Gregori 2008
M. Gregori, "Un altro autografo dei Bari del Caravaggio," in *Caravaggio. I Bari della collezione Mahon*, exhibition catalogue (Forli, Musei San Domenico, 5 April–22 June 2008), edited by D. Benati and A. Paolucci, Cinisello Balsamo 2008, pp. 20–48.

Leone 2008
S. Leone, *The Palazzo Pamphilj in Piazza Navona. Constructing Identity in Early Modern Rome*, London 2008.

Nicolai 2008
F. Nicolai, *Mecenati a confronto. Committenza, collezionismo e mercato dell'arte nella Roma del primo Seicento. Le famiglie Massimo, Altemps, Naro e Colonna*, Rome 2008.

Petrucci 2008
F. Petrucci, *Pittura di ritratto a Roma: il Seicento*, 3 vols., Rome 2008.

2009

Bandera 2009
S. Bandera, "Sala XXIX. Pittura caravaggesca," in *Brera. La Pinacoteca. Storia e capolavori*, Milan 2009, pp. 120–124.

Bann 2009
S. Bann, "Philostratus and the Narcissus of Caravaggio," in *Philostratus*, edited by E. Bowie, J. Elsner, Cambridge 2009, pp. 343–355.

Bellini 2009
F. Bellini, *Melandroni, Fillide*, in *Dizionario Biografico degli Italiani*, Rome 2009, 73, *ad vocem*.

Bellori [1672] 2009
G. P. Bellori, *Le vite de' pittori, scultori e architetti moderni* (1672), edited by E. Borea, Turin 2009.

Cappelletti 2009
F. Cappelletti, *Caravaggio. Un ritratto somigliante*, Milan 2009.

Caravaggio ospita Caravaggio 2009
Caravaggio ospita Caravaggio, exhibition catalogue (Milan, Pinacoteca di Brera 17 January 2009 – 29 March 2009), edited by V. Maderna and A. Pacia, Milan 2009.

Denunzio 2009
A. E. Denunzio, "Per due committenti di Caravaggio a Napoli: Nicolò Radolovich e il viceré VIII conteduca di Benavente (1603–1610)," in *España y Nápoles. Coleccionismo y mecenazgo virreinales en el siglo XVII*, edited by J. L. Colomer, Madrid 2009, pp. 175–193.

Ebert-Schifferer 2009
S. Ebert-Schifferer, *Caravaggio. Sehen – Staunen – Glauben. Der Maler und sein Werk*, Munich 2009.

Gregori 2009
M. Gregori, "Le due cene in Emmaus a confronto," in *Caravaggio ospita Caravaggio* 2009, pp. 29–38.

Marini 2009
M. Marini, "Senso e trascendenza nella Madonna de' Parafrenieri del Caravaggio," in *Artibus et Historiae* XXX, 59, 2009, pp. 135–144.

Moretti 2009
M. Moretti, "Caravaggio e Fantino Petrignani committente e protettore di artisti," in *Da Caravaggio ai caravaggeschi*, edited by M. Calvesi, Rome 2009, pp. 69–21, 441–452.

Papi 2009
G. Papi, "Brevi note sull'attività giovanile di Caravaggio," in *Caravaggio ospita Caravaggio* 2009, pp. 21–27.

Schütze 2009
S. Schütze, *Caravaggio. L'opera completa*, Cologne 2009 (orig. ed. *Caravaggio. Das vollständige Werk*, Cologne 2009; English ed.: *Caravaggio. The Complete Works*, Cologne 2009).

Terzaghi 2009
M. C. Terzaghi, "Le prime copie

da Caravaggio: quando e perché attraverso nuovi documenti Costa," in *Caravaggio e l'Europa. L'artista, la storia, la tecnica e la sua eredità*, proceedings of the international study conference (Milan, 3–4 February 2006), edited by L. Spezzaferro, Cinisello Balsamo 2009, pp. 89–108.

Vannugli 2009
A. Vannugli, "La collezione del segretario Juan de Lezcano. Borgianni, Caravaggio, Reni e altri, nella quadreria di un funzionario spagnolo nell'Italia del primo Seicento," in *Atti dell'Accademia Nazionale dei Lincei. Classe di Scienze morali, storiche, filologiche* CDVI, 2009, pp. 322–539.

Vodret 2009
R. Vodret, *Caravaggio*, Milan 2009.

Wilson 2009
J. Wilson, "An Addition to the Provenance of Caravaggio's 'Taking of Christ'," in *The Burlington Magazine* CLI, 1279, 2009, p. 691.

Zuccari 2009
A. Zuccari, "Cesare Baronio iconografo della Controriforma," in *Studi Romani* LVII, 2009, pp. 182–197.

2009–2010
Sickel 2009–2010
L. Sickel, "Gli esordi del Caravaggio a Roma: una ricostruzione del suo ambiente sociale nel primo periodo romano," in *Römisches Jahrbuch der Bibliotheca Hertziana* 39, 2009–2010, pp. 225–265.

2010
Bastogi 2010
N. Bastogi, "Novità e riflessioni su Caravaggio e sui caravaggeschi negli archivi di Firenze," in *Caravaggio e caravaggeschi* 2010, pp. 336–337.

Benedetti 2010
S. Benedetti, "Cattura di Cristo nell'orto," in *Caravaggio* 2010, pp. 132–139.

Buranelli 2010
F. Buranelli, "Conversione di Saulo," in *Caravaggio* 2010, pp. 106–115.

Calenne 2010
L. Calenne, *Prime ricerche su Orazio Zecca da Montefortino (oggi Artena). Dalla bottega del Cavalier d'Arpino a quella di Francesco Nappi*, Rome 2010.

Caravaggio **2010**
Caravaggio, exhibition catalogue (Rome, Scuderie del Quirinale, 20 February–13 June 2010), edited by C. Strinati, Milan 2010.

Caravaggio e caravaggeschi **2010**
Caravaggio e caravaggeschi a Firenze, exhibition catalogue (Florence, Gallerie degli Uffizi, 24 May 2009–10 January 2010), edited by G. Papi, Florence–Livorno, 2010.

Caravaggio. La bottega del genio **2010**
Caravaggio. La bottega del genio, exhibition catalogue (Rome, Palazzo Venezia, 22 December 2010–29 May 2011), edited by C. Falcucci, Rome 2010.

Cassiani 2010
G. Cassiani, *Il Socrate cristiano. Saggio su Filippo Neri (1515–1595)*, Pisa 2010.

Ebert-Schifferer 2010a
S. Ebert-Schifferer, "Caravaggio e la cortigiana: aspetti sociologici e problemi artistici," in *Le Caravage aujourd'hui et autres études*, in *Bulletin de l'Association des Historiens de l'Art Italien*, 15–16, 2010, pp. 59–74.

Ebert-Schifferer 2010b
S. Ebert-Schifferer, "Santa Caterina d'Alessandria," in *Caravaggio* 2010, pp. 90–95.

Filostrato 2010
Filostrato Maggiore, *La Pinacoteca*, edited by G. Pucci e G. Lombardo, Palermo 2010.

Fried 2010
M. Fried, *The Moment of Caravaggio*, Princeton–Oxford 2010.

Macioce 2010a
S. Macioce, "Caravaggio: il pittore 'colla croce in petto'," in *I Cavalieri di Malta e Caravaggi. La storia, gli artisti, i committenti*, edited by S. Macioce, Rome 2010, pp. 96–122.

Macioce 2010b
S. Macioce, *Michelangelo Merisi da Caravaggio: Documenti, fonti e inventari, 1513–1875,* Rome 2010.

Meraviglie del Barocco **2010**
Meraviglie del Barocco nelle Marche, 1: San Severino e l'Alto Maceratese, exhibition catalogue (San Severino Marche, various venues, 24 July–12 December 2010), edited by V. Sgarbi and S. Papetti, Cinisello Balsamo 2010.

Papi 2010
G. Papi, "Caravaggio, Artemisia e gli altri. Introduzione ai contenuti della mostra," in *Caravaggio e caravaggeschi* 2010, pp. 22–41.

Prodi 2010
P. Prodi, *Il paradigma tridentino. Un'epoca della storia della Chiesa*, Bologna 2010.

Prohaska, Swoboda 2010
W. Prohaska, G. Swoboda, *Caravaggio und der internationale Caravaggismus. Sammlungskatalog der Gemäldegalerie: Rom* I, Cinisello Balsamo 2010.

Sickel 2010
L. Sickel, "Caravaggio, Lanfranco und Reni in der Sammlung Sannesi: Geschicke einer Familie im Spiegel ihres Kunstbesitzes," in *Römisches Jahrbuch der Bibliotheca Hertziana* 38, 2007–2008 (2010), pp. 231–295.

Spear, Sohm 2010
R. E. Spear, P. Sohm, *Painting for Profit. The Economic Lives of Seventeenth-century Italian Painters*, New Haven 2010.

Spezzaferro 2010
L. Spezzaferro, *Caravaggio*, edited by P. Coen, Cinisello Balsamo 2010.

Spike 2010
J. Th. Spike, with the assistance of M. K. Spike, *Caravaggio*, 2nd ed., New York–London 2010.

Terzaghi 2010a
M. C. Terzaghi, "I bari," in *Caravaggio* 2010, p. 43.

Terzaghi 2010b
M. C. Terzaghi, "'Virtuosi illustri del suo tempo': novità e precisazioni per Ottavio Leoni, Caravaggio e i volti della Roma caravaggesca," in *Caravaggio. Mecenati e pittori*, exhibition catalogue (Caravaggio, Palazzo Gallavresi, 25 September–12 December 2010), edited by M. C. Terzaghi, Milan 2010, pp. 15–57.

Terzaghi 2010c
M. C. Terzaghi, "Galanino a Napoli tra Annibale Carracci e Caravaggio," in *Napoli e l'Emilia. Studi sulle relazioni artistiche*, proceedings of the study days (Santa Maria Capua Vetere, 2008), edited by A. Zezza, Naples 2010, pp. 63–86.

2011
Alla ricerca di Ghiongrat **2011**
Alla ricerca di Ghiongrat, studi sui libri parrocchiali romani (1600–1630), edited by R. Vodret, Rome 2011.

Baroncelli 2011
O. Baroncelli, "Caravaggio e l'ospedale di Santa Maria della Consolazione," in *Caravaggio a Roma* 2011, pp. 60–64.

Calvesi 2011
M. Calvesi, "Caravaggio: i documenti e dell'altro," in *Storia dell'arte* 128, January–April 2011, pp. 22–51.

Caravaggio a Roma **2011**
Caravaggio a Roma. Una vita dal vero, exhibition catalogue (Rome, Archivio di Stato, 11 February–15 May 2011), edited by M. Di Sivo and O. Verdi, Rome 2011.

Carofano 2011
P. Carofano, "Un'aggiunta alla fortuna figurativa dei *Musici* Del Monte," in *Atti della Giornata di Studi Francesco Maria del Monte e Caravaggio: Roma, Siena, Bologna. Opera, Biografia, Documenti* (Monte Santa Maria Tiberina, 2 October 2010), edited by P. Carofano, Pontedera 2011, pp. 161–175.

Cavietti, Curti 2011
M. Cavietti, F. Curti, "La bottega di Francesco Morelli pittore: Giovanni Baglione, Vittorio Travagni, Tommaso Salini, tra formazione, parentele, committenze e rivalità all'arrivo di Caravaggio a Roma," in *Roma moderna e contemporanea* XIX, 2, 2011, pp. 373–454.

Cerati 2011
C. Cerati, "Volti e corpi di Caravaggio. La natura dei modelli," in *Caravaggio a Roma* 2011, pp. 137–142.

Cesarini 2011
A. Cesarini, *Il musico, il barbiere, il ferraiolo. Una testimonianza inedita sui primi anni di Caravaggio a Roma,* in *Caravaggio a Roma* 2011, pp. 54–59.

Curti 2011a
F. Curti, "Costantino Spada

'regattiero de quadri vecchi' e l'amicizia con Caravaggio," in *"L'essercitio mio è di pittore"* 2011, pp. 167–197.

Curti 2011b
F. Curti, "Sugli esordi di Caravaggio a Roma. La bottega di Lorenzo Carli e il suo inventario," in *Caravaggio a Roma* 2011, pp. 167–197.

***"L'essercitio mio è di pittore"* 2011**
"L'essercitio mio è di pittore". Caravaggio e l'ambiente artistico romano, edited by F. Curti, M. Di Sivo, O. Verdi, *Roma Moderna e Contemporanea* XIX, 2, 2011.

Flynn 2011
K. Flynn, "More on the Provenance of Caravaggio's 'Taking of Christ'," in *The Burlington Magazine* CLIII, 1301, 2011, p. 529.

Nicolaci, Gandolfi 2011
M. Nicolaci, R. Gandolfi, "Il Caravaggio di Guido Reni: la *Negazione di Pietro* tra relazioni artistiche e operazioni finanziarie," in *Storia dell'arte* 130, 30, August–December 2011, pp. 41–64.

Pampalone 2011a
A. Pampalone, "Caravaggio virtuoso: una leggenda?," in *Caravaggio a Roma* 2011, pp. 46–53.

Pampalone 2011b
A. Pampalone, "Pittori fiorentini a Roma alla fine del Cinquecento. Vittorio Travagni e Nicola Cianchi," in *Annali della Pontificia Insigne Accademia di Belle Arti e Lettere dei Virtuosi al Pantheon* XI, 2011, pp. 415–442.

Sickel 2011
L. Sickel, "Sull'arrivo di Caravaggio a Roma: lo zio Ludovico Merisi e Pandolfo Pucci," in *Caravaggio a Roma* 2011, pp. 77–81.

Soggiu 2011
D. Soggiu, "Prudenzia Bruni e la casa di Caravaggio," in *"L'essercitio mio è di pittore"* 2011, pp. 237–258.

Zuccari 2011
A. Zuccari, *Caravaggio controluce. Ideali e capolavori*, Milan 2011.

2012
Berra 2012
G. Berra, "Il cesto ricolmo di frutta del Vertunno: (noto come il

Fruttaiolo) del Caravaggio," in *Atti della giornata di studi Questioni caravaggesche* (Monte Santa Maria Tiberina, Palazzo Museo Bourbon del Monte, 17 September 2011), edited by P. Carofano, Pontedera 2012, pp. 11–60.

***Caravaggio's Painting* 2012**
Caravaggio's Painting Technique: Proceedings of the CHARISMA Workshop, edited by M. Ciatti and B. Brunetti, Florence 2012.

***Caravaggio tra arte* 2012**
Caravaggio tra arte e scienza, edited by V. Pacelli and G. Forgione, Naples 2012.

Ebert-Schifferer 2012
S. Ebert-Schifferer, *Caravaggio. The Artist and His Work*, Los Angeles 2012.

Fabris 2012a
D. Fabris, "Caravaggio e la musica," in *Caravaggio tra arte* 2012, pp. 201–217.

Fabris 2012b
D. Fabris, "Il "ciclo musicale" di Caravaggio: gioco nascosto di committenti," in *La musica al tempo di Caravaggio*, Proceedings of the International Study Conference (Milan, 29 September 2010), edited by S. Macioce and E. De Pascale, Rome 2012, pp. 73–85.

Moretti 2012 a
M. Moretti, "I Petrignani di Amelia nella Roma di Caravaggio: mecenatismo e committenza," in *Roma al tempo di Caravaggio*, exhibition catalogue (Rome, Museo nazionale di Palazzo Venezia, 16 November 2011–5 February 2012), edited by R. Vodret, Milan 2012, pp. 117–135.

Moretti 2012b
M. Moretti, *I Petrignani di Amelia: fatti, committenze, collezioni tra Roma e l'Umbria,* Isola del Gran Sasso 2012.

Paliaga 2012
F. Paliaga, *Natura in vetro: studi sulla caraffa di fiori di Caravaggio*, Rome 2012.

Papi 2012
G. Papi, "Caravaggio e i ritratti del potere romano," in *Caravaggio tra arte* 2012, pp. 328–345.

Porzio 2012
G. Porzio, "Sulle relazioni tra l'Ordine teatino e il contesto artistico napoletano nel secolo XVII. I casi di Francesco Maria Caselli e Gaspare Del Popolo," in *Sant'Andrea Avellino e i Teatini a Napoli durante il vicereGno spagnolo. Arte, religione, società*, edited by D. A. D'Alessandro, II, Naples 2012, pp. 581–622.

Restaino 2012
C. Restaino, "Potere politico e affermazione tridentina nella decorazione seicentesca delle 'regie cappelle' di San Matteo a Salerno e Sant'Andrea ad Amalfi," in *Tesori del Regno. L'ornamentazione delle cripte delle cattedrali di Salerno e Amalfi nel XVII secolo*, edited by C. Restaino and G. Zampino, Naples 2012, pp. 19–175.

Storey 2012
T. Storey, *Carnal Commerce in Counter–reformation Rome*, Cambridge 2012.

Zuccari 2012
A. Zuccari, *Baronio e l'iconografia del martirio*, in *Cesare Baronio tra santità e scrittura storica*, Proceedings of the international colloquium (Rome, Vallicelliana Library, 25–27 June 2007), edited by F. Scorza Barcellona, R. Michetti, G. A. Guazzelli, Rome 2012, pp. 445–501.

2013
Bolzoni 2013
M. S. Bolzoni, *Il Cavalier Giuseppe Cesari d'Arpino. Maestro del disegno; catalogo ragionato dell'opera grafica*, Rome 2013.

Causa 2013
S. Causa, *Caravaggio tra le camicie nere. La pittura napoletana dei tre secoli. Dalla mostra del 1938 alle grandi esposizioni del Novecento*, Naples 2013.

Margiotta, Travagliato 2013
R. F. Margiotta, G. Travagliato, " '...Lo quale pittore si domanda Sipione Cartaro Gaitano...'. Scipione Pulzone, i Colonna e novità sulla committenza per le chiese cappuccine di Sicilia," in *Opere d'arte nelle chiese francescane. Conservazione, restauro e musealizzazione*, edited by M. C. Di Natale, Palermo 2013, pp. 91–106.

Mariti 2013
L. Mariti, "Roma capitale invisibile del

teatro del Seicento; Teatro pubblico a pagamento e comici improvvisatori. Con un 'campionario' di documenti inediti," in *Teatro e Storia* XXVII, 34, 2013, pp. 93–104, 125–140.

Paganelli 2013
M. Paganelli, *Il Caravaggio negato. "Una musica di alcuni giovani" plagio e scomparsa di un originale celebre*, Arezzo 2013.

Savina 2013
B. Savina, *Caravaggio tra originali e copie, collezionismo e il mercato dell'arte a Roma nel primo Seicento*, Foligno 2013.

Seccaroni 2013
C. Seccaroni, "A New Survey of Caravaggio's Canvases and Preparatory Layers. Materials and Aesthetic Effects," in *Caravaggio's Painting Technique. Proceedings of the Charisma Workshop*, proceedings of the conference (Florence, 17 September 2010), edited by M. Ciatti, B. G. Brunetti, Florence 2013 (Kermes quaderni), pp. 59–67.

Teza 2013
L. Teza, *Caravaggio e il frutto della virtù. Il "Mondafrutto" e l'Accademia degli Insensati*, Milan 2013.

Treffers 2013
B. Treffers, "Sulle orme del Battista: Caravaggio tra morte e vita," in *Vox clamantis in deserto. San Giovanni Battista tra arte, storia e fede,* edited by M. Sodi, Rome 2013, pp. 243–268.

Zuccari 2013
A. Zuccari, "Bellezza reale, bellezza ideale? Il corpo in Caravaggio," in *La Bellezza. Un dialogo tra credenti e non credenti*, edited by M. Forti and L. Mazas, Rome 2013, pp. 61–71.

2014
***I bassifondi del Barocco* 2014**
I bassifondi del Barocco. La Roma del vizio e della miseria, exhibition catalogue (Rome, Accademia di Francia, 7 October 2014–18 January 2015; Paris, Grandes Galeries, 24 February–24 May 2015), edited by A. Lemoine and F. Cappelletti, Milan 2014.

Berra 2014
G. Berra, "Luci, riflessi, ombre e rifrazioni nella caraffa con fiori del *Ragazzo morso da un ramarro del Caravaggio*," in *Atti della giornata di*

studi Quesiti caravaggeschi (Monte Santa Maria Tiberina, Palazzo Museo Bourbon del Monte, 29 September 2012), edited by P. Carofano, Pontedera 2014, pp. 11–71.

Cappelletti 2014
F. Cappelletti, "An Eye on the Main Chance: Cardinals, Cardinal-nephews, and Aristocratic Collectors," in *Display of Art in the Roman Palace 1550–1750*, Los Angeles 2014, pp. 78–88.

***Caravaggio. Reflections* 2014**
Caravaggio. Reflections and Refractions, edited by L. Pericolo and D. M. Stone, Farnham 2014.

Christiansen 2014
K. Christiansen, "Caravaggio's *Portrait of Maffeo Barberini* in the Palazzo Corsini, Florence," in *Caravaggio. Reflections* 2014, pp. 43–58.

Curti 2014
F. Curti, *Dalle botteghe d'arte al palazzo del cardinal del Monte. I primi anni di Caravaggio a Roma*, in *Caravaggio vero*, edited by C. Strinati, Reggio Emilia 2014, pp. 313–327.

D'Anza 2014
D. D'Anza, "Un'occasione perduta. Il Caravaggio di Hartford già in collezione Grioni," in *Ricche minere* I, 1, 2014, pp. 81–95.

Denunzio 2014
A. E. Denunzio, "Caravaggio. 'Martirio di sant'Orsola'", in *Tanzio da Varallo incontra Caravaggio. Pittura a Napoli nel primo Seicento*, exhibition catalogue (Naples, Gallerie d'Italia – Palazzo Zevallos Stigliano, 24 October 2014–11 January 2015), edited by M. C. Terzaghi, Cinisello Balsamo 2014, pp. 138–142.

Fabris 2014
D. Fabris, "Il terzo *Suonatore di liuto* di Caravaggio," in *Grenzüberschreitungen. Musik im interdisziplinären Diskurs. Festschrift für Tilman Seebass zum 75. Geburtstag*, edited by R. Ammann, F. Celestini, L. Christensen, Innsbruck 2014, pp. 23–50.

Koering 2014
J. Koering, "Au miroir de Narcisse: la peinture de Caravage?," in *Poiesis. Überdas Tun in der Kunst*, edited by A. Beyer and D. Gamboni, Berlin 2014, pp. 95–108.

Lemoine 2014
A. Lemoine, "La Roma dei bassifondi, da Caravaggio ai Bentvueghels," in *I bassifondi del Barocco* 2014, pp. 23–41.

Papi 2014a
G. Papi, *Spogliando modelli e alzando lumi. Scritti su Caravaggio e l'ambiente caravaggesco*, Naples 2014.

Papi 2014b
G. Papi, "Caravaggio e i ritratti del potere romani," in Papi 2014a, pp. 66–70.

Porzio 2014
G. Porzio, "Giovanni Bernardino Azzolino, 'Martirio di sant'Orsola'," in *Tanzio da Varallo* 2014, p. 144.

Puccini [ms. 1783] 2014
T. Puccini, [*Diario napoletano*] [ms., 1783], edited by R. Viale, CD-ROM annex to E. Spalletti, R. Viale, *Tommaso Puccini (1749–1811). Conoscitore delle arti e direttore degli Uffizi*, Florence 2014.

Puglisi 2014
C. Puglisi, "Talking pictures. Sound in Caravaggio's Art," in *Caravaggio Reflections* 2014, pp. 105–121.

***Tanzio da Varallo* 2014**
Tanzio da Varallo incontra Caravaggio. Pittura a Napoli nel primo Seicento, exhibition catalogue (Naples, Gallerie d'Italia – Palazzo Zevallos Stigliano, 24 October 2014–11 January 2015), edited by M. C. Terzaghi, Cinisello Balsamo 2014.

2015
Arbasino 2015
A. Arbasino, *Ritratti italiani*, Milan 2015.

***Caravaggio e Mattia Preti* 2015**
Caravaggio e Mattia Preti a Taverna: un confronto possibile, exhibition catalogue (Taverna, Museo Civico, 25 March–3 May 2015), edited by G. Leone and G. Valentino, Rome 2015.

Kimura 2015
T. Kimura, "Analisi iconografica del *San Giovanni Battista nel deserto* del Caravaggio della Galleria Borghese di Roma," in *Artibus et Historiae* LXXII, 2015, pp. 284–304.

Leone 2015
G. Leone, "Il *San Giovanni Battista nel deserto* di Caravaggio nella

Galleria nazionale d'Arte Antica in Palazzo Corsini," in *Caravaggio e Mattia Preti* 2015, pp. 17–33.

Morel 2015
P. Morel, *Renaissance dionysiaque: inspiration bachique, imaginaire du vin et de la vigne dans l'art européen (1430-1630)*, Paris 2015.

Paliaga 2015
F. Paliaga, "'Humilitas occidit superbiam': morte e sofferenza dei dipinti di Caravaggio," in *Interpretazione del dolore nell'arte. Caravaggio*, edited by S. Renzoni, Pisa 2015, pp. 15–45.

Tiozzo 2015
C. B. Tiozzo, *Il San Francesco che riceve le stimmate di Caravaggio nella chiesa di Fagagna (UD)*, Fagagna 2015.

Treffers 2015
B. Treffers, *Caravaggio e il sacro. Dall'arte dell'inganno all'inganno dell'arte*, Rome 2015.

Vodret 2015
R. Vodret, "Il *San Giovanni Battista* Corsini: novità dalla diagnostica," in *Caravaggio e Mattia Preti* 2015, pp. 33–43.

Whitfield 2015
C. Whitfield, "Caravaggio's *Musicians* painted for Cardinal del Monte," in *Una vita per la Storia dell'arte. Scritti in memoria di Maurizio Marini*, edited by P. di Loreto, Rome–Foligno 2015, pp. 401–415.

2016
Baroncini, Collarile 2016
R. Baroncini, L. Collarile, *L'altro Orfeo (1613) e le "nuove musiche" a Venezia*, Rome 2016.

Berra 2016
G. Berra, *Il Ragazzo morso da un ramarro del Caravaggio: l'enigma di un morso improvviso*, Florence 2016.

***Beyond Caravaggio* 2016**
Beyond Caravaggio, exhibition catalogue (London, The National Gallery, 12 October 2016–15 January 2017), edited by L. Treves, London 2016.

Cappelletti 2016
F. Cappelletti, "Northern Artists in Vincenzo Giustiniani's 'Palazzo'. Living in a Baroque Palace in Rome,

1600–38," in *Caravaggio and the Painters of the North*, exhibition catalogue (Madrid, 21 June 2016–18 September 2016), edited by G. J. van der Sman, Madrid 2016, pp. 25–31.

***Caravaggio. Opere a Roma* 2016**
Caravaggio. Opere a Roma. Tecnica e stile, I (essays), II (entries), edited by R. Vodret G. Leone, M. Cardinali, M. B. De Ruggieri, G. S. Ghia, Cinisello Balsamo 2016, 2 vols.

Cardinali 2016
M. Cardinali, "La tecnica pittorica di Caravaggio. Una storia tecnica dell'arte," in *Caravaggio. Opere a Roma* 2016, I, pp. 52–88.

Cardinali *et al.* 2016
M. Cardinali *et al.*, "The Rediscovered Portrait of Prospero Farinacci by Caravaggio," in *Artibus et Historiae* 73, 2016, pp. 249–283.

Cosma 2016
A. Cosma, "Verso un nuovo fedecommesso. Vicende del palazzo e della collezione Corsini tra dispersioni, restauri e riallestimenti (1795–1829)," in *Storie di Palazzo Corsini. Storie di Palazzo Corsini. Protagonisti e vicende nell'Ottocento*, edited by A. Cosma and S. Pedone, Rome 2016, pp. 17–38, 175–218.

Cuppone 2016
M. Cuppone, "Giuditta che taglia la testa a Oloferne," in *Artemisia Gentileschi e il suo tempo*, exhibition catalogue (Rome, Palazzo Braschi, 30 November 2016–7 May 2017), edited by F. Baldassarri, Milan 2016, p. 80.

***Da Caravaggio* 2016**
Da Caravaggio. Il San Giovanni Battista Costa (Studi, scoperte e restauri in Santo Stefano degli Agostiniani a Empoli; 3), Proceedings of the study day (Empoli, 11 April 2015), edited by V. Siemoni, s.l. 2016.

De Marchi 2016
A. G. De Marchi, *Collezione Doria Pamphilj: catalogo generale dei dipinti*, Milan 2016.

De Ruggieri 2016a
M. B. De Ruggieri, "La tecnica pittorica di Caravaggio. Processi compositivi e strutture materiali," in *Caravaggio. Opere a Roma* 2016, I, pp. 88–131.

De Ruggieri 2016b
M.B. De Ruggieri, "San Giovanni Battista. Tecnica pittorica," in *Caravaggio. Opere a Roma: tecnica e stile*, edited by R. Vodret, G. Leone, M. Cardinali, M.B De Ruggieri, G.S. Ghia 2016, Cinisello Balsamo 2016, II, pp. 526–528.

Granata 2016
B. Granata, "Conversione di san Paolo," in *Caravaggio. Opere a Roma* 2016, p. 304.

Leone 2016
G. Leone, "Nella bottega di Lorenzo Carli: precisazioni, riflessioni e una notarella su Caravaggio giovane / The Studio of Lorenzo Carli: Reflections and a Note on the Young Caravaggio," in *Caravaggio. Opere a Roma* 2016, I, pp. 184–209.

Moro 2016
F. Moro, *Caravaggio sconosciuto. Le origini del Merisi, eccellente disegnatore, maestro di ritratti e di "cose naturali"*, Turin 2016.

Negro 2016
A. Negro, "San Giovanni Battista," in *Caravaggio. Opere a Roma* 2016, II, pp. 522–524.

***L'origine della natura morta* 2016**
L'origine della natura morta in Italia. Caravaggio e il Maestro di Hartford, exhibition catalogue (Rome, Galleria Borghese, 16 November 2016–19 February 2017), edited by A. Coliva and D. Dotti, Milan 2016.

Papi 2016a
G. Papi, "Riflessioni sui dipinti di Caravaggio per Ottavio Costa, sulle copie e sulla nuova Giuditta di Giuseppe Vermiglio," in *Da Caravaggio* 2016, pp. 57–63.

Papi 2016b
G. Papi, "Riflessioni sui dipinti di Caravaggio per Ottavio Costa, sulle copie e sulla nuova Giuditta di Giuseppe," in *Entro l'aria bruna d'una camera rinchiusa: scritti su Caravaggio e l'ambiente caravaggesco*, Naples 2016, pp. 8–18.

Spear 2016
R. E. Spear, *Dipingere per profitto: le vite economiche dei pittori della Roma del Seicento*, Rome 2016.

Terzaghi 2016a
M. C. Terzaghi, "Caravaggio. Salomè con la cabeza de San Juan Bautista," in *De Caravaggio a Bernini. Obras Maestras del Seicento italiano en las Collecciónes Reales*, exhibition catalogue (Madrid, Palacio Real, June–October 2016), edited by G. Redín Michaus, Madrid 2016, pp. 122–129.

Terzaghi 2016b
M. C. Terzaghi, "Il 'San Giovanni Battista' e i Caravaggio Costa. Novità e riflessioni," in *Da Caravaggio* 2016, pp. 10–17.

Treves 2016
L. Treves, "Boy Peeling Fruit," in *Beyond Caravaggio* 2016, p. 42.

2017
Atti delle Giornate di Studi 2017
Atti delle Giornate di Studi Caravaggio e i suoi, proceeding of the conference (Monte Santa Maria Tiberina, Palazzo Bourbon del Monte, 8-9 October 2016), edited by P. Carofano, Pisa 2017.

Boccardo 2017
P. Boccardo, *"Vanita vanitatum et omnia vanitas*. Vita, carriere, mecenatismo e collezionismo di Giovan Carlo e Marco Antonio Doria," in *L'ultimo Caravaggio* 2017, pp. 43–57.

Borsellino 2017
E. Borsellino, *La collezione Corsini di Roma dalle origini alla donazione alla Stato Italiano: dipinti e sculture*, 2 vols., Rome 2017.

Cappelletti 2017
F. Cappelletti, *Caravaggio: l'opera oltre la leggenda*, Rome 2017.

***Caravaggio. I Musici* 2017**
Caravaggio. I Musici, exhibition catalogue (Naples, Gallerie d'Italia, Palazzo Zevallos Stigliano, 6 May–16 July 2017), Venice 2017.

***Caravaggio nel patrimonio* 2017**
Caravaggio nel patrimonio del Fondo Edifici di Culto. Il doppio e la copia, exhibition catalogue (Rome, National Galleries of Ancient Art, Palazzo Barberini, 21 June–16 July 2017), edited by G. S. Ghia and C. Strinati, Rome 2017.

Copello 2017
V. Copello, "Nuovi elementi su Vittoria Colonna i cappuccini e i gesuiti," in *Lettere Italiane* LXIX, 2, 2017, pp. 296–327.

Careri 2017
G. Careri, *Caravaggio. La fabbrica dello spettatore*, Milan 2017.

Cuppone 2017
Michele Cuppone, "'Un quadro ch'io gli dipingo'. Nuova luce su Caravaggio per Ottavio Costa, dalla *Giuditta* al *San Giovanni Battista*," in *Atti delle Giornate di Studi* 2017, pp. 59–77.

Curti 2017a
F. Curti, "Caravaggio a Roma tra botteghe d'arte e committenze: il metodo storico e nuovi spunti documentari sui cavalletti e sul quadro 'cum figuris,'" in *Atti delle Giornate di Studi*. 2017, pp. 109–120.

Curti 2017b
F. Curti, "Rivalità di botteghe, rivalità di pittori: un'ipotesi per la nascita dell'inimicizia tra Caravaggio, Giovanni Baglione e Tommaso Salini," in *Dentro Caravaggio* 2017, pp. 269–275.

***Da Caravaggio a Bernini* 2017**
Da Caravaggio a Bernini. Capolavori del Seicento italiano nelle Collezioni Reali di Spagna, exhibition catalogue (Rome, Scuderie del Quirinale, 14 April–30 July 2017), edited by G. Redín Michaus, Milan 2017.

D'Alessandro 2017
D. A. D'Alessandro, "Caravaggio's 'musical' paintings for Cardinal del Monte / I dipinti 'musicali' di Caravaggio per il cardinal del Monte," in *Caravaggio. I Musici* 2017, pp. 49–65.

De Dominici [1742–1743] 2017
B. De Dominici, *Vite de' pittori, scultori ed architetti napoletani* [1742–1743], edited and annotated by F. Sricchia Santoro and A. Zezza [2003–2014], Naples 2017.

***Dentro Caravaggio* 2017**
Dentro Caravaggio, exhibition catalogue (Milan, Palazzo Reale, 29 September 2017–28 January 2018), edited by R. Vodret, Milan 2017.

Denunzio 2017
E. Denunzio, "Caravaggio. Martirio di sant'Orsola," in *L'ultimo Caravaggio* 2017, pp. 100–102.

Di Monte 2017
M. Di Monte, "San Giovanni Battista," in *Dentro Caravaggio* 2017, pp. 124–131.

Fabris 2017
D. Fabris, "I suonatori di liuto di Caravaggio / Caravaggio's the Lute Players," in *Monteverdi e Caravaggio sonar stromenti e figurar la musica*, exhibition catalogue (Cremona, Museo del Violino, 8 April–23 July 2017), Cremona 2017, pp. 133–139.

Falcucci 2017
C. Falcucci, "Come dipingeva Caravaggio? Forse così," in *Dentro Caravaggio* 2017, pp. 305–326.

Gandolfi 2017
R. Gandolfi, "I primi anni di Caravaggio a Roma," in *Dentro Caravaggio* 2017, pp. 249–260.

Morandotti 2017
A. Morandotti, "Da Procaccini a Strozzi. L'alternativa a Caravaggio lungo l'asse Milano–Genova," in *L'ultimo Caravaggio* 2017, pp. 13–18.

Negro, Roio 2017
E. Negro, N. Roio, *Caravaggio e il ritratto*, Rome 2017.

Porzio 2017
G. Porzio, *Bartolomeo Cavarozzi pittore di nature morte. Un nuovo sguardo sulla questione*, in *Bartolomeo Cavarozzi a Genova*, exhibition catalogue (Genoa, Galleria Nazionale di Palazzo Spinola, 6 December 2017–8 April 2018), edited by G. Zanelli, Genoa 2017, pp. 63–77.

Primarosa 2017
Y. Primarosa, *Ottavio Leoni (1578–1630). Eccellente miniator di ritratti. Catalogo ragionato dei disegni e dei dipinti*, Rome 2017.

Rossini 2017
F. Rossini, "Giovan Battista Strozzi il giovane a Roma: la lezione in biasmo della superbia (1611)," in *Aevum* 91, 3, 2017, pp. 733–760

Schütze 2017
S. Schütze, *Caravaggio. L'opera completa*, Cologne 2017, pp. 443–445.

Terzaghi 2017
M. C. Terzaghi, "Caravaggio's *Musici | I Musici* di Caravaggio," in *Caravaggio. I Musici* 2017, pp. 15–47.

***L'ultimo Caravaggio* 2017**
L'ultimo Caravaggio, eredi e nuovi maestri. Napoli, Genova e Milano a confronto. 1610–1640, exhibition catalogue (Milan, Gallerie d'Italia, 30 November 2017–8 April 2018), edited by A. Morandotti, Milan 2017.

Vodret 2017a
R. Vodret, "Dentro Caravaggio," in *Dentro Caravaggio* 2017, pp. 201–236.

Vodret 2017b
R. Vodret, "Giuditta che taglia la testa a Oloferne," in *Dentro Caravaggio* 2017, pp. 88–95.

Zafran 2017
E.M. Zafran, "The Atheneum to the Fore: Hartford and the Italian Baroque," in *Buying Baroque. Italian Seventeenth-Century paintings come to America*, edited by E. P. Bowron, University Park (PA) 2017, pp. 28–39.

2018
***Andare oltre* 2018**
Andare oltre la povertà delle forme. Le ragioni spirituali e materiali della nascita e dello sviluppo dell'Ordine dei Frati Minori Cappuccini, edited by G. Crudo, Rome 2018, pp. 125–138.

Bellori [1672] 2018
G. P. Bellori, *Le vite de' pittori, scultori et architetti moderni* [1672], ed. critica bilingue: *Le vite de' pittori scultori ed architetti moderni | Die Lebensbeschreibungen der modernen Maler, Bildhauer und Architekten*, edited by E. Oy–Marra, T. Weddigen, A. Brug, V: *Vita di Michelangelo Merigi da Caravaggio | Das Leben des Michelangelo Merisi da Caravaggio*, translation by V. von Rosen, edited, commentary and essay by V. von Rosen, translation and commentary with the collaboration of A. Brug, I. Franconi, Göttingen 2018.

Benay 2018
E. E. Benay, *Exporting Caravaggio:* The Crucifixion of Saint Andrew, London 2018.

Berra 2018a
G. Berra, "Il Caravaggio da Milano a Roma: problemi e ipotesi," in *Il giovane Caravaggio* 2018, pp. 30–45.

Berra 2018b
G. Berra, "E il Caravaggio disse che 'tanta manifattura gl'era à fare un quadro buono di fiori, come di figure'," in *L'arte di vivere l'arte: scritti in onore di Claudio Strinati*, edited by P. Di Loreto, Rome 2018, pp. 113–129, 453–479.

Berra 2018c
G. Berra, "Le copie del 'San Francesco in meditazione sulla morte' del Caravaggio," in *Originali, repliche, copie. Uno sguardo diverso sui grandi maestri*, edited by P. Di Loreto, Rome 2018, pp. 117–125.

***Caravage à Rome* 2018**
Caravage à Rome: amis et ennemis, echibition catalogue (Paris, Musée Jacquemart-André, 21 September 2018–28 January 2019), edited by F. Cappelletti, P. Curie, M. C. Terzaghi, Brussels 2018.

Carminati 2018
C. Carminati, *Vita e morte del Cavalier Marino. Edizione e commento della Vita di Giovan Battista Baiacca, 1625, e della Relazione della pompa funerale fatta dall'Accademia degli Umoristi di Roma, 1626*, Bologna 2018.

Causa 2018
S. Causa, *La parola alle cose. Sentieri e scritture della natura morta (1922–1972)*, Naples 2018.

D'Alessandro 2018
D. A. D'Alessandro, "Un madrigale napoletano per Caravaggio. Novità sui 'Musici' Del Monte," in *Ricerche sull'arte a Napoli in età moderna. Saggi e documenti 2017–2018. Annali della Fondazione De Vito*, Naples 2018, pp. 50–85.

Di Tomasi 2018
R. Di Tomasi, *L'eredità di Caravaggio. Nuove ipotesi sull'arrivo a Roma*, Rome 2018.

Gandolfi 2018
R. Gandolfi, "Notizie sul giovane Caravaggio dall'inedita biografia di Gaspare Celio," in *Il giovane Caravaggio* 2018, pp. 20–29.

Gazzara 2018
L. Gazzara, *Giovan Battista Manso promotore delle arti e della cultura nella Napoli del XVII secolo*, in *Manso, Lemos, Cervantes: letteratura, arti e scienza nella Napoli del primo Seicento*, edited by R. Mondola, Naples 2018, pp. 39–67.

***Il giovane Caravaggio* 2018**
Il giovane Caravaggio. "Sine ira et studio", proceedings of the study day (Roma, Sapienza Università di Roma, 1 March 2017), edited by A. Zuccari, Rome 2018.

Papi 2018a
G. Papi, "Il *Narciso* Barberini: da Caravaggio a Spadarino," in G. Papi, *Senza più attendere a studio e insegnamenti*, Rome–Naples 2018, pp. 217–232.

Papi 2018b
G. Papi, "I primi ritratti di Caravaggio. Per la cronologia posticipata della *Giuditta* e del *San Giovanni Battista* Costa," in *Il giovane Caravaggio* 2018, pp. 122–131.

Terzaghi 2018
M. C. Terzaghi, "Tracce per la *Canestra* e la natura morta al tempo di Caravaggio," in *Il giovane Caravaggio* 2018, pp. 108–121.

Teza 2018
L. Teza, "Considerazioni sul *Mondafrutto*, sul *Bacchino malato* e su 'un ritratto di villano'," in *Il giovane Caravaggio* 2018, pp. 56–63.

Vodret 2018
R. Vodret, "La *Buona ventura* della Pinacoteca Capitolina: qualche riflessione sulle analisi tecniche," in *Il giovane Caravaggio* 2018, pp. 74–83.

Zuccari 2018
A. Zuccari, "Le due versioni del *Ragazzo morso da un ramarro* attribuite a Caravaggio," in *Il giovane Caravaggio* 2018, pp. 64–73.

2019
Aiello 2019
P. Aiello, *Caravaggio 1951*, Milan 2019.

***Caravaggio*. Judith et Holopherne 2019**
Caravaggio. Judith et Holopherne, auction catalogue (Toulouse, Labarbe – Cabinet Turquin, 27 June 2019), Paris 2019.

***Caravaggio Napoli* 2019**
Caravaggio Napoli, exhibition catalogue (Naples, Museo e Real Bosco di Capodimonte, 12 April–14 July 2019), edited by M.C. Terzaghi, Milan 2019.

Causa 2019
S. Causa, "Un teatro tutto terreno. Sul significato delle mostre caravaggesche," in *Caravaggio Napoli* 2019, pp. 92–101.

Cecchi 2019
P. Cecchi, "Strozzi Giulio," in *Dizionario Biografico degli Italiani*, Rome 2019, vol. XCIV, *ad vocem*.

Christiansen 2019
K. Christiansen, "Some Thoughts on Caravaggio. The Market, Style, and Chronology," in *Gli amici per Nicola Spinosa* edited by F. Baldassarri and M. Confalone, Rome 2019, pp. 33–42.

Curti 2019
F. Curti, "'Lavorando con Tarquinio et a la sera nelle botteghe': Caravaggio da Ligustri alla casa di Pandolfo Pucci: nuove proposte per i primi tempi romani," in *La luce e i silenzi*, exhibition catalogue (Fabriano, Pinacoteca Bruno Molajoli, 2 August–8 December 2019), edited by A. M. Ambrosini Massari and A. Delpriori, Ancona 2019, pp. 138–145.

Ebert-Schifferer 2019
S. Ebert-Schifferer, *Caravaggio. Sehen, staunen, glauben. Der Maler und sein Werk*, Munich 2019.

Forgione, Magliani 2019
G. Forgione, M. Magliani, *Nostra Signora della Misericordia. Caravaggio*, Verona 2019.

Gazzara 2019
L. Gazzara, "Caravaggio nella prima cappella del Pio Monte della Misericordia," in *Caravaggio Napoli* 2019, pp. 60–69.

Gandolfi 2019
R. Gandolfi, "Il 'turcimanno' del Caravaggio. Prospero Orsi tra pittura e mercato nella Roma del Seicento," in *Le collezioni degli artisti in Italia*, edited by F. Parrilla and M. Borchia, Rome 2019, pp. 85–98.

Haskell 2019
F. Haskell, *Mecenati e pittori. L'arte e la società italiane nell'età barocca*, edited by T. Montanari, Turin 2019.

Papi, Sframeli 2019
G. Papi, M. Sframeli, *La cattura di Cristo da Caravaggio. Un recupero per le Gallerie degli Uffizi*, Livorno 2019.

Porzio 2019
G. Porzio, *Carlo Sellitto. 1580–1614*, Naples 2019.

Schütze 2019
S. Schütze, "Narcissus and the Pathopoeia of the Early Modern Age," in *Caravaggio Bernini. Early Baroque in Rome*, exhibition catalogue (Vienna, Kunsthistorisches Museum, 15 October 2019–19 January 2020; Amsterdam, Rijksmuseum, 14 February–7 June 2020), edited by G. Swoboda and S. Weppelmann, Munich–London–New York 2019, pp. 46–55.

Terzaghi 2019
M. C. Terzaghi, "Caravaggio a Napoli: un percorso," in *Caravaggio Napoli* 2019, pp. 30–59.

2020
Andolina 2020
G. Andolina, "L'Accademia degli Uniti e l'attività teatrale nella bottega del Cavalier d'Arpino," in *Caravaggio e i letterati* 2020, pp. 13–19.

Berger 2020
S. Berger, "From Narcissus to Narcosis," in *Art History* 43, 3, 2020, pp. 612–639.

Berra 2020
G. Berra, "La formazione culturale del Caravaggio: 'Io non me deletto de compor versi ne volgari ne latini'," in *Caravaggio e i letterati* 2020, pp. 20–44.

Caravaggio e i letterati **2020**
Caravaggio e i letterati, proceedings of the interdisciplinary studies conference (Rome, Bibliotheca Hertziana, 20–21 April 2018), edited by S. Ebert–Schifferer and L. Teza, Todi 2020.

Causa 2020
S. Causa, "Il portinaio dell'Ospizio dei Pellegrini. Longhi e i suoi interlocutori al Pio Monte della Misericordia," in *Pio Monte della Misericordia* 2020, I, pp. 45–67.

I marmi Torlonia **2020**
I marmi Torlonia. Collezionare capolavori, exhibition catalogue (Rome, Musei Capitolini, Villa Caffarelli, 14 October 2020–29 June 2021) edited by S. Settis and C. Gasparri, Milan 2020.

Orazio Borgianni **2020**
Orazio Borgianni. Un genio inquieto nella Roma di Caravaggio, exhibition catalogue (Rome, Gallerie nazionali di Arte Antica Palazzo Barberini, 6 March–1 November 2020), edited by G. Papi, Milan 2020.

Papi 2020
G. Papi, "Una proposta per la cena in Emmaus Patrizi di Caravaggio," in *Un misto di grano e di pula. Scritti su Caravaggio e l'ambiente caravaggesco*, Naples–Rome 2020, pp. 8–19.

Peterzano: allievo di Tiziano **2020**
Peterzano: allievo di Tiziano, maestro di Caravaggio, exhibition catalogue (Bergamo, Accademia Carrara, 6 February–17 May 2020), edited by S. Facchinetti, F. Frangi, P. Plebani, M. C. Rodeschini, Milan 2020.

Pio Monte della Misericordia **2020**
Pio Monte della Misericordia. Il patrimonio storico e artistico, edited by P. D'Alconzo and L. P. Rocco di Torrepadula, with the collaboration of L. Gazzara, Naples 2020.

Schütze 2020
S. Schütze, *Caravaggio. The Complete Works,* Cologne 2020.

Terzaghi 2020a
M. C. Terzaghi, "Per le fonti del naturalismo di Caravaggio: il teatro," in *Caravaggio e i letterati* 2020, pp. 79–97.

Terzaghi 2020b
M. C. Terzaghi, *Vermiglio Giuseppe*, *Dizionario Biografico degli Italiani*, vol. 98, Rome 2020, *ad vocem*.

Terzaghi 2020c
M. C. Terzaghi, "Caravaggio 1584–1588: la bottega di Simone Peterzano," in *Peterzano: allievo di Tiziano* 2020, pp. 53–65.

2021
Bassani 2021
R. Bassani, *La donna del Caravaggio. Vita e peripezie di Maddalena Antognetti*, Rome 2021.

Bellini 2021
F. Bellini, "La modella e il 'pittor celebre': una storia in sette quadri," afterword, in R. Bassani, *La donna del Caravaggio. Vita e peripezie di Maddalena Antognetti*, Rome 2021, pp. 199–238.

Berra 2021a
G. Berra "Il 'ramo tagliato' nella corona di spine dell''Ecce Homo' di Madrid attribuito al Caravaggio," in *Aboutartonline.com*, 11 luglio 2021: https://www.aboutartonline.com/il–ramo–tagliato–nella–corona–di–spine–dellecce–homo–di–madrid–attribuito–al–caravaggio/.

Berra 2021b
G. Berra, *Il viaggio della marchesa di Caravaggio Costanza Colonna da Genova a Napoli a bordo di una galera maltese. Lettere inedite*, Heidelberg 2021.

Caravaggio a Napoli **2021**
Caravaggio a Napoli. Nuovi dati e nuove idee, proceedings of the study days (Naples, Museo di Capodimonte 13–14 January 2020), edited by M. C. Terzaghi (Studi di Storia dell'Arte, speciale, 2), Todi 2021.

Caravaggio a Parigi **2021**
Caravaggio a Parigi. Novità e riflessioni sugli anni romani, proceedings of the conference *Caravaggio. Una vita barocca* (Paris, Italian Cultural Institute, 9 January 2019), edited by F. Cappelletti, M. C. Terzaghi, P. Curie, Rome–Naples 2021.

Caravaggio e Artemisia **2021**
Caravaggio e Artemisia: la sfida di Giuditta. Violenza e seduzione nella pittura tra Cinque e Seicento, exhibition catalogue (Rome, Palazzo Barberini, 26 November 2021–27 March 2022), edited by M. C. Terzaghi, Rome 2021.

Causa 2021
S. Causa, "Più Caravaggio di così si muore," in *Il Giornale dell'Arte* 9 April 2021: https://www.ilgiornaledellarte.com/Articolo/Piu–Caravaggio–di–cosi–si–muore.

Cuppone 2021a
M. Cuppone, *Caravaggio. La Natività di Palermo: nascita e scomparsa di un capolavoro*, Rome 2021 (Saggi di storia dell'arte, 64).

Cuppone 2021b
M. Cuppone, "Sul ritorno di Mario Minniti in Sicilia," in *L'archivio di Caravaggio. Scritti in onore di don Sandro Corradini*, edited by P. di Loreto, Rome 2021, pp. 61–65.

Curti 2021
F. Curti, "Gli *Ecce Homo* di Caravaggio nei documenti e nelle fonti letterarie," in Sgarbi 2021, pp. 41–47.

Falcucci 2021
C. Falcucci, "Lo studio della tecnica esecutiva: approcci e metodi scientifici," in Vodret 2021, appendix IV, pp. 102–106.

Forgione 2021
G. Forgione, "Caravaggio e la tradizione. 'L'invenzione di "Nostra Signora della Misericordia'," in *Caravaggio a Napoli.* 2021, pp. 25–38.

Gandolfi 2021
R. Gandolfi, *Le vite degli artisti di Gaspare Celio. "Compendio delle Vite di Vasari con alcune altre aggiunte"*, Florence 2021.

Giani 2021
F. M. Giani, "Il *Martirio di San Pietro* di Carlo Sellitto da Sant'Anna dei Lombardi a Napoli all'Ospedale Sant'Anna a Como," in *Prospettiva* 184, 2021, pp. 83–88.

Giuliano Briganti, Roberto Longhi **2021**
Giuliano Briganti, Roberto Longhi. Incontri. Corrispondenza 1939–1969, edited by L. Laureati, Milan 2021.

Guerrieri Borsoi 2021
M. B. Guerrieri Borsoi, "Alla ricerca di Giovanni Bricci pittore," in *Una rivoluzione silenziosa. Plautilla Bricci pittrice e architettrice*, exhibition catalogue (Rome, Galleria Corsini, 5 November 2021–19 April 2022), edited by Y. Primarosa, Rome 2021, pp. 102–123.

Le Meditationes vitae **2021**
Le Meditationes vitae Christi in volgare secondo il codice Paris, BnF, it. 115, edited by D. Dotto, D. Falvay, A. Montefusco, Venice 2021.

Papi 2021
G. Papi, "Riflessioni sulla *Maddalena* napoletana di Caravaggio," in *Caravaggio a Parigi* 2021, pp. 60–71.

Puddu 2021
P. L. Puddu, "Riflessioni sulla *Flagellazione* di Caravaggio già in collezione Borghese," in *Caravaggio a Napoli* 2021, pp. 101–112.

Pulini 2021
M. Pulini, "'*È il vero* Ecce Homo *di Caravaggio*' pubblichiamo il saggio di Massimo Pulini autore della straordinaria scoperta," in *Aboutartonline.com*, 31 March 2021: https://www.aboutartonline.com/e-il-vero-ecce-homo-di-caravaggio/.

Ricci 2021
S. Ricci, "Caravaggio e i filosofi, nuove considerazioni," in *Caravaggio a Napoli* 2021, pp. 13–23.

Sgarbi 2021
V. Sgarbi, *Ecce Caravaggio. Da Roberto Longhi a oggi*, Milan 2021.

Spina 2021
F. Spina, "Louis Finson e la *Giuditta*. Novità sulla presenza del pittore fiammingo nella Roma di Caravaggio," in *Caravaggio e Artemisia* 2021, pp. 81–84

Terzaghi 2021a
M. C. Terzaghi, *Caravaggio a Roma. Note per un percorso*, in *Caravaggio a Parigi* 2021, pp. 9–25.

Terzaghi 2021b
M. C. Terzaghi, "Caravaggio millennial. Un nuovo *Ecce Homo* del Merisi," in *Caravaggio a Napoli* 2021, pp. 188–210.

Terzaghi 2021c
M. C. Terzaghi, "La *Giuditta* di Caravaggio e i suoi primi interpreti," in *Caravaggio e Artemisia* 2021, pp. 47–79.

Tutini [c. 1664–1666] 2021
C. Tutini, *De' pittori, scultori, architetti, miniatori et ricamatori napolitani e regnicoli* [ms., 1664–1666 c.], edited by L. Giuliano, Matera 2021.

Vincenzo Giustiniani 2021
Vincenzo Giustiniani, Scritti editi e inediti, edited by S. Danesi Squarzina and L. Capoduro, Vatican City 2021.

Vodret 2021a
R. Vodret, *Caravaggio. 1571–1610*, Cinisello Balsamo 2021.

Vodret 2021b
R. Vodret, *Come dipingeva Caravaggio*, in Vodret 2021a, appendix III, pp. 94–101.

Vodret 2021c
R. Vodret, "La *Giuditta che taglia la testa a Oloferne* di Tolosa, considerazioni sulle analisi tecniche e confronti con la prassi esecutiva di Caravaggio," in *Caravaggio a Napoli* 2021, pp. 85–99.

2022
Benati 2022
D. Benati, "Ancora su Guido Reni e il paesaggio: il *Rinaldo Corradini sul mulo*," in *Guido Reni alla Galleria Borghese. Dopo la mostra gli studi*, edited by F. Cappelletti and R. Morselli, Genoa 2022, pp. 30–41.

Caravaggio, ultimo approdo 2022
Caravaggio, ultimo approdo. Un artista in fuga tra incompiuti e repliche, exhibition catalogue (Ragusa, Church of the Badia, 13 May–15 October 2022), edited by P. Carofano, Pontedera 2022.

Cappelletti 2022
F. Cappelletti, "Il *David con la testa di Golia* di Caravaggio dalla collezione al museo," in *Nono dialogo Brera* 2022, pp. 16–33.

Cassiani 2022
G. Cassiani, *Tommaso Bozio. I saperi scientifici e i libri "lincei" (1548–1610)*, Rome 2022.

Costantini 2022
P. Costantini, "Il nostro umile modo di costruire conventi," in *Italia Francescana* 1, 2022, pp. 125–138.

Curti, Verdi 2022
F. Curti, O. Verdi, "Caravaggio, Lena e Maddalena Antognetti. Una storia da riscrivere," in *Storia dell'arte* n.s. 2, 158, 2022, pp. 48–63.

Hodde 2022
J. Hodde, *Ein Bild und sein Doppelgänger. Zur Medialität der Narziss-Darstellung von Caravaggio*, Bielefeld 2022.

Nono dialogo Brera 2022
Nono dialogo Brera. Caravaggio. Cena in Emmaus / David con la testa di Golia, exhibition catalogue (Milan, Pinacoteca di Brera, 21 June–25 September 2022), edited by L. Lodi, Milan 2022.

Papi 2022
G. Papi, *Antiveduto Gramatica. A Rediscovered Concert Scene*, London 2022.

Pinto 2022
A. Pinto, *Raccolta notizie per la storia, arte, architettura di Napoli e dintorni. Parte 1.2: artisti e artigiani m–z*, 2022.

Porzio 2022
G. Porzio, "Alle origini del naturalismo meridionale. Un contributo per Loys Croys e gli esordi di Carlo Sellitto," in *Bollettino d'arte* VII, 50, 2022, pp. 119–124.

Pulini 2022
M. Pulini, *Bartolomeo Mendozzi da Leonessa. Un maestro del Seicento tra l'Incredulità, il caso Ducamps e i nuovi documenti*, Borgo San Giovanni 2022.

Sarti 2022
M. G. Sarti, "Cristo flagellato," in *Tiziano. Venere che benda Amore e i dipinti degli ultimi anni*, edited by M. G. Sarti, Rome 2022, pp. 73–75.

Spagnolo 2022a
D. Spagnolo, "Le libertà del Caravaggio in Sicilia e una traccia sul *Cavadenti*," in *Caravaggio e caravaggeschi. Riflessioni e aggiornamenti*, Messina 2022, pp. 27–41.

Spagnolo 2022b
D. Spagnolo, "Salvatore Mittica, pittore messinese, in versione caravaggesca: una testa di vecchia dal *Cavadenti* e un *Ecce Homo*," in *Studi in onore di Maria Pia Di Dario Guida*, edited by G. Bongiovanni, G. De Marco, M. K. Guida, Naples 2022, pp. 210–216.

Terzaghi 2022a
M. C. Terzaghi, "In fuga. Caravaggio tra Roma e Napoli | On the Run: Caravaggio between Rome and Naples," in *Nono dialogo Brera* 2022, pp. 69–87.

Terzaghi 2022b
M. C. Terzaghi, "Battistello e Caravaggio in context," in *Il patriarca bronzeo dei caravaggeschi. Battistello Caracciolo 1578-1635*, exhibition catalogue (Naples, Museo e Real Bosco di Capodimonte, 9 June–2 October 2022), edited by S. Causa, Naples 2022, pp. 55–69.

Vodret 2022a
R. Vodret, "Per la datazione del *Ritratto di Fillide* 'corteggiana scandalosa'," in *Scritti di donne, 40 studiose per la storia dell'arte*, edited by S. Macioce, Foligno 2022 pp. 431–441.

Vodret 2022b
R. Vodret, "'… *unum quadrum sui retractus manu Michaelis Angeli de Caravagio'*, è di Fillide Melandroni. Una nuova lettura del testamento," in *About art online*, 20 february 2022.

Zuccari 2022a
A. Zuccari, *Cantiere Caravaggio. Questioni aperte, indagini, interpretazioni*, Rome 2022.

Zuccari 2022b
A. Zuccari, "Ricerca scientifica e produzione artistica nella Roma dei primi Lincei," in *Atti dell'Accademia Nazionale dei Lincei, Classe di Scienze morali. Rendiconti* IX, 33, 1–2, 2022, pp. 197–202.

Zuccari 2022c
A. Zuccari, "L'*Ecce Homo* di Madrid: un nuovo Caravaggio?," in Zuccari 2022a, pp. 325–328.

2023
Baglione [1642] 2023
G. Baglione, *Le vite de' pittori, scultori et architetti* [1642], critical edition with commentary, edited by B. Agosti and P. Tosini, Rome 2023.

Cappelletti 2023
F. Cappelletti, "Giardini, marmi e 'belle pitture'. Il primo tempo della Galleria Borghese e le sue metamorfosi," in F. Cappelletti, *Galleria Borghese*, Naples 2023, pp. 21–48.

Caravaggio. L'Ecce Homo svelato 2023
*Caravaggio. L'*Ecce Homo *svelato*, edited by K. Christiansen, G. Papi, G. Porzio, M. C. Terzaghi, scientific direction by M. C. Terzaghi, Venice 2023.

Cecco del Caravaggio 2023
Cecco del Caravaggio. L'allievo modello, exhibition catalogue (Bergamo, Accademia Carrara, 27 January–4 June 2023), edited by G. Papi, Milan 2023.

Christiansen 2023
K. Christiansen, "Riflessioni sull'*Ecce Homo* e sui dipinti di Caravaggio risalenti al periodo post romano," in *Caravaggio. L'*Ecce Homo *svelato* 2023, pp. 111–139.

Cipriani 2023
A. Cipriani, "*Ecce Homo*: l'intervento di restauro," in *Caravaggio. L'*Ecce Homo *svelato* 2023, pp. 141–147.

Cuppone 2023
M. Cuppone, *Caravaggio, la* Natività *di Palermo. Nascita e scomparsa di un capolavoro*, 3rd expanded, revised and updated edition, Rome 2023.

Curti 2023
F. Curti, "'Misesi in una feluca con alcune poche robe': l'ultimo viaggio di Caravaggio," in *Storia dell'arte* 160, 2023, pp. 86–111.

Falcucci 2023
C. Falcucci, "Le indagini diagnostiche e lo studio della tecnica esecutiva: considerazioni e confronti," in *Caravaggio. L'*Ecce Homo *svelato* 2023, pp. 149–165.

***L'immagine sovrana* 2023**
L'immagine sovrana. Urbano VIII e i Barberini, exhibition catalogue (Rome, Gallerie Nazionali di Arte Antica Barberini Corsini, 18 March–30 July 2023), edited by M. Cicconi, F. Gennari Santori, S. Schütze, Rome 2023.

Macioce 2023
S. Macioce, *Michelangelo Merisi da Caravaggio. Documenti, fonti e inventari 1513–1848*, 3rd updated edition, Rome 2023.

Manganelli 2023
G. Manganelli, *Emigrazioni oniriche*, edited by A. Cortellessa, Milan 2023.

***Orazio Gentileschi* 2023**
Orazio Gentileschi e l'immagine di san Francesco. La nascita del caravaggismo a Roma, exhibition catalogue (Rome, Gallerie Nazionali di Arte Antica, Palazzo Barberini, 27 January–10 April 2023), edited by G. Porzio and Y. Primarosa, Rome 2023.

Papa 2023
R. Papa, "Questioni sul *San Giovanni Battista* in Caravaggio," in *L'enigma Caravaggio 1951–2021: nuovi studi a confronto*, edited by S. Rossi and R. Papa, Foligno 2023, pp. 111–121.

Papi 2023a
G. Papi, *Caravaggio's Portrait of a Gentleman with a Ruff*, Florence 2023.

Papi 2023b
G. Papi, *Cecco del Caravaggio*, Florence 2023.

Papi 2023c
G. Papi, "*L'Ecce Homo* di Caravaggio ritrovato a Madrid," in *Caravaggio. L'*Ecce Homo *svelato* 2023, pp. 49–77.

Porzio 2023
G. Porzio, "Caravaggio a Napoli e l'*Ecce Homo* di Madrid," in *Caravaggio. L'*Ecce Homo *svelato* 2023, pp. 79–109.

Sciberras 2023
K. Sciberras, *Art as Life. Caravaggio in Malta*, Valletta 2023.

Terzaghi 2023a
M. C. Terzaghi, "Il *Concerto* di Antiveduto Gramatica: musica e musici al tempo di Caravaggio," conference on the occasion of the study day dedicated to Cecco del Caravaggio (Bergamo, Accademia Carrara, 3 May 2023): https://www.youtube.com/watch?v=6PMhLvgT4wU.

Terzaghi 2023b
M. C. Terzaghi, "L'*Ecce Homo* di Caravaggio: follow up di una scoperta," in *Caravaggio. L'*Ecce Homo *svelato* 2023, pp. 17–47.

Volpe 2023
E. Volpe *I, Caravaggio*, Troy, NY, 2023.

Zuccari 2023
A. Zuccari, "La 'rustica poesia' dei Cappuccini. Nuovi modelli francescani da Girolamo Muziano a Orazio Gentileschi," in *Orazio Gentileschi* 2023, pp. 76–95.

2024
***Caravaggio a Donnaregina* 2024**
Caravaggio a Donnaregina. La Flagellazione, exhibition catalogue (Napoli, Complesso monumentale Donnaregina | Museo diocesano, 28 February–31 May 2024), edited by P. Leone de Castris, Rome 2024.

***Caravaggio e come cercarlo* 2024**
Caravaggio e come cercarlo. Alla Galleria Borghese, a Roma e in giro per il mondo, edited by F. Cappelletti, Naples 2024.

D'Alençon 2024
E. d'Alençon, *Le origini dell'Ordine dei Frati Minori Cappuccini e le gravi difficoltà dei primi anni 1525–1541*, edited by V. Criscuolo, Rome 2024.

Longhi [1951] 2024
R. Longhi, in *Mostra del Caravaggio e dei caravaggeschi. Catalogo*, exhibition catalogue (Milan, Palazzo Reale, April–June 1951), 2nd ed. updated and revised, Florence 1951, now in R. Longhi, *Da Cimabue a Morandi*, edited by C. Acidini and M. C. Bandera, Turin 2024, pp. 901–916.

Longhi [1973] 2024
R. Longhi, *Da Cimabue a Morandi* [1973], edited by C. Acidini e M. C. Bandera, Turin 2024.

Papi 2024
G. Papi, "Sul ritratto di Fillide Melandroni di Caravaggio", in G. Papi, *Di bella et hoscura maniera. Scritti su Caravaggio e l'ambiente caravaggesco*, Rome-Naples 2024, pp. 6-11.

Sorrentino 2024a
V. Sorrentino, "Caravaggio dipinse a Napoli la 'Adorazione dei pastori': spuntano documenti all'Archivio Storico," in *Corriere del Mezzogiorno* 3 December 2024.

Sorrentino 2024b
V. Sorrentino, "Caravaggio 1609. Tre pagamenti inediti e una nuova committente," in *Paragone Arte* LXXV, 897, III, 178, November 2024, pp. 54–73.

Whitlum Cooper 2024
F. Whitlum Cooper, *The Last Caravaggio*, London 2024.

Zappulli 2024
A. Zappulli, "Un prezioso imballaggio e un anticipo da restituire: il *San Giovanni* Borghese di Caravaggio da Napoli a Roma e le tracce di una committenza teatina," in *Fondazione Banco di Napoli. Quaderni dell'Archivio storico* n.s., 8, 2024, pp. 107–114.

2025
Moretti 2025 in press
M. Moretti, "Caravaggio and the Whitewashing of Ethiopians in the *Martyrdom of Saint Matthew*," in *Global Networks in Early Modern Rome: Images, Objects and Diplomacy*, edited by F. Freddolini, Rome 2025.

Terzaghi 2025 in press
M. C. Terzaghi, *Caravaggio e il Maestro di Hartford: natura morta in casa Borghese*, Rome 2025.

Vodret 2025a in press
R. Vodret, *Caravaggio 1571–1610*, English updated edition, Cinisello Balsamo 2025.

Vodret 2025b in press
R. Vodret, "Considerazioni sulla *Vocazione di Matteo* nella Cappella Contarelli," in *In studiis Amicitia. Scritti in onore di Alessandro Zuccari*, edited by M. Moretti, Rome 2025.

Vodret 2025c in press
R. Vodret, "Alcuni elementi per la datazione del David con la testa di Golia della Galleria Borghese," in *Atti della Giornata di Studi in onore di Stefania Macioce* (Rome, Sapienza Università di Roma, 10 May 2023), Rome 2025.

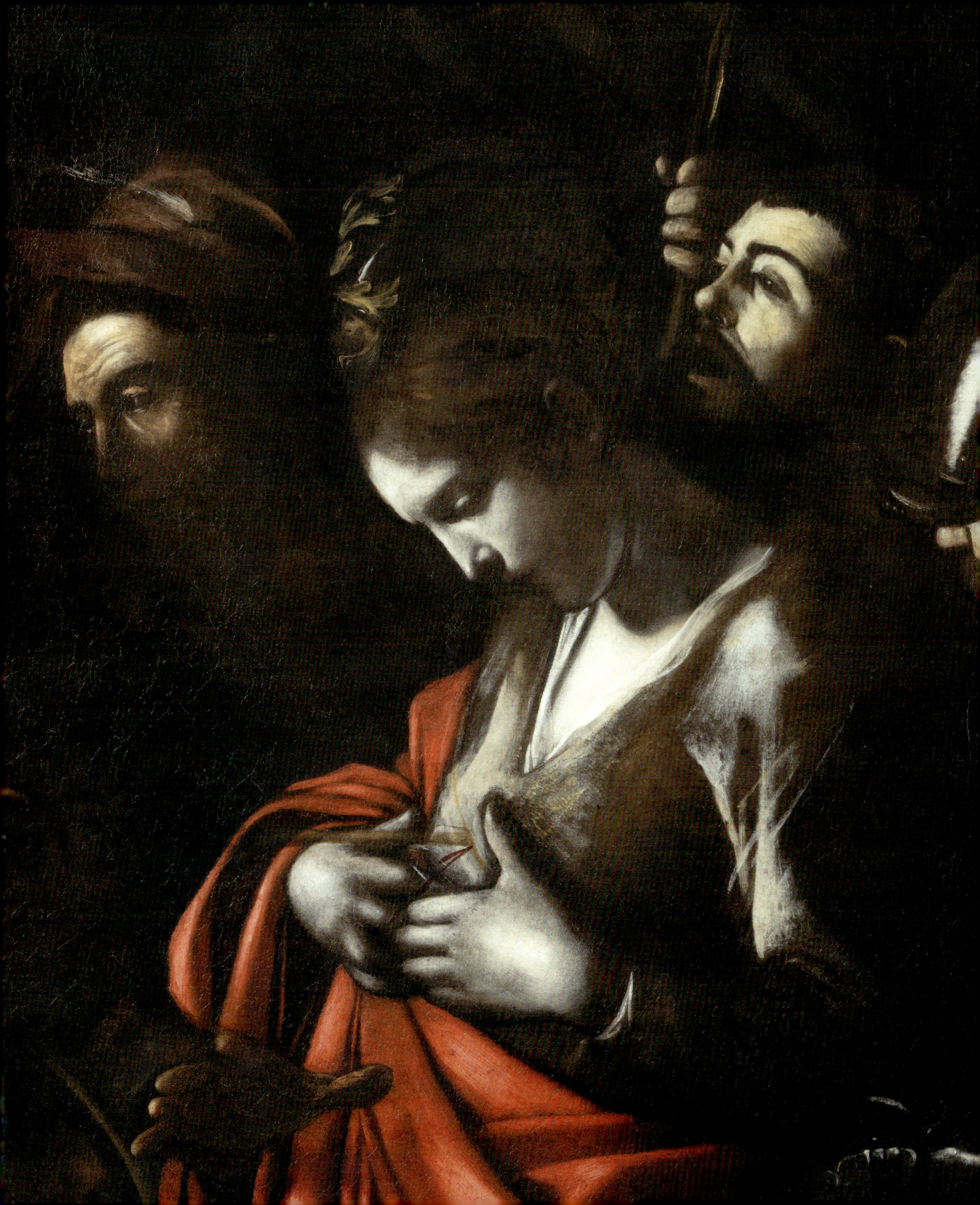

Reproduction and printing
Grafiche Antiga spa, Crocetta
del Montello (TV)
for
Marsilio Arte® srl, Venice